MW00843548

Introduction to Helicopter and Tiltrotor Simulation

Introduction to Helicopter and Tiltrotor Simulation

Mark E. Dreier
Bell Helicopter Textron Inc.
Arlington, Texas

EDUCATION SERIES
Joseph A. Schetz
Series Editor-in-Chief
Virginia Polytechnic Institute and State University
Blacksburg, Virginia

Published by
American Institute of Aeronautics and Astronautics, Inc.
1801 Alexander Bell Drive, Reston, VA 20191

American Institute of Aeronautics and Astronautics, Inc., Reston, Virginia

1   2   3   4   5

Library of Congress Cataloging-in-Publication Data

Dreier, Mark E.
  Introduction to helicopter and tiltrotor simulation / Mark E. Dreier.
    p. cm.—(AIAA education series)
  ISBN-13: 978-1-56347-873-4 (hardcover : alk. paper)
  ISBN-10: 1-56347-873-0
  1. Helicopters—Aerodynamics. I. Title.

  TL716.D65 2007
  629.133′3520113—dc22
          2006035280

Copyright © 2007 by the American Institute of Aeronautics and Astronautics, Inc. All rights reserved. Printed in the United States of America. No part of this publication may be reproduced, distributed, or transmitted, in any form or by any means, or stored in a database or retrieval system, without the prior written permission of the publisher.

Data and information appearing in this book are for information purposes only. AIAA is not responsible for any injury or damage resulting from use or reliance, nor does AIAA warrant that use or reliance will be free from privately owned rights.

MATLAB® and SIMULINK® are trademarks of The MathWorks, Inc. and are used with permission. The MathWorks does not warrant the accuracy of the text or exercises in this book. This book's use or discussion of MATLAB® software or related products does not constitute endorsement or sponsorship by The MathWorks of a particular pedagogical approach or particular use of the MATLAB® software.

VisualBASIC® is a registered trademark of Microsoft® Corporation in the United States and other countries.

This book is dedicated to these giants, upon whose shoulders I stand:
Barnes W. McCormick for showing me what,
John A. Hoffman for showing me how,
Richard L. Bennett for showing me why,
My wife Ruth for showing me support and encouragement beyond measure, and
My mother Edna for everything else.

AIAA Education Series

Editor-in-Chief
Joseph A. Schetz
Virginia Polytechnic Institute and State University

Editorial Board

Takahira Aoki
University of Tokyo

Edward W. Ashford

Karen D. Barker
The Brahe Corporation

Robert H. Bishop
University of Texas at Austin

Claudio Bruno
University of Rome

Aaron R. Byerley
U. S. Air Force Academy

Richard Colgren
University of Kansas

Kajal K. Gupta
*NASA Dryden Flight
Research Center*

Rikard B. Heslehurst
Australian Defence Force Academy

David K. Holger
Iowa State University

Rakesh K. Kapania
*Virginia Polytechnic Institute and
State University*

Brian Landrum
University of Alabama, Huntsville

Tim C. Lieuwen
Georgia Institute of Technology

Michael Mohaghegh
The Boeing Company

Conrad F. Newberry
Naval Postgraduate School

Mark A. Price
Queen's University Belfast

James M. Rankin
Ohio University

David K. Schmidt
*University of Colorado,
Colorado Springs*

David M. Van Wie
Johns Hopkins University

Table of Contents

Software download information can be
found at the end of the book on the
Supporting Materials page.

Preface

Writing this book was a labor of love for the rotorcraft industry, but was motivated by three concerns. First, rotorcraft analysis is not being taught in most engineering schools as part of an aerospace curriculum. At the time of this writing, only a handful of universities offer a rotorcraft curriculum, and only two of them, the Pennsylvania State University and Georgia Institute of Technology, are recognized as Vertical Lift/Research Centers of Excellence. Once the greybeards in our industry retire, there will be a dearth of experienced rotorcraft engineers to design/analyze/build the next generation of these humbling machines. This brings me to my second concern. Rotorcrafts are humbling machines—they challenge the designer, the analyst, and the pilot alike. I would not be surprised to learn that the author of the axiom "It's what you learn after you think you know it all that really counts" was a rotorcraft engineer. To design and analyze rotorcraft, one must be conversant in kinematics, dynamics, aerodynamics, elasticity, vibrations, hydraulics, stability and control, and the list goes on. Then, if one wants to simulate these aircraft, one needs skill in numerical techniques that include integral and differential calculus, fast table look-ups, linear algebra, filtering, computer programming in several languages that include FORTRAN, C++, MATLAB®, SIMULINK®, Ada, and so on. This leads to my third concern. I have been shocked to see graduates and seasoned veterans alike avoid mathematics, rigor, and careful program planning in favor of the quick fix. "Never enough time to do it right, but always enough to do it over" is the mantra of a modeler who shoots from the hip instead of taking careful aim, and then brags about how much easier is trial and error than applying more formal methods. Selective memory is their salvation, but hip shots are a hopeless spiral; if the original model requires enhancement down the road, poor organization makes the furtherance more difficult. This book shows how to approach a problem with rigor; I hope the reader will see how much a little rigor can accomplish, and that the rigor does not need to be painful.

Although much of the information that one needs to write a successful, well-engineered simulation of a rotorcraft already is published, that information is scattered or deeply buried in a number of texts and journal articles. The rest of the information seems to be "tribal knowledge" passed down as oral tradition. It seems that all of the knowledge is encapsulated, that is, the extant islands of important information are separated from each other by oceans of generally understood but poorly documented methods on how to combine the information into a cogent whole. This text bridges the gulfs between these islands with some important tools that are assembled before the reader's eyes. I am not aware of another text that draws to one place all of the disciplines that this book uses to develop a simulation.

This book is rather like one-stop shopping for initial flight-simulation modeling methods, especially for models of rotorcraft.

The text is aimed toward the senior-year-undergraduate or graduate-level engineering student and toward the professional. An aerospace engineering degree that focused on low-to-moderate-speed aerodynamics is preferred, though the text provides a refresher course on fluids, aerodynamics, and the atmosphere that should suffice for those who are not familiar with these topics. The text presents in a straightforward, and what I think is accessible manner, relying on the reader's reminiscences to serve as a foundation for new or refresher material. First principles are supported by linear algebra and undergraduate-level calculus and fleshed out by empirical data. This text also provides numerical methods that are useful to solve the problems that he/she proposes. Flight-simulation engineers are often jacks-of-many-trades. To solve a problem with interesting mathematics, the simulation engineer must understand the physical principles behind the problem and possess the computer science and numerical skills to complete the task.

This text has two important features. First, this text develops models in detail. It is my belief that first principles and a sound mathematical foundation are required to write a flight simulator. In a moment of whimsy, I proposed "It can be shown that . . ." as the "working title" of the text. Several of my school professors invoked this phrase, but the promised threat was never carried out. You will not find that phrase in this book. I err on the side of too much information—you will actually see how equations and models are developed. My sincere hope is that the reader will understand that straightforward application of basic ideas and mathematical methods can and do lead to important capability to model, analyze, and learn. I also hope that the reader comes to see that mathematics is not to be feared.

The other important feature is a tie-in between the chapters and some sophisticated demonstration programs that run with the Windows 2000® or Windows XP® operating system. Software programs include a propeller analysis, a landing-gear demo, a skin-friction experiment using the kinetic theory of gas, a pressure-volume-temperature experiment using the kinetic theory of gas, simple lifting-line and lifting-surface analyses of a wing, and a blade-element rotor analysis program called Rotor Tutor. An important last program, with source code included, is a beginning-to-end simulation of a single main rotor helicopter. It is not general, but it does demonstrate many of the principles that this text describes and thus can be used as a "go-by" for your own simulation models. Each purchaser of this book can download these software programs at http://www.aiaa.org/publications/supportmaterials.

Finally, it is my belief that one will get more from one's job if the job is enjoyable. Therefore, the text includes some light moments and an appendix of humorous axioms and observations about flight. Some of the wisdom of the flying ages is presented there, partly for amusement, partly because pilots that will fly your simulators all know these pearls, and partly because you will need to learn them the easy way if you intend to learn to fly.

I wish all readers delightful flights of fantasy and happy landings.

Mark E. Dreier
January 2007

Foreword

We are extremely pleased to present *Introduction to Helicopter and Tiltrotor Simulation* by Mark E. Dreier. This is a very comprehensive treatment of an important subject area in the aerospace field. The book contains 18 chapters and 12 appendices in more than 600 pages. All the important topics in this subject area are treated in a thorough manner.

Mark Dreier is very well qualified to write on this subject given his extensive industrial experience in the field, and he has written this book in a manner that will make it of interest and utility to both a beginning student as well as an expert in the field. It is with great enthusiasm that we present this new book to our readers.

The AIAA Education Series aims to cover a very broad range of topics in the general aerospace field, including basic theory, applications and design. Information about the complete list of titles can be found on the last page of this volume. The philosophy of the series is to develop textbooks that can be used in a university setting, instructional materials for continuing education and professional development courses, and also books that can serve as the basis for independent study. Suggestions for new topics or authors are always welcome.

Joseph A. Schetz
Editor-in-Chief
AIAA Education Book Series

Acknowledgments

This text evolved from a collection of class notes and handouts churned out over six years of teaching various aspects of helicopter and tiltrotor aerodynamics, dynamics and simulation methods at the University of Texas at Arlington and at Bell Helicopter Textron Incorporated (BHTI). The author had a great many supporters and reviewers, none of whom were shy about suggesting changes. Their input improved this text. In particular, the following people provided much needed constructive criticism, suggestions, and encouragement. I appreciate their input, and I thank each of them greatly.

Meredith Perkins, Chris Jessee, Janice Saylor, and Rodger Williams at the American Institute of Aeronautics and Astronautics (AIAA) told me to look past the jitters that first-time authors often experience. They guided me through the entire publication process. They were right—it was not that scary.

Gavin Grossman waded through the first complete reading of the text. He checked the arithmetic and made numerous suggestions that improved the readability. Richard Bennett provided a significant technical review and reminded me to keep in mind who my audience was. Walter Sonneborn provided a technical review of Dick Bennett's technical review.

Martin Peryea encouraged me to publish what was otherwise a loose confederation of class notes. He also worked the "system" at BHTI for the permission to seek a publisher. Steve Lewis and Craig Lieberman encouraged me to continue writing and to shake out the book by presenting the material at BHTI several times. Craig also found some interesting photographs that I used.

Michael Neal and the rest of the Bell Helicopter visual communications department secured many of the photographic images. Bob Leder helped me obtain permission to use Bell Helicopter photographs.

Gordon Saby of Pratt and Whitney Canada, Robert Wolfersteig of Honeywell Aerospace, and Alex Youngs of Rolls-Royce helped me obtain illustrations and technical data of engines from their respective companies.

Kim Smith and Kay Brackins at the American Helicopter Society provided some permissions information.

Over the years, several friends have encouraged me to continue teaching and have acted as sounding boards when I tried yet another approach to explain a concept or develop a procedure. There are too many to mention them all, but I would be remiss if I did not recognize Brad Roberts, Charles Hogg, Daniel Plata, Ed Smith, Christina Graham, Rossitza Homan, and Emily McAllister.

Among those who suffered under my tutelage are Richard Rauber, Lee Cross, Sam Garcia, Brandon Sprowl, Andrea Pisoni, and Thomas Olesnanik. They all provided insightful and clever solutions to the homework and extra assignment problems I laid out while teaching this course at the University of Texas at Arlington. Their questions in class caused me some embarrassment, prompting me to rewrite some passages in order to explain more clearly some concepts. I have distributed their contributions liberally throughout the text.

Bell Helicopter Textron test pilots Bennie Shields and Jim McCollough provided some of the pearls of wisdom that they earned from a lifetime of flying helicopters.

Eric Bird reminded me that simulation is a subset of reality, not the other way around. Eric Schmidt reminded me that the cost of not training someone was dearer than the cost of training.

The AIAA provided several anonymous reviewers. Their reviews were thorough and thoughtful, their comments were generous and plentiful, and by incorporating their suggestions I feel that the text is more readable and does a better job of getting important points across. Though I do not know your names, please know that I am grateful for your time and effort. Thank you very much.

1
Introduction to the Flight Simulation of Helicopters and Tiltrotors

1.1 Introduction

Flight is without a doubt one of mankind's most remarkable achievements. Nature did not provide mankind with wings, but nature compensated for that oversight with a mind that could work out the details. Spasmodic attempts at flight have been recorded in history for over one thousand years, but only in the last century or so has the dream of flight progressed from a powered, controllable box-kite looking contraption to a journey to the moon.

Much of the early history of flight is filled with stories of great discovery. The history is also filled with stories of mishap and death because manned experimentation preceded analysis or investigations with models. Structural failures, aerodynamic instabilities, ineffective control and simple inexperience with a flying machine were the culprits. This is where simulation enters. Now, instead of bending metal and breaking bones, simulation, especially flight simulation, often reduces a potential disaster to nothing more than a bruised ego.

The author has delivered many lectures on simulation and has always been surprised at the intense interest in simulation by people outside of this discipline. Expressing this thought in a moment of candor, one attendee sent me this explanation of his interest.

> As you noted this morning, you have been pleasantly surprised by the attendance at your lecture series. I believe that you may be underestimating the impact that simulation effort has on all disciplines involved in aircraft design .... Although my discipline is R(eliability) & M(aintainability) and I haven't solved a differential equation since I graduated, the results of simulation are very important to R&M and I wanted at least a basic understanding of how it was accomplished. I am sure many others have this same interest.
>
> I would like to share an example of the impact simulation results have on R&M. I am currently the R&M Lead for Project XXX. Mr. YYY is our control laws expert who is basing much of his work on simulation results. One output of YYY's work is the aircraft CG limits. Our weights engineer has computed the aircraft CG based on equipment location. To keep the CG within limits he makes recommendations where the equipment should be located. What I see as mission significant equipment, he sees as "silicon ballast." As the equipment

1

is moved from compartment to compartment, the compartment operating temperature, vibration environment and accessibility changes. Temperature and vibration levels are key factors in determining electronic equipment reliability. Accessibility has a major impact on ease of maintenance and maintenance times.

What this author took from that letter was that simulation was used for performance calculations, design cycle calculations, and fatigue damage calculations for reliability and maintainability consideration. Many purposes were supported with just one simulation code, although that is not usually the case. Different purposes define the organization, structure, and level of detail of a simulation. However, there is almost universal agreement that simulation helps reduce costs of final products because of the myriad ways in which simulation can be applied at every point in the design, manufacture, test, and refine phases. According to [1], one aerospace firm reported that the single biggest driver of costs was the "test-fail-fix" cycle during development, and that by using simulation to develop process specifications, "engineers could see how variations in manufacturing, materials, quality assurance and flight loads affected the risk to components ...." Reference [1] went on to suggest that

there may be a downside to increased use of simulation. Rodney L. Dreisbach, Boeing Commercial Airplanes senior technical fellow for computational structures technology, is worried about "color-based design," where engineers use graphical design tools that portray high-stress areas as red, low-stress as blue. "Red is bad, blue is good, it can become simple-minded," he said. Ron I. Prihar, an advanced engines structures lead engineer at Pratt & Whitney, agreed. This is something he has observed especially with young engineers. "Most of the time people get blinded by the tool; they're not aware of what's behind it."

The "color-based design" is a valid criticism of simulation and is part of the author's motivation to write this text. In a moment of frivolity, the title "It Can Be Shown That ..." was suggested as the title for this text because one goal of the author was to not leave out important steps when developing or deriving engineering models. If the reader sees the important steps, then blind faith is replaced by settled assurance, and, if need be, assumptions can be questioned, replaced, and even eliminated.

Some common uses of simulation are as follows:

1) *Predesign*: Predesign simulation programs concentrate on aerodynamics and mass properties and are most often used in the initial specification and design of an aircraft. These simulations often include complex tables of weight data, aerodynamic tables of common shapes, engine performance data for several types of engines, etc. Input to these programs includes mission requirements and size and weight constraints, and the outputs are often a physical description of the aircraft. These data can then be used as a starting point for further design.

2) *Performance estimation*: Performance Estimation simulation programs concentrate on the aerodynamics. They use wind-tunnel data, published analytical techniques, and correlation coefficients that the analysts deem necessary, plus geometric data taken from plans, drawings, etc. Geometric data can include

rigid-body information only, or it can incorporate elastic data in the form of modeshapes and eigenvalues. These simulations calculate the trim states, control positions at trim, inertial and aerodynamic loads, stability and control derivatives, and, in some cases, can exercise batch time-domain simulations with control inputs defined by data files. These simulations are designed for maximum flexibility in their ability to model many types or families of aircraft.

3) *Subsystem simulation*: Often, a specific subsystem of an aircraft can be modeled and investigated in detail even if the detail of the aircraft is minimal. For instance, stability and control derivatives can be combined with linear and semilinear models of the kinematics of an aircraft to produce a reasonably good flight simulation. Simple models like these, which are easy to change and inexpensive to run, are just the ticket for a control analyst to begin development of a robust control system for the aircraft.

4) *Procedures and handling-qualities simulation*: A friend of the author, Eric Schmidt, has this quote on his business card: "If you think training is expensive, try ignorance." Simulators used in training can range all of the way from inexpensive foamboard and paper cockpits to very expensive man-in-the-loop, real-time, full-fidelity simulation. In particular, the most sophisticated of the full-fidelity simulations includes all cockpit displays, switches, controls, etc., a visually rich out-the-window display, a moving base with vibration in the floorboard, controls that are hydraulically or electrically loaded to feel as they do in the real aircraft, and a math model that drives all equations of motion, control laws, elastic member equations, etc., in such a way that their answer (behavior) is the same as one would measure on the real aircraft. The good news and bad news is that simulations of this type are usually designed with a specific aircraft or family of aircraft in mind. Representation detail is remarkable, but flexibility is limited. This was true 75 years ago (1930) when Ed Link built his first trainers; it is true today.

One sees that the preceding ordering of the simulation types is not arbitrary. In fact, the first type of simulation could easily provide some data for the second type, which could provide data for the third type and serve as a basis for the fourth type. The dividing line between these types of simulations is not defined precisely. For instance, Bell Helicopter Textron uses a comprehensive rotorcraft performance evaluation program called COPTER, which is a high-fidelity simulation program good for modeling airplanes, helicopters, and tiltrotors in a general sense. It easily calculates trim conditions, general performance, stability and control derivatives, rotor-blade loads, and some maneuver time histories. However, the ability to model the specific control systems and control laws in a given aircraft is limited. This does not preclude its use as a manned simulation, but the overhead costs are greater for COPTER [2] than for a dedicated simulation program such as the Generic Tilt Rotor (GTR) simulation program [3]. GTR is very good at modeling tiltrotors of any given size and weight and is constantly under development to model specific control systems for various applications. It is both a batch and real-time simulation. However, specific loads on the rotor are not calculated because it uses an algebraic rotor model.

A helicopter test pilot once remarked to the author, "A fixed-wing pilot is somebody who is interested in flying, but doesn't have the guts to try it." (Incidentally, the author is a fixed-wing pilot, but takes no insult in that remark. Any fixed-wing pilot who attempts to hover a helicopter for the first time is instantly rewarded with an exhilarating ride by his/her own hand! The real gutsy pilot is one who climbs into the pilot's seat next after witnessing an attempted hover over a spot.) If ever there was a machine invented that challenged piloting skills and many engineering disciplines at the same time, the helicopter and tiltrotor rank near the top. Aerodynamics, dynamics, kinematics, control and stability, mechanical and electrical system models all come into play in a rotorcraft. The engineer who wants to simulate such an aircraft must be conversant in these disciplines, or in the underlying mathematics at a minimum. That is why this text will spend a great amount of time in developing the readers' confidence in mathematics. The author is acquainted with mathematicians who read and write papers that are indecipherable to mere mortals. In some sense, calling the symbolic manipulation that is performed in this text "mathematics" is an insult to mathematicians. However, until a word that is stronger than "arithmetic" but weaker than "mathematics" comes along, we will use the term "mathematics." The appendices review numerical integration techniques and linear algebra. They also provide a useful set of tables to convert units from one system to another. That appendix alone will save the reader an immense amount of time in a developing career.

In chapter two, this text (re-)introduces the reader to the fundamentals of vectors and vector resolution. The text gives special attention to the definition of a vector, the rules of orienting a vector, and some simple rules of thumb when operating on vectors and orientation.

In Chapter 3, axis systems are presented. When one discusses flight simulation, the simulation engineer must be completely comfortable with the plethora of axes needed to describe flight dynamics. These include, but are not limited to, Earth (inertial) axes, aircraft reference axes, body axes, individual element local axes, individual element reference axes, and Euler angles. In later chapters, additional axis systems will be introduced so that rotating and deformable machinery can be described.

Chapter 4 describes kinematics and flight dynamics from the highest level. By the time the reader is finished with that chapter, the four vector equations of rigid-body flight will be as familiar to the reader as any favorite story. One point in particular is worth mentioning specifically. In days gone by, the trigonometric relationships between body-axis angular rates and Euler angle rates were always presented with the caveat that the matrix that related the two was singular at pitch angles of plus or minus 90 degs. Quaternions, an invention of William Hamilton 160 years ago, provide a way to move past the singularity. Quaternions are presented in Chapter 4, but very often the discussions that follow still refer to Euler rates. In the author's experience, it is easier to visualize Euler rates than quaternions. The reader is invited to make his/her own decision on which method is easiest to use.

Chapter 5 opens with a description of the atmosphere and develops the standard atmospheric model in use today. From there, the chapter presents a brief look at the history of the equation that has become a mantra for aerodynamicists—"one-half-rho-vee-squared." Its development by Daniel Bernoulli is clever and has served us well since his first thoughts on the subject after watching a water stream move around a rock. The concepts of viscosity and compressibility are also introduced, though their use will be limited to empirical corrections or tables. This chapter also introduces simple demonstrations of viscosity and the kinetic theory of gas via computer programs. The idea of reinforcing the concepts presented in a chapter using computer programs will be repeated many times. Sometimes the programs are very simple; others have significant sophistication.

Chapter 6 is a collection of odds and ends that are serious business, but not easily pigeonholed. Asking questions such as how high, how fast, and how far seem easy enough to answer. This chapter simply goes over the many different altitudes such as pressure, density, AGL (above ground level), MSL (mean sea level), radar, etc., and shows how they are interconnected. Speed depends on the observer and the instrument. Indicated airspeed is different from true airspeed; ground speed differs from both. How far is straight forward, unless a round Earth is considered.

Chapter 7 lays the final bit of groundwork before physical models are discussed. Specifically, the often overlooked distinction between inertial and aerodynamic velocity is described. This distinction is so important that it makes this chapter one of the few that the author feels is a "must read" before any chapter that follows it.

Chapter 8 offers the first taste of aerodynamic forces with a model of the forces that a body of arbitrary shape develops. Although not as interesting as the chapters to come, this chapter presents an important first look at the nature of aerodynamic forces and empirical modeling. It also adds the realism of a fuselage to the simulations to be developed.

Chapter 9 presents the first exciting look at aerodynamics, the thing that everyone thinks of when talking about flight, wings. Various methods for modeling or estimating wing forces and moments are presented. They range from empirical methods using tables and curve fits to lifting-line and lifting-surface methods. Methods to describe the geometry of wings and important parameters that should be on the tips of tongues are brought out as the models are developed. A very important point also begins its play in the heart of aerodynamic simulation: induced velocity or wash velocity. Any body that generates an aerodynamic force also produces a wash velocity in the opposing direction. This wash interferes with the body itself, but it also interacts with other aerodynamic bodies, essentially coupling the actions of bodies together. This becomes very important when the interaction between rotors, wings, and fuselages is modeled.

Chapter 10 introduces the aerodynamics of rotating machinery. The first of these machines is the propeller. Several well-known methods of analysis are expanded, and extensive use of vector arithmetic and the calculus make propeller models easy to understand. This chapter also has a simple analysis program that the reader may use to explore propellers. It provides an important tool for the simulation engineer—a sanity check when more sophisticated models are used.

Chapter 11 is, admittedly, the author's favorite because it discusses rotors. No other device associated with rotorcraft exemplifies the capabilities of such a craft more so than a rotor. Equally, no other device is more difficult to model. Because the rotor is so important, this is the longest chapter in the book, and it is supported with an appendix that is a must read. A good model of a rotor gives the rotorcraft simulation program a good name and reputation. A bad model will never be lived down. The topics that this chapter discusses include rotor geometry, hub types, hub constraints, control, relative wind, basic dynamics including gyroscopic effects, basic aerodynamics including static and dynamic inflow models, and several modeling options that parallel the redoubtable Gessow and Myers model, or the COPTER, REXOR, and MOSTAB models. This chapter has associated with it a computer program called *RotorTutor*, which employs the strip theory and dynamic wake theory, and presents a transient analysis of a rotor in flight. The user can watch distributed loads develop and change as the blade proceeds around the azimuth. Other views include rotor maps and blade-section views.

The subject of Chapter 12 was alluded to earlier. When bodies produce an aerodynamic force, they also produce a wash. Washes interfere with the "clean" flow of air and can be powerful enough to have significant influence on other bodies in their vicinity. The shape and angular orientation of the washes changes with geometry changes such as when a tiltrotor nacelle changes its orientation. Washes also change shape with flight speed or flight condition. One remarkable video that the author viewed showed how dramatic and instantaneous the change was of a rotor downwash field. In the blink of an eye, the shape of the wash changed from helical column to trailing vortices. Such behavior has been confirmed many times over in the laboratory and with computational fluid dynamics (CFD) investigation.

Chapter 13 is a brief overview of engine models. The chapter begins with a discussion of various levels of model complexity, each building on the previous level. Perfect engines are useful for performance analysis, but must be modified with engine speed dynamics if the model is to be used in a dynamic simulation. Thermodynamic effects further enhance the realism of the engine models, but even these must be modified with dynamic models of engine controls and mechanical properties as well as the electrical system and battery dynamics so that engine starts can be simulated. A method to model the brake horsepower of normally aspirated reciprocating aircraft engines is presented. A fairly detailed flowchart that models the power turbine torque for a turboshaft engine is also provided.

Chapter 14 presents an overview of transmissions and drive trains. Unlike airplanes in which the rule "one engine, one propeller" is the norm, single-engine helicopters and tiltrotors must drive all of the rotors from the single power source. Multi-engine helicopters and tiltrotors have drive systems that let either engine drive all rotors. Thus, the engines share power, backing each other up in the event of an engine failure. This comes as quite a surprise to people unfamiliar with tiltrotors. The chapter provides a cookbook method for assembling a drive train model that has sufficient sophistication to enable power sharing without mountains of "spaghetti code" or other "switchology" that often accompanies uninspired first attempts at writing a drive train model.

Controls are the subject of Chapter 15. Until one actually starts thinking about control, the problem of getting a control input from the fixed (nonrotating) system to the rotating system seems a mere detail. Nothing could be further from the truth. Many rigging issues must be modeled to ensure adequate control over a helicopter. Mast and pylon flexibility reduce control inputs in some cases and introduce uncommanded inputs in other cases. As the mast and pylon change from helicopter to airplane mode, a tiltrotor must wash out cyclic command while scheduling in more and more effectiveness from the elevators, ailerons, and rudders. This chapter does not reveal specific methods of control, but rather prepares the newcomer to some of the problems that will be encountered.

Chapter 16 is surprisingly busy. This chapter discusses landing-gear modeling. At first blush, landing gear would seem to be an easy model—a couple of springs

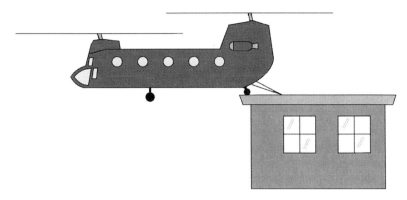

Fig. 1.1 One of many landings that helicopters do routinely and that fixed-wing aircraft may find difficult to do.

and dampers, a bit of rubber and air, a coefficient of friction, and some moment arms should do it. Right? Not exactly. Helicopters and tiltrotors can land in places that fixed-wing aircraft cannot. Figure 1.1 suggests one example. The surfaces may be level or sloped. They may be discontinuous, as in Fig. 1.1, and in some cases the surface may be moving in a somewhat predictable fashion, such as the landing zone on a ship at sea. Even in the most benign of circumstance, each wheel on a tricycle landing gear provides three forces and three moments. But one only needs a total of three forces and three moments at the body center of gravity to trim the aircraft. How does one apportion loads in such an underconstrained system? This chapter suggests some ideas.

Chapter 17 discusses trimming. Trimming is not an art—it is a science—, and it should be approached that way. Yet, the author has witnessed too many times the futile attempts by others to find a static or periodic solution to the balance of forces and moments. So-called "fly-to-trim" methods are the worst, but seem the most attractive because they appear to not require any algebraic techniques. That thinking is a false economy. This chapter describes the redoubtable Jacobian method and the equally strong periodic shooting technique to achieve trims.

Chapter 18 brings all of the pieces together. To this point, the models have assumed the presence of various aircraft states, and the aircraft states are just the time-integrated effects from assembled force-and-moment generators. This implicit loop begs the question—who comes first? This chapter shows where to break the forcing function/aircraft state loop and where to start. The chapter ends with the source code for an alpha-to-omega simulation of a single main rotor helicopter. This code calculates the Euler angles and control positions necessary to trim the helicopter as the velocity sweeps from hover to high forward speed. Flapping angles for the rotors, total power, and other interesting trim facts are printed for each trim condition. The code employs many of the lessons presented in the first 17 chapters. The user is invited to use the code as a "go-by" in writing their simulation program.

Several appendices provide reviews of mathematics including numerical integration, linear algebra, units, and working with nondimensional coefficients. Other important appendices present the momentum law and develop a general solution to the Biot–Savart law as applied to a straight-line vortex filament. One important appendix develops a simple rotor model to serve as the basis for the rigor of Chapter 11.

That is the outline of the text. But before the journey into simulation and modeling begins, learning the language and customs of that new world is appropriate. So, this chapter concludes with some important initial thoughts about simulation in the hope that the reader's appetite for this main course is whetted.

1.2   Elements of a Performance Simulation

Obviously, the desire of the analyst dictates the type of simulation to use or build. One can mix textures (great detail in one area and practically no detail in another), or one can choose to use the same texture throughout. This section discusses some of the details of a simulation that can be used to estimate performance and stability and control derivatives of an existing or planned aircraft.

A performance simulation must be able to perform simple trim calculations. It must also be able to calculate stability and control derivatives and execute the general equations of motion in the time domain. The general equations of motion are driven by aerodynamic, inertial, and reaction loads contributed by all of the independent elements associated with the vehicle. Before the specific calculations are described, consider Fig. 1.2, which is a picture of a single main rotor helicopter and all of the components that are likely to require definition.

Fig. 1.2   Bell Helicopter Textron, Inc. model 407 (courtesy of Bell Helicopter Textron, Inc.).

Table 1.1 contains quite a bit of information that has to be connected together. The task is a little like a puzzle. An edge piece here and part of the wing there give clues on how to assemble the puzzle. In the past, this might have been the way in which models were generated. In today's business and engineering climate a hit-and-miss procedure such as puzzle building is not so acceptable. One of the major goals of this text is to provide insight on how to build a math model from

Table 1.1   List of required models in a simulation

Component	Description
Main rotor, tail rotor	Usually the most complex devices to model correctly. They generate inertial and aerodynamic loads. They have elastic and rigid-body deflections. They are nonlinear.
Transmission/drive train	Models the delivery of torque from the engine to the main and tail rotors, plus any accessories. Includes flexibility in the shafts, inertias of the gears, clutch dynamics, governors, etc.
Control system, engine controls	Includes mechanical, hydraulics, and electronics. Models the stability and control augmentation systems, fuel control systems, linkages to all movable components.
Landing gear	Models the reaction and dynamic loads produced by landing-gear struts, skids, etc. Must be able to work with other than level ground. For applications on ship, the "ground" plane must be able to move in time.
Fuselage	Modeled with simple equations or tables usually. Forces and moments are a function of angles of attack and sideslip, Mach number, and deflections of panels.
Engines	Generally straightforward table look up using control inputs and atmospheric properties to calculate engine speed, torque, temperature. Often, the engine controls are made part of this model.
Wings, winglets, fins	Uses equations or tables to model forces and moments as a function of control deflections, Mach number, sideslip and angle of attack.
Induced velocity and mutual interference effects	These models permit aerodynamic influences of one element on another. Examples include the download on the fuselage from the main rotor, sideload on a vertical fin from a side thrusting tail rotor, swirling wake effects caused by uneven aerodynamic load.
Atmosphere	With elevation and ambient temperature, the air density and Mach number change. This has a profound effect on the aerodynamic loads.

the ground up. In that regard, Chapter 18 could easily be presented first because it lays out a backbone and the information infrastructure.

1.3   Vocabulary of a Performance Simulation

All professions have their own jargon. This specialized language ensures that broad common themes and ideas are transmitted and received with a minimum of effort and time. Often, those who are unfamiliar with the jargon must pick it up on-the-job training (OJT). So, to bring the reader up to speed quickly, Table 1.2

Table 1.2   Conventional names and operations in flight dynamics

Vector	Description
$P_e = \begin{Bmatrix} N \\ E \\ D \end{Bmatrix}$	The position vector of the aircraft center of gravity in inertial (Earth) axes; the elements are the north, east, and down position.
$\alpha_e = \begin{Bmatrix} \phi \\ \theta \\ \psi \end{Bmatrix}$	The vector[a] of angular position of the aircraft body axes with respect to the Earth, resolved to the Earth; the elements are roll angle, pitch angle, and yaw angle. They are usually called the Euler angles. The NASA convention for body axes is this. The origin is the center of gravity. The x axis points to the nose of the aircraft. The y axis points toward the right, and the z axis points down, consistent with a right-hand system.
$V_e = \begin{Bmatrix} \dot{N} \\ \dot{E} \\ \dot{D} \end{Bmatrix} = \dot{P}_e$	The velocity of the aircraft with respect to the Earth, resolved to the Earth; the elements are north-dot, east-dot, and down-dot. Down-dot is usually called the rate of descent.
$\omega_e = \begin{Bmatrix} \dot{\phi} \\ \dot{\theta} \\ \dot{\psi} \end{Bmatrix} = \dot{\alpha}_e$	The time rate of change of the Euler angles.
$R_x(.), R_y(.), R_z(.)$	Rotation matrices about the x, y, and z axes, respectively. They are built with the rules described in the appendices. These matrices are orthonormal.
$T_{BE}(\phi, \theta, \psi) = R_x(\phi) R_y(\theta) R_z(\psi)$	Transformation matrix from Earth to body axes, used for linear velocity terms. This matrix is orthonormal.

Continued

Table 1.2   Conventional names and operations in flight dynamics (Continued)

Vector	Description
$E(\phi,\theta) =$ $$\begin{bmatrix} 1 & 0 & -\sin(\theta) \\ 0 & \cos(\phi) & \sin(\phi)\cos(\theta) \\ 0 & -\sin(\phi) & \cos(\phi)\cos(\theta) \end{bmatrix}$$	Transformation matrix from Earth to body axes for angular velocity terms. This matrix is NOT orthonormal.
$V_b = T_{BE}(\phi,\theta,\psi)V_e = \begin{Bmatrix} u \\ v \\ w \end{Bmatrix}$	Inertial linear velocity of the aircraft, resolved to body axes. The elements are u along the x axis, v along the y axis, and w along the z axis.
$\omega_b = E(\phi,\theta)\omega_e = \begin{Bmatrix} p \\ q \\ r \end{Bmatrix}$	Inertial angular velocity of the aircraft, resolved to body axes. The elements are the roll rate p, the pitch rate q, and the yaw rate r. The E matrix just defined transforms Euler angle rates to body-axis rates.
$F_g = \begin{Bmatrix} -\sin(\theta) \\ \sin(\phi)\cos(\theta) \\ \cos(\phi)\cos(\theta) \end{Bmatrix} \cdot m \cdot g$	The gravity load applied to the aircraft center of gravity in body axes. The column of trigonometric functions is the third column in the T_{BE} matrix, m is the mass, and g is the acceleration of gravity.
$F_{cg} = \begin{Bmatrix} F_x \\ F_y \\ F_z \end{Bmatrix}$	The three-element force vector applied to the aircraft center of gravity, resolved to body axes.
$M_{cg} = \begin{Bmatrix} M_x \\ M_y \\ M_z \end{Bmatrix} = \begin{Bmatrix} L \\ M \\ N \end{Bmatrix}$	The three-element moment vector applied to the aircraft center of gravity, resolved to body axes.
$V_{W_j} = \begin{Bmatrix} u_w \\ v_w \\ w_w \end{Bmatrix}_j$	The three-element column vector of induced velocities at component j. For completeness, this can be extended to six elements to include rotational as well as linear velocities.
$Va_j = Vb_j - V_{W_j}$	The three-element column vector of aerodynamic velocities at component j, resolved to a system of axes parallel to body axes.
$Vb_j = Vb + \omega_b \times r_j$	The three-element inertial velocity vector at component j, resolved to an axis system parallel to the body axes (individual element local axes).
$\dot{V}b_j = \dot{V}b + \dot{\omega}_b \times r_j$	The three-element inertial acceleration vector at component j, resolved to an axis system parallel to the body axes.

Continued

Table 1.2   Conventional names and operations in flight dynamics (*Continued*)

Vector	Description
$r_j = \left\{ \begin{array}{c} x \\ y \\ z \end{array} \right\}$	A three-element position vector measuring from the aircraft center of gravity to the origin of the reference axes of component j. The vector is resolved to body axes.
$Va_{j\|IERA} = R_x(\theta_x)R_y(\theta_y)R_z(\theta_z)Va_j$ $Vb_{j\|IERA} = R_x(\theta_x)R_y(\theta_y)R_z(\theta_z)Vb_j$ $\dot{V}b_{\|IERAj} = R_x(\theta_x)R_y(\theta_y)R_z(\theta_z)\dot{V}b_j$	The three-element vectors of aerodynamic and inertial velocity, and inertial acceleration, resolved to component j's reference axes. The subscript IERA means individual element reference axes, the subscripts x, y, and z refer to the body axes. In these expressions, θ_x, θ_y, and θ_z are general angles of rotation about the x, y, and z axes.
$\dot{V}_b = -\omega_b \times V_b + (F_g + F_{cg})/m$	The body-axis acceleration vector.
$\dot{\omega}_b = I_n^{-1}(-\omega_b \times I_n\,\omega_b + M_{cg})$	The body axis angular acceleration vector. I_n is the inertia matrix.
$C(r_j) = \begin{bmatrix} 0 & -z & y \\ z & 0 & -x \\ -y & x & 0 \end{bmatrix}$	A matrix representation of the cross-product operation. The vector equation $M = r \times f$ can be replaced with the linear algebra expression $M = C(r)f$. Note, because $C^T(r) = -C(r) = C(-r)$ and because $a \times b = -b \times a$, then the angular motion cross product is given by any of these equivalent expressions: $V = \omega \times r = -r \times \omega = C^T(r)\omega = -C(r)\omega.$

[a] Some mechanical engineering purists will balk at this use of the word "vector." Instead, they will say that this is a one-dimensional array. This text employs a broader definition that embraces definitions from the mechanical engineer, the mathematician, and the computer programmer: A vector (single dimensioned array) is a stream of homogeneous data elements [4]. With a bit more detail, Chapter 2 discusses the definition of vectors as this text uses them.

presents many of the vectors and matrix operations that will become second nature by the end of the book.

The usual expression of the equations of motion uses the concept of a state vector. A state vector contains all of the dynamic variables and their time derivatives up to, but not including, the highest derivative. The states are those necessary to define the highest derivatives.

The ordering of the states in the state vector is not important from a mathematical standpoint, although certain computational economies are realized if three-element subvectors remained grouped as just defined. Once the order of the states in the state vector has been selected, the order must be preserved. In this text, the state vector is ordered this way:

$$x = \left\{ \begin{array}{c} P_e \\ V_b \\ \omega_b \\ \alpha_e \end{array} \right\} = \left\{ \begin{array}{c} N \\ E \\ D \\ u \\ v \\ w \\ p \\ q \\ r \\ \phi \\ \theta \\ \psi \end{array} \right\}$$

Therefore, the derivative of the state vector is defined:

$$\dot{x} = \left\{ \begin{array}{c} \dot{N} \\ \dot{E} \\ \dot{D} \\ \dot{u} \\ \dot{v} \\ \dot{w} \\ \dot{p} \\ \dot{q} \\ \dot{r} \\ \dot{\phi} \\ \dot{\theta} \\ \dot{\psi} \end{array} \right\} = \left\{ \begin{array}{c} T_{\mathrm{BE}}^{-1} V_b \\ -\omega_b \times V_b + Mass^{-1}(F_g + F_{cg}) \\ I_n^{-1}(-\omega_b \times I_n\omega_b + M_{cg}) \\ E_e^{-1}\omega_b \end{array} \right\}$$

Note that the state vector is a mixture of body-axes and Earth-axes states. This is not a problem. These are tightly coupled nonlinear differential equations. The F_{cg} and M_{cg} vectors are the focus of the text.

1.4 Component Models

All of the components that generate aerodynamic forces and moments are most easily modeled in a local reference system. In general, the component's local axes are parallel with the body axes and simply displaced from the aircraft center of gravity. On the other hand, the reference or computational axes have arbitrary angular orientation with respect to the body axes. For example, a tiltrotor's nacelles may be rotated from the vertical to the horizontal, and an F-111 wing may be swept forward or backward for efficient slow and high-speed flight, respectively. This not only means that the velocity vectors must be resolved to the local axes, then to reference axes, but the forces and moments developed by an element must be resolved back to the center of gravity. The manner in which the velocity vectors at the center of gravity are transformed to the component local and reference axes is previewed here.

First, the position vector from the center of gravity to the origin of the component's local axes is defined and then used to calculate the full inertial velocity at the origin of the local axes, but still in a system parallel to the body axes. These axes are called the individual element local axes (IELA).

$$V_{b|b} = V_b + \omega_b \times r|_j = V_b + C^T(r)\omega_b|_j$$

The same is done with the acceleration:

$$\dot{V}_{b|b} = \dot{V}_b + \dot{\omega}_b \times r|_j = \dot{V}_b + C^T(r)\dot{\omega}_b|_j$$

Now, the wash velocity vector, which is in the compatible system, is added to get the aerodynamic velocity:

$$V_a = V_b - V_W|_j$$

These vectors can now be manipulated through some rotation matrices to get to the component's reference or modeling axes. These axes are called the individual element reference axes (IERA).

$$V_{a|IERA} = R_x(\theta_x)R_y(\theta_y)R_z(\theta_z)V_a|_j$$
$$V_{b|IERA} = R_x(\theta_x)R_y(\theta_y)R_z(\theta_z)V_b|_j$$
$$\dot{V}_{b|IERA} = R_x(\theta_x)R_y(\theta_y)R_z(\theta_z)\dot{V}_b|_j$$

In general, the angles just mentioned are not fixed. They are incidence angles, tilt angles, etc., which may be under the control of the pilot. Once the vectors are in component reference axes, the equations describing the component loads can be used. The resulting loads are defined in the component reference or modeling axes. Now, the loads must be resolved back to the local axes parallel with the body axes.

$$F|_j = R_z^T(\theta_z)R_y^T(\theta_y)R_x^T(\theta_x)F_{IERA}$$
$$M|_j = R_z^T(\theta_z)R_y^T(\theta_y)R_x^T(\theta_x)M_{IERA}$$

These can then be transformed back to the center of gravity:

$$F_{cg|j} = F|_j$$
$$M_{cg|j} = M|_j + r \times F|_j = M|_j + C(r) \times F|_j$$

Finally, all of the individual forces and moments can be summed to yield the total forces and moments:

$$F_{cg} = \sum_{j=1}^{n} F_{cg|j}$$

$$M_{cg} = \sum_{j=1}^{n} M_{cg|j}$$

This is the process that is required in a performance simulation to calculate a trim, compute a stability or control derivative, and execute in the time domain.

1.5 Be Open to These Concerns

Anyone wishing to work in simulation must constantly remind himself or herself that simulation is a modeling process. Simulation depends on science and engineering and mathematics. Simulation is also an art form. So, keep the following homilies in mind.

No matter how good the simulation is, it will never fool the person in the loop. One only needs to fly a simulator and then jump into an aircraft with the simulated flight fresh in mind to appreciate this fact. This does not mean that simulation is without value. Reference [5] quotes George Box: "All models are wrong: some models are useful." Those words can be interpreted as "fightin' words" by simulation engineers that have built a career "getting it right," but the simple fact is that models are just models and critical feedback is a necessary part of constant improvement, even if feelings are hurt.

The humorous taxonomy holds that reality is just a subset of simulation. Simulations very often answer one question by asking two. Simulations very often suffer from "constants that aren't and variables that don't" (author unknown). Do not expect correct behavior with the first execution. Look for the error. A quote attributed to Chuck Reid says this nicely: "In theory, there is no difference between theory and practice; in practice, there is."

Remember the principle of Occam's razor, also called the principle of parsimony, which states that one should not make any more assumptions than the minimum needed to decide among competing theories or explanations. Choose the simplest explanation—doing so will reduce the chances for redundancy, inconsistency, and ambiguity. But, be careful to not throw the baby out with the bath water. Albert Einstein opined, "Things should be made as simple as possible, but not any simpler."

Remember to have fun and do not fear making mistakes. Again, quoting Albert Einstein, "Anyone who has never made a mistake has never tried anything new." This text makes no claim to be error free, but it does provide some tried-and-true methods for getting results. Use these methods. But, when the time comes that the reader must introduce a new concept, expect that the first shot out of the barrel will have mistakes. Fix them and learn. "Good judgment comes from experience; experience comes from bad judgment" (author unknown).

1.6 Conclusions

This chapter introduced the reader to rest of the text, the raison d'etre for simulation, and the elements of the mathematical language spoken in a performance simulation. The reader should take special notice of the use of vectors and matrices and the component approach that this text uses. The author has found that a significant reduction in analysis and coding errors follows a rigorous approach to modeling. This is a common theme throughout the text.

References

[1] Dornheim, M. A., "Simulation Cuts Development Costs, But Still Needs Improvement," *Aviation Week and Space Technology*, 8 Dec. 2003, p. 60.

[2] Corrigan, J., *Volume 3 Comprehensive Program for the Theoretical Evaluation of Rotorcraft (COPTER – 2000) Engineer's Manual*, Textron Rept. 299-099-376, Rev. A, Bell Helicopter Textron, Inc., Fort Worth, TX, 2004.

[3] Langston, J., "A Generic Simulation Model for Tiltrotor Aircraft," Bell Helicopter Textron, Rept. 901-985-002, Rev. D, Bell-Boeing Joint Program Office, Arlington, VA, Sept. 30, 2003.

[4] Dierks, T., and Allen, C., *The TLS Protocol*, ver. 1.0, Network Working Group, http://www.ietf.org/rfc/rfc2246.txt [retrieved 6 March 2006].

[5] Paulk, Mark C., et al., *The Capability Maturity Model: Guidelines for Improving the Software Process*, Carnegie Mellon Univ., SEI, Addison Wesley Longman, Boston, 2000.

Problems

1.1 Name as many similarities as you can between a simulation video game and an engineering or training simulator.

1.2 Name as many differences as you can between a simulation video game and an engineering or training simulator. Are these differences important, and if so, why?

2
Vectors and Vector Resolution

2.1 Introduction

Vectors are well-defined and well-ordered collections of the values for things. A vector can represent any physical quantity specified by magnitude and direction. Examples of vectors include force, moment, position, velocity, and acceleration. In a larger sense, vectors can also be collections of disparate entities. For instance, a vector can be a collection of dynamic states, each of which may be a scalar. An example of a collection is the state vector for an oscillator. Such a vector contains position and velocity. This text makes use of both senses of a vector, and this chapter introduces the reader to the notation that is used throughout the text.

2.2 Vectors That Specify Magnitude and Direction

The number of elements in a vector defines the length of the vector. Because this text will be using real numbers almost exclusively, a vector in an N-dimensional space will be called an R^N vector. Most of the vectors in this text describe magnitude and direction in either three or six degrees of freedom, so that most vectors are R^3 or R^6.

This text deals almost exclusively with mechanical contrivances that have three dimensions, which are expressed in a Cartesian coordinate system. A Cartesian coordinate system comprises three mutually perpendicular axes that are usually named X, Y, and Z, and have unit vectors along them usually named i, j, and k. Figure 2.1 shows a Cartesian coordinate system.

These three axes meet at one point called the origin, forming three mutually perpendicular planes, XOY, YOZ, and ZOX. It is assumed the reader is familiar with the properties of unit vectors and the concept of right-hand coordinate systems. Of course, there is no requirement for a Cartesian coordinate system to adhere to the right-hand rule. However, the great body of scientific and mathematical work adheres to this rule. The positive sense of the X, Y, and Z vectors is arbitrarily oriented. In the simulation of aircraft, the NACA convention for body axes is to place the origin at the center of gravity, the X axis points forward toward the nose, the Y axis points generally toward the right wing, and the Z axis points generally down toward the floor.

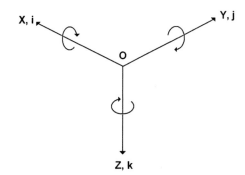

Fig. 2.1   Right-handed Cartesian coordinate system showing the directions of the unit vectors and the names of the directions used throughout this text.

2.3   Defining a Vector—Notation

1) *Vectors represent varying physical quantities.* The name of the vector is arbitrary, of course, but mnemonic devices such as P for position or V for velocity help.

2) *Vectors have a definite direction;* they go or point *from* one place *to* another place. Good notation makes the direction obvious. Throughout this text, vectors will use a to-from naming convention $P_{TO\text{-}FROM}$. For example, the vector P_{A-B} is a vector that points from a point called B to a point called A.

3) *Vectors have an orientation or resolution.* Once the starting and ending points for the vector are known, the axis system in which this vector is measured must also be specified. For instance, the vector in Fig. 2.2 is resolved to two axis systems. It is the same vector in either axis system (physics is independent of the keyhole through which you look), but its coordinate values are very different. In axis system A of Fig. 2.2, the end of the arrow has a position vector with coordinates:

$$P_A = \begin{Bmatrix} 1 \\ 1 \\ 0 \end{Bmatrix}$$

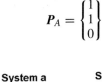

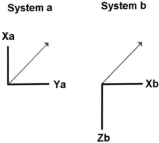

Fig. 2.2   Vector resolved to different axes.

whereas in axis system B the end of the arrow has a position vector with coordinates:

$$P_B = \left\{ \begin{array}{c} 1 \\ 0 \\ -1 \end{array} \right\}$$

Both vectors are the same length, and from the standpoint of a reader who cannot see the A or B axis systems these two vectors point in the same direction. Yet, when the different axis systems are made visible, these vectors have different coordinate values. This is the issue of resolution. A complete definition of a vector requires the answer to four questions, plus notation that shows these answers but is not too cumbersome. The questions are as follows:

1) What kind of vector is it? Examples include force, moment, displacement or position, velocity, magnetic field, vorticity, etc.

2) What is being acted on, or what is moving? Examples include aircraft center of gravity, airfoil center of pressure, landing-gear strut, wing, etc.

3) With respect to what axis system (frame) is the action measured? (The word "frame" is a more modern designation for "axis system." This text will use both phrases.) For instance, you can only measure velocity with respect to some reference point that may or may not be moving. It is relative.

4) To which axis system (frame) is the measurement resolved? Just because we measure with respect to something does not mean we know along which axis the measurement is being taken.

Figure 2.3 offers an example of how these concepts fit together. Three different axis systems are shown. These axes are oriented arbitrarily to each other and do not have coincident origins. Position vectors measure the distance and direction from one point to another in this space. Those points can be the origins of the axes or some point displaced from the axes. The names of the position vectors make the meaning clear. For instance, the vector marked $P_{H-T|T}$ is the position vector P-measuring from the origin of the T system to the point H, with the answer resolved to or expressed in the T system coordinates.

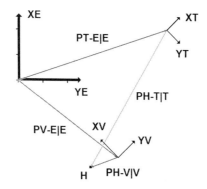

Fig. 2.3   Axis systems and position vectors.

2.4 Orienting a Vector

From Fig. 2.3, one sees that the T system is rotated in a positive sense around the ZE axis, and the V system is rotated about the ZE axis in a negative sense. The method by which a vector is rotated from one axis system to another is through premultiplication by a rotation matrix. A rotation is what is meant by resolution or orientation.

Vectors can be rotated about any axes in any order for any number of times until the final orientation is achieved. Adopting the same TO-FROM notation as with the naming of a vector, a rotation matrix from system E to system D might be named $R_{D\text{-}E}$. Thus, vector $P_{A-B|E}$ in system E can be resolved to system D, that is, $P_{A-B|D}$ through the simple matrix operation:

$$P_{A-B|D} = R_{D\text{-}E}P_{A-B|E} \qquad (2.1)$$

Notice how the subscripts and system names changed. The last symbol in the position vector names the system of resolution, and it must agree with the first or second subscript symbol of the rotation matrix as illustrated.

Rotation matrices are written for R^3 vectors and may rotate a vector around one, two, or all three axes simultaneously. (One can write rotation matrices for any number of dimensions. Modal matrices are an example of higher-dimensional rotation.) It is easiest to understand how these rotation matrices work by considering rotations about one axis at a time.

Rotation about the X axis does not change the component of the vector directed along the X axis, but it does change the y and z components. Consider frames a and b in Fig. 2.4. The X axis for both frames is directed into the page. Now, rotate frame b through the positive angle Φ, measured about the X axis of frame a.

A vector lying on the Ya axis now projects components onto the Yb and negative Zb axes. Similarly, a vector lying on the Za axis now projects onto the Yb and Zb axes. The rotation matrix that does this transformation is

$$R_x(\Phi) = \begin{bmatrix} 1 & 0 & 0 \\ 0 & \cos(\Phi) & \sin(\Phi) \\ 0 & -\sin(\Phi) & \cos(\Phi) \end{bmatrix} \qquad (2.2)$$

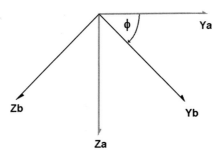

Fig. 2.4   Frame b has been rotated with respect to frame a about the common X axis which is pointing into the page.

In similar fashion, the following matrices perform rotations about a Y axis and a Z axis:

$$R_y(\Theta) = \begin{bmatrix} \cos(\Theta) & 0 & -\sin(\Theta) \\ 0 & 1 & 0 \\ \sin(\Theta) & 0 & \cos(\Theta) \end{bmatrix} \qquad (2.3)$$

$$R_z(\Psi) = \begin{bmatrix} \cos(\Psi) & \sin(\Psi) & 0 \\ -\sin(\Psi) & \cos(\Psi) & 0 \\ 0 & 0 & 1 \end{bmatrix} \qquad (2.4)$$

One measures a rotation angle about (around) the axis of its rotation. If you align your right thumb with the positive direction of the axis, then your fingers curl in the direction of positive angular displacement. The user fixes the location of 0 deg arbitrarily, but once it is fixed it must not vary.

There is an easy way to remember how to build these 3×3 rotation matrices.

1) Put a one in the diagonal position corresponding to the axis you are rotating about. For instance, the R_x matrix has a one in the X-row, X-column position. In the remaining cells of the X row and X column, place zeros.

2) Place the cosine of the rotation angle in the remaining diagonal cells.

3) Place the sine of the rotation angle in the remaining off-diagonal cells.

4) If the rotation is about the X axis or Z axis, put a negative sign in front of the lower sine term. If the rotation is about the Y axis, put a negative sign in front of the upper sine term. Just remember down-up-down. Look at the R_x, R_y, and R_z matrices to see if you can make sense of the preceding four rules.

These matrices are orthonormal, which means the columns in the matrices, if considered vectors, have unity magnitude (normal), and a dot product of column i and j $(i \neq j)$ equals zero (orthogonal). This property has a nice consequence. The inverses of matrices R_x, R_y, and R_z are simply their transposes.

$$R_x^{-1} = R_x^T$$
$$R_y^{-1} = R_y^T$$
$$R_z^{-1} = R_z^T$$

One can also find the inverse by changing the sign on the argument: $R^{-1}(\alpha) = R(-\alpha)$. When inverting a series by transposing, remember to reverse the order of the matrices as well:

$$(R_X R_Y R_Z)^T = R_Z^T R_Y^T R_X^T$$

One can cascade rotations. For example, a rotation about the Z axis in system 1 can be followed by a rotation about the Y axis in system 2 and then about the X axis in system 3. In fact, any number of rotations can be put together in any order. When all is said and done, the resulting cascade can be reduced to a rotation about just three axes. For instance, suppose an analyst performed several rotations on vector

P_1 to end up with vector P_7:

$$P_2 = Rz_{2-1}P_1$$

$$P_3 = Ry_{3-2}P_2$$

$$P_4 = Rz_{4-3}P_3$$

$$P_5 = Rx_{5-4}P_4$$

$$P_6 = Rz_{6-5}P_5$$

$$P_7 = Ry_{7-6}P_6$$

or

$$P_7 = Ry_{7-6}Rz_{6-5}Rx_{5-4}Rz_{4-3}Ry_{3-2}Rz_{2-1}P_1$$

or

$$P_7 = \left[\prod_{j=2-1}^{7-6} R_j(\phi,\theta,\psi)\right]P_1 = \prod P_1 \qquad (2.5)$$

The symbol Π with index notation in expression (2.5) indicates repeated multiplication. The symbol Π without index notation represents the matrix formed by the repeated matrix multiplication. Substituting the expression for P_2 into the expression for P_3, then that result into the expression for P_4, etc. yields the complex expression for P_7. But, all of the matrix multiplications yield a single 3×3 matrix. The entire series of rotations has been reduced to one operation with a single rotation matrix.

In the preceding discussion, the names Φ, Θ, and Ψ were not chosen arbitrarily. In flight dynamics, one encounters a specific order of rotation using angles named Ψ, Θ, and Φ, which represent rotation about the Z axis, the new intermediate Y axis, and the newer X axis, respectively. These angles are the so-called Euler angles, and their naming convention follows NASA standard notation. The matrix that performs this specific action is called an Euler rotation matrix and has this definition:

$$T_{\text{BE}}(\Phi, \Theta, \Psi) = R_x(\Phi)R_y(\Theta)R_z(\Psi) \qquad (2.6)$$

The subscripts B and E stand for "body" and "Earth," respectively. The matrix T_{BE} resolves an Earth-based vector to body axes. Expanding the indicated matrix multiplication, the T_{BE} matrix has these elements:

$$T_{\text{BE}}(\Phi, \Theta, \Psi) = \begin{bmatrix} C_\Theta C_\Psi & C_\Theta S_\Psi & -S_\Theta \\ S_\Phi S_\Theta C_\Psi - C_\Phi S_\Psi & S_\Phi S_\Theta S_\Psi + C_\Phi C_\Psi & S_\Phi C_\Theta \\ C_\Phi S_\Theta C_\Psi + S_\Phi S_\Psi & C_\Phi S_\Theta S_\Psi - S_\Phi C_\Psi & C_\Phi C_\Theta \end{bmatrix} \qquad (2.7)$$

A shorthand notation has been adopted, which is $C_\Theta = \cos(\Theta)$, $S_\Theta = \sin(\Theta)$, etc. If the (1,2), (1,3), and (2,3) elements of the T_{BE} matrix are set equal to the elements of the product matrix Π, then the Euler angles are easily found.

$$\Theta = \sin^{-1}(-\Pi_{1,3})$$

$$\Phi = \sin^{-1}\left[\frac{\Pi_{2,3}}{\cos(\Theta)}\right]$$

$$\Psi = \sin^{-1}\left[\frac{\Pi_{1,2}}{\cos(\Theta)}\right] \qquad (2.8)$$

Therefore, no matter how many rotations are required to resolve a vector into a new system, the result can always be expressed in terms of three Euler angles and the three-axis Euler angle rotation matrix.

2.5   Operations

Given these definitions, there are just a few basic rules to do the work:

1) To change the orientation of a vector expressed in axis system D to axis system C, premultiply the vector by the T_{C-D} matrix.

$$\boldsymbol{P}_{A-B|C} = T_{C-D}\boldsymbol{P}_{A-B|D}$$

2) Of course, to go the other direction, premultiply both sides by the inverse of T_{C-D}. Because T is orthonormal, its inverse is its transpose, so that either operation is correct:

$$\boldsymbol{P}_{A-B|D} = T_{C-D}^{-1}\boldsymbol{P}_{A-B|C} = T_{C-D}^{T}\boldsymbol{P}_{A-B|C}$$

3) To change orientation of a vector in the same axis system, change the sign and reverse the indices of the TO-FROM part of the information:

$$\boldsymbol{P}_{A-B|C} = -\boldsymbol{P}_{B-A|C}$$

4) Vector addition and subtraction must always be in the same axis system, and at least one of the indices must be the same:

$$\boldsymbol{P}_{A-C|D} = \boldsymbol{P}_{A-B|D} + \boldsymbol{P}_{B-C|D}$$

When adding, inner indices (B) must match!

$$\boldsymbol{P}_{A-C|D} = \boldsymbol{P}_{A-B|D} - \boldsymbol{P}_{C-B|D}$$

When subtracting, hind indices (B) must match!

Example 2.1

Problem: Refer to Fig. 2.3. Suppose the position of the point H is desired in the T-axis system. Suppose further that the angular orientations of the V and T axes are known relative to the E system, H is known with respect to, and resolved to the V system, and only the displacement from V to T is known, resolved to the E system. Numerical values of the vectors are given next. To conserve space, the column vectors are presented as row vectors with the transpose operator, superscript T. The transformation matrices T_{V-E} and T_{T-E} use special nomenclature, for example, $T_{X-Y} = T(\Phi, \Theta, \Psi)$.

$$P_{H-V|V} = \begin{pmatrix} 0.7071, & -1.414, & -3 \end{pmatrix}^T$$

$$P_{T-V|E} = \begin{pmatrix} 5, & 2, & 0 \end{pmatrix}^T$$

$$T_{V-E} = T \begin{pmatrix} 0, & 0, & -45\,\text{deg} \end{pmatrix}$$

$$T_{T-E} = T \begin{pmatrix} 0, & 0, & 45\,\text{deg} \end{pmatrix}$$

It is instructive to suppose two other vectors exist. These vectors will not be needed, but will help in the discussion that follows. Those vectors point from the origin of the E system to the V system and from the origin of the E system to the T system. Both are resolved to the E system.

$$P_{V-E|E} = \begin{pmatrix} -3, & -4, & 0 \end{pmatrix}^T$$

$$P_{T-E|E} = \begin{pmatrix} 2, & 6, & 0 \end{pmatrix}^T$$

What is wanted is $P_{H-T|T}$, the position vector to H from the T system origin, resolved to the T system axes.

Solution: A straightforward, if somewhat busy solution is to rotate the vector $P_{H-V|V}$ (the vector that points to H from the origin of the V system) to a system parallel to the E system, then add the vector $P_{V-E|E}$ (the vector from the origin of the E system to the origin of the V system), then subtract the vector $P_{T-E|E}$ (the vector that points from the origin of the E system to the origin of the T system), and finally rotate the result to the T system.

Symbolically,

$$P_{H-V|E} = T_{V-E}^{-1} P_{H-V|V}$$

$$P_{H-E|E} = P_{H-V|E} + P_{V-E|E}$$

$$P_{H-T|E} = P_{H-E|E} + P_{E-T|E} = P_{H-E|E} - P_{T-E|E}$$

$$P_{H-T|T} = T_{T-E} P_{H-T|E}$$

or

$$P_{H-T|T} = T_{T-E} \left(T_{V-E}^{-1} P_{H-V|V} + P_{V-E|E} + P_{E-T|E} \right)$$

By assertion, the vectors $P_{V-E|E}$ and $P_{T-E|E}$ are not known, but $P_{V-T|E}$ is known. The solution can be manipulated as follows:

First, change the addition of the vectors $P_{V-E|E}$ and $P_{E-T|E}$ to a subtraction:

$$P_{V-E|E} + P_{E-T|E} = P_{V-E|E} - P_{T-E|E}$$

Now express the subtraction as

$$P_{V-T|E} = P_{V-E|E} - P_{T-E|E}$$

The vector $P_{V-T|E}$ is the position vector pointing from the T system to the V system, resolved to the E system. Reverse the "to-from" indices by changing the sign:

$$-P_{T-V|E} = P_{V-T|E}$$

and substitute this result into the $P_{H-T|T}$ equation:

$$P_{H-T|T} = T_{T-E}\left(T_{V-E}^{-1}P_{H-V|V} - P_{T-V|E}\right)$$

By using a marching method, two simple rules, and an index matching technique, the rigorous equation involving position and angular resolution has been generated. Given the preceding numerical values, the point H is located at

$$P_{H-T|T} = \begin{bmatrix} \cos(\psi_T) & \sin(\psi_T) & 0 \\ -\sin(\psi_T) & \cos(\psi_T) & 0 \\ 0 & 0 & 1 \end{bmatrix}$$

$$\times \left\{ \begin{bmatrix} \cos(\psi_V) & \sin(\psi_V) & 0 \\ -\sin(\psi_V) & \cos(\psi_V) & 0 \\ 0 & 0 & 1 \end{bmatrix}^{-1} \begin{Bmatrix} 0.7071 \\ -1.414 \\ -3 \end{Bmatrix} - \begin{Bmatrix} 5 \\ 2 \\ 0 \end{Bmatrix} \right\}$$

$$P_{H-T|T} = \begin{bmatrix} 0.7071 & 0.7071 & 0 \\ -0.7071 & 0.7071 & 0 \\ 0 & 0 & 1 \end{bmatrix}$$

$$\times \left\{ \begin{bmatrix} 0.7071 & 0.7071 & 0 \\ -0.7071 & 0.7071 & 0 \\ 0 & 0 & 1 \end{bmatrix} \begin{Bmatrix} 0.7071 \\ -1.414 \\ -3 \end{Bmatrix} - \begin{Bmatrix} 5 \\ 2 \\ 0 \end{Bmatrix} \right\}$$

$$P_{H-T|T} = \begin{Bmatrix} -6.3639 \\ 1.414 \\ -3 \end{Bmatrix}$$

Looking at the diagram and extending the X axis of the T system in the negative direction, it is clear to see that the preceding position vector accurately describes the position of the H point, resolved to the T system.

2.6 Conclusions

This chapter introduced vectors. A vector specifies magnitude and direction when speaking of a single state such as velocity, position, or force. A vector is also a collection of states, which can be vectors themselves or scalar quantities such as temperature or pressure. Four questions must be answered when dealing with vectors that describe the position, velocity, force, or so forth in three degrees of freedom. Vectors are manipulated using straightforward rules of algebra. A good subscript notation makes the manipulation easy. Orientation matrices accomplish vector resolution. Some simple rules of thumb enable the reader to build the orientation matrices. One particular set of orientation matrices uses the NACA convention. The associated angles are the so-called Euler angles, and all of flight simulation uses these same angles in the same order.

Problems

2.1 Describe the distinction between the phrases "with respect to" and "resolved to."

2.2 Attach an axis system to an airplane such that the origin is at the center of gravity of the plane, the x axis points toward the front of the aircraft, and the y axis points in the direction of the right wing tip. The plane defined by the x and y axes should be parallel with the ground plane when the aircraft is sitting on the ground. Answer the following questions.
(a) Using a right-handed system, in what direction does the z axis point?
(b) Rotate the aircraft a positive 90 deg about the body y axis. Now rotate the aircraft a positive 90 deg about the body x axis. Next, rotate the aircraft negative 90 deg about the body y axis, and finally rotate the aircraft negative 90 deg about the body x axis. If the aircraft began parallel to the ground plane, facing directly away from you, which direction is it facing now, and where is the right wing tip relative to its starting point (above, below, forward, aft, left, right)?

2.3 In one step, write the inverse of the following orthonormal rotation matrix:

$$R = \begin{bmatrix} 0.3535 & 0.6124 & -0.7071 \\ -0.5732 & 0.7392 & 0.3536 \\ 0.7392 & 0.2803 & 0.6124 \end{bmatrix}$$

2.4 Find a three-axis rotation (that is, a rotation about the z axis, then the y axis, and finally the x axis) that generates the matrix in the preceding problem. Demonstrate that your answer is correct.

3
Axis Systems

3.1 Introduction

This chapter is quite possibly the most important chapter in this text, because it describes the most significant tool of any good simulation—axis systems. Axis systems provide a reference point or origin and a sense of positive displacement. Without a proper description of the axis system with respect to which a measurement is taken, it is useless to state that your coordinates are $(3, -4, 7)$. Even if you do specify the reference axes in exquisite detail, it may be more convenient to state a position with respect to some other point and oriented in other than some global (or universal) axis system. For instance, as the author writes, he is 5 ft to the east of, 6 ft north of, and 2 ft above the entrance to his work cubicle in Fort Worth. If the center of the universe is taken to be the north entrance to Coventry Lane in Arlington, Texas, the author's actual coordinates can only be estimated as 10,000 ft west of, 52,000 ft north of, and 20 ft above that origin. The same location was described twice, but with respect to two different axis systems. Before continuing with this chapter, the reader is encouraged to review Chapter 2, which presents details of axis system specification and transformation.

3.2 Axis Systems Used in Simulation

Flight simulations require at a minimum two axis systems. The first system is the Earth axes, which serve as an inertial frame. The second system is the body axes, with origin at the body center of gravity and (almost) rigidly attached to the aircraft. In practice, there are usually many other axes that are used to make life for the analyst simpler. The easiest way to show the where, how, and why of these axes is through example. So, begin the journey from the origin of Earth axes, through to the center of pressure on the left winglet of a typical single-main-rotor (SMR) helicopter as shown in Fig. 3.1.

3.3 Earth Axes

Despite overwhelming evidence to the contrary, this text begins with the assumption that the world is flat. The origin of the Earth axes is arbitrary. The origin could be the intersection of the equator, the prime meridian and mean

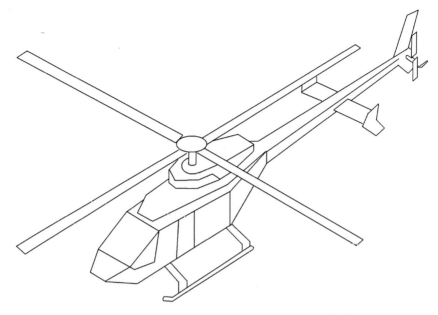

Fig. 3.1   Stylized representation of a single main rotor helicopter.

sea level, or it could be the top of the control tower at some airport of interest. So long as the origin does not move during the course of a time-domain simulation, it is a perfectly adequate inertial reference frame.

Having located the origin, displacement along one or more of a set of orthogonal axes attached rigidly to the origin describes the location of everything else. It is convenient to align these axes with the compass. The three axes are aligned with the axis labeled **N**orth, the axis labeled **E**ast, and the surface normal that points toward the center of the earth, **D**own. These three axes are mutually perpendicular and, when referred to in the order N, E, D, form a right-handed coordinate system. See Fig. 3.2.

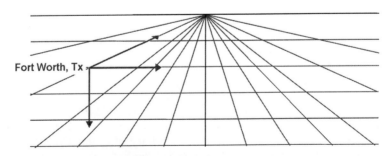

Fig. 3.2   Origin of the universe.

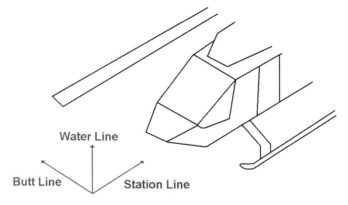

Fig. 3.3   Reference axes (station-line, butt-line, water-line axes).

3.4   Reference Axes

An aircraft has a set of axes assigned to it from which all points on the aircraft are measured. The origin of these axes is not usually located on the aircraft, but rather are forward and below the aircraft, as Fig. 3.3 makes clear.

The reference axes form a right-handed system. The x direction, measuring positive aft, is the *station line*. The y direction, measuring positive out toward the right wing, is the *butt line*. The z direction, measuring positive up, is called the *waterline*. All other parts of the aircraft are located from the origin of these axes. Knowing the location of the parts from the origin means that their distances from each other are also known. In particular, the location of each aircraft part from the center of gravity can be found once the center of gravity is located. This point is very important because the equations of motion for the aircraft are written about the center of gravity. Finding the center of gravity will be covered in a short while.

3.5   Body Axes

The body axes are a set of axes with origin at the center of gravity. The x, y, and z axes form a right-handed system. The x axis lies in the plane of symmetry and generally points forward. (Note: Helicopters do not always have a plane of symmetry, but they nearly do.) The y axis points to the right wing, normal to the plane of symmetry, and the z axis points down. See Fig. 3.4.

The body axes remain fixed to the center of gravity; they do not remain fixed to a particular point on the aircraft. For instance, the V-22 and XV-15 tiltrotor aircraft experience a significant forward shift of the center of gravity as the engine pylons move from helicopter orientation to airplane orientation. The B-1 bomber has a significant shift aft as the wings swing into supersonic cruise configuration. Of course, remembering that the center of gravity moves aft with the wing is mightily important when refueling. One well-known image of the B-1 that circulated on the Internet has the aircraft sitting on its tail, its nose gear a dozen feet in the air after refueling with the wings in the supersonic cruise configuration.

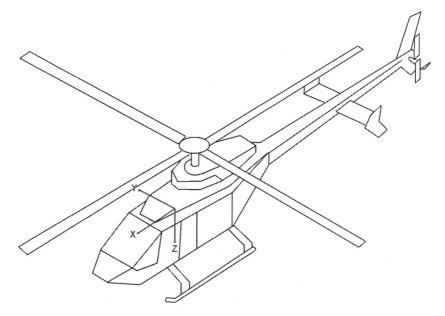

Fig. 3.4   Body axes.

3.6   Euler Angles

Euler angles are an agreed upon triple of angles that are used to transform a vector in Earth axes to a vector in body axes. By convention, the Euler angles perform three rotations in a specific order. First, rotate the aircraft about the body z axis, through the angle Ψ. This is called *yaw*. Per the right-hand convention, a positive rotation about the z axis moves the nose of the aircraft right as illustrated in Fig. 3.5.

Next, rotate the aircraft about the body y axis through the angle Θ. A positive rotation about the y axis raises the nose of the aircraft. This is called *pitch* and is shown in Fig. 3.6.

Finally, rotate the aircraft about its x axis through the angle Φ. A positive rotation about the x axis moves the right wing down and left wing up. This is called *roll*. Figure 3.7 shows a roll of 90 deg about the x axis.

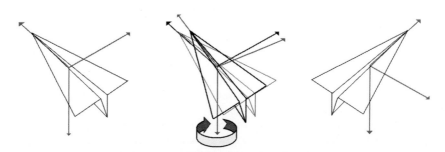

Fig. 3.5   Rotation about Z axis—yaw.

Fig. 3.6   Rotation about *Y* axis—pitch.

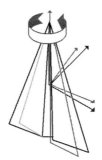

Fig. 3.7   Rotation about *X* axis—roll.

The order of the rotations is very important. Try this experiment at home with a paper airplane. Hold the airplane level, and point it toward some reference point such as the corner of the room. Now, turn the airplane first through 90 deg of yaw, then 90 deg of pitch, then 90 deg of roll, that is, do the rotations pictured. The airplane should be pointing straight up and oriented as if the only rotation had been 90 deg of pitch. Do the same experiment again, but this time rotate through roll first, then pitch, then yaw. The aircraft is now pointing straight down, with the top facing you. So, even though the same amount of angular motion was used around the same axes, the final orientation was very different. Conclusion: order is important. Remember, when going from Earth to body axes, rotate first about the yaw axis through Ψ, then the pitch axis through Θ, and finally the roll axis through Φ. This order is the NASA convention.

3.7   Individual Element Local Axes

Each element on an aircraft has some reference point on it that serves as the collection point for all forces and moments generated by that element. The reference point also serves as a distribution point for motion. By definition, the individual element local axes (IELA) are parallel to the body axes. The origins of the IELA are

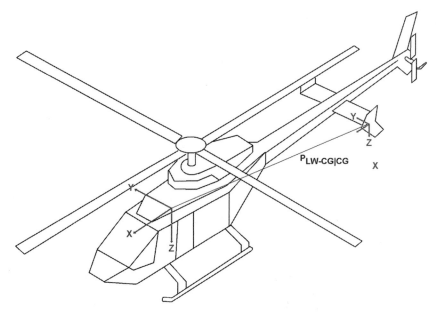

Fig. 3.8　Individual element local axes.

displaced from the body axes origin by a position vector P, which measures from the body-axis origin to the IELA origin. The P vector is used in the calculation of each element's local velocity and acceleration vector and its contribution to the forces and moments at the body axes origin. Figure 3.8 shows a vector measuring from the body axis origin to the IELA for the left winglet. *Remember, the IELA is a translation only from the center of gravity to the element reference point.*

3.8　Individual Element Reference Axes (IERA)

The individual element reference axes (IERA) are the axes that make the analysis most natural or easy to perform. For instance, most people think of a wing situated horizontally, with the x axis pointing toward the leading edge, the z axis pointing *down* toward the pressure side of the wing, and the y axis completing the right-hand system. Sometimes, as in Fig. 3.8, the wing is not situated horizontally. No matter. The same equations work regardless of the orientation of the wing. (The author once heard a second-year engineering student proclaim that Bernoulli's equations only worked on right-side-up wings. When a plane flew upside down, a different set of equations was required. That student eventually dropped out of engineering and ended up as a business major. I swear.) For the analysis to continue, the resolution of the velocity vector must change from the IELA to IERA. Then, the aerodynamics or inertial dynamics can proceed; the forces and moments can be calculated to the satisfaction of the analyst and those results resolved back to the IELA.

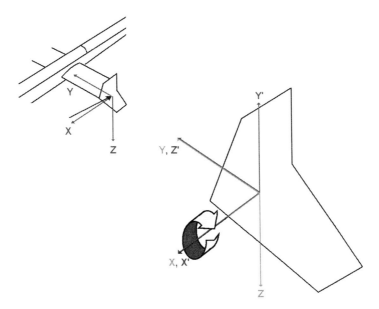

Fig. 3.9   Individual element reference axes.

The IELA and IERA have a common origin, so that only rotations are required. The equations may use as many rotations as desired. As shown in Chapter 2, the final rotation matrix always reduces to a three-axis representation using Euler rotation order. In Fig. 3.9, a rotation of -90 deg about the x axis positions the primed (IERA) axes in a way that puts the z' axis pointing toward the down side of the winglet, and the y' axis going out toward the tip of the winglet.

Remember, the IERA is a rotation only from the IELA to the final angular orientation of the element.

The journey from the Earth axes to the center of pressure on the left winglet of this helicopter is complete. To review, the aircraft's reference axes were measured from the Earth axes. Then, the aircraft's body axes translated from the reference axes. Another translation positions the aircraft's left winglet IELA with respect to the body axes, and finally, a rotation orients the left winglet IERA relative to the IELA. Its reminiscent of the old song about the foot bone being connected to the leg bone, the leg bone connected to the knee bone, etc. The next chapter covers the reason for this rigor.

3.9   Conclusions

As stated in the Introduction, this chapter is quite possibly the most important chapter in this text because it describes the most significant tool of any good simulation—axis systems. The chapter shows a systematic approach to thinking about how to navigate from the inertial axis system to a particular rivet on a whirling blade. The first of the five basic axis systems is the Earth frame, which will be taken as the inertial axes for the remainder of the text. The second basic system is familiar to designers or anyone who has prepared data for an analysis program. It is the reference frame, and it serves as the origin from which every particle of interest on the aircraft is measured. The standard notation is station line, butt line, and water line. The third set of axes is the body axes. Their origin locates the center of mass of the aircraft, so that one must remember that they are not fixed to the aircraft because the center of mass changes with fuel burn, cargo shifts, etc. The equations of motion are written about the body axes, and they are oriented relative to Earth axes with the Euler angles. The order of Euler angle operation is very important. The fourth basic system is the individual element local axes or IELA. The IELA is parallel to the body axes, and its origin is attached to a particle of interest. The IELA is a translation only from the center of gravity to the element reference point. The last axis system is the individual element reference axes or IERA. These axes share a common origin with the IELA, but are oriented so that the analysis for the element to which they are attached is expressed in a familiar way. The IERA is a rotation only from the IELA to the final angular orientation of the element.

Problems

3.1   Using the following figure of the helicopter, identify at least 10 IELA systems that will be needed to model the aircraft.

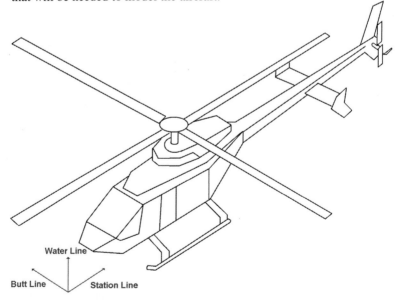

3.2   For each IELA, discuss what rotations you may want to perform to get to the IERA.

4
Kinematics and Flight Dynamics

4.1 Introduction

Simply put, kinematics is the study of motion exclusive of the influences of mass and gravity. In other words, the motion of mechanical linkages, pistons, levers, gears, etc. and how they move, regardless of the rate they move or the accelerations impressed on them, fall under the purview of kinematics. Flight dynamics uses kinematics to build a model of motion under the influence of gravity and other external forces.

Starting with first principles, this chapter shows the development of the six-degrees-of-freedom equations of motion for an aircraft. The text makes significant use of vector mechanics—linear algebra, vector resolution, and differentiation of a vector in a moving frame. These mathematical tools are vitally important in the description of rotors, propellers, and fuselages. The difference between *body axes* and *earth axes* has been explained, but will be revisited in greater detail when aircraft rates are discussed. This chapter is math intensive, and it must be thoroughly understood; otherwise, the best simulation one could hope to write would be an expensive video game that bore little resemblance to real-world behavior.

4.1.1 Euler Angles

The Euler angles Ψ, Θ, and Φ are the agreed-upon triple of angles that rotate a velocity or acceleration vector to body axes from Earth axes. By convention, the rotation is always about the z axis through Ψ, then about the new y axis through Θ, and finally about the newer x axis through Φ. Because this transformation is performed so often, it is given a specific name T_{BE} (read transform to body from Earth). Used in a mathematical sentence, it looks like this:

$$V_b = T_{\mathrm{BE}}(\Phi, \Theta, \Psi)V_e \tag{4.1}$$

where

$$T_{\mathrm{BE}}(\Phi, \Theta, \Psi) = R_x(\Phi)R_y(\Theta)R_z(\Psi) \tag{4.2}$$

Table 4.1   Accepted   names and directions in Earth axes

Symbol	Description
Vn(orth)	X-direction
Ve(ast)	Y-direction
Vd(own)	Z-direction

Table 4.2   Accepted   names and directions in body axes

Symbol	Description
u	X-direction
v	Y-direction
w	Z-direction

or, after expansion

$$T_{BE}(\Phi, \Theta, \Psi) = \begin{bmatrix} C_\Theta C_\Psi & C_\Theta S_\Psi & -S_\Theta \\ S_\Phi S_\Theta C_\Psi - C_\Phi S_\Psi & S_\Phi S_\Theta S_\Psi + C_\Phi C_\Psi & S_\Phi C_\Theta \\ C_\Phi S_\Theta C_\Psi + S_\Phi S_\Psi & C_\Phi S_\Theta S_\Psi - S_\Phi C_\Psi & C_\Phi C_\Theta \end{bmatrix} \quad (4.3)$$

The preceding expression employs a shorthand for the trigonometric functions; $C_\Theta = \cos(\Theta), S_\Phi = \sin(\Phi)$, etc. The inverse of this transformation is the transpose and yields inertial velocities resolved to the Earth if given the body-axis velocities. It is appropriate here to introduce the names usually used in flight dynamics for Earth-axis and body-axis linear velocities.

Tables 4.1 and 4.2 imply these definitions.

$$V_e = \{V_{\text{north}} \quad V_{\text{east}} \quad V_{\text{down}}\}^T = \{\dot{N} \quad \dot{E} \quad \dot{D}\}^T = \dot{P}_e$$
$$V_b = \{u \quad v \quad w\}^T \quad (4.4)$$

Use of the transpose form saves space. The symbol $\dot{P}_e$ emphasizes that V_e is a derivative of position over the face of the Earth. This definition becomes important when assembling the overall state equations of motion.

Example 4.1

An aircraft is moving north at 100 fps, with its nose 10 deg above the horizon. What are the body-axis velocities?

First, write the vector for the velocity of the aircraft in Earth axes:

$$V_e = \left\{ \begin{array}{c} V_{North} \\ V_{East} \\ V_{Down} \end{array} \right\} = \left\{ \begin{array}{c} \dot{North} \\ \dot{East} \\ \dot{Down} \end{array} \right\} = \left\{ \begin{array}{c} 100 \\ 0 \\ 0 \end{array} \right\}$$

where the overdot to indicate differentiation in time will be used exclusively, despite the danger of undesired differentiation performed by flies-joke lifted from [1].

Next, write the vector for the body-axis velocities:

$$V_b = \left\{ \begin{array}{c} u \\ v \\ w \end{array} \right\}$$

Now, write the transformation from Earth to body for a single rotation of 10 deg about the y axis. (Do not forget to convert degrees to radians!):

$$T_{BE}(0, 0.17452, 0) = Rx(0)Ry(0.17452)Rz(0)$$

$$T_{BE}(0, 0.17452, 0) = \begin{bmatrix} \cos(0.17452) & 0 & -\sin(0.17452) \\ 0 & 1 & 0 \\ \sin(0.17452) & 0 & \cos(0.17452) \end{bmatrix}$$

$$= \begin{bmatrix} 0.9849 & 0 & -0.1736 \\ 0 & 1 & 0 \\ 0.1736 & 0 & 0.9849 \end{bmatrix}$$

Finally,

$$V_b = T_{BE}(0, 0.17452, 0)V_e$$

yields

$$\left\{ \begin{array}{c} u \\ v \\ w \end{array} \right\} = \begin{bmatrix} 0.9849 & 0 & -0.1736 \\ 0 & 1 & 0 \\ 0.1736 & 0 & 0.9849 \end{bmatrix} \left\{ \begin{array}{c} 100 \\ 0 \\ 0 \end{array} \right\} = \left\{ \begin{array}{c} 98.49 \\ 0 \\ 17.36 \end{array} \right\}$$

Example 4.2

The airspeed indicator on an aircraft shows 100 kn and the magnetic compass shows a heading of 30° East of North. What is the aircraft's speed in the easterly direction in feet per second? Watch the units!

First, because no pitch or roll information is specified, assume these Euler angles are zero. Also, because no vertical rate or sideward rate is specified, assume these to be zero. Now, the vector for the velocity of the aircraft in fps as measured in body axes is

$$V_b = \left\{ \begin{array}{c} u \\ v \\ w \end{array} \right\} = \left\{ \begin{array}{c} 168.78 \\ 0 \\ 0 \end{array} \right\}$$

Next, write the vector for the velocity of the aircraft in Earth axes:

$$V_e = \left\{ \begin{array}{c} V_{\text{North}} \\ V_{\text{East}} \\ V_{\text{Down}} \end{array} \right\} = \left\{ \begin{array}{c} \dot{North} \\ \dot{East} \\ \dot{Down} \end{array} \right\}$$

Write the transformation from Earth to body for a single rotation of 30 deg about the z axis. (Do not forget to convert degrees to radians!)

$$T_{\text{BE}}(0,0,0.5236) = Rx(0)Ry(0)Rz(0.5236)$$

$$T_{\text{BE}}(0,0,0.5236) = \begin{bmatrix} \cos(0.5236) & \sin(0.5236) & 0 \\ -\sin(0.5236) & \cos(0.5236) & 0 \\ 0 & 0 & 1 \end{bmatrix} = \begin{bmatrix} 0.866 & 0.5 & 0 \\ -0.5 & 0.866 & 0 \\ 0 & 0 & 1 \end{bmatrix}$$

What is required is the transformation from body to Earth axes, which is the inverse or transpose of T_{BE}. The velocity in Earth axes is easily computed.

$$V_e = T^T{}_{\text{BE}}(0,0,0.5236)V_b$$

or

$$\left\{ \begin{array}{c} V_{\text{North}} \\ V_{\text{East}} \\ V_{\text{Down}} \end{array} \right\} = \begin{bmatrix} 0.866 & -0.5 & 0 \\ 0.5 & 0.866 & 0 \\ 0 & 0 & 1 \end{bmatrix} \left\{ \begin{array}{c} 168.78 \\ 0 \\ 0 \end{array} \right\} = \left\{ \begin{array}{c} 146.16 \\ 84.39 \\ 0 \end{array} \right\}$$

The easterly component of aircraft velocity is 84.39 fps.

4.1.2 Euler Rates

The angular orientation of the aircraft changes with time when an aircraft maneuvers. The time integral of the Euler rates defines the Euler angles.

$$\Phi = \int_0^t \dot{\Phi} \, dt$$

$$\Theta = \int_0^t \dot{\Theta} \, dt$$

$$\Psi = \int_0^t \dot{\Psi} \, dt \tag{4.5}$$

Table 4.3   Accepted names and directions in various axes

Symbol	Description
p	X-axis rate commonly called roll rate
q	Y-axis rate commonly called pitch rate
r	Z-axis rate commonly called yaw rate

The Euler rates are a function of the Euler angles and body-axis angular rates. Table 4.3 describes the accepted symbols for body axes.

Euler angles rotate Euler rates into body-axis angular rates. However, the transformation is different from the transformation for linear rates as discussed earlier. The process is complicated by the fact that the Euler angles themselves are involved in the transformation from Euler to body-axis rates. The process proceeds this way. Define the Euler rates as

$$\omega_e = \left\{ \begin{array}{c} \dot{\Phi} \\ \dot{\Theta} \\ \dot{\Psi} \end{array} \right\} = \dot{\alpha}_e \tag{4.6}$$

and the body-axis rates as

$$\omega_b = \left\{ \begin{array}{c} p \\ q \\ r \end{array} \right\} \tag{4.7}$$

The vector ω_e is not a true vector in the vector mechanics sense, but its invention here simplifies the discussions that follow. To get the body-axis rates from the Earth-axis rates, consider the Euler rates individually, resolve them individually to intermediate axes, and then finally to body axes. Define the Euler rate elemental vectors:

$$\omega_{\dot{\Phi}} = \left\{ \begin{array}{c} \dot{\Phi} \\ 0 \\ 0 \end{array} \right\}, \quad \omega_{\dot{\Theta}} = \left\{ \begin{array}{c} 0 \\ \dot{\Theta} \\ 0 \end{array} \right\} \quad \text{and} \quad \omega_{\dot{\Psi}} = \left\{ \begin{array}{c} 0 \\ 0 \\ \dot{\Psi} \end{array} \right\}$$

Rotate the $\omega_{\dot{\Psi}}$ vector through the angle Θ about the y axis, and add the result to the $\omega_{\dot{\Theta}}$ vector. Rotate that sum about the x axis through the angle Φ, and add the result to the $\omega_{\dot{\Phi}}$ vector. The result is the vector of body-axis angular rates.

$$\omega_b = \omega_{\dot{\Phi}} + R_x(\Phi)\lfloor \omega_{\dot{\Theta}} + R_y(\Theta)\omega_{\dot{\Psi}} \rfloor \tag{4.8}$$

Upon some expansion and rearrangement,

$$\omega_b = E(\Phi, \Theta)\omega_e = \begin{bmatrix} 1 & 0 & -\sin(\Theta) \\ 0 & \cos(\Phi) & \sin(\Phi)\cos(\Theta) \\ 0 & -\sin(\Phi) & \cos(\Phi)\cos(\Theta) \end{bmatrix} \omega_e \tag{4.9}$$

To get the Earth-axis rates in terms of body-axis rates, one must invert the transformation matrix E. Unlike the T_{BE} matrix, the inverse of E is not the transpose. Worse yet, the inverse is singular at pitch angles of $+/-90$ deg.

$$E^{-1}(\Phi, \Theta) = \begin{bmatrix} 1 & \sin(\Phi)\tan(\Theta) & \cos(\Phi)\tan(\Theta) \\ 0 & \cos(\Phi) & -\sin(\Phi) \\ 0 & \sin(\Phi)/\cos(\Theta) & \cos(\Phi)/\cos(\Theta) \end{bmatrix} \qquad (4.10)$$

This unfortunate singularity is sometimes called *gimbal lock*, a term familiar to pilots or mechanical engineers designing gyroscopic equipment. A mathematical tool called *quaternions* circumvents the gimbal-lock problem.

4.1.3 Quaternions

In 1843, William Rowan Hamilton found a general solution to the multiplication of triples. In that day and time, however, there were no applications for his elegant solution. He found the proverbial solution in search of a problem!. (The solution occurred to him while walking along the Royal Canal, and his solution so pleased him that he carved it into the stone of Brougham bridge where it is visible to this day.) In these times, quaternions have significant advantages in four-dimensional problems, such as the Minkowski diagrams found in Einstein's general and special theories of relativity and, more to the point of this discussion, rigid-body rotations without gimbal lock. (Gimbal lock occurs when the spin axis of a gyroscope aligns with the pivot axis of one of the outer gimbals. When this happens, unique definition of the direction of the spin axis is lost. Also, the gyroscope cannot break the alignment of the spin axis and the pivot axis, hence the name gimbal lock.) What follows is a cookbook approach to implementing quaternions without the invective brewing between engineers and graphic animators. For more information on quaternions, the interested reader is encouraged to visit the Internet links http://www.ericweisstein.com/encyclopedias/books/Quaternions.html or http://mathworld.wolfram.com/Quaternion.html, or seek Kuipers [2].

A quaternion uses four values to represent a three-dimensional vector. The first value is the scale or magnitude of the vector, and the remaining three values one can liken to the direction cosines. The quadruple is represented thus:

$$q_4 = (e_0, \quad E) \qquad (4.11)$$

where

$$E = \begin{Bmatrix} e_1 \\ e_2 \\ e_3 \end{Bmatrix} \qquad (4.12)$$

The multiplication of two quaternions a and b, where $a = \{a_0, \ a_1, \ a_2, \ a_3\} = \{a_0, \ A\}$ and $b = \{b_0, \ b_1, \ b_2, \ b_3\} = \{b_0, \ B\}$ is given by

$$a^*b = \{a_0 b_0 - A^T B, \quad a_0 B + b_0 A + A \times B\} \qquad (4.13)$$

Obviously, it is also a quadruple. This compact notation leads to a simple expression relating body rates and quaternion elements. First, represent differentiation as an operator by the quaternion equation:

$$D = \left\{ \frac{d}{dt}, \; 0 \right\} = \left\{ \frac{c}{2}, \; \frac{\omega_b}{2} \right\} \tag{4.14}$$

where

$$\omega_b = \left\{ \begin{array}{c} p \\ q \\ r \end{array} \right\} \tag{4.15}$$

The factor c is a defined by the constraint equation $c = 1 - q_4^T q_4$. Next, apply the differentiation operator to the quaternion q_4:

$$q_4 * D = \{e_0, \; E\} * \left\{ \frac{d}{dt}, \; 0 \right\} = \{e_0, \; E\} * \left\{ \frac{c}{2}, \; \frac{\omega_b}{2} \right\} \tag{4.16}$$

This leads to four coupled differential equations:

$$\left\{ \begin{array}{c} \dot{e}_0 \\ \dot{e}_1 \\ \dot{e}_2 \\ \dot{e}_3 \end{array} \right\} = \frac{1}{2} \begin{bmatrix} c & -p & -q & -r \\ p & c & r & -q \\ q & -r & c & p \\ r & q & -p & c \end{bmatrix} \begin{Bmatrix} e_0 \\ e_1 \\ e_2 \\ e_3 \end{Bmatrix} \tag{4.17}$$

The dynamic matrix on the right-hand side (RHS) is skew symmetric and easily remembered. Notice that without computational errors, $c = 0$. The c factor "builds in" an error correction. The initial conditions on the quaternion states are related to the Euler angles.

$$e_0 = \cos\left(\frac{\Phi}{2}\right) \cos\left(\frac{\Theta}{2}\right) \cos\left(\frac{\Psi}{2}\right) + \sin\left(\frac{\Phi}{2}\right) \sin\left(\frac{\Theta}{2}\right) \sin\left(\frac{\Psi}{2}\right)$$

$$e_1 = \sin\left(\frac{\Phi}{2}\right) \cos\left(\frac{\Theta}{2}\right) \cos\left(\frac{\Psi}{2}\right) - \cos\left(\frac{\Phi}{2}\right) \sin\left(\frac{\Theta}{2}\right) \sin\left(\frac{\Psi}{2}\right)$$

$$e_2 = \cos\left(\frac{\Phi}{2}\right) \sin\left(\frac{\Theta}{2}\right) \cos\left(\frac{\Psi}{2}\right) + \sin\left(\frac{\Phi}{2}\right) \cos\left(\frac{\Theta}{2}\right) \sin\left(\frac{\Psi}{2}\right)$$

$$e_3 = \cos\left(\frac{\Phi}{2}\right) \cos\left(\frac{\Theta}{2}\right) \sin\left(\frac{\Psi}{2}\right) - \sin\left(\frac{\Phi}{2}\right) \sin\left(\frac{\Theta}{2}\right) \cos\left(\frac{\Psi}{2}\right) \tag{4.18}$$

At any given time, the quaternion elements generate the following coordinate transformation:

$$T_{BE} = \begin{bmatrix} (e_0^2 + e_1^2 - e_2^2 - e_3^2) & 2(e_1 e_2 + e_0 e_3) & 2(e_1 e_3 - e_0 e_2) \\ 2(e_1 e_2 - e_0 e_3) & (e_0^2 - e_1^2 + e_2^2 - e_3^2) & 2(e_2 e_3 + e_0 e_1) \\ 2(e_1 e_3 + e_0 e_2) & 2(e_2 e_3 - e_0 e_1) & (e_0^2 - e_1^2 - e_2^2 + e_3^2) \end{bmatrix}$$

$$\tag{4.19}$$

whence

$$\Phi = \tan^{-1}\left[\frac{T_{BE}(2,3)}{T_{BE}(3,3)}\right]$$

$$\Theta = \sin^{-1}[-T_{BE}(1,3)]$$

$$\Psi = \tan^{-1}\left[\frac{T_{BE}(1,2)}{T_{BE}(1,1)}\right] \tag{4.20}$$

When quaternions are implemented, the constraint equation is often multiplied by some positive value (32 is a good value) in order to strengthen the constraint by penalizing the error. Also, certain checks for divide-by-zero conditions are employed. These are numeric issues that do not belong in the discussion of theory, but are mentioned as a practical matter. Quaternion usage is encouraged for complete generality in simulation, but the author acknowledges that the Euler-angle development is easier to remember and sufficient for most analyses.

4.1.4   Differentiation in a Moving Axis System

Elementary calculus teaches that the linear velocity of a particle is the time derivative of position:

$$v = \lim_{\Delta t \to 0}\left(\frac{\Delta P}{\Delta t}\right)$$

A second application gives acceleration:

$$a = \lim_{\Delta t \to 0}\left(\frac{\Delta v}{\Delta t}\right)$$

When the motion is rectilinear, these definitions are easy to apply. When the particle follows a curved path, the position vector changes in length and direction. Blakelock [3], among others, derives the first and second derivative in a moving frame.

Let S be the position vector of a particle relative to the origin of a system that is moving with angular rate ω relative to an inertial frame, that is,

$$S = \begin{Bmatrix} x \\ y \\ z \end{Bmatrix} \quad \text{and} \quad \omega = \begin{Bmatrix} \omega_x \\ \omega_y \\ \omega_z \end{Bmatrix} = \begin{Bmatrix} p \\ q \\ r \end{Bmatrix} \tag{4.21}$$

So

$$\frac{\partial S}{\partial t} = \begin{Bmatrix} \dot{x} \\ \dot{y} \\ \dot{z} \end{Bmatrix} = \begin{Bmatrix} u \\ v \\ w \end{Bmatrix} \tag{4.22}$$

The following expressions give the total velocity and acceleration in inertial space:

$$\frac{dS}{dt} = \frac{\partial S}{\partial t} + \omega \times S$$

$$\frac{d^2 S}{dt^2} = \frac{\partial}{\partial t}\left(\frac{dS}{dt}\right) + \omega \times \left(\frac{dS}{dt}\right)$$

$$= \frac{\partial^2 S}{\partial t^2} + 2\omega \times \frac{\partial S}{\partial t} + \frac{\partial \omega}{\partial t} \times S + \omega \times (\omega \times S)$$

Dot notation is now employed. Thus,

$$\frac{dS}{dt} = \dot{S} + \omega_b \times S \tag{4.23}$$

$$\frac{d^2 S}{dt^2} = \ddot{S} + \dot{\omega}_b \times S + 2\omega_b \times \dot{S} + \omega_b \times (\omega_b \times S) \tag{4.24}$$

Expression (4.24) represents the total linear acceleration of a particle of mass with respect to inertial space as it moves in a frame that rotates with respect to inertial space. The individual pieces have these meanings shown in Table 4.4.

The notation shown in most texts for velocity and acceleration comes from the expressions in Table 4.4 after expansion. The expanded versions of the expressions

Table 4.4 Explanation of acceleration terms

Term	Description
$\dfrac{d^2 S}{dt^2}$	Acceleration of the particle as seen by an inertial observer
$\ddot{S} = \begin{Bmatrix} \dot{u} \\ \dot{v} \\ \dot{w} \end{Bmatrix}$	Instantaneous linear acceleration of the particle as seen by the observer in the rotating frame
$\dot{\omega}_b \times S = \begin{Bmatrix} \dot{p} \\ \dot{q} \\ \dot{r} \end{Bmatrix} \times \begin{Bmatrix} x \\ y \\ z \end{Bmatrix}$	Acceleration of the particle as seen by an observer in the rotating frame because of an increase in rotation rate
$2\omega_b \times \dot{S} = 2\begin{Bmatrix} p \\ q \\ r \end{Bmatrix} \times \begin{Bmatrix} u \\ v \\ w \end{Bmatrix}$	So-called Coriolis acceleration
$\omega_b \times (\omega_b \times S) = \begin{Bmatrix} p \\ q \\ r \end{Bmatrix} \times \left(\begin{Bmatrix} p \\ q \\ r \end{Bmatrix} \times \begin{Bmatrix} x \\ y \\ z \end{Bmatrix}\right)$	Centripetal acceleration, which gives rise to centrifugal force

from Table 4.4 are

$$\frac{dS}{dt} = \begin{Bmatrix} v_x \\ v_y \\ v_z \end{Bmatrix} = \begin{Bmatrix} u + qz - ry \\ v + rx - pz \\ w + py - qx \end{Bmatrix} \qquad (4.25)$$

$$\frac{d^2S}{dt^2} = \begin{Bmatrix} a_x \\ a_y \\ a_z \end{Bmatrix} = \begin{Bmatrix} \dot{u} + \dot{q}z - \dot{r}y + 2q\dot{z} - 2r\dot{y} - (q^2 + r^2)x + pqy + prz \\ \dot{v} + \dot{r}x - \dot{p}z + 2r\dot{x} - 2p\dot{z} + pqx - (p^2 + r^2)y + qrz \\ \dot{w} + \dot{p}y - \dot{q}x + 2p\dot{y} - 2q\dot{x} + prx + qry - (p^2 + q^2)z \end{Bmatrix}$$

$$(4.26)$$

The reader easily sees that vector notation is much more compact, and there is significantly less danger of making a sign error in the arithmetic. Find more information on kinematics in Seckel [4] and McCormick [5].

4.2 Mass Properties

Imagine a body divided into infinitesimal elements of mass; call the ith element dm_i. The total mass is the sum.

$$m = \sum_{i=1}^{n} dm_i \qquad (4.27)$$

Mass is the inertial property that resists acceleration. If a body is subjected to a force, it does not instantly arrive at a new velocity. Instead, the object accelerates to a new velocity because of inertial resistance. A familiar example of inertial resistance is a stalled car. Anyone who has pushed a car knows that it is easier to keep the car moving than to start it moving. The resistive property of mass acts the same along all three axes.

A similar inertial resistance exists for angular motion. It is called the inertia tensor, and it is to angular motion what mass is to linear motion, except that the resistance to angular motion varies with the axis that receives the disturbing moment. The tensor is symmetric and is composed of six-different mass integrals.

$$\int (xy)\, dm = I_{xy}$$

$$\int (xz)\, dm = I_{xz}$$

$$\int (yz)\, dm = I_{yz}$$

$$\int (y^2 + z^2)\, dm = I_{xx}$$

$$\int (x^2 + z^2)\, dm = I_{yy}$$

$$\int (x^2 + y^2)\, dm = I_{zz} \qquad (4.28)$$

These integrals comprise the tensor as shown here:

$$I_n = \begin{bmatrix} I_{xx} & -I_{xy} & -I_{xz} \\ -I_{xy} & I_{yy} & -I_{yz} \\ -I_{xz} & -I_{yz} & I_{zz} \end{bmatrix} \qquad (4.29)$$

In aircraft that have a plane of symmetry, usually the X-Z plane, two of the products of inertia, namely, I_{xy} and I_{yz}, are zero.

The expressions for the elements of the inertia tensor are easy enough to recall, but one must also remember to insert negative signs on the off-diagonal terms. Another way exists to make the inertia tensor. Define a position vector $S_j = \begin{Bmatrix} x_j \\ y_j \\ z_j \end{Bmatrix}$ that measures from the center of mass to the jth element of mass.

$$dm_j = \rho_j (dx \cdot dy \cdot dz)$$

The slick, compact expression next builds the inertia tensor with proper signs on all elements in one easy step:

$$I_n = \sum_{j=1}^{n} [(S_j^T S_j)I - S_j S_j^T]\, dm_j \qquad (4.30)$$

4.2.1 Equations of Motion—Linear Motion

The rigid-body motion of all helicopters and airplanes can be described with six differential equations. The necessary tools to write those equations were developed in the preceding sections. But before the equations can be written, there is one more thing that needs review—Newton's three laws of motion.

1) Every object in a state of uniform motion tends to remain in that state of motion unless an external force is applied to it.

2) The relationship between an object's momentum (mv) and the applied force is $F = d(mv)/dt$. Force and momentum are vectors, and the change in momentum induced by the force is in the same direction as the force. When the mass is constant, this expression reduces to the more familiar $F = m(dv/dt) = ma$.

3) For every action there is an equal and opposite reaction.

The consequences of all three laws will be used throughout the remainder of this text. For the rest of this chapter, the most important of these laws is the second law because it permits a quantitative calculation of vehicle dynamics. There is an interesting historical note worth mentioning. The Greek philosopher Aristotle also stated a set of laws of motion. Under Aristotle, a constant force was required to maintain a constant velocity. That is, Aristotle might have written $F = kv$. Certainly, this expression is true for viscous dampers, but it misses the mark otherwise. Newton's brilliance was to recognize that force causes a change in velocity, not velocity itself. In this section the equations of linear and angular motion are presented in a modern context, but are developed from first principles that date back to Newton.

Linear momentum is the product of mass and velocity, and so it is a vector. Force causes momentum to change, and so we say

$$F = \frac{d(mV_b)}{dt} \qquad (4.31)$$

Apply Eq. (4.23) and the chain rule to the preceding expression, and expand the derivative:

$$F = \left(\frac{dm}{dt}\right) V_b + m \left(\frac{\partial V_b}{\partial t} + \omega_b \times V_b\right) = \dot{m} V_b + m \dot{V}_b + \omega_b \times m V_b \qquad (4.32)$$

Burning fuel and dropping stores changes the mass with respect to time. However, the product of the magnitude of the change of mass with time and its current velocity is usually considered small compared to the product of mass and the total acceleration. Equation (4.32) represents the rate of change of linear momentum as a result of applied forces. Those forces are aerodynamics, gravity, and others that can be lumped into a category called externally applied loads. Let the vector F_{ext} represent the external forces:

$$F_{ext} = \begin{Bmatrix} F_x \\ F_y \\ F_z \end{Bmatrix} \qquad (4.33)$$

If the mass is constant, then, **expressed concisely**, *the equation of linear motion is*

$$m \dot{V}_b + \omega_b \times (m V_b) = F_{ext} \qquad (4.34)$$

4.2.2 Equations of Motion—Angular Motion

Seckel [4] demonstrates how to develop the equations of angular motion from the equations of linear motion. What follows is taken from that reference, but expanded to reveal some of the details. Begin with the equation of linear acceleration, repeated here in vector notation and then rearranged slightly differently in expanded notation:

$$\frac{d^2 S}{dt^2} = \ddot{S} + \dot{\omega}_b \times S + 2\omega_b \times \dot{S} + \omega_b \times (\omega_b \times S)$$

After expansion and rearrangement,

$$\ddot{x} = \dot{u} + \dot{q}z - \dot{r}y + q(w + py - qx) - r(v + rx - pz)$$
$$\ddot{y} = \dot{v} + \dot{r}x - \dot{p}z + r(u + qz - ry) - p(w + py - qx)$$
$$\ddot{z} = \dot{w} + \dot{p}y - \dot{q}x + p(v + rx - pz) - q(u + qz - ry)$$

The left-hand side of the preceding expressions, after multiplying both sides by the mass of the jth differential mass element, is an inertial force:

$$(dF_x)_j = dm_j\ddot{x}$$
$$(dF_y)_j = dm_j\ddot{y}$$
$$(dF_z)_j = dm_j\ddot{z} \tag{4.35}$$

If the differential element of mass is located at point S_j, then the mass, besides resisting linear motion, also resists angular force (called a moment) about all three axes. The differential inertial moments are

$$dM_j = s_j \times dF_j$$

or

$$(dM_x)_j = (dF_z)_j y_j - (dF_y)_j z_j$$
$$(dM_y)_j = (dF_x)_j z_j - (dF_z)_j x_j$$
$$(dM_z)_j = (dF_y)_j x_j - (dF_x)_j y_j \tag{4.36}$$

For the duration of this discussion, all forces and moments act on the jth mass particle; summations imply sums over all of the masses, and so the subscript j is dropped.

By definition, the origin of the coordinate system is the center of gravity; therefore,

$$\sum (x)\, dm = 0$$
$$\sum (y)\, dm = 0$$
$$\sum (z)\, dm = 0 \tag{4.37}$$

Apply Eq. (4.37) to Eq. (4.35). What survive are the equations of linear motion:

$$m\ddot{x} = m(\dot{u} + qw - rv)$$
$$m\ddot{y} = m(\dot{v} + ru - pw)$$
$$m\ddot{z} = m(\dot{w} + pv - qu) \tag{4.38}$$

Combine Eqs. (4.28), (4.35–4.37). After tedious expansion, the equations of angular motion appear:

$$L = I_{xx}\dot{p} - I_{xy}\dot{q} - I_{xz}\dot{r} + (I_{zz} - I_{yy})qr + I_{yz}(r^2 - q^2) + I_{xy}pr - I_{xz}pq$$
$$M = -I_{xy}\dot{p} + I_{yy}\dot{q} - I_{yz}\dot{r} + (I_{xx} - I_{zz})pr + I_{xz}(p^2 - r^2) - I_{xy}qr + I_{yz}pq$$
$$N = -I_{xz}\dot{p} - I_{yz}\dot{q} + I_{zz}\dot{r} + (I_{yy} - I_{xx})pq + I_{xy}(q^2 - p^2) + I_{xz}qr - I_{yz}pr \tag{4.39}$$

With effort, this set of equations reduces to a much simpler vector and matrix notation. Let $M_{ext} = \begin{Bmatrix} L \\ M \\ N \end{Bmatrix}$ and recall the definition of body-axis angular velocity vector [Eq. (4.7)]. Then, expressed concisely, *the equation of angular motion is*

$$I_n \dot{\omega}_b + \omega_b \times I_n \omega_b = M_{ext} \tag{4.40}$$

Notice the similarity between the linear equation (4.34) and angular equation (4.40):

$$m\dot{V}_b + \omega_b \times (mV_b) = F_{ext}$$

$$I_n \dot{\omega}_b + \omega_b \times (I_n \omega_b) = M_{ext}$$

Expressions (4.34) and (4.40) are the generalized equations of motion. The 3×1 vectors F_{ext} and M_{ext} are the total external forces and moments respectively that are applied to the body at its center of gravity. In general, F_{ext} and M_{ext} will contain aerodynamic forces, landing-gear reaction loads, sling loads, and so forth. In addition, the F_{ext} vector will contain gravity forces.

4.2.3 Applied Forces and Moments

In essence, the rest of this text devotes itself to the development of the forces and moments that excite the equations of motion. A plethora of loads affects the equations of motion. Table 4.5 names and describes the types of loads that are commonly encountered in flight simulation.

Before the various force and moment models are developed, it is instructive to review the influences that a force and a moment have on a free body.

4.2.4 Effect of Forces

A force can be applied anywhere on a free body in any direction, and it can be pointing toward the center of gravity of the body, or it can be applied as a glancing blow to the body. As shown in Fig. 4.1, forces pointing toward the center of gravity excite linear motion in the direction of the force.

4.2.5 Effect of Moments

Applying a moment to the center of gravity of a body causes the body to rotate. Only if the moment is acting on a principal axis will the rotational acceleration be about that same axis; otherwise, the direction of acceleration will be about all three axes. See Fig. 4.2.

When a force acts on a body in a line that does not pierce the center of gravity, then the force is acting at a distance r, which is normal to the line of force. Figure 4.3 illustrates this. The product of the force and this arm is called a moment, and it produces angular acceleration. The force also causes linear acceleration along a line parallel with the direction of the applied force, but acting through the center of gravity.

Table 4.5 Names and description of various loads applied to the center of gravity

Types of loads	Description
Aerodynamic	Aerodynamics loads are caused by the motion of air around or through a body. Dynamic pressure (a function of velocity and air density), air direction, and body shape all determine the magnitude and direction of the resulting forces and moments.
Inertial	Inertial loads are caused by the acceleration of a body in any axis system. Acceleration comes from change in velocity magnitude and/or direction.
Gravity	Gravity loads are caused by the warp of the space–time continuum, or closer to home, the mutual attraction of two masses as described in classical physics. Gravity is always an attractive force and always acts on every particle in all bodies. The point where gravity acts without inducing angular acceleration is called the center of gravity.
Structural	Structural loads are caused by many things, but usually involve the deformation of a structure, such as landing gear, arresting hook, hub spring, etc. Some structures can store energy; some dissipate energy.
External	"External loads" is a catch-all phrase for just about everything else. The usual suspects include sling loads, magnetic forces, birds, trees, tiedowns, etc. Some device that is not associated usually with the aircraft applies external loads.

If the moment arm r is a three-component position vector of displacements of the force F, itself a three-component vector, then the moment caused by the glancing blow is found using the cross product

$$M = r \times F \qquad (4.41)$$

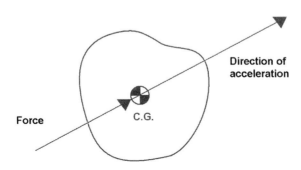

Fig. 4.1 Force applied to an arbitrary body.

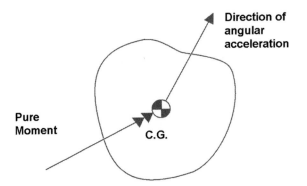

Fig. 4.2   Moment applied to an arbitrary body.

Of course, if a pure moment is applied to the structure as well as a force that causes a moment, then the total moment is

$$M_{\text{tot}} = M_{\text{pure}} + (r \times F) \tag{4.42}$$

Vector notation provides a neat and concise way to express the loads at the center of gravity as a result of loads applied at some other point on the body. Create a 6×1 vector that stores the applied forces and moments. The first three elements of the vector store the three forces in the order F_x, F_y, and F_z, and the second three elements of the vector store the three pure moments in the order M_x, M_y, and M_z. Let the Cartesian coordinates x, y, and z, which measure from point B (the point of interest) to point A (the point of load application), comprise the position vector r. Then the complete load vector at the point of interest is given by

$$P_B = \begin{Bmatrix} F_B \\ M_B \end{Bmatrix} = \begin{bmatrix} I & 0 \\ C(r) & I \end{bmatrix} \begin{Bmatrix} F_A \\ M_A \end{Bmatrix} = G(r)P_A \tag{4.43}$$

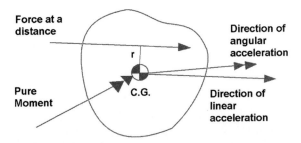

Fig. 4.3   Pure moment and a force applying a glancing blow to an arbitrary body.

where

$$F_A = \begin{Bmatrix} F_x \\ F_y \\ F_z \end{Bmatrix}, \quad M_A = \begin{Bmatrix} M_x \\ M_y \\ M_z \end{Bmatrix} \quad \text{and} \quad r = \begin{Bmatrix} x \\ y \\ z \end{Bmatrix} \quad (4.44)$$

The skew-symmetric cross-product operator was defined earlier. It is repeated here for convenience:

$$C(r) = \begin{bmatrix} 0 & -z & y \\ z & 0 & -x \\ -y & x & 0 \end{bmatrix} \quad (4.45)$$

I represents the 3×3 identity matrix, and P_A and P_B are the 6×1 vectors of forces and moments whose arrangement is obvious from the context of the preceding expression. The 6×6 G matrix is a geometric matrix that transmits local loads to some other point. In the preceding case, local loads applied at point A are transmitted to the point B on the body.

If more than one load is applied, the total body load is simply summed.

$$P_B = \sum_{i=1}^{n} G(r)_i P_{A_i} \quad (4.46)$$

A computationally clean way to express this is to place all of the 6×6 G matrices in a giant $6 \times 6n$ G matrix, and stack all of the corresponding loads vectors (each a 6×1 vector) in a $6n \times 1$ column vector, then do the simple calculation shown:

$$G = [G(r)_1 \quad G(r)_2 \quad \cdots \quad G(r)_n]$$

$$P_A = \begin{Bmatrix} P_{A1} \\ P_{A2} \\ \vdots \\ P_{An} \end{Bmatrix}$$

$$P_B = G P_A \quad (4.47)$$

4.2.6 Resolution of Forces and Moments

The preceding material assumed that the forces and moments were resolved to axes that are parallel to the aircraft body axes, which is not usually the case. For instance, a vertical fin may have its z axis pointing to the right, and a propeller may have its z axis pointing aft. The loads expressed in those axes must be resolved to axes that are parallel to the body axes before they can be summed at the body-axes origin. It is instructive to remember that the loads each element develops are a result of velocities and accelerations that started out in body axes and were transferred to the individual element reference axes or IERA, which are described in Chapter 3. The loads are computed in the IERA, and then are transformed back to the body-axes origin. Here are the steps to transfer velocities and accelerations from the body axes to the IERA, and then transfer the forces and moments from the IERA back to the body axes:

1) Linear velocities transfer directly from the origin of body axes to the origin of the individual element local axes, which Chapter 3 describes. That is, the velocity of the body with respect to the Earth resolved to body axes transfers directly to the origin of the IELA and is resolved to the IELA because these are parallel to the body axes:

$$V_{\text{IELA}-\text{E}|\text{B}} = V_{\text{B}-\text{E}|\text{B}}$$

2) Likewise, angular velocities transfer directly from the origin of the body axes to the IELA origin:

$$\omega_{\text{IELA}-\text{E}|\text{IELA}} = \omega_{\text{B}-\text{E}|\text{B}}$$

3) Angular velocities also contribute to linear velocities via a cross product with the position vector $R_{\text{IELA}-\text{B}|\text{B}}$, measuring from body axes to the IELA, resolved to body axes:

$$V_{\text{TOT:IELA}-\text{E}|\text{IELA}} = V_{\text{IELA}-\text{E}|\text{IELA}} + \omega_{\text{IELA}-\text{E}|\text{IELA}} \times R_{\text{IELA}-\text{B}|\text{B}}$$

4) Linear velocities undergo a vector resolution transformation from IELA to IERA:

$$V_{\text{TOT:IERA}-\text{E}|\text{IERA}} = T_{\text{IERA}-\text{IELA}}(\alpha_x, \alpha_y, \alpha_z)V_{\text{TOT:IELA}-\text{E}|\text{IELA}}$$

5) Angular velocities undergo a vector resolution transformation from IELA to IERA:

$$\omega_{\text{IERA}-\text{E}|\text{IERA}} = T_{\text{IERA}-\text{IELA}}(\alpha_x, \alpha_y, \alpha_z)\omega_{\text{IELA}-\text{E}|\text{IELA}}$$

6) Compute the forces and moments at that element. By definition, the forces and moments are resolved to the IERA.

7) Forces undergo a vector resolution transformation from IERA to IELA:

$$F_{\text{IELA}|\text{IELA}} = T_{\text{IERA}-\text{IELA}}^{T}(\alpha_x, \alpha_y, \alpha_z)F_{\text{IERA}|\text{IERA}}$$
$$= T_{\text{IELA}-\text{IERA}}(\alpha_x, \alpha_y, \alpha_z)F_{\text{IERA}|\text{IERA}}$$

8) Moments undergo a vector resolution transformation from IERA to IELA:

$$M_{\text{IELA}|\text{IELA}} = T_{\text{IERA}-\text{IELA}}^{T}(\alpha_x, \alpha_y, \alpha_z)M_{\text{IERA}|\text{IERA}}$$
$$= T_{\text{IELA}-\text{IERA}}(\alpha_x, \alpha_y, \alpha_z)M_{\text{IERA}|\text{IERA}}$$

9) Moments transfer directly to the body axes origin from the IELA origin:

$$M_{\text{B}|\text{B}} = M_{\text{IELA}|\text{IELA}}$$

10) Forces transfer directly to the body axes origin from the IELA origin:

$$F_{B|B} = F_{IELA|IELA}$$

11) Forces also contribute to moments via a cross product with the position vector measuring from the body axes to the IELA, resolved to body axes:

$$M_{TOT:B|B} = M_{B|B} + R_{IELA-B|B} \times F_{B|B}$$

The transformation matrix in steps 4, 5, 8, and 9 is a general three-angle Euler transformation. All of these steps are expressed very neatly and concisely if the linear and angular velocities and loads are stacked, and the cross-product operator is introduced:

$$V_{B,6} = \begin{Bmatrix} V_{B-E|B} \\ \omega_{B-E|B} \end{Bmatrix} \tag{4.48}$$

$$V_{IELA,6} = G^T(R_{IELA-B|B})V_{B,6} = \begin{bmatrix} I & C^T(R_{IELA-B|B}) \\ 0 & I \end{bmatrix} V_{B,6} \tag{4.49}$$

$$V_{IERA,6} = \begin{bmatrix} T_{IERA-IELA}(\alpha_x,\alpha_y,\alpha_z) & 0 \\ 0 & T_{IERA-IELA}(\alpha_x,\alpha_y,\alpha_z) \end{bmatrix} V_{IELA,6} \tag{4.50}$$

or

$$V_{IERA,6} = T_{IERA-IELA,6}(\alpha_x,\alpha_y,\alpha_z)V_{IELA,6}$$

$$P_{IERA} = \begin{Bmatrix} F_{IERA} \\ M_{IERA} \end{Bmatrix} = \begin{Bmatrix} \text{Elemental} \\ \text{Equations} \end{Bmatrix} \tag{4.51}$$

$$P_{IELA} = \begin{bmatrix} T_{IERA-IELA}^T(\alpha_x,\alpha_y,\alpha_z) & 0 \\ 0 & T_{IERA-IELA}^T(\alpha_x,\alpha_y,\alpha_z) \end{bmatrix} P_{IERA} \tag{4.52}$$

or

$$P_{IELA} = T_{IERA-IELA,6}^T(\alpha_x,\alpha_y,\alpha_z)P_{IERA}$$

$$P_{B|B} = G(R_{IELA-B|B})P_{IELA} = \begin{bmatrix} I & 0 \\ C(R_{IELA-B|B}) & I \end{bmatrix} P_{IELA} \tag{4.53}$$

$$\begin{Bmatrix} F_{B|B} \\ M_{TOT:B|B} \end{Bmatrix} = P_{B|B} \tag{4.54}$$

Because $C(R_{IELA-B|B})$ is skew symmetric, $C^T(R_{IELA-B|B}) = C(-R_{IELA-B|B})$. Also, because this formula was first mentioned in connection with forces and moments, it is defined in the sense already given rather than its negative, which would be the case if it were defined with velocities in mind. That is, the cross-product operator uses the left vector in a cross product as its argument. The subscript 6 used throughout Eqs. (4.48–4.54) indicates that the vector or transformation applies to a six-degrees-of-freedom vector or matrix.

4.2.7 Static vs Dynamic

Neither the mass nor the inertia tensor is constant. As an aircraft flies, it burns fuel. Furthermore, the pilot may drop off some passengers or pick up an external load. Mass changes; therefore, the inertia tensor changes. Even if mass remained constant for the duration of the simulation, variable geometry aircraft such as the V-22 with its movable pylons or the B-1 bomber with its swing wing move significant amounts of weight from one position to another. This weight shift changes the position arm of the pylon or wing with respect to the center of gravity; the shift also moves the center of gravity and changes the inertia tensor with time. Any good simulation must be able to account for these effects.

Having asserted these time effects, the equations of motion should actually be written:

$$\dot{m}V_b + m\dot{V}_b + \omega_b \times (mV_b) = F_{\text{ext}}$$

$$\dot{I}_n\omega_b + I_n\dot{\omega}_b + \omega_b \times (I_n\omega_b) = M_{\text{ext}} \tag{4.55}$$

or, after rearranging:

$$m\dot{V}_b + \omega_b \times (mV_b) = F_{\text{ext}} - \dot{m}V_b$$

$$I_n\dot{\omega}_b + \omega_b \times (I_n\omega_b) = M_{\text{ext}} - \dot{I}_n\omega_b \tag{4.56}$$

However, although the change in mass and inertia is important, usually the rate of change of these quantities is small when compared to the perturbing forces and moments. Therefore, it is customary and acceptable to simply drop the terms involving the time derivatives of the mass properties. An important exception to this statement comes with missile or rocket equations of motion. These topics are specifically uninvited to this party.

4.3 Overall States of an Aircraft

These are the equations of linear and angular motion, as derived earlier, with one small change.

$$M_b\dot{V}_b + \omega_b \times (mV_b) = F_{\text{ext}}$$

$$I_n\dot{\omega}_b + \omega_b \times (I_n\omega_b) = M_{\text{ext}} \tag{4.57}$$

M_b is the mass matrix. It is diagonal and has the same value of mass along the diagonal. Expression (4.2) showed how the body-axis linear velocities relate to Earth-axis velocities:

$$V_b = T_{\text{BE}}(\Phi, \Theta, \Psi)V_e \quad \text{and} \quad V_e = T_{\text{BE}}^{-1}(\Phi, \Theta, \Psi)V_b = \dot{P}_e \tag{4.58}$$

The so-called Euler angles Ψ, Θ, and Φ are the agreed-upon triple of angles that rotate to body axes a vector initially resolved to Earth axes. The Euler angles are not constant. They change as the aircraft rolls, loops, and spins; they are the time integral of the Euler rates:

$$\alpha_e = \begin{Bmatrix} \Phi \\ \Theta \\ \Psi \end{Bmatrix} = \begin{Bmatrix} \int_0^t \dot{\Phi}\,dt \\ \int_0^t \dot{\Theta}\,dt \\ \int_0^t \dot{\Psi}\,dt \end{Bmatrix} \tag{4.59}$$

The time derivative of Eq. (4.59), combined with expressions (4.6), (4.7), (4.9), and (4.10) give the relationship between body-axis angular rates and Euler rates:

$$\dot{\alpha}_e = \omega_e = E^{-1}(\Phi,\Theta)\omega_b \tag{4.60}$$

Recall that the $E^{-1}(\Phi,\Theta)$ matrix is singular at $\Theta = \pm\pi/2$. If necessary, quaternions can be used instead to find Euler angles as the integral of body rates.

Now comes a stunning demonstration of the convenience of linear algebra. The complete set of 12 equations that describes the motion of the six-degrees-of-freedom aircraft is contained in just four differential vector expressions!

$$\begin{aligned}
\dot{P}_e &= T_{BE}^{-1}(\Phi,\Theta,\Psi)V_b = T_{BE}^{-1}(\alpha_e)V_b \\
\dot{V}_b &= M_b^{-1}[F_{ext} - \omega_b \times (mV_b)] \\
\dot{\omega}_b &= I_n^{-1}[M_{ext} - \omega_b \times (I_n\omega_b)] \\
\dot{\alpha}_e &= E^{-1}(\Phi,\Theta)\omega_b = E^{-1}(\alpha_e)\omega_b
\end{aligned} \tag{4.61}$$

This notation for the equations of motion is compact, n'est pas? And in this format, the equations do not look nearly so formidable. This is not to say that the solution of these equations is a trivial matter. Even when the equations are forced into simple form by assuming a plane of symmetry and confining motion to the X-Z plane, these equations are nonlinear and intractable. Digital and/or analog computation is almost always required. However, if the equations are cast correctly, the reader is reasonably assured that the solution is an acceptable simulation of aircraft motion.

In the next two sections, linearized forms of Eqs. (4.61) present an homage to classical analysis of longitudinal and lateral motion.

4.3.1 Longitudinal Equations of Motion

If the aircraft under study has a plane of symmetry, usually the X-Z plane, then some convenient things happen. First, the I_{xy} and I_{yz} moments of inertia are zero; therefore, the inertia matrix reduces to

$$I_n = \begin{bmatrix} I_{xx} & 0 & -I_{xz} \\ 0 & I_{yy} & 0 \\ -I_{xz} & 0 & I_{zz} \end{bmatrix} \tag{4.62}$$

From the third of Eqs. (4.61), the moment equation about the Y axis reduces to the simple expression:

$$I_{yy}\dot{q} = M_y = M \tag{4.63}$$

(Do not confuse the italicized M, which represents the pitching moment, with the M_b before it, which stands for the mass matrix.) This expression means that roll and yaw rates and accelerations are decoupled from pitch rate and acceleration—motion about the roll and yaw axes does not cause, nor is it caused by, motion about the pitch axis. Because of this fact, angular motion may be constrained to lie in the X-Z plane with little regret, that is, roll and yaw rates and accelerations are constrained to be zero. Also, because motion only in the X-Z plane is allowed, the Y direction equation of linear motion is ignored, which reduces the force equations along the X and Z axes to the simple expressions:

$$m\dot{u} = -mqw + F_x$$
$$m\dot{w} = mqu + F_z \tag{4.64}$$

The conversion of body-axis pitch rate to Euler pitch rate simplifies to

$$\dot{\Theta} = q\cos\Phi \tag{4.65}$$

If the roll angle starts at zero, it remains at zero, and the Euler pitch rate becomes

$$\dot{\Theta} = q \tag{4.66}$$

At this point, the X and Z direction forces need some embellishment. Gravity and aerodynamic forces comprise the F_x and F_z terms. Weight points toward the center of the Earth. Resolved to body axes, the X- and Z-gravity components are

$$G_x = -mg\sin(\Theta)$$
$$G_z = mg\cos(\Phi)\cos(\Theta) \tag{4.67}$$

Near a reference point, a Taylor series truncated after the first term models the gravity equations nicely. Let Φ_0 and Θ_0 represent the reference values of roll and pitch angle, and let $\Delta\Phi$ and $\Delta\Theta$ be the small excursions from the reference point. Then

$$G_x = -mg\sin(\Theta_0) - mg\cos(\Theta_0)\Delta\Theta$$
$$G_z = mg\cos(\Phi_0)\cos(\Theta_0) - mg\sin(\Phi_0)\cos(\Theta_0)\Delta\Phi$$
$$- mg\cos(\Phi_0)\sin(\Theta_0)\Delta\Theta \tag{4.68}$$

Likewise, a Taylor-series expansion about the same reference point provides a reasonable model of the aerodynamic forces and moments. For instance, to show that the X force is a function of body-axis velocities u and w, then the following expansion works:

$$X = X_0 + \frac{\partial X}{\partial u}\Delta u + \frac{\partial X}{\partial w}\Delta w$$

For ease and clarity, the literature often expresses the partial derivatives with a shorthand notation, of which the following is an example:

$$X_u = \frac{\partial X}{\partial u}$$

This text will adopt that shorthand. The Taylor-series aerodynamic force and moment model becomes

$$X = X_0 + X_u \Delta u + X_w \Delta w + X_q \Delta q + X_\Theta \Delta \Theta + X_{c_i} \Delta c_i$$
$$Z = Z_0 + Z_u \Delta u + Z_w \Delta w + Z_q \Delta q + Z_\Theta \Delta \Theta + Z_{c_i} \Delta c_i$$
$$M = M_0 + M_u \Delta u + M_w \Delta w + M_q \Delta q + M_\Theta \Delta \Theta + M_{c_i} \Delta c_i \tag{4.69}$$

The c_i vector represents an unspecified number of controls. The other partial derivatives are defined similarly. Assembling all of these pieces, the simplified *longitudinal equations of motion* are

$$m\dot{u} = -mqw - mg \sin \Theta + X_0 + X_u \Delta u + X_w \Delta w + X_q \Delta q + X_\Theta \Delta \Theta + X_{c_i} \Delta c_i$$
$$m\dot{w} = mqu + mg \cos \Phi \cos \Theta + Z_0 + Z_u \Delta u + Z_w \Delta w + Z_q \Delta q$$
$$+ Z_\Theta \Delta \Theta + Z_{c_i} \Delta c_i$$
$$I_{yy}\dot{q} = M_0 + M_u \Delta u + M_w \Delta w + M_q \Delta q + M_\Theta \Delta \Theta + M_{c_i} \Delta c_i$$
$$\dot{\Theta} = q \cos \Phi \tag{4.70}$$

These equations are extremely useful for sanity checks and stability analysis. A similar set exists for the lateral equations, derived next.

4.3.2 Lateral Equations of Motion

Again, assume the aircraft has a plane of symmetry. The rolling-, pitching-, and yawing-moment equations are:

$$I_{xx}\dot{p} - I_{xz}\dot{r} - I_{xz}pq - (I_{yy} - I_{zz})qr = M_x = L$$
$$I_{yy}\dot{q} + (I_{xx} - I_{zz})pr + I_{xz}(p^2 - r^2) = M_y = M$$
$$I_{zz}\dot{r} - I_{xz}\dot{p} - (I_{xx} - I_{yy})pq + I_{xz}qr = M_z = N \tag{4.71}$$

The text uses L, M, and N as the names of the moments about the X, Y, and Z axes, which follows NASA convention. Context eliminates confusion about whether L means lift or rolling moment, and whether M means mass or pitching moment.

The pitch acceleration equation is decoupled from the roll, yaw acceleration equations, and so is ignored for the remainder of this development. Because roll rate and yaw rate are usually small, their product is even smaller, and so the pitch-moment equation is safely discarded, and Eq. (4.71) reduce to

$$I_{xx}\dot{p} - I_{xz}\dot{r} = L$$
$$I_{zz}\dot{r} - I_{xz}\dot{p} = N \tag{4.72}$$

or, after inversion, and expansion

$$\dot{p} = \frac{(I_{zz}L + I_{xz}N)}{(I_{xx}I_{zz} - I_{xz}^2)}$$
$$\dot{r} = \frac{(I_{xz}L + I_{xx}N)}{(I_{xx}I_{zz} - I_{xz}^2)} \tag{4.73}$$

The Y-direction force equation is the only force represented in the lateral equations:

$$m\dot{v} = -mru + mpw + F_y \qquad (4.74)$$

The conversion of body roll and yaw rate to Euler roll and yaw rate simplifies to

$$\dot{\Phi} = p + r \cos \Phi \tan \Theta$$

$$\dot{\Psi} = r \left(\frac{\cos \Phi}{\cos \Theta} \right) \qquad (4.75)$$

For small angles, the Euler roll and yaw rates are

$$\dot{\Phi} \approx p + r\Theta \approx p$$

$$\dot{\Psi} \approx r \qquad (4.76)$$

Gravity contributes only to the Y-force equation and is found using the T_{BE} matrix:

$$G_y = mg \sin \Phi \cos \Theta \qquad (4.77)$$

Expanding the aerodynamic forces and moments in a Taylor series,

$$Y = Y_0 + Y_u \Delta u + Y_w \Delta w + Y_q \Delta q + Y_\Phi \Delta \Phi + Y_\Psi \Delta \Psi + Y_{c_i} \Delta c_i$$
$$L = L_0 + L_u \Delta u + L_w \Delta w + L_q \Delta q + L_\Phi \Delta \Phi + L_\Psi \Delta \Psi + L_{c_i} \Delta c_i$$
$$N = N_0 + N_u \Delta u + N_w \Delta w + N_q \Delta q + N_\Phi \Delta \Phi + N_\Psi \Delta \Psi + N_{c_i} \Delta c_i \qquad (4.78)$$

Assembling all of these pieces, the simplified *lateral equations of motion* are

$$\dot{v} = -ru + pw + g \sin \Phi \cos \Theta + \frac{Y}{m}$$

$$\dot{p} = \frac{(I_{zz}L + I_{xz}N)}{(I_{xx}I_{zz} - I_{xz}^2)}$$

$$\dot{r} = \frac{(I_{xz}L + I_{xx}N)}{(I_{xx}I_{zz} - I_{xz}^2)}$$

$$\dot{\Phi} = p + r \cos \Phi \tan \Theta$$

$$\dot{\Psi} = r \frac{\cos \Phi}{\cos \Theta} \qquad (4.79)$$

These equations are also useful for sanity checks and stability analysis.

N.B.: Equations (4.70) and (4.79) are not the linearized equations used in stability analysis. They are partially decoupled, nonlinear equations in which some attempt has been made to combine linearized aerodynamics with nonlinear dynamic and kinematic relationships. To get the linearized equations, the gravity terms must be expanded in a Taylor series. The trim aerodynamic forces then exactly cancel the gravity terms. The total velocity terms in the centripetal acceleration must be expanded as, for instance, $u = u_0 + \Delta u$, and products of perturbation variables discarded as being higher order. Also, all angles are presumed small, and trim longitudinal angles do not affect lateral dynamics and vice versa. (The assumptions required for classical linearized equations of motion almost seem crippling. Despite the assumptions, control laws based on these assumptions fair well.) What remains are the classical linearized equations of motion:

$$m\dot{u} = \Delta X - mqw_0 - mg(\cos\Theta_0)\Delta\Theta$$
$$m\dot{w} = \Delta Z + mqu_0 - mg(\sin\Theta_0)\Delta\Theta$$
$$I_{yy}\dot{q} = \Delta M$$
$$\dot{\Theta} = q$$

where

$$\Delta X = X_u\Delta u + X_w\Delta w + X_q\Delta q + X_\Theta\Delta\Theta + X_{c_i}\Delta c_i$$
$$\Delta Z = +Z_u\Delta u + Z_w\Delta w + Z_q\Delta q + Z_\Theta\Delta\Theta + Z_{c_i}\Delta c_i$$
$$\Delta M = M_u\Delta u + M_w\Delta w + M_q\Delta q + M_\Theta\Delta\Theta + M_{c_i}\Delta c_i$$

and

$$m\dot{v} = -mru_0 + mpw_0 + mg(\cos\Phi_0)\Delta\Phi + \Delta Y$$
$$I_{xx}\dot{p} - I_{xz}\dot{r} = \Delta L$$
$$I_{zz}\dot{r} - I_{xz}\dot{p} = \Delta N$$
$$\dot{\Phi} = p$$
$$\dot{\Psi} = r$$

where

$$\Delta Y = Y_u\Delta u + Y_w\Delta w + Y_q\Delta q + Y_\Phi\Delta\Phi + Y_\Psi\Delta\Psi + Y_{c_i}\Delta c_i$$
$$\Delta L = L_u\Delta u + L_w\Delta w + L_q\Delta q + L_\Phi\Delta\Phi + L_\Psi\Delta\Psi + L_{c_i}\Delta c_i$$
$$\Delta N = N_u\Delta u + N_w\Delta w + N_q\Delta q + N_\Phi\Delta\Phi + N_\Psi\Delta\Psi + N_{c_i}\Delta c_i$$

The decoupled equations of motion are presented out of respect for history. Helicopters rarely possess a plane of symmetry. Even if one does exist from the mass perspective, single main rotor helicopters exhibit aerodynamic coupling between the longitudinal and lateral equations. Thrust from the main rotor is directed primarily *along* the z axis (longitudinal equation). The rotor generates a torque, which is measured *about* the z axis (lateral equation). For this reason and the convenience of linear algebra, the fully coupled equations will be used the majority of the time.

The great challenge lies in finding the expressions for the external forces and moments. Some expressions are mind-numbingly simple. Gravity is a no-brainer. Rockets, jets, and propellers are fairly straightforward. Fuselage models are a bit more complex, especially if they are flexible. Landing-gear models fall into this category as well. Wings are much more complex, owing to their unique aerodynamic properties. Helicopter rotor dynamics and aerodynamics are the coin of the realm for mathematical masochists. A large portion of the remainder of this text is devoted to deriving the dynamic models for each of these elements and others as the need occurs.

4.4 Conclusions

Kinematics is the study of motion exclusive of the influences of mass and gravity. Flight dynamics uses kinematics to model the motion of a mass under the influence of gravity and other external forces. This chapter started with first principles to develop the six-degrees-of-freedom equations of motion for an aircraft. Along the way, the reader was reminded of Euler angles. The difference between Euler rates and body angular rates was discussed, and their interconnection using the classical formulation and with quaternions was presented. Differentiation in a moving axis system preceded the development of the linear and angular equations of motion in body axes. The reader will appreciate that all important effects are included in the equations of motion when vector methods are employed. Finally, the forcing functions for the equations of motion are the real challenge, and so the remaining chapters are devoted to deriving them.

References

[1]Rainville, Earl D., *Elementary Differential Equations*, Macmillan, New York, 1958, p. 141.

[2]Kuipers, J. B., *Quaternions and Rotation Sequences: A Primer with Applications to Orbits, Aerospace, and Virtual Reality*, Princeton Univ. Press, Princeton, NJ, 1998.

[3]Blakelock, J. H., *Automatic Control of Aircraft and Missiles*, Wiley, New York, 1965, pp. 296–297.

[4]Seckel, E., *Stability and Control of Airplanes and Helicopters*, Academic Press, New York, 1964, pp. 44–47.

[5]McCormick, B. W., *Aerodynamics, Aeronautics and Flight Mechanics*, Wiley, New York, 1979, pp. 591–594.

Problems

4.1 A ground observer measures your speed over the ground at 100 kn and measures your rate of climb at 500 ft per minute. Your aircraft has a nose-down pitch angle of 5 deg. What are the body-axis velocities u, v, and w in feet per second?

4.2 You are in a standard rate turn (3 deg/s) to the right, as observed by someone on the ground. Your pitch angle is 5 deg nose up, and your roll angle is 10 deg right wing down. What are your body-axis angular rates in rad/s?

4.3 Using expression (4.34), determine the instantaneous acceleration of a body with the following properties, states, and applied forces.

$$m = 6, \quad V = \begin{Bmatrix} 100 \\ 50 \\ 25 \end{Bmatrix}, \quad \omega = \begin{Bmatrix} -1 \\ -2 \\ -3 \end{Bmatrix}, \quad F_{\text{ext}} = \begin{Bmatrix} 1000 \\ 0 \\ -1000 \end{Bmatrix}$$

4.4 Using expression (4.40), determine the instantaneous angular accelerations of a body with the following properties, states, and applied moments.

$$I_n = \begin{bmatrix} 1000 & 0 & -100 \\ 0 & 2000 & 0 \\ -100 & 0 & 2000 \end{bmatrix}, \quad \omega = \begin{Bmatrix} -1 \\ -2 \\ -3 \end{Bmatrix}, \quad M_{\text{ext}} = \begin{Bmatrix} 1000 \\ 0 \\ -1000 \end{Bmatrix}$$

4.5 The assertion that the mass and inertia tensors remain constant during a simulated flight was briefly discussed. Give at least two examples of when the weight change is large and rapid and may make the constancy assertion invalid.

5
Atmosphere

5.1 Introduction

The 20th century philosopher William Cosby once pondered, "Why is there air?" His answer was that air exists to blow up volleyballs and basketballs. With all due respect, Cosby completely missed the point. Air is used to hold up airplanes and helicopters. The study of air in motion and how this motion generates forces is called aerodynamics.

Aerodynamic forces are the result of dynamic pressure, some angle of attack, and geometric manipulation. Air has weight; it is viscous, and its properties or states change with altitude and temperature. A fundamental understanding of the medium through which aircraft fly is essential.

5.2 Static Properties of Air—Standard-Day Definition

Aerodynamicists use the properties listed in Table 5.1 as the definition of a standard day.

A standard day establishes a reference point from which the performance of an aircraft can be measured on other days. The definition of the standard day also includes the important phrase "measured at mean sea level." Stop the motion of all of the oceans, and draw a line in the sand where the sea meets the shore— that line marks mean sea level. As one moves above or below this line, the properties of the atmosphere change. Dommasch et al. [1] and Abbott and Von Doenhoff [2] provide the mathematical models in great detail. What follows is a lay description.

Imagine a square column of air one unit wide, one unit deep, and as high as the sensible atmosphere. Look at an infinitesimal chunk of it, dh units high, taken from somewhere in the column. The product of the infinitesimal volume of that chunk and ρ, the density of the air within, is the mass. In anticipation of pressure variation with altitude, the pressure P acting on the lower face of the volume changes to $P + dP$ acting on the upper face. Figure 5.1 shows this chunk with all of the pressure and gravity forces acting on it.

The chunk weighs

$$mg = \rho g(dh)(1)(1) \tag{5.1}$$

Table 5.1　Some properties of the standard day

Property	SSL value	Description
Pressure	2116.217 lbs/ft^2 101325 N/m^2	Weight of a column of air divided by its 　base area, as measured at mean sea level
Density	0.0023768 slugs/ft^3 1.22596 kgm/m^3	Mass of one cubic foot of air, measured at 　mean sea level
Temperature	518.67 R	Temperature above absolute zero, in 　degrees Rankine
Kinematic viscosity	1.5723×10^4 ft^2/s 1.4607×10^3 m^2/s	Viscosity divided by density. This is a 　measure of the "stickiness" of the air
Speed of sound	1116.89 ft/s 340.428 m/s	Speed of sound at sea level on a standard 　day

Sum the vertical forces, and set them equal to zero for a static atmosphere.

$$\sum Fz = -P(1)(1) + (P + dP)(1)(1) + \rho g(dh)(1)(1) = 0$$

$$\therefore dP = -\rho g(dh) \tag{5.2}$$

The equation of state for a gas relates pressure, density, and temperature with a universal gas constant usually given the name R. (See the Home Experiments section at the end of this chapter for an exciting demonstration of this equation.) The equation is

$$P = \rho RT \tag{5.3}$$

or, solving for the density

$$\rho = \frac{P}{RT}$$

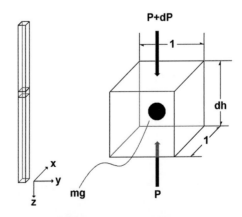

Fig. 5.1　Chunk of air showing pressures acting on it.

Substitute this expression for density into Eq. (5.2), and rearrange so that all references to pressure are on the left-hand side.

$$\frac{dP}{P} = -\frac{g(dh)}{RT} \tag{5.4}$$

Experimental observation suggests that, up to 36,089 ft, the variation of the air temperature with altitude is a constant, or nearly so, and has the symbol a. The industry name for this variation is *lapse rate*.

$$\frac{dT}{dh} = a$$

Multiply and divide the right-hand side (RHS) of expression (5.4) by dT and regroup. The variation of pressure from some reference value is known if the variation of temperature from some reference is known:

$$\frac{dP}{P} = -\frac{g(dT)(dh)}{RT(dT)} = -\frac{g}{Ra}\frac{dT}{T} \tag{5.5}$$

The values of the constants are as follows:

$$g = 9.80665 \, \text{m/s}^2 = 32.1742 \, \text{ft/s}^2$$

$$R = 287.053 \, \text{m}^2/\text{s}^2\text{-K} = 1716.562 \, \text{ft}^2/\text{s}^2\text{-}{}^\circ\text{R}$$

$$a = -6.5 \, \text{K}/1000 \, \text{m} = -3.566 \, {}^\circ\text{F}/1000 \, \text{ft}$$

Substitute these values into Eq. (5.5).

$$\frac{dP}{P} = 5.2561\frac{dT}{T}$$

Integrate both sides, and then take the exponential of both sides:

$$\frac{P_2}{P_1} = \left(\frac{T_2}{T_1}\right)^{5.2561} \tag{5.6}$$

Thus, *this equation relates any two points in the atmosphere.* The literature gives the symbol δ to the pressure ratio.

$$\delta = \frac{P_2}{P_1} \tag{5.7}$$

The temperature ratio has the symbol Θ.

$$\Theta = \frac{T_2}{T_1} \tag{5.8}$$

The ratio symbols express concisely the relationship between pressure and temperature ratio:

$$\delta = \Theta^{5.2561} \tag{5.9}$$

Very often, P_1 is the standard sea-level value of $14.7\,\text{lb/in.}^2$ or $2117\,\text{lb/ft}^2$ or $101{,}325\,\text{N/m}^2$ and T_1 is the standard-day value of $518.67\,^\circ\text{R}$.

Because the equation of state for a gas holds for all temperatures, pressures, and densities that low-speed aircraft will encounter, then

$$P = \rho R T$$

$$P_0 = \rho_0 R T_0$$

or

$$\frac{P}{P_0} = \frac{\rho}{\rho_0} \frac{R}{R} \frac{T}{T_0}$$

Let the symbol σ be the density ratio. Therefore,

$$\delta = \sigma \Theta$$

This leads to

$$\sigma = \frac{\delta}{\Theta} = \Theta^{4.2561} \tag{5.10}$$

Finally, the temperature ratio as a function of altitude is

$$\Theta = 1 - 0.000006875 h \tag{5.11}$$

when h is measured in feet. The symbol h can have two different subscripts to indicate two different types of altitude important to pilots. Sectional maps indicate floors and ceilings of airspace and the tops of obstructions in feet measured from mean sea level. A barometric altimeter measures the altitude above mean sea level. This altitude is the pressure altitude and has the symbol h_p. The other important altitude is the density altitude, which has the symbol h_ρ. Density altitude is not measured; it is derived. Given a certain pressure and outside air temperature (OAT), the air will have a certain density. One can search the standard-atmosphere table to determine what the altitude on a standard day would have to be to have this same density. This is the density altitude, and it determines the performance of the engine and affects takeoff and landing distances. Customary practice is to apply subscript 0 to the pressure, temperature, and density when describing the standard day, as shown in these examples.

Example 5.1

At $h_0 = 1000$, what are the temperature, pressure, and density of the standard atmosphere?

$$\Theta_0 = 1 - (0.000006875)(1000) = 0.993125$$

$$T_{h=1000} = \Theta_0 T_{\text{SSL}} = 0.993125(59 + 459.67) = 515.12\,^\circ\text{R} = 55.43\,^\circ\text{F}$$

$$\sigma_0 = \Theta_0{}^{4.2561} = 0.9931254.2561 = 0.97107$$

$$\delta_0 = \Theta_0{}^{5.2561} = 0.9931255.2561 = 0.96439$$

$$\rho = \sigma_0\rho_0 = 0.97107 * 0.002378 = 0.002309 \, \text{slug/ft}^3 = 1.191 \, \text{kgm/m}^3$$

$$P = \delta_0 P_0 = (0.96439)(2117.) = 2041.6 \, \text{lb/ft}^2 = 14.18 \, \text{lb/in.}^2 = 97767.7 \, \text{N/m}^2$$

The appendix on units provides some handy conversions for temperature. They are repeated here for convenience:

$$C = (F - 32)(5/9)$$

$$C = K - 273.15$$

$$F = C(9/5) + 32$$

$$F = K(9/5) - 459.67$$

$$R = F + 459.67$$

$$R = K(9/5)$$

Mother Nature rarely provides, and flight-test engineers rarely desire, standard-day atmospheres. Usually the temperature, pressure, and altitude are very different from the standard day. Here then is an additional example of how the atmosphere parameters are computed.

Example 5.2

At $h = 1000$ ft, the OAT (outside air temperature) is 95°F. What are the pressure and density? What is the density altitude?

The standard-day temperature ratio is

$$\Theta_0 = 1.0 - (0.000006875)(1000.0) = 0.993125$$

The standard-day pressure ratio is

$$\delta_0 = \Theta_0{}^{5.256} = 0.993125^{5.256} = 0.96439$$

The actual temperature ratio is

$$\Theta_{\text{ACT}} = \frac{T_{\text{ACT}}}{T_{\text{SSL}}} = \frac{(459.67 + 95.0)}{(459.67 + 59.0)} = \frac{554.57}{518.67} = 1.0694$$

The density ratio for this nonstandard day is, therefore,

$$\sigma' = \frac{\delta_0}{\Theta_{\text{ACT}}} = \frac{0.96439}{1.0694} = 0.9018$$

The pressure is

$$P = P_0\delta_0 = (2117.0)(0.96439) = 2041.6 \, \text{lb/ft}^2 = 14.177 \, \text{lb/in.}^2 = 97747 \, \text{N/m}^2$$

The density is

$$\rho = \rho_0\sigma' = (0.002378)(0.9018) = 0.002145 \, \text{slug/ft}^3 = 1.1064 \, \text{kgm/m}^3$$

Calculating the density altitude is a little tricky. Because the fundamental relationship between pressure, density, and temperature ratios must always hold, and the temperature ratio is to be related to the density altitude, then

$$\sigma' = \frac{\delta_{\text{ACT}}}{\Theta_{\text{ACT}}} = \frac{\Theta_{\text{ACT}}^{5.256}}{\Theta_{\text{ACT}}} = \Theta_{\text{ACT}}^{4.256} = (1.0 - .000006875h_\rho)^{4.256}$$

Solving for h_ρ (density altitude) gives

$$h_\rho = \frac{(1.0 - 0.9018^{1/4.526})}{6.875 \cdot 10^{-6}} = 3490 \, \text{ft} = 1063.75 \, \text{m}$$

Example 5.3

What are the temperature and pressure of the air mass surrounding an aircraft flying at a pressure altitude of h_{aircraft} if the temperature, pressure, and altitude of the airport directly beneath it are T_{airport}, P_{airport}, and h_{airport}, respectively?

The temperature ratio is the ratio between any two temperatures and is based on the assumed standard lapse rate of $-3.57°F/1000$ ft. The only thing that changes on a nonstandard day is the offset, that is, the y intercept of the standard-day temperature equation is the only thing that moves. So, determine how different this day is from the standard day. Find the ΔT between this day and the standard day this way. Set up the temperature ratio equation to read:

$$\frac{T_{\text{airport}} + 459.688 - \Delta T}{59.0 + 459.688} = (1.0 - 0.000006875h_{\text{airport}})$$

Solve this equation for ΔT:

$$\Delta T = T_{\text{airport}} + 459.688 - 518.688 * (1.0 - 0.000006875h_{\text{airport}})$$

Now, write the temperature ratio equation with the aircraft temperature and altitude instead:

$$\frac{T_{\text{aircraft}} + 459.688 - \Delta T}{59.0 + 459.688} = (1.0 - 0.000006875h_{\text{aircraft}})$$

Solve for T_{aircraft}:

$$T_{\text{aircraft}} = \Delta T - 459.688 + 518.688 * (1.0 - 0.000006875h_{\text{aircraft}})$$

This collapses to

$$T_{\text{aircraft}} = T_{\text{airport}} - 0.00357 * (h_{\text{aircraft}} - h_{\text{airport}})$$

Of course, this equation is intuitively obvious in hindsight. The pressure follows from the expression for the pressure ratio:

$$\frac{P_{\text{aircraft}}}{P_{\text{airport}}} = \left(\frac{T_{\text{aircraft}}}{T_{\text{airport}}}\right)^{5.2561}$$

Do not forget, the temperatures must be measured from absolute zero, and so they must be Rankine or Kelvin.

5.3 Bernoulli's Equation

The story goes that Daniel Bernoulli watched water flowing in a stream and noticed something curious about the speed of the water in the vicinity of a large rock. Lifting the rock out of the stream, Bernoulli saw the average local velocity of the water decrease. Replacing the rock, the velocity increased. As with Newton's apple, this story may be urban myth, but anyone can try the experiment and see that it works. Stimulated by this observation, Bernoulli investigated fluid flow mathematically. His contribution is that the pressure in a fluid changes as the velocity changes, but the total "head" must be a constant. Here is how he determined this.

Imagine a wire box filled with an incompressible fluid that is moving at a steady rate through the wire faces. (The assumption that the fluid is incompressible is just the first in a series needed to make the study of fluids tractable.) The wire box has dimensions dx, dy, and dz, measured from the origin. Velocities in the x, y, and z directions are called u, v, and w, respectively. We can imagine that something may act on the fluid (such as a constriction) so that the velocity changes with distance along all three axes. For the sake of clarity, a change only in the x direction is shown in Fig. 5.2, but it is not difficult to see the other two directions work the same.

Because the velocity U is just dx/dt, then the volume of fluid entering the wire box in the x direction in unit time is $(dx)(dy)(dz)/dt = U(dy)(dz)$. Similar statements follow for the y and z directions.

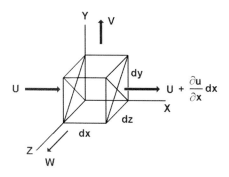

Fig. 5.2   Chunk of fluid.

To a first order, the amounts of fluid leaving the wire box per unit time in the x, y, and z directions are

$$\left(u + \frac{\partial u}{\partial x}\, dx\right)(dy)(dz)$$

$$\left(v + \frac{\partial v}{\partial y}\, dy\right)(dx)(dz)$$

$$\left(w + \frac{\partial w}{\partial z}\, dz\right)(dx)(dy)$$

Because the fluid is incompressible and because fluid is neither created or destroyed as it passes through the box, the total volume of fluid entering the box must equal the total volume leaving the box. Subtract the fluid entering from the fluid leaving, and sum the answers in all three directions:

$$\frac{\partial u}{\partial x} + \frac{\partial v}{\partial y} + \frac{\partial w}{\partial z} = 0 \tag{5.12}$$

This is the equation of continuity for an incompressible fluid. When applied in one dimension, this can be written as

$$d(uA) = 0$$

At any two points along a streamtube, the preceding expression implies

$$\rho A_1 u_1 = \rho A_2 u_2 \tag{5.13}$$

Newton's law states that the force applied to a body causes a change in momentum of the body. This can be a change in velocity in unit time, or a change in mass in unit time, or a combination of both. The fluid in the wire box has three dimensions, and so three equations are written:

$$X = \rho \frac{Du}{Dt}(dx)(dy)(dz)$$

$$Y = \rho \frac{Dv}{Dt}(dx)(dy)(dz)$$

$$Z = \rho \frac{Dw}{Dt}(dx)(dy)(dz) \tag{5.14}$$

The terms X, Y, and Z are the forces in the x, y, and z directions, and t is time. The derivatives are taken following the motion of the fluid (another assumption). For axes that are stationary with respect to the observer, the components of velocity are generally functions of time and space. So,

$$\frac{Du}{Dt} = \frac{\partial u}{\partial t} + \frac{\partial u}{\partial x}\frac{\partial x}{\partial t} + \frac{\partial u}{\partial y}\frac{\partial y}{\partial t} + \frac{\partial u}{\partial z}\frac{\partial z}{\partial t} = \frac{\partial u}{\partial t} + u\frac{\partial u}{\partial x} + v\frac{\partial u}{\partial y} + w\frac{\partial u}{\partial z}$$

$$\frac{Dv}{Dt} = \frac{\partial v}{\partial t} + u\frac{\partial v}{\partial x} + v\frac{\partial v}{\partial y} + w\frac{\partial v}{\partial z}$$

$$\frac{Dw}{Dt} = \frac{\partial w}{\partial t} + u\frac{\partial w}{\partial x} + v\frac{\partial w}{\partial y} + w\frac{\partial w}{\partial z} \tag{5.15}$$

Neglecting gravity, the only forces acting on the fluid are pressure forces. So, regarding Fig. 5.2, the force acting on the left face of the wire box is $p(dy)(dz)$, and the force acting on the right face is $[p + (dp/dx)dx](dy)(dz)$. Similar arguments apply for the other two directions. The resulting force acting on the fluid is therefore

$$X = -\frac{dp}{dx}(dx)(dy)(dz)$$

$$Y = -\frac{dp}{dy}(dx)(dy)(dz)$$

$$Z = -\frac{dp}{dz}(dx)(dy)(dz) \tag{5.16}$$

Combine the nine preceding equations:

$$-\frac{dp}{dx} = \rho\left(\frac{\partial u}{\partial t} + u\frac{\partial u}{\partial x} + v\frac{\partial u}{\partial y} + w\frac{\partial u}{\partial z}\right)$$

$$-\frac{dp}{dy} = \rho\left(\frac{\partial v}{\partial t} + u\frac{\partial v}{\partial x} + v\frac{\partial v}{\partial y} + w\frac{\partial v}{\partial z}\right)$$

$$-\frac{dp}{dz} = \rho\left(\frac{\partial w}{\partial t} + u\frac{\partial w}{\partial x} + v\frac{\partial w}{\partial y} + w\frac{\partial w}{\partial z}\right) \tag{5.17}$$

Now, consider a particle of fluid moving in a streamtube in the x-y plane, at some arbitrary angle and constant velocity. The particle has a u velocity and a v velocity. As the particle moves some distance dx, it rises some distance dy. Clearly, the following equality holds:

$$\frac{dy}{dx} = slope = \frac{v}{u}$$

or

$$\frac{dx}{u} = \frac{dy}{v} = \left(\frac{dz}{w}\right) \tag{5.18}$$

The term in parentheses was added to show that this idea extends into three dimensions.

Multiply the first of Eqs. (5.17) by dx, multiply the second of Eqs. (5.17) by dy and so forth, and limit the discussion to steady flow so that the time derivative is zero (the third assumption). The pressure equations in the three directions are now

$$-\frac{dp}{dx}dx = \rho\left(u\frac{\partial u}{\partial x}dx + v\frac{\partial u}{\partial y}dx + w\frac{\partial u}{\partial z}dx\right)$$

$$-\frac{dp}{dy}dy = \rho\left(u\frac{\partial v}{\partial x}dy + v\frac{\partial v}{\partial y}dy + w\frac{\partial v}{\partial z}dy\right)$$

$$-\frac{dp}{dz}dz = \rho\left(u\frac{\partial w}{\partial x}dz + v\frac{\partial w}{\partial y}dz + w\frac{\partial w}{\partial z}dz\right) \qquad (5.19)$$

or

$$-\frac{dp}{dx}dx = \rho\left(u\frac{\partial u}{\partial x}dx + u\frac{\partial u}{\partial y}dy + u\frac{\partial u}{\partial z}dz\right) = \rho\left[d\left(\frac{u^2}{2}\right)\right]$$

$$-\frac{dp}{dy}dy = \rho\left(v\frac{\partial v}{\partial x}dx + v\frac{\partial v}{\partial y}dy + v\frac{\partial v}{\partial z}dz\right) = \rho\left[d\left(\frac{v^2}{2}\right)\right]$$

$$-\frac{dp}{dz}dz = \rho\left(w\frac{\partial w}{\partial x}dx + w\frac{\partial w}{\partial y}dy + w\frac{\partial w}{\partial z}dz\right) = \rho\left[d\left(\frac{w^2}{2}\right)\right]$$

Add the last three equations together to get

$$-dp = \frac{\rho}{2}d(u^2 + v^2 + w^2) = \frac{\rho}{2}d(V^2) \qquad (5.20)$$

The V is the magnitude of the velocity vector. Integrate both sides to get Daniel Bernoulli's famous equation:

$$p + \frac{1}{2}\rho V^2 = H \qquad (5.21)$$

The H is the constant of integration. It is also called the head. Because H is a constant, this equation shows that as the velocity of the fluid increases in a streamtube, its local pressure decreases. The consequences of this equation are used throughout the remainder of this text. This equation explains why flight is possible.

5.4　Viscosity

Viscosity is a measure of the "stickiness" of a fluid or gas. The exact nature of viscosity is probably a molecular level electrochemical attraction, though it can be partially explained as a transfer of momentum between adjacent layers of moving fluid. To see this, begin with a simple description of gas as a collection of molecules. Each molecule has its own velocity $V_g = V_\infty + C_i$, which is the vector sum of the freestream velocity V_∞ (the same for all molecules) and C_i, the instantaneous velocity of the ith gas molecule measured by some device that is moving with the fluid. If the fluid is not moving, this device records that the molecules move in random directions. The chunk of gas does not have a preferred direction to creep, but the mean magnitude of the velocity is definitely not zero. Any given molecule travels only a short distance before colliding with another molecule. This short distance is called the mean freepath length. The collision is perfectly elastic—no energy or momentum is lost, only transferred. Over the long haul, the average velocities of the molecules tend to equalize, and from a macroscopic point of view, the flow velocity is uniform.

Now, imagine two adjacent layers of fluid moving in the same direction, but at slightly different flow velocities, as illustrated in Fig. 5.3.

The figure shows all of the particles moving along parallel, nonintersecting paths, though in reality some of the molecules in each lamina will have vertical components of velocity that cause them to mix with neighboring lamina. At the interface of the two lamina, the molecules of the upper, faster moving lamina, having higher kinetic energy than their subordinate neighbors, will tend to inject energy into the lower lamina and increase the speed of the lower lamina molecules when crossing the boundary. Likewise, the slower moving molecules in the lower layer will tend to reduce the velocity of the faster moving molecules in the upper layer. After sufficient time, the two layers will be moving with the same flow velocity, the momentum and energy transfers having successfully equalized the mean velocities. The momentum transfer between the two layers is called viscosity, and the viscous force per unit area is called the *shear stress*.

At a solid boundary, the molecules in the lamina just above the boundary will collide with the immovable boundary. A perfectly elastic collision will occur. The normal component of the momentum of the molecules is what is recorded as pressure. If the boundary were perfectly smooth, there would be no other forces recorded. However, no surface is perfectly smooth. Even the most highly polished

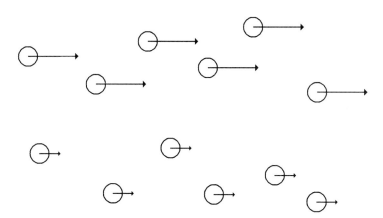

Fig. 5.3   Two layers of air. Both layers are moving to the right, but the upper layer moves slightly faster.

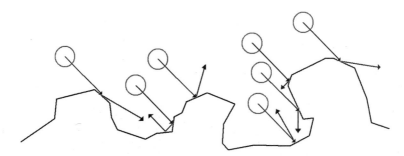

Fig. 5.4   Molecules colliding with a rough surface.

surface has irregularities at least the size of the molecules of gas. As Fig. 5.4 illustrates, even a perfectly aligned stream of molecules rebounds in random directions because of this surface roughness.

Because the flow in the lamina has a preferred direction, the momentum exchange is biased in one direction. This bias force is recorded as viscous drag.

If many moving lamina are stacked upon each other, and the stack is in contact with a solid boundary, the lamina immediately in contact with the boundary can be considered stopped. The next lamina has marginal "permission" to move, the next after that has a bit more room to move, and so forth. Lamina removed sufficiently far from the surface move with the freestream velocity. Viewed edge on, the mean velocity of the lamina forms a velocity profile similar to the one shown in Fig. 5.5.

The slope of the gradient at the solid boundary is a measure of the shear stress in the fluid or gas. By definition, a Newtonian fluid is one in which the shear stress is linearly related to the velocity gradient:

$$\tau = \mu \frac{\mathrm{d}u}{\mathrm{d}y} \tag{5.22}$$

The proportionality constant is the viscosity.

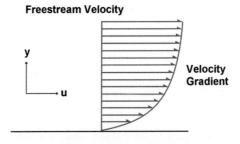

Fig. 5.5   Velocity profile as a result of viscosity.

5.4.1 Home Experiments

The program GasModel, which is included with this text, uses the momentum exchange argument to model skin friction and demonstrate the generation of the velocity gradient. When it executes, several hundred molecules of air acquire random initial positions and velocities and a uniform field velocity on top of that. They are flowing past a flat plate. When you execute the Skin Friction option, watch as the molecules collide with each other and with the flat plate, which is the bottom of the red box. All collisions are perfectly elastic. But, the plate sends the molecules back at a random angle, simulating the rough nature of the plate surface. At three positions along the plate, a velocity rake measures the velocity of every particle passing the rake, and an average velocity is computed. After a time, the flow stops, and the velocity gradients appear.

Run the program a second time, and watch the overall flow, not just an individual particle. One can almost see a swirling of the gas as it moves along. As evident from the velocity profiles generated, the gas flows faster as it gets farther away from the plate surface. Imagine the direction normal to the surface divided into evenly spaced lamina. Model the lamina by placing the palms of your two hands together and moving them. If the upper hand and the lower hand move at the same rate, then a pencil pinched between them will move with translational velocity only, as seen in Fig. 5.6a. On the other hand, so to speak, if the upper hand moves faster than the lower hand, then the pencil pinched between them will move with translational velocity and rotational velocity. This is seen in Fig. 5.6b.

This phenomenon is called vorticity, and more will be said about it later.

The preceding description is admittedly simple minded. Many an author has struggled to describe fluid flow with viscosity mathematically. Some of the best references are Batchelor [3] and Kuethe and Chow [4].

A second home experiment demonstrates the equation of state for an ideal gas. The kinetic theory option in the GasModel program uses kinetic theory and simple elastic collisions between particles and with the walls of a unit depth box in order to calculate pressure. An elastic collision with a wall changes the momentum of a molecule. The rate at which the molecules change momentum is a force. When the

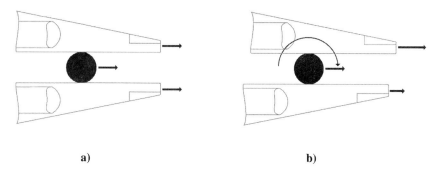

a)   b)

Fig. 5.6 Simple demonstration of vorticity: a) these hands are moving at the same speed, and b) the upper hand is moving at higher speed than the lower hand.

area of the wall that the molecule struck divides the force, a pressure is measured. Let P be the pressure in the box of volume V. The number of molecules is n, and the temperature is T. Because temperature is a measure of kinetic energy, T is proportional to the square of the molecular velocity. K is a constant of proportionality. The equation of state that this experiment attempts to verify is

$$PV = nKT \qquad (5.23)$$

See the homework problems for the experiment that will demonstrate whether the kinetic theory of gas has any validity.

5.5 Compressibility

The pressure in the vicinity of a wing varies as the wing moves through the air. In subsonic flight, the variations in pressure are small compared to the absolute pressure. However, as the speed of the wing increases, the changes in dynamic pressure increase at an increasing rate until their ratio with ambient pressure is no longer negligible, invalidating subsonic wing theory. At this point, the wing characteristics will not agree with experimental results or theoretical prediction. Compressibility effects cause these differences. The measure of compressibility is the ratio of the local speed to the speed of sound, the familiar Mach number.

One way to appreciate the sonic phenomenon is to recall the common experience of listening to a horn or whistle on a car or train as it approaches and then retreats. As the sound source passes, one notes the frequency drop. This is the Doppler effect, which is caused by the sound pressure wave being crowded by the approaching train, but relaxed after it passes. Pressure pulses from a stationary source propagate in all directions at the same speed and cause the air to change its pressure and velocity very little. That is, the changes to the air are continuous. Now, as the source begins to move, the pressure waves propagating in the same direction as the source are being "chased" by the source. When the source speed is much lower than the sonic speed, the pressure and velocity changes are small and continuous. However, as the source speed approaches the speed of sound, the pressure waves have not had time to move ahead of the source. That is, the source catches the pressure waves almost before they have been emitted. This means the velocity and pressure of the air ahead of the source remain unaffected by the oncoming source. This limited upstream influence gives rise to discontinuous rises in pressure and velocity, and a sonic boom results.

Starting with Bernoulli's equation and the adiabatic equation of state, one can show that the speed of propagation of a sound wave is equal to

$$V_{\text{sound}} = \sqrt{\frac{\mathrm{d}p}{\mathrm{d}\rho}} = \sqrt{\frac{\gamma P}{\rho}} \qquad (5.24)$$

In the preceding expression, P, ρ, and γ are the pressure, density, and ratio of the coefficient of specific heat at constant pressure to the coefficient of specific heat at constant volume, respectively. The ratio of the local velocity (vehicle velocity) to the speed of sound is called the Mach number, after Ernst Mach.

$$M = \frac{V}{V_{sound}} \tag{5.25}$$

The intent of this section is not to develop the theory of compressibility, but rather to indicate some of its effects.

5.5.1 Compressibility and Wing Lift

One of the two most important first-order effects of compressibility is called the Glauert–Prandtl rule, which relates the lift coefficient or lift-curve slope to the Mach number:

$$\frac{Cl_c}{Cl_i} = \frac{a_c}{a_i} = \frac{1}{\sqrt{1 - M^2}}$$

The subscripts c and i stand for "compressible" and "incompressible," respectively (notation taken from [1]). This relation also holds for moment coefficient and pressure coefficient. Others have developed the correction further to account for thickness and arbitrary, but symmetrical profiles of wing section. What this expression means is the lift-curve slope gets steeper with increasing Mach number so that the wing generates more lift at the same angle of attack.

5.5.2 Compressibility and Wing Drag

When some point on the airfoil exceeds Mach 1 (supersonic), even when the wing itself is traveling at less than Mach 1, this is called the critical Mach number. As the speed increases past the critical Mach number, marked changes in airfoil characteristics occur. This is called drag divergence, and the Mach number at which these significant changes take place is called the drag-divergence Mach number. At this Mach number, the drag increases sharply and considerably more force is required to overcome the drag. The interaction of thickness effects and compressibility takes the theoretical development beyond the scope of this text. The effects are important; they will be handled by empirical methods when the time comes.

5.6 Conclusions

This chapter began with a development of the standard atmosphere model. The reader sees that the pressure, temperature, and density are intimately linked via the universal gas law. A simple experiment using the demonstration computer program called GasModel shows how the basic properties of a gas are explained using a kinetic model of the collisions of hundreds of gas molecules in a closed vessel. The skin-friction option of the same program shows how a mechanical model of gas molecules colliding with a rough surface explains skin friction or viscosity. Using first principles, this chapter also derives Bernoulli's famous equation that relates pressure and the velocity of a gas. Finally, vorticity and compressibility are introduced.

References

[1]Dommasch, Daniel O., Sherby, Sydney S., and Connolly, Thomas F., *Airplane Aerodynamics*, 4th ed., Pitman, New York, 1967, pp. 13–22, 115–120.

[2]Abbott, Ira H., and Von Doenhoff, Albert E., *Theory of Wing Sections*, 2nd ed., Dover, New York, 1959, pp. 32–35.

[3]Batchelor, G. K., *An Introduction to Fluid Dynamics*, Cambridge Univ. Press, London, 1967, pp. 141–151.

[4]Kuethe, A. M., and Chow, C. Y., *Foundations of Aerodynamics: Bases of Aerodynamic Design*, 3rd ed., Wiley, New York, 1976, p. 297.

Problems

5.1 Assume a standard day. The pressure altitude is 10,000 ft. Find the density altitude in feet, the air pressure in lbs/ft² and lbs/in.², the density in slugs/ft³, and the outside air temperature (OAT) in °F, °C, °R, and K.

5.2 Water is pouring in a funnel at the rate of 1 gall per minute. If the water level in the funnel has stabilized, at what rate is the water leaving the funnel?

5.3 Run the skin friction option of the GasModel program using the default settings. Sketch the velocity profiles after 600 problem time units. What do you notice about the shapes of the three velocity profiles, especially with regard to the slope of the profile near the surface?

5.4 Run the kinetic theory option of the GasModel program, and perform the following experiments using the values from the following table. After each run, record the pressure value. Based on the results, how well does the kinetic theory of gas match the ideal gas law (Pressure $*$ Volume $=$ # of molecules $*$ R $*$ Temp)?

Number of molecules	Number of time points	Velocity of molecules	Size scale factor	Pressure
150	300	10	1.0	
300	300	10	1.0	
150	300	20	1.0	
150	300	10	0.5	

6
How High, How Fast, How Far

6.1 Introduction

The title of this chapter asks questions that are more involved than at first they appear. For instance, when one asks "How high are you flying?" the answer is not simply "X feet." Altitude is measured against agreed-upon references, some of which are, quite literally, fluid. "Controlled flight into terrain" is avoided when the pilot knows the aircraft altitude above the ground. Altitude also interests the pilot because aircraft performance is dependent on air density and density is a function of altitude.

Likewise, when one asks "How fast are you flying?," the answer may be expressed relative to several frames of reference and may be corrected for temperature and installation errors. There is a great difference between true airspeed, indicated airspeed, equivalent airspeed, and calibrated airspeed, and each of these airspeeds means something different. Add to this the effects of wind so that ground speed can be computed, and one sees that speed does not have a simple answer.

"How far are you flying?" is probably the easiest question to answer because distances between departure point and arrival point either do not change (airport to airport) or are easily computed (airport to ship). The only difficulties come in simple trigonometry, conversion of changes in longitude and latitude to displacement in other units, and consistent use of units.

This chapter, although brief, is essential for making a simulation useful as a training device and an engineering design tool.

6.2 How High?

What could be easier than stating your height?

Pressure altitude: Pressure altitude is the altitude measured above an agreed-upon datum called mean sea level (msl). Pressure altitude is expressed in feet, msl. When preparing to fly, a pilot sets the barometric altimeter to the height of the field. As flight progresses to another airport, the local weather might be different, and so an update to the barometric altimeter will be required. Pilots use this value to avoid cummulo-granite clouds and controlled flight into terrain.

Altitude above ground level: Altitude above ground level (AGL) is sometimes called wheel height, skid height, etc. It is the vertical distance from some point on the aircraft to the ground, and it is reported in feet, AGL. Altitude above the ground is unaffected by variations in the pressure, density, or temperature of the atmosphere. That is, regardless of the weather, a plumb line dropped from the top of the Eiffel Tower to its bottom will read the same always. Radar altimeters report altitude above the ground.

Density altitude: Given a standard day, the pressure and density go down as an aircraft goes up. Because engine performance and dynamic pressure are dependent on the density of the air, knowledge of the density is vitally important for take-off and landing distance calculations and climb/cruise performance calculations. Density of the air can be determined with some of the expressions in the chapter on atmosphere. Given a temperature and pressure altitude, a density can be found. That value can then be compared to the standard atmosphere to determine what the altitude on a standard day would have to be to have this same density. This is the density altitude.

The differences between pressure altitude and altitude above ground are illustrated in the following example.

Example 6.1

The top of a tower is known to be 1000 ft AGL. The tower is located near an airport situated by a cliff that overlooks the ocean. The airport, whose altitude above mean sea level is 100 ft, broadcasts an Automatic Terminal Information Service (ATIS) report, labeled Information Whiskey, which reports that the local altimeter setting is 29.92 in. (of Mercury). Unfortunately, that information has not been updated recently. In the time since information Whiskey was recorded, the barometric pressure has dropped 0.5 in. Describe the next few minutes of the pilot's life if the pilot is flying toward the tower at a pressure altitude of 1500 ft using the old barometric pressure.

Answer: Draw a picture of the situation. See Fig. 6.1.

The field is 100 ft above the water, that is, the field elevation is 100 ft msl. The top of the tower is 1000 ft above the ground, or 1000 ft AGL. This means the top of the tower is 1100 ft msl. The pilot's rule of thumb is that a drop in pressure equal to 1 in. of mercury equals a rise in pressure altitude of 1000 ft. The pilot is flying at an indicated pressure altitude of 1500 ft msl with the assumption that the barometric

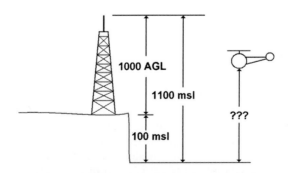

Fig. 6.1   What is the altitude of the helicopter?

pressure is 29.92 in. of mercury. However, the barometric pressure has dropped 0.5 in. Because an altimeter only reports a pressure, calibrated in feet, the altimeter interprets a drop in pressure as an increase in altitude. If the pilot maintained a constant *indicated* altitude, he would have descended to counter the "apparent" altitude increase. That is, the pilot's actual altitude is 500 ft less than the indicated altitude, or 1000 ft msl. (Silly as it seems, pilots use rhymes to remember some of the most important safety rules. The rhyme that the author learned is, "High pressure to low, look out below; low pressure to high, clear blue sky!" Thank you Cathy B.) Unless the pilot makes an evasive maneuver, he will strike the tower 100 ft below its top.

6.3 How Fast?

What is your speed? Two types of instruments in the aircraft report speed; they are the airspeed indicator and some radio or satellite navigation equipment. The airspeed indicator is an air data device that measures the dynamic pressure and reports the answer in units of speed. Recall Bernoulli's equation, which for this discussion reads:

$$\Delta P = \frac{1}{2}\rho V^2 = \frac{1}{2}\rho_0 \sigma V^2 \tag{6.1}$$

Solve for velocity.

$$V = \sqrt{\frac{2\Delta P}{\rho_0 \sigma}} \tag{6.2}$$

The indicated airspeed is a function of some pressure difference and density ratio, which is a function of altitude and outside air temperature. The pressure difference is measured between a pitot tube, which is a tube aligned with the freestream air, and a static port, which is an opening on the side of the fuselage, normal to the freestream air. If the opening of the pitot tube is a stagnation point, then the pressure it senses is the total pressure. The static port sees a velocity normal to its opening and thus senses the total head reduced by the dynamic pressure. The difference between the two ports is therefore the dynamic pressure, which is a function of airspeed. Because the dynamic pressure is also a function of density, altitude and temperature will introduce some "errors" in the value of airspeed that is indicated. Furthermore, compressibility effects begin to be important above Mach values of 0.3. The location of the pitot tube and the static port can have a significant effect on the reported speed if their positions on the aircraft preclude an accurate reading of the pressure difference between the static pressure and the dynamic pressure. This source of error is called *installation error* or *position error*. The airspeed indicator might have mechanical errors that are labeled collectively as *instrument error*.

With so many sources of error and types of corrections, a systematic naming convention and means of accounting for them are required. The names and meanings of the various airspeeds are described in Table 6.1.

For a more complete understanding of the airspeeds, the reader is encouraged to review [1] and [2].

Table 6.1   Airspeed names and descriptions

Airspeed	Description/meaning
VT(RUE)	True airspeed: this is the speed of the aircraft relative to the air mass and is the value needed to calculate the dynamic pressure. $$V_T = \sqrt{u^2 + v^2 + w^2}$$
VEAS	Equivalent airspeed: this is the true airspeed corrected for density variation from msl value. It is the value assuming the air is incompressible. This is close to what the airspeed indicator reports. $$V_e = V_T\sqrt{\sigma}$$
VCAS	Calibrated airspeed: this is the equivalent airspeed corrected for compressibility effects. $$V_{cas} = V_{sound}\left[5\left(\left\{\delta\left[\left(1 + \frac{M^2}{5\theta}\right)^{\gamma/\gamma-1} - 1\right] + 1\right\}^{\gamma-1/\gamma} - 1\right)\right]^{1/2}$$ $$M = \frac{V_T}{V_{sound}}$$
VIAS	Indicated airspeed: this is the calibrated airspeed corrected for installation or position error. The correction equation is often a simple polynomial. $$V_{IAS} = c_0 + c_1 V_{CAS} + c_2 V_{CAS}^2$$ The coefficients are determined in flight test.
VI	Cockpit instrument reading: Any errors in the mechanicals of the instrument are absorbed here. It is this value that the pilot sees in the cockpit.

6.4   How Far?

Navigation distances are measured in some unit large enough to express great distances with a manageable number. Statute and nautical miles usually serve the purpose. Close in to an object, feet or meters can be used instead. If the simulation involves a round Earth and travel over great distances, the digital maps use longitude and latitude. Here are some quick conversions.

A distance of 1 n mile is defined as an arc length of 1 min on the surface of the Earth at 40° latitude. This means that the circumference of the Earth is estimated to be 21600 n miles (= 360 ∗ 60). A nautical mile, a statute mile, and feet are related by the conversions in Table 6.2.

Selby [3] reports the equatorial radius of the Earth is 20,926,435 ft. The latitude λ and longitude ψ measured from a known starting point are computed from the

Table 6.2 Conversion table

Multiply this	By this	To get this
Nautical mile	1.150779	Statute mile
Nautical mile	6076.115	Feet
Statute mile	0.868976	Nautical mile
Statute mile	5280.0	Feet
Feet	0.0001645788	Nautical mile
Feet	0.0001893934	Statute mile

following expressions:

$$\lambda = \frac{North}{R_{\text{earth}}} + \lambda_0$$

$$\psi = \frac{East}{R_{\text{earth}} \cos(\lambda)} + \psi_0$$

These are the simplest of expressions and do not address how an aircraft must pitch while flying parallel to a line of latitude. (An aircraft that maintains the horizon at the same spot on the windshield is pitching nose down at a very slow rate so that the gravity vector remains pointing toward the floorboard. Because performance simulations rarely require great distances to be traveled, the Earth is assumed to be flat, and so the center of the Earth is infinitely deep below the surface. Thus, the horizon will remain where it started with respect to the windshield no matter how far one flies. If the aircraft absolutely did not pitch with respect to an inertial frame, then after it had flown 1/4 of the distance around the Earth, it would be pointing straight up!) For a more complete treatment of how inertial space, Earth axes, geographic axes, and body axes are related to each other, the reader is directed to Zipfel [4].

6.5 Conclusions

Things are not always as they seem. Altitude is dependent on the frame of reference (AGL vs msl) and even temperature (density altitude). Speed is true when measured by a radar gun mounted in the inertial frame. An equivalent airspeed accounts for density variations, a calibrated airspeed corrects the equivalent airspeed for Mach-number effects, indicated airspeed modifies calibrated airspeed for position and installation error, and instrument airspeed is what the pilot reads from the instrument panel. Distances are probably the easiest measurement to make, but beware the dragon named units. Also, if a conversion to latitude and longitude is required, remember that longitude depends on latitude but not vice versa.

References

[1]*Aeronautical Vest-Pocket Handbook*, 18th ed., 29th printing, Pratt and Whitney Aircraft of Canada, Ltd., Pratt and Whitney Aircraft of West Virginia, June 1978, pp. 150–151.

[2]Dommasch, D. O., Sherby, S. S., and Connolly, T. F., *Airplane Aerodynamics*, 4th ed., Pitman, New York, 1967, pp. 49–56.

[3]Selby, S. M., *CRC Standard Mathematical Tables*, Chemical Rubber Co., Cleveland, OH, 1973, p. 7.

[4]Zipfel, P. H., *Modeling and Simulation of Aerospace Vehicle Dynamics*, AIAA, Reston, VA, 2000, pp. 69–83.

Problems

6.1 Given an msl altitude in feet above the surface of the Earth, how far away is the horizon, in miles? Assume the Earth is perfectly smooth. Hint: the line of sight from the cockpit is tangent to the Earth at the horizon.

6.2 Starting at the intersection of the prime meridian and the equator, how many miles north and east (or is it west?) is the Royal Observatory in London? Hint: the latitude is 51°, 33 min, and 28 s North.

7
Aerodynamic Velocity, Inertial Velocity, Wash Velocity, and Gusts

7.1 Introduction

Bodies exposed to moving air generate aerodynamic forces. In general, they also change the magnitude of the velocity and the direction of the oncoming air. It does not make a difference whether the body is moving relative to still air, if the air is rushing past a still body, or if the air and the body are moving with respect to some inertial reference. Moving air impinging on a body generates aerodynamic force. The moving air is called the aerodynamic velocity. It is not just the speed of the air caused by a body's motion relative to some inertial reference. It is a vector sum of several components. This chapter, although short, is very important because in so many cases modelers have ignored the difference between aerodynamic and inertial velocity with horrible consequences. [A case in point is a simulation program with which the author has some experience. Previous programmers added wind and gust velocities directly to inertial velocity values using a replacement statement similar to $U = U + U_{wind}$. At this point, U is the aerodynamic velocity and could be used to calculate aerodynamic forces. But, when the equations of motion were assembled for an upcoming integration step, the wind and gust velocities had to be subtracted out temporarily so that centripetal acceleration terms could be correctly calculated, e.g., $dw/dt = q(U - U_{wind}) - p(V - V_{wind}) + \ldots$. Then, when the velocities for the next frame were calculated, the old wind and gust had to be permanently removed, only to be replaced by new values: $U = U + U_{wind} - U_{wind\_last\_pass}$. This kind of coding is messy and confusing from a physics standpoint.] Here then are important differences in inertial, aerodynamic, and wash velocities.

7.2 Inertial Velocity

Inertial velocity is the velocity that a body moves with respect to the North Star or some other suitable inertial reference frame. Consider a lone particle of air and a body moving toward it along the body's positive x axis. From the standpoint of the body, the air particle seems to move past it in the negative x direction. So, the positive sense of inertial velocity resolved to the body, that is, the positive U, V, and W elements of velocity point in the negative X-axis, Y-axis, and Z-axis directions, respectively.

85

7.3 Wash Velocity

Turn on a fan, and feel a breeze. Put that fan on a frictionless surface, and it begins to move in the direction opposite from the breeze that it creates. A force called thrust causes that breeze. The breeze is a *wash velocity* often called induced velocity.

Further your understanding of wash velocity by trying this experiment. While a friend drives, put your hand out the window and turn it so that the palm is normal to the oncoming air. You feel the wind trying to push your hand back. Also, obviously, the wind is not penetrating your hand. The force you feel is aerodynamic drag, and apparently, that drag has something to do with decelerating the oncoming wind so that the wind does not penetrate your hand. That "something" is the generation of wash velocity.

So, is it true that thrust accelerates air and drag decelerates air? The answer is not that simple, though the same basic model of wash velocity explains both observations. The wash velocity increases with increasing aerodynamic force, and the wash velocity always points in a direction opposite that force. In general,

$$w = -K * F \qquad (7.1)$$

K is not a constant. The functional form of K can be estimated using the Buckingham Pi theorem. If A is a characteristic area of the body that generates the force, $|V_a|$ is the magnitude of the total aerodynamic velocity vector impinging upon the body, and ρ is the density of the air, then, in general, the functional form follows this expression:

$$K \approx \frac{1}{\rho A \, |V_a|} \qquad (7.2)$$

By convention, a positive force points along the positive axes. So, a positive force produces a wash velocity with a positive sense along the negative axes of the body.

7.4 Gust/Wind Velocity

Stand in an open field, and feel the breeze. Hold a kite, and the kite wants to move with the wind. Run with the kite, and it produces the same aerodynamic force that we saw when discussing the inertial velocity. So, gusts and wind have the same sign sense as inertial velocity.

7.5 Aerodynamic Velocity

Aerodynamic velocity is the total velocity of the air particles as they approach a body. Because positive inertial velocity is directed toward the negative body axes, and it is usually associated with a drag force in the same direction, and because the wash velocity is in opposition to the drag force, then the vector sum for aerodynamic velocity is the unsurprising expression:

$$V_a = V_I - w + v_{\text{gust}} \qquad (7.3)$$

where all vectors above are R^6 in general with three linear and three angular components.

Note: Aerodynamic force is a function of aerodynamic velocity. Aerodynamic velocity is a function of the wash velocity. Wash velocity is a function of the aerodynamic velocity and aerodynamic force. An implicit loop is born. Except for the simplest of models, this implicit model is intractable. Iteration is the solution method of first resort, and serious examples will present themselves soon.

7.6 Why Are These Distinctions Important?

Consider the general equation of linear motion for an aircraft, which the preceding chapter presented, and the expression for aerodynamic velocity:

$$m(\dot{V}_I + \omega_I \times V_I) = F_{grav} + F_{aero}[V_a] \tag{7.4}$$
$$V_a = V_I - w + v_{gust}$$

(Here, the subscript is I rather than b in order to emphasize that the velocity components are inertial. They are still resolved to body axes.) The square brackets on the term $F_{aero}[V_a]$ mean that F_{aero} is a function of V_a. Substitute the expression for aerodynamic velocity into equation for linear motion and solve for the acceleration:

$$\dot{V}_I = m^{-1}\left(F_{grav} - m\omega_I \times V_I + F_{aero}\left[V_I - w + v_{gust}\right]\right) \tag{7.5}$$

The reader can glean two important observations from this expression:

1) Aerodynamic velocity depends on inertial velocity, wash velocity and gust velocity directly.

2) Inertial velocity is stimulated by gusts, but the gust velocity does not add directly to the inertial velocity. Instead, it modifies the aerodynamic velocity. That changes the aerodynamic forces, generating acceleration and in that way changing the inertial velocity.

The second point cannot be stressed enough. When you write a flight simulation, carry a minimum of four velocity vectors—one for inertial velocity, one for wash velocity, one for winds and gusts, and one for aerodynamic velocity. The distinctions are necessary for proper physics. Enforcing these distinctions also will improve readability and maintainability of your code.

7.7 Dynamic Pressure

As developed in the chapter on atmospheric modeling, the equation relating pressure and the velocity of moving fluid is

$$P + \frac{\rho V_a^2}{2} = H \tag{7.6}$$

H is the pressure head, and is a constant, P is the pressure in the fluid, V_a is the velocity of the fluid, and ρ is the fluid density. Because the head is a constant, the pressure must decrease if the fluid velocity increases. The combination of terms $\frac{1}{2}\rho V_a^2$ occurs regularly in flight simulation and aerodynamics. It is the *dynamic pressure*, and the symbol q is often shorthand for it. Most often V_a is the magnitude of the entire three-dimensional velocity vector $\boldsymbol{V_a} = \sqrt{u_a^2 + v_a^2 + w_a^2}$; other times, one or two of the velocity components may be excluded.

7.8   Angles of Attack and Sideslip

Aerodynamic forces are dependent on the dynamic pressure, the configuration of the body, and the angle at which the air is striking the body. Consider the perspective drawing of a tubular fuselage in Fig. 7.1.

Two angles describe the direction of the oncoming air. The first angle α is measured in the X-Z plane and is called the *angle of attack*. The other angle β is measured in the X-Y plane and is called the *angle of sideslip*. The reader should carefully note that a positive sideslip angle is achieved when the y direction component of velocity comes from the right side of the aircraft.

For fuselages or other blunt bodies, and for wings, the convention for calculating these two angles is

$$\alpha = \tan^{-1}\left(\frac{w_a}{u_a}\right)$$

$$\beta = \sin^{-1}\left(\frac{v_a}{\sqrt{u_a^2 + v_a^2 + w_a^2}}\right) \tag{7.7}$$

Sometimes the wind-tunnel test procedure forces an alternative definition:

$$\alpha = \sin^{-1}\left(\frac{w_a}{\sqrt{u_a^2 + w_a^2}}\right)$$

$$\beta = \tan^{-1}\left(\frac{v_a}{u_a\sqrt{1 + w_a^2/u_a^2}}\right) \tag{7.8}$$

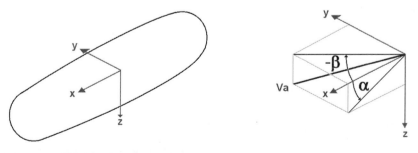

Fig. 7.1   Tubular fuselage with body axes attached, and the velocity vector showing the angles of sideslip and attack.

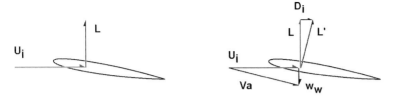

Fig. 7.2   Consequences of using aerodynamic velocity instead of inertial velocity when calculating aerodynamic forces.

Expressions (7.8) and (7.8) define aerodynamic angles of attack and sideslip respectively because they use components of the aerodynamic velocity vector. If components of inertial velocity had been used instead, the angles so calculated would be kinematic angles. Though somewhat premature for our discussion of wings, Fig. 7.2 demonstrates graphically the difference between the two types of angles and one of the consequences of not recognizing the difference. Both wing sections are at the same geometric pitch angle relative to the inertial velocity U_i. Both are developing lift L. However, w_w, the downwash caused by lift, has been added to the inertial velocity seen by the wing section on the right. This small addition has these three effects. First, the aerodynamic velocity V_a has a slightly greater magnitude than U_i alone. This means the dynamic pressure will be a bit higher. Second, the V_a vector has been rotated such that the angle of attack between it and the chord line of the airfoil has decreased. A reduction in angle of attack means that the lift will change. In the example shown, the lift likely will decrease despite the increase in dynamic pressure. Third, because lift is defined to be normal to the relative velocity vector, a small component of lift is directed aft. This component is called the induced drag D_i.

The conclusion to take from this example is that the geometric pitch angle is not the angle to use when calculating the aerodynamic forces; neither is the kinematic angle. Only aerodynamic velocity should be used to calculate aerodynamic forces.

7.9   Conclusions

The lesson to take from this short chapter is this. The motion of the aircraft is usually specified with respect to some inertial reference. The velocities and accelerations can be expressed in inertial axes or body axes, but they are independent of the atmosphere. These velocities are called inertial velocities. When an aerodynamic body generates an aerodynamic force, a necessary consequence is a wash velocity, which is directed exactly opposite to the resultant aerodynamic force vector. The vector sum of the inertial velocity and wash velocity is the aerodynamic velocity. It is this velocity that should be used to calculate aerodynamic forces.

Problems

7.1 A well-known induced velocity model for a helicopter rotor obeys this formula:

$$w_w = -\frac{F_z}{2\rho\pi R^2 \sqrt{u_i^2 + (w_i - w_w)^2}}$$

Subscript i indicates inertial, and subscript w indicates wash. R is the rotor radius, and F_z is the thrust the rotor is making. Because w_w is on both sides of this equation, this is an implicit equation. Implicit equations can sometimes be solved algebraically, but often require iteration. Solve the equation for w_w algebraically or iteratively at 11 evenly distributed values of inertial velocity ranging from $u_i = 0$ (hover) to $u_i = 200$ fps (high forward speed). Plot your results with u_i as the abscissa and w_w as the ordinate. Assume a standard day at sea level. Use the following parameters: $F_z = -6000$ lb, $w_i = 0$ fps, and $R = 22.0$ ft. What conclusion about the nature of a rotor's induced velocity do you draw from this exercise?

7.2 The nonlinear equation of motion of an airplane is modeled with the equation:

$$m\dot{u}_i = -\frac{\rho(u_i + u_{\text{wind}})^2 S C_d}{2} + T$$

When the wind is zero and thrust T equals the product $\rho u_i^2 S C_d / 2$, the acceleration is zero, and the airplane is moving at a trim velocity of u_i through the air and over the ground. If the wind speed builds to u_{wind} but the thrust does not change, what is the final value of the inertial speed? What does this say about how pilots account for the effect of wind when planning a flight?

8
Aerodynamics of Arbitrary Shapes

8.1 Introduction

The earliest aircraft had fuselages. Joseph Michael and Jacques Etienne Montgolfier were the inventors of the first practical balloon, which was made of silk and lined with paper to trap the heated air. On 21 September 1783, they demonstrated their aircraft to Louis XVI and Marie Antoinette, successfully lifting a sheep, duck, and rooster aloft for 8 min. The basket they hung beneath the balloon set the precedent—it seems no one wants to fly without some sort of fuselage now (hang-gliding and ultralight enthusiasts excepted, of course).

Like wings, rotors, and propellers, fuselages are aerodynamic bodies subject to the same basic tenets of force and moment generation. An area, exposed to some dynamic pressure and attenuated by a coefficient, generates forces and moments that act at the origin of the so-called individual element reference axes (IERA). The coefficient is dependent on geometry and the angle the wind strikes the body. But that is where the similarity abruptly ends. Where wings and rotors have easy-to-use airfoil sections and precious little else, a fuselage is a monstrous affair not easily given to analytical treatment. Nevertheless, the fuselage influences greatly the handling qualities and performance of the aircraft, often making an otherwise stable arrangement of wings and rotors expensive to fly and unstable about some axes.

8.2 Basic Geometry—Fuselages

A fuselage is a volume of irregular shape, usually, but not necessarily symmetric in the X-Z plane. A fuselage generates three forces and three moments that are usually measured at a reference point. Because they have such unusual shapes, owing to their need to house passengers, engines, transmissions, controls, fuel, etc., there is no handy reference describing the aerodynamics of all of the shapes. In the last quarter of a century, computing power, computer speed, engineering algorithms, and the understanding of fluid flows have all dramatically increased. This means that computational fluid dynamics (CFD) is relied upon more heavily for initial aerodynamic load estimates. This increase in CFD use is good because computing is far less expensive than wind-tunnel experimentation. However, CFD still eats much more time than can be swallowed by real-time simulation. For this reason, the most common method to model a fuselage resorts to tables or curve fits of wind-tunnel data, flight-test data, and CFD data. Here then is an introduction to modeling arbitrary shapes, fuselages, and bluff bodies in general.

The first rule of fuselage modeling should be this: model the fuselage as a body only. No wing-like structures, such as vertical or horizontal stabilizers, winglets, etc, should be included as part of the fuselage aerodynamics. Further, the landing gear and pylon (the aerodynamic fairing surrounding the mast and pitch links) should not be included as part of the fuselage model. Five good reasons recommend this strategy:

1) Wind-tunnel tests are usually performed this way. Additional wind-tunnel tests may add on just a stabilizer, or a fin, etc., building up to a complete fuselage. This is done so that the interference drag can be estimated.

2) Modeling this way removes stall and other sharp aerodynamic breaks from the data. One finds that the fuselage models are generally well behaved without wing structures.

3) Modifying the model for wings of different size, shape, placement, or static/dynamic orientation is easier.

4) Landing gear is retractable in some cases, or can change from skid to wheeled configuration. In the retractable case, the drag changes dramatically during extension/retraction. This is better handled as part of the landing gear "object." Of course, this argument extends to other elements that can change shape in flight.

5) Maintaining the main rotor hub and pylon (the structure surrounding the mast and control rods) separate from the fuselage is recommended because tiltrotors move the pylon through as much as 95 deg of rotation, which varies the pylon drag considerably.

The second rule of fuselage modeling is that a good axis system is fundamental to good analysis. Look at the body in Fig. 8.1.

The axes shown here are the IERA. The origin is at the fuselage reference point, found in the aircraft's interior. The reference point is the point at which the wind-tunnel measurements were taken or resolved; it is probably not at the center of mass. However, when the aircraft moves with linear velocity and angular velocity, those velocities are measured at the aircraft center of gravity. Therefore, the velocities at the center of mass must be translated to the fuselage reference point. Using the following expressions and including the effects of wash velocity, the aerodynamic velocity at the reference point is calculated:

$$V_{a|cg} = V_{b|cg} - V_{w|cg}$$
$$\omega_{a|cg} = \omega_{b|cg} - \omega_{w|cg}$$
$$V_f = V_{a|cg} + \omega_{a|cg} \times r_{f-cg|cg}$$
$$\omega_f = \omega_{a|cg} \tag{8.1}$$

where

$$V_f = \begin{Bmatrix} u_f \\ v_f \\ w_f \end{Bmatrix} \quad \text{and} \quad \omega_f = \begin{Bmatrix} p_f \\ q_f \\ r_f \end{Bmatrix} \tag{8.2}$$

The subscripts a, b, f, and w mean *aerodynamic, body, fuselage,* and *wash*, respectively. The subscript cg indicates the vectors are resolved to the body axes with

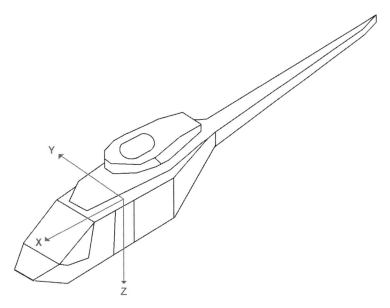

Fig. 8.1　Fuselage and reference axes.

origin at the *center of gravity* of the complete aircraft. All of these velocities are with respect to an inertial frame. At this point, the goals of the model suggest a major modeling decision, namely, that 1) the mathematical model should take advantage of wind-tunnel or CFD data when available (preferential advantage should be given to the wind tunnel data, as it is the prevalent source) and 2) the mathematical model should be valid for all orientations of the fuselage with respect to the wind. The first point seems obvious. The alternate approach of estimating forces and moments builds up a complex shape from simple shapes and then tunes that shape with best estimates of interference drag. There is considerable art and license in this technique. Absent any measured data, this might be the only method available. In that case, the not completely unreasonable answers might prove good enough, though the end user of such a model should keep in mind the limitations of the data.

Regarding the second point, some simulation codes (see [1]) divide the force and moment models into detailed treatments for nominal forward flight conditions and less detailed treatments for large aerodynamic angle flight. Other codes require the same texture at all angles, even if the texture is coarse (see [2]). Dividing the problem into nominal flight conditions and so-called high-angle conditions leads to another can of worms. It is true that most flight is conducted at small angles, and that this is where the majority of the wind-tunnel and/or flight-test data reside. Finding data at high angles, or certain coupled conditions (high pitch and yaw at the same time), are problematic, so that concentrating on small angle conditions seems reasonable. But, helicopters, tiltrotors, and other V/TOL aircraft can and do fly sideways, backwards, and vertically regularly, so that high-angle models are required. If the various regimes are modeled with low-order polynomial functions of aerodynamic angles, then one must also find a method to smoothly blend the various regimes with other interpolating polynomials. The number of coefficients in the polynomials could exceed the number of data points actually available!

In the end, the modeler should recognize that the selection of model type is often dictated by corporate culture, and that when a better model becomes available, it can always be introduced as a new option. That being said, the remainder of this chapter assumes that the fuselage model uses either aerodynamic equations or aerodynamic data tables. Tables accurately represent data taken in a wind tunnel, though cross coupling and large angles are not always available. Equations make parametric studies easy and are well suited to cases where little or no data are available.

8.3   Reference System

The reference system is more than just the placement and orientation of some origin for a set of axes. Aerodynamics are wrought in several different axes: wind, stability, and body. The differences are important. Stability axes are orthogonal axes that remain fixed with respect to the relative wind in pitch, but that rotate with the aircraft in yaw. Body axes are also orthogonal axes that remain fixed to the body and therefore rotate with it in roll, pitch, and yaw. Wind axes are aligned with the oncoming wind and resolved to the body axes through two angles normally named α and β.

Wind-tunnel tests, at a minimum, will hold angle of attack constant at zero and sweep yaw from -90 to $+90$ deg. Then yaw will be held constant at zero while angle of attack is swept from -90 to $+90$ deg. A sting, attached to the aircraft, measures the forces and moments, which by definition are in the wind axes. Figure 8.2 shows some results for a model fuselage. (The units have been normalized by an arbitrary factor to conceal competition sensitive data.)

Fuselage Normalized Aerodynamic Coefficients

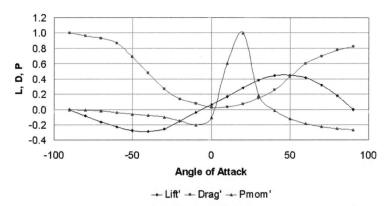

Fig. 8.2   Example of aerodynamic coefficients for a model fuselage.

Because most available data comes from wind-tunnel tests, it makes sense to model the fuselage aerodynamics assuming wind axes. The angle of attack and sideslip angle must be calculated from the body-axis velocities. This is an easy task. Wind-tunnel data present as straight-line wind directed along the long axis of the tunnel. When the wind-tunnel data were being generated, the fuselage was angled first through sideslip, then through angle of attack. In general, three body-axis velocities impinged upon the fuselage. Let Eq. (8.3) express the magnitude of the wind-tunnel velocity, also known as flight-path velocity for reasons explained shortly:

$$V_{\text{fp}} = \sqrt{V_f^T V_f} \tag{8.3}$$

Expression (8.4) relates V_{fp} and the body-axis velocity components. Expression (8.4) also provides the necessary relationships to calculate the angle of attack and angle of sideslip knowing the body-axis velocity components:

$$V_f = \begin{Bmatrix} u_f \\ v_f \\ w_f \end{Bmatrix} = R_y(\alpha_w)R_z(-\beta_w) \begin{Bmatrix} V_{\text{fp}} \\ 0 \\ 0 \end{Bmatrix} = \begin{Bmatrix} V_{\text{fp}} \cos\alpha_w \cos\beta_w \\ V_{\text{fp}} \sin\beta_w \\ V_{\text{fp}} \sin\alpha_w \cos\beta_w \end{Bmatrix} \tag{8.4}$$

Expression (8.4) provides these solutions for the wind angles.

$$\alpha_w = \tan^{-1}\left(\frac{w_f}{u_f}\right), \qquad\qquad -180\,\text{deg} < \alpha < 180\,\text{deg}$$

$$\beta_w = \sin^{-1}\left(\frac{v_f}{V_{\text{fp}}}\right), \qquad\qquad -90\,\text{deg} < \beta < 90\,\text{deg} \tag{8.5}$$

The companion expressions (8.5) point out an important mathematical constraint that exists between the two rotation angles. If one of the angles uses the arctangent function, which is good between -180 and $+180$ deg then the other angle must be defined with the arcsine function, which limits the range of the angle between -90 and $+90$ deg. Another set of equations that defines the angles of attack and sideslip can be derived from Eqs. (8.3) and (8.4)

$$\alpha_w = \sin^{-1}\left(\frac{w_f}{\sqrt{u_f^2 + w_f^2}}\right), \qquad\qquad -90\,\text{deg} < \alpha < 90\,\text{deg}$$

$$\beta_w = \tan^{-1}\left(\frac{v_f}{u_f\sqrt{1 + w_f^2/u_f^2}}\right), \qquad\qquad -180\,\text{deg} < \beta < 180\,\text{deg} \tag{8.6}$$

Either of the preceding companion sets of equations can be used; the manner in which the wind-tunnel test was conducted drives the choice.

The preceding angles are the aerodynamic pitch and yaw angles and are identical to the wind-tunnel pitch and yaw angles. They are independent and can be used in the force and moment calculations. Note carefully that if $V_{fp} = 0$, then both angles are undefined. However, because this happens only if all three velocity components are zero, then the angles can be set to zero with impunity because the dynamic pressure is also zero, and therefore no aerodynamic forces are being generated. If $u_f = w_f = 0$ and $v_f \neq 0$, then the pitch angle is undefined. Because the aircraft meets this condition only when it is flying sideways ($\psi_w = \pm\pi/2$), the pitch angle matters not and can be set to zero.

Often, the wind-tunnel data will be incomplete, which requires the modeler to decide how to fill in the missing data. The easiest approach would be to use existing data and assume some sort of symmetry. For instance, consider the drag curve in Fig. 8.2. If one simply reflected the data from 0 to 90 deg about the 90-deg line, and in similar fashion reflected the data from 0 to −90 deg about the −90-deg breakpoint, then a reasonable *and continuous* drag curve results. A similar procedure could also be applied to the lift and pitch moment, though one should expect that the reflected data of the lift curve should also have the sign reversed. The result is shown in Fig. 8.3.

The inverse trigonometric functions are only required if the fuselage model uses tables or equations that require the angles. Examining the fuselage curves in Fig. 8.3, one sees that the lift and drag curves seem very smooth and sinusoidal in nature. In fact, very reasonable approximations to the lift and drag curves over the complete range of angle of attack (−180 to +180) are expressed with these simple equations:

$$L = L_0 + L_{1S2} \sin(2\alpha_w) \tag{8.7}$$

and

$$D = D_0 + D_{1S1} \sin(\alpha_w) + D_{2C1} \cos^2(\alpha_w) \tag{8.8}$$

The subscripts are interpreted this way: a zero indicates a steady value, an S or C is shorthand for a sine or cosine function, an integer that precedes an S or C indicates

Derived Fuselage Coefficients Using Reflection

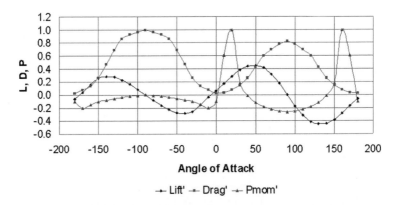

Fig. 8.3   Example of reflection method to extend wind-tunnel data.

Comparison of Measured Lift and Harmonic Curve Fit

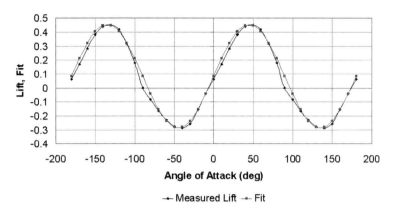

Fig. 8.4   Correlation of measured data and curve fit model for fuselage lift.

the exponent of the function, and an integer that follows indicates the harmonic. The fuselage lift and drag coefficients listed as Eq. (8.9) were determined with simple harmonic analysis and some trial and error.

$$L_0 = 0.084$$

$$L_{1S2} = 0.37$$

$$D_0 = 0.9$$

$$D_{1S1} = -0.1$$

$$D_{2C1} = -0.875 \tag{8.9}$$

The results shown in Figs. 8.4 and 8.5 speak for themselves.

Comparison of Measured Drag and Harmonic Curve Fit

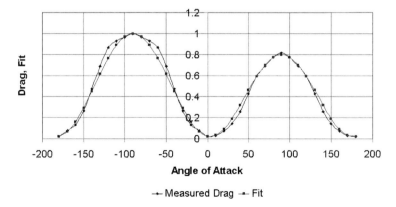

Fig. 8.5   Correlation of measured data and curve fit model for fuselage drag.

The pitching-moment equation would require many higher harmonic terms to get an adequate fit.

These simple examples serve to illustrate two points. First, curve fitting is a reasonable method to handle regular data. Second, the inverse trigonometric functions could be eliminated; trigonometric functions can be used instead. Specifically, the first harmonic functions are

$$\sin \alpha_w = \frac{w_f}{\sqrt{u_f^2 + w_f^2}} \cdot \text{sign}(u_f) = \frac{w_f}{u_f \sqrt{1 + (w_f/u_f)^2}}$$

$$\cos \alpha_w = \frac{|u_f|}{\sqrt{u_f^2 + w_f^2}}$$

$$\sin \beta_w = -\frac{v_f}{V_{fp}}$$

$$\cos \beta_w = \frac{\sqrt{u_f^2 + w_f^2}}{V_{fp}} \cdot \text{sign}(u_f) = \frac{u_f \sqrt{1 + (w_f/u_f)^2}}{V_{fp}} \qquad (8.10)$$

The higher harmonic functions are easily constructed using the rules of trigonometry.

8.4   Building the Force and Moment Equations

All of the pieces are in place to build an aerodynamic model of the fuselage. The fuselage is modeled without the vertical and horizontal stabilizers, the stabilizer winglets, the landing gear, and the main rotor hub. The reasons were cited earlier.

The body has attached to it a reference point where all forces and moments will be considered to act. This reference point does not have to be at the center of gravity of the body, and in fact it usually is not. The origin of this reference point is found first by translation of the individual element local axes (IELA) from the aircraft center of gravity. The IELA are parallel to the body axes by definition. The IERA share the same origin, but are rotated for a final alignment to ensure that the wind-tunnel data tables or curve fits agree with the orientation of the fuselage.

The fuselage moves with six body-axis velocities u_b, v_b, w_b, p_b, q_b, and r_b. Wash velocities are subtracted from them to yield the fuselage aerodynamic velocity vector. From this, the fuselage angle of attack and fuselage yaw angle are determined using the expressions derived earlier.

The fuselage angles of attack and sideslip determine the aerodynamic coefficients, usually expressed as F/q_{tot} and M/q_{tot}, where F and M are force and moment, respectively, and q_{tot} is the dynamic pressure. This means that the coefficients are in units of area for force and area times a characteristic length for moment. This is standard practice in the industry. The amount of computer memory that is available, the speed with which a coefficient must be found, and the availability of data dictate the computational relationship between the angles and the coefficients. The usual methods that relate the angles and the coefficients are multidimensional tables and analytical/empirical expressions. The more daring among the readers may propose using artificial neural networks or polynomial neural networks such as the group method of data handling as a compact way to surface fit the wind-tunnel data. If the angles of attack and sideslip are guaranteed to be small (obviously not good for hovering simulation) or if the accuracy need not be great, Eq. (8.11) provide a simple and effective model [3].

$$X_f = \frac{\rho}{2} \left[C_{Xuu} u_f |u_f| + C_{Xvu} v_f u_f + C_{Zwu} w_f u_f \right]$$

$$Y_f = \frac{\rho}{2} \left[C_{Yuv} u_f v_f + C_{Yvv} v_f |v_f| + C_{Ywv} w_f v_f \right]$$

$$Z_f = \frac{\rho}{2} \left[C_{Zuw} u_f w_f + C_{Zvw} v_f w_f + C_{Zww} w_f |w_f| \right]$$

$$L_f = 0$$

$$M_f = \frac{\rho}{2} \left[C_{Muu} u_f |u_f| + C_{Muw} u_f w_f + C_{Muq} u_f q_f \right]$$

$$N_f = \frac{\rho}{2} \left[C_{Nuv} u_f v_f + C_{Nuq} u_f r_f \right] \tag{8.11}$$

The coefficients in Eq. (8.11) are not derivatives; they are curve-fit coefficients. The roll-moment equation is identically zero. No matter what roll attitude the aircraft takes on, the fuselage does not generate a rolling moment. (A wing at some incidence angle may generate a rolling moment, but the supposition going in was that the fuselage model did not have wings.) As with the curve-fit method, the coefficients in the force and moment equations have units of area and area times a length, respectively. The reader should expect variations of Eq. (8.11) in the literature (for example, see [4]).

Finally, if the tables or equations express forces and moments in wind axes, rotate the forces and moments back to fuselage IERA.

$$\left\{ \begin{array}{c} X_f \\ Y_f \\ Z_f \end{array} \right\}_{IERA} = R_y(\alpha_w) R_z(-\beta_w) \left\{ \begin{array}{c} -Drag \\ Yf \\ -Lift \end{array} \right\}_{wind} \tag{8.12}$$

A similar expression is written for moments. Once the forces and moments are available in IERA, rotate them to the IELA, and finally translate them to the aircraft center of gravity.

8.5 Conclusions

Fuselages are irregularly shaped bodies that generate aerodynamic forces and moments. The aerodynamic coefficients come from wind-tunnel data, CFD analysis, flight test, and rough estimation using similarly shaped bodies. Often, the data are presented in tables as a function of some angles that orient the oncoming wind. At other times, the data are represented by polynomials, harmonic functions, and even artificial neural networks. The angles of attack and sideslip work together and must be defined so that a unique pointing vector is defined by the trigonometric functions calculated from the angles. The data itself might be incomplete, requiring the user to apply some judgment on how to fill in the missing data. Although the fuselage might not be the most exciting thing about rotorcraft, it is responsible for some of the greatest modeling difficulty. Do not ignore its influence.

References

[1]Corrigan, J., *Comprehensive Program for Theoretical Evaluation of Rotorcraft (COPTER) User's Guide (Vol. 2)*, Rep. 299-099-376, Bell Helicopter Textron, Inc., Fort Worth, TX, Oct. 1993, pp. 4.19–4.44.

[2]Talbot, P. D., Tinling, B. E., Decker, W. A., and Chen, R. T. N., "A Mathematical Model of a Single Main Rotor Helicopter for Piloted Simulation," NASA TM 84281, Sept. 1982, pp. 5–6, 32–34.

[3]Heffley, R. K., "ROTORGEN Minimal-Complexity Simulator Math Model with Application to Cargo Helicopters (U)," NASA CR 196705, March 1997, p. 20.

[4]Hoffman, J. A., and Dreier, M. E., *User's Manual for the Modular Stability Derivative Program High Frequency Version (MOSTAB)*, Paragon Pacific, Inc., El Segundo, CA, May 1979, pp. B-8–B-10.

Problems

8.1 Discuss the strengths and weaknesses of harmonic and polynomial functions when applied to curve fits of fuselage aerodynamic data.

8.2 Compare and contrast the use of tables vs analytical functions when applied to the modeling of fuselage aerodynamic data.

Aerodynamics of Airfoils, Wings, and Fins

9.1 Introduction

Save for spasmodic jumping, humankind's motion in space was limited to forward, backward, side to side, and down when falling. Sustained upward motion was not possible until enterprising observers and experimenters devised means for flight. Interestingly, some of the first attempts at flight did not try to emulate birds. In China, in the late third century B.C.E., imperfectly sealed ceremonial bamboo tubes filled with saltpeter, sulphur, and charcoal formed the first rockets. Nineteen centuries later, Wan-Hu, a clever inventor of the Ming Dynasty, estimated the journey to the moon to be no more than 47 tubes worth. Strapping himself and said arsenal to a wicker chair and setting the rockets alight, he was determined to predate the Armstrong and Aldrin landing by 400 years. The ensuing explosion was spectacular; the results were less than stellar.

In ancient Greek mythology, and more to the point of atmospheric flight, King Minos commanded an Athenian artisan named Daedalus to construct a labyrinth to imprison the king's wife Pasiphae and their hideous child, the minotaur. Daedalus did the work, but then sought to leave Crete because he did not trust Minos. He fashioned wings made of wax to which he stuck feathers. One set he wore, and one set he gave to his son Icarus. Despite his father's advice, Icarus flew too close to the sun. The wax melted, feathers started flying, and Icarus stopped flying; his wings disassembled, sending him plunging into the sea to drown.

Other attempts to achieve flight have often focused on wings, especially moving wings. After all, this is how birds fly, is it not? Yes and no. Atmospheric flight is achieved with wings, sometimes moving wings. [Yes, the Darwin Awards speak of the anti-Einstein that strapped a couple of jet-assisted takeoff (JATO) bottles to his automobile and unintentionally achieved a low Earth orbit, culminating in a collision with a cumulo-granite cloud. However, this text is limited to the scientific method, not the "hold my beer and watch this" method. By the way, the story of the rocket car has been debunked as urban myth.] This chapter presents the mathematics and physics behind wings and several methods for modeling them. This chapter also looks at fins, which this chapter defines as partial-span wings. Fins are most often used as stabilizer surfaces or endplates. The mathematics used to model fins is essentially the same as the mathematics used on wings. The location of the reference axes is usually the difference, but this is not a confusing factor.

9.2   Basic Geometry—Airfoils

A wing or fin is a three-dimensional device that generates lift. An airfoil (section) is an infinitesimally thin two-dimensional slice through the wing or fin created by two parallel vertical planes as shown in Fig. 9.1.

The study of wings and fins begins here at the airfoil section. Viewed from the side, an airfoil section resembles the top view of a trout. A straight line, which joins the leading edge to the trailing edge, is called the chord line and is given the symbol c. It is the reference line for several other important measurements.

For the purposes of analysis, an airfoil is decomposed into three pieces (Fig. 9.2a) The thickness distribution (Fig. 9.2b) describes how thick the airfoil is at any point measured along the chord. The thickness distribution is always symmetric. The camber line (Fig. 9.2c) is the locus of points midway between the upper and lower surfaces of the airfoil, measured from the chord. For symmetric airfoils, this line is straight. Finally, the flat plate (Fig. 9.2d) is the straight line that is used as a reference line to measure the aerodynamic angle of attack. It is usually the chord line.

For symmetric airfoils, the chord line and the zero lift line are coincident. Relative wind blowing parallel to the chord line will produce no lift. If the airfoil has camber as shown in Fig. 9.2, then relative wind blowing parallel to the chord line will produce lift toward the top of the page. Let this direction be called "away from the crown." In the discussions that follow, assume airfoil sections are symmetric, unless otherwise noted.

The airfoil must have an axis system attached to it in order to make sense of the aerodynamic data and to properly report the forces and moment that it generates. A convention stemming from analysis and experimentation places the airfoil reference axes at the quarter-chord point, which is the point on the chord line one-fourth of the way back from the leading edge. All airfoil tables with which the author is aware use the quarter-chord point as the reference point. This text will position the airfoil reference axes at the quarter-chord point and the x axis coincident with the chord line and pointing toward the leading edge. The direction

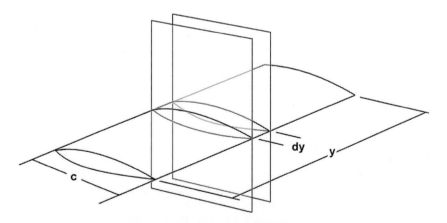

Fig. 9.1   Airfoil section of a wing or fin.

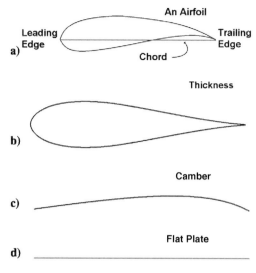

Fig. 9.2 Decomposition of a wing.

of the z axis is difficult to define without resorting to a "conventional" sense of orientation. Without belaboring the point, if the conventional orientation of an airfoil is such that lift is directed toward the top of the page when the wind attacks from beneath, then the positive z axis points toward the bottom of the page, which is the high-pressure side of the airfoil. This is illustrated in Fig. 9.3. What is most important is this. Once a reference axis has been attached to the airfoil, it must remain attached no matter what the orientation of the airfoil. If the airfoil is rotated about the y axis through some angle, then the reference axes are rotated through that angle.

Airfoils can be of constant shape, or they can have various devices that extend from their surface to augment their lift. Figure 9.3 also shows an airfoil with a simple flap. A positive flap deflection lowers the flap and increases the lift. A penalty in drag and pitching moment is the price. Flaps come in many flavors. Slats that extend from the leading edge also have several variations. A third device

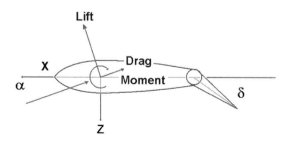

Fig. 9.3 Airfoil section with a simple flap.

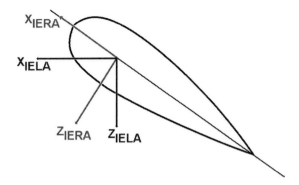

Fig. 9.4   Airfoil with IELA, IERA attached.

called a spoiler deploys from the center of the upper surface and, as its name implies, causes the lift to decrease and the drag to increase dramatically.

9.3   Individual Element Reference Axes, Individual Element Local Axes Orientation—Airfoils

Figure 9.4 shows an airfoil with individual element reference axes (IERA) and individual element local axes (IELA). The x axis of the IERA is coincident with the chord line, the origin lies at the quarter-chord point, and the positive direction points toward the leading edge. The y axis points into the page, and the z axis is arranged according to the right-hand rule. If the airfoil has an angle of incidence, that angle is introduced by rotating the IERA relative to the IELA. See the chapter on axis systems for a reminder of the definitions of the IERA and IELA.

9.4   Generation of Aerodynamic Forces and Moments on Airfoils

An airfoil generates two forces and one moment. The forces are resolved to the x and z axes of the IERA, and the moment is resolved about the y axis. There are two principal methods to estimate these forces and moments. Most of the time, the reader will use the empirical method. However, the analytical method is useful when data are not available or when the user must estimate interference effects and three-dimensional effects.

9.4.1   Empirical Method for Airfoils

An airfoil moving through the air produces the same forces and moments as one that is stationary but experiencing a wind moving by it. It is customary to analyze the airfoil as if it were stationary. In the two-dimensional analysis, the aerodynamic velocity of the air is given by two components u_a and w_a along the x and z axes of the IELA, respectively. The total velocity vector is the vector sum of these individual components, which form an inflow angle ϕ that measures from

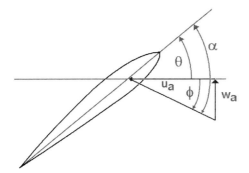

Fig. 9.5   Airfoil at an angle of attack.

the local horizon. By convention, positive u_a and w_a components (along the x and z axes, respectively) produce a positive ϕ, even though this is a negative rotation about the y axis. (When vector resolution becomes important, this convention will rear its ugly head, but will be dealt with rigorously.) The airfoil section IERA rotates through the pitch angle θ with respect to the local horizon or IELA. At this point the usual method is to add the two angles together to produce the angle of attack α. The pitch angle θ is purely geometry; the inflow angle ϕ is purely an aerodynamic function. The angle of attack is not the pitch angle, nor is it the inflow angle; it is the sum of both. This distinction is very important. Figure 9.5 illustrates the distinction.

For two-dimensional analysis, simple addition of the two angles suffices, but in preparation for three-dimensional analysis the rigor of formal vector resolution is necessary. Resolve the components of the total velocity vector, currently expressed in IELA, to the airfoil chord line or IERA by rotating through the incidence angle θ. Calculate the angle of attack from the components u_c and w_c thus created.

$$\begin{Bmatrix} u_c \\ w_c \end{Bmatrix} = \begin{bmatrix} \cos\theta & -\sin\theta \\ \sin\theta & \cos\theta \end{bmatrix} \begin{Bmatrix} u_a \\ w_a \end{Bmatrix} \tag{9.1}$$

$$\alpha = \tan^{-1}\left(\frac{w_c}{u_c}\right) \tag{9.2}$$

$$\phi = \tan^{-1}\left(\frac{w_a}{u_a}\right) \tag{9.3}$$

It is an easy exercise to show that the angle of attack in expression (9.2) equals the sum of the pitch angle and the inflow angle of expression (9.3).

Now comes the empiricism. Knowing the angle of attack, Mach number, Reynolds number, and flap deflection, the lift, drag, and moment coefficients are calculated using tabulated data. That is, the coefficients of lift, drag, and moment are given by

$$C_l = C_l(\alpha, M, \text{Re}, \delta)$$
$$C_d = C_d(\alpha, M, \text{Re}, \delta)$$
$$C_m = C_m(\alpha, M, \text{Re}, \delta) \tag{9.4}$$

Usually, airfoil tables for aircraft large enough to carry humans neglect the Reynolds number because the airspeeds and characteristic lengths are such that the Reynolds numbers are well past the point of conversion from laminar to turbulent boundary layers. Unless otherwise noted, this text will ignore it.

When writing a simulation program, one should anticipate three-dimensional table look-up for wings.

Define the total aerodynamic velocity and dynamic pressure as

$$V_a^2 = (u_c^2 + w_c^2)$$

$$q_{tot} = \frac{1}{2}\rho V_a^2 \tag{9.5}$$

Use coefficients (9.4) and the dynamic pressure to calculate the differential lift, drag, and pitching moment:

$$\frac{dLift}{dy} = \frac{dL}{dy} = \frac{1}{2}\rho V_a^2 cC_l$$

$$\frac{dDrag}{dy} = \frac{dD}{dy} = \frac{1}{2}\rho V_a^2 cC_d$$

$$\frac{dMoment}{dy} = \frac{dM}{dy} = \frac{1}{2}\rho V_a^2 c^2 C_m \tag{9.6}$$

This text adopts the shorthand dL/dy for $dLift/dy$, etc., which makes the reading easier. Please note that the differential lift, drag, and moment are measured in lb/ft, lb/ft, and ft-lb/ft, respectively—they are measured in terms of a distributed amount. Also, note that the lift and drag are positive when pointing primarily in the negative z and negative x directions, respectively. This is an issue of emotion instead of science. This convention will not be bucked here. However, the simulation engineer must remember to account for the signs when resolving the forces to other axes.

The lift vector is perpendicular to the aerodynamic velocity vector, and the drag vector is parallel to the aerodynamic velocity vector by definition. Most likely, these forces will be desired in the IELA; therefore, they must be rotated through the negative of the inflow angle. That is,

$$\begin{Bmatrix} \dfrac{dF_x}{dy} \\ \dfrac{dF_z}{dy} \end{Bmatrix} = \begin{bmatrix} \cos(-\phi) & \sin(-\phi) \\ -\sin(-\phi) & \cos(-\phi) \end{bmatrix} \begin{Bmatrix} -\dfrac{dD}{dy} \\ -\dfrac{dL}{dy} \end{Bmatrix} \tag{9.7}$$

Just so that it is clear, the negative sign in front of the $\sin(-\phi)$ term in the (2,1) position of this rotation matrix accounts for the rotation through the negative of the

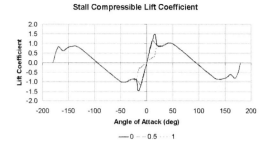

Fig. 9.6   Effects of Mach number on lift coefficient.

inflow angle. The negative sign in front of the angle name itself accounts for the fact that the inflow angle is defined positive when u_a and w_a are positive, but should be negative as shown in the diagram. (This is the aforementioned ugly head.) The negative signs preceding the differential drag and lift terms on the right-hand side (RHS) account for the emotion of desiring lift to be positive when an airplane goes up. There are so many negative signs in Eq. (9.7), that it is worthwhile to go over this equation and this paragraph repeatedly until the signs make sense.

The coefficients of lift, drag, and moment have been tabulated or presented graphically in Abbott and Von Doenhoff [1] for a wide variety of airfoils over a narrow range of angle of attack. Crtizos et al. [2] present a detailed summary of a wind-tunnel investigation of the aerodynamic characteristics of a symmetric, 12% thick airfoil, the well-known NACA 0012. (Such texts and reports are not the only source of this data. Computational fluid dynamics (CFD) also provides the data for these graphs.) In Figs. 9.6 and 9.7 the lift and drag coefficients for the NACA 0012 are shown as functions of angle of attack and Mach number. Note that the lift coefficient seems unaffected by the Mach number after stall, which is not true. Closer to the truth, the data-gathering process was rigorous only for the Mach = 0 case. Other cases ended after an angle of attack of 20 deg, and the results were simply faired into the Mach = 0 case. The reader is well served to remember that data gathering is expensive; therefore, not all tables are complete.

In Figs. 9.8–9.10, the lift, drag, and moments for the same airfoil are examined more closely, in the so-called linear range. Here, the effect of flap deflection

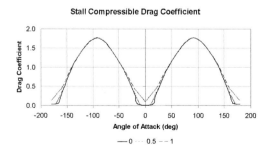

Fig. 9.7   Effects of Mach number on drag coefficient.

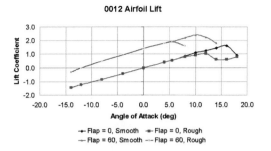

Fig. 9.8   Flap and roughness effect on lift coefficient.

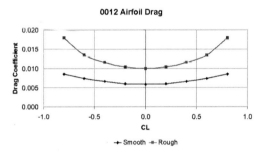

Fig. 9.9   Flap and roughness effect on drag coefficient.

and roughness is also shown. If the flap hinge is parallel to the y axis, which is positive into the page, then a positive flap deflection rotates the flap so that the trailing edge moves toward the positive z axis. Figure 9.3 shows an airfoil with a positively deflected flap. Figure 9.8 shows the effect such a deflection has on the lift coefficient.

Figure 9.9 presents the drag coefficient as a function of lift coefficient. Such a presentation is called a drag polar.

Figure 9.10 confirms thin airfoil theory that with no flap deflection a symmetrical airfoil has no moment regardless of the angle of attack when it operates in the linear range. However, when the flap is lowered, a significant moment develops.

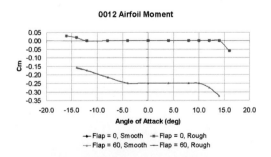

Fig. 9.10   Flap and roughness effect on moment coefficient.

The preceding discussion laid out the method used to calculate the distributed lift, drag, and moment produced by an airfoil. The empirical nature of the coefficients adds realism to the answers one achieves, but sometimes makes analysis intractable. The quick and dirty (QD) method is often employed for quick estimates. (Sometimes the desired data are not available. In that case, experience may be relied upon.) In the absence of data, the following rules of thumb are reasonable.

1) Assume the airfoil will operate in the linear range, with angles of attack between plus and minus 15 deg. Rotorcraft stabilizers, wings, and rotors routinely bust this assumption.
2) The slope of the lift curve is 5.73 C_l/radian or 2π C_l/radian for thin airfoil analysis.
3) The drag coefficient can be considered constant over that entire range. Values of 0.010 to 0.015 are not too bad.
4) The moment coefficient is zero, unless you know a better value.
5) From [3], the angle of attack increases with flap deflection by the value $\tau\delta$, where δ is the flap deflection angle in radians, τ is an effectiveness factor estimated (roughly) by the expression $\tau = 1 - (\theta_f - \sin\theta_f)/\pi$, and $\theta_f = \cos^{-1}(1 - \frac{x_f}{c/2})$, c is the chord of the airfoil, and x_f is the distance back from the leading edge of the airfoil to the leading edge of the flap.

9.4.2 Analytic Method for Airfoils

Several analytic methods exist that calculate airfoil performance. Most depend on a computer to do the serious number crunching. CFD methods are by far the most rigorous, but also require the most time and computer resources to do the job. A reasonable alternative is the distributed vorticity method. In this method, the camber line is replaced with one or more vortices whose filaments are normal to the plane of the airfoil. Then, the induced velocity at other points on the camber line is calculated, and the strengths of the vortices are adjusted so that the freestream velocity is deflected just enough to guarantee no penetration of the camber line. Once the distributed vorticity is known, the lift and moment are calculated. The following example makes this idea clear.

Model the airfoil as a flat plate at some angle of attack, as in Fig. 9.11.

Position a vortex filament at the $\frac{1}{4}$-chord point, and position a control point at the $\frac{3}{4}$-chord point. If the freestream velocity is not to penetrate the airfoil at the control point, then the vortex must induce a velocity w_i of sufficient magnitude and direction to turn the oncoming air by the angle of attack. This concept is the essence of a technique by Weissinger, as described in McCormick [3]. (In a more sophisticated analysis, the camber line replaces the flat plate, and the no-penetration requirement is enforced at several points on the camber line.) The geometry of this problem is seen in Fig. 9.11. For small angles, the tangent of the angle is the angle in radians. Therefore we write

$$\frac{w_i}{V_\infty} = \alpha \qquad (9.8)$$

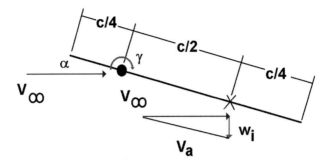

Fig. 9.11   Weissinger's approximation of an airfoil.

From the Biot–Savart law, an infinitely long, straight-line vortex filament induces a velocity in the plane normal to the filament equal to

$$w_i = \frac{\gamma}{2\pi r} \tag{9.9}$$

where γ is the vortex strength or vorticity. So, the induced velocity at the $\frac{3}{4}$-chord point is just

$$w_i = \frac{\gamma}{2\pi(3c/4 - c/4)} = \frac{\gamma}{\pi c} \tag{9.10}$$

Restricting the analysis to linear aerodynamics, the distributed lift is given by

$$\frac{dL}{dy} = \frac{1}{2}\rho V_a^2 c C_l = \frac{1}{2}\rho V_a^2 c a_0 \alpha = \frac{1}{2}\rho V_a^2 c a_0 \left(\frac{\gamma}{\pi c V_a}\right) \tag{9.11}$$

The term a_0 is the lift-curve slope when the wing is operating in the linear range. From thin airfoil theory, the lift-curve slope equals 2π, that is, $a_0 = 2\pi$. Divide the preceding expression by the dynamic pressure and the chord to get the airfoil section lift coefficient. Thus,

$$C_l = a_0\left(\frac{\gamma}{\pi c V_a}\right) = \frac{2\gamma}{c V_a} \tag{9.12}$$

or

$$\gamma = \frac{1}{2}cV_a C_l = \frac{1}{2}cV_\infty C_l \tag{9.13}$$

A simple sanity check shows that this is the correct value for vortex strength. The two-dimensional version of the Kutta–Joukowski law, which relates lift and vorticity, is

$$\frac{dL}{dy} = \rho V_\infty \gamma \tag{9.14}$$

Substitute Eq. (9.13) into Eq. (9.14). The result is

$$\frac{dL}{dy} = \frac{1}{2}\rho V_\infty^2 c C_l \qquad (9.15)$$

Everything balances.

All by itself, this result is not terribly remarkable. However, if the camber line is divided into several pieces, and each piece is given its own vortex and control point, then the chordwise distribution of lift can be calculated. Because flap deflection is just a local change of camber line, this procedure is useful in estimating the lift and moment of the airfoil at an angle of attack and with flap deflection, as demonstrated next.

9.4.3 Chordwise Distribution of Lift

Refer to Fig. 9.12. Imagine the same airfoil as before, but now let it be divided into n equally sized segments. Each segment acts as a little airfoil. Deflect the last segment(s) down through the (small) angle δ, representing the deflection of a flap. On each segment, place a vortex at its $\frac{1}{4}$-chord point and a control point on its $\frac{3}{4}$-chord point. Now, each vortex not only induces a velocity at the control point of the airfoil segment with which it is associated, it also induces velocities at all of the other airfoil segments as well. Assuming the positive direction of vorticity to be clockwise, then control points to the right of a vortex experience a downward induced velocity while control points to the left see an upward induced velocity. The problem, of course, is to find the vortex strengths so that the no-penetration requirement is satisfied at all control points; that is, one must solve n simultaneous equations for n vortex strengths. The following example clarifies this problem.

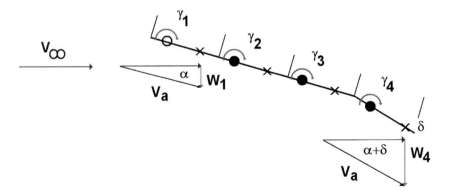

Fig. 9.12   Weissinger's approximation for chordwise distribution of lift.

Example 9.1

Consider the airfoil that has been divided into four smaller airfoils, as shown in Fig. 9.12. Further, deflect the trailing edge of the last subairfoil down by an angle δ, simulating a deflected flap.

Note: For clarity, Fig. 9.12 does not show w_2 or w_3, but they are there. At each of the control points, the induced velocity must turn the freestream velocity to run parallel to the local chord line. Each chord segment is $c/4$ long. The following four equations can be written relating the local turning to all of the vortices:

$$\frac{\gamma_1}{2\pi(cV/8)} - \frac{\gamma_2}{2\pi(cV/8)} - \frac{\gamma_3}{2\pi(3cV/8)} - \frac{\gamma_4}{2\pi(5cV/8)} = \frac{w_1}{V} = \alpha_1$$

$$\frac{\gamma_1}{2\pi(3cV/8)} + \frac{\gamma_2}{2\pi(cV/8)} - \frac{\gamma_3}{2\pi(cV/8)} - \frac{\gamma_4}{2\pi(3cV/8)} = \frac{w_2}{V} = \alpha_2$$

$$\frac{\gamma_1}{2\pi(5cV/8)} + \frac{\gamma_2}{2\pi(3cV/8)} + \frac{\gamma_3}{2\pi(cV/8)} - \frac{\gamma_4}{2\pi(cV/8)} = \frac{w_3}{V} = \alpha_3$$

$$\frac{\gamma_1}{2\pi(7cV/8)} + \frac{\gamma_2}{2\pi(5cV/8)} + \frac{\gamma_3}{2\pi(3cV/8)} + \frac{\gamma_4}{2\pi(cV/8)} = \frac{w_4}{V} = \alpha_4 + \delta \tag{9.16}$$

A matrix and a couple of vectors present these equations compactly:

$$\begin{bmatrix} 1 & -1 & -1/3 & -1/5 \\ 1/3 & 1 & -1 & -1/3 \\ 1/5 & 1/3 & 1 & -1 \\ 1/7 & 1/5 & 1/3 & 1 \end{bmatrix} \begin{Bmatrix} \gamma_1 \\ \gamma_2 \\ \gamma_3 \\ \gamma_4 \end{Bmatrix} = \frac{2\pi cV}{8} \begin{Bmatrix} \alpha_1 \\ \alpha_2 \\ \alpha_3 \\ \alpha_4 + \delta \end{Bmatrix} \tag{9.17}$$

If the airfoil has camber, then the slope of the camber line at each control point can be added (or subtracted as appropriate) to the local angles of attack. Inverting the matrix and postmultiplying the result by the local angle of attack, which includes flap deflection, find the distributed vorticity:

$$\begin{Bmatrix} \gamma_1 \\ \gamma_2 \\ \gamma_3 \\ \gamma_4 \end{Bmatrix} = \frac{2\pi cV}{8} \begin{bmatrix} 0.6836 & 0.4102 & 0.4102 & 0.6836 \\ -0.2930 & 0.5273 & 0.2930 & 0.4102 \\ -0.0586 & -0.3164 & 0.5273 & 0.4102 \\ -0.0195 & -0.0586 & -0.2930 & 0.6836 \end{bmatrix} \begin{Bmatrix} \alpha_1 \\ \alpha_2 \\ \alpha_3 \\ \alpha_4 + \delta \end{Bmatrix} \tag{9.18}$$

so

$$\begin{Bmatrix} dL_1 \\ dL_2 \\ dL_3 \\ dL_4 \end{Bmatrix} = \rho V \left(\frac{2\pi cV}{8} \right) \begin{bmatrix} 0.6836 & 0.4102 & 0.4102 & 0.6836 \\ -0.2930 & 0.5273 & 0.2930 & 0.4102 \\ -0.0586 & -0.3164 & 0.5273 & 0.4102 \\ -0.0195 & -0.0586 & -0.2930 & 0.6836 \end{bmatrix} \begin{Bmatrix} \alpha_1 \\ \alpha_2 \\ \alpha_3 \\ \alpha_4 + \delta \end{Bmatrix} \tag{9.19}$$

The individual dL_i values are the lift of the individual segments of airfoil, acting at the $c/4$ point of each of the segments. The total lift is simply the sum of the individual lifts. One sees immediately that the pressure peak is at the leading edge and the distributed pressure decreases rapidly toward the trailing edge. This result is in good agreement with experimental observation.

The chordwise distributed lift permits the calculation of a pitching moment. Sum the moments at the quarter-chord of the entire airfoil:

$$M = dL_1 \left(\frac{4c}{16} - \frac{c}{16} \right) + dL_2 \left(\frac{4c}{16} - \frac{5c}{16} \right) + dL_3 \left(\frac{4c}{16} - \frac{9c}{16} \right)$$
$$+ dL_4 \left(\frac{4c}{16} - \frac{13c}{16} \right) \tag{9.20}$$

The lift and moment coefficients are found from the expressions:

$$C_l = \frac{\sum_{j=1}^{4} dL_j}{\frac{1}{2}\rho V^2 c} \quad \text{and} \quad C_m = \frac{M}{\frac{1}{2}\rho V^2 c^2} \tag{9.21}$$

The text provides a simple program named AIRFOIL1 that divides the camber line into many segments (up to 20). A flat plate, a circular arc airfoil, or the camber line data from an arbitrary airfoil define the positions of the vortex centers and the control points. From the camber data for a NACA 4412 airfoil, the lift and moment coefficient as a function of angle of attack and flap deflection (flap chord equal to 20% of the airfoil chord) are shown in the Figs. 9.13 and 9.14.

The lift coefficient as a function of angle of attack is reasonably accurate in the linear range. However, stall is not represented; hence, the grossly exaggerated C_l at high angles of attack. The moment coefficient also appears to be overestimated. More segments would not significantly change the overall behaviors seen here. Real-world effects that account for viscosity, adverse pressure gradients, etc. must also be introduced to predict stall and improve the moment predictions, but by then the benefits of this simple analysis are obviated.

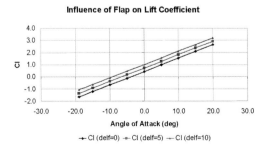

Fig. 9.13   Lift coefficient as a function of flap deflection.

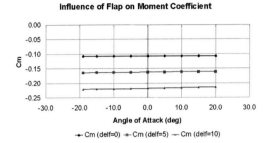

Fig. 9.14   Moment coefficient as a function of flap deflection.

9.4.4   *Mutual Interference of Two Airfoils*

When two airfoils are in close proximity, the wash from each affects the other as well as their own selves. This mutual interference has a significant effect on trim attitude and handling qualities. A simple estimate of the mutual interference is made easily with an adaptation of Weissinger's approximation, which follows.

Assume two airfoils of chord c_1 and c_2, with quarter-chord points separated by a distance d. Let the airfoils be acting at angles of attack α_1 and α_2. The induced velocities at the 3/4-chord point on each airfoil are

$$w_1 = \frac{\gamma_1}{2\pi\, c_1/2} - \frac{\gamma_2}{2\pi\,(d - c_1/2)} = V\alpha_1$$

$$w_2 = -\frac{\gamma_1}{2\pi\,(d + c_2/2)} + \frac{\gamma_2}{2\pi\, c_2/2} = V\alpha_2 \qquad (9.22)$$

Solve the simultaneous equations for the vortex strengths:

$$\begin{Bmatrix} \gamma_1 \\ \gamma_2 \end{Bmatrix} = \pi V c_1 \frac{[4f^2 + 2f(k-1) - k]}{[4f^2 + 2f(k-1)]} \begin{bmatrix} 1 & \dfrac{k}{2f-1} \\[2ex] \dfrac{-1}{2f+k} & 1 \end{bmatrix} \begin{Bmatrix} \alpha_1 \\ \alpha_2 \end{Bmatrix} \qquad (9.23)$$

where $k = c_2/c_1$ and $f = d/c_1$. The lift coefficients of the fore and aft airfoils follow immediately.

$$C_{l1} = \frac{2\gamma_1}{c_1 V}$$

$$C_{l2} = \frac{2\gamma_2}{c_2 V}$$

Example 9.2

Let two airfoils of equal chord operate in proximity to each other. Each airfoil is operating at the same kinematic angle of attack, that is, $\alpha_1 = \alpha_2$. How does the

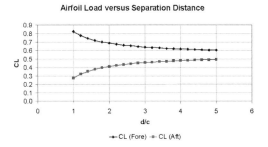

Fig. 9.15 Lift coefficient of two wings operating in close proximity.

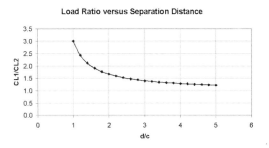

Fig. 9.16 Effort ratio of two wings operating in close proximity.

lift of each airfoil vary as the nondimensional distance between the $\frac{1}{4}$-chord points increases from $f = 1$ to $f = 5$? Let the angle of attack be 5 deg.

Solution: Substitute the appropriate values into the solution expression for the vorticity, and multiply both equations by $2/Vc$ to get the lift coefficients.

$$\begin{Bmatrix} C_{l1} \\ C_{l2} \end{Bmatrix} = 2\pi \frac{(4f^2 - 1)}{(4f^2)} \begin{bmatrix} 1 & \dfrac{1}{2f-1} \\ \dfrac{-1}{2f+1} & 1 \end{bmatrix} \begin{Bmatrix} 1 \\ 1 \end{Bmatrix} \alpha \qquad (9.24)$$

A simple calculation on a spreadsheet shows that the forward airfoil is always lifting more that the aft airfoil, but as the distance between them increases, the disparity between them decreases. The results are illustrated in Figs. 9.15 and 9.16.

The point is that airfoils (and wings and fins) communicate with each other through aerodynamics, which is quite important when systems of wings or fins are considered.

9.5 Basic Geometry—Wings

As alluded to in Fig. 9.1, a wing is a collection of infinitesimally thin airfoils or blade sections placed side by side. The distance from the left tip to the right tip is called the span, which usually is given the symbol b. At any given position along the span, the distance from the leading edge to the trailing edge is the chord, and that usually has the name c. The wing root is found at midspan, and the chord there is called the root chord. Its symbol is c_{root}. The leading and trailing edges may have lift augmentation devices such as slats, flaps, and ailerons. The primary function of these devices is to change the lift coefficient without changing the angle of attack. A wing can also have panels that deploy on the upper surface in such a way as to severely disrupt the airflow and spoil the lift. They are called spoilers.

A wing is a single element; therefore, it has just one IERA. The origin of the IERA is located at the quarter-chord point of the midspan chord, and it is coincident with the origin of the IELA. The IERA x axis is coincident with the root-chord line and points toward the leading edge. The y axis points generally toward the right wing; the z axis points toward the lower surface.

In general, a wing has mirror symmetry in the x-z plane. That is, if the wing has sweep or dihedral, the left tip will be just as high and far behind the IERA origin as the right tip. This symmetry does not preclude analysis of aircraft such as the x wing because the IERA can also be rotated about the z axis. The effects of sweep, dihedral, and twist are handled through the use of empirical corrections or simple analysis. More sophistication may be employed using strip theory; that theory will be presented later in the chapter.

Sometimes, only a portion of a wing needs to be analyzed. Examples include the horizontal or vertical stabilizers that do not have equal areas on either side of a fuselage or boom, or endplates on main wings or horizontal stabilizers. Wings of this type are referred to as fins in this text. Generally, fins are uncontrolled. An easy method to model a fin when one is encountered is to assume that it is some portion (usually one-half) of a wing. Throughout this text, the word fin will mean one-half of a wing. The same arithmetic that is used for the full wing is used for a fin, with the exception that only the appropriate amount of the wing is modeled.

Wings employ lift-augmentation devices, twist, taper, sweep, and elevation (dihedral or anhedral) to achieve desired performance. Airfoil sections and thickness can change along the span. The skin itself may be porous to control the boundary layer or destabilize the tip vortex. The number of techniques employed to modify performance fills volumes, and so is beyond the scope of this text. This section will attempt to discuss wing highlights from a modeling perspective, leaving specific modifications to be defined by the application and attended by the engineer.

Consider Fig. 9.17, which shows the right half of an unswept, tapered wing in planform.

The IERA attach to the root end (midspan) of the wing at the $\frac{1}{4}$-chord point. The wing chord tapers from C_{root} to C_{tip} over the semispan $b/2$. A partial-span flap, of span length b_f, is located somewhere along the trailing edge. The flap has a chord of c_f. Standing at the root end of the wing and looking toward the tip, the wing is twisted through the wash-out angle θ_{wo}. The twist rate has a negative sign, that is, the incidence angle of sections further out from the root is less than the incidence angle of the root.

The half-wing of Fig. 9.17 is shown in perspective in Fig. 9.18 with the flap deflected through the positive angle δ.

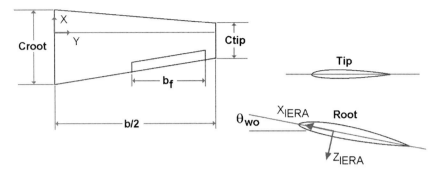

Fig. 9.17   Typical elements of a three-dimensional wing half (fin).

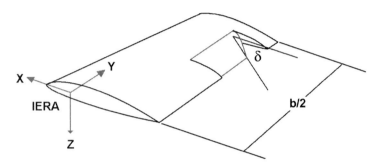

Fig. 9.18   Right half of a wing showing flap deflection.

Four important integrals characterize the geometry. The first is the area of the half-wing, and it is given by

$$S_{(1/2)} = \int_0^{b/2} c(y) \, dy \tag{9.25}$$

The distance y measures from root to tip in the IERA. The parenthetical subscript reminds the reader that this is the area of a half-wing. When the chord is an analytical function of y, then the area can be found exactly. Very often, the analytical function is linear taper, with the taper ratio given by

$$\lambda = \frac{C_{tip}}{C_{root}} \tag{9.26}$$

whence

$$c(y) = C_{root} \left[1 + (\lambda - 1) \frac{2y}{b} \right] \tag{9.27}$$

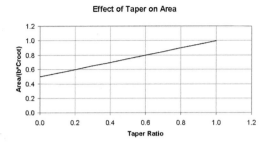

Fig. 9.19   Wing area as a function of taper ratio.

and

$$S_{(1/2)} = \int_0^{b/2} c(y)\, dy = bC_{\text{root}} \frac{(1 + \lambda)}{4}$$

$$S = S_{(\text{total})} = 2S_{(1/2)} \tag{9.28}$$

In Fig. 9.19, the area is normalized with the area of a rectangular wing of dimension $b \cdot C_{\text{root}}$.

The second important integral is the mean aerodynamic chord. According to NACA nomenclature, the mean aerodynamic chord is "the chord of an imaginary airfoil which would have force vectors throughout the flight range identical with those of the actual wing or wings." In practice, the mean geometric chord usually replaces the mean aerodynamic chord, so it can be thought of as an "average" value of wing chord for an equivalent rectangular wing of the same area and span. McCormick [4] shows the analytical expression for mean aerodynamic chord, repeated next without development.

$$\bar{c} = \int_0^{b/2} c^2(y)\, dy \Big/ S_{(1/2)} = \frac{2C_{\text{root}}}{3} \frac{(\lambda^2 + \lambda + 1)}{(\lambda + 1)} \tag{9.29}$$

The mean aerodynamic chord is normalized with the root chord in Fig. 9.20.

The location of the 1/4-chord point of the mean aerodynamic chord is the subject of the other two integrals. For the moment, assume the wing has no sweep

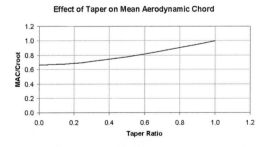

Fig. 9.20   Mean aerodynamic chord as a function of taper.

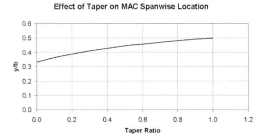

Fig. 9.21   Spanwise location of MAC as a function of taper.

or dihedral. All of the calculations take place in the x-y plane of the IERA. The y axis is the wing reference line as Fig. 9.17 shows. For a full wing, the location of the mean aerodynamic chord is the wing root. If the wing is decomposed into a left and right wing half (or fin), then the spanwise location of the right wing mean aerodynamic chord is

$$s_{mac} = \int_0^{b/2} y \cdot c(y)\, dy \Big/ S_{(1/2)} \tag{9.30}$$

which, after evaluation, gives

$$s_{mac} = \frac{b\,(2\lambda + 1)}{6\,(\lambda + 1)} \tag{9.31}$$

The mean aerodynamic chord for the left wing half would be located at

$$s_{mac} = -\frac{b\,(2\lambda + 1)}{6\,(\lambda + 1)} \tag{9.32}$$

The spanwise location of the centroid is called s_{mac} to help the reader differentiate it from the coordinate y_{mac}, which will be defined and developed shortly.

Because by supposition the wing reference line lies on the y axis, the coordinate $x(y)$ is zero. Thus, using the formal definition of x_{mac}, the chordwise location of the wing centroid is

$$x_{mac} = \int_0^{b/2} x(y)c(y)\, dx \Big/ S_{(1/2)} = 0 \tag{9.33}$$

For more generality, add the effects of sweep and dihedral. Again, the reference line for the wing lies on the 1/4-chord line. The sweep angle is Λ; a positive value means the leading edge at the tip is downstream from the leading edge at the root. Dihedral is Γ; a positive value raises the tip chord higher than the root chord. Now, the point location of the mean aerodynamic chord can be found using the inverse of the standard rotations from the IERA to some wing reference axes:

$$\begin{Bmatrix} x_{mac} \\ y_{mac} \\ z_{mac} \end{Bmatrix}_{RightWing} = R_{\bar{z}}^T(\Lambda)R_x^T(-\Gamma) \begin{Bmatrix} 0 \\ s_{mac} \\ 0 \end{Bmatrix} \tag{9.34}$$

Figure 9.21 shows y_{mac} as a function of taper when dihedral is zero. The arclength measure, as well as the sweep and dihedral angles, will have opposite signs for the left wing:

$$\begin{Bmatrix} x_{mac} \\ y_{mac} \\ z_{mac} \end{Bmatrix}_{LeftWing} = R_z^T(-\Lambda)R_x^T(\Gamma)\begin{Bmatrix} 0 \\ -s_{mac} \\ 0 \end{Bmatrix} \tag{9.35}$$

The effects of taper ratio and sweep on the chordwise location of the mean aerodynamic center are shown in Fig. 9.22. As sweep angle increases and taper ratio increases, the MAC moves farther aft. This has an important effect on the pitching moment at the aircraft center of gravity.

Another important geometric parameter that influences the performance of the wing is the aspect ratio; if b is the span and S is the area, then the definition of aspect ratio is

$$A_R = \frac{b^2}{S} \tag{9.36}$$

The aspect ratio is a measure of the fineness of the wing, that is, how closely is resembles a two-dimensional airfoil. The higher the aspect ratio, the more like a two-dimensional airfoil the wing behaves. Aspect ratio affects lift and induced drag. So far as lift is concerned, the linear lift-curve slope is affected approximately as

$$a_{03-D} = a_{02-D}\frac{A_R}{A_R + 2(A_R + 4/A_R + 2)} \tag{9.37}$$

Induced drag, which adds to viscous drag, is affected approximately as

$$C_{Di} = \frac{C_L^2}{\pi e A_R} \tag{9.38}$$

and is caused by the backward tilt of the lift vector caused by the trailing vortex system pushing the resultant velocity vector down. The e is called Oswald's efficiency factor, and is 1.0 for an elliptically loaded wing, and decreases from there

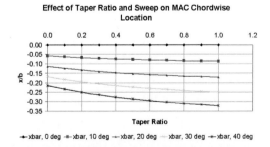

Fig. 9.22   Chordwise location of MAC as a function of taper.

for various planforms. Oswald's efficiency factor is a function of taper ratio, twist, and sweep. The induced velocity is mentioned here for historical perspective. If the rigorous vector treatment presented next is used, the induced drag need not be calculated explicitly. It will already be accounted for through force resolution and wash velocity.

9.6   Generation of Aerodynamic Forces and Moments on Wings

A wing generates three forces and three moments. The forces carry the names drag, lift, and side force. The moments are named for their principal direction: roll, pitch, and yaw. These loads are calculated using several different methods, which are presented here in increasing order of complexity.

9.6.1   Point-Load Method

The point-load method estimates the action of the entire wing as equal to a fictitious wing with the same area and mean aerodynamic chord. Flap effectiveness is included in the C_L, C_D, and C_M tables. Although obviously bad for distributed loads estimation, the point-load method is a very fast and effective way to get the total loads that eventually drive the airframe.

Using the methods outlined in the chapter on kinematics, calculate the three linear aerodynamic velocities and three angular aerodynamic velocities at the wing IELA. These velocities are stored in the two three-element vectors V_{IELA} and ω_{IELA}. Start with body-axis velocities, and translate them to IELA through the distance $R_{\text{wing}-\text{cg}|\text{cg}}$.

$$V_{\text{IELA}} = V_B + \omega_B \times R_{\text{wing}-\text{cg}|\text{cg}} = \begin{Bmatrix} u_a \\ v_a \\ w_a \end{Bmatrix}$$

$$\omega_{\text{IELA}} = \omega_B = \begin{Bmatrix} p_a \\ q_a \\ r_a \end{Bmatrix} \tag{9.39}$$

Because the IELA locates the quarter-chord point of the midspan chord, and because this is the origin of the IERA, there is no vector measuring from the IELA to the IERA.

Rotate V_{IELA} and ω_{IELA} to the reference axes, and call the new vectors V_{IERA} and ω_{IERA}. That is, if the reference axes have an orientation angle of ϕ_z about the z axis of the IELA, then an orientation angle of ϕ_y about the new y axis, and then an orientation angle of ϕ_x about the newest x axis, then expressions (9.40) provide V_{IERA} and ω_{IERA}.

$$V_{\text{IERA}} = R_x(\phi_x)R_y(\phi_y)R_z(\phi_z)V_{\text{IELA}} = T(\phi_x, \phi_y, \phi_z)V_{\text{IELA}}$$

$$\omega_{\text{IERA}} = R_x(\phi_x)R_y(\phi_y)R_z(\phi_z)\omega_{\text{IELA}} = T(\phi_x, \phi_y, \phi_z)\omega_{\text{IELA}} \tag{9.40}$$

One may be tempted to use the reference-axis orientation angles to provide sweep, dihedral, and incidence, but beware. That idea may work for a fin, which does not have mirror symmetry in the x-z plane of the IERA, but it fails for a wing. For instance, using $\phi_x = -\Gamma$ for dihedral would certainly lift the right-hand tip of the wing, but it would lower the left tip. In the author's experience, it is best to use the additional dihedral, incidence, and sweep angles in another set of rotation matrices for these effects.

Now, use expressions (9.34) and (9.35) to find the centroid of the right and left wing panels. These expressions are the proper place to introduce dihedral, incidence, and sweep effects. The position vectors so calculated point from the origin of the IERA to the panel centroid and are resolved to the IERA:

$$R_{\text{LWmac--IERA|IERA}} = \begin{Bmatrix} x_{\text{mac}} \\ y_{\text{mac}} \\ z_{\text{mac}} \end{Bmatrix}_{\text{Left}} \quad \text{and} \quad R_{\text{RWmac--IERA|IERA}} = \begin{Bmatrix} x_{\text{mac}} \\ y_{\text{mac}} \\ z_{\text{mac}} \end{Bmatrix}_{\text{Right}}$$

$$(9.41)$$

From here, the process is the same for the left and right wing panels, and so the arithmetic for the right panel only will be developed. Figure 9.23 clarifies all of the upcoming axis system rotations through an example of a wing with incidence angle only; the text presents the process with dihedral, incidence, and sweep angles.

The velocity at the computation points is measured in an axis system parallel to the IERA. Thus,

$$V_{\text{RWmac|IERA}} = V_{\text{IERA}} + \omega_{\text{IERA}} \times R_{\text{RWmac--IERA|IERA}}$$

$$\omega_{\text{RWmac|IERA}} = \omega_{\text{IERA}} \qquad (9.42)$$

To get these velocities aligned with the wing-reference-axis (WRA) system, rotate these vectors through the dihedral angle $\alpha_x = \Gamma$, the incidence angle $\alpha_y = \theta$, and the sweep angle $\alpha_z = \Lambda$. In general, anticipate a three-axis transformation from the IERA to the WRA.

$$V_{\text{RWmac|WRA}} = T(\alpha_X, \alpha_Y, \alpha_Z) V_{\text{RWmac|IERA}}$$

$$\omega_{\text{RWmac|WRA}} = T(\alpha_X, \alpha_Y, \alpha_Z) \omega_{\text{RWmac|IERA}} \qquad (9.43)$$

Figure 9.23a shows the representative airfoil section at an incidence angle of $\alpha_y = \theta$ and velocity components u_a and w_a from the vector $V_{\text{RWmac|IERA}}$. In Fig. 9.23b, the velocity components take the names u_c and w_c after rotation to the chord line, which represents the WRA; they are the components of the vector $V_{\text{RWmac|WRA}}$. Equation (9.43) describes that resolution.

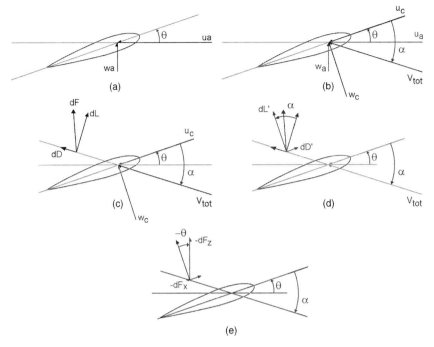

Fig. 9.23   Illustration of the series of velocity and force resolution steps used to model a wing. a) An airfoil at some pitch angle with horizontal and vertical components of aerodynamic velocity resolved to the IERA; b) the same airfoil with the aerodynamic velocity components resolved to the WRA, which defines the angle of attack; c) the lift and drag in wind axes; d) resolve the lift and drag to the WRA by rotating through the negative of the angle of attack; and e) resolve the forces to the IERA by rotating through the negative of the pitch angle.

Vector and matrix notation expresses concisely, and with cleaner subscripts, this entire set of operations:

$$V_{B6} = \left\{ \begin{matrix} V_B \\ \omega_B \end{matrix} \right\}$$

$$V_{\text{IELA6}} = G^T(R_{\text{wing-cg|cg}})\, V_{B6} = \begin{bmatrix} I & C^T(R_{\text{wing-cg|cg}}) \\ 0 & I \end{bmatrix} V_{B6}$$

$$V_{\text{IERA6}} = T_6(\phi_x, \phi_y, \phi_z)V_{\text{IELA6}}$$

$$V_{\text{RW|IERA6}} = G^T(R_{\text{RWmac|IERA}})V_{\text{IERA6}} = \begin{bmatrix} I & C^T(R_{\text{RWmac-IERA|IERA}}) \\ 0 & I \end{bmatrix} V_{\text{IERA6}}$$

$$V_{\text{RW|WRA}} = T_6(\alpha_x, \alpha_y, \alpha_z)V_{\text{RW|IERA6}}$$

$$\left\{ \begin{matrix} V_{\text{a|WRA}} \\ \omega_{\text{a|WRA}} \end{matrix} \right\} = \left\{ \begin{matrix} V_{\text{RWmac|WRA}} \\ \omega_{\text{RWmac|WRA}} \end{matrix} \right\} = V_{\text{RW|WRA}} \qquad (9.44)$$

The final velocity vectors contain the linear and angular velocities resolved to the WRA at the computation point. That is,

$$V_{a|\text{WRA}} = \begin{Bmatrix} u_c \\ v_c \\ w_c \end{Bmatrix}$$

$$\omega_{a|\text{WRA}} = \begin{Bmatrix} p_c \\ q_c \\ r_c \end{Bmatrix} \qquad (9.45)$$

The additional matrices are

$$C(x, y, z) = \begin{bmatrix} 0 & -z & y \\ z & 0 & -x \\ -y & x & 0 \end{bmatrix}$$

$$T_6(\alpha_x, \alpha_y, \alpha_z) = \begin{bmatrix} T(\alpha_x, \alpha_y, \alpha_z) & 0 \\ 0 & T(\alpha_x, \alpha_y, \alpha_z) \end{bmatrix} \qquad (9.46)$$

The skew-symmetric C matrix is the so-called cross-product operator, defined so that the matrix expression $C(R)f$ represents the cross-product operation $R \times f$. The T_6 matrix is simply the three-axis transformation matrix through the indicated angles repeated in block-diagonal form for the linear and angular velocities.

The angle of attack is given by

$$\alpha = \tan^{-1}\left(\frac{w_c}{u_c}\right) \qquad (9.47)$$

Remember, this is the angle that the wind makes with the chord. The lift is normal to the oncoming wind, and the drag is parallel to it as shown in Fig. 9.23c. If δ is the flap deflection, M is the Mach number, and Re is the Reynolds number, then the aerodynamic forces are calculated from the following expressions:

$$Drag = \frac{\rho V_{a|\text{WRA}}^T V_{a|\text{WRA}} S_{(1/2)}}{2} C_D(\alpha, \delta, M, Re)$$

$$Lift = \frac{\rho V_{a|\text{WRA}}^T V_{a|\text{WRA}} S_{(1/2)}}{2} C_L(\alpha, \delta, M, Re)$$

$$My = \frac{\rho V_{a|\text{WRA}}^T V_{a|\text{WRA}} S_{(1/2)}}{2} C_m(\alpha, \delta, M, Re) \qquad (9.48)$$

Note: Because only the right-hand side of the wing is being analyzed, only half of the area of the wing is used in the force and moment calculation. Translate and rotate these loads to the IELA for wash velocity calculations, and then translate and rotate the loads back to the aircraft center of gravity for the flight-dynamics problem. Begin the process by creating force and moment vectors at the computation point in an axis system parallel to the final aerodynamic velocity vector axes. Call them F and M:

$$F = \begin{Bmatrix} -Drag \\ 0 \\ -Lift \end{Bmatrix}, \quad M = \begin{Bmatrix} 0 \\ My \\ 0 \end{Bmatrix} \tag{9.49}$$

Stack them into a load vector called P_6:

$$P_6 = \begin{Bmatrix} F \\ M \end{Bmatrix} \tag{9.50}$$

Rotate P_6 parallel to the WRA through the angle of attack α. Note, because this means "undoing" the rotation of the velocity vector through the angle of attack, use the transpose of a T_6 matrix:

$$P_{\text{WRA}} = T_6^T(0, -\alpha, 0)P_6 \tag{9.51}$$

The minus sign in front of the angle of attack acknowledges that the positive sense of the angle of attack is actually a negative rotation about the y axis. Figure 9.23d shows this rotation. From here, rotate the loads to an axis system parallel to the IERA, as in Fig. 9.23e.

$$P_{\text{RW|IERA6}} = T_6^T(\alpha_x, \alpha_y, \alpha_z)P_{\text{WRA}} \tag{9.52}$$

The forces are located at the $\frac{1}{4}$-chord of the mean aerodynamic chord. A moment caused by those forces develops when they are transferred to the IELA.

$$P_{\text{IERA6}} = \begin{bmatrix} I & 0 \\ C(R_{\text{RWmac|IERA}}) & I \end{bmatrix} P_{\text{RW|IERA6}} = G(R_{\text{RWmac|IERA}})P_{\text{RW|IERA6}} \tag{9.53}$$

Rotate these loads to the IELA:

$$P_{\text{IELA6}} = T_6^T(\phi_x, \phi_y, \phi_z)P_{\text{IERA6}} \tag{9.54}$$

Finally, transfer the loads to the center of gravity of the aircraft:

$$P_{\text{wing|B}} = \begin{bmatrix} I & 0 \\ C(R_{\text{wing-cg|cg}}) & I \end{bmatrix} P_{\text{IELA6}} = G(R_{\text{wing-cg|cg}})P_{\text{IELA6}} \tag{9.55}$$

The path from center of gravity to wing and back is rigorous, and this text will use the same method many times. It is straightforward and should not present much of a challenge. Exercises at the end of this chapter help to reinforce the procedure.

Model the left-hand side of the wing with the same process as the right side, with the only difference being the position vector from the IELA to the computation point for the left and right sides. Each wing will calculate three forces and three moments. Example 9.3 calculates the three forces and moments generated by the right-hand side of a wing. The reader is encouraged to find the loads on the left-hand side.

Example 9.3

Find the three forces and three moments applied to the aircraft center of gravity by a right half of a wing that has a total span of 20 ft, a root chord of 2.0 ft, tapering linearly to 1.5 ft at the tip. The wing has no twist, $\theta_{wo} = 0$, nor does it have any sweep, $\Lambda = 0$, but it does have an incidence angle of $\theta = 5$ deg nose up and a dihedral angle of $\Gamma = 10$ deg, tip up. The wing has no flap. The IELA for the wing is located 10 ft back and 2 ft above the aircraft center of gravity. The aerodynamic velocity vector at the aircraft center of gravity is $u_a = 100$ ft/s, $v_a = 0.0$ ft/s, $w_a = 10.0$ ft/s, $p_a = 0.1$ rad/s, and $q_a = r_a = 0.0$ rad/s. Assume standard sea level (SSL) atmospheric conditions, a linear lift-curve slope of 5.73 C_L/radian, a constant drag coefficient of 0.10, and a symmetric airfoil. Figure 9.24 shows a three-view of this wing.

The taper ratio is

$$\lambda = \frac{1.5}{2.0} = 0.75$$

The area of the half-wing is given by

$$S_{(1/2)} = bC_{\text{root}}\frac{(1+\lambda)}{4} = (20.0)(2.0)\frac{(1+0.75)}{4} = 17.5\,\text{ft}^2$$

The mean aerodynamic chord is

$$\bar{c} = \frac{2C_{\text{root}}}{3}\frac{(\lambda^2 + \lambda + 1)}{(\lambda + 1)} = \frac{2(2.0)(0.75^2 + 0.75 + 1)}{3(0.75 + 1)} = 1.762\,\text{ft}$$

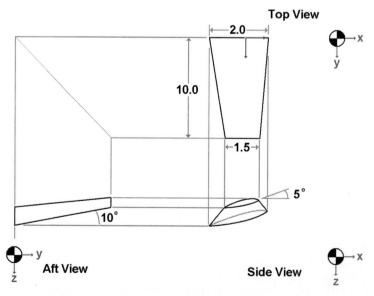

Fig. 9.24   Three view of the wing in the example problem.

The location of the mean aerodynamic chord (mac) is

$$s_{mac} = \frac{b}{6}\frac{(2\lambda + 1)}{(\lambda + 1)} = 4.76 \text{ ft}$$

$$\begin{Bmatrix} x_{mac} \\ y_{mac} \\ z_{mac} \end{Bmatrix}_{RW} = R_Z^T(0)R_X^T\left(-\frac{10}{57.295}\right)\begin{Bmatrix} 0 \\ 4.76 \\ 0 \end{Bmatrix} = \begin{Bmatrix} 0 \\ 4.69 \\ -.827 \end{Bmatrix}$$

The position vector that points from the aircraft center of gravity to the wing IELA, resolved to the c.g., is

$$R_{wing-cg|cg} = \begin{Bmatrix} -10 \\ 0 \\ -2 \end{Bmatrix}$$

The position vector that points from the IELA to the location of computation point is

$$R_{RWmac|IERA} = \begin{Bmatrix} x_{mac} \\ y_{mac} \\ z_{mac} \end{Bmatrix}_{RW} = \begin{Bmatrix} 0.0 \\ 4.69 \\ -0.827 \end{Bmatrix}$$

Following the steps just outlined, the velocity at the wing IERA, resolved to the IELA, is

$$V_{B6} = \begin{Bmatrix} V_B \\ \omega_B \end{Bmatrix} = \begin{Bmatrix} 100.0 \\ 0.0 \\ 10.0 \\ 0.1 \\ 0.0 \\ 0.0 \end{Bmatrix}$$

$$V_{IELA6} = \begin{bmatrix} 1 & 0 & 0 & 0 & -2.0 & 0.0 \\ 0 & 1 & 0 & 2.0 & 0 & -10.0 \\ 0 & 0 & 1 & 0.0 & 10.0 & 0 \\ 0 & 0 & 0 & 1 & 0 & 0 \\ 0 & 0 & 0 & 0 & 1 & 0 \\ 0 & 0 & 0 & 0 & 0 & 1 \end{bmatrix} \begin{Bmatrix} 100.0 \\ 0.0 \\ 10.0 \\ 0.1 \\ 0.0 \\ 0.0 \end{Bmatrix} = \begin{Bmatrix} 100.0 \\ 0.2 \\ 10.0 \\ 0.1 \\ 0.0 \\ 0.0 \end{Bmatrix}$$

$$V_{IERA6} = T_6(0,0,0)V_{IELA6}$$

$$V_{RW|IERA6} = \begin{bmatrix} 1 & 0 & 0 & 0 & -0.8269 & -4.690 \\ 0 & 1 & 0 & 0.8269 & 0 & 0.0 \\ 0 & 0 & 1 & 4.690 & 0.0 & 0 \\ 0 & 0 & 0 & 1 & 0 & 0 \\ 0 & 0 & 0 & 0 & 1 & 0 \\ 0 & 0 & 0 & 0 & 0 & 1 \end{bmatrix} \begin{Bmatrix} 100.0 \\ 0.2 \\ 10.0 \\ 0.1 \\ 0.0 \\ 0.0 \end{Bmatrix}$$

$$= \begin{Bmatrix} 100.0 \\ 0.2827 \\ 10.469 \\ 0.1 \\ 0.0 \\ 0.0 \end{Bmatrix}$$

Use the incidence angle to rotate the velocity vector to the WRA:

$$T_{WRA-IERA}(-\Gamma, \theta, \Lambda) = R_x(-\Gamma)R_y(\theta)R_z(\Lambda)$$

With the values provided, the transformation matrix is

$$T_{WRA-IERA}(-10, 5, 0) = \begin{bmatrix} 0.9962 & 0.0 & -0.0872 \\ -0.0151 & 0.9848 & -0.1730 \\ 0.0858 & 0.1737 & 0.9811 \end{bmatrix}$$

So the T_6 matrix is

$$T_{WRA-IERA,6}(-10, 5, 0)$$

$$= \begin{bmatrix} 0.9962 & 0.0 & -0.0872 & 0.0 & 0.0 & 0.0 \\ -0.0151 & 0.9848 & -0.1730 & 0.0 & 0.0 & 0.0 \\ 0.0858 & 0.1737 & 0.9811 & 0.0 & 0.0 & 0.0 \\ 0.0 & 0.0 & 0.0 & 0.9962 & 0.0 & -0.0872 \\ 0.0 & 0.0 & 0.0 & -0.0151 & 0.9848 & -0.1730 \\ 0.0 & 0.0 & 0.0 & 0.0858 & 0.1737 & 0.9811 \end{bmatrix}$$

The velocity vector in IERA axes, resolved to WRA axes, is

$$V_{RW|WRA} = T_{WRA-IERA,6}(\alpha_x, \alpha_y, \alpha_z)V_{RW|IERA6}$$

$$V_{RW|WRA} = \begin{Bmatrix} 98.707 \\ -3.046 \\ 18.903 \\ 0.0996 \\ -0.0015 \\ 0.0086 \end{Bmatrix}$$

The angle of attack is

$$\alpha = \tan^{-1}\left(\frac{w_{a|\text{WRA}}}{u_{a|\text{WRA}}}\right) = \tan^{-1}\left(\frac{19.1448}{98.707}\right) = 0.189$$

Although the angle of attack is positive in this case, it is very important to note that the angle is measured from the x-y plane and in fact represents a negative rotation about the y axis, which will be important when the forces are being resolved back to the IELA.

The aspect ratio is

$$AR = \frac{b^2}{S} = \frac{20.0^2}{35} = 11.4286$$

This equation gives an estimate of the wing lift-curve slope of

$$a_{0,3D} = 5.73\frac{11.4286}{11.4286 + 2(11.4286 + 4/11.4286 + 2)} = 4.7708$$

The dynamic pressure is

$$q_{\text{tot}} = \frac{\rho\|V_{a|\text{WRA}}\|^2}{2} = \frac{0.002378 * [98.707^2 + (-3.046)^2 + 18.903^2]}{2}$$

$$= 12.0204\,\text{lb/ft}^2$$

The lift, drag, and moment coefficients are

$$C_L = a_0 * \alpha = 4.7708 * 0.189 = 0.903$$
$$C_D = 0.1$$
$$C_M = 0.0$$

The lift, drag, and moment are

$$Drag = q_{\text{tot}}S_{(1/2)}C_D(\alpha, \delta, R_n) = (12.02)(35)(0.01) = 21.04$$
$$Lift = q_{\text{tot}}S_{(1/2)}C_L(\alpha, \delta, R_n) = (12.02)(35)(0.9140) = 189.89$$
$$My = q_{\text{tot}}S_{(1/2)}C_m(\alpha, \delta, R_n) = (12.02)(1.762)(35)(0.0) = 0.0$$

Place these loads in to the F and M vectors as discussed earlier:

$$F = \left\{\begin{array}{c} -21.04 \\ 0.0 \\ -189.89 \end{array}\right\}, \quad M = \left\{\begin{array}{c} 0.0 \\ 0.0 \\ 0.0 \end{array}\right\}$$

Stack them into a load vector called P_6:

$$P_6 = \begin{Bmatrix} F \\ M \end{Bmatrix} = \begin{Bmatrix} -21.04 \\ 0.0 \\ -189.89 \\ 0.0 \\ 0.0 \\ 0.0 \end{Bmatrix}$$

Rotate P_6 back to the IERA through the angle of attack α. Note, because this means undoing the rotation of the velocity vector through the angle of attack, use the transpose of a y-axis rotation matrix:

$$P_{WRA} = T_6^T(0, -\alpha, 0)P_6 = \begin{bmatrix} C_{(-\alpha)} & 0 & S_{(-\alpha)} & 0 & 0 & 0 \\ 0 & 1 & 0 & 0 & 0 & 0 \\ -S_{(-\alpha)} & 0 & C_{(-\alpha)} & 0 & 0 & 0 \\ 0 & 0 & 0 & C_{(-\alpha)} & 0 & S_{(-\alpha)} \\ 0 & 0 & 0 & 0 & 1 & 0 \\ 0 & 0 & 0 & -S_{(-\alpha)} & 0 & C_{(-\alpha)} \end{bmatrix} P_6$$

so

$$P_{WRA} = \begin{bmatrix} 0.9822 & 0 & -0.1881 & 0 & 0 & 0 \\ 0 & 1 & 0 & 0 & 0 & 0 \\ 0.1881 & 0 & 0.9822 & 0 & 0 & 0 \\ 0 & 0 & 0 & 0.9822 & 0 & -0.1881 \\ 0 & 0 & 0 & 0 & 1 & 0 \\ 0 & 0 & 0 & 0.1881 & 0 & 0.9822 \end{bmatrix} \begin{Bmatrix} -21.04 \\ 0.0 \\ -189.89 \\ 0.0 \\ 0.0 \\ 0.0 \end{Bmatrix}$$

or

$$P_{WRA} = \begin{Bmatrix} 15.06 \\ 0.0 \\ -190.46 \\ 0.0 \\ 0.0 \\ 0.0 \end{Bmatrix}$$

From here, the loads must be rotated to an axis system parallel to the IELA:

$$T^T_{\text{WRA}-\text{IERA},6}(-10,5,0)$$

$$= \begin{bmatrix} 0.9962 & -0.0151 & 0.0858 & 0.0 & 0.0 & 0.0 \\ 0.0 & 0.9848 & 0.1737 & 0.0 & 0.0 & 0.0 \\ -0.0872 & -0.1730 & 0.9811 & 0.0 & 0.0 & 0.0 \\ 0.0 & 0.0 & 0.0 & 0.9962 & -0.0151 & 0.0858 \\ 0.0 & 0.0 & 0.0 & 0.0 & 0.9848 & 0.1737 \\ 0.0 & 0.0 & 0.0 & -0.0872 & -0.1730 & 0.9811 \end{bmatrix}^T$$

$$P_{\text{RW}|\text{IERA6}} = T^T_{\text{WRA}-\text{IERA},6}(\alpha_x, \alpha_y, \alpha_z)P_{\text{WRA}} = \begin{Bmatrix} -1.35 \\ -33.08 \\ -188.17 \\ 0.0 \\ 0.0 \\ 0.0 \end{Bmatrix}$$

The forces are located at the $\frac{1}{4}$-chord of the mean aerodynamic chord. A moment caused by those forces develops when they are transferred to the IELA.

$$P_{\text{IERA6}} = \begin{bmatrix} I & 0 \\ C(R_{\text{RWmac}|\text{IERA}}) & I \end{bmatrix} P_{\text{RW}|\text{IERA6}} = G(R_{\text{RWmac}|\text{IERA}})P_{\text{RW}|\text{IERA6}}$$

$$P_{\text{IERA6}} = \begin{bmatrix} 1 & 0 & 0 & 0 & 0 & 0 \\ 0 & 1 & 0 & 0 & 0 & 0 \\ 0 & 0 & 1 & 0 & 0 & 0 \\ 0 & 0.8269 & 4.690 & 1 & 0 & 0 \\ -0.8269 & 0 & 0 & 0 & 1 & 0 \\ -4.690 & 0 & 0 & 0 & 0 & 1 \end{bmatrix} \begin{Bmatrix} -1.35 \\ -33.08 \\ -188.17 \\ 0.0 \\ 0.0 \\ 0.0 \end{Bmatrix} = \begin{Bmatrix} -1.35 \\ -33.08 \\ -188.17 \\ -909.76 \\ 1.12 \\ 6.32 \end{Bmatrix}$$

Rotate the loads to the IELA:

$$P_{\text{IELA6}} = T^T_6(\phi_x, \phi_y, \phi_z)P_{\text{IERA6}}$$

Finally, transfer the loads to the center of gravity of the aircraft:

$$P_{\text{wing}|B} = \begin{bmatrix} I & 0 \\ C(R_{\text{wing}-\text{cg}|\text{cg}}) & I \end{bmatrix} P_{\text{IELA6}} = G(R_{\text{wing}-\text{cg}|\text{cg}})P_{\text{IELA6}}$$

$$P_{\text{wing}|B} = \begin{bmatrix} 1 & 0 & 0 & 0 & 0 & 0 \\ 0 & 1 & 0 & 0 & 0 & 0 \\ 0 & 0 & 1 & 0 & 0 & 0 \\ 0 & 2.0 & 0 & 1 & 0 & 0 \\ -2.0 & 0 & 10.0 & 0 & 1 & 0 \\ 0 & -10.0 & 0 & 0 & 0 & 1 \end{bmatrix} \begin{Bmatrix} -1.35 \\ -33.07 \\ -188.17 \\ -909.76 \\ 1.12 \\ 6.32 \end{Bmatrix} = \begin{Bmatrix} -1.35 \\ -33.07 \\ -188.17 \\ -975.9 \\ -1877.8 \\ 337.06 \end{Bmatrix}$$

Remember, this is the load vector generated by the right side of the wing. You must employ a similar process to get the forces and moments from the left side. This example was fairly complex, designed to show the reader many of the details involved in simulating a wing in motion. It is easy to see that writing a core set of matrix and vector functions makes programming such a wing model easy. The appendix on linear algebra suggests a minimum set of such subroutines.

9.6.2 Strip-Theory Method

To improve the estimates of wing performance and move into the realm of distributed loads and hinge moments, abandon the point method, and employ strip theory instead. Strip theory is a natural extension, easily implemented. Its only drawback is that it requires numerical integration. In years past, numerical integration spent precious computing cycles on something that was easily estimated with some analytical integration. For airplanes, which always move in one direction only, this was fine. But for helicopters, which can fly in any direction and hover, the airflow over the wings is in serious violation of the usual small-angle assumptions. The current state of the art in computing is such that computer speed has passed the sophistication of the mathematical models. Therefore, use of strip theory is now a viable option.

As with the point-load method example just presented, consider the right half of a wing and a small strip taken in the chordwise direction. The strip is a two-dimensional airfoil, and so the usual methods that are applied to airfoils can be used.

The analysis begins by calculating the linear and angular velocity of the IELA using methods described earlier. Let $R_{\text{wing}-\text{cg}|\text{cg}}$ be a three-dimensional position vector that measures from the aircraft center of gravity to the wing IELA, resolved to the body axes.

$$V_{\text{IELA}} = V_B + \omega_B \times R_{\text{wing}-\text{cg}|\text{cg}} = \begin{Bmatrix} u_a \\ v_a \\ w_a \end{Bmatrix}$$

$$\omega_{\text{IELA}} = \omega_B = \begin{Bmatrix} p_a \\ q_a \\ r_a \end{Bmatrix} \qquad (9.56)$$

Again, the origins of the IELA and IERA are coincident; the position vector from the IELA to the IERA is null. Now, rotate the vectors to the IERA through the orientation angles:

$$V_{\text{IERA}} = T(\phi_x, \phi_y, \phi_z)V_{\text{IELA}}$$

$$\omega_{\text{IERA}} = T(\phi_x, \phi_y, \phi_z)\omega_{\text{IELA}} \qquad (9.57)$$

These operations are expressed concisely with the following statements:

$$V_{B6} = \begin{Bmatrix} V_B \\ \omega_B \end{Bmatrix}$$

$$V_{\text{IELA6}} = G^T(R_{\text{wing-cg|cg}})V_{B6} = \begin{bmatrix} I & C^T(R_{\text{wing-cg|cg}}) \\ 0 & I \end{bmatrix} V_{B6}$$

$$V_{\text{IERA6}} = T_6(\phi_x, \phi_y, \phi_z)V_{\text{IELA6}} \tag{9.58}$$

Now, imagine a WRA that runs along the quarter-chord line of the wing, that is, the WRA is the locus of origins of a series of airfoil section axes. The y axis of the airfoil section axes (ASA) is tangent to the wing reference line and points generally toward the tip. The x axis is normal to the reference line, pointing toward the leading edge, and parallel with the zero-lift line of the airfoil at that station. The z axis completes a right-handed triad.

In strip theory, one sweeps from the root to the tip of the wing along the reference line. *Imagine then that this statement marks the beginning of a loop over all blade stations along the wing reference axis.*

First, the chord and angular orientation angles are functions of position along the reference line. Let s be the position coordinate. Dihedral and sweep are usually constant while the incidence angle changes as a result of the twist of the wing.

$$c(s) = C_{\text{root}}\left[1 + (\lambda - 1)\frac{2s}{b}\right]$$

$$\theta(s) = \theta_{\text{root}} + \theta_{\text{twist}}\frac{2s}{b} \tag{9.59}$$

The orientation of the reference line is found by rotating through the sweep and dihedral angles, which may be functions of spanwise location.

$$R(s)_{\text{ASA\_IERA|IERA}} = R_Z^T[\Lambda(s)]R_X^T[-\Gamma(s)]\begin{Bmatrix} 0 \\ s \\ 0 \end{Bmatrix} \tag{9.60}$$

Notice that a negative sign precedes the dihedral angle; a positive dihedral is a negative rotation about the x axis. Equation (9.58) describes the position vector from the IERA to the origin of the airfoil section axes.

Next, construct the matrix that rotates velocities from the IERA to the ASA. Because the reference line is along the y axis, the transformation matrix through the incidence angle was not required in Eq. (9.60). However, for aerodynamic calculations that use velocities along all three axes, incidence is required. The total transformation matrix is

$$T(-\Gamma_x, \theta_y, \Lambda_z) = R_x[-\Gamma(s)]R_y[\theta(s)]R_z[\Lambda(s)] \tag{9.61}$$

and its six-dimensional form is

$$T_6(-\Gamma_x, \theta_y, \Lambda_z) = \begin{bmatrix} T(-\Gamma_x, \theta_y, \Lambda_z) & 0 \\ 0 & T(-\Gamma_x, \theta_y, \Lambda_z) \end{bmatrix} \tag{9.62}$$

Find the velocity in airfoil section axes by transferring the IELA velocity vector to the origin of the airfoil section axes, then rotating them to those axes:

$$V(s)_{\text{ASA6|IERA}} = \begin{bmatrix} I & C^T[R(s)_{\text{ASA-IELA|IELA}}] \\ 0 & I \end{bmatrix} V_{\text{IERA6}}$$

$$V(s)_{\text{ASA}} = T_6(-\Gamma_x, \theta_y, \Lambda_z)V(s)_{\text{ASA6|IERA}}$$

$$\begin{Bmatrix} V_{a|\text{ASA}} \\ \omega_{a|\text{ASA}} \end{Bmatrix} = V(s)_{\text{ASA}} \tag{9.63}$$

Once the velocity vector in the airfoil section axes is known, the aerodynamic calculations proceed as before. The angle of attack, which is a function of spanwise location, is given by

$$\alpha(y) = \tan^{-1}\left(\frac{w_{a|\text{ASA}}}{u_{a|\text{ASA}}}\right) \tag{9.64}$$

Remember, this angle is the angle that the wind makes with the chord, and a positive value for it is actually a negative rotation about the y axis. Again, lift is normal to this line, and drag is parallel to this line. The *distributed* aerodynamic forces are calculated from the following expressions:

$$dDrag(s) = \frac{\rho V^2 c(s)}{2} C_D[\alpha(s), \delta, M, R_n]\, ds$$

$$dLift(s) = \frac{\rho V^2 c(s)}{2} C_L[\alpha(s), \delta, M, R_n]\, ds$$

$$dMy(s) = \frac{\rho V^2 c^2(s)}{2} C_m[\alpha(s), \delta, M, R_n]\, ds$$

$$V^2 = V(s)_{a|\text{ASA}}^T V(s)_{a|\text{ASA}} \tag{9.65}$$

These distributed loads are stacked into a three-dimensional force vector and a three-dimensional moment vector:

$$dF(s) = \begin{Bmatrix} -dDrag(s) \\ 0 \\ -dLift(s) \end{Bmatrix}, \quad dM(s) = \begin{Bmatrix} 0 \\ dMy(s) \\ 0 \end{Bmatrix} \tag{9.66}$$

Stack these two vectors into a six-dimensional distributed loads vector called dP_{ASA6}:

$$dP(s)_{\text{ASA6}} = \begin{Bmatrix} dF(s) \\ dM(s) \end{Bmatrix} \tag{9.67}$$

Rotate this vector back through the angle of attack to get the loads in a system parallel with the IERA:

$$dP(s)_6 = T_6^T[0, -\alpha(s), 0]\, dP(s)_{\text{ASA6}}$$

$$dP(s)_{\text{IERA}} = T_6^T(-\Gamma_x, \theta_y, \Lambda_z)\, dP(s)_6 \tag{9.68}$$

The minus sign on the angle of attack acknowledges the fact mentioned earlier that a positive angle of attack is actually measured as a negative rotation about the y axis. Account for the moment arm from the origin of the IERA to the ASA.

$$dP(s)_{IERA6} = \begin{bmatrix} I & 0 \\ C[R(s)_{ASA-IERA|IERA}] & I \end{bmatrix} \tag{9.69}$$

$$dP(s)_{IERA} = G[R(s)_{ASA-IERA|IERA}] \, dP(s)_{IERA}$$

Rotate the distributed load to the IELA:

$$dP(s)_{IELA6} = T_6^T(\phi_x, \phi_y, \phi_z) \, dP(s)_{IERA6} \tag{9.70}$$

This is the bottom of the loop that marches along the wing. In essence, a spatial integration from wing root to wing tip takes place. Adding all of the individual incremental loads yields the loads in the IELA. Formally,

$$P_{IELA6} = \int_0^{b/2} dP(s)_{IELA6} \, ds \tag{9.71}$$

Of course, the integration is numerical. Finally, transfer those loads back to the aircraft center of gravity for the flight-dynamics problem.

$$P_{wing|B} = \begin{bmatrix} I & 0 \\ C(R_{wing-cg|cg}) & I \end{bmatrix} P_{IELA6} = G(R_{wing-cg|cg})P_{IELA6} \tag{9.72}$$

Example 9.4

Because of the great number of calculations, the text includes a simple computer program called WING1 that demonstrates this method. The half-wing is divided into 10 segments. The default data are the same as in the point load method. It is interesting to see how similar and how different are the answers between the two methods.

9.6.3 Derivative Method

An empirical blend of the point-load method, strip theory, and/or experimental results is often used. The point-load technique determines forces and moments caused by linear velocities. For loads caused by angular rates, derivatives are used as a linear model. These derivatives are determined from experiment or strip theory. Furthermore, the derivatives from strip theory can be found analytically or numerically. Also, the derivatives are usually expressed at the IELA, not the aircraft center of gravity. Because the full methods of strip theory and point load have already been demonstrated, the derivative method is shown here in simplified fashion, calculating the rolling moment and lift caused by roll rate, and then applying them to the loads calculations.

9.6.3.1 Numerical Derivative Method   The WING1 analysis program offers the option of calculating the stability derivatives. (Because that wing model does not have a flap, no control derivatives are calculated, though in general they would also be calculated.) The stability derivatives are generated numerically by using the central difference technique, which works like this.

1) Establish some flight condition. Set a reference value for the linear and angular velocities. Refer to this flight condition as the *subscript-zero* or simply *set-point* condition.

2) Determine the forces and moments at the IELA using strip theory or point load method. Call these loads the subscript-zero values.

3) Add a small (perturbation) value to a subscript-zero linear or angular velocity.

4) Determine the forces and moments at the IELA. Call these loads the *forward* values.

5) Subtract a small (perturbation) value from a subscript-zero linear or angular velocity.

6) Determine the forces and moments at the IELA. Call these loads the *backward* values.

7) Subtract the backward values from the forward values, and divide the result by two times the perturbation value. The result is a numerical approximation to the derivatives of the forces and moments with respect to the linear or angular velocity that was perturbed.

8) Repeat steps 3 through 7 for every linear or angular velocity.

Obviously, the central-difference derivative technique is easily implemented in a digital computer; this is exactly the method used in WING1.

9.6.3.2 Analytical-Derivative Method   There is little to be gained except experience and hand cramps by going through a complete development of analytical derivatives. However, a simple example provides valuable insight to both the analytical and numerical methods. So, start again with the simple wing in Fig. 9.25, and consider the small strip taken in the chordwise direction. The strip is a two-dimensional airfoil, and so the usual methods applied to airfoils can be used. To simplify this discussion, the airfoil is assumed symmetric, possessing a linear lift curve and free of drag. The wing is unswept, untwisted, and not tapered.

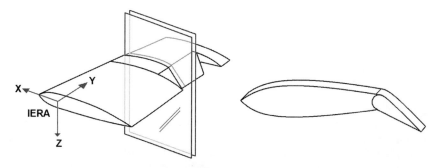

Fig. 9.25   Perspective of a wing with a deflected flap used in strip theory.

The analysis begins by assuming the availability of the linear and angular velocity of the IELA.

The origins of the IELA and IERA are coincident, so that

$$V_{B6} = \begin{Bmatrix} V_B \\ \omega_B \end{Bmatrix}$$

$$V_{\text{IELA6}} = G^T(R_{\text{wing}-\text{cg}|\text{cg}})V_{B6} = \begin{bmatrix} I & C^T(R_{\text{wing}-\text{cg}|\text{cg}}) \\ 0 & I \end{bmatrix} V_{B6} \qquad (9.73)$$

The reference line runs along the quarter-chord line of the wing, with the origins of a continuous system of airfoil section axes attached to it as described in the Strip Theory section.

As stated, the wing is untapered and untwisted, so that the chord and incidence angles are constant.

$$c(y) = C_{\text{root}}$$
$$\theta(y) = \theta_{\text{root}} \qquad (9.74)$$

The orientation of the reference line is found by rotating through the sweep and dihedral angles. By supposition, this wing has no dihedral or sweep, so that the position vector pointing to the airfoil section axes from the IELA is simply

$$R(y)_{\text{ASA\_IELA|IELA}}(y) = R_Z^T(\Lambda)R_X^T(-\Gamma)\begin{Bmatrix} 0 \\ y \\ 0 \end{Bmatrix} = \begin{Bmatrix} 0 \\ y \\ 0 \end{Bmatrix} \qquad (9.75)$$

Because the reference line is along the y axis, the transformation matrix through the incidence angle is not required. However, for aerodynamic calculations that use velocities along all three axes, incidence is required. The total transformation matrix is

$$T(-\Gamma_x, \theta_y, \Lambda_z) = R_x(-\Gamma)R_y(\theta)R_z(\Lambda) \qquad (9.76)$$

and the six-dimensional form of the preceding transformation matrix is

$$T_6(-\Gamma_x, \theta_y, \Lambda_z) = \begin{bmatrix} T(-\Gamma_x, \theta_y, \Lambda_z) & 0 \\ 0 & T(-\Gamma_x, \theta_y, \Lambda_z) \end{bmatrix} \qquad (9.77)$$

Again, by supposition, the wing has only a root incidence, and so the T_6 matrix is

$$T_6 = \begin{bmatrix} C_\theta & 0 & -S_\theta & 0 & 0 & 0 \\ 0 & 1 & 0 & 0 & 0 & 0 \\ S_\theta & 0 & C_\theta & 0 & 0 & 0 \\ 0 & 0 & 0 & C_\theta & 0 & -S_\theta \\ 0 & 0 & 0 & 0 & 1 & 0 \\ 0 & 0 & 0 & S_\theta & 0 & C_\theta \end{bmatrix} \qquad (9.78)$$

If that wing has a root incidence of zero radians, then T_6 is the identity matrix. For this discussion, let the root incidence be zero. Find the velocity in airfoil section axes by transferring the IELA velocity vector to the origin of the airfoil section axes, and then rotating the airfoil section axes to the IERA:

$$V_{ASA6|IERA} = \begin{bmatrix} I & C^T(R_{ASA-IERA|IERA}) \\ 0 & I \end{bmatrix} V_{IELA6}$$

$$V_{IERA6} = T_6(\Gamma, \theta, \Lambda) V_{ASA6|IERA}$$

$$\begin{Bmatrix} V_{a|IERA} \\ \omega_{a|IERA} \end{Bmatrix} = V_{IERA6} \qquad (9.79)$$

With all of the assumptions about wing geometry that have been made, the expressions for the aerodynamic velocity can be written out exactly:

$$u_{a|ASA} = u_{IELA} - r_{IELA} y$$

$$v_{a|ASA} = v_{IELA}$$

$$w_{a|ASA} = w_{IELA} + p_{IELA} y$$

$$p_{a|ASA} = p_{IELA}$$

$$q_{a|ASA} = q_{IELA}$$

$$r_{a|ASA} = r_{IELA} \qquad (9.80)$$

The angle of attack, which is a function of spanwise location, is given by

$$\alpha = \tan^{-1}\left(\frac{w_{a|ASA}}{u_{a|ASA}}\right) \qquad (9.81)$$

For small angles, this becomes

$$\alpha = \frac{w_{IELA} + p_{IELA} y}{u_{IELA} - r_{IELA} y} \qquad (9.82)$$

Remember, α is the angle that the wind makes with the chord, and a positive value of α is actually a negative rotation about the y axis. The lift is normal to this line, and the drag is parallel to this line. For small angles, the lift will just be in the negative z direction. The *distributed* aerodynamic forces are calculated from the following expressions:

$$dDrag = \frac{\rho V^2 c(y)}{2} C_D(\alpha, \delta, M, R_n)\, dy$$

$$dLift = \frac{\rho V^2 c(y)}{2} C_L(\alpha, \delta, M, R_n)\, dy$$

$$dMy = \frac{\rho V^2 c^2(y)}{2} C_m(\alpha, \delta, M, R_n)\, dy \qquad (9.83)$$

With the assumptions about the aerodynamics, the distributed loads reduce to

$$dDrag = 0$$

$$dLift = \frac{\rho}{2}(u_{\text{IELA}}^2 + w_{\text{IELA}}^2)ca_0 \left(\frac{w_{\text{IELA}} + p_{\text{IELA}}y}{u_{\text{IELA}} - r_{\text{IELA}}y} \right) dy$$

$$dMy = 0 \qquad (9.84)$$

Certain products of p and r have been eliminated as higher-order terms. Further simplifications are possible. Setting the velocity vector reference to these values:

$$u_{\text{IELA}} = u_{\text{IELA}}$$

$$v_{\text{IELA}} = 0$$

$$w_{\text{IELA}} = 0$$

$$p_{\text{IELA}} = p_{\text{IELA}}$$

$$q_{\text{IELA}} = 0$$

$$r_{\text{IELA}} = 0 \qquad (9.85)$$

The distributed lift becomes

$$dLift = \frac{\rho u_{\text{IELA}}^2}{2} ca_0 \left(\frac{p_{\text{IELA}}y}{u_{\text{IELA}}} \right) dy = \frac{1}{2}\rho ca_0\, u_{\text{IELA}}\, p_{\text{IELA}}\, y\, dy \qquad (9.86)$$

Stack the distributed loads into three-dimensional force and moment vectors:

$$dF = \left\{ \begin{array}{c} 0 \\ 0 \\ -\dfrac{1}{2}\rho ca_0\, u_{\text{IELA}}\, p_{\text{IELA}}\, y\, dy \end{array} \right\}, \quad dM = \left\{ \begin{array}{c} 0 \\ 0 \\ 0 \end{array} \right\} \qquad (9.87)$$

Stack these into a six-dimensional distributed loads vector called $d\boldsymbol{P}_{\text{ASA6}}$:

$$d\boldsymbol{P}_{\text{ASA6}} = \left\{ \begin{array}{c} d\boldsymbol{F} \\ d\boldsymbol{M} \end{array} \right\} \qquad (9.88)$$

Rotate this vector back through the angle of attack to get the loads in a system parallel with the IERA:

$$d\boldsymbol{P}_6 = T_6^T(0, -\alpha, 0)\, d\boldsymbol{P}_{\text{ASA6}} \qquad (9.89)$$

Because this example admits the use of small angles and the objects of the example are the lift and roll-moment derivatives, the preceding T_6 matrix is safely assumed to be the identity matrix. Next, the moment arm from the origin of the IERA to the ASA generates a rolling moment from lift. Formally,

$$d\boldsymbol{P}_{\text{IERA6}} = \begin{bmatrix} I & 0 \\ C(\boldsymbol{R}_{\text{ASA-IERA|IERA}}) & I \end{bmatrix} d\boldsymbol{P}_6 = G(\boldsymbol{R}_{\text{ASA-IERA|IERA}})\, d\boldsymbol{P}_6 \qquad (9.90)$$

The distributed $d\mathbf{P}_{\text{IERA6}}$ can be expanded:

$$
d\mathbf{P}_{\text{IERA6}} =
\begin{bmatrix}
1 & 0 & 0 & 0 & 0 & 0 \\
0 & 1 & 0 & 0 & 0 & 0 \\
0 & 0 & 1 & 0 & 0 & 0 \\
0 & 0 & y & 1 & 0 & 0 \\
0 & 0 & 0 & 0 & 1 & 0 \\
-y & 0 & 0 & 0 & 0 & 1
\end{bmatrix}
\left\{
\begin{array}{c}
0 \\
0 \\
-\dfrac{1}{2}\rho c a_0\, u_{\text{IELA}}\, p_{\text{IELA}}\, y\, dy \\
0 \\
0 \\
0
\end{array}
\right\}
\tag{9.91}
$$

After expansion,

$$
d\mathbf{P}_{\text{IERA6}} =
\left\{
\begin{array}{c}
0 \\
0 \\
-\dfrac{1}{2}\rho c a_0\, u_{\text{IELA}}\, p_{\text{IELA}}\, y \\
-\dfrac{1}{2}\rho c a_0\, u_{\text{IELA}}\, p_{\text{IELA}}\, y^2 \\
0 \\
0
\end{array}
\right\}
dy
\tag{9.92}
$$

Next, rotate the distributed load to the IELA:

$$
d\mathbf{P}_{\text{IELA6}} = T_6^T(\Gamma, \theta, \Lambda)\, d\mathbf{P}_{\text{IERA6}}
\tag{9.93}
$$

Because it has already been established that the rotation matrix is the identity matrix in this particular example, $d\mathbf{P}_{\text{IELA6}} = d\mathbf{P}_{\text{IERA6}}$. A spatial integration from the root of the wing to the tip gives the lift and rolling moment with all other forces and moments equal to zero.

$$
\mathbf{P}_{\text{IELA6}} = \int_0^b d\mathbf{P}_{\text{IELA6}}\, dy =
\left\{
\begin{array}{c}
0 \\
0 \\
-\dfrac{1}{2}\rho c a_0\, u_{\text{IELA}}\, p_{\text{IELA}}\, \dfrac{b^2}{2} \\
-\dfrac{1}{2}\rho c a_0\, u_{\text{IELA}}\, p_{\text{IELA}}\, \dfrac{b^3}{3} \\
0 \\
0
\end{array}
\right\}
\tag{9.94}
$$

$$
\mathbf{P}_{\text{wing}|\text{B}} =
\begin{bmatrix}
I & 0 \\
C(\mathbf{R}_{\text{wing}-\text{cg}|\text{cg}}) & I
\end{bmatrix}
\mathbf{P}_{\text{IELA6}} = G(\mathbf{R}_{\text{wing}-\text{cg}|\text{cg}})\mathbf{P}_{\text{IELA6}}
\tag{9.95}
$$

Recall, the initial objective was to calculate the derivatives of lift and rolling moment with respect to roll rate p. The derivatives are easily determined:

$$L_p = \frac{\partial Lift}{\partial p_{\text{body}}} = -\frac{1}{4}\rho c a_0 u_{\text{IELA}} b^2$$

$$M_{xp} = \frac{\partial M_x}{\partial p_{\text{body}}} = -\frac{1}{6}\rho c a_0 u_{\text{IELA}} b^3 \tag{9.96}$$

Derivatives are presented often in nondimensional form. To make the preceding dimensional derivatives nondimensional, first divide force derivatives by the product of the dynamic pressure and a characteristic area (usually wing area), and divide the moment derivatives by the product of the dynamic pressure, a characteristic area, and a characteristic length (usually the mean aerodynamic chord). Then for derivatives with respect to a linear velocity, multiply by a characteristic velocity (usually the forward velocity), and for derivatives with respect to an angular velocity, multiply by a characteristic velocity, and divide by a characteristic length (usually the semispan). Going through this arithmetic makes the derivatives nondimensional, but it requires that the linear velocities be divided by the same characteristic velocity and the angular velocities be multiplied by the same characteristic length and divided by the same characteristic velocity. In the example about to conclude, the nondimensional lift and rolling moment are

$$C_{L\bar{p}} = \frac{L_p}{(\rho u_{\text{IELA}}^2 bc/2)}\left(\frac{2u_{\text{IELA}}}{b}\right) = -a_0 \tag{9.97}$$

$$C_{Mx\bar{p}} = \frac{M_{xp}}{(\rho u_{\text{IELA}}^2 bc^2/2)}\left(\frac{2u_{\text{IELA}}}{b}\right) = -\frac{2a_0 b}{3c} \tag{9.98}$$

The correct use of the derivatives requires the linear and angular velocities be made nondimensional. Generate the nondimensional linear velocity by dividing by the characteristic velocity. Generate the nondimensional angular velocity by dividing by the characteristic velocity and multiplying by the characteristic length. Multiply the derivatives by the nondimensional velocities, and then reconstitute the dimensional force or moment by appropriate multiplication by the dynamic pressure, area, and characteristic length as required.

$$\bar{p} = \left(\frac{pb}{2u_{\text{IELA}}}\right)$$

$$Lift = C_{L\bar{p}}\left(\frac{\rho u_{\text{IELA}}^2 bc}{2}\right)\bar{p}$$

$$Mx = C_{Mx\bar{p}}\left(\frac{\rho u_{\text{IELA}}^2 bc^2}{2}\right)\bar{p} \tag{9.99}$$

Expand the preceding equations to confirm that the lift and rolling moment are recovered.

9.6.4   Other Methods

There are several other methods to calculate the forces and moments that wings generate. These methods include, but are not limited to lifting line, lifting surface, or vortex lattice, and computational fluid dynamics (CFD).

The vortex-lattice (VL) method covers a surface with closed trapezoids of circulation and a trailing system of horseshoe vortices. The goal is to calculate the circulation strengths of the trapezoidal circuits and the horseshoes so that at every control point (one for each vortex) the freestream wind does not penetrate the wing surface. A series of simultaneous equations (one for each vortex) must be solved for each condition.

The CFD methods use numerical techniques to solve the partial differential equations of fluid flow over an aerodynamic body. These equations are known as the Navier–Stokes equations. Such methods can solve both static and time-dependent problems. But to get a sufficiently detailed and stable solution, a very fine mesh is required, and this means a great amount of computer time is required.

Both the VL and CFD methods are very expensive in a computational sense and are not suited for real-time simulation. On the other hand, the computational burden of the lifting-line method is significantly lower than the VL or CFD methods and may in fact offer a real-time solution. The lifting-line method uses one or more horseshoe vortices that interact with each other and is especially useful in estimating the induced drag of a wing and the distributed lift. What is more, this method also provides an estimate of the wake, which is important when aerodynamic interference (coupling) or "wake turbulence" is modeled. Therefore, a brief discussion of the lifting-line method is warranted.

9.6.4.1   Lifting-Line Method   A horseshoe vortex consists of two vortices that trail from the quarter-chord point on the tips of the wing to infinity. These vortices are called the trailing tip vortices. A bound vortex segment, which is the locus of quarter-chord points along the span of the wing, joins the endpoints of the trailing tip vortices. Obviously, all three parts of this horseshoe vortex have the same strength. Figure 9.26 illustrates a simple horseshoe system.

The dot is a point of interest for the calculations about to happen. Each segment of this horseshoe contributes to induced velocity at this (and every other) point.

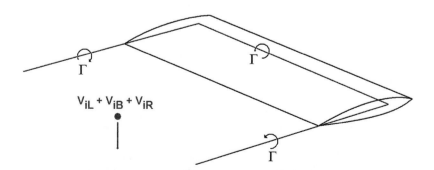

Fig. 9.26   Horseshoe vortex system attached to a wing.

Closed-form solutions of the Biot–Savart law for straight-line segments are well known and available in the literature. One general solution for vortex segments in three dimensions is found in the appendix. A less general solution for a segment is given without development next:

$$v_z = \frac{\gamma}{4\pi h} \left[\frac{x_2}{\sqrt{x_2^2 + h^2}} - \frac{x_1}{\sqrt{x_1^2 + h^2}} \right] \tag{9.100}$$

This equation gives the induced velocity normal to the plane that contains the vortex segment and the control point. The geometry is explained in Fig. 9.27.

All three segments of the horseshoe contribute to the induced velocity at the control point. If the control point is located in the plane of the wing/horseshoe system at midspan, then with these solutions one can estimate the induced velocity at the control point. That solution is

$$v_z = \frac{\gamma}{\pi b'} \left[\frac{\sqrt{\eta^2 + 1}}{\eta} + 1 \right] \tag{9.101}$$

where

$$\eta = \frac{2d}{b'} \tag{9.102}$$

and d is the downstream distance from the $\frac{1}{4}$-chord of the wing and b' is the effective wing span. For elliptically loaded wings, the effective span (and separation of the trailing tip vortices) is

$$\frac{b'}{b} = \frac{\pi}{4} \tag{9.103}$$

The Kutta–Joukowski theorem states

$$L = \rho V \times \Gamma \tag{9.104}$$

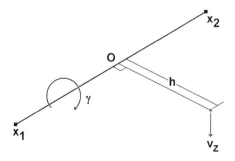

Fig. 9.27   Segment of a straight-line vortex filament.

In this expression, ρ is the density of air, V is the freestream velocity, and Γ is the vortex strength. For two-dimensional flow, this equation becomes

$$L = \rho V \Gamma \tag{9.105}$$

The lift in the preceding expression is actually distributed lift. If only one vortex is used along the effective span, then the total lift is

$$L = \rho V \Gamma b' \tag{9.106}$$

Recall the definition of the aspect ratio $A_R = b^2/S$. Because only one vortex is expressed in the preceding model $\gamma = \Gamma$. Finally, if one makes the induced velocity nondimensional by dividing by the freestream velocity, the result is the downwash angle (for small angles).

$$\varepsilon_H = \frac{8C_L}{\pi^3 A_R} \left[\frac{\sqrt{\eta^2 + 1}}{\eta} + 1 \right] \tag{9.107}$$

Dommasch et al. [5] state an empirical formula for downwash angle:

$$\varepsilon_D = \frac{20C_L}{57.3} \left(\frac{3c}{d} \right)^{\frac{1}{4}} \frac{\lambda^{0.3}}{A_R^{0.725}} \tag{9.108}$$

The term λ is the inverse of the taper ratio with which the reader is familiar, that is, it is the root chord divided by the tip chord. In Fig. 9.28, the simple horseshoe model described in McCormick [4] is compared against the Dommasch et al. [5] model for two values of downstream distance and various values of aspect ratio. A rectangular wing was modeled in all cases.

Presented in this way, the comparison looks surprisingly good, considering how crude the horseshoe model is. The analytical model seems to consistently predict a downwash angle greater than the empirical model. If one adds the complexity of elevation out of the plane of the wing, then the analytical model becomes

$$\varepsilon_H = \frac{8C_L}{\pi^3 AR} \left[\frac{\eta}{\sqrt{\eta^2 + \theta^2 + 1}} \left(\frac{1}{1 + \theta^2} + \frac{1}{\eta^2 + \theta^2} \right) + \frac{1}{1 + \theta^2} \right] \tag{9.109}$$

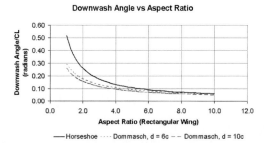

Fig. 9.28   Effect of aspect ratio on downwash.

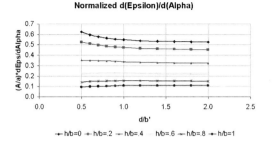

Fig. 9.29   Change in downwash angle as a function of downstream distance.

where

$$\theta = \frac{2\,h}{b'} \tag{9.110}$$

The term h is the height above the plane of the wing. The downwash characteristic curves shown in Fig. 9.29 were obtained by differentiating the preceding downwash expression with respect to α, and multiplying both sides by A_R/a, where a is the lift-curve slope.

The lifting line just described assumes that the distributed lift is a constant across the span of the wing. This is not true in the general case. A more sophisticated estimate can be obtained by stacking horseshoes, as in Fig. 9.30.

Now the vorticity is a function of spanwise location. The vortex sheet leaving the trailing edge rolls up into two distinct trailing tip vortices in very little distance, so that as a first approximation the concept of the single horseshoe is not too bad for interference calculations. A photograph of the "smoke angel" produced by a C-17 Globemaster as the smoke from flares is organized by the trailing tip vortices argues this point nicely.

The method whereby the distributed vortex strengths are calculated is outside the scope of this text. The interested reader is encouraged to consult McCormick [4] for a simple but very useful approach for the case of straight-and-level flight.

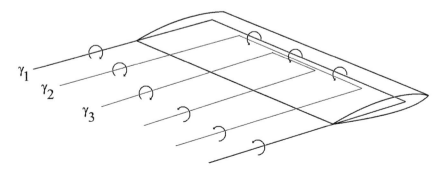

Fig. 9.30   Multiple horseshoe vortices—the lifting line approach.

Fig. 9.31 **"Smoke angel" visualizes the genesis of the trailing tip vortices from a C-17 (U.S. Air Force photograph by Tech. Sgt. Russell E. Cooley IV).**

Finally, because most aircraft have d/c ratios of no more than five or six, the simple horseshoe model seems to be lacking. Therefore, bear in mind that one can use the theory to gain insight into trends, but empirical data gleaned from flight-test data, wind-tunnel data, and the like should be trusted. Do not fall into the trap of mistrusting your data because it disagrees with your preconceived notions. In this regard, it is interesting to note the philosophy of Wilbur Wright. In the two-volume collection by Marvin McFarland titled *The Papers of Wilbur and Orville Wright* [6], Wilbur expressed his concern on the fairing of data by Samuel Langley. In a letter to Octave Chenute dated 1 December 1901, Wright wrote, "... I have myself sometimes found it difficult to let the lines run where they will, instead of running them where I think they ought to go. My conclusion is that it is safest to follow the observations exactly, and let others do their own correcting if they wish." This remarkable insight led the Wright brothers to recognize wing stall.

9.7 Odds and Ends

The text includes three demonstration programs. The AIRFOIL1 program demonstrates the use of the Weissinger approximation in airfoil analysis. The WING1 program demonstrates the strip-theory method and point-load method. The WINGSURF2 program calculates wing performance using the vortex-lattice method.

9.8 Conclusions

Airfoils are two dimensional; fins and wings have three dimensions. Analysis and modeling of airfoils, fins, and wings uses CFD techniques such as stream functions, velocity potentials, distributed vorticity, lifting-line methods, lifting-surface methods, the computational solution to the Reynolds-averaged Navier–Stokes equation, wind-tunnel data, and flight-test data. The geometry of airfoils is described fully with a chord line, a camber line, and a thickness schedule. The geometry of wings requires a definition of its sweep, dihedral, twist, and taper. Airfoil sections and wings may have various devices called flaps, slats, and spoilers to give the pilot additional command over the lift, drag, and pitching moment. Airfoils and wings have a region where the lift varies linearly with a change in the angle of attack. After a critical angle, the wing stalls—the lift drops rapidly, and the drag rises dramatically. The aerodynamic coefficients are functions of angle of attack, Mach number, flap deflection, and Reynolds number. Wings operating near each other influence each other by virtue of the trailing tip vortices. The point-load method, strip-theory method, and derivative method are popular and easily written methods to model wing and fm aerodynamics.

References

[1]Abbott, Ira H., and Von Doenhoff, Albert E., *Theory of Wing Sections*, Dover, New York, 1959, Appendix IV, pp. 449–687.

[2]Crtizos, C. C., Heyson, H. H., and Boswinkle, B. W., "*Aerodynamic Characteristics of NACA 0012 Airfoil Section at Angles of Attack from 0° to 180°*," NACATN 3361, Jan. 1955.

[3]McCormick, Barnes W., *Aerodynamics of V/STOL Flight*, Academic Press, New York, 1967, pp. 69, 168–170.

[4]McCormick, B. W., *Aerodynamics, Aeronautics and Flight Mechanics*, Wiley, New York, 1979, pp. 130–142, 485–488.

[5]Dommasch, Daniel O., Sherby, Sydney S., and Connolly, Thomas F., *Airplane Aerodynamics*, Pitman, New York, 1967, pp. 443–444.

[6]McFarland, Marvin, "*The Papers of Wilbur and Orville Wright including the Chenute–Wright Letters and other papers of Octave Chenute*," Volume I 1899–1905, Volume II 1906–1948, McGraw-Hill Book Co., Inc., New York, Toronto, London, 1953, p. 171.

Problems

9.1 Consider a rectangular wing. *Derive* an expression for the induced velocity midspan at the $\frac{3}{4}$-chord point using the Biot–Savart law. The wing is not elliptically loaded; let $b = b'$. Then, use the Kutta–Joukowski law to relate the vortex strength to the lift on the wing. Finally, express the answer in terms of the freestream velocity, the angle of attack, and the aspect ratio only. Vary the aspect ratio from two to 20 in increments of two, and plot the ratio of induced velocity divided by the freestream velocity. Assume the angle of attack is unity. What do you observe? How does the result influence the geometry of glider wings?

9.2 An untwisted wing is mounted with a cantilever attachment to the left side wall of a wind tunnel as observed by someone standing downwind of the wing. The span is 5 ft, the root chord is 2 ft, and the taper ratio is 0.5. The incidence angle at the wing root is 5 deg. The airfoil is the NASA 0012. Assume $C_D = 0.010$. The wind tunnel is operating at SSL conditions, and the wind speed is 100 kn. What are the three forces and three moments at the root end of the wing resolved to the IELA and IERA? Use the point-load method. Show your work, and use the Wing1.exe program to check your results.

9.3 Using expressions (9.1), (9.2), and (9.3), prove that the angle of attack for an airfoil equals the sum of the pitch angle and the inflow angle.

10
Aerodynamics of Propellers

10.1 Introduction

The Wright brothers had been flying for several years before their famous flight on 17 December 1903. What made that date special is that they did it with power. Before then, favorable winds, tethers, and long gentle slopes were required to stay aloft. But on that day, they used a device of their own design that drew their airplane forward against its own drag. That device was a propeller [1].

A propeller is, at its core, a high-aspect-ratio wing that has been pinned at one tip and is spinning about that pin. The spinning motion moves air over the propeller, giving rise to dynamic pressure and lift. Of course, that lift does not come free. As with any wing, there is profile and induced drag associated with lift. Multiplied by an appropriate moment arm, the drag produces torque and the propeller is said to absorb this torque (or power). This all seems reasonable, and with the wing theory just presented, this seems tractable.

However, there is a phenomenon that has not been discussed in detail yet, but one with which everyone is familiar. Turn on a fan, and feel a breeze. That breeze is called induced velocity. It is a consequence of thrust. The speed of the induced velocity depends on the axial speed of the propeller and the amount of thrust the propeller produces. A fourth-order polynomial describes the speed of the induced velocity for many cases. It comes from the momentum theory, and that theory will be visited time after time throughout the remainder of this text. Propellers made powered flight possible. This chapter brings to the table some fundamental material needed to model propellers.

10.2 Momentum Theory

Newton's second law states that an applied force changes the momentum of a system in a finite time. That is,

$$F = \frac{\mathrm{d}(mv)}{\mathrm{d}t} \tag{10.1}$$

149

When the mass is constant, this reduces to the familiar refrain:

$$F = m\frac{dV}{dt} = ma \qquad (10.2)$$

A propeller produces thrust by accelerating a great mass of air through a relatively small change in velocity. The first of the theories behind this is called the Rankine–Froude actuator disk theory. It is also commonly referred to as the Glauert momentum model. It develops like this.

Imagine a disk with an infinite number of infinitesimally narrow blades arranged around the hub of the propeller. This is an actuator disk. Now, looking from the side, draw a tubular control volume around the propeller large enough to capture all of the air being "sucked" into it, and extending far enough downstream of the propeller to account for the wake contraction. (This clairvoyant knowledge is hard to explain. The author has seen it visualized, but did Glauert? Prouty [2] suggests a nice way to visualize wake contraction. Pour some syrup from a pitcher onto a pancake. At the pitcher, the cross-sectional area of the syrup flow is some size and is flowing at some rate. Because no additional syrup is entering the system, the amount of syrup hitting the pancake equals the amount leaving the pitcher. But, gravity is adding energy to the syrup, so that at the pancake the syrup has a higher velocity, and must therefore have a smaller cross-sectional area as required by the continuity equation. Thus, there is some reason to think that the streamtube will constrict because the propeller is increasing the velocity of the air.) The control volume is porous. Also, draw the streamtube that just surrounds the propeller disk, but expands enough to capture all of the air being sucked into the propeller, and shrinks downstream of the propeller, again accounting for wake contraction. Figure 10.1 illustrates the control volume and streamtube.

Upstream of the propeller, the pressure is P_0, and the wind approaching the rotor is V_0. At the plane of the propeller, which is producing thrust T evenly distributed over area A, the pressure rises to a value of P as the velocity increases to V_1. A discontinuous rise in pressure dP takes place as the propeller produces thrust. Far behind the propeller, the air mass in the streamtube is flowing with velocity V_2, but has relaxed back to pressure P_0. The appendix on the momentum

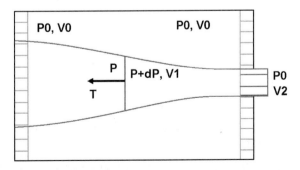

Fig. 10.1   Control volume, slipstream, and actuator disk viewed edge on.

law finishes the development, and the reader is encouraged to review it. The salient results are these:

1) The thrust is related to the velocity far upstream and in the wake far downstream by the expression: $T = \rho \pi r^2 V_2 (V_2 - V_0)$.

2) The air velocity through the disk is the average of the velocities far upstream and far downstream in the wake, that is, $V_1 = (V_2 + V_0)/2$.

3) The increment that is added to the freestream velocity at the rotor disk is called the induced velocity, $w = V_1 - V_0$.

4) The Glauert momentum model relates the induced velocity to the thrust with this expression: $T = \rho A (V_0 + w) 2w$.

Rearrange the preceding thrust equation to the following form, which gives an estimate of the induced velocity for a given forward speed and thrust. This is the common expression of the Glauert momentum model:

$$w = \frac{T}{2\rho A \|V\|} \tag{10.3}$$

where in this case $\|V\| = \sqrt{(V_0 + w)^2}$.

When the rotor is in hover, the freestream velocity is zero, and the induced velocity is given by

$$w_{w0} = \sqrt{\frac{T}{2\rho A}} = \sqrt{\frac{1}{2\rho}} \sqrt{DiskLoading} \tag{10.4}$$

The power that the propeller absorbs is

$$P_{\text{ideal}} = T(V_0 + w) \tag{10.5}$$

The useful power is

$$P_{\text{use}} = T V_0 \tag{10.6}$$

and so the efficiency of the propeller, which is given the symbol η, is

$$\eta = \frac{P_{\text{use}}}{P_{\text{ideal}}} = \frac{V_0}{V_0 + w} = \frac{1}{1 + w/V_0} \tag{10.7}$$

One sees immediately that the propeller (or rotor) is most efficient if it is pushing a large mass of air at low induced velocities. Efficient propellers (from an aerodynamic standpoint) have low disk loadings. One also sees that expression (10.7) breaks down at zero forward airspeed. The chapter on rotors introduces the figure of merit, which presents an alternate definition of efficiency that does not blow up with zero airspeed.

10.3 Momentum Theory Expanded for Disk Plane Angle of Attack and Rate of Descent

The expression relating thrust and induced velocity appears to be second order in the induced velocity and also appears to be good only for axial flight. One finds

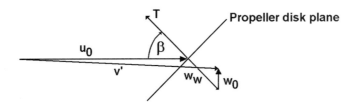

Fig. 10.2   Disk plane at an angle of attack.

a somewhat more general version of the momentum equation if the propeller is placed at an angle with respect to the oncoming wind and if a rate of descent is introduced, as pictured in Fig. 10.2. Let the propeller generate thrust T perpendicular to the disk plane. The disk plane is normal to the shaft, which is at an angle β with the horizon. The forward speed is u_0, and the rate of descent is w_0. The propeller generates a wash velocity w_w caused by the thrust.

Rewriting Eq. (10.3), the thrust-induced velocity relationship at the plane of the propeller is

$$T = -2\rho A V' w_w \tag{10.8}$$

Note the negative sign in expression (10.8). The direction of the wash velocity is exactly opposite the direction of thrust. From Fig. 10.2 and the Pythagorean theorem, the general velocity V' is given by the expression

$$V' = [(u_0 + w_w \cos \beta)^2 + (w_0 - w_w \sin \beta)^2]^{1/2} \tag{10.9}$$

Substitute Eq. (10.9) into Eq. (10.8), and employ these normalizing factors with the aid of expression (10.4):

$$\hat{w} = \frac{w_w}{w_{w0}}$$

$$\hat{\mu} = \frac{u_0}{w_{w0}}$$

$$\hat{\eta} = \frac{w_0}{w_{w0}} \tag{10.10}$$

The result is a fourth-order polynomial:

$$\hat{w}^4 + 2(\hat{\mu} \cos \beta - \hat{\eta} \sin \beta)\hat{w}^3 + (\hat{\mu}^2 + \hat{\eta}^2)\hat{w}^2 - 1 = 0 \tag{10.11}$$

The Newton–Raphson method or eigenanalysis easily solves this polynomial for $\hat{w}$, which is the non-dimensional wash velocity. It is instructive to look at two limiting cases. If the rate of descent is zero and the forward velocity is varied from zero to some high value, then the solution of Eq. (10.11) appears as shown in Fig. 10.3.

Two things are immediately obvious. First, the induced velocity decreases rapidly with forward speed, before asymptotically approaching zero. Second, the effect of the mast angle (90 deg is helicopter mode, 0 deg is airplane mode) is not

Induced Velocity as a Function of Mast Angle and
Forward Speed

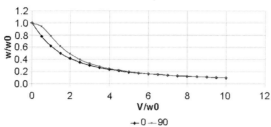

Fig. 10.3   Variation of induced velocity with forward speed and mast angle.

Induced Velocity as a Function of Vertical Velocity

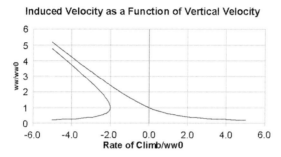

Fig. 10.4   Variation of induced velocity with rate of climb (negative rate of descent).

profound when it comes to the strength of the induced velocity. However, it is very important when power for a given thrust is considered.

In the other limiting case, vary the rate of descent while holding the forward speed to zero. If the propeller is oriented in "helicopter" mode (90 deg of mast angle), then the solution of Eq. (10.11) is shown in Fig. 10.4.

Presenting this second curve is a bit premature; it will appear again in the chapter on rotors. Nevertheless, some very important results are immediately obvious. Over the entire climbing portion of the solution, and over some of the descending portion (down to -2.0), the solution is single valued when confined to the positive values of induced velocity. However, when the normalized descent rate becomes more negative than -2.0, the solution has three positive roots. As discussed in the chapter on rotors, this is the difference between powered descent and autorotation. All three solutions have physical meaning, though only the lowest or highest is usually achieved.

10.4   Propeller Analysis

The following analysis differs from classical approaches for two reasons. First, in an effort to retain a uniform approach to modeling, the rigor of the IELA and IERA are applied. In the long run, this rigor will enable the modeler to place the propeller at arbitrary angles to the oncoming wind, and the propeller can have a curved reference line. Second, simulation is more than just performance. It is also behavior. The estimation of propeller performance is very important, of course, but that is a static measure taken on the thrust axis when the oncoming wind is purely axial. In real life, as any pilot knows, a propeller at an angle of attack develops what is sometimes called p-factor [3], a moment normal to the spin axis. This moment causes the aircraft to yaw during climb. (The direction of yaw is dependent on the direction of propeller spin. Propellers on single-engine aircraft spin clockwise when viewed from the cockpit. This creates a left yawing moment, which must be countered with right rudder pedal. The moment is not small. In fact, in many (but not all) multi-engine aircraft, both propellers spin the same direction. The phrase, "critical engine out," means that the left engine has been cut. The pilot must contend with the yaw moment caused by thrust of the right propeller, which has a significant moment arm, and the p-factor, which is adding yaw moment in the same direction. The black humor often applied to critical-engine-out performance is that the good engine flies you to the scene of the accident.) Simple performance equations do not reveal this. However, with just a bit of rigor, the effects of off-axis wind and angular rates are easily determined. As with wing analysis, begin with the IELA.

10.4.1   Individual Element Local Axes

The IELA is parallel with the aircraft body axes, but translated to the location of the propeller hub. The origin of the IELA lies in the plane of, and at the center of, the spinning blades assuming the blades are coplanar. Otherwise, the IELA contains the apex of the cone swept by the spinning blades.

10.4.2   Individual Element Reference Axes

The IERA shares its origin with the IELA, but is rotated primarily about the y axis of the IELA such that x axis of the IERA points down, and the z axis points generally downstream, as shown in Fig. 10.5. The IERA does not spin with the propeller.

If $R_{\text{prop}-\text{cg}|\text{cg}}$ measures from the aircraft center of gravity to the propeller IELA, resolved to the center of gravity, then the linear and angular inertial velocities of the IELA are

$$V_{\text{IELA}} = V_B + \omega_B \times R_{\text{prop}-\text{cg}|\text{cg}} = \begin{Bmatrix} u_i \\ v_i \\ w_i \end{Bmatrix} \qquad (10.12)$$

$$\omega_{\text{IELA}} = \omega_B = \begin{Bmatrix} p_i \\ q_i \\ r_i \end{Bmatrix} \qquad (10.13)$$

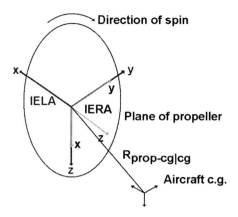

Fig. 10.5 Propeller IELA and IERA.

Because the origins of the IELA and IERA are coincident, then the IERA velocities, resolved to the IELA, are

$$V_{\text{IERA}|\text{IELA}} = V_{\text{IELA}}$$
$$\omega_{\text{IERA}|\text{IELA}} = \omega_{\text{IELA}} \tag{10.14}$$

The IERA are rotated relative to the IELA. If the spin axis of the propeller is defined to lie on the z axis of the IERA, then the rotation matrix is defined by the angular orientation of the transmission/engine and is usually fixed once installed. The velocity in the IERA is thus:

$$V_{\text{IERA}} = T(\theta_x, \theta_y, \theta_z)V_{\text{IERA}|\text{IELA}}$$
$$\omega_{\text{IERA}} = T(\theta_x, \theta_y, \theta_z)\omega_{\text{IERA}|\text{IELA}} \tag{10.15}$$

The arguments in the transformation matrix are general orientation angles. For instance, one would set

$$\theta_x = \theta_z = 0 \qquad \text{and} \qquad \theta_y = -\frac{\pi}{2}$$

in Fig. 10.5. Induced velocity was described earlier. From the standpoint of a stand-alone model, induced velocity is most easily understood when described in the IERA. However, if the downwash from the propeller is to affect the aerodynamic velocity at other points on the aircraft, then it is best to "keep the books" in the IELA. This makes transformations into other axes less wearisome. Given this, the induced velocity in the IELA is also transformed to the IERA in similar fashion.

$$w_{\text{IELA}} = \begin{Bmatrix} u_w \\ v_w \\ w_w \end{Bmatrix} \tag{10.16}$$

$$\boldsymbol{\omega}_{w|\text{IELA}} = \begin{Bmatrix} p_w \\ q_w \\ r_w \end{Bmatrix} \qquad (10.17)$$

$$\boldsymbol{w}_{\text{IERA}|\text{IELA}} = \boldsymbol{w}_{\text{IELA}}$$

$$\boldsymbol{\omega}_{w|\text{IERA}|\text{IELA}} = \boldsymbol{\omega}_{w|\text{IELA}} \qquad (10.18)$$

$$\boldsymbol{w}_{\text{IERA}} = T(\theta_x, \theta_y, \theta_z)\boldsymbol{w}_{\text{IERA}|\text{IELA}}$$

$$\boldsymbol{\omega}_{w|\text{IERA}} = T(\theta_x, \theta_y, \theta_z)\boldsymbol{\omega}_{w|\text{IERA}|\text{IELA}} \qquad (10.19)$$

10.4.3 Hub Axes

The coordinate system that spins with the propeller is called the hub system. The hub axes and the IERA have a common origin, and their z axes are coincident. See Fig. 10.6.

Because the hub axes spin with the propeller, the linear and angular velocities seen at the hub are dependent on the azimuth angle of the propeller. In addition, the rotational speed of the propeller adds to the angular velocity vector. Note that the angular speed of the rotor is a negative about the z axis of the IERA. Propellers spin clockwise as seen from the cockpit. The zero azimuth angle may be defined anywhere, but it will be convenient to describe it as the angle when the number 1 blade is pointing in the negative x-axis direction of the IERA. The chapter on rotors will explain this. Define the azimuthal resolution matrix thus:

$$\boldsymbol{T}_\psi = \begin{bmatrix} \cos\psi & -\sin\psi & 0 \\ \sin\psi & \cos\psi & 0 \\ 0 & 0 & 1 \end{bmatrix} \qquad (10.20)$$

and the propeller spin rate vector as

$$\boldsymbol{E}_z(-\Omega) = \begin{Bmatrix} 0 \\ 0 \\ -\Omega \end{Bmatrix} \qquad (10.21)$$

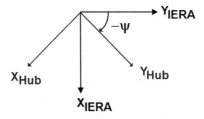

Fig. 10.6   Hub axes rotated from IERA through the azimuth angle. This would be the view from the cockpit—the z axis of both systems points out of the page toward the reader.

Then, the hub velocities are

$$V_h = R_z(\psi)V_{\text{IERA}} = T_\psi V_{\text{IERA}}$$
$$\omega_h = T_\psi \omega_{\text{IERA}} + E_z(-\Omega) \tag{10.22}$$

Note: T_ψ uses a negative angle ψ about the z axis. This is because the azimuth angle ψ, which measures about the negative z axis, is defined by the integral expression $\psi = \int \Omega \, dt$, and human desire dictates that rotor speed Ω has a positive value. This same argument will show up again in the chapter on rotors.

Wash velocities are also transformed in the same way. Thus, the total aerodynamic velocities are

$$V_{a_h} = V_h - w_h$$
$$\omega_{a_h} = \omega_h - \omega_{w_h} \tag{10.23}$$

Imagine now a blade reference line moving out along blade 1. The reference line attaches to the 1/4-chord points of the individual blade sections, and so it spins with the propeller. Figure 10.7 shows a propeller with a blade reference line running through the quarter-chord points of the blade sections and one section excised.

The simplest of the blade reference lines, which describes a straight blade in the shaft normal plane, is given by

$$R_{\text{bl}}(s) = \begin{Bmatrix} -s \\ 0 \\ 0 \end{Bmatrix} \tag{10.24}$$

The symbol s rather than r is used for the radial position for two reasons. First, it eliminates confusion between radial station and angular rate r, and second it reminds the user that this is an arclength measure. Other examples of reference line are as shown in Fig. 10.8.

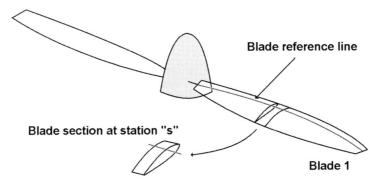

Fig. 10.7   Propeller with blade section shown.

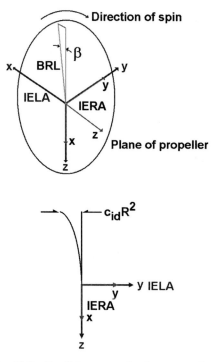

Fig. 10.8 Possible geometries for a propeller.

a) *Blades coned in the thrust direction*:

$$R_{bl}(s) = \left\{ \begin{array}{c} -s\cos\beta \\ 0 \\ -s\sin\beta \end{array} \right\}$$

b) *Curved blades*:

$$R_{bl}(s) = \left\{ \begin{array}{c} -s \\ -c_{id}s^2 \\ 0 \end{array} \right\}$$

In the example of coning, the angle β represents the angular displacement of the blade out of the shaft normal plane. In the curved blade example, the coefficient for inplane displacement C_{id} is a scaling factor set so that at the tip of the blade the maximum in-plane displacement is $C_{id}R^2$, where R is the propeller radius. The negative sign in the y direction means that the blade tip is "behind" the blade root in the direction of spin.

The aerodynamic velocity at the blade section local axes is

$$V_{a_{bl}} = V_{a_h} + \omega_{a_h} \times R_{bl} \tag{10.25}$$

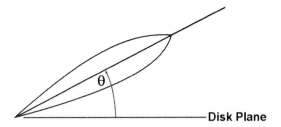

Fig. 10.9   End view of a blade section.

In general, each blade section is twisted out of the shaft normal plane by some angle θ as illustrated in Fig. 10.9.

Velocities in the disk (shaft normal) plane must be resolved to the chord line of the blade section. At the risk of losing some generality, the discussion from here on out will focus on an unconed, straight blade, aligned with the negative x axis in the IERA. This means the aerodynamic velocity in the blade-section reference axes is

$$V_{br} = T_x(\theta_B)V_{a_{bl}} = \begin{Bmatrix} u_{br} \\ v_{br} \\ w_{br} \end{Bmatrix} \qquad (10.26)$$

where, for the "ideally" twisted blade, the twist angle is given by

$$\theta_B = \theta_{Root} + \frac{\theta_{Twist}}{x}$$

$$x = \frac{s}{R} \qquad (10.27)$$

and

$$T_x(\theta_B) = \begin{bmatrix} 1 & 0 & 0 \\ 0 & \cos\theta_B & -\sin\theta_B \\ 0 & \sin\theta_B & \cos\theta_B \end{bmatrix} \qquad (10.28)$$

Because s increases in the negative x direction, the rotation about the x axis has the opposite sign from the conventional transformation matrix. In addition, the root angle is usually less than zero, and the twist angle is positive. (The usual presentation has the root angle greater than zero, and the twist angle negative. The rigor of the axes conventions here reverses these signs.)

The aerodynamic angle of attack at the blade section is

$$\alpha = \tan^{-1}\left(\frac{w_{br}}{v_{br}}\right) \qquad (10.29)$$

If the blade section is not symmetric, which is usually the case, then the angle from the chord line to the zero-lift line must be added to the angle of attack just given. Table look-up will automatically take care of this, and that approach will be assumed for the remainder of this presentation. The blade-section total velocity and Mach number are simply

$$V_{\text{Tot}}^2 = v_{\text{br}}^2 + w_{\text{br}}^2$$

$$M = \frac{V_{\text{Tot}}}{V_{\text{sound}}} \tag{10.30}$$

The distributed lift and drag are then

$$dL = \frac{1}{2}\rho V_{\text{Tot}}^2 c(s) Cl(\alpha, M)\, ds$$

$$dD = \frac{1}{2}\rho V_{\text{Tot}}^2 c(s) Cd(\alpha, M)\, ds \tag{10.31}$$

Recall, these forces are perpendicular and parallel to the total velocity vector. It is desired to resolve these forces into hub axes. Do this by rotating them through the negative of the angle of attack to get them into blade-section axes, then rotating that resultant through the blade-section pitch angle:

$$d\boldsymbol{F}_{\text{bl}} = T_x(-\alpha) \begin{Bmatrix} 0 \\ -dD \\ -dL \end{Bmatrix}$$

$$d\boldsymbol{F}_h = T_x^T(\theta_B)\, d\boldsymbol{F}_{\text{bl}} \tag{10.32}$$

where

$$T_x(-\alpha) = \begin{bmatrix} 1 & 0 & 0 \\ 0 & \cos\alpha & -\sin\alpha \\ 0 & \sin\alpha & \cos\alpha \end{bmatrix}$$

The distributed moment is found with the cross product of the blade reference line and the distributed forces in hub axes.

$$d\boldsymbol{M}_h = \boldsymbol{R}_{\text{bl}}(s) \times d\boldsymbol{F}_h \tag{10.33}$$

The average value of the forces and moments in the IERA are then

$$\boldsymbol{F}_{\text{IERA}} = \frac{1}{2\pi} \int_0^{2\pi} T_\psi^T \int_0^R d\boldsymbol{F}_h\, d\psi$$

$$\boldsymbol{M}_{\text{IERA}} = \frac{1}{2\pi} \int_0^{2\pi} T_\psi^T \int_0^R d\boldsymbol{M}_h\, d\psi \tag{10.34}$$

Finally, the forces and moments in body axes are

$$\boldsymbol{F}_{\text{IELA}} = T^T(\theta_x, \theta_y, \theta_z)\boldsymbol{F}_{\text{IERA}}$$

$$\boldsymbol{M}_{\text{IELA}} = T^T(\theta_x, \theta_y, \theta_z)\boldsymbol{M}_{\text{IERA}} \tag{10.35}$$

That completes the story about the loads. The story about the wash calculation continues. Recall the Glauert model defines thrust in terms of the inertial and induced velocity. However, the problem is more generally expressed as finding the induced velocity as an implicit function of induced velocity, inertial velocity, and thrust:

$$w = \frac{T}{2\rho A(V + w)}$$

In keeping with the axis system rigor presented thus far, the induced velocity model is, in the IELA,

$$u_{w|\text{IELA}} = 0$$

$$v_{w|\text{IELA}} = 0$$

$$w_{w|\text{IELA}} = \frac{-F_{Z|\text{IELA}}}{2\rho A V'}$$

$$p_{w|\text{IELA}} = 0$$

$$q_{w|\text{IELA}} = 0$$

$$r_{w|\text{IELA}} = 0$$

$$V' = \sqrt{V_{a_h}^T V_{a_h}} \qquad (10.36)$$

The angular wake elements are all set to zero in this presentation. More sophisticated models acknowledge that the blades drag the air in a circular fashion. Define the ratio of total blade planform area to disk area as the solidity $\sigma = n_b c / \pi R$, and let the drag coefficient at a radial station be C_d. Prouty [2] introduces induced and parasite drag using these definitions and derives an expression for wake rotation about the thrust axis.

$$r_{w|\text{IELA}} = \Omega \left[\frac{\sigma C_d}{4 w_{w|\text{IELA}}} + 1 - \sqrt{\frac{1 - 2C_T}{(r/R)^2}} \right] \qquad (10.37)$$

One notices immediately that the swirling wake is a function of the linear induced velocity. One also notices that the swirl is a function of radial station.

Because the induced velocity function is implicit, there is no escaping the requirement for iteration. One effective technique is to guess a value of induced velocity (even zero works!) and perform the arithmetic just shown. After a value for thrust has been generated, the Glauert model is used to calculate the induced velocity. The new value and the original value are combined in some proportion (perhaps 50-50, or 70-30), and the entire process is repeated. This iteration continues until the induced velocity values converge to some comfortable error.

10.4.4 Simplified Performance Estimation

The preceding model estimates the three forces and three moments of the propeller resolved to the IELA. The price paid is numerical integration along the blade

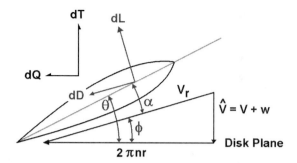

Fig. 10.10   Blade section with velocity triangle.

and around the azimuth, as well as table look-ups for lift and drag coefficient. These are computationally expensive. If all that is desired is a simple estimation of the thrust and torque, then the following analysis from McCormick [4] and Houghton and Brock [5] may be helpful. Consider the blade section shown in Fig. 10.10.

The propeller is spinning with rotational speed $2\pi n = \Omega$, and so at some radial station r the tangential speed is $2\pi nr = \Omega r$. The propeller sees oncoming wind $\hat{V} = V + w$. The wash velocity is w, and V is the axial velocity. The angle formed by the resultant velocity vector and the tangential velocity is the inflow angle and has the symbol ϕ. The blade section is elevated at this station by the angle θ, which is a function of radial station and pilot input. A simple, but representative function describing the blade-section pitch angle is

$$\theta = \Delta\theta_{\text{Root}} + \frac{\theta_{\text{Tip}}}{x} \tag{10.38}$$

with

$$x = \frac{r}{R}$$

R is the radius of the blade, θ_{Tip} is the geometric pitch angle of the blade at the tip when the pilot sets the propeller to "flat" pitch, and $\Delta\theta_{\text{Root}}$ is the additional pitch that the pilot and/or the rpm governor can input. The difference between the pitch angle and the inflow angle is the angle of attack, which when multiplied by the lift-curve slope a_0 yields the lift coefficient. An average drag coefficient of $\overline{C}_d$ is sufficient for this simply analysis. The differential lift and drag are

$$dL = \frac{1}{2}\rho\left[(\Omega r)^2 + \hat{V}^2\right] ca_0 \left[\Delta\theta_{\text{Root}} + \frac{\theta_{\text{Tip}}}{x} - \tan^{-1}\left(\frac{\hat{V}}{\Omega r}\right)\right] dr$$

$$dD = \frac{1}{2}\rho\left[(\Omega r)^2 + \hat{V}^2\right] c\overline{C}_d dr \tag{10.39}$$

It is convenient to work with nondimensional parameters whenever possible. Normalize the velocities with $V_T = \Omega R$ and the radial station with R. Let

$\varepsilon = \overline{C}_d / a_0$. Define the inflow ratio as $\lambda = V/V_T$, and introduce the convenient fiction that the inflow angle is small over the entire radius. This yields

$$dL = \frac{1}{2}\rho V_T^2 cRa_0 \left[x^2 + \lambda^2\right]\left(\Delta\theta_{\text{Root}} + \frac{\theta_{\text{Tip}}}{x} - \frac{\lambda}{x}\right)dx$$

$$dD = \frac{1}{2}\rho V_T^2 cRa_0 \left[x^2 + \lambda^2\right]\varepsilon \, dx \qquad (10.40)$$

The forces must be resolved to the shaft normal plane. Multiply the in-plane force by the radial station r to get the differential torque:

$$dT = dL\cos\phi - dD\sin\phi$$

$$dQ = (dL\sin\phi + dD\cos\phi)r \qquad (10.41)$$

The trigonometric functions are

$$\cos\phi = \frac{x}{\left[x^2 + \lambda^2\right]^{1/2}}$$

$$\sin\phi = \frac{\lambda}{\left[x^2 + \lambda^2\right]^{1/2}} \qquad (10.42)$$

After making the indicated substitutions, and applying these integrals,

$$\int_0^1 \left[x^2 + \lambda^2\right]^{1/2} dx = \frac{1}{2}\left[\left(1 + \lambda^2\right)^{1/2} + \lambda^2 \ell n\left(\frac{1 + \sqrt{1 + \lambda^2}}{\lambda}\right)\right] = g(\lambda)$$

$$\int_0^1 x \left[x^2 + \lambda^2\right]^{1/2} dx = \frac{1}{3}\left[\left(1 + \lambda^2\right)^{3/2} - \lambda^3\right] = f(\lambda)$$

$$\int_0^1 x^2 \left[x^2 + \lambda^2\right]^{1/2} dx = \frac{1}{8}\left(1 + \lambda^2\right)^{1/2}\left(2 + \lambda^2\right)$$

$$- \frac{\lambda^4}{8}\ell n\left(\frac{1 + \sqrt{1 + \lambda^2}}{\lambda}\right) = h(\lambda) \qquad (10.43)$$

the thrust and torque are

$$T = \frac{b}{2}\rho V_T^2 cRa_0 \left\{f(\lambda)\Delta\theta_{\text{Root}} + g(\lambda)\left[\theta_{\text{Tip}} - (1 + \varepsilon)\lambda\right]\right\}$$

$$Q = \frac{b}{2}\rho V_T^2 cR^2 a_0 \left\{f(\lambda)\lambda\Delta\theta_{\text{Root}} + g(\lambda)\lambda\left[\theta_{\text{Tip}} - (1 + \varepsilon)\lambda\right] + h(\lambda)\varepsilon\right\}$$

$$P = Q\Omega \qquad (10.44)$$

Manufacturers usually express propeller performance in terms of thrust and power coefficients, efficiency and an advance ratio, which Table 10.1 defines. The symbol D is the diameter of the propeller.

Table 10.1 Definition of common propeller coefficients

Symbol	Definition	Expression
C_T	Thrust coefficient	$C_T = T/\rho n^2 D^4$
C_P	Power coefficient	$C_P = Q\Omega/\rho n^3 D^5$
η	Efficiency	$\eta = C_T J/C_P$
J	Advance ratio	$J = V/nD$

In the preceding development, the axial flow that defined the inflow ratio used only the speed of the oncoming wind. If the inflow ratio included the induced velocity, that is, if $\lambda = \hat{V}/V_T$, then the induced power and total power absorbed would increase, in accordance with measured data. However, that correction requires an iterative loop because the induced velocity is a function of thrust, which is a function of induced velocity. A slightly less rigorous approach simply adds an empirical correction that McCormick [4] teaches. Without development, that correction in coefficient form is

$$C_{P_i} = 1.12\frac{C_T}{2}\left[-J + \left(J^2 + \frac{8C_T}{\pi}\right)^{1/2}\right] \tag{10.45}$$

Thus, the total power is

$$C_{P_{Total}} = \frac{P\Omega}{\rho n^3 D^5} + C_{P_i} \tag{10.46}$$

10.4.5 Results of a Simple Analysis

A simple computer program that performs a propeller analysis based on the rigorous equations given at the beginning of this section was written. The program is available as part of this text. A sample propeller is provided as internal data. The user may override this internal table with his/her own data. See the appendix for the user's guide. The sample propeller has the following characteristics shown in Table 10.2.

The following performance results were obtained, and are shown in Figs. 10.11 through 10.14.

The thrust coefficient increases with increased blade pitch—no surprise there. The term dTheta is the increment added to the root pitch and is the $\Delta\theta_{root}$ in Eq. (10.38). The thrust coefficient decreases with forward speed for a given blade pitch. At first, this might seem surprising, but with reflection one realizes that the velocity of the oncoming wind can be so high that the propeller is actually coming close to windmilling. In such a case, the angle of attack goes negative, and so does the thrust.

The power coefficient behavior is a bit more complex. For a given speed, it increases with increased blade pitch. This is because increased thrust means increased induced velocity at a given forward speed, but as forward speed increases

Table 10.2 Physical characteristics of sample propeller

Item	Value	Units	Description
Nb	3	None	Number of blades
R	4.0	Feet	Propeller radius
Xhub	0.2	N.D.	Hub cutout to account for spinner
RPM	1800	rpm	Speed of rotor
$r(i); i = 1, 11$	0.0 to 4.0	Feet	Radial stations; they are not necessarily evenly distributed
$\theta(i); i = 1, 11$	Various	Radians	Distributed blade pitch; tip values are typically small, while root values are theoretically $\pi/2$
$c(i); i = 1, 11$	Various	Feet	Distributed chord; the example propeller does not have a constant chord, so that these values vary
$a0$	6.0	CL/radian	Lift-curve slope, Cl/radian
$cd0, cd1, cd2$	0.006225, −0.003, 0.01	N.D.	Drag polar coefficients, forming a polynomial of the form: $Cd = cd0 + Cl^*(cd1 + Cl^*cd2)$
VINF1, VINF2, VINFSTEP	0.0, 500.0, 50.0	Feet/sec	Starting, ending, and increment values of the freestream velocity used in the speed sweep
NTHETA	7	None	Number of root pitch increments to use in blade pitch sweep; each increment is 5 deg

the induced velocity decreases. As thrust goes negative, the power will go negative. Again, this is windmilling.

The ratio $\eta = JC_T/C_P$ defines the efficiency of the propeller. It is the ratio of induced (ideal) power to total power. One sees that a propeller is a remarkably

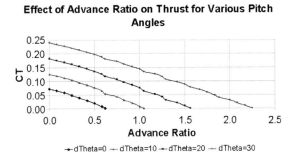

Fig. 10.11   Thrust coefficient.

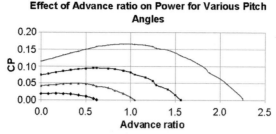

Fig. 10.12   Power coefficient.

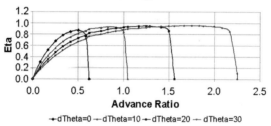

Fig. 10.13   Propeller efficiency.

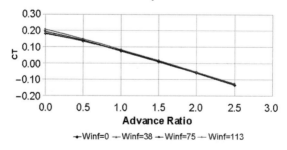

Fig. 10.14   Thrust coefficient.

efficient device over a wide range of advance ratios; however, they do require quite a bit of power to turn.

As stated before, one of the strengths of simulation is the estimation of behavior as well as performance. The preceding results are performance estimates. The following results are behavior estimates of the example propeller at a single pitch angle, but at various values of vertical velocity, as one might encounter during

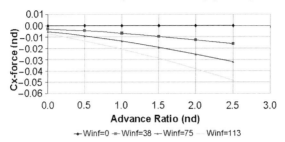

Fig. 10.15   X-force (up force) coefficient.

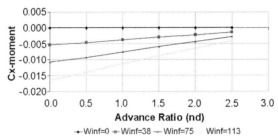

Fig. 10.16   Yaw moment (p factor) coefficient.

climbout. The thrust, X force resolved to the IERA, and X-moment (i.e., p factor) resolved to the IERA are shown in Figs. 10.15 and 10.16.

One sees that the thrust coefficient is relatively unaffected by off-axis velocity. This should probably not be too much of a surprise. The ratio of vertical velocity to tip speed ranges from 0 to 0.2, and the effects of such an in-plane velocity affect the thrust coefficient by the square of that ratio.

The effect of off-axis velocity on X force is more interesting. First, be certain what force is being discussed. Recall, the IERA is the axis system with z axis along the propeller shaft. The x axis is generally pointing to the ground. Thus, this graph shows that as the vertical component of freestream wind increases (from the bottom), the x force becomes increasingly negative, that is, the x force is pointing up, in the direction opposite the in-plane direction of motion.

The effect of off-axis velocity on X moment is what was described earlier as p factor. From this graph, one sees that during a climbout, when the vertical component of the freestream is pointing up, the rotor is developing a nose-left moment. This moment decreases with increased forward speed.

10.5   Conclusions

The propeller is a high-aspect ratio wing pinned at one end, spinning about that pin. Propellers are generally twisted, with the flattest pitch near the tip, and the greatest pitch angle near the center of rotation. Analysis requires familiarity with the momentum theory for axial flow, which requires the solution to a second-order polynomial, and off-axis flow, which requires the solution to a fourth order polynomial. Often, propeller analysis or models present only the on-axis or performance equations. Those analyses will model most behaviors, but they will miss the effects of in-plane flow, which include a very strong and sometimes dangerous effect called p factor. To analyze a propeller, the reader must be conversant in numerical integration techniques, three-dimensional corrections to blade element analysis, and resolution of wind vectors through several axis systems, some rotating and some fixed to the aircraft body.

References

[1] Lienhard, J. H., "Engines of Our Ingenuity, No. 1867, The Wright Brother's Propellers," http://www.uh.edu/engines/epi1867.htm [retrieved 17 Dec. 2004].

[2] Prouty, R. W., *Helicopter Performance, Stability and Control*, Krieger, Malabar, FL, 1995, pp. 3–5, 48–52.

[3] *Manual of Flight*, Jeppesen and Co., Denver, 1978, pp. 2.13–2.14.

[4] McCormick, B. W., *Aerodynamics of V/STOL Flight*, Academic Press, New York, 1967, pp. 347–366.

[5] Houghton, E. L., and Brock, A. E., *Aerodynamics for Engineering Students*, 2nd ed., Butler and Tanner, Ltd., London, 1970, pp. 105–125.

Problems

10.1 The designer of a lightweight, single-engine aircraft proposes to use a three-bladed fixed-pitch propeller with a constant chord of 3.0 in. and a twist schedule that varies with radius according to the equation: $\theta = (\pi/2)e^{-0.687r}$. The radius of the propeller is 3.0 ft, the nondimensional hub cutout (i.e., hub cutout/propeller radius) is 0.2, and the nominal propeller speed is 2300 rpm. Cruise speed will be 118 kn at sea level. The airfoil coefficients for $a0$, $cd0$, $cd1$, and $cd2$ are 6.000, 0.006225, −0.003, and 0.01, respectively. Use the propeller program. Sweep the velocity from 0.0 to 260 ft/s in increments of 20.0, and then determine the following items of interest:

(a) What power will the propeller absorb, and what is the thrust at the design cruise speed when the root pitch is increased 5 deg? (Hint: Use the preceding pitch equation to generate the manufactured twist, and then run the program with ntheta equal to 2. The data corresponding to dtheta = 5 are the data you desire.)

(b) Using the same configuration as in the first part, that is, dtheta = 5, at what advance ratio is the maximum power and what is that power? To what forward speed does this advance ratio correspond? What are the thrust and propeller efficiency at that power?

Power should be expressed in horsepower; thrust should be expressed in pounds.

11
Aerodynamic and Dynamic Modeling
of Rotors

11.1 Introduction

The rotor without a doubt is the feature that defines a helicopter or tiltrotor. Rotors do double duty, serving as the primary lifting device and as the primary propulsive device, Fig. 11.1. A rotor enables a helicopter to fly in any direction, hover in place, and ascend or descend. Rotors can have from one to more than a dozen blades, though most main rotors have two to seven. (Yes, one blade, though why anyone would build such a rotor is a mystery. It is true there would be a savings on the cost of blades and the mechanism for controlling blade pitch. However, the counterweight required to offset the centrifugal force of the unmatched blade would add nothing to the performance of the aircraft. Yet, such a helicopter was built and tested. That it is not seen in production speaks volumes about its utility as a boat anchor.) Rotors behave elastically. In fact, elastic or mechanical deformation is the key to the successful use of rotors. Rotors generate thrust, side forces, and moments under the pilot's control. Rotors are more than just propellers facing up. The loads that rotors apply to the top of the mast are as much a function of aerodynamics as dynamics or gyroscopic forces. The aerodynamic environment in which rotors operate is messy, for lack of a better word.

One of the earliest designs of a rotor was the product of DaVinci's fertile mind, Fig. 11.2. The resemblance to a screw is not a surprise—it is reminiscent of Archimedes screw for lifting water. What is especially interesting is that DaVinci's design included guy wires and supports to make the screw rigid. This design philosophy continued right through to the first serious attempts at helicopter and autogiro design. Also, this design philosophy kept the rotors from working successfully until Juan de la Cierva determined that blade flexibility was necessary.

It is probably fair to say that each helicopter company, each academic center, and each analyst of rotors has a favorite level of detail. This author is not an exception. This chapter presents a representative sample of the diverse number of problems one encounters when modeling a rotor. With so many disciplines working in concert, it is often difficult to know where to begin. Aerodynamics? Dynamics? Control? Basic mathematics? Rotor models can be so complex that they easily become the biggest computational module in a rotorcraft simulation. Because rotors require so many diverse bits of knowledge, they are one of the most rewarding of modeling challenges.

169

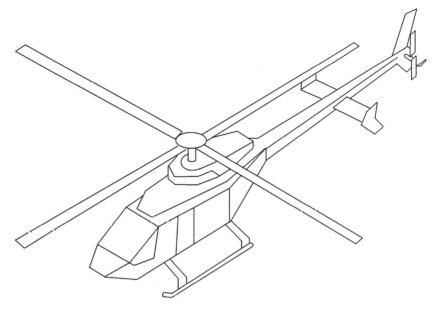

Fig. 11.1   A single main rotor (SMR) helicopter with four blades on the main rotor.

Fig. 11.2   DaVinci's helicopter.

11.2   Basic Rotor Modeling Concepts

One does not eat the entire elephant all at once. Neither should one try to write the performance equations for the general case of a helicopter rotor without appreciating the simplest cases first. Before proceeding with the rest of this chapter, the reader should read Appendix J, which describes the basic techniques used in modeling simply articulated rotors by employing a paddle at the end of a zero-thick rod. These lessons are learned there.

1) At hover, a one-to-one correspondence exists between longitudinal flapping and longitudinal cyclic. This is the so-called equivalence of flapping and feathering.

2) As airspeed increases, the longitudinal flapping-to-feathering ratio is amplified.

3) Forward flight causes aft flapping.

4) Lateral flapping and lateral cyclic are in one-to-one correspondence over the entire velocity range.

5) Longitudinal flapping, which is a cosine term, is produced by a sine term in the forcing function. Likewise, lateral flapping, which is a sine term, is produced by a cosine term in the forcing function. The flapping *LAGS* the forcing function by 90 deg.

These observations serve as a stable of sanity checks.

The techniques used in Appendix J are straightforward, but may be confusing to the first-time reader. It is very important that the reader becomes comfortable with the algebraic and trigonometric manipulations that are used in rotor modeling. With Appendix J as a foundation, the reader can add more sophistication to the rotor models.

11.3   Basic Rotor Geometry

Improvements to the paddle blade model begin with enhanced geometry of the blade and its attachment to the mast.

11.3.1   Full-Span Blade

The first improvement to the paddle blade model is to extend the blade to full span, that is, the blade runs from the centerline of the mast to the blade tip. The blades of a rotor are generally "nice" in shape—straight, constant, or simply tapered chord, and moderately twisted. The planform shape is driven by manufacturing cost as much as for any aerodynamic or dynamic reason; however, the blade twist is most definitely a result of aerodynamic considerations. The twist is generally such that the pitch angle of the root-chord line is greater than the pitch angle of the tip-chord line when both are measured from the shaft normal plane, which is an imaginary plane perpendicular to and atop the rotating shaft. Figure 11.3 shows a twisted blade such that $\theta_{\text{Root}} > \theta_{\text{Tip}}$.

Actual twist is usually not linear, but quite often it is modeled as such. When $\theta_{\text{Root}} > \theta_{\text{Tip}}$, the blade is said to have negative twist, which is the norm.

Now, divide the blade into infinitesimally thin slices. Each slice is a blade section that is located a distance s from the center of rotation along a blade reference line (BRL). The symbol s is used because it evokes a connection to arclength and it will eliminate confusion with the body-axes angular velocity r. A blade section is also shown in Fig. 11.3. The analysis of this three-dimensional blade uses two-dimensional aerodynamics. This technique is often called blade-element theory. When the wash velocity is calculated using the momentum theory, the combination is called *combined blade-element/momentum theory analysis*.

The blade reference line is assumed to pierce the quarter-chord point on each blade section. Each blade section is assumed to have a mass distributed over the width ds. Thus, one speaks of the section mass $dm = \overline{m}\,ds$, where $\overline{m}$ is the running or distributed mass and has units of slugs/ft for instance.

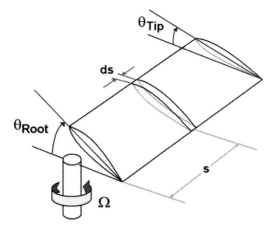

Fig. 11.3   Full-span blade showing twist and a blade section.

The instantaneous position of the section mass is located in three dimensions knowing the location on the blade reference line and the dynamic deformation angles. A blade deforms as it is subjected to aerodynamic and inertial forces. Deformation is necessary. In the analysis that follows, the blade is assumed to be infinitely stiff in bending and torsion, so that deformation is accommodated by means of hinges near the root end. The first, and primary, deformation is *out-of-plane flapping*, and the name β is usually assigned to this angle. The secondary deformation is the *in-plane* or *lead-lag* deflection. The literature is less specific about this name. Often, ε and γ are used. The third deformation is *torsion*, and again the literature is not settled on a single name. A perspective view of an untwisted blade flapping out of plane is shown in Fig. 11.4a. A schematic of a blade section viewed from the negative y_r axis is seen in Fig. 11.4b. In both views the flapping angle is clearly seen. (In more sophisticated analyses, the position requires knowledge of all of the kinematics and dynamic responses of the *elastic* blade modes. In this simple development, the only deformation is assumed to be out-of-plane flapping defined with just the flapping angle.)

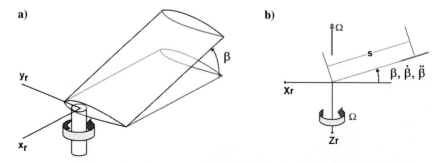

Fig. 11.4   Full-span flapped blade shown a) in perspective and b) in schematic.

11.3.2 Hub Types

The second improvement to the paddle blade model concerns the attachment to the mast. As stated earlier, a flapping hinge can be used to accommodate out-of-plane flapping. A cantilever attachment to the mast with a flexible section near the root end of the blade can also act as a hinge because of elastic deformation. In-plane motion is permitted in a similar fashion with hinges or elastic deformation. Torsion in this simple example is not modeled. If one wished to add this mode, the motion would take place along the pitch or *feathering* axis, with the pitch link and pitch horn providing the necessary stiffness.

The following figures show some of these attachment configurations. In all of the diagrams, the viewer is above the rotors, and the rotors are spinning counterclockwise. The Xs indicate the location of the feathering axis bearings.

11.3.2.1 Articulated Hub   The most straightforward arrangement to analyze is the simply articulated blade (Fig. 11.5), which has a flapping hinge at the center of rotation. The motion of a given blade does not influence any other blade. The schematic shows the blade reference line viewed from the left side. It is flapped "up."

11.3.2.2 Fully Articulated Hub   A slightly more complete arrangement includes a flapping hinge and an in-plane or lead-lag hinge (Fig. 11.6). Again, the flapping motion of this blade does not influence any other blade. The in-plane motion of this blade is similarly uncoupled from other blades. The top schematic shows the blade flapped up, and the bottom schematic shows the blade lagging.

11.3.2.3 Articulated Hub with Hinge Offset   This configuration is identical to the simply articulated blade except that the flapping hinge is now displaced from the center of rotation (Fig. 11.7). Such a hinge allows the rotor to transmit a moment to the top of the mast. Also, this hinge affects the dynamic response of the blade.

11.3.2.4 Articulated Hub with Hub Spring   The arrangement in Fig. 11.8 is a simply articulated blade with the addition of a spring that generates a moment that resists flapping motion. As with the hinge offset, this arrangement transmits a moment to the top of the mast, and it affects the dynamic response.

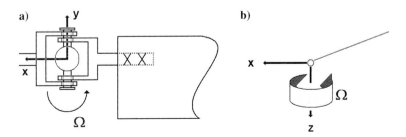

Fig. 11.5   Articulated hub a) from above and b) schematically from side.

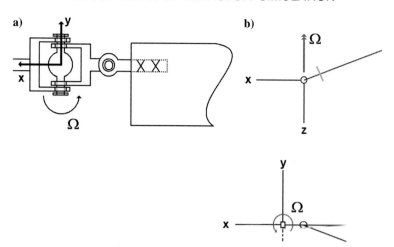

Fig. 11.6   Fully articulated hub a) from above and b) schematically from above and side.

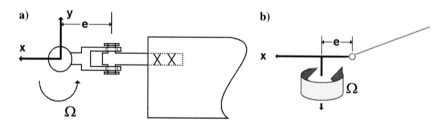

Fig. 11.7   Articulated hub with hinge offset a) from above and b) schematically from side.

11.3.2.5   Teetering Hub   Figure 11.9 shows a two-bladed teetering rotor. Clearly, as the right blade flaps up, the left blade flaps down. No out-of-plane moment is transmitted to the top of the mast. The pin that forms the flapping hinge penetrates the collar to which the blades are attached and the mast about which

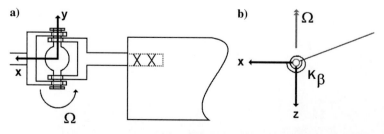

Fig. 11.8   Articulated hub with a spring a) from above and b) schematically from side.

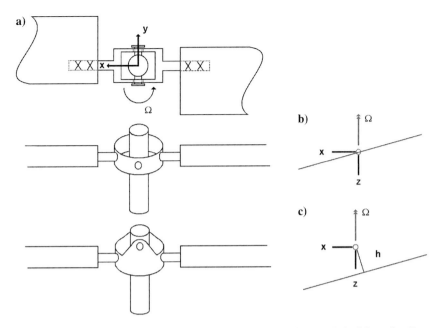

Fig. 11.9 Teetered hub a) from above, b) without undersling, and c) with undersling.

the blades spin. If that pin is above the plane of the blades, then the hub is said to have undersling. The schematics on the right make this arrangement easier to see. Undersling is employed to eliminate the Coriolis forces, which can cause great in-plane stress.

11.3.2.6 Delta-3 Figure 11.10 shows a two-bladed teetering rotor system with an effect called *delta-3*. (Someone is bound to ask why the name "delta-3." The author is unsure of the exact reason, though it is not hard to imagine that because delta-0, delta-1, and delta-2 were already used to describe the drag polar, and because this arrangement produces a change (delta) to the blade pitch, the next available delta was used. Just a guess, but not a bad one.) As the right blade flaps up using this system, one can see that the leading edge of the right blade would pitch down.

There are two methods to introduce the delta-3 effect; the virtual method and the real method. The virtual method uses a cocked flapping hinge. When the blade flaps up, the blade pitches nose down, but without exercising the feathering-axis bearings. The real method achieves feathering because of pitch control—if the end of the pitch horn that is attached to the control rods does not move as the blade flaps up, the blade will pitch nose down. The effect is the same as the virtual method, but causes extra wear on the feathering-axis bearings.

Attached to either the leading or trailing edge, and near the root end, a pitch horn mechanically muscles the blade to different pitch values. Pitch control has a steady value and cyclic value that varies once per revolution. The pitch control is

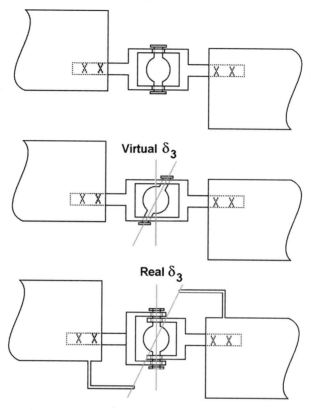

Fig. 11.10　Hub without delta-3, with virtual delta-3, and with real delta-3.

commanded by the pilot and transmitted from the nonrotating system to the rotating system through a swashplate, of which more will be written shortly. Of course, there are other methods to change blade lift including 1) tabs on the trailing edge that are flown by the pilot and that act like trim tabs on an elevator, and 2) circulation control achieved through the use of hollow blades and pressurized air issuing out slots located near the leading and trailing edges.

Some exotic methods such as active twist and higher harmonic control have also been investigated, either analytically or experimentally. Again, the focus of this text is introduction, and so the venerable swashplate, control rod, and pitch horn will serve as the basic form of blade pitch control. With this issue settled, Fig. 11.11, adapted from an original work in Gessow and Myers [1] illustrates one method that transfers pitch control commanded by a pilot sitting in a nonrotating environment to a blade that is operating in a rotating frame of reference.

Figure 11.11 schematically demonstrates how the fore/aft (longitudinal) cyclic, the lateral cyclic, and the collective affect the pitch of a rotor blade as it traverses the azimuth. In particular, the reader should note the apparent out-of-phase connections with the cyclic. For instance, if the cyclic is pushed forward, the side of

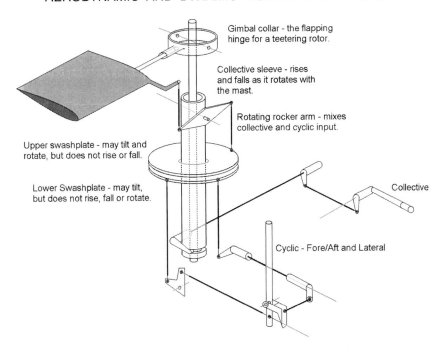

Gimbal collar - the flapping hinge for a teetering rotor.

Collective sleeve - rises and falls as it rotates with the mast.

Rotating rocker arm - mixes collective and cyclic input.

Upper swashplate - may tilt and rotate, but does not rise or fall.

Lower Swashplate - may tilt, but does not rise, fall or rotate.

Collective

Cyclic - Fore/Aft and Lateral

Fig. 11.11   Schematic of a simple swashplate mechanism.

the lower swashplate closest to the reader moves down, pushing the side furthest away up. That motion passes through the rocker arm pulling down on the pitch horn of the blade that is shown. This pitch change decreases the lift of the blade when the blade is on the side of the aircraft nearest the reader. Intuitively, one would think that the thrust should increase behind the aircraft and decrease in front of the aircraft so that a pitching moment would develop, rather than decrease on the advancing side and increasing on the retreating side. This is not the case, as will be shown later in this chapter.

This was not an exhaustive introduction to rotor blades or controls. However, mastering these diagrams will position the reader with a general understanding of rotor geometry.

11.4   Basic Wind Geometry

Six fundamental diagrams that describe relative wind and blade position are presented in Appendix J. They are repeated here with a brief description. Figure 11.12 shows a view of an American-made rotor system from overhead. The convention for zero azimuth angle is indicated.

Figure 11.13 indicates the positive direction of longitudinal flapping of the tip-path plane. The component of thrust in the shaft normal plane is called H-force. The same tip-path plane may also be tilted to the side. The positive

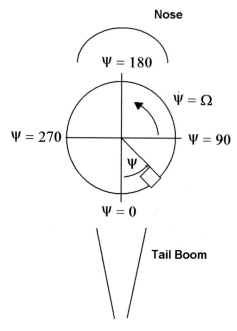

Fig. 11.12   Overhead view of rotor disk. The "helicopter" is flying toward the top of the page.

direction of lateral flapping is indicated in Fig. 11.14. The shaft normal component of thrust in the y direction is called Y-force.

Recall, the axes that are labeled with the subscript "hub" do not spin with the rotor. These axes form the IERA. They can be installed with tilt or even moved to some other angular orientation, but they are part of the so-called *fixed system*. In this context, the *fixed system* is industry jargon for the fuselage. In general, the fixed system is the frame of reference from which the rotation of the rotor is measured, be it the fuselage, a pylon or nacelle, or a sting in a wind tunnel.

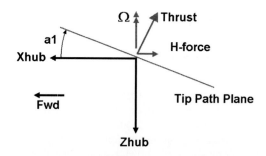

Fig. 11.13   Left-side view of tip-path plane.

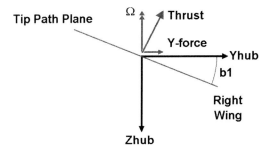

Fig. 11.14 Aft view of tip-path plane.

In Fig. 11.15, the rotating system axes are viewed from the left side, from a point on the negative Yr axis looking toward the origin. Axes labeled with the subscript r indicate that they spin with the rotor. One differential element of the blade is seen a distance s from the origin.

The Greek symbols β, $\dot{\beta}$, $\ddot{\beta}$ are used for flapping angle, flapping rate, and flapping acceleration, respectively, and are measured in the rotating system.

Finally, a blade section is seen in Fig. 11.16 as viewed from an observer on the blade reference line looking toward the hub. An important angle called the inflow angle ϕ is easily discerned. The inflow angle measures the angular displacement of the aerodynamic velocity vector with respect to the shaft normal plane and is resolved to the shaft normal plane. The inflow angle is by definition the arctangent of the ratio of vertical velocity to in-plane velocity. Also visible are the differential lift and drag forces. The blade section is at a geometric pitch angle θ, which, except for twist, is under pilot control. The angle of attack is clearly the sum of the geometric and inflow angles.

Two of the three axes of the blade-section axes are shown in Fig. 11.16. The origin of the blade-section axes is attached to the BRL. The positive x_b axis lies on the BRL and points generally toward the hub. The positive y_b axis points from the BRL to the leading edge and lies on or parallel to the chord. The positive z_b axis is normal to the y_b axis, in the plane of the page, and oriented to complete a right-handed system.

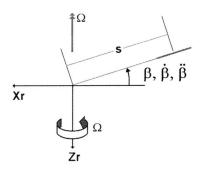

Fig. 11.15 Basic geometry in rotating axes.

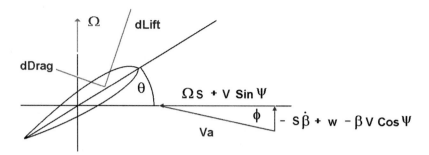

Fig. 11.16   End view of blade section.

11.5   Simple Rotor Math Model

The math model develops in the same manner as Appendix J. Aerodynamics follows dynamics, and again, only a simple rotor model is sought. Later in the chapter, the added sophistication of an aeroelastic rotor is outlined.

11.5.1   Simplified Dynamics of a Full-Span Rotor

Assume the blade mass is uniformly distributed along a straight BRL, which is coincident with the quarter-chord points of the blade sections. The BRL is inextensible, and no elastic deformation is permitted. Positions along the BRL are located in three dimensions with the scalar parameter s, which is an arclength measure along the blade.

Body rates used in the dynamic model are inertial rates, and to emphasize this, a subscript i is used. The rotor spins with respect to the fuselage with speed Ω about the negative z axis of the IERA and can accelerate at a rate of $\dot{\Omega}$. The hub of the rotor can move with linear and angular degrees of freedom. These motions introduce cyclic variations that excite blade dynamics and aerodynamics.

The hub-axes angular velocity is given by

$$\boldsymbol{\omega}_{i|\text{hub}} = \begin{Bmatrix} p_i \\ q_i \\ r_i \end{Bmatrix} \tag{11.1}$$

This vector is resolved to the rotor axes through the azimuthal transformation matrix:

$$T_\psi = \begin{bmatrix} \cos(\psi) & -\sin(\psi) & 0 \\ \sin(\psi) & \cos(\psi) & 0 \\ 0 & 0 & 1 \end{bmatrix} \tag{11.2}$$

The angular velocities in rotor axes are

$$\boldsymbol{\omega}_{i|\text{rotor}} = T_\psi \boldsymbol{\omega}_{i|\text{hub}} = \begin{Bmatrix} p_i \cos(\psi) - q_i \sin(\psi) \\ p_i \sin(\psi) + q_i \cos(\psi) \\ r_i \end{Bmatrix} \tag{11.3}$$

The preceding transformation matrix does not violate the original rules about where the sign on the sine goes. The azimuth angle is measured positively about the negative z axis, so that the negative sign goes on the upper sine. One other subtle point about ψ requires attention. The azimuth angle is the angle between the BRL and a line on the fixed system—usually a line on the tail boom. If the fixed system is spinning about a vertical axis with spin rate r_i, then the derivative of the azimuth angle with time must account for the fuselage spin rate. This fact will manifest itself in just a moment. The total hub angular velocity must also include the rotational rate of the hub, resolved to the hub.

$$\omega_{\text{rotor|hub}} = \begin{Bmatrix} 0 \\ 0 \\ -\Omega \end{Bmatrix} \tag{11.4}$$

Therefore, the total rotor velocity resolved to rotor axes is

$$\omega_{\text{rotor|rotor}} = \omega_{\text{i|rotor}} + \omega_{\text{rotor|hub}} = \begin{Bmatrix} p_i \cos(\psi) - q_i \sin(\psi) \\ p_i \sin(\psi) + q_i \cos(\psi) \\ -\Omega' \end{Bmatrix} \tag{11.5}$$

where

$$\Omega' = \Omega - r_i \tag{11.6}$$

Recall ψ is the azimuth angle, and its derivative is the rotor speed. Therefore, the time derivative of the rotor angular velocity is

$$\dot{\omega}_{\text{rotor|rotor}} = \begin{Bmatrix} (\dot{p}_i - q_i \Omega') \cos(\psi) - (\dot{q}_i + p_i \Omega') \sin(\psi) \\ (\dot{p}_i - q_i \Omega') \sin(\psi) + (\dot{q}_i + p_i \Omega') \cos(\psi) \\ -\dot{\Omega}' \end{Bmatrix} \tag{11.7}$$

The preceding derivatives use Ω' as defined in expression (11.6).

Referring to Fig. 11.15, the blade-element reference line and its time derivatives are given by the following three-dimensional vectors. The velocity and acceleration of the position are found by direct differentiation. Use small angles, and drop higher-order terms as outlined in Appendix J:

$$s \cong \begin{Bmatrix} -s \\ 0 \\ -s\beta \end{Bmatrix} \tag{11.8}$$

$$\dot{s} \cong \begin{Bmatrix} 0 \\ 0 \\ -s\dot{\beta} \end{Bmatrix} \tag{11.9}$$

$$\ddot{s} \cong \begin{Bmatrix} 0 \\ 0 \\ -s\ddot{\beta} \end{Bmatrix} \tag{11.10}$$

The acceleration of the blade section mass, resolved to rotor axes, is given by

$$a = \ddot{s} + 2\omega_{\text{rotor|rotor}} \times \dot{s} + \dot{\omega}_{\text{rotor|rotor}} \times s$$

$$+ \omega_{\text{rotor|rotor}} \times (\omega_{\text{rotor|rotor}} \times s) + T_\psi a_{\text{hub}} \qquad (11.11)$$

The last term in expression (11.11) is the hub acceleration expressed in rotor axes. It will be developed in more detail later. For now, accept that a_{hub} is a three-dimensional vector. The total acceleration is

$$a = \left\{ \begin{array}{c} s(\Omega')^2 + Ca_x - Sa_y \\ s\dot{\Omega}' + Sa_x + Ca_y \\ -s\ddot{\beta} + s(\dot{p}_i - q_i\Omega')S + s(\dot{q}_i + p_i\Omega')C + s(p_i\Omega'C - q_i\Omega'S) + a_z \end{array} \right\}$$

$$(11.12)$$

A shorthand of sorts has been adopted in the preceding expression: $S = \sin(\psi)$ and $C = \cos(\psi)$.

The differential inertial load is given by

$$\mathrm{d}fi = -\overline{m}a \qquad (11.13)$$

The variable $\overline{m}$ just shown is distributed mass given in units of slugs/ft for instance. The preceding expression leads to the differential inertial forces. Differential inertial moments are found by crossing the position vector into the differential force.

$$\mathrm{d}Mi = s \times \mathrm{d}fi \qquad (11.14)$$

Expanding this expression,

$$\mathrm{d}Mi = \begin{vmatrix} i & j & k \\ -s & 0 & -s\beta \\ \mathrm{d}fxi & \mathrm{d}fyi & \mathrm{d}fzi \end{vmatrix} \qquad (11.15)$$

From this, the y moment (flapping moment) is

$$\mathrm{d}Myi = -(s\beta)\,\mathrm{d}fxi + (s)\,\mathrm{d}fzi \qquad (11.16)$$

After expansion and dropping higher-order terms,

$$\mathrm{d}Myi = \overline{m}s^2[(\Omega')^2\beta + \ddot{\beta} - \dot{p}_iS - \dot{q}_iC - 2p_i\Omega'C + 2q_i\Omega'S]$$

$$+ \overline{m}s(\beta a_xC - \beta a_yS - a_z) \qquad (11.17)$$

Integrate expression (11.22) from the blade root to the blade tip to obtain the inertial contribution to the flapping moment:

$$Myi = I_b\left[(\Omega')^2\beta + \ddot{\beta} - \dot{p}_iS + 2q_i\Omega'S - \dot{q}_iC - 2p_i\Omega'C \right]$$

$$+ M_1\left[\beta a_xC - \beta a_yS - a_z \right] \qquad (11.18)$$

where

$$I_b = \int_0^R s^2(\overline{m})\,ds \qquad \text{and} \qquad M_1 = \int_0^R s(\overline{m})\,ds \qquad (11.19)$$

I_b is called the blade flapping inertia with units of slug-ft^2 and M_1 is the first mass moment of the blade with units of slug-ft.

With the benefit of 20/20 hindsight, Eq. (11.18) is modified to account for hub restraint such as hinge offset, hub springs, and delta-3. These restraints are employed in order to transmit a moment to the top of the mast or change the dynamic response. For the moment, accept the following modification to the Myi equation. Substitute ω_n^2 for $(\Omega')^2$ in the first term inside the parentheses. (In general, $\omega_n \geq \Omega'$.) Appendix J explains the mathematics to model these changes.

$$Myi = I_b[\omega_n^2\beta + \ddot{\beta} - \dot{p}_iS + 2q_i\Omega'S - \dot{q}_iC - 2p_i\Omega'C]$$
$$+ M_1\left[\beta a_x C - \beta a_y S - a_z\right] \qquad (11.20)$$

This equation is the simplified dynamic model of a flapping rotor blade. The left-hand side represents the total inertial moment at the flapping hinge. The first term on the right-hand side is a restoring moment arising from centrifugal force. The second term represents inertial resistance to out-of-plane flapping. The next four terms are gyroscopic moments that arise when the rotor hub has angular rates and accelerations imposed upon it. The last three terms are moments caused by linear accelerations imposed upon the hub from the fixed system.

11.5.2   Simplified Aerodynamic Model of a Full-Span Rotor

Though crude, much can be learned from a simple rotor model that uses linear aerodynamics. What follows in this section is an extension of the work of [2 and 3].

The first step is to derive an expression for the inertial velocity at a blade station. Subtracting the wash velocity later will yield the aerodynamic velocity at the blade station.

The inertial velocity in hub axes is

$$V_{\text{hub}-i|\text{hub}} = \begin{Bmatrix} u_i \\ v_i \\ w_i \end{Bmatrix} \qquad (11.21)$$

Resolve this vector to the rotating system using the azimuthal transformation $T_z(\psi)$, Fig. 11.17a, then to the flapped blade axes, Fig. 11.17b.

Use the small-angle approximation to flapping about the y axis,

$$T_y(\beta) = \begin{bmatrix} 1 & 0 & \beta \\ 0 & 1 & 0 \\ -\beta & 0 & 1 \end{bmatrix} \qquad (11.22)$$

to get

$$V_{\text{rotor}-i|\text{blade}} = T_y(\beta)T_z(\psi)V_{\text{hub}-i|\text{hub}} \qquad (11.23)$$

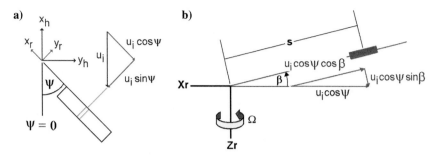

Fig. 11.17   Transformation to a) rotating axes and b) flapped blade axes.

This vector is added to the velocity of the blade because of its flapping motion and its angular motion with respect to inertial space:

$$V_{i\,\text{blade}|\text{blade}} = V_{\text{rotor}-i|\text{blade}} + \dot{s} + \boldsymbol{\omega}_{\text{rotor}|\text{rotor}} \times s \qquad (11.24)$$

or

$$V_{i\,\text{blade}|\text{blade}} = \left\{ \begin{array}{c} u_i C - v_i S + w_i \beta \\ u_i S + v_i C + \Omega' s \\ -u_i \beta C + v_i \beta S + w_i - s\dot{\beta} + s p_i S + s q_i C \end{array} \right\} \qquad (11.25)$$

Recall, the definition of aerodynamic velocity:

$$V_a = V_i - V_w \qquad (11.26)$$

V_w is the wash velocity. This expression holds for both linear and angular velocities. In general, the rotorcraft community uses only the axial wash velocity, with perhaps a truncated cylinder of air spinning about the y axis (fixed frame). In this text, all six elements of the aerodynamic velocity are presumed to have inertial and wash contributions. That is,

$$u_a = u_i - u_w$$
$$v_a = v_i - v_w$$
$$w_a = w_i - w_w$$
$$p_a = p_i - p_w$$
$$q_a = q_i - q_w$$
$$r_a = r_i - r_w \qquad (11.27)$$

Similar to Eq. (11.6), an aerodynamic rotor speed is defined:

$$\Omega_a = \Omega - r_a$$

The same azimuthal transformations applied to the inertial velocities are also applied to the wash velocities, and so the result is easily written:

$$V_a = \begin{Bmatrix} u_a C - v_a S + w_a \beta \\ u_a S + v_a C + \Omega_a s \\ -u_a \beta C + v_a \beta S + w_a - s\dot{\beta} + s p_a S + s q_a C \end{Bmatrix} \qquad (11.28)$$

Because the reader now knows that the aerodynamic velocity of a blade section is resolved to blade-section axes, the formal subscripting is relaxed for clarity. Carrying the side velocity around is cumbersome. If one rotates the zero azimuth angle to align itself with the oncoming wind, solves the problems in that wind-mast axis system, and rotates back after all of the hard work, then the side velocity can be dropped. That technique is used here. The transformation to and from the wind-mast axes is shown later. With the lateral velocity v_a dropped, the aerodynamic velocity at a blade section is

$$V_a = \begin{Bmatrix} u_a C + w_a \beta \\ u_a S + \Omega_a s \\ -u_a \beta C + w_a - s\dot{\beta} + s p_a S + s q_a C \end{Bmatrix} = \begin{Bmatrix} U_r \\ U_t \\ U_p \end{Bmatrix} \qquad (11.29)$$

The subscripts r, t, and p on the velocity elements on the right-hand side stand for radial, tangential, and perpendicular. These names are used often in the rotorcraft community.

Appendix J defined several velocity ratios, which are repeated here with a slight modification for angular aerodynamic velocity.

$$\mu = \frac{u_i}{V_{\text{Ta}}} \approx \frac{u_a}{V_{\text{Ta}}}$$

$$\lambda_i = \frac{w_i}{V_{\text{Ta}}}$$

$$\lambda_w = \frac{w_w}{V_{\text{Ta}}}$$

$$\lambda_a = \frac{w_a}{V_{\text{Ta}}} = \lambda_i - \lambda_w \qquad (11.30)$$

where

$$V_{\text{Ta}} = \Omega_a R \qquad (11.31)$$

The nondimensional parameter μ is the advance ratio, which is the ratio of the advancing speed to the tip speed V_{Ta}. Typical ratio values lie between 0 (hover) and 0.3 to 0.4 for high-speed flight. The other three ratios are the inflow caused by inertial velocity, the inflow caused by downwash, and the total inflow ratio. Using these expressions and factoring out the tip speed, the tangential and perpendicular velocities *at any blade section* are given by

$$U_t = V_a(y) = V_{Ta}(\mu S + x)$$

$$U_p = V_a(z) = V_{Ta}(-\mu\beta C + \lambda_a - x\frac{\dot{\beta}}{\Omega_a} + x\hat{p}_a S + x\hat{q}_a C) \qquad (11.32)$$

where

$$\hat{p}_a = \frac{p_a}{\Omega_a}, \quad \hat{q}_a = \frac{q_a}{\Omega_a}, \quad \text{and} \quad x = \frac{s}{R} \qquad (11.33)$$

Therefore, the inflow angle *at any blade section* is given by

$$\phi = \arctan\frac{U_p}{U_t} \approx \frac{U_p}{U_t} = \frac{[-\mu\beta C + \lambda_a - x(\dot{\beta}/\Omega_a) + x\hat{p}_a S + x\hat{q}_a C]}{(\mu S + x)} \qquad (11.34)$$

Figure 11.16 showed that the blade-section angle of attack depends on the inflow angle and the geometric pitch angle, which is under pilot control. Appendix J introduced the reader to three components of blade pitch. The first was the collective angle θ_0, which is a steady amount transmitted to all blades at the same time. This angle is often controlled with a collective lever found near the pilot's left hand. The second angle is the lateral cyclic A_1, which introduces a once-per-revolution (one-P or one-per-rev) variation in the blade pitch such that the tip-path plane will tilt to the left or right, pointing the thrust vector slightly left or right through the lateral flapping angle b_1. The third angle is the longitudinal cyclic B_1, which introduces a one-P variation in blade pitch so that the tip-path plane tilts forward or aft, pointing the thrust vector likewise through the longitudinal flapping angle a_1.

A fourth component called blade twist is now incorporated for the full-span blade. The twist angle has the name θ_T. Twist is usually negative in value, meaning that when the root is at some positive nose-up pitch angle, the tip is at a lesser nose-up angle. For helicopters, the twist is very nearly linear and is usually a small angle less than 15 deg. For tiltrotors, which use the rotor as a propeller in airplane mode, and as a rotor in helicopter mode, the twist is in the neighborhood of 45 deg. This is no longer a small angle. Twist is usually thought of as static and simply a function of radial station that is manufactured into the blade and does not change. However, in recent years the concept of dynamic twist has been investigated. That work is beyond the scope of this text, but what is presented may offer some ideas on the introduction of twist that varies cyclically and collectively. Also, in this introduction the blade is assumed to be stiff in torsion, that is, neither aerodynamic nor inertial loads can warp or change the blade twist. In reality, the blade undergoes significant warping. Methods to deal with that are deferred to a later section of this chapter. Blade twist, illustrated in Fig. 11.3, adds directly to the other three for the final blade pitch, which is now a function of time (azimuth) and space (radial). So, the blade pitch is given by

$$\theta = \theta_0 + \theta_T x + A_1 \cos(\psi) + B_1 \sin(\psi) \qquad (11.35)$$

When the geometric pitch angle and inflow angle are known, the angle of attack *at any blade section* is

$$\alpha = \theta + \phi \approx \theta_0 + \theta_T x + A_1 \cos(\psi) + B_1 \sin(\psi)$$
$$+ \frac{[-\mu\beta C + \lambda_a - x(\dot{\beta}/\Omega_a) + x\hat{p}_a S + x\hat{q}_a C]}{(\mu S + x)} \tag{11.36}$$

So far, this expression is not much more difficult than the expression found in Appendix J. Twist, the contributions caused by angular velocity, and variations caused by radial position are the only new components.

Assume that $U_t \gg U_p$, so that the magnitude of the aerodynamic velocity vector is

$$\|V_a\| = \sqrt{U_t^2 + U_p^2} \cong U_t \tag{11.37}$$

Putting this all together, the differential lift of a given section is

$$dL = \frac{1}{2}\rho V_{\mathrm{Ta}}^2 R c a_0 (\mu S + x)^2 \left[\theta_0 + \theta_T x + A_1 C + B_1 S \right.$$
$$\left. + \left(\frac{-\mu\beta C + \lambda_a - x(\dot{\beta}/\Omega_a) + x\hat{p}_a S + x\hat{q}_a C}{\mu S + x} \right) \right] dx \tag{11.38}$$

The differential drag is

$$dD = \frac{1}{2}\rho V_{\mathrm{Ta}}^2 R c a_0 (\mu S + x)^2 \varepsilon_0 \, dx \tag{11.39}$$

where

$$\varepsilon_0 = \frac{\overline{C}_D}{a_0} \tag{11.40}$$

These two distributed forces lead to thrust and in-plane forces. (A cambered airfoil introduces two extra wrinkles to this work. A blade-section pitching moment must be accounted for, and an offset to the zero lift line must be included in the lift calculation. In this simple development, the airfoil is assumed symmetric.) In addition, these forces cause the rotor to absorb torque and can lead to moments at the top of the mast, depending on the hub type. As written, the forces are resolved to blade-section axes. The distributed lift is in the negative z_b direction, and the distributed drag is in the negative y_b direction. These forces must be resolved to the rotor axes by rotating them about the x_b axis through the inflow angle, then about the y_b axis through the flapping angle. Note, the twist angle does not play a part in the orientation of the aerodynamic forces, but it does affect the magnitude of the forces. Because these transformations are rotations going from the final blade axes back to the initial rotor axes, the direction of rotation will be opposite the usual sense. Also, because we are using small angles, the rotation matrices become very easy to describe. The aerodynamic forces in the rotor (rotating) axis system are

$$
\mathrm{d}\mathbf{F}a_r = T_y^T(\beta)T_x^T(\phi)
\begin{Bmatrix}
0 \\
-\mathrm{d}D \\
-\mathrm{d}L
\end{Bmatrix}
=
\begin{Bmatrix}
\beta\,\mathrm{d}L \\
-\mathrm{d}D + \phi\,\mathrm{d}L \\
-\phi\,\mathrm{d}D - \mathrm{d}L
\end{Bmatrix}
=
\begin{Bmatrix}
\mathrm{d}Fxa_r \\
\mathrm{d}Fya_r \\
\mathrm{d}Fza_r
\end{Bmatrix}
\qquad (11.41)
$$

Notice that higher-order terms (HOT) have been dropped. In the hub or mast (fixed) axes, the differential forces are

$$
\mathrm{d}\mathbf{F}a_{\mathrm{mast}} = T_\psi^T\,\mathrm{d}\mathbf{F}a_r
\qquad (11.42)
$$

Integrating expression (11.42) in space at a given azimuth angle will generate the instantaneous values of force in the X, Y, and Z directions. These forces are known as the H, Y, and T forces, respectively. Integrating these forces once around the azimuth (in time or azimuth angle) will generate the average H, Y, and T forces. Of course, these values are for one blade. For all blades, multiply by the number of blades. Those expressions will be given later in this chapter.

As with the inertial model, the aerodynamic moments at the top of the mast in rotor axes are given by the cross product of the BRL and the distributed load:

$$
\mathrm{d}\mathbf{M}a_r = s \times \mathrm{d}\mathbf{F}a_r
\qquad (11.43)
$$

Expanding this expression,

$$
\mathrm{d}\mathbf{M}a_r =
\begin{vmatrix}
i & j & k \\
-s & 0 & -s\beta \\
\mathrm{d}Fxa_r & \mathrm{d}Fya_r & \mathrm{d}Fza_r
\end{vmatrix}
=
\begin{Bmatrix}
s\beta(\mathrm{d}Fya_r) \\
-s\beta(\mathrm{d}Fxa_r) + s(\mathrm{d}Fza_r) \\
-s(\mathrm{d}Fya_r)
\end{Bmatrix}
\qquad (11.44)
$$

The y component of the distributed moment is usually called the flapping moment. Substituting the expressions for $\mathrm{d}Fxa_r$ and $\mathrm{d}Fya_r$ into the flapping moment gives

$$
\mathrm{d}Mya_r \cong s(-\phi\,\mathrm{d}D - \mathrm{d}L)
\qquad (11.45)
$$

Higher-order terms have been cast aside. Substitute the expressions for $\mathrm{d}L$, $\mathrm{d}D$, and ϕ into the preceding equation. After some algebra and factoring, the aerodynamic flapping moment becomes

$$
\mathrm{d}Mya_r = -\frac{1}{2}\rho V_{\mathrm{Ta}}^2 R^2 ca_0(\mu S + x)^2 x\Big[\theta_0 + \theta_T x + A_1 C + B_1 S
$$
$$
+ \left(\frac{-\mu\beta C + \lambda_a - x(\dot{\beta}/\Omega_a) + x\hat{p}_a S + x\hat{q}_a C}{\mu S + x}\right)(1 + \varepsilon_0)\Big]\mathrm{d}x
\qquad (11.46)
$$

Integrating from root to an effective tip B_T (the so-called tip loss factor, which is discussed later in this chapter), the aerodynamic moment is

$$
Mya_r = \int_0^{B_T} (\mathrm{d}Mya_r)\,\mathrm{d}x
\qquad (11.47)
$$

or

$$Mya_r = -\frac{1}{2}\rho V_{Ta}^2 R^2 c a_0 \dots$$

$$
\left[
\begin{aligned}
&\left(\frac{B_T^4}{4} + \frac{2\mu B_T^3 S}{3} + \frac{\mu^2 B_T^2 S^2}{2} \right) \Theta_0 \\
&+ \left(\frac{B_T^5}{5} + \frac{2\mu B_T^4 S}{4} + \frac{\mu^2 B_T^3 S^2}{3} \right) \Theta_T \\
&+ \left(\frac{B_T^4}{4} + \frac{2\mu B_T^3 S}{3} + \frac{\mu^2 B_T^2 S^2}{2} \right) A_1 C \\
&+ \left(\frac{B_T^4}{4} + \frac{2\mu B_T^3 S}{3} + \frac{\mu^2 B_T^2 S^2}{2} \right) B_1 S \\
&- \left(\frac{B_T^3}{3} + \frac{\mu B_T^2 S}{2} \right) (1 + \varepsilon_0)(\mu\beta C - \lambda_a) \\
&- \left(\frac{B_T^4}{4} + \frac{\mu B_T^3 S}{3} \right) (1 + \varepsilon_0) \left(\frac{\dot{\beta}}{\Omega_a} \right) \\
&+ \left(\frac{B_T^4}{4} + \frac{\mu B_T^3 S}{3} \right) (1 + \varepsilon_0)\hat{p}_a S \\
&+ \left(\frac{B_T^4}{4} + \frac{\mu B_T^3 S}{3} \right) (1 + \varepsilon_0)\hat{q}_a C
\end{aligned}
\right]
\tag{11.48}
$$

At the flapping hinge, the aerodynamic and inertial moments must add to zero because a hinge cannot support a moment. Add the two moments, and set the result to zero. Define the nondimensional Lock number:

$$\gamma = \frac{\rho c a_0 R^4}{I_b} \tag{11.49}$$

Factor the result and rearrange. The result is the classical flapping equation, extended for angular rates:

$$\ddot{\beta} + \frac{\gamma \Omega_a^2}{2} \left(\frac{B_T^4}{4} + \frac{\mu B_T^3 S}{3} \right) (1 + \varepsilon_0)\frac{\dot{\beta}}{\Omega_a}$$

$$+ \left[\omega^2 + \frac{\gamma \Omega_a^2}{2} \left(\frac{B_T^3}{3} + \frac{\mu B_T^2 S}{2} \right) (1 + \varepsilon_0)\mu C + \frac{M_1}{I_b}(a_x C - a_y S) \right] \beta$$

$$= \frac{\gamma \Omega_a^2}{2} \left[\begin{array}{l} \left(\dfrac{B_T^4}{4} + \dfrac{2\mu B_T^3 S}{3} + \dfrac{\mu^2 B_T^2 S^2}{2} \right) \Theta_0 \\[3mm] + \left(\dfrac{B_T^5}{5} + \dfrac{2\mu B_T^4 S}{4} + \dfrac{\mu^2 B_T^3 S^2}{3} \right) \Theta_T \\[3mm] + \left(\dfrac{B_T^4}{4} + \dfrac{2\mu B_T^3 S}{3} + \dfrac{\mu^2 B_T^2 S^2}{2} \right) A_1 C \\[3mm] + \left(\dfrac{B_T^4}{4} + \dfrac{2\mu B_T^3 S}{3} + \dfrac{\mu^2 B_T^2 S^2}{2} \right) B_1 S \\[3mm] + \left(\dfrac{B_T^3}{3} + \dfrac{\mu B_T^2 S}{2} \right) (1 + \varepsilon_0) \lambda_a \\[3mm] + \left(\dfrac{B_T^4}{4} + \dfrac{\mu B_T^3 S}{3} \right) (1 + \varepsilon_0) \hat{p}_a S \\[3mm] + \left(\dfrac{B_T^4}{4} + \dfrac{\mu B_T^3 S}{3} \right) (1 + \varepsilon_0) \hat{q}_a C \end{array} \right]$$

$$+ \dot{p}_i S - 2q_i \Omega' S + \dot{q}_i C + 2p_i \Omega' C + \frac{M_1}{I_b} a_z \qquad (11.50)$$

Notice that the second term on the left-hand side is not reduced, that is,

$$\frac{\gamma \Omega_a^2}{2} \left(\frac{B_T^4}{4} + \frac{\mu B_T^3 S}{3} \right) (1 + \varepsilon_0) \frac{\dot{\beta}}{\Omega_a}$$

was not reduced to

$$\frac{\gamma \Omega_a}{2} \left(\frac{B_T^4}{4} + \frac{\mu B_T^3 S}{3} \right) (1 + \varepsilon_0) \dot{\beta}$$

The reader will discover that maintaining the normalization $\dot{\beta}/\Omega_a$ will ease the arithmetic to come.

Equation (11.50) is linear with time-varying, periodic coefficients. Left in this form, the stability of the rotor system with periodic coefficients can be examined using Floquet methods. For performance analysis, the next section discusses two popular methods that solve this equation.

11.6   Method to Solve the Flapping Equation

The flapping equation is linear with time-varying, periodic coefficients. Two methods are usually employed to solve Eq. (11.50). The first method is time integration using any good integration technique such as Runge–Kutta, Adams–Bashforth, or improved Euler. The second method is the quasi-static method in which a pre-sumed form of the solution is substituted into the equation, and the result is factored into several algebraic equations after azimuthal integration eliminates the periodic coefficients. Because time integration is straightforward, it is not discussed here. The second method provides many important insights into rotor behavior, and so some time will be spent on it.

The quasi-static solution employs several assumptions:

1) The blade flaps in simple harmonic motion, limited to the first harmonic and a steady term.

2) The coefficients describing the simple harmonic motion are constant.

3) The quasi-static solution assumes that the system operates at a high enough frequency and with high enough damping that all transients decay rapidly and that the so-called infinite time solution is acceptable even in the presence of time-varying inputs.

4) The quasi-static solution presumes that the periodic coefficients in the equation do not affect the stability of the system appreciably. Floquet or root-perturbation methods confirm this assumption. These assumptions are embodied by the expressions for flapping, flapping rate, flapping acceleration, and the trigonometric expressions shown here:

$$\beta = \beta_0 - a_1 C - b_1 S$$

$$\dot{\beta} = (a_1 S - b_1 C) \frac{d\psi}{dt} = (a_1 S - b_1 C)\Omega'$$

$$\ddot{\beta} = (a_1 C + b_1 S)(\Omega')^2$$

$$S^2 = \frac{1}{2} - \frac{C_2}{2}$$

$$C^2 = \frac{1}{2} + \frac{C_2}{2}$$

$$SC = \frac{1}{2}S_2$$

$$S^2 C = \frac{C}{4} - \frac{C_3}{4}$$

$$SC^2 = \frac{S}{4} + \frac{S_3}{4}$$

$$S^3 = \frac{3S}{4} - \frac{S_3}{4} \tag{11.51}$$

The S and C represent sine and cosine functions of azimuth angle, and the sub-script represents the harmonic. Thus, $S_3 = \sin(3\psi)$, etc. The three constants in the assumed flapping response, namely, β_0, a_1, and b_1 represent the coning angle, the fore/aft or longitudinal flapping angle, and the lateral flapping angle, respec-tively. Substitute these expressions into the flapping equation. There just are not any easy ways to reduce the arithmetic involved short of investing in a symbolic manipulation package or writing your own program to do that. The author wrote a simple text substitution program to assist in the expansions, and then checked the results against known solutions. Retain only the steady and first harmonic elements, and write three algebraic equations. The first equation has only the steady terms, the second equation has only the sine terms, and the third equation has only the cosine terms. The three equations are conveniently gathered into a matrix level expression, given here:

$$
\begin{bmatrix}
P^2 & \dfrac{\gamma}{2}F_{a_1} & 0 \\[2ex]
0 & \dfrac{\gamma}{2}A_{a_1} & (1-P^2) \\[2ex]
\dfrac{\gamma}{2}B_{\beta_0} & (1-P^2) & -\dfrac{\gamma}{2}B_{b_1}
\end{bmatrix}
\begin{Bmatrix}
\beta_0 \\[1ex] a_1 \\[1ex] b_1
\end{Bmatrix}
$$

$$
= \begin{bmatrix}
\dfrac{\gamma}{2}F_0 & \dfrac{\gamma}{2}F_T & 0 & \dfrac{\gamma}{2}F_{B_1} \\[2ex]
\dfrac{\gamma}{2}A_0 & \dfrac{\gamma}{2}A_T & 0 & \dfrac{\gamma}{2}A_{B_1} \\[2ex]
0 & 0 & \dfrac{\gamma}{2}B_{A_1} & 0
\end{bmatrix}
\begin{Bmatrix}
\theta_0 \\[1ex] \theta_T \\[1ex] A_1 \\[1ex] B_1
\end{Bmatrix}
+ \begin{bmatrix}
\dfrac{\gamma}{2}F_\lambda & \dfrac{\gamma}{2}F_p & 0 \\[2ex]
\dfrac{\gamma}{2}A_\lambda & \dfrac{\gamma}{2}A_p & 0 \\[2ex]
0 & 0 & \dfrac{\gamma}{2}B_q
\end{bmatrix}
\begin{Bmatrix}
\lambda_a \\[1ex] \hat{p}_a \\[1ex] \hat{q}_a
\end{Bmatrix}
$$

$$
+ \begin{bmatrix}
0 & 0 & 0 & 0 & -\dfrac{M_1 R a_1}{2 I_b} & \dfrac{M_1 R b_1}{2 I_b} & \dfrac{M_1 R}{I_b} \\[2ex]
0 & -2 & 1 & 0 & 0 & -\dfrac{M_1 R \beta_0}{I_b} & 0 \\[2ex]
2 & 0 & 0 & 1 & \dfrac{M_1 R \beta_0}{I_b} & 0 & 0
\end{bmatrix}
\begin{Bmatrix}
\hat{p}_i \\[1ex] \hat{q}_i \\[1ex] \dot{p}_i/\Omega'^2 \\[1ex] \dot{q}_i/\Omega'^2 \\[1ex] a_x/R\Omega'^2 \\[1ex] a_y/R\Omega'^2 \\[1ex] a_z/R\Omega'^2
\end{Bmatrix}
$$

$$(11.52)$$

The coefficients are defined here:

$$
F_0 = F_\Omega^2 \left(\frac{B_T^4}{4} + \frac{B_T^2 \mu^2}{4} \right) \qquad
F_T = F_\Omega^2 \left(\frac{B_T^5}{5} + \frac{B_T^3 \mu^2}{6} \right)
$$

$$
F_\lambda = F_\Omega^2 \left(\frac{B_T^3}{3} \right)(1 + \varepsilon_0) \qquad
F_{B1} = F_\Omega^2 \left(\frac{B_T^3 \mu}{3} \right)
$$

$$
F_p = F_\Omega^2 \left(\frac{B_T^3 \mu}{6} \right)(1 + \varepsilon_0) \qquad
F_{a1} = F_\Omega^2 \left(\frac{\mu B_T^3}{6 F_\Omega} \right)(1 + \varepsilon_0)(1 - F_\Omega) \quad (11.53)
$$

$$
A_0 = F_\Omega^2 \left(\frac{2 B_T^3 \mu}{3} \right) \qquad
A_T = F_\Omega^2 \left(\frac{B_T^4 \mu}{2} \right)
$$

$$A_\lambda = F_\Omega^2 \left(\frac{B_T^2 \mu}{2} - \left\langle \frac{\mu^3}{8} \right\rangle \right) (1 + \varepsilon_0) \quad A_{B1} = F_\Omega^2 \left(\frac{B_T^4}{4} + \frac{3 B_T^2 \mu^2}{8} \right) \quad (11.54)$$

$$A_p = F_\Omega^2 \left(\frac{B_T^4}{4} \right) (1 + \varepsilon_0) \quad A_{a_1} = F_\Omega^2 \left(\frac{B_T^4}{4 F_\Omega} - \frac{B_T^2 \mu^2}{8} \right) (1 + \varepsilon_0)$$

$$B_{\beta_0} = F_\Omega^2 \left(\frac{B_T^3 \mu}{3} \right) (1 + \varepsilon_0) \quad B_{A_1} = F_\Omega^2 \left(\frac{B_T^4}{4} + \frac{B_T^2 \mu^2}{8} \right)$$

$$B_q = F_\Omega^2 \left(\frac{B_T^4}{4} \right) (1 + \varepsilon_0) \quad B_{b_1} = F_\Omega^2 \left(\frac{B_T^4}{4 F_\Omega} + \frac{B_T^2 \mu^2}{8} \right) (1 + \varepsilon_0) \quad (11.55)$$

The factor P is the nondimensional ratio of flapping frequency to inertial rotor speed; the factor F_Ω is the ratio of aerodynamic rotor speed to inertial rotor speed. The inertial roll and pitch rates are made nondimensional by dividing by inertial rotor speed:

$$P = \frac{\omega}{\Omega'}$$

$$F_\Omega = \frac{\Omega_a}{\Omega'}$$

$$\hat{p}_i = \frac{p_i}{\Omega'}$$

$$\hat{q}_i = \frac{q_i}{\Omega'} \quad (11.56)$$

The term $(1 + \varepsilon_0)$, which amplifies coefficients of the flapping angles and inflow ratio, is very nearly unity. If the average drag coefficient is 0.015 and the lift-curve slope is 5.73, then this term has a value of 1.00262. That is to say, this term will change the flapping moment by no more than 0.262% over what would be calculated if we ignored the drag contribution. For this reason, it is safe to ignore ε_0 and set the term $(1 + \varepsilon_0)$ to unity in the flapping moment coefficients above. However, the drag contribution to thrust and torque will be retained. In expressions (11.54), the A_λ equation has a term in angle braces. This is a correction for reverse flow and is included in derivations by McCormick [2] and Dreier [3]. Its development is beyond the current scope. Interested readers are encouraged to consult [2] and [4]. In expression (11.52), the coefficients multiplying the hub accelerations are functions of the flapping angles, which are the values that are sought. This is an implicit loop that must be solved iteratively. The equation could be rearranged so that two of the hub accelerations are made part of the coefficient matrix on the left-hand side (LHS). This would eliminate the implicit loop, but it would separate a_x and a_y from a_z, which would still be on the right-hand side (RHS). This is not a very neat solution.

It is instructive to examine the flapping solution for the case of a one-per-rev flapping frequency rotor operating with $r_i = r_w = 0$, that is, $P = 1$ and $F_\Omega = 1$. For ease, let the hub accelerations be zero. In that case, after inversion, the three equations for coning, longitudinal, and lateral flapping are

$$
\begin{Bmatrix} \beta_0 \\ a_1 \\ b_1 \end{Bmatrix} =
\begin{bmatrix}
\dfrac{\gamma}{2}F_0 & \dfrac{\gamma}{2}F_T & 0 & \dfrac{\gamma}{2}F_{B_1} \\[2mm]
\dfrac{A_0}{A_{a_1}} & \dfrac{A_T}{A_{a_1}} & 0 & \dfrac{A_{B_1}}{A_{a_1}} \\[2mm]
\dfrac{\gamma}{2}\dfrac{B_{\beta_0}}{B_{b_1}}F_0 & \dfrac{\gamma}{2}\dfrac{B_{\beta_0}}{B_{b_1}}F_T & -\dfrac{B_{A_1}}{B_{b_1}} & \dfrac{\gamma}{2}\dfrac{B_{\beta_0}}{B_{b_1}}F_{B_1}
\end{bmatrix}
\begin{Bmatrix} \theta_0 \\ \theta_T \\ A_1 \\ B_1 \end{Bmatrix}
$$

$$
+
\begin{bmatrix}
\dfrac{\gamma}{2}F_\lambda & \dfrac{\gamma}{2}F_p & 0 \\[2mm]
\dfrac{A_\lambda}{A_{a_1}} & \dfrac{A_p}{A_{a_1}} & 0 \\[2mm]
\dfrac{\gamma}{2}\dfrac{B_{\beta_0}}{B_{b_1}}\Gamma_\lambda & \dfrac{\gamma}{2}\dfrac{B_{\beta_0}}{B_{b_1}}F_p & -\dfrac{R_q}{B_{b_1}}
\end{bmatrix}
\begin{Bmatrix} \lambda_a \\ \hat p_a \\ \hat q_a \end{Bmatrix}
+
\begin{bmatrix}
0 & 0 \\[2mm]
0 & -\dfrac{4}{\gamma A_{a_1}} \\[2mm]
-\dfrac{4}{\gamma B_{b_1}} & 0
\end{bmatrix}
\begin{Bmatrix} \hat{\dot p}_i \\ \hat{\dot q}_i \end{Bmatrix}
$$

$$
\tag{11.57}
$$

Now consider two speed cases. If the helicopter is hovering, the advance ratio is zero. The equations describing coning, longitudinal, and lateral flapping become

$$
\beta_0 = \frac{\gamma}{2}\left(\frac{B_T^4}{4}\theta_0 + \frac{B_T^5}{5}\theta_T + \frac{B_T^3}{3}\lambda_a \right)
$$

$$
a_1 = \frac{p_a}{\Omega'} - \frac{16}{\gamma\Omega'}q_i + \frac{8}{\gamma(\Omega')^2}\dot p_i + B_1
$$

$$
b_1 = -\frac{q_a}{\Omega'} - \frac{16}{\gamma\Omega'}p_i - \frac{8}{\gamma(\Omega')^2}\dot q_i - A_1
\tag{11.58}
$$

These are sanity check equations. Clearly, for a rotor in hover these statements can be made:

1) Coning is unaffected by roll rate or pitch rate. Coning angle is linearly related to the collective angle and the inflow angle. Increasing collective increases the coning. However, thrust also increases, and so the inflow increases, and the coning angle increase is attenuated.

2) The rotor flaps in the direction opposite of an inertial angular rate by the amount $16/\gamma\Omega'$. Therefore, a positive roll rate causes negative lateral flapping (left wing down), and a positive pitch rate causes negative longitudinal (forward) flapping.

3) Positive roll rate or negative swirling wake about the x axis causes aft flapping.

4) Positive pitch rate or negative swirling wake about the y axis causes left-wing-down flapping.

5) The rotor flaps one unit for every unit of cyclic input. That is, one degree of longitudinal cyclic yields one degree of longitudinal flapping. The same holds for the lateral response. This result is the so-called equivalence of flapping and feathering.

6) Longitudinal flapping, which is a cosine term, is produced by a sine term in the forcing function. Likewise, the lateral flapping, which is a sine term, is

produced by a cosine term in the forcing function. The flapping LAGS the forcing function by 90 deg. Strictly speaking, the pitch and roll acceleration terms should be dropped because the flapping equation is assumed to be a steady-state solution and these accelerations would be transient excitations.

Most of the solution terms are easier to see than they are to develop mathematically. For instance, as the rotor is rolled to the right at steady rate, the advancing blade is being pushed down, which means that the blade is seeing additional velocity striking its bottom. This generates additional lift, which begins to raise the blade. Ninety degrees later, that additional lift has flapped the blade up in the front. This is aft flapping (statement 3). A similar argument holds for a steady pitch rate, which generates lateral flapping.

The so-called damping derivative $16/\gamma\Omega'$ is not as easy to see. This derivative is, in fact, the gyroscopic term. The aerodynamic-type term (the Lock number) appears by virtue of the way in which the equations were solved, but the derivative came from the inertial part of the equation. You may think of it as a gyroscope that is not completely free to maintain its alignment in inertial space because of some aerodynamic moment. Still, if the fuselage beneath the rotor is pitching nose up, relative to the fuselage the rotor tip-path plane will appear to be pitching nose down. A well-known video clip on the Internet shows a CH-53 chopping off its own refueling probe. Careful examination of the clip reveals that the fuselage flew into the rotor, and not the other way around.

The other speed case to consider is a moderate advance ratio while holding cyclic and collective constant and holding roll and pitch rates and accelerations to zero. In this case, the equations for coning, longitudinal, and lateral flapping become

$$
\begin{Bmatrix} \beta_0 \\ a_1 \\ b_1 \end{Bmatrix} =
\begin{bmatrix}
\dfrac{\gamma}{2}F_0 & \dfrac{\gamma}{2}F_T & 0 & \dfrac{\gamma}{2}F_{B_1} & \dfrac{\gamma}{2}F_\lambda \\[2mm]
\dfrac{A_0}{A_{a_1}} & \dfrac{A_T}{A_{a_1}} & 0 & \dfrac{A_{B_1}}{A_{a_1}} & \dfrac{A_\lambda}{A_{a_1}} \\[2mm]
\dfrac{\gamma}{2}\dfrac{B_{\beta_0}}{B_{b_1}}F_0 & \dfrac{\gamma}{2}\dfrac{B_{\beta_0}}{B_{b_1}}F_T & -\dfrac{B_{A_1}}{B_{b_1}} & \dfrac{\gamma}{2}\dfrac{B_{\beta_0}}{B_{b_1}}F_{B_1} & \dfrac{\gamma}{2}\dfrac{B_{\beta_0}}{B_{b_1}}F_\lambda
\end{bmatrix}
\begin{Bmatrix} \theta_0 \\ \theta_T \\ A_1 \\ B_1 \\ \lambda_a \end{Bmatrix}
$$

(11.59)

Three relationships in particular are very interesting. If one substitutes the expressions for the coefficients into the preceding matrix, one finds the following:

1) Longitudinal flapping increases linearly (or nearly so) with advance ratio at a given collective setting. The partial derivative

$$
\frac{\partial a_1}{\partial \theta_0} = \frac{8B_T\mu}{3(1-\mu^2/2)}
$$

is a speed stability term that directs the flapping aft with forward speed.

2) The equivalence of flapping and feathering holds for longitudinal flapping out to moderate speeds. The partial derivative

$$
\frac{\partial a_1}{\partial B_1} = \frac{(B_T^2 + 3\mu^2/2)}{(B_T^2 - \mu^2/2)}
$$

is 20% greater than unity for advance ratios of 0.3. For lateral flapping, the partial derivative $\partial b_1/\partial A_1 = 1$ for all advance ratios.

3) Coning causes flapping. The greater the thrust for a given rotor, the greater the aft flapping tendency.

These equations are sanity checks for a rotor in forward flight.

A fun experiment the reader can try at home reinforces the results described by Eq. 11.58. The 90-deg phase lag between control inputs and flapping output may seem mysterious at first, but it is real. The phase lag is the reason one sees the swashplate rigged as it is in the diagram earlier in this chapter. A simple experiment that costs about a dime to prepare drives home this relationship in a way the reader will never forget. Poke a small hole through the center of a paper plate with a thumbtack. Then, press the tack through the hole in the plate and into the eraser of a pencil so that you end up with the configuration pictured here:

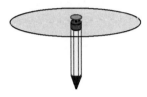

Do not push the tack all of the way down to the top of the eraser. You want the rotor (plate) to spin easily and wobble easily. Now, hold the pencil with your left hand, and use your right hand to spin the plate counterclockwise (if viewed from above). If the plate does not spin easily, pull the tack out a little and also widen the hole in the plate a little. Once the plate is spinning, position your finger under the plate, pointing up, parallel to the pencil, close to the center of rotation, but slightly to the right. See the following diagram:

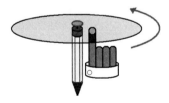

Now, push lightly on the spinning plate. What you should see is the plate will "flap" in such a way as to have the edge nearest you move down and the edge farthest away from you move up. In other words, 90 deg later in the direction of rotation, the plate will move up in response to the upward force provided by your finger! This is called gyroscopic precession, and all helicopter rotors behave this way. You can try other variations on this experiment. For instance, try taping four pennies to the plate, all equally distant from the center, and evenly spaced around the plate. Perform the same experiment. Did the 90-deg phase change at all?

11.7 Hub Forces and Moment

Rotor flapping is only half the fun. The forces and moments at the top of the mast are what make a rotor useful. The forces are developed first.

In the preceding section, the aerodynamic forces in the rotating system, shaft normal plane were stated broadly:

$$dF a_r = \left\{ \begin{array}{c} \beta \, dL \\ -dD + \phi \, dL \\ -\phi \, dD - dL \end{array} \right\} \tag{11.60}$$

These loads are resolved to the fixed system through the inverse of the azimuth transformation matrix:

$$dF a_h = \begin{bmatrix} \cos(\psi) & \sin(\psi) & 0 \\ -\sin(\psi) & \cos(\psi) & 0 \\ 0 & 0 & 1 \end{bmatrix} \left\{ \begin{array}{c} \beta \, dL \\ -dD + \phi \, dL \\ -\phi \, dD - dL \end{array} \right\} = \left\{ \begin{array}{c} (\beta C + \phi S) \, dL - (S) \, dD \\ (\phi C - \beta S) \, dL - (C) \, dD \\ -\phi \, dD - dL \end{array} \right\} \tag{11.61}$$

Substitute the expressions derived earlier for the differential lift and drag, the inflow angle, and the flapping angle into the preceding equations and expand. Integrate once around the azimuth and then out along the blade. Finally, multiply the answer by the number of blades. After normalization, the nondimensional equations for X-force, Y-force, and thrust in hub axes are your reward. *This step is extremely tedious*, and it is very easy to introduce arithmetic errors, usually an incorrect sign. The following equations were developed with a symbolic manipulation program and have been checked against the source code of a well-known computer program. The nondimensional expressions are

$$\frac{2C_x}{\sigma a_0} = \left\{ \begin{array}{l} -\left(\dfrac{B_T^2 \mu}{2}\right)\varepsilon_0 + \left(\dfrac{B_T \mu}{2}\lambda_a - \dfrac{B_T^3}{3}a_1\right)\theta_0 \\[2ex] +\left(\dfrac{B_T^2 \mu}{4}\lambda_a - \dfrac{B_T^4}{4}a_1\right)\theta_T + \left(\dfrac{B_T^3}{6}\beta_0\right)(A_1 + b_1) \\[2ex] +\left(\dfrac{B_T^2}{4}\lambda_a - \dfrac{B_T^2 \mu}{4}a_1\right)B_1 - \dfrac{3B_T^2}{4}\lambda_a a_1 - \dfrac{B_T^2}{4}(\beta_0^2 + a_1^2)\mu \\[2ex] +\left(\dfrac{B_T^3}{6}\theta_0 + \dfrac{B_T^4}{8}\theta_T + \dfrac{B_T^2}{2}\lambda_a + \dfrac{3B_T^2 \mu}{16}B_1 + \dfrac{B_T^2 \mu}{16}a_1\right)\hat{p}_a \\[2ex] +\left(\dfrac{B_T^3}{6}\beta_0 + \dfrac{B_T^2 \mu}{16}A_1 + \dfrac{B_T^2 \mu}{16}b_1\right)\hat{q}_a \end{array} \right\} \tag{11.62}$$

$$\frac{2C_y}{\sigma a_0} = \left\{ \begin{array}{l} \left[\left(\frac{B_T^3}{3} + \frac{B_T \mu^2}{2} \right) b_1 - \frac{3B_T^2 \mu}{4} \beta_0 \right] \theta_0 \\[2ex] + \left[\left(\frac{B_T^4}{4} + \frac{B_T^2 \mu^2}{4} \right) b_1 - \frac{B_T^3 \mu}{2} \beta_0 \right] \theta_T \\[2ex] + \left(\frac{B_T^2}{4} \lambda_a + \frac{B_T^2 \mu}{4} a_1 \right) A_1 \\[2ex] + \left[-\left(\frac{B_T^3}{6} + \frac{B_T \mu^2}{2} \right) \beta_0 + \frac{B_T^2 \mu}{2} b_1 \right] B_1 \\[2ex] + \left(\frac{3B_T^2}{4} b_1 - \frac{3B_T \mu}{2} \beta_0 \right) \lambda_a \\[2ex] + \left(+\frac{B_T^3}{6} \beta_0 + \frac{B_T^2 \mu}{4} b_1 - B_T \mu^2 \beta_0 \right) a_1 \\[2ex] + \left(\frac{B_T^2 \mu}{16} A_1 - \frac{B_T^3}{6} \beta_0 + \frac{5B_T^2 \mu}{16} b_1 \right) \hat{p}_a \\[2ex] + \left(\frac{B_T^3}{6} \theta_0 + \frac{B_T^4}{8} \theta_T + \frac{B_T^2}{2} \lambda_a + \frac{B_T^2 \mu}{16} B_1 + \frac{7B_T^2 \mu}{16} a_1 \right) \hat{q}_a \end{array} \right\} \tag{11.63}$$

$$\frac{2C_z}{\sigma a_0} = -\left\{ \begin{array}{l} \left(\frac{B_T^3}{3} + \frac{\mu^2 B_T}{2} \right) \theta_0 + \left(\frac{B_T^4}{4} + \frac{\mu^2 B_T^2}{4} \right) \theta_T \\[2ex] + \left(\frac{B_T^2}{2} + \left\langle \frac{\mu^2}{4} \right\rangle \right) (1 + \varepsilon_0) \lambda_a + \left(\frac{\mu B_T^2}{2} + \left\langle \frac{\mu^3}{8} \right\rangle \right) B_1 \\[2ex] + \left(\frac{B_T^2 \mu}{4} (1 + \varepsilon_0) \right) \hat{p}_a \end{array} \right\} \tag{11.64}$$

The symbol $\sigma = bc/\pi R$ and is called the solidity. Solidity is the ratio of blade area to disk area. The symbol for the number of blades is b, the thrust-weighted chord is c, and the rotor radius is R. The dimensional forces are recovered by multiplying C_x, C_y, and C_z by $\rho \pi R^2 V_{Ta}^2$. In the literature, one often finds mention of H-force. This is nothing more than the negative of the X-force already developed.

Usually, the only hub moment found using this method is the torque because the hub moments about the hub x and y axes are either zero (owing to a hinge), or can be found with the tip-path plane flapping angles and the equivalent hub spring rate. However, in some cases, aerodynamic moments produced by the rotor drive swirling wakes about the x and y hub axes. All three aerodynamic moments are calculated here using the cross product of the BRL vector and the aerodynamic forces. The x-axis and y-axis moments are shown in terms of rotor states, aircraft states, and swashplate inputs.

$$C_{mx} = \frac{\sigma a_0}{2} \left\{ \begin{array}{l} -\left(\frac{B_T^3 \mu}{3}\right)\theta_0 - \left(\frac{B_T^4 \mu}{4}\right)\theta_T - \left(\frac{B_T^2 \mu}{4}\right)\lambda_a - \left(\frac{B_T^4}{8}\right)\hat{p}_a \\ \\ -\left(\frac{B_T^4}{8} + \frac{3B_T^2 \mu^2}{16}\right)B_1 + \left(\frac{B_T^4}{8} - \frac{B_T^2 \mu^2}{16}\right)a_1 \end{array} \right\} \tag{11.65}$$

$$C_{my} = \frac{\sigma a_0}{2} \left\{ \left(\frac{B_T^3 \mu}{6}\right)\beta_0 - \left(\frac{B_T^4}{8}\right)\hat{q}_a - \left(\frac{B_T^4}{8} + \frac{B_T^2 \mu^2}{16}\right)A_1 \right. $$
$$\left. - \left(\frac{B_T^4}{8} + \frac{B_T^2 \mu^2}{16}\right)b_1 \right\} \tag{11.66}$$

Compare the preceding expressions with Eqs. (11.52–11.55). With some algebra, the aerodynamic moments are shown to balance inertial accelerations and phasing caused by flapping of a rotor with a natural flapping frequency other than one-per-rev. Specifically,

$$\left\{ \begin{array}{c} C_{mx} \\ C_{my} \end{array} \right\} = \frac{\sigma a_0}{2\gamma} \begin{bmatrix} 0 & -(1-P^2) & 0 & -2 & 1 & 0 & 0 & -\dfrac{M_1 R \beta_0}{I_b} \\ -(1-P^2) & 0 & 2 & 0 & 0 & 1 & \dfrac{M_1 R \beta_0}{I_b} & 0 \end{bmatrix}$$

$$\bullet \left\{ \begin{array}{c} a_1 \\ b_1 \\ \hat{p}_i \\ \hat{q}_i \\ \dot{p}_i/R\Omega'^2 \\ \dot{q}_i/R\Omega'^2 \\ a_x/R\Omega'^2 \\ a_y/R\Omega'^2 \end{array} \right\} \tag{11.67}$$

If the rotor is unaccelerated, then only phased flapping generates aerodynamic moments:

$$\left\{ \begin{array}{c} C_{mx} \\ C_{my} \end{array} \right\} = \frac{\sigma a_0}{2\gamma} \begin{bmatrix} 0 & -(1-P^2) \\ -(1-P^2) & 0 \end{bmatrix} \left\{ \begin{array}{c} a_1 \\ b_1 \end{array} \right\} \tag{11.68}$$

If the rotor is teetered, then $P = 1$, and no aerodynamic moments are generated, as is expected.

The torque expression is quite complicated, and so it is presented in several parts.

$$C_{Q0} = \frac{\sigma a_0}{2} \left\{ \begin{array}{l} Q_\varepsilon \varepsilon_0 - Q_\lambda \lambda_a - Q_{\beta_0^2}\beta_0^2 - Q_{a_1^2}a_1^2 - Q_{b_1^2}b_1^2 \\ + Q_{\beta_0 b_1}\beta_0 b_1 - Q_{a_1 \lambda}a_1 \lambda_a \end{array} \right\} \tag{11.69}$$

where

$$Q_\varepsilon = \left(\frac{B_T^4}{4} + \frac{B_T^2\mu^2}{4}\right) \quad Q_{\lambda_a} = \left(\frac{B_T^3}{3}\right)\theta_0 + \left(\frac{B_T^4}{4}\right)\theta_T + \left(\frac{B_T^2}{2}\right)\lambda_a$$

$$Q_{\beta_0^2} = \left(\frac{B_T^2\mu^2}{4}\right) \quad Q_{a_1^2} = \left(\frac{B_T^4}{8} + \frac{3B_T^2\mu^2}{16}\right)$$

$$Q_{b_1^2} = \left(\frac{B_T^4}{8} + \frac{B_T^2\mu^2}{16}\right) \quad Q_{\beta_0 b_1} = \left(\frac{B_T^3\mu}{3}\right)$$

$$Q_{a_1\lambda} = \left(\frac{B_T^2\mu}{2}\right) \tag{11.70}$$

In addition, there is an extra amount that accounts for cyclic input. Those terms are

$$C_{Q\text{cyclic}} = \frac{\sigma a_0}{2}\{Q_{B_1a_1}B_1a_1 - Q_{B_1\lambda}B_1\lambda_a + Q_{A_1\beta_0}A_1\beta_0 - Q_{A_1b_1}A_1b_1\} \tag{11.71}$$

where

$$Q_{B_1a_1} = \left(\frac{B_T^4}{8} - \frac{B_T^2\mu^2}{16}\right) \quad Q_{B_1\lambda} = \left(\frac{B_T^2\mu}{4}\right)$$

$$Q_{A_1\beta_0} = \left(\frac{B_T^3\mu}{6}\right) \quad Q_{A_1b_1} = \left(\frac{B_T^4}{8} + \frac{B_T^2\mu^2}{16}\right) \tag{11.72}$$

Finally, a portion caused by roll and pitch rate is defined.

$$C_{Qpq} = \frac{\sigma a_0}{2}\{Q_p\hat{p}_a + Q_q\hat{q}_a\} \tag{11.73}$$

where

$$Q_p = \left(-\frac{B_T^4}{8}B_1 - \frac{B_T^3\mu}{6}\theta_0 - \frac{B_T^4\mu}{8}\theta_T - \frac{B_T^4}{8}\hat{p}_a + \frac{B_T^4}{4}a_1\right)$$

$$Q_q = \left(-\frac{B_T^4}{8}A_1 + \frac{B_T^3\mu}{3}\beta_0 - \frac{B_T^4}{8}\hat{q}_a - \frac{B_T^4}{4}b_1\right) \tag{11.74}$$

The total nondimensional torque is just the sum of these three pieces $C_Q = (C_{Q0} + C_{Q\text{cyclic}} + C_{Qpq})$. The dimensional moments are recovered by multiplying C_{mx}, C_{my}, and C_Q by $\rho\pi R^3 V_{\text{Ta}}^2$.

11.8 Hub Restraints and Their Influence on Flapping

Hub restraints are mechanical devices that are used to provide moment at the hub and/or influence the magnitude and phase of the flapping. Hub restraints usually reduce the rotor flapping and move the frequency of the flapping equation. This frequency change may be an important design consideration if the flapping frequency is very close to the frequency of a physically connected system. If the damping in that other system is low, destructive resonance can result. (The Tacoma Narrows Bridge, a.k.a. Galloping Gurdy, is a dramatic example of resonance leading to a very bad day for one unlucky dog.)

Three restraints are examined. Two of them are strictly inertial or mechanical, and one uses aerodynamics.

11.8.1 Hinge Offset

This purely mechanical contrivance uses the inertial properties of a flapping blade with an offset hinge. Look at Fig. 11.18.

The position vector in the rotating system for a given point on the blade is specified for two cases: when the arclength position is inboard of the flapping hinge and when it is outboard. Thus, when $s \le e$,

$$s = \left\{ \begin{array}{c} -s \\ 0 \\ 0 \end{array} \right\}, \quad \dot{s} = \left\{ \begin{array}{c} 0 \\ 0 \\ 0 \end{array} \right\}, \quad \ddot{s} = \left\{ \begin{array}{c} 0 \\ 0 \\ 0 \end{array} \right\} \qquad (11.75)$$

and when $s > e$,

$$s = \left\{ \begin{array}{c} -s \\ 0 \\ -(s-e)\beta \end{array} \right\}, \quad \dot{s} = \left\{ \begin{array}{c} 0 \\ 0 \\ -(s-e)\dot{\beta} \end{array} \right\}, \quad \ddot{s} = \left\{ \begin{array}{c} 0 \\ 0 \\ -(s-e)\ddot{\beta} \end{array} \right\} \qquad (11.76)$$

The spin vector is

$$\omega = \left\{ \begin{array}{c} 0 \\ 0 \\ -\Omega \end{array} \right\} \qquad (11.77)$$

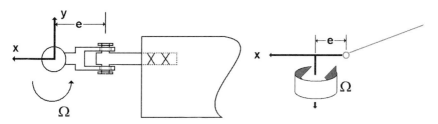

Fig. 11.18   Hinge offset.

The acceleration of the particle in inertial space and the attending inertial force are

$$a = \ddot{s} + 2\omega \times \dot{s} + \dot{\omega} \times s + \omega \times (\omega \times s) \qquad (11.78)$$

so

$$a = \begin{Bmatrix} s\Omega^2 \\ 0 \\ 0 \end{Bmatrix} \quad \text{when} \quad s \le e, \quad \text{and} \quad a = \begin{Bmatrix} s\Omega^2 \\ 0 \\ (s-e)\ddot{\beta} \end{Bmatrix} \quad \text{when} \quad s > e$$

$$(11.79)$$

The differential inertial force is

$$df_i = -a(dm)\,ds \qquad (11.80)$$

The inertial moment can be calculated in the usual way. Sum the moments at the flapping hinge, not the center of rotation. This gives

$$dM_{\text{hinge}} = s_{s>e} \times df_i = \begin{vmatrix} i & j & k \\ -(s-e) & 0 & -(s-e)\beta \\ (dm)s\Omega^2\,ds & 0 & -(dm)(s-e)\ddot{\beta}\,ds \end{vmatrix} \qquad (11.81)$$

or

$$dM_{\text{hinge}-y} = (\overline{m})(s-e)^2\ddot{\beta}\,ds + (\overline{m})s(s-e)\Omega^2\beta\,ds = 0 \qquad (11.82)$$

A useful substitution is to let $x = s - e$. Then $x + e = s$ and $dx = ds$. Integrating the two mass integrands gives

$$\int_0^{R-e} (\overline{m})(s-e)^2\,ds = \int_0^{R-e} (\overline{m})x^2\,dx = \frac{(\overline{m})(R-e)^3}{3} = I_b \qquad (11.83)$$

and

$$\int_0^{R-e} (\overline{m})s(s-e)\,ds = \int_0^{R-e} (\overline{m})(x+e)x\,dx$$

$$= (\overline{m})\left[\frac{(R-e)^3}{3} + \frac{(R-e)^2 e}{2}\right] = i_b \qquad (11.84)$$

In the preceding integrals, the mass is distributed uniformly. This is not the case usually; the integrals are perhaps best calculated numerically. Using the mass integrals, the inertial part of the flapping equation becomes

$$I_b\ddot{\beta} + \Omega^2 i_b\beta = 0 \qquad (11.85)$$

or

$$\ddot{\beta} + \omega_n^2\beta = 0 \qquad (11.86)$$

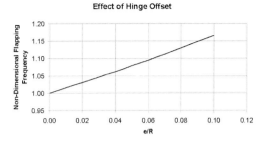

Fig. 11.19   Flapping frequency as a function of hinge offset.

where

$$\omega_n^2 = (P\Omega)^2 = \Omega^2 \left[1 + \frac{3}{2} \frac{e/R}{(1 - e/R)} \right] \qquad (11.87)$$

P is the nondimensional frequency given in units of per rev, that is, if the natural flapping frequency were 30.0 rad/s and the rotor speed were 25 rad/s, then the nondimensional frequency would be $P = 30.0/25.0 = 1.2$ per rev. The amount by which the natural flapping frequency increases with hinge offset is illustrated in Fig. 11.19.

11.8.2   Hub Spring

The hub spring is also a mechanical contrivance, consisting of a spring that resists flapping motion. The spring can deform in translation or rotation and can be constructed of metal or an elastomeric material.

Though shown in Fig. 11.20 attached to an articulated blade, the spring may also work with teetering or gimbaled rotors and blades that have hinge offset. Means to measure the influence of the spring are straightforward. The inertial model has added to it a spring that resists flapping motion. Now the flapping equation becomes

$$I_b \ddot{\beta} + I_b \Omega^2 \beta = -K_\beta \beta + \cdots \qquad (11.88)$$

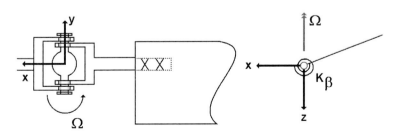

Fig. 11.20   Blade with a flapping spring.

or

$$\ddot{\beta} + \left(\Omega^2 + \frac{K_\beta}{I_b}\right)\beta = \cdots \tag{11.89}$$

where

$$\omega_n^2 = (P\Omega)^2 = \left(\Omega^2 + \frac{K_\beta}{I_b}\right) \tag{11.90}$$

Obviously, a spring can only raise the natural flapping frequency. Figure 11.21 shows the effect of spring stiffness on flapping frequency. The product of the flapping inertia and the square of the rotor speed has normalized the spring stiffness—in essence the flapping moment as a result of centrifugal force. With no spring rate, the flapping frequency is exactly one per rev.

11.8.3 Delta-3 Effect

The third hub restraint we will examine is the so-called delta-3 effect. Regardless of whether the delta-3 is real or virtual, its effect is the same—the blade pitch is coupled to the blade flapping. Figure 11.10 illustrates both types; virtual delta-3 alone is illustrated in Figure 11.22.

In this configuration, the blade pitch decreases (leading edge goes down) as the blade flaps up (out of the plane). This is called positive delta-3. The influence from delta-3 is calculated in three steps. First, evaluate the change to the blade-section pitch equation. Next, evaluate the aerodynamic flapping moment caused by this change and then finally move its influence to the LHS.

The blade-pitch equation is modified to read:

$$\theta = \theta_0 + \theta_T x + A_1 \cos(\psi) + B_1 \sin(\psi) - \tan(\delta_3)\beta \tag{11.91}$$

This definition modifies the aerodynamic flapping moment to read:

$$\frac{M_a}{I_b} = \frac{\gamma\Omega^2}{8}\left[\theta_0 + \frac{4}{5}\theta_T + \cdots - \tan(\delta_3)\beta\right] \tag{11.92}$$

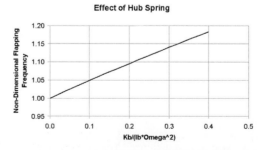

Fig. 11.21 Flapping frequency as a function of hub spring rate.

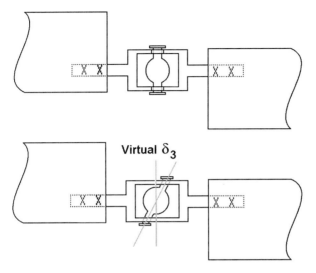

Fig. 11.22   Virtual delta-3.

The far right term on the RHS can be moved to the LHS, yielding

$$\ddot{\beta} + \Omega^2 \beta + \frac{\gamma}{8}\Omega^2 \tan(\delta_3)\beta = \cdots \tag{11.93}$$

or

$$\ddot{\beta} + \omega_n^2 \beta = \cdots \tag{11.94}$$

where

$$\omega_n^2 = (P\Omega)^2 = \Omega^2 \left[1 + \frac{\gamma}{8}\tan(\delta_3) \right] \tag{11.95}$$

Figure 11.23 shows the effect of delta-3 for various values of Lock number. Recall, the Lock number is a measure of the relative influence of aerodynamic forces to inertial forces. The higher the Lock number is, the higher the relative importance of aerodynamic forces. Also note that it is possible to find a combination of Lock number and delta-3 that produces a divergent solution.

11.8.4   Undersling

Undersling is introduced to reduce the Coriolis accelerations by keeping the center of gravity of the blade a (nearly) constant distance from the center of rotation. Undersling is purely mechanical, using inertial properties of a flapping blade that has a hinge offset in the vertical direction. Look at Fig. 11.24.

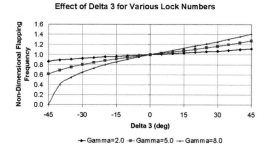

Fig. 11.23   Flapping frequency as a function of delta-3.

The position, velocity, and acceleration vectors in rotating axes and the rotational vector for a given point on the blade are specified thus:

$$
s = \left\{ \begin{array}{c} -s - h\beta \\ 0 \\ h - s\beta - s\beta_0 \end{array} \right\}, \quad
\dot{s} = \left\{ \begin{array}{c} -h\dot{\beta} \\ 0 \\ -s\dot{\beta} \end{array} \right\}, \quad
\ddot{s} = \left\{ \begin{array}{c} -h\ddot{\beta} \\ 0 \\ -s\ddot{\beta} \end{array} \right\} \tag{11.96}
$$

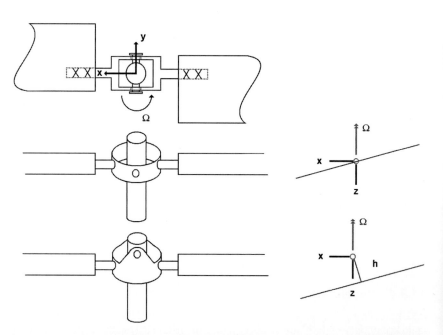

Fig. 11.24   Three views of a teertering rotor: top view, side view with no undersling, and side view with undersling.

and

$$\omega = \begin{Bmatrix} 0 \\ 0 \\ -\Omega \end{Bmatrix}$$

The term β_0 is called the precone. Precone is a constant coning angle introduced to alleviate steady bending moments. The undersling value is called h and is usually a small number on the order of a few percent of rotor radius. The acceleration in inertial space of a particle of rotor and the attending inertial force are

$$a = \ddot{s} + 2\omega \times \dot{s} + \dot{\omega} \times s + \omega \times (\omega \times s) \tag{11.97}$$

so that

$$a = \begin{Bmatrix} -h\ddot{\beta} + s\Omega^2 + \Omega^2 h\beta \\ 2\Omega h\dot{\beta} \\ -s\ddot{\beta} \end{Bmatrix} \tag{11.98}$$

Using Eq. (11.98), the inertial force is $df_i = -a(\overline{m})ds$, from which the inertial moments are calculated.

$$d\mathbf{M}_{\text{hinge}} = \mathbf{s}_{s>e} \times d\mathbf{f}_i$$

$$= \begin{vmatrix} i & j & k \\ -s - h\beta & 0 & h - s\beta - s\beta_0 \\ -(\overline{m})(-h\ddot{\beta} + s\Omega^2 + h\Omega^2\beta)\,ds & -(\overline{m})(2\Omega h\dot{\beta})\,ds & (\overline{m})s\ddot{\beta}\,ds \end{vmatrix}$$

$$\tag{11.99}$$

The moment about the flapping hinge is

$$d\mathbf{M}_{\text{hinge}-y} = (\overline{m})(s^2 + h^2)\ddot{\beta}\,ds + (\overline{m})(s^2 - h^2)\Omega^2\beta\,ds + (\overline{m})(s^2\beta_0 - sh)\Omega^2 \tag{11.100}$$

Discard higher-order terms. The steady moment on the right-hand side will be canceled by an equal term from all other blades in the rotor, so that we may safely ignore it. Besides, the steady moment does not affect the flapping frequency. Define the following two integrals:

$$\int_0^R (\overline{m})(s^2 + h^2)\,ds = \frac{(\overline{m})(R^3 + 3Rh^2)}{3} = I_b$$

and

$$\int_0^R (\overline{m})(s^2 - h^2)\,ds = \frac{(\overline{m})(R^3 - 3Rh^2)}{3} = i_b \tag{11.101}$$

This means the inertial part of the flapping equation becomes

$$I_b\ddot{\beta} + \Omega^2 i_b\beta = \cdots \tag{11.102}$$

or

$$\ddot{\beta} + \omega_n^2 \beta = \cdots$$

where

$$\omega_n^2 = (P\Omega)^2 = \Omega^2 \left[\frac{1 - 3(h/R)^2}{1 + 3(h/R)^2}\right] \qquad (11.103)$$

Because $h \ll R$, the preceding expression shows that undersling does not affect flapping frequency significantly, so that it can be added with impunity and ignored in the frequency calculation.

In summary, hub restraints change the flapping equation to this more complete form:

$$\ddot{\beta} + \Omega^2 \left\{ 1 + \left[\frac{3}{2}\frac{e/R}{(1 - e/R)}\right] + \left(\frac{K_\beta}{I_b\Omega^2}\right) + \left[\frac{\gamma}{8}\tan(\delta_3)\right] \right\}\beta = M_{\text{aero}} \quad (11.104)$$

so that the expression for the natural flapping frequency is

$$\frac{\omega_n^2}{\Omega^2} = \left\{ 1 + \left[\frac{3}{2}\frac{e/R}{(1 - e/R)}\right] + \left(\frac{K_\beta}{I_b\Omega^2}\right) + \left[\frac{\gamma}{8}\tan(\delta_3)\right] \right\} \qquad (11.105)$$

11.9   Methods to Solve the Thrust/Induced Velocity Loop

Through all of the preceding development the total inflow, λ_a has been treated as a constant, which of course, it is not. The induced velocity is a function of the thrust, forward speed, and vertical speed, but thrust is a function of induced velocity. An implicit relationship is born that is fourth order in the general case and has no simple algebraic solution. This relationship was introduced in the chapter on propellers. The salient features are repeated here for convenience.

A rotor at an angle of attack is shown in Fig. 11.25 with horizontal and vertical velocities.

At the plane of the propeller, the thrust-induced velocity relationship is

$$T = 2\rho A V' w_w \qquad (11.106)$$

The general velocity V' is given by the expression

$$V' = [(u_0 + w_w \cos \beta)^2 + (w_0 - w_w \sin \beta)^2]^{1/2} \qquad (11.107)$$

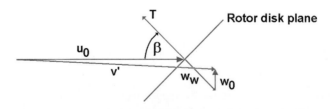

Fig. 11.25   Propeller disk plane with arbitrary mast angle.

Use the definition of the hover induced velocity

$$w_{w_0} = \sqrt{\frac{T}{2\rho \pi R^2}} \qquad (11.108)$$

to define the nondimensional general induced velocity, forward inertial velocity, and vertical inertial velocity, respectively:

$$\hat{w} = \frac{w_w}{w_{w_0}}, \quad \hat{\mu} = \frac{u_0}{w_{w_0}}, \quad \text{and} \quad \hat{\eta} = \frac{w_0}{w_{w_0}} \qquad (11.109)$$

Substitute Eq. (11.107) into Eq. (11.106), and employ Eq. (11.109). The result is the momentum-theory fourth-order polynomial representing the induced velocity in vertical and horizontal flight at arbitrary incidence to the oncoming wind.

$$\hat{w}^4 + 2(\hat{\mu} \cos \beta - \hat{\eta} \sin \beta)\hat{w}^3 + (\hat{\mu}^2 + \hat{\eta}^2)\hat{w}^2 - 1 = 0 \qquad (11.110)$$

This expression covers the gamut from hover to high forward speed, climb, moderate descent, and windmill brake state. In particular, let the mast angle $\beta = 90$ deg, the usual orientation for helicopters. After some rearranging, the polynomial reduces to

$$\hat{w}^2 \left[\hat{\mu}^2 + (\hat{w} - \hat{\eta})^2 \right] - 1 = 0 \qquad (11.111)$$

The well-known diagram in Fig. 11.26 illustrates the solution to the momentum theory in vertical flight, at zero forward speed. Also shown are representative experimental data taken from Taghizad et al. [5]. Note, the velocities are normalized to hover induced velocity.

Comparing the theoretical solution to the observed data, it is obvious that the momentum model begins to break down in the region where the magnitude of the descent speed is approximately one-half that of the hover induced velocity. This region is the so-called vortex ring state (VRS). One method to deal with this is simply to fit a curve through the experimental data or find an analytical expression that fits it. A very good discussion of VRS is found in Brand et al. [6].

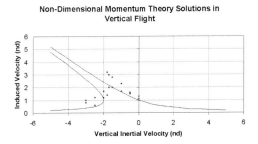

Non-Dimensional Momentum Theory Solutions in
Vertical Flight

Fig. 11.26   Classical presentation of induced velocity as a function of vertical inertial velocity.

In general, iterative procedures are required to find the solution to this polynomial. (The special case is hover with no horizontal or vertical speed. In that case, the induced velocity is just $w_w = \sqrt{T/2\rho A}$.) Four iterative procedures are described next. Each procedure has its strengths and weaknesses.

11.9.1 Method 1—Newton–Raphson

Create a function of the induced velocity. Call it $f(\hat{w})$:

$$f(\hat{w}) = \hat{w}^4 + 2(\hat{\mu}\cos\beta - \hat{\eta}\sin\beta)\hat{w}^3 + (\hat{\mu}^2 + \hat{\eta}^2)\hat{w}^2 - 1 \qquad (11.112)$$

Calculate its derivative and call it $F(\hat{w})$:

$$F(\hat{w}) = 4\hat{w}^3 + 6(\hat{\mu}\cos\beta - \hat{\eta}\sin\beta)\hat{w}^2 + 2(\hat{\mu}^2 + \hat{\eta}^2)\hat{w} \qquad (11.113)$$

The goal is to find a value of $\hat{w}$ such that the function $f(\hat{w})$ goes to zero. Start with some estimate for the induced velocity, and construct a Taylor series around the presumed solution, setting the result to zero.

$$f(\hat{w} + \Delta\hat{w}) = 0 = f(\hat{w}) + F(\hat{w})\Delta\hat{w} \qquad (11.114)$$

Solve this equation for the change in induced velocity:

$$\Delta\hat{w} = -\frac{f(\hat{w})}{F(\hat{w})} \qquad (11.115)$$

Add this change to the current estimate to generate the next estimate. Repeat this procedure until the function is within an acceptable distance from zero. The Newton–Raphson method is a very good method, especially if the derivative can be written analytically, as here. The drawback to this method is if the zero is the maximum or minimum of the function, for then the derivative is also zero and special branching is required, a distasteful annoyance.

11.9.2 Method 2—Simple Iterative Feedback with Caution

Equation (11.64) gives the coefficient of Z-force, which is just the negative of the thrust coefficient C_T. Equation (11.30) defines the nondimensional wash velocity and the inertial vertical and horizontal velocities λ_w, λ_0, and μ_a, respectively. Equations (11.106) and (11.107), when combined and normalized with the factor $\rho\pi R^2 V_{\text{Tip}}^2$ yield the implicit, nondimensional thrust-induced velocity relationship. Left in nondimensional form, the induced velocity problem looks like this:

$$C_T[i] = \frac{\sigma a_0}{2}[T_0\theta_0 + \cdots + T_\lambda(\lambda_0 - \lambda_w[i])]$$

$$\lambda_w[i+1] = \frac{C_T[i]}{2[\mu_a^2 + (\lambda_0 - \lambda_w[i])^2]^{1/2}}$$

$$\lambda_w[i+1] = \frac{(\hat{\lambda}_w[i+1] + \lambda_w[i])}{2} \qquad (11.116)$$

The indices in square brackets indicate the iteration upon which one is operating. Start the process with some initial guess for the induced velocity, calculate the thrust, and then use that value to come to a new guess for the induced velocity. If necessary, the average of the new guess and the old guess can be used as the improved new guess. This average guess is the caution used in iteration of "stiff" systems. The advantage of this method is that the engineering equations have not disappeared. The disadvantages are that a nonzero estimate for the induced velocity is required at hover, and this entire system is undefined at zero thrust and zero forward speed (such as at engine start).

11.9.3 Method 3—Bisection

The bisection method rewrites the thrust/induced velocity equations so that no divisions are ever used. In the present example, create a functional (a function with more than one equation—a subroutine if you will) that rearranges the two following expressions into a system with no divisions.

Original system [from Eq. (11.116), with square brackets removed] is

$$C_T = \frac{\sigma a_0}{2}[T_0\theta_0 + \cdots + T_\lambda(\lambda_0 - \lambda_w)]$$

$$\lambda_w = \frac{C_T[i]}{2(\mu_a^2 + (\lambda_0 - \lambda_w)^2)^{1/2}}$$

Rewritten system is

$$F(\lambda_w) = \begin{cases} C_T = \dfrac{\sigma a_0}{2}[T_0\theta_0 + \cdots + T_\lambda(\lambda_0 - \lambda_w)] \\ f(\lambda_w) = 2\lambda_w\left[\mu_a^2 + (\lambda_0 - \lambda_w)^2\right]^{1/2} - C_T \end{cases} \qquad (11.117)$$

The functional $F(\lambda_w)$ takes the value of the second equation in braces, but must execute both equations with every invocation. Now comes the bisection, which is easiest to describe in algorithmic form:

1) Set a maximum number of iterations and initialize an iteration counter.

2) Choose the left-most (or greatest negative) value for λ_w, call it λ_L, and evaluate the function at that point. Call that value F_L.

3) Choose the right-most (or greatest positive) value for λ_w, call it λ_R, and evaluate the function at that point and call it F_R.

4) Ensure that F_L and F_R have opposite signs. If F_L and F_R do not, either no root has been bracketed, or an even number of roots have been bracketed. Unfortunately, no a priori knowledge informs of which situation exists. In all cases with which the author is familiar, if the starting values are set such that $\lambda_R = 20\lambda_{Hover}$ and $\lambda_L = -\lambda_R$, then the desired root is bracketed.

5) Find the midpoint value for λ_w, call it $\lambda_M = \lambda_L + \lambda_R/2$, and evaluate the function at that point. Call this value F_M.

6) If $F_M = 0$. (or within an acceptable tolerance), then exit this routine with $\lambda_w = \lambda_M$ as the desired value. If the iteration counter reaches the maximum value, exit this routine with $\lambda_w = \lambda_M$ as the desired value. If neither condition is met, go to the next step.

7) F_M is not zero. Compare the sign of F_M to F_L. If the signs are the same, then go to step 8; otherwise, go to step 9.

8) The root is known to lie between F_M and F_R. Set $\lambda_L \leftarrow \lambda_M$ and $F_L \leftarrow F_M$, then increment the iteration counter and go back to step 5.

9) The root is known to lie between F_L and F_M. Set $\lambda_R \leftarrow \lambda_M$ and $F_R \leftarrow F_M$, then increment the iteration counter, and go back to step 5.

A slight variation on this routine suggests that the test of acceptable tolerance be ignored. Instead, just go a set number of iterations. Doing so ensures that the answer lies within $(\lambda_{R_0} - \lambda_{L_0})/2^n$ of the actual answer. If $n = 20$, then the answer has converged to one part in one million. The upside of this method is that divisions by zero are completely eliminated, and so a continuous passage from negative thrust to positive thrust is possible. The downside is that one must ensure the initial left and right estimates bracket one and only one root.

11.9.4 Method 4—Dynamic Modeling

Several dynamic models of the rotor wake exist. They include axial flow and truncated cylinders spinning about the roll and pitch axes. What follows is a simple example of how a dynamic model can be designed. It is highly suggested for the sake of engineering "correctness" that the established models of Pitt and Peters [7] and others be used for production efforts.

The Glauert momentum model, Eq. (11.106), is of the form:

$$T = 2\rho A|V_a|w_w$$

This model says that thrust is equal to the momentum flux. Now, imagine a sphere centered on the rotor. Let the radius of the sphere be some fraction k of the radius of the rotor. If one suggests that the mass in the sphere is accelerated by the thrust, then Glauert's model can be modified to read:

$$T = 2\rho A|V_a|w_w + \frac{4}{3}\pi(kR)^3\rho\dot{w}_w \qquad (11.118)$$

Normalize the equation by dividing both sides by $\rho A V_T^2$. The result, after some reduction, is

$$\tau\dot{\lambda}_w = -2\frac{|V_a|}{V_T}\lambda_w + C_T \qquad (11.119)$$

where $\tau = 4k^3/3$ and $\dot{\lambda}_w = \dot{w}_w/\Omega^2 R$.

Values of k between 0.74 and 0.86 bring this model into line with the Pitt–Peters model [7], of which more will be said later. Once a trim value for the induced velocity is found, subsequent values during the maneuver phase of a simulation are found by solving this differential equation along with the aircraft equations of motion. More will be said about dynamic wakes later in this chapter.

11.10 Tip Loss Factor

There is an important refinement to all of the work that has been presented thus far, which is that the lift on a blade cannot discontinuously disappear at the tip. Unless a rigorous lifting-line or lifting-surface model is used, the method commonly used to account for a continuous drop-off of blade distributed lift is the tip loss factor. When using this method, one assumes that the lift distribution is what it is, but that the limits of integration when evaluating the aerodynamics do not extend to the tip, but rather, they go to some point slightly inboard of the tip. This multiplier of the radius is the tip loss factor and is usually given the symbol B_T. Analytical and experimental investigations have been performed to determine the value of this factor. Prandtl and the Goldstein–Lock calculations for lightly loaded rotors produced this empirical expression that is most often used:

$$B_T = 1 - \frac{\sqrt{2C_T}}{b} \qquad (11.120)$$

where b is the number of blades. Although this expression is dependent on the thrust coefficient, one will find that a tip loss factor of 0.97 is commonly used. The correction is applied to the radial integration on the lift contributions only (talk about a fudge factor!). This factor can mean as much as 9% difference in thrust and H and Y force given the same control settings. In power, the difference is somewhat smaller because the overhead of profile power is paid fully whether or not the rotor is producing any lift.

11.11   Summary of Quasi-Static Closed-Form Method

The model just presented has been used in industry with good results for many years. (Or one just like it. Every helicopter firm has its closely guarded and trusted models. What has been presented is typical of the closed-form models. Modifications to these models include drag polars that are a function of thrust coefficient, accommodations for large twist angles, tapered blades, tip sweep, unusually shaped tips, and high inflow. Modifications to account for nonuniform wake are also included in some models. The equations presented here already allow for that modification via the swirling wake.) Refinements have improved the correlation to flight-test results. But, it is instructive to review the assumptions that are present in this model and their implications.

First, flapping angles are assumed small. In general, this is not a bad assumption. If the rotor is flapping more than 15 deg, there is a serious problem. Products of the flapping angle and its derivatives will also be small and will generally not be significant players. There is one exception. Think of the rotor as a lumped mass at the end of a mass-less rod, hinged at or near the center of rotation. The angular momentum is $h = m(R \cos \beta)^2 \Omega^2$. An applied torque changes the angular momentum in time. That is, $M = \dot{h} = -2m(R^2 \cos \beta \sin \beta \dot{\beta} \Omega^2) \cong -2mR^2\Omega^2 \beta \dot{\beta}$. This moment is the so-called Coriolis load, which is an in-plane bending moment caused by out-of-plane flapping and is a large load that must be accounted for in design. Coriolis load does not show up in aerodynamic performance equations because it is inertial. It does not show up in simple inertial models because of the (almost cavalier) discard of supposedly higher-order terms.

Second, blade pitch angles are assumed small, and the twist angle is assumed small and linear. For most helicopters, the collective and cyclic inputs are small, so that these assumptions are not unreasonable. However, for tiltrotors the collective angle input can be large. The twist angles for helicopters are usually small as well, any nonlinear twist effects are near the root where dynamic pressures are low and do not contribute much to loads. Again, tiltrotors violate that assumption, with nonlinear twists amounting to 45 deg or more.

Third, the assumption of uniformly distributed downwash is a convenient fiction used to make the mathematics tractable. At the very least, a cyclic and radial variation should be modeled. The preceding development admits such a model, if only the relationship between moment and swirling wake can be written. A momentum-based wake that is reactive to local blade loading is even better, and a CFD model would be best—but alas there is not enough time in the day.

Fourth, the blade is assumed to be infinitely stiff, with the in-plane, out-of-plane, and torsional deflection coming only at conveniently placed hinges. Many years ago, some enterprising engineers mounted a camera at the hub of a rotor and pointed the lens toward the tip. As the blade whirled around while the aircraft was in forward flight, the camera recorded the decidedly elastic deflection of the blade. The deflection was multimodal, involving motion in every direction. For the most part, the motion would affect blade bending moments more than rotor aerodynamic performance, hence the apparent success of a simple, articulated blade model.

Fifth, the geometry of the rotor blade is assumed to be simple with constant chord, straight lines, and no tip treatment. An equivalent chord, called a thrust-weighted chord, is used in the preceding model. The thrust-weighted chord is found by evaluating the following integral expression:

$$c_{\text{thrust-weighted}} = \frac{\int_0^R c(s)s^2 \, ds}{\int_0^R s^2 \, ds} \qquad (11.121)$$

A power-weighted chord may be desired instead. It is found through a similar expression:

$$c_{\text{power-weighted}} = \frac{\int_0^R c(s)s^3 \, ds}{\int_0^R s^3 \, ds} \qquad (11.122)$$

To account for blade reference lines that deviate from straight lines, a polynomial may be substituted for the x, y, and z components in the BRL vector, and the analysis repeated. This substitution and analysis is a great amount of work. To account for tip treatments, some "correlation" factors on lift-curve slope and drag polar are required.

Sixth, linear aerodynamics are used. Small angles of attack are assumed around the azimuth. On the advancing blade, this assumption is probably reasonable. On the retreating blade, the flow actually reverses inboard of a region defined by $\mu R \sin \psi$ and is at large angles of attack over most of the retreating blade, increasing with increased airspeed. In addition, the Mach-number effects on lift and drag curves are not easily accounted for with linear aerodynamics.

There is a way to combat some of these problems, which is the subject of the next section.

11.12 Blade Element Aeroelastic Rotor Modeling

A blade-element approach is required when modeling a rotor with elasticity and nonlinear aerodynamics. As before, the math model for a rotor divides into two pieces, dynamics and aerodynamics. Numerical integration will be the only way to calculate the loads and solve the flapping equation. Even the flapping equation will be developed an entirely new way. Although the amount of computing that goes into the rotor performance calculations increases by several orders compared to the quasi-static solution given in the preceding sections, the actual math model is easier to express because expansions are not performed. Here is one representative description of an aeroelastic blade-element rotor model. It is simple in comparison to, but similar in development to, the rotor model found in programs in [8] and [9].

11.12.1 Assumptions

Let a position vector measure from the center of rotation to some point on a blade. This vector is the blade reference line or BRL. The BRL is assumed infinitely stiff in tension (inextensible), but in every other respect is as free to move as a piece of wet spaghetti. The infinitesimally wide blade section at any point has a mass equal to $\overline{m}(y)\,dy$ and distributed inertia tensor equal to $dI(y)$. As what is to follow is expository only, the assumption is made that the aerodynamic center and section center of gravity are colocated on the BRL and only the linear (as opposed to angular) inertial and aerodynamic loads will be developed. Absent the accelerations that cause angular blade motion, well-known effects like the "tennis-racket moment" are not present in this model. For greater sophistication, the reader is encouraged to consult [8] and [9].

The normal-modes approach is used to model the elastic behavior, which is assumed to be a perturbation from a prescribed geometry. Prescribed geometry includes manufactured shapes such as twist, precone, and tip shape, plus any prescription from the pilot through collective or cyclic control. Programs such as Myklestad or NASTRAN provide the normal modes. In the general case, the modes are a function of collective position, type of hub, pitch link stiffness, and rpm. Assume that capability here, though it will not be explicitly dealt with.

11.12.2 Elastic (Normal Modes) Model of a Rotor

The position vector has six elements in it; three are linear positions, and three are angular positions. The vector is ordered as shown here:

$$
\boldsymbol{P}_{\mathrm{bf}}(s,t) = \left\{
\begin{array}{l}
x_{\mathrm{bf}}(s,t) \\
y_{\mathrm{bf}}(s,t) \\
z_{\mathrm{bf}}(s,t) \\
\phi x_{\mathrm{bf}}(s,t) \\
\phi y_{\mathrm{bf}}(s,t) \\
\phi z_{\mathrm{bf}}(s,t)
\end{array}
\right\}
\qquad (11.123)
$$

The linear coordinates are x_{bf}, which lies on and is tangent to the BRL, pointing generally toward the hub; y_{bf}, which lies parallel to the chord line and points

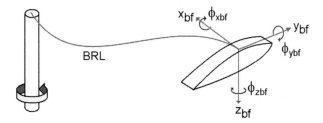

Fig. 11.27 Blade-reference-line and blade-section coordinates.

toward the leading edge; and z_{bf}, which points in a direction so as to complete a right-hand system. The angular coordinate ϕx_{bf} measures an angle around the x_{bf} axis, positive leading edge down. This angular coordinate is commonly the pitch angle. The angular coordinate ϕy_{bf} measures an angle about the local y_{bf} axis, and so this is the local flapping angle. The positive direction would be flapping down. The coordinate ϕz_{bf} measures an angle that the blade section leads and lags. The positive sense is in the lag direction. The subscript f means full or final. Figure 11.27 shows these coordinates.

As just stated, elastic analysis is usually conducted using the normal-modes approach, which is a perturbation model. What follows is the modeling method used in Hoffman and Dreier [8] and Anderson et al. [9]. This method, while appearing busy, has a distinct advantage over other, classical, normal-modes approaches. In the classical methods, the inertial model is expanded, and those terms that comprise the elastic-beam problem are put on the left-hand side while the kinematic accelerations, which form part of the forcing function, are placed on the right. That is, the equations are expanded and rearranged by hand, with the hope that no terms were dropped or "double dipped." In the method of [8], the inertial model is retained intact and remains on the right-hand side as part of a complete nonlinear forcing function for a linear deformation equation, which is manufactured on the left-hand side. Because no hand expansions are required, the potential for double dipping and/or dropping terms reduces significantly.

The perturbation is measured from a prescribed position vector. A manufactured (static) shape and a pilot-controlled alteration to the shape comprise the prescribed position vector. The alterations are partial derivatives of the BRL coordinates with respect to a parameter, here named $\theta(t)$. The symbol $\theta(t)$ is chosen out of historical perspective as most rotor modelers use $\theta(t)$ for the blade-pitch angle. The most obvious specification for $\theta(t)$ is the expansion $\theta(t) = \theta_0 + A_1 \cos(\Omega t) + B_1 \sin(\Omega t)$. Let θ_{ref} be the reference value for the parameter $\theta(t)$, taken, perhaps, at zero cyclic and hover trim value of collective.

$$\boldsymbol{P}_{bp}(s,t) = \begin{Bmatrix} x_{bp}(s,t) \\ y_{bp}(s,t) \\ z_{bp}(s,t) \\ \phi x_{bp}(s,t) \\ \phi y_{bp}(s,t) \\ \phi z_{bp}(s,t) \end{Bmatrix} = \begin{Bmatrix} x_{b0}(s) \\ y_{b0}(s) \\ z_{b0}(s) \\ \phi x_{b0}(s) \\ \phi y_{b0}(s) \\ \phi z_{b0}(s) \end{Bmatrix} + \begin{Bmatrix} \partial x_b(s)/\partial\theta \\ \partial y_b(s)/\partial\theta \\ \partial z_b(s)/\partial\theta \\ \partial \phi x_b(s)/\partial\theta \\ \partial \phi y_b(s)/\partial\theta \\ \partial \phi z_b(s)/\partial\theta \end{Bmatrix} [\theta(t) - \theta_{ref}]$$

$$(11.124)$$

The pilot or control system provides inputs to $\theta(t)$. The preceding subzero vector is a function only of space, as is the partial derivative vector. Because the partial derivative vector is a function of space, the model has the capability of doing partial-span pitch changes defined simply by data. An example of the prescribed position vector function is

$$
\boldsymbol{P}_{b0}(s) = \left\{ \begin{array}{c} -s\cos\beta_0 \\ 0 \\ -s\sin\beta_0 \\ -\theta_{\text{root}} + \theta_T \dfrac{s}{R} \\ -\beta_0 \\ 0 \end{array} \right\}, \quad \frac{\partial \boldsymbol{P}_b(s)}{\partial\theta} = \left\{ \begin{array}{c} 0 \\ 0 \\ 0 \\ -1 \\ 0 \\ 0 \end{array} \right\} \tag{11.125}
$$

One sees immediately that the fourth element of $\boldsymbol{P}_{b0}$ is the manufactured twist of the blade, and that the fourth element of $\partial \boldsymbol{P}_b(s)/\partial\theta$ adds the pilot controls $\theta(t) = \theta_0 + A_1\cos(\Omega t) + B_1\sin(\Omega t)$ directly to the twist schedule to arrive at the prescribed and instantaneous pitch angle of the blade section.

Define the perturbation vector so that it has the sense of

$$
\delta_p = \boldsymbol{P}_{\text{bf}} - \boldsymbol{P}_{\text{bp}} = \left\{ \begin{array}{c} x_{\text{bf}} - x_{\text{bp}} \\ y_{\text{bf}} - y_{\text{bp}} \\ z_{\text{bf}} - z_{\text{bp}} \\ \phi_x \\ \phi_y \\ \phi_z \end{array} \right\} \tag{11.126}
$$

for the first three elements. The second three elements of δ_p (the angular perturbations) are defined so that a vector is transformed from prescribed axes to final axes via

$$
V_f = R_x(\phi_x)R_y(\phi_y)R_z(\phi_z)V_p \tag{11.127}
$$

A full, distributed load is a function of inertia and aerodynamic loads, which are functions of the blade position, rate and acceleration, and control inputs. That is,

$$
\mathrm{d}\boldsymbol{F}_f = \left\{ \begin{array}{c} \mathrm{d}F_{xf} \\ \mathrm{d}F_{yf} \\ \mathrm{d}F_{zf} \\ \mathrm{d}M_{xf} \\ \mathrm{d}M_{yf} \\ \mathrm{d}M_{zf} \end{array} \right\} = \mathrm{d}\boldsymbol{F}_f(\boldsymbol{P}_{\text{bf}}, \dot{\boldsymbol{P}}_{\text{bf}}, \ddot{\boldsymbol{P}}_{\text{bf}}, \theta, \dot{\theta}, \ddot{\theta}) \tag{11.128}
$$

Likewise, a prescribed distributed load is

$$
\mathrm{d}\boldsymbol{F}_p = \left\{ \begin{array}{c} \mathrm{d}F_{xp} \\ \mathrm{d}F_{yp} \\ \mathrm{d}F_{zp} \\ \mathrm{d}M_{xp} \\ \mathrm{d}M_{yp} \\ \mathrm{d}M_{zp} \end{array} \right\} = \mathrm{d}\boldsymbol{F}_p(\boldsymbol{P}_{\mathrm{bp}}, \dot{\boldsymbol{P}}_{\mathrm{bp}}, \ddot{\boldsymbol{P}}_{\mathrm{bp}}, \theta, \dot{\theta}, \ddot{\theta}) \tag{11.129}
$$

The difference between the two load vectors is a function of inertial acceleration, spin stiffening, and all other aerodynamic loads:

$$
\delta\,\mathrm{d}\boldsymbol{F} = \mathrm{d}\boldsymbol{F}_f - \mathrm{d}\boldsymbol{F}_p = \delta\,\mathrm{d}\boldsymbol{F}(\delta p, \delta\dot{p}, \delta\ddot{p}, \theta, \dot{\theta}, \ddot{\theta}) = \mathrm{d}\boldsymbol{F} - \int m\delta\ddot{p}\,\mathrm{d}s - \int k_s\delta p \tag{11.130}
$$

The claim is that a "spring" term multiplied by the elastic deformation represents this force. That is,

$$
\delta\,\mathrm{d}\boldsymbol{F} = \int k_e\delta q \tag{11.131}
$$

Equating these two expressions leads to a definition of dF:

$$
\int m\delta\ddot{p}\,\mathrm{d}s + \int K\delta p = \mathrm{d}\boldsymbol{F} \tag{11.132}
$$

where

$$
K = k_s + k_e
$$

The k_s and k_e matrices obey Maxwell's reciprocity theorem, so that $k_s^T = k_s$ and $k_e^T = k_e$. Combine this expression with the expression that relates dF to perturbation loads (repeated here in slightly rearranged form):

$$
\mathrm{d}\boldsymbol{F} = \mathrm{d}\boldsymbol{F}_f - \mathrm{d}\boldsymbol{F}_p + \int m\delta\ddot{p}\,\mathrm{d}s + \int k_s\delta p \tag{11.133}
$$

to get

$$
\int m\delta\ddot{p}\,\mathrm{d}s + \int K\delta p\,\mathrm{d}s = \mathrm{d}\boldsymbol{F}_f - \mathrm{d}\boldsymbol{F}_p + \int m\delta\ddot{p}\,\mathrm{d}s + \int k_s\delta p \tag{11.134}
$$

Now, utilizing the separation of variables technique, the perturbation displacement, velocity, and acceleration are

$$
\delta p(s, t) = Q(s)\beta(t)
$$
$$
\delta\dot{p}(s, t) = Q(s)\dot{\beta}(t)
$$
$$
\delta\ddot{p}(s, t) = Q(s)\ddot{\beta}(t) \tag{11.135}
$$

The $Q(s)$ matrix is the collection of modeshapes. Substitute these modeshapes into the preceding integrodifferential equation, premultiply the result by $Q^T(s)$, and integrate that result along the blade:

$$\iint Q^T(s)m(s)Q(s)\,ds\ddot{\beta}(t) + \iint Q^T(s)KQ(s)\,ds\beta(t)$$
$$= \int Q^T(s)(dF_f - dF_p)\,ds + \iint Q^T(s)m(s)Q(s)\,ds\ddot{\beta}(t)$$
$$+ \iint Q^T(s)k_sQ(s)\,ds\beta(t) \tag{11.136}$$

The first double integral is called the generalized inertia. Premultiply the entire preceding expression by the inverse of the generalized inertia matrix. The result is a diagonal system of linear, second-order differential equations with a nonlinear forcing function representing the elastic deflection of a rotor blade:

$$\ddot{\beta}(t) + \omega^2\beta(t) = M_g^{-1}\int Q^T(s)(dF_f - dF_p)\,ds + \ddot{\beta}(t) + M_g^{-1}K_s\beta(t) \tag{11.137}$$

Notice the similarity with the simplified flapping equation presented earlier. This modal equation is used in several aeroelastic analysis programs. The appearance of $\ddot{\beta}$ on the RHS distresses readers the first time they encounter it. Nevertheless, that term belongs there because it exactly cancels a $-\ddot{\beta}$ term that arises in the first integral on the RHS. Because the spin-stiffening matrix k_s is not known a priori, the K_s matrix cannot be calculated directly. Instead, recognize that K_s is really a linearized residual (derivative) of the RHS with respect to β. Therefore, the K_s matrix is calculated via numerical differentiation:

$$K_s = \frac{\partial[\int Q^T(s)(dF_f - dF_p)\,ds]}{\partial\beta} \tag{11.138}$$

An example of this calculation will be provided later.

The advantage of doing things this way is that the inertial model and aerodynamic model can be treated with equal rigor, and without engineering judgment about what terms should be retained, and on which side should they be placed. All that is left now is to write expressions for dF_f and dF_p.

11.12.3 Inertial Model for the Aeroelastic Rotor

Much of the inertial model for the aeroelastic rotor has already been developed for the simple rotor model. The missing pieces are the hub motion contributions. The more complete model is summarized next. True to the spirit of working with linear algebra, this model is not expanded. The result will be an expression for the differential force. A radial integration gives the hub load.

The top of the mast (the hub) has linear and angular velocity. These vectors are resolved to the hub axes, which are parallel to the body axes; that is, the IELA.

$$V_{i|hub} = \begin{Bmatrix} u_h \\ v_h \\ w_h \end{Bmatrix} \quad \text{and} \quad \omega_{i|hub} = \begin{Bmatrix} p_h \\ q_h \\ r_h \end{Bmatrix} \tag{11.139}$$

Likewise, the hub has accelerations also resolved to the IELA:

$$\dot{V}_{i|hub} = \begin{Bmatrix} \dot{u}_h \\ \dot{v}_h \\ \dot{w}_h \end{Bmatrix} \quad \text{and} \quad \dot{\omega}_{i|hub} = \begin{Bmatrix} \dot{p}_h \\ \dot{q}_h \\ \dot{r}_h \end{Bmatrix} \tag{11.140}$$

All velocities and accelerations are resolved to hub axes (IELA). Using Coriolis theorem, the total acceleration at the hub caused by mast motion is

$$\frac{dV_{i|hub}}{dt} = \dot{V}_{i|hub} + \omega_{i|hub} \times V_{i|hub} \tag{11.141}$$

One must resolve this vector to the rotating system. The total linear acceleration caused by hub motion is

$$\frac{dV_{i|r}}{dt} = T_\psi \frac{dV_{i|hub}}{dt} \tag{11.142}$$

(Formally, each of the vectors that went into that expression should have been resolved to the hub axes independently, and then the cross product and addition should have been evaluated. Fortunately, the rules of algebra show that the preceding faster method yields the same result.) The rotor axes spin with rate Ω_z about the z axis resolved to hub axes. Add Ω_z to the hub angular velocity, and resolve the sum to rotor axes.

$$\omega_{r|r} = T_\psi (\omega_{i|hub} + \Omega_z) \tag{11.143}$$

Note: The vector

$$\Omega_z = \begin{Bmatrix} 0 \\ 0 \\ -\Omega \end{Bmatrix}$$

which keeps this development on track with the previous work. The derivative of the angular velocity in rotor axes is found by direct differentiation:

$$\dot{\omega}_{r|r} = T_\psi (\dot{\omega}_{i|hub} + \omega_{i|hub} \times \Omega_z + \dot{\Omega}_z) \tag{11.144}$$

The blade position vector is

$$P_{bf}(s,t) = P_{b0}(s) + \left[\frac{\partial P_b(s)}{\partial \theta} \right] [\theta(t) - \theta_{ref}] + Q(s)\beta(t) \tag{11.145}$$

The blade position rate and acceleration are

$$\dot{\boldsymbol{P}}_{bf}(s,t) = \left[\frac{\partial \boldsymbol{P}_b(s)}{\partial \theta}\right]\dot{\theta}(t) + Q(s)\dot{\beta}(t) \tag{11.146}$$

and

$$\ddot{\boldsymbol{P}}_{bf}(s,t) = \left[\frac{\partial \boldsymbol{P}_b(s)}{\partial \theta}\right]\ddot{\theta}(t) + Q(s)\ddot{\beta}(t) \tag{11.147}$$

The linear part of the position vector is all that is needed for the inertial model:

$$\boldsymbol{P}_{bf3}(s,t) = \begin{Bmatrix} x_{bf}(s,t) \\ y_{bf}(s,t) \\ z_{bf}(s,t) \end{Bmatrix} \tag{11.148}$$

The derivatives are similarly defined. All of the pieces required for the acceleration of a blade mass particle are now known. The total acceleration is

$$\frac{dV_b}{dt} = \frac{dV_{i|r}}{dt} + \ddot{\boldsymbol{P}}_{bf3} + 2\boldsymbol{\omega}_{r|r} \times \dot{\boldsymbol{P}}_{bf3} + \dot{\boldsymbol{\omega}}_{r|r} \times \boldsymbol{P}_{bf3} + \boldsymbol{\omega}_{r|r} \times (\boldsymbol{\omega}_{r|r} \times \boldsymbol{P}_{bf3}) \tag{11.149}$$

This equation is the acceleration of a blade particle in inertial space, resolved to rotor axes. The inertial load it produces is simply

$$d\boldsymbol{F}_i = -\overline{m}\frac{dV_b}{dt}\,ds \tag{11.150}$$

The $\overline{m}$ is a distributed mass with units of mass/length.

11.12.4 Aerodynamic Model for the Aeroelastic Rotor

The aeroelastic rotor model employs classical, steady, two-dimensional (strip) theory aerodynamics. Modifications for spanwise blowing, unsteady airfoil theory and the like are beyond the scope of this text, but are certainly admissible in this development.

Distributed aerodynamic loads are developed in blade-section axes and then resolved to rotor axes. Begin with a calculation of the velocity in three dimensions at a blade section. The linear and angular hub velocities are given by Eq. (11.139), repeated here for convenience:

$$\boldsymbol{V}_{i|hub} = \begin{Bmatrix} u_h \\ v_h \\ w_h \end{Bmatrix} \quad \text{and} \quad \boldsymbol{\omega}_{i|hub} = \begin{Bmatrix} p_h \\ q_h \\ r_h \end{Bmatrix}$$

These vectors are just inertial quantities. For aerodynamics, the aerodynamic velocities are required. The linear and angular wash velocities are

$$\boldsymbol{V}_{wash|hub} = \begin{Bmatrix} u_w \\ v_w \\ w_w \end{Bmatrix} \quad \text{and} \quad \boldsymbol{\omega}_{wash|hub} = \begin{Bmatrix} p_w \\ q_w \\ r_w \end{Bmatrix} \tag{11.151}$$

Thus, the aerodynamic velocities are

$$V_{a|hub} = V_{i|hub} - V_{wash|hub} + V_{gust|hub} \qquad (11.152)$$

and

$$\boldsymbol{\omega}_{a|hub} = \boldsymbol{\omega}_{i|hub} - \boldsymbol{\omega}_{wash|hub} + \boldsymbol{\omega}_{gust|hub} \qquad (11.153)$$

Both aerodynamic vectors must be resolved to rotor axes. As before, the rotor axes spin with rate $\boldsymbol{\Omega}_z$ about the z axis resolved to hub axes. This must be added to the hub angular velocity before resolution to rotor axes.

$$V_{a|r} = T_\psi V_{a|hub} \qquad (11.154)$$

$$\boldsymbol{\omega}_{a|r} = T_\psi (\boldsymbol{\omega}_{a|hub} + \boldsymbol{\Omega}_z) \qquad (11.155)$$

The linear velocity is added to the velocity caused by blade elastic deformation and angular motion with respect to the hub.

$$V_{bf|r} = V_{a|r} + \dot{P}_{bf} + \boldsymbol{\omega}_{a|r} \times P_{bf} \qquad (11.156)$$

Finally, the aerodynamic velocity is transformed from the shaft normal plane to the final blade-section axes, the IERA of each section. This transformation is performed in two steps. First, transform to the prescribed blade-section axes, and then rotate again through the perturbations.

$$V_{bf|bf} = T(\phi_x, \phi_y, \phi_z) T(\phi_{0_x}, \phi_{0_y}, \phi_{0_z}) V_{bf|r} \qquad (11.157)$$

The prescribed blade-section transformation is given by the series of large angle rotations:

$$T(\phi_{0_x}, \phi_{0_y}, \phi_{0_z}) = R_x(\phi_{0_x}) R_y(\phi_{0_y}) R_z(\phi_{0_z}) \qquad (11.158)$$

whereas the rotation through the perturbation (small) angles is adequately described by

$$T(\phi_x, \phi_y, \phi_z) = \begin{bmatrix} 1 & \phi_z & -\phi_y \\ -\phi_z & 1 & \phi_x \\ \phi_y & -\phi_x & 1 \end{bmatrix} \qquad (11.159)$$

The three elements of $V_{bf|bf}$ are the oft-named radial, tangential, and perpendicular components in final blade axes. This text uses the word "normal" instead of "perpendicular" so that the subscript n can be used. This nomenclature is necessary in order to distinguish dF_n (the normal force, a scalar) from dF_p (the prescribed force, a three-dimensional vector).

$$V_{bf|bf} = \begin{Bmatrix} U_r \\ U_t \\ U_n \end{Bmatrix} \qquad (11.160)$$

From here, all of the basic and advanced aerodynamics can be written. The section angle of attack, dynamic pressure, and Mach number are

$$\alpha = \arctan\left(\frac{U_n}{U_t}\right)$$

$$q_{bf} = \frac{\rho(U_t^2 + U_n^2)}{2}$$

$$M_{bf} = \frac{\sqrt{V_{bf|bf}^T V_{bf|bf}}}{V_{sound}} \tag{11.161}$$

The lift, drag, and moment coefficients are found through table look up or curve fits. In general, the functional forms of these coefficients are

$$C_l = C_l(\alpha, M_{bf})$$
$$C_d = C_d(\alpha, M_{bf})$$
$$C_m = C_m(\alpha, M_{bf}) \tag{11.162}$$

The perpendicular and tangential forces and blade pitching moment in final blade axes are

$$dF_t = -q_{bf}c(-C_l \sin\alpha + C_d \cos\alpha)\,ds$$
$$dF_n = -q_{bf}c(+C_d \sin\alpha + C_l \cos\alpha)\,ds$$
$$dM_a = -q_{bf}c^2(C_m)\,ds \tag{11.163}$$

The two distributed forces are resolved to rotor axes by first placing them into a generic aerodynamic force vector and then rotating back from final blade axes to rotor axes:

$$d\mathbf{F}_{a|r} = T^T(\phi_{0_x}, \phi_{0_y}, \phi_{0_z})T^T(\phi_x, \phi_y, \phi_z)\begin{Bmatrix} 0 \\ dF_t \\ dF_n \end{Bmatrix} \tag{11.164}$$

The distributed moment is left in final blade-section axes as required by the perturbation model for the modal equation. When hub loads are needed, then the same transformation will be applied. That completes the equations for the aerodynamic loads. All that is left is to derive expressions for the hub loads and the full, distributed loads required in the modal equation.

11.12.5 Hub Loads and Full Distributed Loads

The full, distributed load function first mentioned during the development of the modal equation is now defined as

$$d\mathbf{F}_f = \begin{Bmatrix} d\mathbf{F}_{a|r} + d\mathbf{F}_i \\ d\mathbf{M}_{a|bf} + d\mathbf{M}_i \end{Bmatrix} \tag{11.165}$$

The dM_i vector was not derived in this model. It can simply be set to zero. The preceding vector is the load used in the modal equation, which has all contributions from aerodynamics and dynamics. Note: No engineering judgment was required about which terms to retain on the forcing function side and which were to be moved to the LHS.

The hub loads in rotor axes are just

$$F_{a|r} = \int_0^{BR} dF_{a|r} \, ds \qquad (11.166)$$

and

$$M_{a|bf} = \int_0^{BR} T^T(\phi_{0_x}, \phi_{0_y}, \phi_{0_z}) T^T(\phi_x, \phi_y, \phi_z) \left[P_{bf} \times \left\{ \begin{matrix} 0 \\ dF_t \\ dF_n \end{matrix} \right\} + \left\{ \begin{matrix} dM_{a|bf} \\ 0 \\ 0 \end{matrix} \right\} \right] ds \qquad (11.167)$$

These equations are easily resolved to the nonrotating system by

$$F_{hub} = T_\psi^T F_{a|r}$$

$$M_{hub} = T_\psi^T M_{a|bf} \qquad (11.168)$$

The x-axis element in F_{hub} is the negative of the so-called H-force, the y-axis element is the Y-force, and the negative of the z-axis element is the thrust. The z-axis element of the M_{hub} vector is the torque absorbed by the rotor.

11.12.6 Accounting for All Blades

A rotor has nb (in the literature, b is sometimes used) blades. It is not necessary that the blades be equally spaced around the azimuth, though in most circumstances they are. Number the blades 1 to nb, placing blade 1 over the tail boom, at azimuth 0.0 deg. Blade 2 follows blade 1 over the tail, so that, with the convention of counterclockwise rotation, blade two is $\Delta\psi_2$ away from blade 1, measured *clockwise*. Blade 3 is $\Delta\psi_3$ away from blade 1, measured clockwise, and so on. Figure 11.28 shows the numbering for a four-bladed rotor. Obviously, $\Delta\psi_1$ always equals zero.

The only complication this adds to what has been presented is now each blade has its own azimuth transformation matrix. So, when rotating from the fixed system to the rotating system, instead of using

$$T(\psi) = \begin{bmatrix} \cos(\psi) & -\sin(\psi) & 0 \\ \sin(\psi) & \cos(\psi) & 0 \\ 0 & 0 & 1 \end{bmatrix} \qquad (11.169)$$

one must now use

$$T(\psi_k) = \begin{bmatrix} \cos(\psi + \Delta\psi_k) & -\sin(\psi + \Delta\psi_k) & 0 \\ \sin(\psi + \Delta\psi_k) & \cos(\psi + \Delta\psi_k) & 0 \\ 0 & 0 & 1 \end{bmatrix} \qquad (11.170)$$

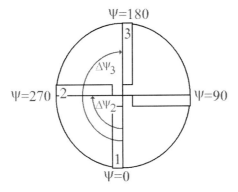

Fig. 11.28   Numbering and spacing all blades around the azimuth.

Index k is the blade number. Likewise, the resolution from the rotating system back to the fixed system must be conducted through the transpose of this matrix.

11.12.7   Calculation of the Prescribed Load

The definition of the prescribed loads is that column of distributed loads that will drive the modal forcing function to zero in a vacuum chamber. This means that the modal parameters $\beta, \dot{\beta}, \ddot{\beta} = 0$. Also, the full, distributed load is composed only of inertial terms. Start with the modal equation (11.137).

$$\ddot{\beta}(t) + \omega^2 \beta(t) = M_g^{-1} \int Q^T(s)(dF_f - dF_p)\,ds + \ddot{\beta}(t) + M_g^{-1} K_s \beta(t)$$

and apply the preceding requirements. The surviving terms generate this definition of the prescribed load.

$$\int Q^T(s)\,dF_i\,ds = \int Q^T(s)\,dF_p\,ds \qquad (11.171)$$

By far, the easiest function to imagine is a constant or perhaps a triangular distribution. So, for the jth mode, propose a triangular prescribed load function of the form:

$$dF_p = \begin{Bmatrix} Px_0 \\ Py_0 \\ Pz_0 \end{Bmatrix}_j \frac{s}{R} \qquad (11.172)$$

where Px_0, Py_0, and Pz_0 have units of distributed force, for example, lb/ft. No modal response (and no rotor speed change) means the inertial load reduces to

$$dF_i = -\overline{m}[\omega_r \times (\omega_r \times P_{bf3})]\,ds \qquad (11.173)$$

The user provides the modeshapes. Substitute Eqs. (11.172) and (11.173) into Eqs. (11.171), and solve for the constants in the prescribed load function:

$$\left(\int \Delta_x^T \frac{s}{R} \, ds \right) P_x + \left(\int \Delta_y^T \frac{s}{R} \, ds \right) P_y + \left(\int \Delta_z^T \frac{s}{R} \, ds \right) P_z = -\Omega^2 \int \overline{m} s \Delta_x^T \, ds$$

$$(11.174)$$

The Δ are the individual rows of the modeshape function and have units of length.

Engineering judgment is invited at this point. The LHS has three constants, whereas the RHS has just one term. How to solve for three constants with one equation is a black art. However, a rule of thumb is available. The first flapping mode is without doubt the most important. Because the z-direction forces drive it primarily, set $P_x = P_y = 0$, and solve for P_z:

$$P_z = -\Omega^2 \frac{\int \overline{m} s \Delta_x^T \, ds}{\int \Delta_z^T (s/R) \, ds} \qquad (11.175)$$

For in-plane and torsional modes, similar rules of thumb exist, though it is the author's experience that setting $P_x = P_y = 0$ and showing concern for just the first flapping model is all that is required for good results.

Example 11.1

If the rotor is simply articulated, then the position vector is

$$\boldsymbol{P}_b(s) = \begin{Bmatrix} -s \cos \beta \\ 0 \\ -s \sin \beta \end{Bmatrix}$$

One can imagine building a Taylor series about a preconed shape.

$$\boldsymbol{P}_b(s) = \begin{Bmatrix} -s \cos \beta_0 \\ 0 \\ -s \sin \beta_0 \end{Bmatrix} + \begin{Bmatrix} s \sin \beta_0 \\ 0 \\ -s \cos \beta_0 \end{Bmatrix} \beta = \boldsymbol{P}_{b0}(s) + \begin{Bmatrix} \Delta_x \\ \Delta_y \\ \Delta_z \end{Bmatrix} \beta$$

If the blade has a uniform mass distribution, then

$$P_z = -\Omega^2 \overline{m} \frac{\sin \beta_0}{\cos \beta_0} \frac{\int_0^R s^2 \, ds}{\int_0^R -(s^2/R) \, ds} = \overline{m} R \Omega^2 \tan \beta_0 \approx \overline{m} R \Omega^2 \beta_0$$

11.12.8 Calculation of the K_s Matrix

The definition of the K_s matrix is given by Eq. (11.138), repeated here for convenience:

$$K_s = \frac{\partial \left[\int Q^T(s)(dF_f - dF_p) \, ds \right]}{\partial \beta}$$

In general, the analytic expression for K_s would be prohibitively long, and its computation overhead would overshadow its value. A value, determined by numerical differentiation about some midrange, midspeed operating point, and averaged around the azimuth is generally good enough.

A calibration of sorts is available using the simple analysis at the beginning of this chapter. The inertial load for a simply articulated rotor was given by the expression (11.13), supported by Eq. (11.12):

$$d\mathbf{f}i = -(\overline{m})\mathbf{a}$$

$$\mathbf{a} = \left\{ \begin{array}{c} s(\Omega')^2 \\ s\dot{\Omega}' \\ -s\ddot{\beta} + s(\dot{p}_i - q_i\Omega')S + s(\dot{q}_i + p_i\Omega')C + s(p_i\Omega'C - q_i\Omega'S) \end{array} \right\}$$

Notice, the hub accelerations are set to zero and the inertial load has no dependence on β.

By definition and Eq. (11.172), the prescribed load has no dependence on β either. This lack of dependence leaves just the aerodynamic load, which from Eqs. (11.38–11.41) is

$$dL = \frac{1}{2}\rho V_T^2 Rca_0(\mu S + x)^2 \left\{ \Theta_0 + \Theta_T x + A_1 C + B_1 S \right.$$

$$+ \left[\frac{-\mu\beta C + \lambda_a - x(\dot{\beta}/\Omega') + x\hat{p}_a S + x\hat{q}_a C}{\mu S + x} \right] \right\} dx$$

$$dD = \frac{1}{2}\rho V_T^2 Rca_0(\mu S + x)^2 \varepsilon_0 \, dx$$

$$\varepsilon_0 = \frac{\overline{C}_D}{a_0}$$

$$d\mathbf{F}a_r = \left\{ \begin{array}{c} \beta dL \\ -dD + \phi \, dL \\ -\phi \, dD - dL \end{array} \right\} = \left\{ \begin{array}{c} dFxa_r \\ dFya_r \\ dFza_r \end{array} \right\}$$

The drag has no dependence on β, and so it can be safely discarded leaving

$$d\mathbf{F}a_r = \left\{ \begin{array}{c} \beta \, dL \\ \phi \, dL \\ -dL \end{array} \right\} = \left\{ \begin{array}{c} dFxa_r \\ dFya_r \\ dFza_r \end{array} \right\} \tag{11.176}$$

Again, assume a simply articulated rotor

$$\left\{ \begin{array}{c} \Delta_x \\ \Delta_y \\ \Delta_z \end{array} \right\} = \left\{ \begin{array}{c} s \sin \beta_0 \\ 0 \\ -s \cos \beta_0 \end{array} \right\} \tag{11.177}$$

and substitute the expressions into the K_s equation. After some algebra, one obtains the following expression for K_s:

$$M_g^{-1} K_s = \beta_0^2 \Omega^2 P + \beta_0 \frac{\gamma \Omega^2}{2} \left(\frac{B^3 \mu}{3} \right) a_1 \qquad (11.178)$$

The product has nothing but higher-order terms. This convenient result means the $M_g^{-1} K_s$ term can be safely discarded.

11.13   Nonuniform Wake and Wake Rotation

The wake in the vicinity of the rotor plane is not uniform. The wake reacts to local blade loading, and so it is natural to assume that the wake is a function of radial position and azimuth position. Several different methods are used to model the wake. Computational-fluid-dynamics methods model the wake using the Navier–Stokes equations. The results are very good, but the method takes minutes to hours of clock time to achieve a solution of only several problem seconds. This technique is obviously not applicable for real-time analysis.

Lifting-line, lifting-surface, prescribed-wake, and free-wake-vortex solutions have also been used with success to estimate the wake in the vicinity of the rotor. Unfortunately, these models are also computationally expensive. Again, real-time analysis does not benefit.

Generalized dynamic-wake theories, like those of Pitt and Peters [7], and static-wake models such as those described by Azuma and Kawachi [6], Prouty [4], and others are more amenable to real-time solution. Two models are presented next. The first is a static-wake model that achieves radial and azimuthal variation via two truncated cylinders and a uniform inflow. The second model is the dynamic inflow model of Pitt and Peters [7].

11.13.1   Static Wake—Truncated Cylinders

Imagine a cylinder of air with diameter just large enough to swallow a rotor and with its long axis along the x axis of the rotor IELA (hub) (Fig. 11.29). An infinitesimally wide strip runs vertically from the top of the great circle to the bottom at a point y out from the origin. A differential thrust and induced velocity are associated with that strip. If the thrust varies along the radius, the induced velocity does as well. Subtracting out the average (uniform) wake and equating the remaining wake to the truncated cylinder, a swirling wake is established. The angular velocity of the rigid-body swirl can be estimated by two different methods. The first method uses a momentum approach.

The induced velocity and the differential thrust are related by Glauert's hypothesis, where the distributed loading summed over all blades dT/dA replaces the disk loading T/A.

$$w = \frac{-dT}{2\rho |V_a| \, dA} \qquad (11.179)$$

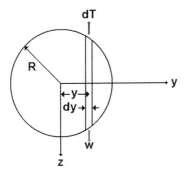

Fig. 11.29   Relating incremental thrust and induced velocity.

The differential area is given by

$$dA = 2R^2\sqrt{1 - \left(\frac{y}{R}\right)^2}\,d\left(\frac{y}{R}\right) = 2R^2\sqrt{1 - \eta^2}\,d\eta \qquad (11.180)$$

Propose that the steady value of thrust is removed. That is, the thrust is cyclic and causes a rolling moment only. (Obviously, the same arguments apply to a pitching moment as well.) The induced velocity associated with this thrust then is also cyclic and causes only a swirling wake.

$$w = p_w y = p_w R\eta$$
$$dM_x = y(dT) = R(dT)\eta \qquad (11.181)$$

Substitute Eqs. (11.180) and (11.181) into Eqs. (11.179), rearrange, and integrate from one side of the rotor disk to the other:

$$\frac{M_x}{p_w} = -4\rho R^4 |V_a| \int_{-1}^{1} \eta^2 \sqrt{1 - \eta^2}\,d\eta \qquad (11.182)$$

The result, after some further rearranging and integration, is

$$p_w = \frac{-M_x}{2\rho(\pi R^4/4)|V_a|} \qquad (11.183)$$

This equation is the desired model; it relates the swirling wake p_w to the hub *aerodynamic* rolling moment M_x.

A second approach is the so-called impulse method. Here, the impulsive, differential thrust is matched to the sector of rotor disk over which it acts. Start with Eq. (11.179), but now substitute $dA = r\,dr\,d\psi$:

$$w = \frac{-dT}{2\rho(r\,dr\,d\psi)|V_a|} \qquad (11.184)$$

As before, relate the induced velocity to the rigid-body swirl and the differential thrust to a differential rolling moment. The swirl velocity now looks like this:

$$p_w = \frac{-dM_x}{2\rho(r^3\,dr\,d\psi)|V_a|} \tag{11.185}$$

Rearrange and integrate both sides over the rotor radius and around the azimuth:

$$p_w = \frac{-M_x}{2\rho(\pi R^4/2)|V_a|} \tag{11.186}$$

This equation has the same form as the preceding method, but the swirl speed is half as great. In general, the truncated cylinder model has the form:

$$p_w = \frac{-M_x}{2\rho[(\pi R^4/4)\kappa]|V_a|} \tag{11.187}$$

where $1 \leq \kappa < 2$ and $\kappa = 1$ for strip theory while $\kappa = 2$ for impulse theory.

11.13.2 Dynamic Wake—Pitt–Peters Model

The Pitt–Peters [7] model is a perturbation model that introduces dynamics via an apparent mass of the air influenced by thrust variations. Start with the Glauert model. The steady thrust is

$$T_s = 2\rho A(u_0^2 + w^2)^{\frac{1}{2}}w_i \tag{11.188}$$

where $w = w_0 + w_i$ and the subscripts 0 and i indicate inertial and induced quantities, respectively, and the subscript s indicates steady. Please note that the induced velocity in the Pitt–Peters model has the opposite sense of the induced velocity used throughout this text. The thrust near this steady value is then

$$\frac{T_s + \Delta T}{2\rho A} = (u_0^2 + w^2)^{1/2}w_i + \left[-\left(u_0^2 + w^2\right)^{-1/2}ww_i + (u_0^2 + w^2)^{1/2}\right]\Delta w_i \tag{11.189}$$

Solve for the perturbation equation:

$$\frac{\Delta T}{2\rho A} = \left[-\left(u_0^2 + w^2\right)^{-1/2}ww_i + \left(u_0^2 + w^2\right)^{1/2}\right]\Delta w_i \tag{11.190}$$

Define the nondimensional total inflow, change in induced velocity, trim induced velocity, and advance ratio and substitute them into Eq. (11.190).

$$\bar{\lambda} = \frac{w}{V_T}, \quad v_0 = \frac{\Delta w_i}{V_T}, \quad \bar{v} = \frac{w_i}{V_T}, \quad \mu = \frac{u_0}{V_T}$$

Rearranging slightly, one ends with this expression:

$$2\left[\frac{\mu^2 + \bar{\lambda}(\bar{\lambda} + \bar{v})}{\sqrt{\mu^2 + \bar{\lambda}^2}}\right]v_0 = \Delta C_T \tag{11.191}$$

This is a static expression. The dynamics are introduced by means of apparent mass, which is a function of loading. The development involves elliptic integrals and is beyond the scope of this book. With the "mass" term included, the dynamic wake is

$$\left(\frac{8}{3\pi}\right)\frac{d\upsilon_0}{d\psi} + 2\left[\frac{\mu^2 + \bar{\lambda}(\bar{\lambda} + \bar{\upsilon})}{\sqrt{\mu^2 + \bar{\lambda}^2}}\right]\upsilon_0 = \Delta C_T \tag{11.192}$$

Depending on constraints as described in [7], the mass term can also take the value $(125/75\pi)$. The derivative is interpreted as nondimensional time. To recover dimensional time, substitute $\psi = \Omega t$ and regroup:

$$\left\{\begin{matrix}\left(\dfrac{8}{3\pi\Omega}\right)\\ \text{or}\\ \left(\dfrac{125}{75\pi\Omega}\right)\end{matrix}\right\}\frac{d\upsilon_0}{dt} + 2\left[\frac{\mu^2 + \bar{\lambda}\left(\bar{\lambda} + \bar{\upsilon}\right)}{\sqrt{\mu^2 + \bar{\lambda}^2}}\right]\upsilon_0 = \Delta C_T \tag{11.193}$$

The Pitt–Peters dynamic model includes swirling components as well. The static model was already derived. It is repeated here for convenience:

$$p_w = \frac{-M_x}{2\rho[(\pi R^4/4)\kappa]|V_a|}$$

In the Pitt–Peters model, the apparent mass is a function of loading and is solved using elliptic integrals. A "street" estimate of the apparent mass (or, more correctly, moment of inertia) is the volume of air contained in a sphere of radius kR, where R is the rotor radius. This evaluates to

$$I_p = \frac{2}{5}\left(\rho\frac{4}{3}\pi R^3 k^3\right)R^2 k^2 = \frac{8}{15}\rho\pi R^5 k^5 \tag{11.194}$$

whence

$$\left(\frac{8}{15}\rho\pi R^5 k^5\right)\dot{p}_w + \left[2\rho\left(\frac{\pi R^4}{4}\kappa\right)|V_a|\right]p_w = -M_x \tag{11.195}$$

Set $\kappa = 1$, and normalize this equation with $\rho(\pi R^3)V_T^2$:

$$\left(\frac{8}{15}k^5\right)\frac{\dot{p}_w}{\Omega^2} + \left(\frac{|V_a|}{2V_T}\right)\frac{p_w}{\Omega} = -C_m \tag{11.196}$$

The equivalent Pitt–Peters expression reads

$$\left\{\begin{matrix}\left(\dfrac{256}{945\pi}\right)\\ \text{or}\\ \left(\dfrac{16}{45\pi}\right)\end{matrix}\right\}\frac{\dot{p}_w}{\Omega^2} + \left(\frac{|V_a|}{2V_T}\right)\frac{p_w}{\Omega} = -C_m \tag{11.197}$$

Set the value of $k = 0.71$ in Eq. (11.196) to make the poor man's estimate fall between the extremes of the Pitt–Peters model. This is not quite as satisfying as the axial-flow agreement, but this crafty expedient is not too bad either.

11.13.3 Nonuniform Distribution Caused by Local Blade Loading

Another nonuniform downwash model starts by equating the distributed thrust to the wash in a circular lamina determined by the Glauert momentum principle. This technique is described in Prouty [4] for a simple rotor with no cyclic input at hover. The extension to forward speed is obvious, tedious, and must be solved iteratively. Its usefulness is in doubt in light of what the hover model will show.

Using notation in this text, and discarding cyclic input because it contributes nothing to the average value of thrust in hover, the expression for the distributed lift is

$$dT = \frac{b}{2}\rho(\Omega s)^2 ca_0 \left(\theta_0 + \theta_T \frac{s}{R} - \frac{w}{\Omega s}\right) ds \tag{11.198}$$

This simple development assumes the blade lift is parallel to the thrust. The number of blades is b. If the thrust expressed by Eq. (11.198) is used to force the air through an infinitesimally thin-walled annular ring of average radius r, then the Glauert momentum principle defines the downwash at the radial station:

$$dT = 2\rho(2\pi s \, ds)w^2 \tag{11.199}$$

Define the nondimensional radial station, tip speed, and solidity with the following expressions:

$$x = \frac{s}{R}$$

$$V_T = \Omega R$$

$$\sigma = \frac{bc}{\pi R}$$

Equate Eqs. (11.198) and (11.199), and solve for w:

$$w = \frac{a_0 \sigma V_T}{16} \left[-1 + \sqrt{1 + \frac{32(\theta_0 x + \theta_T x^2)}{a_0 \sigma}} \right] \tag{11.200}$$

These expressions were programmed on a spreadsheet twice: one rotor employed a uniform distribution and the other used the nonuniform distribution. The collective was adjusted so that both rotors produced the same thrust. The difference between the two collective values was less than 0.05 deg out of 15 deg. The results are shown in Figs. 11.30–11.32. The downwash as a function of radius has the characteristic look of a square-root function in the nonuniform application. Curiously,

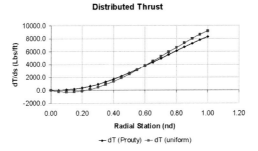

Fig. 11.30   Effect of nonuniform wash on distributed thrust.

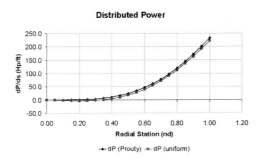

Fig. 11.31   Effect of nonuniform wash on distributed power.

the distributed lift and power curves look almost the same for both rotors. Careful inspection shows that the distributed power for the nonuniform inflow case is slightly higher than for the uniform case. In this particular example, to lift 12800 lb, the rotor with uniform downwash required 891 hp, whereas the rotor with the nonuniform distribution of downwash required 933 hp—an increase of 5% for the same thrust.

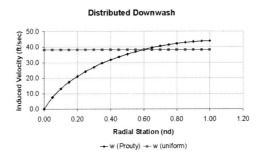

Fig. 11.32   Distributed downwash reacting to local loading function.

One can conclude the following:

1) From the standpoint of average thrust calculations, an assumption of uniform distribution of downwash is reasonable. No significant differences in control settings are noted for thrust, at least not in the hover case.

2) For a given thrust, the rotor with nonuniform downwash requires slightly more power. That is, a uniform distribution is optimistic in power requirements—actual power is likely to be higher. The Prandtl tip loss factor is one method to account for this difference.

3) Use of the uniform distribution of downwash makes solutions tractable and much cleaner in appearance.

11.14   Final Thoughts on Rotors

Writing a title like "Final Thoughts on Rotors" is a little like writing "Final Thoughts on the Universe!" There are an incredible number of aspects to rotor modeling that simply cannot be covered in any single text, let alone any single chapter. Investigators have worked a century on rotating wing aerodynamics. This chapter has presented the bare-bones minimum for understanding rotors and rotor modeling. In earlier parts of this chapter, some topics were deferred to a later time. The chickens come home to roost here.

11.14.1   Wind-Mast Axis System

Eliminating the y-axis linear velocity reduces the arithmetic complexity in the closed-form, quasi-static rotor model. The method is outlined here. First, "rotate" the equations so that the oncoming wind is in the X–Z plane. The angle of rotation is $\psi_{\text{wind–mast}} = \tan^{-1}(v/u)$. This is about the z_{mast} axis. Rotate the linear velocities, the angular velocities, the flapping angles from the previous pass, and the cyclic control inputs. Next, use these rotated values as the standard named variables in the quasi-static model. Solve the flapping equation and then find the hub forces and moments. Finally, rotate the hub forces and moments and the new flapping angles back to the mast axes through the negative of the wind-mast transformation angle.

11.14.2   Hub Moments

If the hub is a teetering or focused gimbal type, then no out-of-plane flapping moments are transmitted to the mast. If the teetering or gimbaled hub has a hub spring, then the moment is simply determined by the product of the hub spring rate and the tip-path plane flapping angles a_1 and b_1. If the hub is cantilevered and has a hinge offset, then the effective spring rate, multiplied by the tip-path plane flapping angles a_1 and b_1 give the pitch and roll moments:

$$\begin{Bmatrix} M_x \\ M_y \end{Bmatrix} = \frac{b}{2}\left[e\int_0^R mr\Omega^2\,dr\right]\begin{Bmatrix} b_1 \\ a_1 \end{Bmatrix} \tag{11.201}$$

If the more sophisticated model is used, the modal analysis package will also provide bending moment coefficients, which can be used in place of the roll- and pitch-moment calculations.

11.14.3   Reverse Flow Corrections in the Quasi-Static Model

As the rotor moves forward, inboard portions of the retreating blade actually see air moving from the trailing edge to the leading edge. This is the so-called *reverse-flow* region. Investigators have developed corrections to the flapping equation and the load equations to account for the losses.

Integration around the azimuth is decomposed into three parts as shown here:

$$\int_0^{2\pi} \int_0^R f(\psi)\,dr\,d\psi = + \int_0^{\pi} \int_0^R f(\psi)\,dr d\psi - \int_{\pi}^{2\pi} \int_0^{-\mu R \sin \psi} f(\psi)\,dr d\psi$$

$$+ \int_{\pi}^{2\pi} \int_{-\mu R \sin \psi}^R f(\psi)\,dr\,d\psi \qquad (11.202)$$

The first part is the integration over the half-circle on the advancing side. The second part is the reverse-flow region, which runs from the hub to a circular boundary defined by $-\mu R \sin \psi$. The third part is the region on the retreating side outside of the reverse-flow region.

It is true that this region has a strong effect on handling qualities and, ultimately, the maximum speed that the rotor can fly forward. However, the quasi-static equations as presented do a reasonable job for low to moderate advance ratios, say, out to 0.3.

11.14.4   Transient Response of the Quasi-Static Model

The quasi-static model is not dynamic by definition. If one uses this model in a simulation, one may expect reasonable answers in static performance calculations, but much too rapid a response in maneuvering flight. One method to overcome this problem is described and developed in Appendix K.

11.14.5   Mach-Number Effects

A rotor blade sees aerodynamic velocities anywhere from zero (and actually negative values—see reverse flow) to nearly transonic. As the Mach number increases, the drag begins an accelerated rise, and the lift-curve slope in the linear range increases. Also, the center of pressure moves aft from the quarter-chord point. This will increase the nose-down pitching moment on the blade. If the quasi-static model is used, a simple table look-up or polynomial fitting the linear lift-curve slope and average drag coefficient as a function of Mach number can be employed. The quasi-static model did not use the moment, and so it needs no correction. If the blade-element model is used, then these terms should already be in the lift, drag, and moment coefficient tables.

11.14.6   Ground Effect

When a rotor operates near the ground, the downwash "splashes" back into the rotor, providing some "free" lift. Another way to say this is that for a given lift, ground effect reduces the induced power. The same sort of phenomenon happens with wings. Developing an analytical expression for ground effect is problematic because the rotor usually operates near a fuselage, which negates some of the benefit. Also, modeling the air circulation in the vicinity of a rotor operating near the ground is very difficult, even for the simple hover case. Nevertheless, if one pretends the rotor is a wing and it is operating near the ground, then using a simple horseshoe vortex for the rotor and the "image" rotor below the ground, one can estimate the induced drag of the rotor in ground effect. Specifically, if the control point on the wing is at midspan on the bound vortex, then the induced drag outside of ground effect (OGE) is

$$D_{iOGE} = 2L\frac{w}{V} = 2\frac{L}{V}\frac{\gamma}{4\pi(b/2)} = 2\frac{L}{V}\frac{\gamma}{2\pi b} \qquad (11.203)$$

The image vortex provides upwash equal in strength to

$$w_{upwash} = \frac{\gamma}{4\pi\sqrt{(b/2)^2 + (2h)^2}}\left(\frac{b/2}{\sqrt{(b/2)^2 + (2h)^2}}\right) \qquad (11.204)$$

If this upwash is subtracted off of the OGE downwash, after some algebra, the ratio of induced velocities (and thus power) is

$$\frac{P_{iIGE}}{P_{iOGE}} = \frac{(16h^2/b^2)}{1 + (16h^2/b^2)}$$

One can refine this a little by setting the span equal to $R\sqrt{2}$ (which is the diameter of the streamtube after contraction). Then, the ratio of induced power inside of ground effect (IGE) to OGE is

$$\frac{P_{iIGE}}{P_{iOGE}} = \frac{(8h^2/R^2)}{1 + (8h^2/R^2)} \qquad (11.205)$$

This relationship is plotted next. The graph shows that when the rotor is one-half of a rotor radius above the ground plane, there is a 33% reduction in induced power. One full rotor radius above the ground, the reduction is 11%. More than one-and-a-half radii above the ground the reduction in induced power is essentially nil. This ground effect model is simple and does not account for forward speed. In fact, the usefulness of this model at hover should be suspect. Nevertheless, the model illustrates a well-known phenomenon and can serve as a first approximation.

A second curve in Fig. 11.33 shows the estimated ratio of induced power IGE to OGE using a somewhat more sophisticated analysis involving vortex rings emitted at blade passage frequency acting upon a blade-element rotor motor. There is little surprise that those results are a bit more conservative but show the same trend.

11.14.7 Autorotation

Helicopters come equipped with a clutch that disengages the rotor from the transmission in the event the engine quits. If the pilot lowers the collective immediately after the engine failure, the helicopter will begin to descend, and air will

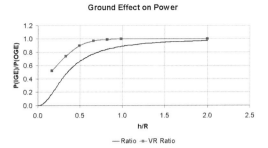

Fig. 11.33   Simple model of ground effect.

rush up through the rotor disk causing the rotor to windmill. This is called *autorotation*. If the pilot fails to reduce the collective quickly enough, the rotor speed will decay to the point where the blades have stalled and useful thrust has evaporated and a bad day ensues. A simple study of the rotor speed decay and loss in altitude can be obtained with the following model. The first-order equation for rotor speed is

$$J\dot{\Omega} = Q_{\text{eng}} - Q_{\text{rotor}} \tag{11.206}$$

where the torque supplied by the engine and torque absorbed by the rotor are as indicated. In trim flight, the right-hand side of this expression adds to zero, meaning the rotor acceleration is zero. Let the rotor torque and thrust be modeled as

$$Q_{\text{rotor}} = \left(\frac{\Omega}{\Omega_0}\right)^2 Q_0 \tag{11.207}$$

and

$$T = \left(\frac{\Omega}{\Omega_0}\right)^2 W \tag{11.208}$$

where W is the aircraft weight and the collective was set so that thrust was equal to weight. Substitute Eq. (11.207) into Eq. (11.206), and set $Q_{\text{eng}} = 0$ to model a complete engine failure. The rotor speed equation becomes

$$J\dot{\Omega} = -\left(\frac{\Omega}{\Omega_0}\right)^2 Q_0 \tag{11.209}$$

This is called a Bernoulli equation. Its solution is

$$\Omega = \frac{\Omega_0}{1 + Q_0 t/J\Omega_0} \tag{11.210}$$

The equation of motion in the vertical direction is

$$\ddot{y} = g\left(1 - \frac{T}{W}\right) = g\left[1 - \left(\frac{\Omega}{\Omega_0}\right)^2\right] \tag{11.211}$$

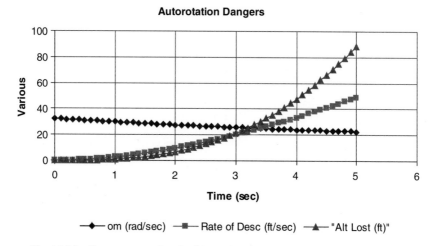

Fig. 11.34   Dangers associated with not lowering collective after power loss.

Integrate once for velocity (rate of descent) and again for loss of altitude:

$$v = g \left\{ t + \frac{J\Omega_0}{Q_0} \left[\left(1 + \frac{Q_0 t}{J\Omega_0} \right)^{-1} - 1 \right] \right\}$$

$$h = g \left[\frac{t^2}{2} + \left(\frac{J\Omega_0}{Q_0} \right)^2 \ln \left(1 + \frac{Q_0 t}{J\Omega_0} \right) - \frac{J\Omega_0 t}{Q_0} \right] \tag{11.212}$$

An example helicopter was programmed with these equations. The following parameters were used: $W = 6600\,\text{lb}$, $R = 22\,\text{ft}$, $C = 1.25\,\text{ft}$, $g = 32.2\,\text{ft/s/s}$, $Vtip = 715\,\text{ft/s}$, $B = 2$, $Cd = 0.010$, $J = 2804\,\text{slug-ft}^2$, and SSL. The controls were not moved. The plots in Fig. 11.34 show how rapidly rotor speed and altitude are lost, and how rapidly descent rate increases.

11.14.8   Rotor Acceleration

One can also calculate rotor acceleration with the same equation for rotor speed. The problem becomes a little more difficult because the torque available from the engine might not be known analytically as a function of rotor speed. A solution to the limiting case of a step input of engine torque is found thus. First, write the rotor acceleration equation in terms of a reference or target rotor speed:

$$J\dot{\Omega}(t) = Q_{\text{eng}} - \left(\frac{\Omega(t)}{\Omega_{\text{ref}}} \right)^2 Q_{\text{ref}} \tag{11.213}$$

Define $F = Q_{\text{eng}}/J$ and $K = Q_{\text{ref}}/J\Omega_{\text{ref}}^2$. The general solution of Eq. (11.213) to a step input is

$$\Omega(t) = a \left[\frac{\tanh(t\sqrt{FK}) + \Omega(0)/a}{1 + \tanh(t\sqrt{FK})(\Omega(0)/a)} \right] \tag{11.214}$$

This solution is easily verified by substituting it and its derivative into the original differential equation.

11.14.9 Figure of Merit

A rotor at hover may be performing a useful function, but it is not performing any work, and so its efficiency is zero. To measure the efficiency of a rotor in hover, practitioners define the *figure of merit* as the ratio of ideal power at hover ($P_i = Tw$) to the total power ($P_{\text{total}} = P_i + P_{\text{parasite}}$):

$$M = \frac{P_i}{P_{\text{total}}}$$

$$P_{\text{total}} = P_i + \Delta P \tag{11.215}$$

so

$$M = \left(1 + \frac{\Delta P}{P_i}\right)^{-1} \tag{11.216}$$

The standard definitions for the thrust coefficient, the power coefficient, and the solidity, σ will be useful.

$$C_T = \frac{T}{\rho \pi R^2 V_T^2}$$

$$C_P = \frac{P}{\rho \pi R^2 V_T^3}$$

$$\sigma = \frac{Bc}{\pi R}$$

It is hardly an easy task to arrive at "typical" numbers for these quantities, but for the sake of calibration, consider the two types of aircraft in Table 11.1.

Table 11.1 Thrust, power and solidity coefficients for two rotorcraft

Entity	Light twin	Tiltrotor
C_T	0.00357	0.0149
C_P	0.000151	0.00128
σ	0.0578	0.075

Recall that the induced velocity at hover is given by $w = \sqrt{T/2\rho\pi R^2} = V_T\sqrt{C_T/2}$. Thus, the ideal power equals

$$P_i = \frac{T^{3/2}}{\sqrt{2\rho\pi R^2}} \tag{11.217}$$

so that

$$M = \left(1 + \frac{\Delta C_p\sqrt{2}}{C_T^{3/2}}\right)^{-1} \tag{11.218}$$

Now, because ΔC_p does not change much with thrust coefficient, as thrust coefficient gets larger the figure of merit approaches one. This suggests that to compare two rotors you must compare them at equal thrust coefficients. Though often spoken, it is true that a rotor never stalls. Blades do. If one wants to measure the maximum capability of a rotor, or to measure properly its efficiency, one should not use disk loading, but rather should use blade loading.

Look at the thrust and power using average values of lift coefficient and drag coefficient. Calculate the thrust from all blades by integrating the product of the blade-section dynamic pressure, chord, and lift coefficient from the root to the tip, and multiplying by the number of blades B:

$$T = B\int_0^R \frac{1}{2}\rho(\Omega r)^2 c\overline{C}_L \, dr$$

$$T = \frac{B\rho\Omega^2 R^3 c\overline{C}_L}{6} = \frac{B\rho V_T^2 Rc\overline{C}_L}{6} \tag{11.219}$$

whence

$$C_T = \frac{T}{\rho\pi R^2 V_T^2} = \frac{\overline{C}_L\sigma}{6} \tag{11.220}$$

or

$$\overline{C}_L = \frac{6C_T}{\sigma} \tag{11.221}$$

Now, look at the power. Power has two contributors. The power associated with induced velocity is called *induced power*. The power caused by dragging a blade through the air is called *profile power*. The expression for induced power has already been given. The profile power is estimated using an average drag coefficient. Integrating the product of the local blade-section dynamic pressure, chord, radial station, and drag coefficient, and then multiplying that answer by the number of blades yields

$$Q_{\text{prof}} = B\int_0^R \frac{1}{2}\rho(\Omega r)^2 rc\overline{C}_D \, dr = \frac{B\rho\Omega^2 R^4 c\overline{C}_D}{8} = \frac{B\rho V_T^2 R^2\overline{C}_D}{8} \tag{11.222}$$

and

$$P_{\text{prof}} = Q_{\text{prof}}\Omega = \frac{Bc\rho V_T^3 R\overline{C}_D}{8}$$

So

$$C_{Pprof} = \frac{P}{\rho \pi R^2 V_T^3} = \frac{\sigma \overline{C}_D}{8} \tag{11.223}$$

or

$$\overline{C}_D = \frac{8 C_{Pprof}}{\sigma} \tag{11.224}$$

Thus, the profile power is the delta power aforementioned. Using the definitions of average lift and drag coefficient as just calculated, along with the definition of solidity and tip speed, the figure of merit is expressed as a function of blade lift and drag:

$$M = \left(1 + \frac{3}{4} \frac{V_T}{w} \frac{\overline{C}_D}{\overline{C}_L}\right)^{-1} \tag{11.225}$$

Rotors are designed to run their blades at an average lift coefficient of 0.5. Measurements on typical airfoils show that the average drag coefficient is about $C_d = 0.009 + 0.0125 \cdot C_l^2 = 0.01213$. The ratio of induced velocity to tip speed (at hover) is $\sqrt{C_T/2}$. Therefore, $w/V_T = 1/20$, which makes the figure of merit for rotors in hover approximately 0.73. One must be careful not to use the figure of merit as a means of comparing two different rotors. Just because one rotor has a higher figure of merit does not mean it is better or more efficient. It may just be acting at a higher thrust coefficient, which means that the induced power is higher. Strictly speaking, the figure-of-merit parameter is not necessary for a rotor model. It is desired as a method of measuring rotor efficiency, and so is reported post facto. It is presented here for historical interest.

11.15 Rotor Model Explorer

This text comes with a rotor model that uses the blade-element method to calculate rotor loads and the flapping equation for a single flapping degree of freedom. The program is called Rotor Tutor. In Rotor Tutor, the user may specify basic rotor geometry parameters, hub parameters, flight parameters, maneuver parameters, display desires, and trim requirements. Output displays include a perspective of the rotor blade as it rotates with distributed lift and drag shown, radial and azimuth rotor maps of lift, drag, out-of-plane displacement and angle of attack, time histories of thrust, induced velocity and flapping, and moving section analysis showing the U_P and U_T velocities. Appendix L is the user's guide.

11.16 Conclusions

There is no more intricate modeling problem than the rotor(s) on a helicopter, tiltrotor, or other rotorcraft. One needs a strong understanding of aerodynamics; momentum theory, vortex theory, two-and three-dimensional effects are all required. Rotor precession and rotor flapping or blade deformation are described by the dynamics of rotating machinery. The manner of attachment of the blades to the hub has a significant influence on the loads that the rotor transmits to the airframe because of the presence or absence of a hinge and because of the variation in natural frequency of vibration. The blades can be twisted, tapered, and swept. The blade-pitch angle is controlled from the fixed system by way of a swashplate. Blades deform elastically and/or mechanically in response to the pitch commands as well as the periodic variation in velocity caused by forward flight. The flapping equation is all but intractable except for the simplest case of hover. Investigators usually solve the flapping equation using numerical methods that include harmonic balance and open integration schemes. Rotor wake modeling is difficult with time and space dependencies and nonlinear velocity field equations. Several models were presented.

References

[1] Gessow, A., and Myers, Jr., G. C., *Aerodynamics of the Helicopter*, Frederick Ungar Publishing Co., New York, 1978, p. 27.

[2] McCormick, Barnes W., *Aerodynamics of V/STOL Flight*, Academic Press, New York, 1967, pp. 128–134.

[3] Dreier, Mark E., "The Influence of a Trailing Tip Vortex on a Thrusting Rotor," Masters Thesis, Aerospace Engr. Dept., Univ. of Pennsylvania, University Park, 1977, March 1977.

[4] Prouty, Raymond W., *Helicopter Performance, Stability and Control*, Krieger, Malabar, FL, 1995, pp. 201–205.

[5] Taghizad, A., Jimenez, J., Binet, L., and Heuze, D., "Experimental and Theoretical Investigations to Develop a Model of Rotor Aerodynamics Adapted to Steep Descents," Presented at the 58th Annual Forum of the American Helicopter Society, June 2002.

[6] Brand, A., Kisor, R., Blyth, R., Mason, D., and Host, C., "V-22 High Rate of Descent (HROD) Test Procedures and Long Record Analysis," Presented at the 60th Annual Forum of the American Helicopter Society, June 2004.

[7] Pitt, D. M., and Peters, D. A., "Theoretical Evaluation of Dynamic Inflow Derivatives," *Vertica*, Vol. 5, No. 1, 1980, pp. 21–34, Pergamon Press, Ltd.

[8] Hoffman, J. A., and Dreier, M. E. *User's Manual for the Modular Stability Derivative Program High Frequency Version (MOSTAB)*, PPI-5300-1, Paragon Pacific, Inc., El Segundo, CA, 1977, pp. 3.70–3.80.

[9] Anderson, W. P., Conner, F., Kretsinger, P., and Reaser, J. S., *REXOR Rotorcraft Simulation Model, Vol. 1—Engineering Documentation*, UASSMRDL-TR-76-28A, Lockheed, Burbank, CA, 1976.

[10] Azuma, A., and Kawachi, K., "Local Momentum Theory and Its Application to the Rotary Wing," *Journal of Aircraft*, Vol. 16, No. 1, 1979, pp. 6–13.

Problems

11.1   Use the differential expression of the Biot–Savart law (found in the appendices) to calculate the induced velocity at the center of a square with sides of length R. The sides of the square are vortex filaments, and each side has the same vortex strength Γ (why?). Assign the positive direction of the filaments such that the induced velocity at the center of the square blows toward you.

11.2 Use the differential expression of the Biot–Savart law (found in the appendices) to calculate the induced velocity at the center of a vortex ring with radius R and strength Γ. Assign the positive direction of the filament such that the induced velocity at the center of the ring blows toward you.

11.3 Repeat problem 2, but approximate the ring with regular polygons of increasing rank, that is, a square (4), a pentagon (5), a hexagon (6), etc. up to decagon (10). In all cases, let the vertices lie on the circle. Based on the results, how many sides are required to find an approximation of the analytical solution that has no more than 5% error?

11.4 Imagine an untwisted, unswept, rotor blade of radius R, constant chord c, and with its flapping hinge at the center of rotation. The rotor is spinning at constant speed Ω, counterclockwise when viewed from above, and is not subject to any other linear or angular velocities or accelerations. The rotor has a Lock number of 6. The collective is set to θ_0, and the longitudinal cyclic is set to 5 deg. Prove that the angle of attack at any given radial station is constant. Find an expression for that angle. Use small-angle approximations.

11.5 Use the quartic expression for induced velocity to calculate the induced velocity of a rotor at 11 evenly spaced values of forward speed from hover to five times the induced velocity at hover. (Hint: The quartic expression might have to be solved iteratively.) Assume $\beta = 90$ deg and $w_0 = 0$.

11.6 Use the Rotor Tutor program to analyze a rotor that has rectangular blades with a radius of 22 ft, a constant chord of 24 in., two blades, linear twist of -11.0 deg, a Lock number of 6.0, a rotational speed of 310 rpm, and an articulated hub. For 13 evenly distributed velocities from hover to 120 kn, trim the rotor to zero longitudinal flapping, zero lateral flapping, and 6000 lb of thrust, and then execute the simulation to verify that the rotor achieves the desired flapping and thrust. Plot the average torque as a function of advance ratio.

11.7 Continuing with problem 6, you should have noticed that the advancing side blade showed negative thrust on the outer 10%. What one modification could you make to the geometry of the blade to eliminate the negative thrust on the tip but still achieve the desired thrust and flapping. What did the change do to the required torque?

12
Aerodynamic Interference

12.1 Introduction

One early lesson in airplane aerodynamics is the notion of downwash angle, usually given the symbol ε, and the rate of change of downwash angle with angle of attack of the main wing, usually given the symbol $\partial\varepsilon/\partial\alpha$. Downwash changes the angle of attack at the horizontal tail in such a way that an increment of lift develops in the positive z direction, body axes. At high angles of attack, the tail can be rendered ineffective as the wash from the main wing spills off and immerses the tail in turbulent flow. Another source of coupling on fixed-wing aircraft is the swirling wake from the propeller impinging on the horizontal and vertical tail. Such action produces a rolling moment that becomes a function of power absorbed by the engine.

Helicopters and tiltrotors present many more opportunities for aerodynamic interference. Consider the single main rotor helicopter shown in Fig. 12.1.

Immediately, one sees the wash from the main rotor pushing down on the fuselage in hover. As forward speed increases, the downwash migrates back along the thinner tail boom, but along the way encounters a horizontal stabilizer, where the wash is great enough to require pilot-controlled variable incidence in some cases. The motion of the air over the tail boom can be augmented with flow from within the boom to produce a Coanda effect antitorque device. The NOTAR® system is such as device. If the helicopter is equipped with a tail rotor, it can push against or pull away from a vertical fin, but in either case it induces flow past the fin. The main rotor induces flows on itself beyond the axial flow normally considered. The fuselage pushes air out of its way in forward flight. Some of that air is pushed into the main rotor. The number of examples grows like topsy.

Aerodynamic coupling is one of the most important aspects of helicopter and tiltrotor modeling and one of the most difficult to model. It is so important, in fact, that the reader must always make a distinction between aerodynamic and inertial velocity so that the aerodynamic interference model can evolve without programming interference. A detailed treatment using the Navier–Stokes equations would be unrealistic for real-time simulation. It is not necessary either. With just a

245

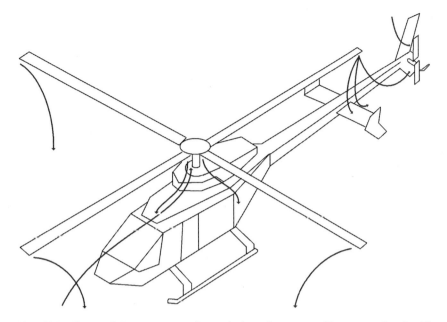

Fig. 12.1 Some of the many aerodynamic interference problems associated with helicopters.

few handfuls of couplings, the principal effects on handling qualities may be well represented. This chapter outlines some of the basic interferences.

12.2   Self-Induced Interference

The basic aerodynamic elements presented in preceding chapters are presented now with the notion of self-induced interference. Once the basic models of self-influence are understood, then mutual influence is presented. Also, each wash model is shown as a static model—dynamics can be added later.

Most important, remember that *the wash models are developed in the individual element reference axes* (IERA), but ultimately stored in the individual element local axes (IELA). This will be very important when mutual interference is modeled. For instance, the primary induced velocity from a rotor will always be directed along the *z* axis. Orienting the rotor like a propeller positions the induced velocity parallel to the body *x* axis. Figure 12.2 illustrates this. Note: The origins of the IELA and IERA are coincident. They are shown slightly displaced for clarity.

12.2.1   Basic Wash Model

For propeller models, a good generic wash model is the Rankine–Froude (or Glauert) expression for induced velocity generated by an actuator disk. That is, if an actuator disk of radius R is generating thrust T along the negative z axis of the IERA while moving forward with speed V, then the induced velocity w_w along

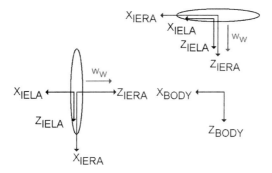

Fig. 12.2   Wash modeled in IERA is resolved to IELA.

the positive z axis of the IERA satisfies Eq. (9.3) of Chapter 9, rewritten here with due regard to sign convention:

$$T = -2\rho(\pi R^2)(V - w_w)w_w \tag{12.1}$$

The negative signs acknowledge that induced velocity and generating force are oppositely directed. This expression is good for one-dimensional axial flow. From previous insistence, the difference $(V - w_w)$ is called the *aerodynamic velocity*.

One can extend expression (12.1) to three dimensions. Let V_i and V_w be three-dimensional inertial and velocity vectors respectively that replace their scalar counterparts V and w_w. Define the norm of the aerodynamic velocity vector:

$$|V_a| = \sqrt{(V_i - V_w)^T (V_i - V_w)} \tag{12.2}$$

Replace the thrust with a general three-dimensional force vector F, and substitute a general area A for the specific area (πR^2). Rearrange (12.1) to form an implicit expression for V_w:

$$V_w = \left(\frac{-1}{2\rho|V_a|}\right)\left(\frac{1}{A}\right)F \tag{12.3}$$

The area A in the preceding wash expression implies a characteristic area that may actually have units of $L(\text{ength})^2$, L^3, or L^4. This is a reasonable wash model, which will we will refer to as the standard wash model.

It is instructive to discuss a philosophical point here. Expression (12.3) says that any aerodynamic force generates a wash. The author argues that in a broad sense this is a perfectly reasonable statement. For instance, consider the occasion when a large truck passes by you at high speed. You feel a buffeting wind as the truck pushes the air out of its way because the air cannot penetrate the impermeable surface of the truck. This push is the aerodynamic drag that the truck is overcoming, and it caused the air near the truck to move. That movement of air is a wash. Computational fluid techniques such as the panel method or a vortex-lattice method enforce the no-penetration requirement, formally $V \cdot n = 0$, by creating a field that generates velocity in opposition to the oncoming wind. In that sense, the wash seems to be a convenient mathematical contrivance to decelerate the oncoming wind. Yet the example of the buffeting wind from a passing truck argues that the wash is quite real. On the other hand, a fan, propeller, rotor, or wind turbine adds to or subtracts energy from the wind as modeled by the momentum theory, and that is a very real breeze. Ultimately, the surface of the arbitrary body does not permit the air to pass through it, and so the individual molecules of air bounce off the surface. This change in momentum of the molecule imparts a force on the body called *drag*; the reflected wind is the *wash*.

12.2.2 Rotor Self-Influence

The major influence the rotor has on itself is the axial induced velocity. However, the rotor produces H-force and Y-force, which also generate washes. The suggested characteristic area for all three forces is the rotor disk, and so the induced velocity in three dimensions is

$$\begin{Bmatrix} u_w \\ v_w \\ w_w \end{Bmatrix} = \left(\frac{-1}{2\rho|V_a|} \right) \begin{bmatrix} 1/\pi R^2 & 0 & 0 \\ 0 & 1/\pi R^2 & 0 \\ 0 & 0 & 1/\pi R^2 \end{bmatrix}_r \begin{Bmatrix} F_x \\ F_y \\ F_z \end{Bmatrix} \tag{12.4}$$

If the user does not wish to include the x- or y-direction induced velocities, then the corresponding coefficients in the 3 × 3 matrix can be set to zero. The forces and wash velocities are resolved to the IERA at this point.

As discussed in the chapter on rotors, aerodynamic rolling and pitching moments at the hub also cause the air to swirl in the vicinity of the rotor. Modeled as truncated cylinders, the angular wakes are related to the hub aerodynamic moments by the expression:

$$\begin{Bmatrix} p_w \\ q_w \\ r_w \end{Bmatrix} = \left(\frac{-1}{2\rho|V_a|} \right) \begin{bmatrix} 4/\pi R^4 \kappa_x & 0 & 0 \\ 0 & 4/\pi R^4 \kappa_y & 0 \\ 0 & 0 & 4\pi R^4 \kappa_z \end{bmatrix} \begin{Bmatrix} M_x \\ M_y \\ M_z \end{Bmatrix} \tag{12.5}$$

where $1 \leq \kappa_{x,y,z} < 2$ and $\kappa_{x,y,z} = 1$ for strip theory while $\kappa_{x,y,z} = 2$ for impulse theory. Of course, κ may be given any value that the analyst wants if it improves the correlation to measured data. (A term like κ is often called a "fudge factor." A sense of authority may be implied if terms like those are renamed "correlation coefficients." A rose by any other name. . . .) As with expression (12.4), the moments and the angular washes of expression (12.5) are resolved to the IERA at this point. *Also, the forces and moments on the right-hand side of Eqs. (3–5) are aerodynamic only— inertial loads do not generate wakes.*

Drees [1] and Ruddell [2], as reported in Prouty [3], document a local induced velocity model that is equivalent to a truncated cylinder superimposed on a uniform distribution, namely,

$$v(r, \psi) = v_0 \left(1 + K \frac{r}{R} \cos \psi \right) \tag{12.6}$$

In this expression, Prouty suggests a constant value of unity for the K factor (also known as the distortion factor). In [2], Ruddell shows that the value of K varies from 0 at hover to nearly 2 at the bottom of the power bucket. Ruddell also points out that the ABC rotor is a very rigid rotor, that is, its hub supports a moment and thus M_y may be nonzero over the entire flight envelope. With this in mind, it is immediately obvious that the preceding expression is equivalent to generating the two wake components:

$$
\left\{ \begin{array}{c} w_w \\ q_w \end{array} \right\} = \left(\frac{-1}{2\rho|V_a|} \right) \begin{bmatrix} \dfrac{1}{\pi R^2} & 0 \\ 0 & \dfrac{4}{\pi R^4 \kappa_y} \end{bmatrix} \left\{ \begin{array}{c} F_z \\ M_y \end{array} \right\} \tag{12.7}
$$

From the chapter on rotors, the aerodynamic moment about the y axis varies with the product of coning and advance ratio and can be nonzero, even with a 1/rev rotor. The influence of this swirl wake has a significant effect on lateral flapping. This is an important refinement to the usual induced velocity models.

In general, the induced velocity model for the rotor is expressed in this form:

$$
\left\{ \begin{array}{c} u_w \\ v_w \\ w_w \\ p_w \\ q_w \\ r_w \end{array} \right\} = \left(\frac{-1}{2\rho|V_a|} \right) \begin{bmatrix} a_{11} & a_{12} & \cdot & \cdot & \cdot & a_{16} \\ a_{21} & a_{22} & & & & \cdot \\ \cdot & & & & & \cdot \\ \cdot & & & & & \cdot \\ \cdot & & & & & \cdot \\ a_{61} & \cdot & \cdot & \cdot & \cdot & a_{66} \end{bmatrix} \left\{ \begin{array}{c} F_x \\ F_y \\ F_z \\ M_x \\ M_y \\ M_z \end{array} \right\} \tag{12.8}
$$

or

$$
V_w = \left(\frac{-1}{2\rho|V_a|} \right) [A]P
$$

This form is the six-degrees-of-freedom version of the standard form and will be useful for all types of aerodynamic models, not just rotor models. The A matrix is usually sparse and predominantly diagonal. In fact, even the worst model, in which the only nonzero element is the single diagonal element that is associated with the axial induced velocity, will do a creditable job.

12.2.3 Wing Self-Influence

A wing with an elliptic distribution of circulation has uniformly distributed induced velocity along the span. If Γ_0 is the circulation strength at midspan, then the strength of the induced velocity satisfies the expression

$$
2bw = \Gamma_0 \tag{12.9}
$$

The lift is elliptically distributed as well:

$$dL = \frac{2\rho V \Gamma_0}{b} \sqrt{\frac{b^2}{4} - y^2}\, dy \qquad (12.10)$$

Substitute the expression for circulation strength into the preceding distributed lift equation, and integrate along the span to get the lift in terms of the induced velocity, that is,

$$L = \frac{2\rho V(2bw)}{b} \int_{-b/2}^{b/2} \sqrt{\frac{b^2}{4} - y^2}\, dy = 2\rho V \left(\frac{\pi b^2}{4}\right) w \qquad (12.11)$$

This expression can be rearranged into the standard form. With proper regard for signs, the linear wash velocities are

$$\begin{Bmatrix} u_w \\ v_w \\ w_w \end{Bmatrix} = \left(\frac{-1}{2\rho|V_a|}\right) \begin{bmatrix} 4/\pi b^2 & 0 & 0 \\ 0 & 4/\pi b^2 & 0 \\ 0 & 0 & 4/\pi b^2 \end{bmatrix} \begin{Bmatrix} F_x \\ \Gamma_y \\ F_z \end{Bmatrix} \qquad (12.12)$$

One derives the model for the angular components of induced velocity using strip or momentum theory. If p_i is the inertial rotational rate expressed in IERA, then strip theory expresses the rolling moment in IERA accounting for roll wake by expression (12.13):

$$M_x = -\frac{1}{2}\rho U^2 c a_0 \left(\frac{p_i - p_w}{U}\right) \int_{-b/2}^{b/2} y^2\, dy = -\frac{1}{2}\rho U a_0 \frac{b^4}{12 A_R}(p_i - p_w) \qquad (12.13)$$

Expression (12.13) assumes a rectangular wing planform, and the definition of aspect ratio $A_R = b^2/S$ has been invoked. Use the rotor model as a "go by" to calculate a rolling wake of strength p_w, in IERA.

$$p_w = -M_x/2\rho U \left(\frac{\pi b^4 \kappa_x}{64}\varepsilon\right) \qquad (12.14)$$

The value of 64 comes from substituting $b/2$ for R as found in the rotor-wake model. The correlation coefficient ε provides an adjustment for nonrectangular planforms. Following Etkin [4], substitute $2\pi K = a_0$ to account for theoretical and actual lift-curve slopes. Also, substitute the expression for p_w into expression (12.13) and solve for M_x:

$$M_x = \left(\frac{\rho U (2\pi K) b^4}{24 A_R}\right) p_i \bigg/ \left(1 + \frac{8K}{3 A_R \kappa_x \varepsilon}\right) \qquad (12.15)$$

Effect of Aspect Ratio on Rolling Moment Derivative

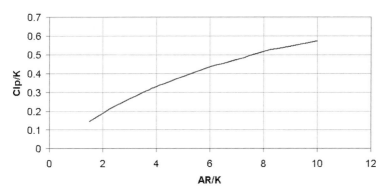

Fig. 12.3   Aspect-ratio effect on rolling moment.

Take the derivative of M_x with respect to p_i, and make the answer nondimensional by dividing by $\rho US(b^2/4)$:

$$\frac{CM_{x,p}}{K} = \frac{\pi(A_R/K)\kappa_x\varepsilon}{3(A_R/K)\kappa_x\varepsilon + 8} \qquad (12.16)$$

Calibrate this model using the relationship between the rolling-moment derivative with roll rate vs the aspect ratio of the wing as described in [4]. Etkin provides data that lead to Fig. 12.3.

Figure 12.3 provides a range of values for ε. For example, if $A_R/K = 6$, then $CM_{x,p}/K = 0.435$. (In Etkin, the derivative of rolling moment with respect to rolling rate is named Clp/K.) Using strip theory, $\kappa_x = 1$; thus, $\varepsilon = 0.316$. If momentum theory had been employed, then $\kappa_x = 2$, and then $\varepsilon = 0.158$. The product of the two terms remains the same however. So, if ε absorbs the κ_x factor, the angular wash model becomes

$$\begin{Bmatrix} p_w \\ q_w \\ r_w \end{Bmatrix} = \left(\frac{-1}{2\rho|V_a|}\right) \begin{bmatrix} 64/\pi b^2\varepsilon & 0 & 0 \\ 0 & 64/\pi b^2\varepsilon & 0 \\ 0 & 0 & 64/\pi b^2\varepsilon \end{bmatrix} \begin{Bmatrix} M_x \\ M_y \\ M_z \end{Bmatrix} \qquad (12.17)$$

and $\varepsilon = 0.316$. This factor varies with sweep angle, planform, Mach number, etc., and so may need to be reevaluated as speed varies or geometry changes. It is also a very powerful factor. When equal to 0.316, the roll-damping derivative is reduced by as much as 57% compared to strip theory without the swirling wake. When $\varepsilon = 1.0$, the roll-damping derivative is reduced as much as 30%.

Once again, the general form for induced velocity is sufficient to model the wing wash on itself:

$$\begin{Bmatrix} u_w \\ v_w \\ w_w \\ p_w \\ q_w \\ r_w \end{Bmatrix} = \left(\frac{-1}{2\rho|V_a|} \right) \begin{bmatrix} a_{11} & a_{12} & \cdot & \cdot & \cdot & a_{16} \\ a_{21} & a_{22} & & & & \cdot \\ \cdot & & \cdot & & & \cdot \\ \cdot & & & \cdot & & \cdot \\ \cdot & & & & \cdot & \cdot \\ a_{61} & \cdot & \cdot & \cdot & \cdot & a_{66} \end{bmatrix} \begin{Bmatrix} F_x \\ F_y \\ F_z \\ M_x \\ M_y \\ M_z \end{Bmatrix} \tag{12.18}$$

or

$$V_w = \left(\frac{-1}{2\rho|V_a|} \right) [A]P$$

12.2.4 Bluff-Body Self-Influence

Many stability and control analyses define an airspeed efficiency factor that attenuates the freestream velocity at the empennage. That is, the bluff body causes the freestream wind to decay by a factor:

$$u_e = \eta u \tag{12.19}$$

This decay can be used to estimate the (long axis) x-direction characteristic area. Following Hoffman and Dreier [5], let the drag of the fuselage be given by

$$D_f = -\frac{\rho V_a^2 f}{2} \tag{12.20}$$

The f term is the equivalent flat-plate area. Using the developing self-influence model, the wash velocity in the x direction is a function of the undetermined influence area A.

$$u_w = \left(\frac{-1}{2\rho|V_a|} \right) \left(\frac{1}{A} \right) D_f \tag{12.21}$$

Substitute D_f into the expression for u_w:

$$u_w = \frac{V_a f}{4A} \tag{12.22}$$

The velocity at the empennage reduces to $u_e = \eta u$ because of friction and other interferences. Thus,

$$\eta u = u_e = u - u_w = u - \frac{V_a f}{4A} \approx u - \frac{uf}{4A} \tag{12.23}$$

The approximation sign supports the idea that the fuselage is flying with small angles of attack and sideslip. Solve the following expression for A:

$$A = \frac{f}{4(1 - \eta)} \tag{12.24}$$

Obviously, the flat-plate area f and the efficiency factor η can both be functions of aerodynamic angle of attack and angle of sideslip. Nevertheless, the preceding characteristic area fits nicely into the induced-velocity model:

$$\begin{Bmatrix} u_w \\ v_w \\ w_w \end{Bmatrix} = \left(\frac{-1}{2\rho |V_a|} \right) \begin{bmatrix} 4(1-\eta)/f & 0 & 0 \\ 0 & 0 & 0 \\ 0 & 0 & 0 \end{bmatrix} \begin{Bmatrix} F_x \\ F_y \\ F_z \end{Bmatrix} \qquad (12.25)$$

Of course, the other diagonal terms can be developed in a similar fashion, though it is probably true that these terms are very close to zero.

12.2.5 General Self-Influence

By now, the convenience of the self-influence model is established. For the fuselage, landing gear, pylon, etc., the same form of the wash model may be employed. The greatest challenge is determining the characteristic length to use in the inverse area calculation. Absent any measured data, a good rule of thumb is this.

Table 12.1   Candidate characteristic lengths for a fuselage

Direction	Length candidate	Discussion
X	One-half of the greater of fuselage height or width	This is the drag direction. The normalizing area for the drag tables will most likely be projected frontal area. The area produced by the L candidate will therefore be close to this value. This area may be adjusted for measured empennage losses as described
Y	One-half of the distance from the fuselage nose to the far end of the tail boom, or far end of the fuselage if no tail boom	This will generate a very large area and thus a very small wash value. An alternative, especially for helicopters with thin tail booms, is to model the fuselage in two sections. Use the length of the passenger compartment as the L candidate for the forward section and the length of the tail boom as the L candidate for the boom
Z	Same candidate as the Y direction	Same discussion as the Y direction
Mx	One-half of the greater of fuselage height or width	This is the rolling direction. Because the rolling moment for the fuselage is generally considered zero, the inverse area can just be set to zero
My	Same candidate as the Y direction	Same discussion as the Y direction
Mz	Same candidate as the Y direction	Same discussion as the Y direction

Surround the aerodynamic body with a circle, and then use half of the diameter as the characteristic length. As wind-tunnel, CFD, or flight-test data become available, introduce a correlation coefficient that attenuates the basic model. If the general form of the wash model is taken to be

$$w = \frac{-1}{2\rho|V_a|}\left(\frac{1}{\pi L^2}\right)F \tag{12.26}$$

for forces, and

$$\omega = \frac{-1}{2\rho|V_a|}\left(\frac{4}{\pi L^4}\right)M \tag{12.27}$$

for moments, then Tables 12.1 and 12.2 and the following discussion summarize reasonable guesses for the characteristic lengths of fuselages and pylons. All directions are given in the IERA for the element being discussed.

12.2.5.1 Fuselage Areas
The IERA for the fuselage is assumed to lie as shown in Fig. 12.4.

The x axis lies along the long axis of the fuselage, the y axis is normal to the plane of symmetry, and the z axis completes a right-handed coordinate system.

12.2.5.2 Pylon Area
The IERA of the pylon is best modeled with the x axis pointing along the long axis or the axis that is most closely parallel to the

Table 12.2 Candidate characteristic lengths for a pylon

Direction	L candidate	Discussion
X	One-half of the major-axis dimension of the projected area of the pylon normal to the x axis	An alternative is to use the projected area of the pylon normal to the x axis to back out an L candidate that fits the model
Y	One-half of the maximum length of the pylon measured along the x axis	An alternative is to use the projected area of the pylon normal to the y axis to back out an L candidate that fits the model
Z	Same candidate as the Y direction	An alternative is to use the projected area of the pylon normal to the z axis to back out an L candidate that fits the model
Mx	Same candidate as the X direction	Same discussion as the X direction
My	Same candidate as the Y direction	Same discussion as the Y direction
Mz	Same candidate as the Z direction	Same discussion as the Y direction

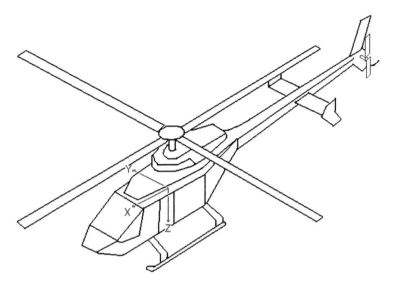

Fig. 12.4   IERA for the fuselage.

shaft. This means that in most cases the x axis will be pointing up and the z axis will be pointing forward. An obvious exception is a tiltrotor or tilt-wing aircraft, in which the pylon is free to pivot. In airplane mode, the x axis will point forward and the z axis down.

12.3 Mutual Interference

A principal power penalty paid by helicopters in hover is downwash. The downwash from a rotor impinges upon the fuselage, striking it almost normally. On a tiltrotor, the downwash blasts the main wing normally, or at any angle between normal and streamwise, and in some cases may even oppose the streamwise direction. The horizontal tail of the tiltrotor may be immersed in downwash in hover and low forward speed; the tendency of a tiltrotor to pitch up with sideslip in helicopter mode is explained partially by rotor downwash. The main wings on a tilt-wing are immersed completely in the slipstream from the rotors. With forward speed, the wake decreases in strength and moves aft toward the tail. The horizontal and vertical tails experience significant attenuation and reorientation of the downwash with airspeed. The tail rotor (if so equipped) also experiences extraordinary changes in the strength and direction of the main (or forward) rotor downwash.

The rotor is not the only wash generator though. The main wing on a tiltrotor or tilt-wing aircraft develops significant downwash with forward speed as it takes over the lifting job from the rotors. That downwash affects the empennage. The fuselage itself also decelerates or redirects the moving air, influencing all other bodies attached to it. (The author has experience with horizontal-axis wind turbines, which are just autorotating rotors mounted on a horizontal axis atop a tower. The tower, regardless of whether it is upwind or downwind of the rotor, introduces a pronounced impulse because of its aerodynamic "shadow," which is easily modeled with a potential flow about a circular cylinder.)

The point is, all elements affect all other elements aerodynamically, though in some cases it is easy, or at least reasonable, to argue that the influence is minimal and can be safely ignored. In this section, some methods for determining the aerodynamic effect of one body on another are presented. The methods listed here are by no means the only methods, nor are they necessarily the best methods. One should always trust wind-tunnel or flight-test data over some theory or model. (Pandora's box time: Many are familiar with the old saying, "No one believes the analysis except the analyst; everyone believes the test data except the test engineer." In simulation, one enjoys the best (or worst) of both worlds—flavoring first principles with empirical data, or alternatively, structuring measured data with a mathematical foundation. Take your pick—we can all get along.) But, if no data of this sort are available, these techniques will work in a pinch. There are three basic steps. Align the wash velocities, determine the amount of their influence, and then add them as indicated.

12.3.1   Aligning the Wash Velocities

As stated in the preceding section, the wash models are developed in the IERA systems for each aerodynamic element. Because each element can in theory influence every other element, it makes sense to find a common orientation in which to express all of the washes so that the inter-IERA transformations are straightforward. That common orientation is the collection of IELA systems. Recall, all IELA are parallel to the body axes. Given the IERA orientation angles each aerodynamic body has, it is a simple matter to rotate the washes to the IELAs.

$$V_{w|IELA} = T^T(\theta_x, \theta_y, \theta_z) V_{w|IERA} \qquad (12.28)$$

The matrix $T(\theta_x, \theta_y, \theta_z)$ uses the equivalent orientation angles to rotate a vector from the IELA to the IERA. (Recall that any number of rotations can be used to accomplish the desired orientation of a body, but that in the end all of the transformations can be represented by an equivalent set of just three rotations through three angles. That is what is meant by "equivalent orientation angles.") This same expression works for all elements, and so requires no further elaboration.

12.3.2   Determine the Level of Influence

As the reader has become aware, the induced velocity of the rotor has a value of w at the disk and $2w$ in the ultimate wake. The influence of the wing changes with proximity to the quarter-chord as well. In general, all wakes change with distance. Viscous effects and dissipation rates confound the analyst that tries to use theory to determine how much, and in what direction, the wakes change. This problem must rely heavily on empirical data. However, theory may still guide strength estimates. Here then are some rules of thumb for use with the form of wash model being presented.

12.3.2.1   Rotor Influence   When assessing the effect of rotor wash on some other point, determine the distance between the IELA of the rotor and the IELA of the other body. Use expression (12.29), developed by McCormick [6] to estimate the induced velocity at some distance downstream (or upstream) of the rotor disk:

$$\frac{v_i(d)}{v_i(0)} = 1 + \frac{(d/R)}{\sqrt{1 + (d/R)^2}} \tag{12.29}$$

Combine with the continuity equation to estimate the radius of the streamtube:

$$\frac{R(d)}{R(0)} = \sqrt{\frac{\sqrt{1 + (d/R)^2}}{(d/R) + \sqrt{1 + (d/R)^2}}} \tag{12.30}$$

(Because the induced velocity ratio was developed assuming no contraction, the preceding expressions must be viewed with some skepticism. Generally, the results agree with more elaborate theories, measurements, and pictures. This suggests the expressions can be used with some expectation of an acceptable answer. Caveat emptor.)

12.3.2.2   Rotor Influence on Wing   Use velocity vectors to determine if a body is influenced by the rotor wake. Consider the example of a rotor and a horizontal wing near it. In the hover case, (Fig. 12.5), the rotor wake does not interact with the horizontal stabilizer. Notice that the wake contraction has been considered, though it would not have mattered much here.

Now, let this simple combination begin flying toward the left, as shown in the following. In Fig. 12.6a, the wake still does not envelope the horizontal stabilizer because the wake has contracted. In Fig. 12.6b, wake contraction has been ignored. Thus, some of the wake has impinged on the tail. This kind of effect is very important for pitch and roll trim correlation with flight test when making critical azimuth calculations. But even this is not enough, for the wake is seen to be departing the rotor disk at the same angle as it is intersecting the horizontal stabilizer.

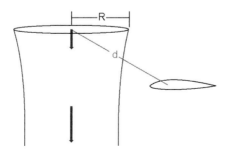

Fig. 12.5   Wake contraction.

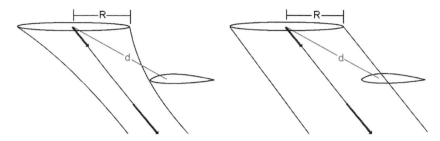

Fig. 12.6   (a) Wake with contraction. (b) Wake without contraction.

A further refinement considers the curvature of the midline of the streamtube. The departure angle χ measured from the horizontal is given by

$$\chi = \tan^{-1}\left(\frac{-w_a}{u_a}\right) \tag{12.31}$$

At hover, the value for w_a is the induced velocity w_w, and u_a is 0. The departure angle is 90 degs at the disk and all along the midline of the streamtube. As the forward speed increases, the departure angle begins to move away from the vertical. Because the induced velocity in the ultimate wake increases to $2w$, the wake angle will change. Figures 12.7a and 12.7b show the consequence of ignoring this acceleration.

Less of the wing is enveloped by the wake if the departure angle variation is accounted for. In reality, the wake has already begun to dissipate. The line between when the tail is in the wake and when it is not is not as sharp as these images. Rigid insistence to the contrary is to partake of the marvelous.

There is another way in which the rotor wake may come to the horizontal stabilizer. In the case of tiltrotors and tilt-wings, the shaft axis is tilted by pilot control. In that case, wake coverage is a function of mast angle, airspeed, and wake contraction. Figure 12.8 shows a typical encounter.

In Figs. 12.8a and 12.8b, the mast has been rotated to approximately the wake departure angle. Significantly more horizontal tail area is immersed in the main

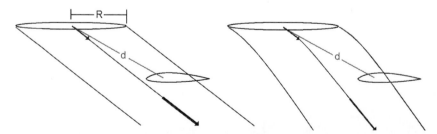

Fig. 12.7   (a) Wake acceleration not taken into account. (b) Wake acceleration taken into account.

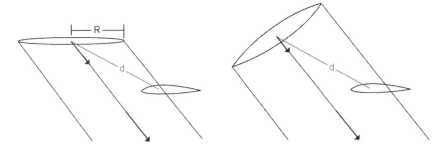

Fig. 12.8 (a) Before mast tilt. (b) After mast tilt.

rotor wake. How does one account for all of these variations on a theme? Not easily. But, the following points may help:

1) Use the $v_i(d)/v_i(0)$ ratio to estimate the induced velocity at the distance d from the rotor hub. Call this ratio Rv.

2) Use the radius contraction ratio $R(d)/R(0)$ to estimate the wake radius at the distance d from the rotor hub.

3) Resolve the body-axis velocities into mast axes. Add the axial induced velocity to get the aerodynamic velocity at the hub and several downstream positions measured in the axial direction. Calculate the departure angle at each of these stations. The off-axis displacement of the midline is estimated by the integral

$$e = \int_0^d (\chi) \, ds,$$

where s is measured along the mast axis. This is a busy calculation, but it can be precalculated because $\chi(s)$ is ultimately a function only of u_a, w_a, and d (or s). Figure 12.9 graphically illustrates this step.

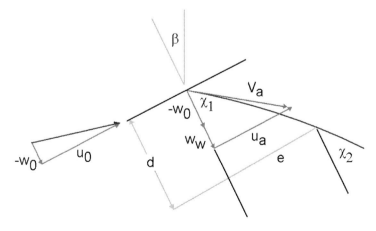

Fig. 12.9 Velocity vectors in the vicinity of a rotor.

4) The wake radius is introduced, centered on the midline, and normal to a line parallel to the mast. The reader is free to disagree and invent his/her own geometry argument.

5) The influence coefficient can be based on area ratios, such as the ratio of the area of the horizontal tail that is wetted by the wake to the cross-sectional area of the wake at this point. The influence can also be based strictly on nondimensional strength of wake Rv at a location d from the hub. Perhaps, the influence coefficient is the product of the area ratios and the velocity ratios.

12.3.2.3 Rotor Influence on Fuselage   The rotor wake impinges on the fuselage almost all of the time, with the possible exception of flight at high forward speed, high sideward speed, or high descent rate. A tiltrotor or tilt-wing may not be so lucky even then. This wake causes "drag" in the vertical direction, which is called *download*. Typically, the download adds 3–5% onto the thrust requirement of a single main rotor helicopter.

Use the velocity vectors to determine if the main rotor wets the projected vertical area of the fuselage. If so, determine how much of the fuselage area is wetted by the downwash (Fig. 12.10). Then, calculate the induced velocity at the fuselage top a distance d below the rotor using the Rv ratio $[= v_i(d)/v_i(0)]$. The dynamic pressure on the top of the fuselage can be determined. Multiply that by the wetted area of the fuselage and an estimated drag coefficient in the vertical direction to get the download.

12.3.2.4 Fuselage Interference on Rotor   As the fuselage plows through the air, the air above the fuselage is pushed up out of the way. The air also is retarded directly in front of the fuselage, but accelerated in the x direction over the top of the fuselage. The retardation for a single main rotor helicopter is small, but can be estimated using the empennage loss method described earlier. The accelerated flow over the top of the fuselage and the z-direction effect is not as easily estimated. A potential flow model of the fuselage is one method to estimate the effect. Keuthe and Chow [7] describe a numerical method to estimate the potential flow using finite panels.

12.3.3 Linking the Wakes

Evidently, the element wakes are functions of flight condition and controlled geometry. A few of the many methods to describe the influence of one element

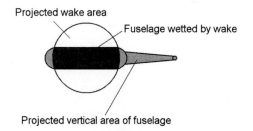

Fig. 12.10   Area of fuselage wetted by downwash.

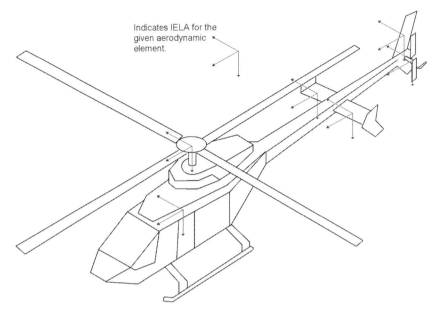

Indicates IELA for the
given aerodynamic
element.

Fig. 12.11   Some IELA locations for the example problem.

on another have been set forth. The final step is to link all of the wakes. This
task is best described as an overall matrix-vector multiplication, but is probably
most easily grasped in the context of an example. Therefore, consider the example
helicopter in Fig. 12.11.

Six elements have been located with six IELA systems. (There are many more
than six elements. The number was reduced to keep the size of the example
manageable.) Let them be numbered as shown in Table 12.3.

Each element has a 6×1 column vector of wake velocities owing to self-
influence. The velocities are numbered 1 to 6, corresponding to u, v, w, p, q, and r.
The mutual interference is then described with a simple index table. Review
Table 12.4 for one interference proposal.

**Table 12.3   Aerodynamic elements of example
problem**

Index	Element
1	Fuselage
2	Main rotor
3	Right horizontal stabilizer
4	Left horizontal stabilizer
5	Vertical stabilizer
6	Tail rotor

Table 12.4 Wake coupling matrix identifying possibly important interferences

Element being influenced	Wake direction being influenced	Element doing the influencing	Wake direction doing the influencing	Strength of influence	Description
1	1	1	1	1	Fuselage self-influence u
1	2	1	2	1	Fuselage self-influence v
1	3	1	3	1	Fuselage self-influence w
2	1	2	1	1	Rotor self-influence u
2	2	2	2	1	Rotor self-influence v
2	3	2	3	1	Rotor self-influence w
2	4	2	4	1	Rotor self-influence p
2	5	2	5	1	Rotor self-influence q
3	1	3	1	1	Left hor. stabilizer self-influence u
3	2	3	2	1	Left hor. stabilizer self-influence v
3	3	3	3	1	Left hor. stabilizer self-influence w
4	1	4	1	1	Right hor. stabilizer self-influence u
4	2	4	2	1	Right hor. stabilizer self-influence v
4	3	4	3	1	Right hor. stabilizer self-influence w
5	1	5	1	1	Vertical stabilizer self-influence u
5	2	5	2	1	Vertical stabilizer self-influence v
5	3	5	3	1	Vertical stabilizer self-influence w
6	1	6	1	1	Tailrotor self-influence u
6	2	6	2	1	Tailrotor self-influence v
6	3	6	3	1	Tailrotor self-influence w

3	2	3	Varies with flight and geometry	Main rotor downwash on left hor. stab. in z direction
4	2	3	Varies with flight and geometry	Main rotor downwash on left hor. stab. in z direction
5	2	3	Varies with flight and geometry	Main rotor downwash on vertical fin in x direction
1	2	3	Varies with flight and geometry	Main rotor downwash on fuselage in z direction
5	6	2	1	Tail rotor downwash (note it is pointing in y direction) on vertical fin; this is a sideload

This table certainly does not cover all of the possible links. It is merely expository.

One can imagine a simple method to do all of the summations. If each element has a 6×1 column of wakes associated with it, and these vectors were stacked according to the index of the elements, then the global wake vector would have $6*N$ elements in it. In this example, the self-influence wake vector would have 36 elements in it, arranged as

$$V_{w|\text{self}} = \begin{Bmatrix} \{6x1\}\textit{fuselage} \\ \{6x1\}\textit{mainrotor} \\ \ldots \\ \{6x1\}\textit{tailrotor} \end{Bmatrix} \tag{12.32}$$

Any individual element could be found with the simple successor formula:

$$wake\_index_{\text{global}} = wake\_index_{\text{local}} + (body\_index - 1) * 6 \tag{12.33}$$

So, the w wake velocity (local wake index 3) of the left horizontal stabilizer (body index 4) is found at location

$$wake\_index_{\text{global}} = 3 + (4 - 1) * 6 = 21 \tag{12.34}$$

The wake velocity vector considering all mutual interference effects, or what this text calls simply the V_w vector, is

$$V_w = [X]V_{w|\text{self}} \tag{12.35}$$

and X is a sparse matrix $6N \times 6N$ in size, with coefficients placed in the array positions given by the global wake index. (Because the X matrix is so sparse, it is recommended that the formality of the matrix-vector multiplication be abandoned for sparse matrix arithmetic.)

12.4 Conclusions

The problem of correctly modeling aerodynamic interference in a rotocraft is as much art as it is science. This chapter presented some ideas starting with a basic wash model that relates the strength of the induced velocity to the aerodynamic force that generated it. The wash velocity adds as a vector to the intertial velocity to create the aerodynamic velocity, which produces aerodynamic forces that generate the washes. And so the circle continues. Every element that produces an aerodynamic force produces a wash that at the least influences itself. This chapter presented models for rotor, wing, and body self-influence. The same elements and washes also influence nearby elements. The rotor downwash pushes down on the top of the fuselage and horizontal stabilizer. The tailrotor pushes sideways on the vertical fin. The fuselage decelerates the flow before it reaches the empennage. This chapter also presented a workable linking scheme to aid in the bookkeeping of the most common mutual interferences one is likely to encounter.

References

[1]Drees, J. M., "A Theory of Airflow Through Rotors and Its Applications to Some Helicopter Problems," Journal of the Helicopter Society of Great Britain, Vol. 3, No. 3, 1949.

[2]Ruddell, "Advancing Blade Concept Development," Journal of the American Helicopter Society, Vol. 22, No. 1, 1977.

[3]Prouty, R. W., *Helicopter Performance, Stability and Control*, Krieger, Malabar, FL, 1995, p. 124.

[4]Etkin, B., *Dynamics of Flight, Stability and Control*, J. Wiley, New York, 1959.

[5]Hoffman, J. A., and Dreier, M. E., *User's Manual for the Modular Stability Derivative Program High Frequency Version (MOSTAB)*, PPI-5300-1, Paragon Pacific, Inc., El Segundo, CA, May 1979, pp. 4.6–4.8.

[6]McCormick, B. W., *Aerodynamics of V/STOL Flight*, Academic Press, New York, 1967, pp. 96–98.

[7]Keuthe, A. M., and Chow, C. Y., *Foundations of Aerodynamics: Bases of Aerodynamic Design*, 3rd ed., J. Wiley, New York, 1976, pp. 107–115.

Problem

12.1 A tiltrotor has two rotors mounted near the tips of a main wing. The rotors can and do tilt forward from the vertical to horizontal and also tilt backward, but no more than 5 deg. The wing is mounted on top of the fuselage, which also has a horizontal tail and one to three vertical tails. The landing gear is retractable. Create a table similar to Table 12.4 for a tiltrotor. Of all of the interferences that you identify, which do you feel are the most important and why?

13
Engines

13.1 Introduction

The two principal types of engines used on helicopters are the reciprocating engine and the turbine engine. (Brief forays into ramjets or rockets mounted on blade tips have not shown promise. This introductory text will confine itself to conventional methods.) Reciprocating engines are reasonably priced, inexpensive to maintain, and very reliable, but they are also relatively heavy, have a low power-to-weight ratio, and have hundreds of moving parts. Gas turbines, on the other hand, are light, have a high power-to-weight ratio, are very reliable, and have essentially one or two moving parts, but they are also expensive to buy and maintain. TANSTAAFL (There ain't no such thing as a free lunch).

Unlike automobile engines, helicopter engines are operated at constant rpm, which is achieved by 1) vigilant pilot control on the throttle, 2) mechanical techniques that add or subtract from the throttle as the collective is manipulated, 3) a governor that controls the throttle and/or blade pitch, or 4) a full-authority digital engine control (FADEC).

Analysis and models of engines run the gamut from simple to complex; the models usually fall into one of the following categories:

1) *Perfect engines* match the power required by the rotors, propellers, accessories, etc. exactly and instantaneously, up to some limit. Perfect engines are used only when static performance is important.

2) *Perfect engines with lead-lag compensators and washout filters* act to model the engine and governors, spool-up time constants, delays, and lead signals from collective or power lever manipulation. When engine dynamics are important to handling qualities but details of a particular engine are unavailable, reasonable estimates for various gains and time constants can do a respectable job.

3) *Thermodynamic models* are based on static performance charts, which show power as a function of rpm, manifold air pressure, throttle, exhaust gas temperature, air density or density ratio, temperature ratio, etc. These models provide quite realistic estimates of the power available from an engine given the aforementioned variables. The estimated power is instantaneously available.

4) *Thermodynamic/dynamic models* are based on static performance charts *and* presumed dynamics of a system with inertia, engine control units (ECU) and hydromechanical units (HMU). These are the most complex of the models, but provide the users with extra capability such as dynamic simulation of engine starts.

Even the best thermodynamic/dynamic models are not completely adequate for a full fidelity simulation. For instance, a dynamic model of the electrical system is important, especially for turbine simulations, so that battery drain can be modeled during an attempted engine start. This is important because turbine rpm must steadily increase during a start, even past the ignition point, in order to avoid damage to an engine from over heating; a so-called hot start can ruin turbine blades and "burn" an engine rapidly. Fuel flow models are desired so that engine acceleration, smoothness of engine operation, and weight burn can be calculated. FADEC simulations model the engine controller.

This chapter begins with the simplest representation of an engine and connects it to a simple power-absorbing device via an infinitely stiff shaft. Then, the simple engine is modified so that it emulates the dynamic behavior of real engines. The chapter continues by starting over, representing the engine as a thermodynamic/dynamic model. Both reciprocating and turbine engines are examined.

13.2   Fundamental Test-Bed Architecture

The torque or power absorbed by the rotors, accessories, hanger bearings, the transmission, etc., (collectively, torque absorbers) is calculated in every frame of a time-domain simulation. The torque requirement is applied to one end of an ideal drive train. The engine output is applied to the other end. Call this arrangement the bench test setup. Figure 13.1 illustrates the bench test arrangement.

So far as an analytic model for the bench test is concerned, the ideal drive train is an infinitely stiff shaft, and the ideal torque absorber (subscript TA in what follows) is a constant multiplied by the square of the rotational speed. Let Q_{eng} be the torque that the engine supplies, and let Q_{TA} be the torque that the torque absorber requires. Let J be the polar moment of inertia of the rotor or torque absorber, and let Q_{Ω^2} be a multiplier of the square of the rotor speed, which is Ω. The rotor accelerates at the rate $\dot{\Omega}$, and, with an engine in place, the differential equation of motion that describes rotor acceleration is

$$J\dot{\Omega} = Q_{eng} - Q_{TA} \qquad (13.1)$$

As written in Eq. (13.1), both Q_{eng} and Q_{TA} are positive. When Q_{eng} equals Q_{TA}, then the rotor spins at constant speed, and the system is said to be in trim; otherwise, the rotor will accelerate or decelerate depending on the sign of the right-hand side

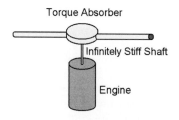

Torque Absorber

Infinitely Stiff Shaft

Engine

Fig. 13.1   Bench test.

of Eq. (13.1). This observation leads to a simple proposal for a control system that governs rotor speed by operating on both terms on the right-hand side of Eq. (13.1). First, the reader's experience suggests that increasing or decreasing fuel flow rate will increase or decrease the engine torque, which will increase or decrease rotor speed according to Eq. (13.1). Therefore, one method to control rotor speed is to modify the engine torque by linking an error between actual and desired rotor speed to the fuel flow rate into the engine. That is, create a Taylor series for engine torque that has as an independent variable the fuel flow rate $\dot{w}_f$. If the steady-state value of fuel flow rate is $\dot{w}_{f0}$, then a first-order equation for engine torque with a controller is

$$Q_{eng} = Q_{eng_0} + \left.\frac{\partial Q_{eng}}{\partial \dot{w}_f}\right|_{\Omega=\Omega_0} (\dot{w}_f - \dot{w}_{f0}) \qquad (13.2)$$

The controller equation would be

$$\dot{w}_f = \dot{w}_{f0} + K_{\dot{w}_f}(\Omega - \Omega_0) \qquad (13.3)$$

Assuming the derivative

$$\left.\frac{\partial Q_{eng}}{\partial \dot{w}_f}\right|_{\Omega=\Omega_0} > 0$$

then the fuel flow gain $K_{\dot{w}_f}$ must be less than zero for system stability. (Can the reader see why?)

The second method to change the rotor speed is to link an error between the actual and desired rotor speed to the amount of torque the rotor absorbs. An effective control is the collective. If the rotor is developing thrust, then increasing the collective causes the rotor to absorb more torque, but do not forget that increasing the collective also causes the rotor to increase its thrust. Decreasing the collective has the opposite effect. As with the engine, create a Taylor-series model of the rotor torque that has collective as the independent variable. However, the absorbed torque is also a function of the square of the rotor speed. Thus, if the reference value of collective is θ_0, then a reasonable first-order model for rotor torque with a controller is

$$Q_{TA} = (Q_{\Omega^2}|_{\theta=\theta_0,\Omega=\Omega_0})\Omega^2 + \left.\frac{\partial Q_{TA}}{\partial \theta}\right|_{\Omega=\Omega_0}(\theta - \theta_0) \qquad (13.4)$$

The controller equation takes the form

$$\theta = \theta_0 + K_{\theta\Omega}(\Omega - \Omega_0) \qquad (13.5)$$

Assuming

$$\left.\frac{\partial Q_{TA}}{\partial \theta}\right|_{\Omega=\Omega_0} > 0$$

then the collective gain $K_{\theta\Omega}$ must be greater than zero for a stable system. The rotor torque model $(Q_{\Omega^2}|_{\theta=\theta_0,\Omega=\Omega_0})\Omega^2$ can be estimated from the torque equations in the rotor chapter.

Of course, control laws that combine both schemes are also used because each alone has some limitations. The point is, a discussion of engine models necessarily includes a discussion of the governor system as the coming models will show.

13.3   Simplest Engine Representation

The simplest engine model is simply a device that delivers the required torque instantaneously. Figure 13.2 illustrates this setup.

There are no equations of motion in this representation because there are no dynamic elements. (Alternatively, one could say that the gains $K_{\dot{w}_f}$ and $K_{\theta\Omega}$ are very large in magnitude so that the error in rotor speed is corrected with what amounts to a very short time constant. In practice, one asserts the desired torque.) The output of the engine model is set equal to the required torque or power. As much as anything else, personal preference dictates whether the output of the engine model should be power or torque. The two are related by the constitutive equation $P = Q\Omega$, where P is power, Q is torque, and Ω is the engine speed. Sometimes available models make the decision for you. For instance, accessory losses are often presented in terms of power. An equivalent torque requirement can be calculated, but that calculation leads to a division by zero at startup. In the author's experience, torque is the preferred engine model output. Power, if needed, can then be calculated by multiplication. In this way, division by zero is avoided.

Equation (13.6) represents the simplest engine model and really is not reasonable for anything except static performance calculations.

$$Q_{\text{eng}} = Q_{\text{TA}} \tag{13.6}$$

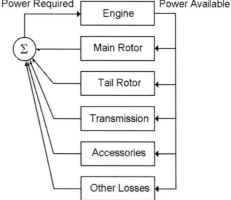

Fig. 13.2   **Simplest engine model matches power required with power available instantly.**

However, incorporating a simple limiter adds a modicum of realism:

$$Q_{eng} = \max[\min(Q_{TA}, Q_{upper}), Q_{lower})] \tag{13.7}$$

Further embellishment of this simple model recalls the lesson of the silk purse/sow's ear.

13.4 Time-Constant Models

Near the nominal operating point, turbine engines behave like simple first-order systems. Given a step input in available fuel, the fireball in the combustion chamber instantly increases pressure. The pressure difference across the power turbine rotor increases, and this increases the available torque. (If increased torque demand is absent, the power turbine accelerates to a higher speed via a first-order Bernoulli equation.) The torque model of Eq. (13.2) can be improved by including the acceleration of the engine itself. A transfer function or its equivalent differential equation states the improved model concisely:

$$Q_{eng} = \left[\frac{K_{eng}}{1 + \tau_{eng}s} \right] \Delta \dot{w}_f \tag{13.8}$$

or

$$\tau_{eng} \dot{Q}_{eng} = -Q_{eng} + K_{eng} \Delta \dot{w}_f$$

In the preceding expressions, $\Delta \dot{w}_f$ is the change in fuel flow from the reference fuel flow. Fuel flow is usually expressed in units of weight per unit time, for example, lb/s. The gain $K_{eng} = \partial Q_{eng}/\partial \dot{w}_f$ and the time constant τ_{eng} may be constant or functions of engine torque.

The fuel flow is a function of throttle setting and a controller that uses main rotor speed. A generic proportional, integral, and derivative (PID) control law with the architecture of Eq. (13.9), which is an embellishment of Eq. (13.3), covers all bases.

$$\Delta \dot{w}_f = \dot{w}_f - \dot{w}_{f0} = \left(K_P + \frac{K_I}{s} + sK_D \right) \Delta\Omega$$

$$\Delta\Omega = \Omega - \Omega_0 \tag{13.9}$$

The torque, rotor speed error, and integral of the rotor speed error comprise the states of three coupled first-order differential equations, which are expressed in standard state-space format in Eq. (13.10):

$$\begin{Bmatrix} \dot{Q}_{eng} \\ \Delta\dot{\Omega} \\ \Delta\dot{\alpha} \end{Bmatrix} = \begin{bmatrix} -K_{eng}K_D/\tau_{eng}J & -K_{eng}K_P/J & -K_{eng}K_I/\tau_{eng} \\ 1/J & 0 & 0 \\ 0 & 1 & 0 \end{bmatrix} \begin{Bmatrix} Q_{eng} \\ \Delta\Omega \\ \Delta\alpha \end{Bmatrix}$$

$$+ \begin{bmatrix} K_{eng}K_D/\tau_{eng}J \\ -1/J \\ 0 \end{bmatrix} Q_{rotor} \tag{13.10}$$

Note: The equation $\Delta\dot{\alpha} = \Delta\Omega$ appears in Eq. (13.10) to accommodate the time integral of $\Delta\Omega$, which is required by the K_I gain.

The actual rotor speed and engine power are then

$$\Omega = \Omega_0 + \Delta\Omega$$

$$P = Q_{eng}\Omega \qquad (13.11)$$

The power expressed in units of horsepower is $Hp = Q_{eng}\Omega/550$ if the product $Q_{eng}\Omega$ has units of ft-lb/s.

An improvement on the representation of the governor is available if 'feedforward' information on collective motion is added to the fuel flow control law. If θ_{Coll} is the position of the collective pitch on the rotor, then Eq. (13.9) may be changed to anticipate the motion of the collective:

$$\Delta\dot{w}_f = \left(K_P + \frac{K_I}{s} + sK_D\right)\Delta\Omega + \left[\frac{\tau_1 s + K_C}{\tau_2 s + 1}\right]\theta_{Coll} \qquad (13.12)$$

The particular form of the collective feedforward term is called a lead-lag filter. It has these attributes:

1) The amount of fuel commanded by the collective has a simple proportional gain K_C. K_C is knowable from static performance requirements.

2) The time constant in the denominator determines how rapidly the system settles on the final value. The rule of thumb is four time constants to get to 98% of final value.

3) The time constant in the numerator determines the magnitude of the initial reaction to collective change. Given a step input the output overshoots initially and decays to the final value if $\tau_1 > \tau_2$. If $\tau_1 < \tau_2$, then the output has an immediate nonzero output and rises to the final value.

It is well known that the time constant and gain in the engine torque expression are strong functions of the set point, so that unless the gains are themselves a function of the current operating condition this model is only satisfactory over a narrow range of operating conditions. Nevertheless, models of this form are used with great success. References [1–3] are examples. Expanded realism requires a thermodynamic model that has rotor dynamics, engine control units, and hydromechanical units.

13.5 Thermodynamic Models

At a minimum, a thermodynamic model is based on static performance charts that show power as a function of engine speed, manifold pressure, throttle, exhaust gas temperature, air density or density ratio, temperature ratio, etc. When the dynamics of the fireball are coupled with the dynamics of a cascade of rotor/stator stages that have inertia, ECU, and hydromechanical units, then the model can be used for flight regimes that run the gamut from ground idle to maximum continuous power. Combine this model with a representation of the dynamics of a power supply (battery or ground cart) and the torque curves during startup, and the engine model may also qualify for procedure training.

Two principle types of engine are in use today. The first type is the reciprocating aircraft engine that operates much like the engine you find in your automobile. The second type of engine is the turboshaft engine, which is a jet engine with a very low speed exhaust. A brief look at each type is presented next.

13.5.1 Reciprocating Engines

The first aircraft engines were reciprocating. They were air-cooled, in-line, and had low power-to-weight ratios. Advances in materials and supercharging improved the power-to-weight ratio and kept the costs down. Today, reciprocating engines are the mainstay of fixed-wing general aviation. Reciprocating engines are also in helicopter use.

The power from an engine is a function of engine speed, intake manifold pressure, inlet air temperature, and pressure altitude. The data are typically arranged on a two-page engine performance chart, an example of which is shown in Fig. 13.3.

These engine performance charts are represented by multivariable tables or curve fits. Smith and Dreier [4] describe the application of the least-squares method to fitting the power charts. From there, corrected brake horsepower is found using the following scheme, also taken from [4].

The brake horsepower at altitude is a function of manifold air pressure (MAP) and engine rpm. This is the value found on the right-hand side of the engine power charts at point **A**. Call this value BHP_{altitude}. Also, make a note of the value of the density ratio found at the bottom of the chart, and call it σ_A. Note, σ_A represents the density ratio corresponding to the measured MAP and rpm. It does not reflect the ambient conditions of temperature and pressure.

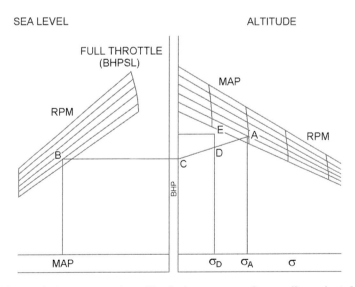

Fig. 13.3   Typical representation of brake horsepower of normally aspirated reciprocating aircraft engine.

Find the corresponding engine power at sea level given the same rpm and MAP by consulting the left-hand-side charts. This is point **B** on the charts. Call this value *BHPB*.

An original term gleaned from the left-hand-side charts is the brake horsepower at sea level with full throttle. This is apparently a function only of rpm. Call this power BHP_{sealevel}.

A relationship between brake horsepower at sea level and at altitude for full throttle and constant rpm was established in Hamlin [5]. That relationship is expressed here:

$$\frac{BHP_{\text{altitude}}}{BHP_{\text{sealevel}}} = \frac{\sigma - 0.117}{0.883} \tag{13.13}$$

Solve Eq. (13.13) for the density ratio:

$$\sigma = 0.117 + 0.883\frac{BHP_{\text{altitude}}}{BHP_{\text{sealevel}}}$$

The effects of the ambient conditions of actual air temperature and air pressure are reflected in the density ratio σ_D, which is found from the perfect-gas law:

$$\sigma_D = \frac{\delta_D}{\theta_D}$$

The temperature ratio θ_D and pressure ratio δ_D are given by the well-known expressions

$$\theta_D = \frac{459.67 + T}{519.0}$$

$$\delta_D = (1 - 0.000006875h)^{5.256}$$

(For a review of the industry standard symbols in the atmosphere model, revisit Chapter 5). The temperature T is the actual temperature in degrees Fahrenheit and the pressure altitude h is measured in feet.

Connect points BHP_{altitude} and *BHPB* with a straight line, and then find point *BHPD* given the density ratio σ_D and the equation for the straight line. This is point **D** on the chart:

$$BHPD = BHPB + (BHP_{\text{altitude}} - BHPB)\left(\frac{1 - \sigma_D}{1 - \sigma_A}\right) \tag{13.14}$$

Finally, correct BHPD for the nonstandard day temperature, point **E**. This procedure is found on the charts:

$$BHP_{\text{Corrected}} = BHPD\sqrt{\frac{459.67 + T_s}{459.67 + T}} = BHPD\sqrt{\frac{1 - 0.000006875h}{\theta_D}} \tag{13.15}$$

The corrected brake horsepower is the power delivered to the transmission and eventually to the rotors, accessories, etc.

Of course, the normally aspirated engines may also get boosts from superchargers, turbosuperchargers, or a compound arrangement utilizing the exhaust gases to drive the supercharger and the engine shaft. Dommasch et al. [6] report engine thermal efficiencies of 35% are possible with such an arrangement.

13.5.2 Gas Turbine Engines

A jet used in fixed-wing aircraft produces thrust by accelerating a significant amount of air at high pressure out the exhaust port. A turboshaft engine, on the other hand, derives its power by expanding that exhaust to low pressure, capturing the energy when the exhaust gas turns a turbine. Figure 13.4 shows a cutaway drawing of a 6000-shaft-horsepower-class turboshaft engine used on aircraft such as the V-22 and, with some modifications, on the C-130J and Saab 2000 regional passenger jet.

The AE1107 employs a FADEC for engine control. Power output is 6150 shp, and the weight is 971 lb, giving a power-to-weight ratio of 6.33 hp/lb. The 14-stage axial compressor has a pressure ratio of 16.7. Output speed is 15,000 rpm, and all of this comes in a package measuring 78.1 in. in length and 34.2 in. in diameter. For more information about the AE1107, the reader is directed to Nourse [7].

Figure 13.5 shows another approach in power extraction used in the Pratt and Whitney Canada PT6C series engine. Figure 13.6 shows a cutaway of Honeywell's T-55 engine.

The schematic in Fig. 13.7 illustrates the basic process in a coaxial turboshaft engine.

Fig. 13.4   Cutaway of the AE1107 engine showing the compressor, the combustion chamber, and the power turbine. (Photo courtesy of and © Rolls-Royce.)

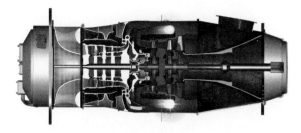

Fig. 13.5   Cutaway of the PT6C engine showing the compressor, the combustion chamber, and the power turbine. (Image courtesy of Pratt and Whitney Canada. Reprinted with permission.)

A compressor draws in air at ambient temperature and pressure. Passing through several stages of rotor/stator combinations, the air is pressurized and heated to several hundred degrees Fahrenheit. The compressed air is directed to the combustion chamber where it is mixed with fuel. The fuel vaporizes when it contacts the hot air, and then it burns. The combustion gases are forced into the turbine sections by the high pressure at the compressor outlet. To start the engine, an igniter is required. Once the fireball is established, the igniter is no longer needed. The so-called N1 turbine takes some of the energy and converts it into rotary motion that drives the compressor. The N2 turbine extracts much of the remaining energy. This turbine turns a pinion gear that turns a power gear. The power gear drives the rest of the gears in the transmission and delivers power to the rotors, accessories, etc.

T55 TURBOSHAFT ENGINE

Fig. 13.6   Cutaway of the T-55 engine showing the compressor, the combustion chamber, and the power turbine. (Image courtesy of Honeywell International, Inc.)

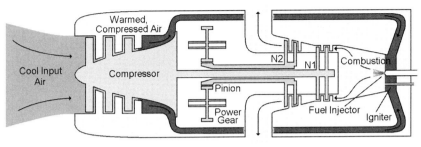

Fig. 13.7   Schematic of a turboshaft engine.

The following data, provided by Pratt and Whitney Canada, may calibrate the reader. At a typical operating condition, the PT6C has an inlet mass flow rate of 11 lb/s. The compressor speed is 38,000 rpm, and the compressor pressure ratio is 12 : 1. The compressor has increased the temperature of the air to 700 °F. The interturbine temperature (ITT) is 1400 °F, and the exhaust temperature is 1000 °F.

A typical implementation of a turboshaft engine model is shown in the following figures. The engine model depends on tables of measured torque as a function of fuel flow and gas generator speed. These tables, which are provided by the manufacturers, are static; that is, a given combination of fuel flow and gas generator speed was introduced to a real engine, and after the transients died, the torque was recorded. Perturbations from these referred values serve to add some robustness to the model.

In Fig. 13.8, the commanded gas compressor speed N1 is compared to the actual gas compressor speed. Any error is converted into fuel flow command that is limited between a minimum amount required to keep the engine running and a maximum amount permitted. A simple lag is introduced to account for the dynamics of the fuel valve. The commanded fuel flow is compared to the referred steady-state value, and any difference is multiplied by a gain that represents the partial derivative of gas compressor torque with respect to fuel flow. That torque, divided by the inertia of the compressor turbine, accelerates the turbine. That acceleration, integrated in

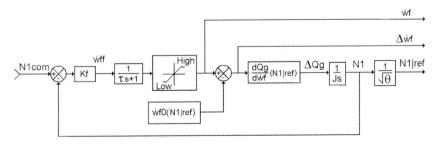

Fig. 13.8   Generation of fuel flow command and referred gas compressor speed.

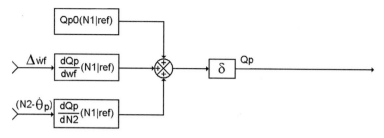

Fig. 13.9   Power turbine torque schematic.

time, gives the gas compressor speed that was used at the start of this loop. The gas compressor speed is also corrected to atmospheric temperature ratio; the corrected value is called the *referred speed*.

Fuel flow also affects the torque output from the power turbine. In Fig. 13.9, the difference between actual fuel flow and referred steady-state fuel flow is multiplied by the partial derivative of power turbine torque with respect to fuel flow. That delta in torque is added to the steady-state value and to a contribution caused by any difference between the reference (desired) speed of the power turbine N2 and the actual power turbine speed. This sum, after correction for pressure ratio, is the power turbine torque.

The pilot has some input into the power control. That influence may be presented as a gas compressor speed command or a power command. Consider first a gas compressor command. The pilot manipulates a power lever and, in so doing, commands a gas compressor speed $N_{1|pl}$. The command is compared to the actual compressor speed N_1, and the difference is converted by a simple gain K_g into a candidate compressor acceleration value. Consider now a power command or torque command after division by an appropriate speed. Compare torque commanded $Q_{p|pl}$ to actual power turbine torque Q_p. The difference is converted by another simple gain to another candidate compressor acceleration value. Similar comparisons between actual power turbine speed $\dot{\theta}_p$ and reference speed $N_{2|ref}$ and other reference values, for example, $N_{gaccel|(N1|ref)}$, which is a function of pressure ratio, may also become candidate acceleration values. Typically, the minimum value of all candidates is chosen, and winner is compared to a deceleration limit. The maximum value here is checked for sign. Only positive values are propagated, and then only after confirmation that fuel flow demand is above the minimum required to keep the engine running. If all conditions are met, this acceleration is integrated in time. The commanded gas compressor speed feeds back to Fig. 13.8. Figure 13.10 illustrates how the commanded gas compressor speed is generated.

Finally, the power turbine must react to its own load, which is a damping term, and to the load that the rotor places on it. The accelerating torque is compared to the actual power turbine torque and any difference, after division by the power turbine inertia is the definition of the power turbine acceleration. After integration, the power turbine speed is compared to the rotor speed, which is resisted by case damping and spool wind-up. A clutch prevents the engine from dragging the rotor speed down in the event of engine failure. This step will be examined in more detail in the chapter on drive systems. Figure 13.11 shows the final loop.

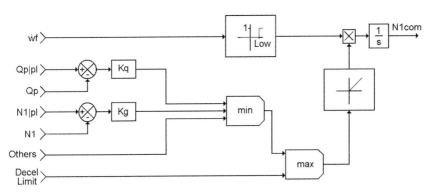

Fig. 13.10   Genesis of the gas compressor command.

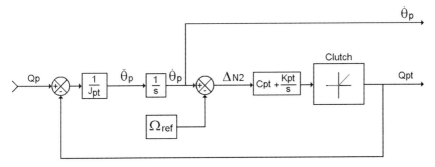

Fig. 13.11   Power turbine speed loop.

The reader is cautioned that the preceding description is illustrative only. Each engine manufacturer has its own spin on engine modeling and control. If and when the reader is asked to simulate an engine, the manufacturer will have to supply this information as well.

13.6   Conclusions

Though trying to get engine manufacturers to supply any detailed information about their product is a little like pulling teeth, this chapter did present a foundation for engine modeling that accepts measured data or "gut feel" values that produce realistic behavior from an engine model. Different levels of texture from the perfect engine to a dynamic/thermodynamic model provide latitude in the level of sophistication. A brief explanation of reciprocating engine modeling preceded a more detailed look at turboshaft engine operation. Finally, the chapter presented a flowchart that explained engine behavior and control in broad strokes.

References

[1] Talbot, P. D., Tinling, B. E., Decker, W. A., and Chen, R. T. N., "*A Mathematical Model of a Single Main Rotor Helicopter for Piloted Simulation*," NASA TM-84281, 1982.

[2] Heffley, R. K., "*ROTORGEN Minimal Complexity Simulator Math Model with Application to Cargo Helicopters (U)*," NASA CR 196705, March 1997.

[3] Corrigan, J., *Comprehensive Program for Theoretical Evaluation of Rotorcraft (COPTER) User's Guide, Vol. 2*, Rep. 299-099-376, Bell Helicopter Textron, Inc., Fort Worth, TX, Oct. 1993, pp. 3.149–3.152.

[4] Smith, H. C., and Dreier, M. E., "*A Computer Technique for the Determination of Brake Horsepower Output of Normally-Aspirated Reciprocating Aircraft Engines*," Society of Automotive Engineers, 770465, Warrendale, PA, March 1977.

[5] Hamlin, B., *Flight Testing Conventional and Jet-Propelled Airplanes*, MacMillan, New York, 1946.

[6] Dommasch, D. O., Sherby, S. S., and Connolly, T. F., *Airplane Aerodynamics*, 4th ed., Pitman, New York, 1967, pp. 253–258.

[7] Nourse, J. G., "*AE1107 Growth Paths and Methodologies*," Presented at the 58th Annual Forum of the American Helicopter Society, June 2002.

Problems

13.1   Draw a block diagram (information flow diagram) that covers Eqs. (13.1–13.5). Show the integrator as a Laplacian block, and use a multiplier to square the rotor speed.

13.2   Find the analytical solution to the ideal torque absorbed when the engine torque is suddenly set to zero, that is, find the analytical solution to $J\dot{\Omega} = -Q_{\Omega_0^2}\Omega^2$ given some initial rotor speed $\Omega(t = 0) = \Omega_0$.

13.3   Continue with problem 2. Let $J = 1000$, $Q_{\Omega_0^2} = 1.0$, and $\Omega_0 = 30$. Use the analytical solution to calculate the instantaneous rotor speed at 11 equally spaced points from $t = 0$ to $t = 5$ and then plot the solution as a function of time. Next, solve the differential equation numerically using any integration scheme you want, but using the same Δt as with the points determined from the analytical solution. Plot the numerical answer as well.

14
Drive Trains

14.1 Introduction

One or more engines power the rotors, generators, air conditioners, and other auxiliary equipment. How that power is distributed is the function of the drive train, which comprises transmissions, gearboxes, drive shafts, clutches, and sometimes the power turbine drive shaft of the engine. In the simplest sense, a static equation can model a drive train. At the other end of the spectrum, a dynamic drive train model takes account of the inertia of every main and pinion gear, the stiffness of all shafts, losses caused by friction between gears and between the shafts and various bearings, and power losses caused by auxiliary equipment. The level of detail is entirely the user's choice, though at a minimum main and tail rotor gear ratios and a clutch are required.

If one wishes to analyze dynamic loads in the rotors, drive shafts, generators, and so forth, the use of a dynamic drive train model is indicated. Dynamic loads in the main rotor are of special interest because structure to resist or absorb such loads has a direct bearing on the weight of the rotor and the useful load of the aircraft. However, if the user wishes to explore only performance issues, then the simpler static equations suffice. This chapter outlines the fundamental elements of a drive train and describes several methods to construct the differential equations that model the drive train. Without a drive train, power from the engine does not get transmitted to the rotors and other power-absorbing devices.

14.2 Fundamental Architecture

The power of one or more engines is transferred in a transmission to one or more drive shafts, which then redistributes that power to the rotors and accessories. Overriding clutches are placed between the engines and the drive shafts so that in the event of an engine failure remaining engines, if any, will continue to supply power to the rotors without wasting energy turning dead engines. In the case of single main rotor helicopters, the main rotor in autorotation also provides power to keep the tail rotor turning. Very simple schematics of some fundamental drive train architectures are shown in the following diagrams.

Figure 14.1 shows how a single engine drives the main and tail rotors and the accessories. The placement of the clutch permits the main rotor in autorotation to backdrive the tailrotor in the event of engine failure.

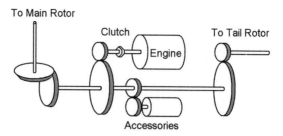

Fig. 14.1   Single main rotor and one engine.

Figure 14.2 illustrates how a single main rotor and tail rotor are powered by two engines. (The accessories are not shown for clarity.) Each engine has a clutch. A similar arrangement is used to power both rotors of a tandem helicopter.

A tiltrotor aircraft presents an additional factor in the drive train. The rotors spin in opposite directions, but the engines spin in the same direction. An idler gear, as shown in Fig. 14.3, reverses the spin direction of one of the engines. Because the

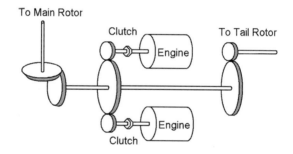

Fig. 14.2   Single main rotor with two engines.

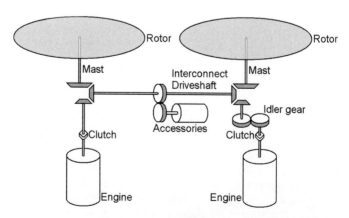

Fig. 14.3   Typical two-rotor, two-engine arrangement in a tiltrotor.

engines are housed in the pods at the ends of the wings underneath the rotors, two prop-rotor gearboxes are required. Accessories are driven at the midwing gearbox by tapping into the interconnect drive shaft. Again, the reader can appreciate that the location of the clutches, and the interconnect drive shaft isolates a dead engine while permitting the remaining engine to turn both rotors in the event of a failure of the other engine. (A common misconception about tiltrotors is that each engine turns only the rotor directly above it, as is the case on a multi-engine fixed-wing airplane. The interconnect drive shaft ensures that power is available to both rotors even when one engine is inoperative.)

14.3 Building Blocks

Several basic building blocks comprise a drive train model. Table 14.1 lists the blocks with their schematics and descriptions.

Linear constitutive equations accompany some of the schematics shown in Table 14.1. The equations need not be linear, nor do the coefficients need to be constant. Almost always, the reader will use a combination of a main gear, a pinion gear, and a flexible shaft with structural damping and damping to ground. This combination appears so often that it is convenient to name it as a fundamental building block called a drive train element. Figure 14.4 shows a drive train element.

The symbols c_s and k_s represent the shaft damping and stiffness, respectively. The pinion gear is massless, but the main gear has polar inertia J_m. The main gear can also exhibit case drag, represented by the product $b\dot\theta_m$. When the shaft experiences dynamic deformation, an internal torque Q_s develops. An external torque Q_{ext} is the forcing function. It comes from the engine, the rotor, or other load,

Table 14.1   Elements of a drive train analysis

Building block	Schematic	Description
Gears with mass	θ $\dot\theta = \Omega$ $J\ddot\theta = J\dot\Omega = Q$	Gears with mass have a polar moment of inertia J. The independent degree of freedom is an angular measurement. The first two derivatives are also required for dynamic analysis. The gear is accelerated with a torque applied axially. Positive torque produces positive acceleration.
Pinion gears	θ $\dot\theta = \Omega$ $\ddot\theta = \dot\Omega$	Pinion gears are assumed massless and therefore have no inertia. The angular degree of freedom is not independent. It is driven by a true independent degree of freedom from a dynamic element in the gearbox.

Continued

Table 14.1   Elements of a drive train analysis (*Continued*)

Building block	Schematic	Description
Gear ratios	$\theta_2 = \eta_{12}\theta_1$ $\dot{\theta}_2 = \eta_{12}\dot{\theta}_1$ $\ddot{\theta}_2 = \eta_{12}\ddot{\theta}_1$	A ratio of the rotational speeds of a driving gear and a driven gear is the gear ratio. For gears, the ratio is a negative number because gears change the direction of rotation. For sheaves, the ratio is a positive number. If the absolute value of the ratio is greater than one, then the driven gear is spinning faster than the driving gear. The ratio applies to the angular displacement and acceleration as well.
Shafts	θ_1 θ_2 Q_s Q_s $Q_s = c_s(\theta_1 - \theta_2) + k_s(\theta_1 - \theta_2)$	Shafts transmit torque between points through deformation. When the two ends of the shaft have an angular displacement between them, the product of that displacement and the shaft stiffness equals the torque. Damping may also contribute.
Case damping	Q_s $Q_s = c_c\dot{\theta}$	Gears, sheaves, and shafts are supported in the gearbox case by bearings. Despite lubrication, some drag exists, which manifests as a velocity dependent torque.
Clutches	Driver Driven	Clutches work as diodes. When the driver side shaft spins in the preferred direction, the driven side spins at the same speed. If the driver side spins the other direction, the driven side does not spin (or spins minimally caused by some drag).
Constitutive equations	$J\ddot{\theta} + D\dot{\theta} + K\theta = Q$	Constitutive equations relate torque to the mechanical action of angular displacement, velocity, and acceleration.
Generalized torque	Q	The dynamics of a drive train are excited by torques generated externally and propagated internally. The positive sense of torque is indicated with a double-headed arrow.

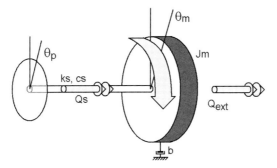

Fig. 14.4   Drive train element.

and because drive train elements have an interface with each other. Equation (14.1) is the dynamic model of the drive train element:

$$J_m\ddot{\theta}_m = Q_s + Q_{ext} - b\dot{\theta}_m \tag{14.1}$$

Equation (14.2) is the shaft torque:

$$Q_s = c_s(\dot{\theta}_p - \dot{\theta}_m) + k_s(\theta_p - \theta_m) \tag{14.2}$$

The positive sense of direction of external torque and shaft torque accelerates the main gear in the direction of positive displacement θ_m. Here is an easy way to remember how to formulate the shaft torque. Imagine that the main gear is frozen in position. Grasp the pinion gear and twist it in the direction of positive displacement θ_p and hold it there. The shaft will produce a torque resisting the motion of the pinion gear. If the main gear is suddenly released, the pent-up energy will accelerate the main gear, relieving the shaft of the internal torque. Obviously then, a spring term multiplied by a positive θ_p produces a positive shaft torque Q_s, and that same spring term multiplied by a negative θ_m reduces the shaft torque. The same argument is made for the damping term. Damping to the case always resists the direction of positive $\dot{\theta}_m$.

14.4   Model Construction with Building Blocks

Assembling a dynamic model is as easy as assembling a plastic model. Reduce the blueprint to schematic drive train elements, connect them as shown, and then expand the resulting equations. An example makes this process clear.

Consider the drive train for a twin engine, single main rotor helicopter. At the simplest level, the engine power shafts will feed a train of gears (with inertia) that reduce the engine speed down to rotor speed. The reduced speed output of the gear train is directed to the mast for the main rotor and the mast plus drive shaft for the tail rotor. The power shafts will lose some power to case damping, as will the gear train. The main rotor mast probably will not experience case damping, nor will the tail rotor mast. The tail rotor drive train likely will experience some case damping as a result of the hanger bearings.

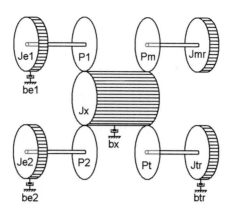

Fig. 14.5 Schematic of two-engine SMR drive train.

Step 1: Draw a schematic of the system. One such schematic is shown in Fig. 14.5. Label the main gears, the pinion gears, and the case damping elements. It is useful to name the main gears with a symbol that represents the inertia of the gear. For example, J_x is the name for the transmission gear and represents the value of its inertia.

This schematic is in its infancy. It shows and names only the dynamic elements. The case damping is shown explicitly; the shaft stiffness and shaft structural damping are not shown for the sake of clarity.

Step 2: Indicate the positive direction of the external and internal torques and name them. When a pinion and a main gear contact each other, the internal torque should be shown in both directions at the interface. In the example, main gear 1 (J_{e1}) and pinion gear 1 (P_1) are connected by shaft 1. Pinion gear 1 is also in contact with main gear 2 (J_x). The internal torque between P_1 and J_{e1} points to the left. An equal and opposite torque, which acts on J_x, points to the right. It will be very beneficial to indicate the contact torque that is applied to a main gear from a pinion gear with some symbol, a tilde for instance. Figure 14.6 shows the internal and external torques and how the internal torques reverse direction at the interface of a main gear and a pinion gear.

Step 3: Use the right-hand rule to determine the positive direction for every main gear and pinion gear in the diagram. Note that the gear train, indicated as a single massive gear, apparently has no preferred direction. Choose one. The equations will work themselves out. The positive directions the author chose for every gear are shown in Fig. 14.7.

Step 4: Write the dynamic equation for each drive train element. Use only the inertia of the main gear, the case damping term, and the external and internal torques. Also, write the constitutive equation relating the internal torque to the difference in end-to-end displacements and velocities:

$$J_{e1}\ddot{\theta}_{e1} = Q_{e1} + Q_{p1} - b_{e1}\dot{\theta}_{e1}$$
$$Q_{p1} = c_{pe1}(\dot{\theta}_{p1} - \dot{\theta}_{e1}) + k_{pe1}(\theta_{p1} - \theta_{e1}) \tag{14.3}$$

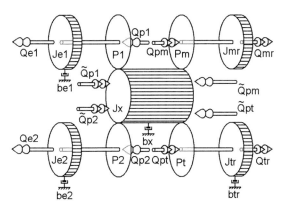

Fig. 14.6   Schematic showing external and internal torques.

$$J_{e2}\ddot{\theta}_{e2} = Q_{e2} + Q_{p2} - b_{e2}\dot{\theta}_{e2}$$

$$Q_{p2} = c_{pe2}(\dot{\theta}_{p2} - \dot{\theta}_{e2}) + k_{pe2}(\theta_{p2} - \theta_{e2}) \qquad (14.4)$$

$$J_{mr}\ddot{\theta}_{mr} = Q_{mr} + Q_{pm} - b_{mr}\dot{\theta}_{mr}$$

$$Q_{pm} = c_{mr}(\dot{\theta}_{pm} - \dot{\theta}_{mr}) + k_{mr}(\theta_{pm} - \theta_{mr}) \qquad (14.5)$$

$$J_{tr}\ddot{\theta}_{tr} = Q_{tr} + Q_{pt} - b_{tr}\dot{\theta}_{tr}$$

$$Q_{pt} = c_{tr}(\dot{\theta}_{pt} - \dot{\theta}_{tr}) + k_{tr}(\theta_{pt} - \theta_{tr}) \qquad (14.6)$$

The dynamic equation for the massive gear representing the gear train requires extra attention. Consider the torque Q_{p1}, which turns in the positive direction of θ_{p1}, and torque $\tilde{Q}_{p1}$, which turns in the positive direction of θ_x. At the point where the pinion gear associated with θ_{p1} contacts the main gear named J_x, the direction

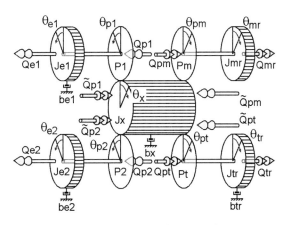

Fig. 14.7   Schematic showing everything required to write the drive train equations.

of spin reverses. So, the influence of $\tilde{Q}_{p1}$ on J_x leads to the expression

$$J_x\ddot{\theta}_x = \tilde{Q}_{p1} \tag{14.7}$$

The equation of motion can also be written as

$$J_x\ddot{\theta}_x = \eta_{x-p1}Q_{p1} = -Q_{p1} \tag{14.8}$$

On the other hand, the torque Q_{pm} that turns θ_{pm} in the positive direction pairs with $\tilde{Q}_{pm}$, which decelerates J_x. One can write the Q_{pm} contribution to the equation of J_x motion directly:

$$J_x\ddot{\theta}_x = -\tilde{Q}_{pm} = \eta_{x-pm}Q_{pm} = -Q_{pm} \tag{14.9}$$

Compare Eq. (14.8) to Eq. (14.9). Notice that the tilde performed a sign change on Q_{pm}, but that the direction factor η_{x-pm} changed the sign again. This is often confusing for the first-time modeler. Some formality will reduce the "sign chase" to a recipe. In general, the direction factor η_{b-a} depends on three factors, which when multiplied together give the sign of η_{b-a}. The first factor is defined by observing in which direction the driver and driven gears are affected by the internal torques Q and $\tilde{Q}$. If Q is aligned so that positive Q accelerates gear a, then the first factor has a value of $+1$; otherwise, it has a value of -1. If $\tilde{Q}$ is aligned so that positive $\tilde{Q}$ accelerates gear b, then the second factor has a value of $+1$; otherwise, it has a value of -1. If the contact between gear a and gear b shows a reversal of spin direction, the third factor has a value of -1; otherwise, the third factor equals $+1$. So, the general equation for the driven gear is

$$J_b\ddot{\theta}_b = \eta_{b-a}Q_a \tag{14.10}$$

In the specific example of the contact between gear P_1 and gear J_x, the η_{x-p1} factor is

$$\eta_{x-p1} = \text{sign}(Q_{p1} \quad \text{on} \quad P_1) * \text{sign}(\tilde{Q}_{p1} \quad \text{on} \quad J_x) * \text{sign(contact)}$$
$$= (+1)(+1)(-1) = -1 \tag{14.11}$$

Thus,

$$J_x\ddot{\theta}_x = \eta_{x-p1}Q_{p1} = -Q_{p1} \tag{14.12}$$

In the specific example of the contact between gear P_m and gear J_x, the η_{x-pm} factor is

$$\eta_{x-pm} = \text{sign}(Q_{pm} \quad \text{on} \quad P_m) * \text{sign}(\tilde{Q}_{pm} \quad \text{on} \quad J_x) * \text{sign(contact)}$$
$$= (+1)(-1)(+1) = -1 \tag{14.13}$$

Thus,

$$J_x\ddot{\theta}_x = \eta_{x-pm}Q_{pm} = -Q_{pm} \tag{14.14}$$

Therefore, the total dynamic equation for the θ_x degree of freedom is

$$J_x \ddot{\theta}_x = -Q_{p1} - Q_{p2} - Q_{pm} - Q_{pt} - b_x \dot{\theta}_x \qquad (14.15)$$

Step 5: Write the constraint equations. The constraint equations have no dynamics; they are algebraic relationships that link the motion of two gears to each other. In the example, the constraint equations relate the motion of the gear train main gear θ_x to the motion of the four pinion gears that contact it.

$$\theta_{p1} = \theta_{p2} = \theta_{pm} = \theta_{pt} = \theta_x \qquad (14.16)$$

The first derivatives of the pinion displacements are defined similarly. Note: There is no mention of gear ratios yet. Often, many or all of the drive train dynamic elements are referenced to a given speed, so that gear ratios do not show up in the dynamic equations. However, the gear ratios are required to scale the rotational speed of the pinion gears for the main rotor and tail rotor to bring them up to their physical speeds. Also, the gear ratios are required to reference the torques absorbed by the main rotor and the tail rotor to the reference stiffness and damping.

Step 6: Substitute the constraint equations into the constitutive equations, and then substitute the constitutive equations into the dynamic equations. (Hand expansion could be avoided here. All of the drive train elements, each consisting of a main gear, flexible shaft, case damping term, and pinion gear can be assembled into a matrix level quadratic equation automatically, provided the user can specify the gear ratios and contact constraints. However, such a method leads to either a generalized mass matrix or a generalized stiffness matrix that is degenerate in rank by 1. A method of reducing the resulting equations to a system of full rank exists, but is beyond the scope of this text. The interested reader is invited to consult [1].) Also, refer the physical speeds Ω_{mr} and Ω_{tr} of the main rotor and the tail rotor respectively to the drive train speeds, and refer the measured torque values absorbed by the main rotor and the tail rotor to the drive train torques. (Physical speed is the speed an observer measures with a clock. This is different from the speed in the drive train model, which is a dynamically scaled speed referred to some base speed; likewise, the physical torque measured at the mast of a rotor is referred to the drive train model via the gear ratio.)

$$J_{e1} \ddot{\theta}_{e1} = Q_{e1} + c_{pe1} (\dot{\theta}_x - \dot{\theta}_{e1}) + k_{pe1} (\theta_x - \theta_{e1}) - b_{e1} \dot{\theta}_{e1}$$

$$Q_{p1} = c_{pe1} (\dot{\theta}_x - \dot{\theta}_{e1}) + k_{pe1} (\theta_x - \theta_{e1}) \qquad (14.17)$$

$$J_{e2} \ddot{\theta}_{e2} = Q_{e2} + c_{pe2} (\dot{\theta}_x - \dot{\theta}_{e2}) + k_{pe2} (\theta_x - \theta_{e2}) - b_{e2} \dot{\theta}_{e2}$$

$$Q_{p2} = c_{pe2} (\dot{\theta}_x - \dot{\theta}_{e2}) + k_{pe2} (\theta_x - \theta_{e2}) \qquad (14.18)$$

$$J_{mr} \ddot{\theta}_{mr} = Q_{mr} + c_{mr} (\dot{\theta}_x - \dot{\theta}_{mr}) + k_{mr} (\theta_x - \theta_{mr}) - b_{mr} \dot{\theta}_{mr}$$

$$Q_{pm} = c_{mr} (\dot{\theta}_x - \dot{\theta}_{mr}) + k_{mr} (\theta_x - \theta_{mr})$$

$$\Omega_{mr} = \eta_{mr} \dot{\theta}_{mr}$$

$$Q_{mr} = \eta_{mr} Q_{mr-\text{measured}} \qquad (14.19)$$

$$J_{tr}\ddot{\theta}_{tr} = Q_{tr} + c_{tr}(\dot{\theta}_x - \dot{\theta}_{tr}) + k_{tr}(\theta_x - \theta_{tr}) - b_{tr}\dot{\theta}_{tr}$$

$$Q_{pt} = c_{tr}(\dot{\theta}_x - \dot{\theta}_{tr}) + k_{tr}(\theta_x - \theta_{tr})$$

$$\Omega_{tr} = \eta_{tr}\dot{\theta}_{tr}$$

$$Q_{tr} = \eta_{tr}Q_{tr-measured} \tag{14.20}$$

$$J_x\ddot{\theta}_x = \begin{Bmatrix} -c_{pe1}(\dot{\theta}_x - \dot{\theta}_{e1}) - k_{pe1}(\theta_x - \theta_{e1}) \\ -c_{pe2}(\dot{\theta}_x - \dot{\theta}_{e2}) - k_{pe2}(\theta_x - \theta_{e2}) \\ -c_{mr}(\dot{\theta}_x - \dot{\theta}_{mr}) - k_{mr}(\theta_x - \theta_{mr}) \\ -c_{tr}(\dot{\theta}_x - \dot{\theta}_{tr}) - k_{tr}(\theta_x - \theta_{tr}) - b_x\dot{\theta}_x \end{Bmatrix} \tag{14.21}$$

Equations (14.17–14.21) are the dynamic equations of motion of the drive train. The external forcing functions are the torques generated by the expanding gases in the engines and the torques absorbed by the main and tail rotors.

At this point, the equations could be coded for a real-time simulation. Each second-order equation represents two coupled first-order equations, which means a total of ten simultaneous differential equations model this system. However, there are two enhancements that will make these equations easier to work with and provide some additional insight into the dynamic behavior of the transmission. These are discussed in the next two steps.

Step 7: Write Eqs. (14.17–14.21) in matrix form, preferably state space. Create a solution vector z, which contains all of the degrees of freedom. One possible ordering is shown here:

$$z = \begin{Bmatrix} \theta_{e1} \\ \theta_{e2} \\ \theta_x \\ \theta_{mr} \\ \theta_{tr} \end{Bmatrix} \tag{14.22}$$

First and second derivatives of z are obvious. The mass, damping, and stiffness matrices are given by

$$J = \begin{bmatrix} J_{e1} & 0 & 0 & 0 & 0 \\ 0 & J_{e2} & 0 & 0 & 0 \\ 0 & 0 & J_x & 0 & 0 \\ 0 & 0 & 0 & J_{mr} & 0 \\ 0 & 0 & 0 & 0 & J_{tr} \end{bmatrix} \tag{14.23}$$

$$C = \begin{bmatrix} (b_{e1} + c_{pe1}) & 0 & -c_{pe1} & 0 & 0 \\ 0 & (b_{e2} + c_{pe2}) & -c_{pe2} & 0 & 0 \\ -c_{pe1} & -c_{pe2} & (b_x + c_{mr} + c_{tr} + c_{pe1} + c_{pe2}) & -c_{mr} & -c_{tr} \\ 0 & 0 & -c_{mr} & (b_{mr} + c_{mr}) & 0 \\ 0 & 0 & -c_{tr} & 0 & (b_{tr} + c_{tr}) \end{bmatrix} \tag{14.24}$$

$$K = \begin{bmatrix} k_{pe1} & 0 & -k_{pe1} & 0 & 0 \\ 0 & k_{pe2} & -k_{pe2} & 0 & 0 \\ -k_{pe1} & -k_{pe2} & (k_{mr} + k_{tr} + k_{pe1} + k_{pe2}) & -k_{mr} & -k_{tr} \\ 0 & 0 & -k_{mr} & k_{mr} & 0 \\ 0 & 0 & -k_{tr} & 0 & k_{tr} \end{bmatrix} \quad (14.25)$$

The forcing function is

$$f = \begin{Bmatrix} Q_{e1} \\ Q_{e2} \\ 0 \\ Q_{mr} \\ Q_{tr} \end{Bmatrix} \quad (14.26)$$

The state-space expression is

$$\dot{x} = Ax + Bu \quad (14.27)$$

where

$$A = \begin{bmatrix} 0 & I \\ -J^{-1}K & -J^{-1}C \end{bmatrix}$$

$$B = \begin{bmatrix} 0 \\ J^{-1} \end{bmatrix} \quad (14.28)$$

and

$$x = \begin{Bmatrix} z \\ \dot{z} \end{Bmatrix}, \quad u = f \quad (14.29)$$

The 0 and I symbols in expression (14.28) represent null and identity matrices of size 5×5, respectively. The advantage of expressing the equations in the form of Eq. (14.27) is this. An eigenanalysis of the A matrix will yield stability information and thus provide a sanity check of the equations. In addition, the highest frequency (the largest imaginary part of any of the eigenvalues) will guide the reader's selection of the step time used in the time-domain solution of the drive train equations. (The highest frequency has the smallest period $T = 2\pi/\Omega$, where Ω is measured in rad/s. A good rule of thumb is to use $1/10$th of the smallest period as the integration time step for good numerical accuracy. Never use less than $1/5$th of the period of the highest frequency mode—numerical instability will ensue.)

Step 7: Calculate the initial conditions of all of the state variables. One is tempted to set $\dot{x} = 0$ in Eq. (14.27) and then invert the A matrix to solve for x. Symbolically, the inverse of the A matrix is given by the expression:

$$A^{-1} = \begin{bmatrix} -K^{-1}C & -K^{-1}J \\ I & 0 \end{bmatrix} \quad (14.30)$$

Unfortunately, the stiffness matrix K is singular, so that the A matrix is also singular. This singularity is sometimes called a free zero, which is identified by an eigenvalue that equals zero exactly. One can "boil out" the free zero using the method described in Williamson et al. [1], but that method is numerically intensive and does not lead to easy physical interpretation. Instead, use a physics-based approach tempered with engineering judgment as described next.

When the system is in trim, all second derivatives are zero, that is, $\ddot{\theta}_{e1} = \ddot{\theta}_{e2} = \ddot{\theta}_{mr} = \ddot{\theta}_{tr} = \ddot{\theta}_x = 0$. Furthermore, all angular velocities are steady and are related to some reference speed. Two natural candidates for the reference speed are the main rotor speed and the engine speed. For the sake of example, let the engine speed be the reference. This means the time derivatives of constraint Eqs. (14.16) completely define the angular velocities of the pinion gears in the drive system. The main gears have the same velocity as their associated pinion gears:

$$\begin{aligned}
\dot{\theta}_{p1} &= \dot{\theta}_x & \dot{\theta}_{e1} &= \dot{\theta}_{p1} \\
\dot{\theta}_{p2} &= \dot{\theta}_x & \dot{\theta}_{e2} &= \dot{\theta}_{p2} \\
\dot{\theta}_{pm} &= \dot{\theta}_x & \dot{\theta}_{mr} &= \dot{\theta}_{pm} \\
\dot{\theta}_{pt} &= \dot{\theta}_x & \dot{\theta}_{tr} &= \dot{\theta}_{pt}
\end{aligned} \qquad (14.31)$$

The first of the four constraint equations is written with the transmission speed on the right-hand side to emphasize that the engine speed is the reference and that all other speeds are based on it. Because the accelerations equal zero at trim and constraint equations (14.31) define all of the angular velocities, Eqs. (14.19) and (14.20) reduce to

$$\alpha_{mx} = \dot{\theta}_x - \dot{\theta}_{mr} = \frac{(b_{mr}\dot{\theta}_{mr} - Q_{mr})}{k_{mr}}$$

$$Q_{pm} = k_{mr}(\theta_x - \theta_{mr}) = k_{mr}\alpha_{mx} \qquad (14.32)$$

$$\alpha_{tx} = \dot{\theta}_x - \dot{\theta}_{tr} = \frac{(b_{tr}\dot{\theta}_{tr} - Q_{tr})}{k_{tr}}$$

$$Q_{pt} = k_{tr}(\theta_x - \theta_{tr}) = k_{tr}\alpha_{tx} \qquad (14.33)$$

Because the torques from the main rotor and tail rotor are known, the derived variables α_{mx} and α_{tx} are known, which leads to values for Q_{pm} and Q_{pt}.

Also, because the accelerations are zero, Eq. (14.15) can be rewritten as

$$Q_{p1} + Q_{p2} = Q_{pm} + Q_{pt} + b_x\dot{\theta}_x \qquad (14.34)$$

At this point, a bit of engineering judgment is required. Let the shaft torques from the engines be defined as fractions of the total torque required. The fractions define the load-sharing relationship between the engines. In other words, define the engine shaft torques as shown here:

$$Q_{p1} = \gamma Q_{ptotal}$$

$$Q_{p2} = (1 - \gamma)Q_{ptotal} \qquad (14.35)$$

If the engines are performing equally, then $\gamma = \frac{1}{2}$, and $Q_{p1} = Q_{p2} = Q_{ptotal}/2$. If only engine one is operating, then $\gamma = 1$, and $Q_{p1} = Q_{ptotal}$ and $Q_{p2} = 0$, and so forth. Obviously, Eq. (14.34) is a definition for Q_{ptotal}, specifically,

$$Q_{ptotal} = Q_{pm} + Q_{pt} + b_x \dot{\theta}_x \qquad (14.36)$$

Another bit of engineering judgment is introduced here. Usually, when an aircraft simulation is trimmed, the power or torque required by the rotors and accessories is calculated, and this specifies the requirements on the engines. This means that dynamic equations (14.17) and (14.18) are actually definitions for engine torque at trim. Using the known constraints, reduce and rearrange Eqs. (14.17) and (14.18) to the following static equations:

$$Q_{e1} = b_{e1}\dot{\theta}_{e1} - Q_{p1} = b_{e1}\dot{\theta}_{e1} - \gamma Q_{ptotal}$$
$$Q_{p1} = \gamma Q_{ptotal} = k_{pe1}(\theta_x - \theta_{e1}) \qquad (14.37)$$
$$Q_{e2} = b_{e2}\dot{\theta}_{e2} - Q_{p2} = b_{e2}\dot{\theta}_{e2} - (1-\gamma)Q_{ptotal}$$
$$Q_{p2} = (1-\gamma)Q_{ptotal} = k_{pe2}(\theta_x - \theta_{e2}) \qquad (14.38)$$

Recall, the K matrix is singular with rank 4 out of 5 degrees of freedom. Therefore, one of the angular degrees of freedom must be specified. The θ_x degree of freedom appears in Eqs. (14.32), (14.33), (14.37), and (14.38), so that it seems a natural candidate. Without loss of generality, it can be set to zero. Thus, the initial conditions equations are as follows:

$$\dot{\theta}_{p1} = \text{specified} \qquad \theta_x = 0$$
$$\dot{\theta}_x = \dot{\theta}_{p1} \qquad \theta_{mr} = \left(Q_{mr} - b_{mr}\dot{\theta}_{mr}\right)/k_{mr}$$
$$\dot{\theta}_{p2} = \dot{\theta}_x \qquad \theta_{tr} = \left(Q_{tr} - b_{tr}\dot{\theta}_{tr}\right)/k_{tr}$$
$$\dot{\theta}_{pm} = \dot{\theta}_x \qquad \theta_{e1} = -\gamma Q_{ptotal}/k_{pe1}$$
$$\dot{\theta}_{pt} = \dot{\theta}_x \qquad \theta_{e2} = -(1-\gamma)Q_{ptotal}/k_{pe2} \qquad (14.39)$$

An important point about numerics must be made. The set of equations for this example has 10 states; however, one state is a free zero. Which state is free is of little consequence, because that state represents how many revolutions a gear has made since the beginning of the simulation. Because the same main gear drives so many pinion gears, think of the main gear angular displacement as the free zero. Being a free zero means that the angular displacement of the main gear will grow with time forever. Other angular displacements will grow accordingly. This is not bad, in and of itself, because only the difference between angular displacements (and in some cases angular rates) is all that is required to estimate the internal torques. However, because computers only carry finite precision, and because what is important is the *small* difference of numbers that will eventually become large, numerical precision will be lost, and the torque calculations and numerical stability will suffer. There is a way around the problem of finite precision and the small difference of large numbers. Careful examination of Eq. (14.21) invites the creation of a new independent variable called α_{xe1}, defined as follows:

$$\alpha_{xe1} = \theta_x - \theta_{e1}$$

Rewrite Eqs. (14.17) using α_{xe1}:

$$J_{e1}\ddot{\theta}_{e1} = Q_{e1} + c_{pe1}\dot{\alpha}_{xe1} + k_{pe1}\alpha_{xe1} - b_{e1}\dot{\theta}_{e1}$$
$$Q_{p1} = c_{pe1}\dot{\alpha}_{xe1} + k_{pe1}\alpha_{xe1}$$
$$\dot{\alpha}_{xe1} = \dot{\theta}_x - \dot{\theta}_{e1} \qquad (14.40)$$

Rewrite Eqs. (14.18–14.21) in similar fashion:

$$J_{e2}\ddot{\theta}_{e2} = Q_{e2} + c_{pe2}\dot{\alpha}_{xe2} + k_{pe2}\alpha_{xe2} - b_{e2}\dot{\theta}_{e2}$$
$$Q_{p2} = c_{pe2}\dot{\alpha}_{xe2} + k_{pe2}\alpha_{xe2}$$
$$\dot{\alpha}_{xe2} = \dot{\theta}_x - \dot{\theta}_{e2} \qquad (14.41)$$

$$J_{mr}\ddot{\theta}_{mr} = Q_{mr} + c_{mr}\dot{\alpha}_{mmr} + k_{mr}\alpha_{mmr} - b_{mr}\dot{\theta}_{mr}$$
$$Q_{pm} = c_{mr}\dot{\alpha}_{mmr} + k_{mr}\alpha_{mmr}$$
$$\dot{\alpha}_{mmr} = \dot{\theta}_x - \dot{\theta}_{mr} \qquad (14.42)$$

$$J_{tr}\ddot{\theta}_{tr} = Q_{tr} + c_{tr}\dot{\alpha}_{ttr} + k_{tr}\alpha_{ttr} - b_{tr}\dot{\theta}_{tr}$$
$$Q_{pt} = c_{tr}\dot{\alpha}_{ttr} + k_{tr}\alpha_{ttr}$$
$$\dot{\alpha}_{ttr} = \dot{\theta}_x - \dot{\theta}_{tr} \qquad (14.43)$$

$$J_x\ddot{\theta}_x = \begin{Bmatrix} -c_{pe1}\dot{\alpha}_{xe1} - k_{pe1}\alpha_{xe1} - c_{pe2}\dot{\alpha}_{xe2} - k_{pe2}\alpha_{xe2} \\ -c_{mr}\dot{\alpha}_{mmr} - k_{mr}\alpha_{mmr} - c_{tr}\dot{\alpha}_{ttr} - k_{tr}\dot{\alpha}_{ttr} - b_x\dot{\theta}_x \end{Bmatrix} \qquad (14.44)$$

Equations (14.40–14.44) have two very nice properties. First, the number of differential equations has been reduced from 10 to nine. Second, the problem associated with the small difference of large numbers is eliminated.

Finally, beginning with Eqs. (14.5) and (14.6), and tracking their evolution to Eqs. (14.42) and (14.43), the main rotor torque Q_{mr} and tailrotor torque Q_{tr} would seem to accelerate the main rotor gear and tail rotor gear, respectively. Indeed, if the values for Q_{mr} and Q_{tr} were positive, they would. However, torque absorbed by the rotors is a negative quantity usually, so that the physical sense that these torques should decelerate the rotors is preserved.

14.5 Model Construction with Information Flow Diagram

Another method that organizes quite well the equations of motion of a drive train (or any dynamic system) might be called the information flow diagram method. The equations are drawn in frames using stylized analog computing elements. Arrowheads indicate information available to all pages of the diagram, whereas arrow tails indicate information coming in from another page of the overall diagram. For instance, consider Eqs. (14.17), repeated here for convenience:

$$J_{e1}\ddot{\theta}_{e1} = Q_{e1} + c_{pe1}(\dot{\theta}_x - \dot{\theta}_{e1}) + k_{pe1}(\theta_x - \theta_{e1}) - b_{e1}\dot{\theta}_{e1}$$
$$Q_{p1} = c_{pe1}(\dot{\theta}_x - \dot{\theta}_{e1}) + k_{pe1}(\theta_x - \theta_{e1})$$

This equation describes the genesis of variables θ_{e1} and Q_{p1}. The diagram in Fig. 14.8 shows how this equation can be drawn using the popular MATLAB® tool [2].

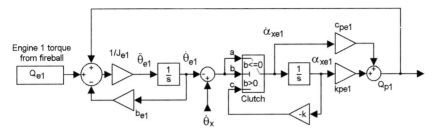

Fig. 14.8   Equation (14.17) shown schematically.

One sees that the only "external" signal is the transmission speed $\dot{\theta}_x$. The diagram makes the shaft torque of the power turbine Q_{p1} available to other diagrams. The difference $\dot{\alpha}_{xe1} = \dot{\theta}_x - \dot{\theta}_{e1}$ is defined per the preceding method. One notes the appearance of a clutch symbol. The clutch has three inputs and one output. The inputs are the two continuous variables $\dot{\theta}_x - \dot{\theta}_{e1}$ and $-K\alpha_{xe1}$, which plug into the first and third input slots, respectively. The middle input is the signal used to choose which of the two inputs is directed to the output. In this case, the switch logic signal is also the continuous variable $\dot{\theta}_x - \dot{\theta}_{e1}$. If the value of $\dot{\theta}_x - \dot{\theta}_{e1}$ is less than or equal to zero, the output of the clutch is $\dot{\theta}_x - \dot{\theta}_{e1}$; otherwise, the output of the clutch is $-K\alpha_{xe1}$. What this accomplishes is this: when $\dot{\theta}_x - \dot{\theta}_{e1}$ is less than or equal to equal to zero, the clutch acts as a rigid link, but when $\dot{\theta}_x - \dot{\theta}_{e1}$ is greater than zero, the engine has slowed relative to the transmission, and so freewheeling is required. The high-gain negative feedback $-K\alpha_{xe1}$ permits the power turbine shaft to relax to zero internal torque when freewheeling is required.

Equation (14.18), repeated here for convenience is shown schematically in Fig. 14.9.

$$J_{e2}\ddot{\theta}_{e2} = Q_{e2} + c_{pe2}(\dot{\theta}_x - \dot{\theta}_{e2}) + k_{pe2}(\theta_x - \theta_{e2}) - b_{e2}\dot{\theta}_{e2}$$

$$Q_{p2} = c_{pe2}(\dot{\theta}_x - \dot{\theta}_{e2}) + k_{pe2}(\theta_x - \theta_{e2})$$

In a similar fashion, Eqs. (14.19), (14.20), and (14.15), repeated next, are diagrammed in Figs. 14.10, 14.11, and 14.12, respectively.

$$J_{mr}\ddot{\theta}_{mr} = Q_{mr} + c_{mr}(\dot{\theta}_x - \dot{\theta}_{mr}) + k_{mr}(\theta_x - \theta_{mr}) - b_{mr}\dot{\theta}_{mr}$$

$$Q_{pm} = c_{mr}(\dot{\theta}_x - \dot{\theta}_{mr}) + k_{mr}(\theta_x - \theta_{mr})$$

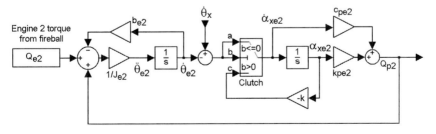

Fig. 14.9   Equation (14.18) shown schematically.

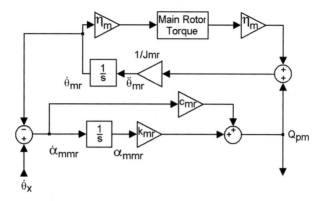

Fig. 14.10   Equation (14.19) shown schematically.

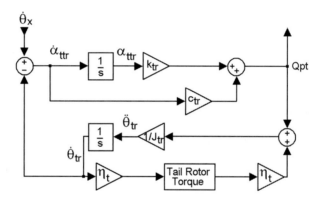

Fig. 14.11   Equation (14.20) shown schematically.

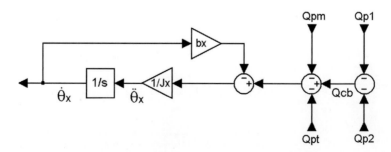

Fig. 14.12   Equation (14.15) shown schematically.

$$J_{tr}\ddot{\theta}_{tr} = Q_{tr} + c_{tr}(\dot{\theta}_x - \dot{\theta}_{tr}) + k_{tr}(\theta_x - \theta_{tr}) - b_{tr}\dot{\theta}_{tr}$$

$$Q_{pt} = c_{tr}(\dot{\theta}_x - \dot{\theta}_{tr}) + k_{tr}(\theta_x - \theta_{tr})$$

$$J_x\ddot{\theta}_x = -Q_{p1} - Q_{p2} - Q_{pm} - Q_{pt} - b_x\dot{\theta}_x$$

All of these diagrams can be "glued" together into a system diagram. Figure 14.13 shows the results of such an effort.

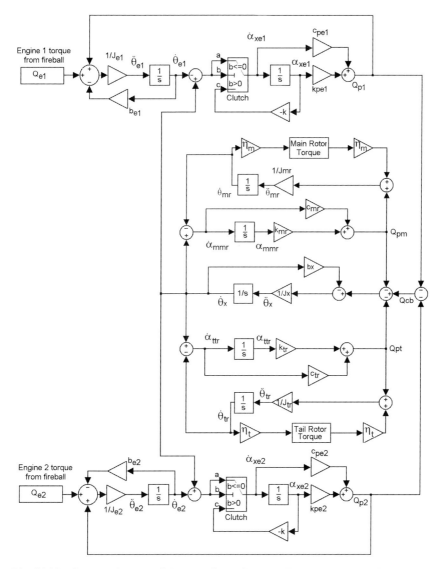

Fig. 14.13   System diagram of the equations of motion for the example drive system.

Of course, Fig. 14.13 was reverse engineered from the equations that were developed in the preceding section. Quite often, diagrams like those of Fig. 14.13 are the first thing provided by transmission specialists, and it will be the reader's job to correctly develop the dynamic equations of motion. That process is easy.

1) Locate every integrator and name the outputs, and then name the inputs with an overdot to indicate the input is the time derivative of the output.

2) Locate and name the output from every summing junction.

3) Name intermediate variables when it helps to track important physical variables or variables that are used in an unusual manner.

4) Write the algebraic equations for information flowing into the summing junctions.

5) Write the dynamic equations for information flowing into the integrators.

6) Treat special cases, such as clutches as a fix-up step.

A certain amount of finesse is permitted, even desired, if it improves readability of the documentation and/or the code.

14.6   Other Sanity Checks

Regardless of the number of engines, a transmission and drive train permit freewheeling in the event of partial or complete power loss. On such occurrences, the pilot enters autorotation; the main rotor continues to spin, and it also backdrives the tail rotor. A good drive train model should do the same. A MATLAB® model exercised the example drive train. In the figures that follow, the abscissa is time, measured in seconds. When the ordinate is torque, the units are foot-pounds; when the ordinate is displacement, the units are radians; and when the ordinate is speed, the units are radians/second. (Do not forget that these equations were written with scaled velocity and scaled displacement!)

At 0.5 s, engine 1 suddenly stops. At 1.0 s, the output of engine 2 doubles. This is shown in Fig. 14.14. The behavior of the engine models is completely unrealistic, but it does stimulate the rest of the drive train model.

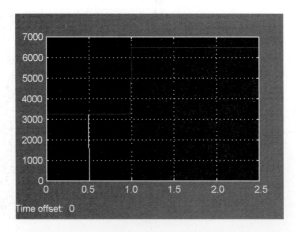

Fig. 14.14   Engine 1 cutoff, engine 2 doubling torque output.

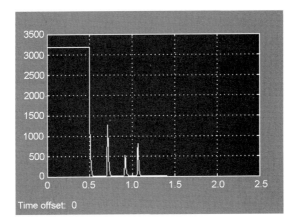

Fig. 14.15   Power turbine shaft torque Qpc1.

In Fig. 14.15, one observes the power turbine torque Qpc1 drops almost instantly to zero as engine 1 fails. Close inspection shows that the torque drops exponentially at very high rate. This is the effect of the high gain feedback of the clutch model shown in Fig. 14.9. The chatter that follows immediately after comes from the very stiff, lightly damped power turbine shaft ringing. As it oscillates, the clutch momentarily engages and disengages.

The angular output of the clutch is visualized in Fig. 14.16. It matches the torque of Fig. 14.15 to within a constant multiplier.

The main speed of the transmission Nxm is shown in Fig. 14.17. Clearly, when engine 1 fails, the system begins to decelerate. Such an impulsive failure also sets up a significant amount of ringing. When the output torque of engine 2 doubles in order to compensate, the deceleration arrests, and a slow acceleration back to speed begins.

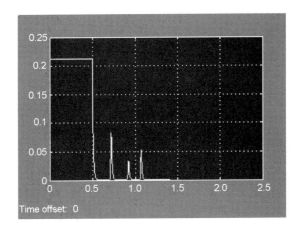

Fig. 14.16   Angular output of the clutch.

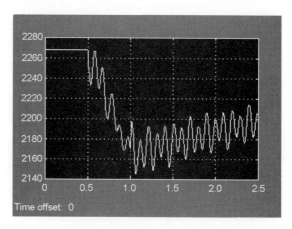

Fig. 14.17   Main transmission speed Nxm.

The torque of the main rotor in the MATLAB® model is a linear function of the rotor speed. This is not realistic for large excursions in rotor speed, but it is not too bad for small perturbations. In Fig. 14.18, the torque absorbed by the main rotor decreases almost linearly. Because the main rotor has very high inertia, it slows smoothly in response to the engine failure. When the second engine torque doubles impulsively, some ringing is introduced, but it also is of low amplitude.

Compare the behavior of the main rotor torque with the tail rotor torque, shown in Fig. 14.19. The rotor slows when engine 1 fails, but its response is considerably more erratic than the main rotor response. This is a result of a combination of factors, which includes the much smaller polar moment of inertia of the tail rotor, its higher spin rate, the stiffness of the tail rotor mast and drive shaft, the case

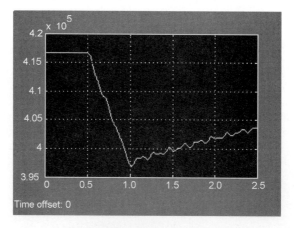

Fig. 14.18   Main rotor torque.

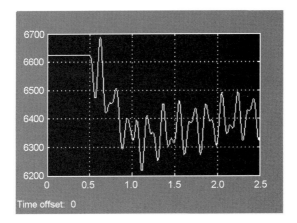

Fig. 14.19 Tail rotor torque.

damping, and the aerodynamic damping. A good simulation model will help the drive train operators see the dynamic effects of the engine failures.

14.7 Conclusions

This chapter presented a generic approach to the problem of mechanical power distribution and absorption. A set of fundamental building blocks is shown to be sufficient to construct a sophisticated drive system model that features nonlinear stiffness and damping characteristics and clutches and can easily interface with rigorous models of engines, rotors, and accessories. The assembly method that this chapter discusses is straightforward, if not a little tedious, but it does illustrate how to write the coupled differential equations that model the drive train. The assembly method also shows how to reduce the equation count and, very important, how to write the equations so that small differences of large numbers are avoided.

References

[1]Williamson, D. R., Hoffman, J. A., and Henninger, W. C., "*Mathematical Methods Incorporated in the Wind Energy System Coupled Dynamics Analysis Methodology: Wind Turbine Linear Analysis Software System (WINDLASS)*", Paragon Pacific, Inc., Rept. PPI-1018-7, El Segundo, CA, 1977.

[2]*MATLAB® High-Performance Numeric Computation and Visualization Software*, The MathWorks, Inc., Natick, MA, 1996.

Problems

14.1 Look at Fig. 14.8. Why is the feedback from α_{xe1} to the clutch important? What consequences would the drive train model suffer if the clutch merely opened and closed without the feedback? Is this a physically reasonable way to model the clutch and the shafts that attach to it?

14.2 Look at Fig. 14.13. Pretend that engine number two shut down instantly. Describe the behavior of the drive train for the first several seconds after the shutdown. In particular, explain why the main rotor and tail rotor continue to spin even though only engine number one continues to operate.

14.3 Look at Fig. 14.13. If both engines fail, the pilot will initiate an autorotation in which the main rotor begins to windmill and supply torque rather than absorb torque. Assume a steady-state autorotation has been achieved. Answer the following questions: Will the tail rotor continue to spin? Does it need to? What steady-state value does Q_{pm} reach, expressed in terms of QMR (main rotor torque—not shown but equal to the value coming out of the main rotor torque box)? Hint: With both engines dead, $Q_{cb} = 0$, and the problem is reduced to actions only of Figs. 14.10–14.12.

15
Controls

15.1 Introduction

A pilot wishes to clear a tall tree looming ahead. In a fixed-wing airplane, the pilot pulls back on the control column and pushes forward on the throttle or power lever. In a helicopter, the pilot pulls back on the fore/aft cyclic, pulls up on the conventional collective, and rotates the throttle grip to get more power. In a tiltrotor, the pilot pulls back on the fore/aft cyclic, and, depending on the rigging, pushes forward or pulls up on the power lever/collective. The discerning reader observed that the motion of the cyclic or control column was always the same. The motion of the power lever or collective was not. [This statement is a powerful argument for the need to simulate. Helicopter pilots learn early on that lowering the collective quickly is how one enters autorotation or plants the aircraft on the ground after landing. This motion requires pilots to extend their arms. In the commercial version of the tiltrotor, the collective/power lever is rigged to follow this natural convention. In the military version of the tiltrotor, the power lever is rigged in the opposite direction, designed to behave more like a fixed-wing power lever (ala Harrier jet) than a collective. This dichotomy in rigging can lead to inappropriate control application. Flight simulation is a very good method to train that behavior out of a pilot. The only thing bruised in a simulated crash is one's ego.] How much, and in what direction should a pilot move the controls to achieve desired accelerations, rates, and attitudes is the subject of control theorists and regulatory mandate. The subject of simulation answers the question, Will the aircraft achieve the desired/mandated performance?

With controls, aircraft work in their element, to our benefit and delight. Without controls, an aircraft is just another pretty shape that sits on the ground. Controls are essential to flight and to the simulation of flight. This chapter introduces the concepts of control from the standpoint of actuator actions as a result of pilot inputs. This chapter also examines control mixing and fading. However, control theory and stability and control augmentation are discussed only briefly, because those subjects, although an important part of full-up simulation, are very involved and are covered in detail in other excellent texts.

15.2 Fundamental Rigging Issues

A single main rotor helicopter and a tandem rotor helicopter are rigged differently. Tiltrotors and tiltwings are rigged differently from each other and certainly differently from helicopters. Here are some basic rigging concepts to use when modeling the control system.

15.2.1 Single Main Rotor Helicopter Arrangement

The single main rotor helicopter sans hydraulic boost is the simplest arrangement to discuss. The pilot has four controls that are directly linked through control tubes and bellcranks to the lower swashplate and a collective sleeve or plunger. The four controls are the main rotor collective, fore/aft or longitudinal cyclic, the lateral cyclic, and the tail rotor collective.

Collective raises or lowers the collective sleeve or plunger, changing the pitch on all blades in the rotor the same amount at the same time. The collective is rigged so that about 1 ft of motion changes the blade pitch a total of about 15–20 deg. Obviously, these measurements are all give-or-take. The pilot's pedals operate the tail rotor collective. Generally, the throw is 2 or 3 in. either pedal, which will change the tail rotor collective angle 25–30 deg. The collective controls are generally rigged with an offset. That is, the full-down position of the collective may mean the root of the blade is still at a positive geometric angle of attack, but the tip is not owing to twist. The full-up position will have the root end of the blade at a very high pitch angle and the tip at a more moderate positive angle.

The cyclic controls are generally rigged symmetrically, with +/−4 to 5 in. of cyclic input at the pilot's hand translating into +/−10 to 15 deg of cyclic blade pitch. Cyclic moves the lower swashplate, which does not spin with the rotor. Riding on a bearing, and constrained to follow the tilt of the lower swashplate, the upper swashplate spins with the rotor. The same point on the blade is always over a given spot on the upper swashplate. Attached to the upper swashplate, the pitch links transfer the tilt (which has defined a plane in space not necessarily normal to the shaft) to the blades in such a manner as to change the pitch of the blades. The pitch horn may be a leading-edge or trailing-edge pitch horn, and the pitch (feathering) bearing may be a real bearing, or it may be an elastomeric bearing manipulated by a pitch sleeve.

The pedals are simply the collective control over the tail rotor. The tail rotor is not rigged symmetrically. Generally, the pedals are rigged to require more left pedal at hover and approximately neutral displacement at cruise speed. (This is a natural consequence of a tail fin developing sufficient side force at speed to perform the antitorque function of the tail rotor. At higher speeds, the tail rotor takes on more of the characteristics of a rudder alone.)

Through a system of bellcranks, pulleys, control rods, and control lines, the mechanical advantage of the pilot is manipulated to ensure sufficient controllability, without overcontrolling the aircraft. In practice, all of the linkage from pilot input to swashplate motion is not modeled. Instead, a simple model, usually linear, establishes the linkage between pilot inputs expressed in units of linear displacement like inches and actuator or surface outputs often expressed in degrees. This model must also introduce control phasing to compensate for flapping frequencies other than one per rev and swirling wakes that introduce aerodynamic cyclic. A typical control model develops in stages, starting with the link from the pilot to the fixed-system collective and cyclic inputs ahead of the phasing:

$$\theta_0' = \theta_{0|\text{LowLimit}} + (\theta_{0|\text{HighLimit}} - \theta_{0|\text{LowLimit}}) \left(\frac{Coll - Coll_{\text{LowLimit}}}{Coll_{\text{HighLimit}} - Coll_{\text{LowLimit}}} \right)$$

$$A_1' = A_{1|\text{LowLimit}} + (A_{1|\text{HighLimit}} - A_{1|\text{LowLimit}})$$
$$\times \left(\frac{Lateral - Lateral_{\text{LeftLimit}}}{Lateral_{\text{RightLimit}} - Lateral_{\text{LeftLimit}}} \right)$$

$$B_1' = B_{1|\text{LowLimit}} + (B_{1|\text{HighLimit}} - B_{1|\text{LowLimit}})$$
$$\times \left(\frac{ForeAft - ForeAft_{\text{LeftLimit}}}{ForeAft_{\text{RightLimit}} - ForeAft_{\text{LeftLimit}}} \right)$$

$$\theta_{\text{ped}}' = \theta_{\text{ped|LowLimit}} + (\theta_{\text{ped|HighLimit}} - \theta_{\text{ped|LowLimit}})$$
$$\times \left(\frac{Ped - Ped_{\text{LowLimit}}}{Ped_{\text{HighLimit}} - Ped_{\text{LowLimit}}} \right) \tag{15.1}$$

The subscripts LowLimit and HighLimit have obvious definitions. The terms *Coll, Lateral, ForeAft,* and *Ped* refer to the displacements of the collective stick, the lateral cyclic stick, the longitudinal cyclic stick, and the pedals, respectively. The terms θ_0, A_1, B_1, and θ_{ped} are the angular inputs to the main and tail rotor models. A prime superscript indicates that the value is interpolated. A stability and control augmentation system (SCAS) may intervene at this point, adding to the pilot's controls.

$$\theta_0^{Com} = \theta_0' + \theta_0^{SCAS}$$
$$A_1^{Com} = A_1' + A_1^{SCAS}$$
$$B_1^{Com} = B_1' + B_1^{SCAS}$$
$$\theta_{\text{ped}}^{Com} = \theta_{\text{ped}}' + \theta_{\text{ped}}^{SCAS} \tag{15.2}$$

The superscript Com means Command, indicating that this signal either will command a swashplate directly or command a hydraulic boost actuator. If boost is available, it is in the fixed system. The actuators are usually very high in frequency and so are often modeled as static, linear equations. Sometimes, a small amount of lag may be introduced. A second-order system is almost always sufficient. For instance, a typical transfer function for the collective actuator is

$$\left(s^2 + 2\omega_n \zeta_n s + \omega_n^2 \right) \theta_0'' = K\theta_0^{Com} \tag{15.3}$$

Similar expressions are used for the other three controls. The damping ratio is usually high enough to ensure little, if any, overshoot. A good default is 0.7. The natural frequency is also usually very high, which will necessitate an inner loop when performing the time integration. Because the frequency, damping ratio, and scaling K

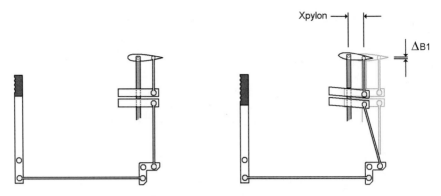

Fig. 15.1   Effect of structural deformation on cyclic input.

are all constants, a good choice for integrating techniques is the Tustin (bilinear) transformation method or the state transition matrix method. If the actuator models are to include rate and displacement limiting, then a Runge–Kutta, or improved Euler method is the better bet.

The next wrinkle is the introduction of the fixed-system phasing. Phasing is usually represented with a matrix that has lateral and longitudinal phasing angles. Phasing affects only the cyclic input. However, the collective control is carried along to emphasize the idea that three controls are available to the rotor.

$$\begin{Bmatrix} \theta_0''' \\ A_1''' \\ B_1''' \end{Bmatrix} = \begin{bmatrix} 1 & 0 & 0 \\ 0 & -\sin(\psi_{Lat}) & \sin(\psi_{Long}) \\ 0 & \cos(\psi_{Lat}) & -\cos(\psi_{Long}) \end{bmatrix} \begin{Bmatrix} \theta_0'' \\ A_1'' \\ B_1'' \end{Bmatrix} \tag{15.4}$$

Notice that the preceding operation is not a rotation in the usual sense. At this point, effects such as structural deformation can be introduced. For instance, if the pylon tilts, twists, or bends, the pitch links might not bend the same amount. Relative to the top of the pylon, the pitch input will change. Figure 15.1 illustrates how structural deformation enters the picture.

In the figure, the pylon (not shown) has moved the swashplate and mast forward through a distance of x_{pylon}. Because the pitch link is inextensible, the trailing-edge pitch horn is pulled down, which generates an increment in longitudinal cyclic that increases the pitch of the blade. A mathematical representation of the structural deformation is shown here.

$$\begin{Bmatrix} \theta_0^c \\ A_1^c \\ B_1^c \end{Bmatrix} = \begin{Bmatrix} \theta_0''' \\ A_1''' \\ B_1''' \end{Bmatrix} + \begin{bmatrix} \dfrac{\partial \theta_0}{\partial \varphi_p} & \dfrac{\partial \theta_0}{\partial \theta_p} & \dfrac{\partial \theta_0}{\partial \psi_p} & \dfrac{\partial \theta_0}{\partial x_p} & \dfrac{\partial \theta_0}{\partial y_p} & \dfrac{\partial \theta_0}{\partial z_p} \\[2mm] \dfrac{\partial A_1}{\partial \varphi_p} & \dfrac{\partial A_1}{\partial \theta_p} & \dfrac{\partial A_1}{\partial \psi_p} & \dfrac{\partial A_1}{\partial x_p} & \dfrac{\partial A_1}{\partial y_p} & \dfrac{\partial A_1}{\partial z_p} \\[2mm] \dfrac{\partial B_1}{\partial \varphi_p} & \dfrac{\partial B_1}{\partial \theta_p} & \dfrac{\partial B_1}{\partial \psi_p} & \dfrac{\partial B_1}{\partial x_p} & \dfrac{\partial B_1}{\partial y_p} & \dfrac{\partial B_1}{\partial z_p} \end{bmatrix} \begin{Bmatrix} \varphi_{pylon} \\ \theta_{pylon} \\ \psi_{pylon} \\ x_{pylon} \\ y_{pylon} \\ z_{pylon} \end{Bmatrix}$$

$$\tag{15.5}$$

The derivatives indicate how much the inputs change because of structural deformation. The vector $\{\varphi_{pylon}, \theta_{pylon}, \psi_{pylon}, x_{pylon}, y_{pylon}, z_{pylon}\}$ gives the pylon deformation. The product of the vector and the matrix of partial derivatives is the change to the input as a result of pylon deformation. All of the partial derivatives in Eq. (15.5) depend on the structural properties of the pylon, including the flexibility of the material and the deliberate or accidental flexibility built into the geometry of the pylon. Thus, a general expression for the derivatives is not possible. Equation (15.5) demonstrates one method to account for structural deformation.

The pitch command to individual blades undergoes additional phasing because of rigging and indexing in the rotating frame. (Indexing refers to the azimuthal displacement of the root of the ith blade from blade number one.) Again, the phasing only affects the cyclic input, but the collective is carried along to complete the set. A control phasing variable γ_c and an indexing variable ψ_c model these effects:

$$\begin{Bmatrix} \theta_0' \\ A_{1s}' \\ B_{1s}' \end{Bmatrix} = \begin{bmatrix} 1 & 0 & 0 \\ 0 & \cos(\psi_c - \gamma_c) & -\sin(\psi_c - \gamma_c) \\ 0 & \sin(\psi_c - \gamma_c) & \cos(\psi_c - \gamma_c) \end{bmatrix} \begin{Bmatrix} \theta_0^c \\ A_1^c \\ B_1^c \end{Bmatrix} \qquad (15.6)$$

The mast bends and winds up while rotating. This changes the pitch in the rotating frame. Let $\{\varphi_{mast}, \theta_{mast}, \psi_{mast}, x_{mast}, y_{mast}, z_{mast}\}$ be a vector of (small) angular and translational deformations of the mast resolved to the body axes. Then, with derivatives approximated from any linear theory, an expression similar to Eq. (15.5) describes the effect of mast deformation:

$$\begin{Bmatrix} \theta_0 \\ A_{1s} \\ B_{1s} \end{Bmatrix} = \begin{Bmatrix} \theta_0' \\ A_{1s}' \\ B_{1s}' \end{Bmatrix} + \begin{bmatrix} \dfrac{\partial \theta_0}{\partial \varphi_m} & \dfrac{\partial \theta_0}{\partial \theta_m} & \dfrac{\partial \theta_0}{\partial \psi_m} & \dfrac{\partial \theta_0}{\partial x_m} & \dfrac{\partial \theta_0}{\partial y_m} & \dfrac{\partial \theta_0}{\partial z_m} \\ \dfrac{\partial A_1}{\partial \varphi_m} & \dfrac{\partial A_1}{\partial \theta_m} & \dfrac{\partial A_1}{\partial \psi_m} & \dfrac{\partial A_1}{\partial x_m} & \dfrac{\partial A_1}{\partial y_m} & \dfrac{\partial A_1}{\partial z_m} \\ \dfrac{\partial B_1}{\partial \varphi_m} & \dfrac{\partial B_1}{\partial \theta_m} & \dfrac{\partial B_1}{\partial \psi_m} & \dfrac{\partial B_1}{\partial x_m} & \dfrac{\partial B_1}{\partial y_m} & \dfrac{\partial B_1}{\partial z_m} \end{bmatrix} \begin{Bmatrix} \varphi_{mast} \\ \theta_{mast} \\ \psi_{mast} \\ x_{mast} \\ y_{mast} \\ z_{mast} \end{Bmatrix}$$

$$(15.7)$$

["... derivative approximated from any linear theory" is not meant to sound cavalier. The intent is to show that the linear model, Eq. (15.7), admits a wide range of effects, including no effects. These derivatives can come from bending beam theory, rotating shaft theory, empirical data, etc.]

The reader can appreciate that Eqs. (15.4–15.7) work equally well with a tail rotor if the cyclic pitch controls are simply set to zero.

15.2.2   Tandem Rotor Helicopter Arrangement

Helicopters like the CH-46 and CH-47 have collective and cyclic control on both the forward and aft rotors. The pilot, however, is presented with just the same four controls as are found in the single main rotor helicopter. The pilot's four hand (and foot) controls manipulate six blade-pitch controls through the use of a

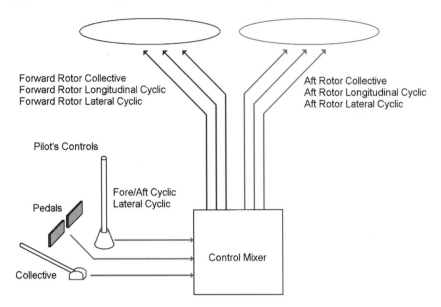

Fig. 15.2   Schematic of pilot inputs mixing before going to the rotors.

control mixing stage, shown in the schematic in Fig. 15.2 and Eq. (15.8). Note, the structural deformation effects are not shown explicitly. The fixed-system phasing, SCAS, rigging, and indexing corrections are not shown either, though their effects are there.

Rigging and piloting strategy are both considered in the design of the control mixer. For instance, the pilot may want the hovering tandem helicopter to yaw about the center of the aircraft, or closer to the centerlines of either the forward or aft rotors. One strategy that accomplishes this applies opposing lateral cyclic for yawing motion about the center of the aircraft, or applies lateral cyclic to the forward rotor only for yaw motion centered on the aft rotor, and vice versa for yaw motion centered on the forward rotor. Fuselage pitch control can be effected through differential collective pitch introduced by the fore/aft cyclic stick. The other degrees of freedom are excited through different combinations of collective and cyclic blade pitch on both rotors.

The control mixer may be a purely mechanical device, electromechanical or hydromechanical. The rigging may be constant, or it may be gain scheduled with control displacement or airspeed for example. In addition, though not shown in the schematic, the pilot inputs may also cause the incidence angle on a stabilizer to change. A flying tail (seen on a UH-60 for example) is used to control fuselage pitch in all regimes of flight.

It is not hard to imagine a general scheme for control mixing based on the discussion thus far. The inputs to a control mixer are the pilot inputs, constant or constraint values for some control outputs, and possibly airspeed and other pilot-controlled geometry functions indicated by (V, β) in Eq. (15.8). The outputs are the collective and cyclic pitch for the rotors, plus incidence angles or flap angles of various surfaces.

$$
\begin{Bmatrix}
\begin{Bmatrix} \theta_0 \\ A_{1s} \\ B_{1s} \end{Bmatrix}_{\text{Rotor1}} \\
\begin{Bmatrix} \theta_0 \\ A_{1s} \\ B_{1s} \end{Bmatrix}_{\text{Rotor2}} \\
\vdots \\
\begin{Bmatrix} \varphi \\ \theta \\ \psi \\ \delta \end{Bmatrix}_{\text{Wing}(j)}
\end{Bmatrix}
=
\begin{bmatrix}
K^{R1}_{\theta 0/\text{Coll}} & K^{R1}_{\theta 0/\text{Long}} & K^{R1}_{\theta 0/\text{Lat}} & K^{R1}_{\theta 0/\text{Ped}} \\
K^{R1}_{A1/\text{Coll}} & \ddots & & \vdots \\
K^{R1}_{B1/\text{Coll}} & & \ddots & \vdots \\
K^{R2}_{\theta 0/\text{Coll}} & \ddots & & \\
K^{R2}_{A1/\text{Coll}} & & \ddots & \\
K^{R2}_{B1/\text{Coll}} & & & \\
\vdots & & & \\
K^{Wj}_{\varphi/\text{Coll}} & \ddots & & \\
K^{Wj}_{\theta/\text{Coll}} & & \ddots & \\
K^{Wj}_{\psi/\text{Coll}} & & & \\
K^{Wj}_{\delta/\text{Coll}} & \cdots & \cdots & K^{Wj}_{\delta/\text{Ped}}
\end{bmatrix}_{(V,\beta)}
$$

$$
* \begin{Bmatrix} Coll \\ Fore/\text{Aft} \\ Lateral \\ Pedal \end{Bmatrix}
+
\begin{Bmatrix}
\begin{Bmatrix} Const \\ Const \\ Const \end{Bmatrix}_{\text{Rotor1}} \\
\begin{Bmatrix} Const \\ Const \\ Const \end{Bmatrix}_{\text{Rotor2}} \\
\vdots \\
\begin{Bmatrix} Const \\ Const \\ Const \\ Const \end{Bmatrix}_{\text{Wing}(j)}
\end{Bmatrix}
\tag{15.8}
$$

The gains in the model of Eq. (15.8) may be constant, or they may be functions of velocity, mast angle β, or some other parameter(s). No matter how general one tries to make the model, someone will dream a scheme that does not fit it. The preceding model is certainly broad in scope. Just as certainly, however, what seems to be a basic element to someone will be missing from this model. The intent of Eq. (15.8) is to show that with some forethought a quite capable model may be rendered within a manageable size.

15.2.3 Tiltrotor Arrangement

The tiltrotor aircraft represents a significant challenge to the control system designer. The pilot has control over the usual rotor inputs and now the rudders, elevators, flaps, rotor rpm, and pylon tilt as well. In some tiltrotor aircraft, the controls are mixed mechanically. In others, the control mixing and control laws are intertwined, driving surface and swashplate actuators in concert. In some tiltrotors, all of the conventional aircraft surfaces are available in addition to the rotors. In two tiltrotor configurations, rudders are not even used!

The most recognizable feature of the tiltrotor is its pylon tilt. Figures 15.3 and 15.4 show the BA609 in helicopter mode and airplane mode.

Much like the tandem rotor configuration described earlier, the aircraft is manipulated with various combinations of collective and cyclic input. For instance, in helicopter mode roll control is accomplished with differential collective pitch on the two rotors. In airplane mode, the flaperons control rolling moment. In helicopter mode, yaw control is handled with differential longitudinal cyclic. In airplane mode, the rudders do the job, though differential collective could be used (and is on the BA-609 and the Eagle Eye). In helicopter mode, fuselage pitch control is achieved with cooperative longitudinal cyclic, while in airplane mode the elevator controls pitching moment. Of course, during conversion, one method of control is washed out as another control washes in. Several functions are useful for blending or washing out effects. Almost all of the functions use the mast angle as the primary argument. Simple linear interpolation is the easiest to introduce, though it is not always the best. A slightly more exotic function still uses linear interpolation, but places the breakpoints interior to the extremes of the input argument range.

Fig. 15.3   Bell-Agusta BA609 in helicopter mode. (Courtesy of Bell Helicopter Textron, Inc.)

Fig. 15.4 Bell-Agusta BA609 in airplane mode. (Courtesy of Bell Helicopter Textron, Inc.)

Very often, the sine and cosine function, or powers of those functions, are used. For example, imagine the need to distribute the fore/aft pilot input to the rotor longitudinal cyclic input and to the elevator depending on the mast angle the pilot selects. Figure 15.5 shows a schematic.

Let the longitudinal cyclic washout and elevator cyclic washout be functions of the mast angle, which is defined so that helicopter mode is 90 degs and airplane mode is 0 degs. Tables 15.1 and 15.2 list sample functions that fit the washout boxes.

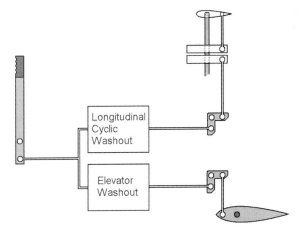

Fig. 15.5 Schematic of longitudinal control mixing.

Table 15.1   Functions that wash out as pylon goes from helicopter to airplane mode

Application	Name	Scheme
Longitudinal cyclic washout	Linear up	
Longitudinal cyclic washout	Semilinear up	
Longitudinal cyclic washout	$[1 - \cos(2\theta)]/2$	

Sometimes the trigonometric functions are raised to the second and even third power. Other functions are used, and some of those are expressed as tables. In the preceding example, the tables show complimentary functions for the cyclic and elevator washout, which is not at all a requirement and in some cases may create dreadful handling qualities.

The pilot has direct control over the flap extension and the pylon tilt. Usually, the flap controls are set for automatic extension and retraction, as defined by the conversion corridor. [The conversion corridor is a band found on a plot of mast angle vs airspeed. At zero forward airspeed, the mast had better be vertical or nearly so, depending on the center-of-gravity location and maximum pitching moment available from maximum allowable flapping. As airspeed increases, the wings take over an increasing part of the lifting task, enabling the mast to tilt more toward the horizontal until finally the mast is horizontal. At any airspeed in conversion, there is a range of permissible mast angles. The high side (more vertical) is governed by the drag of the aircraft, which defines the power required, which in turn is limited by the transmission rating. The low side (more horizontal)

Table 15.2   Functions that washout as pylon goes from airplane to helicopter mode

Application	Name	Scheme
Elevator washout	Linear down	
Elevator washout	Semilinear down	
Elevator washout	$[1 + \cos(2\theta)]/2$	

is set by the applicable margin above stall speed.] The pylons, while still under the pilot's thumb (literally), are constrained by conversion corridor parameters as well. Rotor rpm is a new control feature when modeling tiltrotors. In helicopter mode, the rotor spins at some rate typical of helicopters. This rotor speed is maintained during conversion all of the way to airplane configuration. Only after the pylon is locked down is the rpm reduced to airplane mode. The pilot's control over rpm is not profound, but it does exist.

It is not hard to see how the programmable gains in Eq. (15.8) represent the washout functions shown in Table 15.2. In fact, Fig. 15.2 and Eq. (15.8) are useful control models for tiltrotor aircraft as well as tandem rotor helicopters.

15.3 Basic Control Diagram

In preparation for the chapter on trim procedures, a conceptual list of pilot controls as independent arguments is presented in Table 15.3.

Table 15.3   Conceptual list of controls available to the pilot

Pilot control	Operation
Collective	The collective lever is the principal means of controlling collective blade pitch on main rotor of a single main rotor helicopter or both rotors of a tandem helicopter or tiltrotor.
Fore/aft cyclic	The fore/aft cyclic stick controls longitudinal cyclic blade pitch of a single main rotor helicopter or tiltrotor and differential collective blade pitch of a tandem helicopter. In airplane mode of a tiltrotor, this control also affects the elevator angle.
Lateral cyclic	The lateral cyclic stick controls lateral cyclic blade pitch of a single main rotor helicopter or the forward rotor of a tandem helicopter and differential collective blade pitch of a tiltrotor in helicopter mode and differential flaperon deflection of a tiltrotor in airplane mode.
Pedal	The pedals control collective blade pitch of the tail rotor on a single main rotor helicopter, lateral cyclic blade pitch on the aft rotor of a tandem helicopter, differential longitudinal cyclic blade pitch on a tiltrotor in helicopter mode, and differential collective blade pitch and/or rudder displacement on a tiltrotor in airplane mode.
Power lever	In tiltrotor aircraft, this lever is the collective/power lever. It commands collective blade-pitch angle in helicopter mode and power in airplane mode.
Throttle	Usually ganged with collective or power lever, the throttle controls fuel flow to the engines, thereby regulating potential power.
Mast angle	Unique to tiltrotor aircraft, the pylons (and therefore the masts) can be tilted forward from 90 to 0 deg, or aft to 95 deg. The mast angle is a very powerful pilot control. Control phasing, mixing, and washout are all governed by this angle and airspeed.
Wing angle	Unique to tiltwing aircraft, the entire wing can be tilted forward from 90 to 0 deg. Rotor downwash helps maintain the wing at small angles of attack despite the apparent large geometric angles. In tiltwing aircraft, the angle of the wing governs control mixing, phasing, and washout.
Rotor rpm	The pilot has limited control over the rotor rpm, usually restricted to some nominal speed plus or minus a small range. Tiltrotors and tiltwings have two nominal values, one for helicopter mode and one for airplane mode. The pilot's control over these values is limited.
Flaps	Tiltrotors and tiltwings are equipped with flaps or flaperons on the main wing. A lever in the cockpit controls the flaps, or, if available, the flaps may be set automatically by the control laws depending on airspeed and mast angle.
LTM	Lateral translation mode is sometimes provided in tiltrotor aircraft. This is nothing more than lateral cyclic blade pitch introduced by the pilot via a small thumbwheel mounted on the collective lever head.

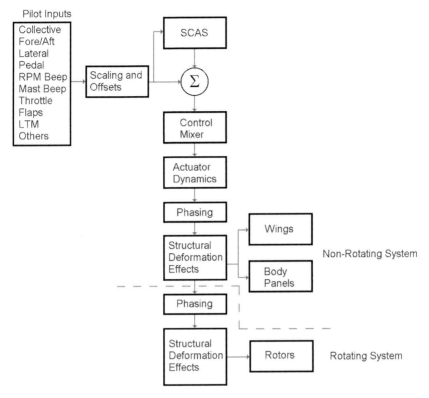

Fig. 15.6   Major components of a control system model.

Figure 15.6 brings together all of the control system concepts presented thus far. Control of an aircraft begins with a conscious decision by the pilot followed by a deliberate manipulation of one or more controls. The controls are usually expressed in units that a pilot would use in conversation—inches of forward cyclic, aft mast beep, etc. These pilot control values are then converted through scaling and offsets to linear and angular command values. A SCAS provides shaping to the pilot input and important stability enhancement. SCAS output is added to the command values and mixed. The outputs of the mixer are the command values to the actuators throughout the aircraft. Fixed-system phasing and fixed system structural effects are introduced next, and the final fixed system actuator commands are distributed to the wings, body panels, etc. If the output goes to a rotor or propeller, additional effects as a result of structural deformation and phasing in the rotating system are added before the rotor or propeller gets its final commands.

The reader's favorite nuances may have been left out of Fig. 15.6. The preceding control system model is a suggested framework, but it is not the only way to get pilot input to the various element models. Regard Fig. 15.6 as a roadmap. The roadmap certainly points the way, but it does not preclude the use of unmarked side streets and detours.

15.4   Stability and Control Augmentation Systems

Stabilization and control enhancement routines known collectively by the moniker SCAS (and other names) use pilot inputs and aircraft states to improve the stability and controllability of the aircraft. Many references on control law design are available. Blakelock [1] is one such reference.

Control systems have two main functions. The first is regulation or stabilization. The second is control. These functions are achieved through a variety of strategies. This section will introduce both functions and a few of the methods in common use.

15.4.1   Regulation/Stabilization

Regulation forces a dynamic system to be stable. A stable dynamic system returns to a given state (set point) after being perturbed. A trace of the system states as a function of the independent variable, usually time, may be oscillatory with diminishing amplitude or purely convergent. Plants (another name for a dynamic system) may be naturally stable, or they may be neutrally stable or completely unstable. A neutrally stable dynamic system oscillates around a given state or remains a given distance from a given state after perturbation. An unstable system continues to move away from a given state after perturbation. That motion can be oscillatory with ever-increasing amplitude, or purely divergent.

A regulator works independently of a pilot or controller. A regulator reads some or all of the observable states of a plant and combines them after passing them through various gains. The output of a regulator is the input to the plant. If the gains are correct, the resulting behavior of the plant is stable. If the regulator has all of the states of the plant available to it, then this is known as full state feedback. This is shown in Fig. 15.7. If the plant is linear, it has a state-space representation given in Eq. (15.9):

$$\dot{x} = Ax + Bu$$
$$y = Cx + Du \tag{15.9}$$

A is the dynamics matrix, B the control matrix, C the observation matrix, and D the feedforward matrix. Notice that the matrices of Eq. (15.9) are constant. The vector of plant dynamic states is x, while those that are measured and reported are contained in y. The control inputs to the plant are stacked in the u vector. If the plant has n states, then n states must be fed back, though the coefficients acting on some of the states may be zero. One way to do this is to set C to the unity

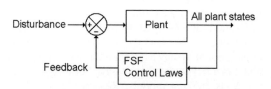

Fig. 15.7   Full state feedback regulator.

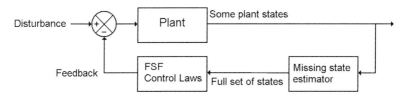

Fig. 15.8   Partial state feedback regulator.

matrix and D to the null matrix. That action makes the y vector equal to the plant
state vector exactly. Then, in the simplest application of full state feedback, the
closed-loop model looks like this:

$$\dot{x} = Ax + B(d + u_f)$$
$$y = Cx + Dd$$
$$u_f = -Ky \qquad (15.10)$$

The K matrix is a simple matrix of gains. The disturbance is introduced in the d
vector.

   If the regulator does not have all of the states available to it, then a partial
state feedback system exists. In such a case, the control system must estimate
the missing states so that full state feedback techniques may be used. Figure 15.8
shows where the estimator is inserted.

   The underobserved plant is also represented in state-space notation with
Eq. (15.9). However, the C matrix is no longer the identity matrix. In fact, it
is most likely not square, having fewer rows than columns. Now, before the loop
can be closed, the missing states must be estimated so that a full complement
of states may be fed back. Several techniques are available, and they range from
simple to complex. An example of a simple estimator is a numerical differentiator
or integrator to supply a missing velocity or displacement term.

$$\dot{x}_{\text{est}} = \frac{(x_t - x_{t-\Delta t})}{\Delta t} \qquad (15.11)$$

or

$$x_t = x_{t-\Delta t} + \dot{x}_t \Delta t \qquad (15.12)$$

A more complex and robust estimator is the Kalman filter in which the reduced
set of observed states in the y vector is passed through a Kalman filter gain matrix
yielding an estimated plant state vector:

$$x_{\text{est}} = Hy \qquad (15.13)$$

Admitting that the state estimator might require current and past values of the y and
u vectors, let the following symbolic notation describe the function of estimation:

$$x_{\text{est}} = H(y_0, y_{-1}, u_0, u_{-1}) \qquad (15.14)$$

Now, the simple linear regulator can be represented by Eq. (15.15):

$$\dot{x} = Ax + B(d + u_f)$$
$$y = Cx + Dd$$
$$u_f = -KH\left(y_0, y_{-1}, u_0, u_{-1}\right) \tag{15.15}$$

The subscripts on the y and u vectors indicate that the current (0) and past (-1) values might be required.

15.4.2 Control

Regulators drive a plant back toward a set point after a perturbation has upset it. Controllers allow the user to move the set point, overcoming regulation long enough so that the user is not fighting the regulator. [The author is constantly reminded of one of the Wright brothers' many contributions to controlled flight. Contemporaries of the Wrights seemed convinced that the way to make an airplane flyable was to make it unconditionally stable. But this meant that the pilots would constantly struggle against the tendency of the plant to resist perturbation. The Wrights chose to allow the airplane to remain unstable (in lateral dynamics), but controllable.] Many control algorithms exist. Two algorithms that work well are the model-follower and the model-based compensator.

15.4.2.1 Model Follower   A model-follower control system compares the plant behavior to a desired behavior and then calculates the input required to drive the plant toward the desired trajectory. Figure 15.9 illustrates the basic idea.
It is instructive to analyze the model follower in LaPlace space. The following equations are written by inspection:

$$y_m(s) = M(s)u_{\text{pilot}}(s)$$
$$\bar{u}_p(s) = P^{-1}(s)y_m(s)$$
$$u_m(s) = H(s)y_m(s)$$
$$u_p(s) = \bar{u}_p(s) + u_m(s) - u_y(s)$$

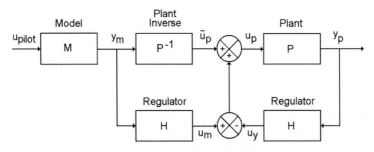

Fig. 15.9   Basic model follower.

$$y_p(s) = P(s)u_p(s)$$

$$u_y(s) = H(s)y_p(s) \tag{15.16}$$

After a few substitution steps, the output as a function of input is seen to be

$$y_p(s) = P(s)\left[P^{-1}(s)M(s)u_{\text{pilot}}(s) + H(s)M(s)u_{\text{pilot}}(s) - H(s)y_p(s)\right] \tag{15.17}$$

One further algebra step reduces this equation to the simple transfer function:

$$\frac{y_p(s)}{u_{\text{pilot}}(s)} = \frac{M(s)}{I} \tag{15.18}$$

The upside of this technique is that the plant follows the model exactly! The downside is that the plant must be known exactly so that the inverse of the plant can be calculated. Full state observation is assumed.

15.4.2.2 Model-Based Compensator
Sometimes all of the states of the plant cannot be observed. More often than not, the pilot has an insufficient number of controls to control all of the plant states. This does not mean the plant cannot be controlled. But, before control is possible, a control strategy must be devised that assigns a control to a state and estimates unassigned states. A model-based compensator is one such strategy.

Figure 15.10 shows the structure of a model based compensator and how it interfaces with the plant.

The compensator relies on two cleverly constructed gains. The first is the H matrix, which is the Kalman filter gain. Its function is to accept the difference between the observed states generated by the model and the plant and estimate the unobserved states. The vector coming out of the Kalman filter is at the same time an error vector and a perturbation vector for the model. The other gain is the G matrix, which is a linear quadratic regulator (LQR). An LQR is a full state feedback control law designed to drive the acceleration vector of the model to zero. The same control signal sent to the model is also sent to the plant, which drives the plant to follow the model.

Again, there is good news and bad news. In theory, the model can be made to follow a desired state trajectory exactly. However, in order to design a model-based compensator, one must have a good model of the plant.

15.4.2.3 Other Methods
As presented, the preceding methods are not too robust. When the plant changes as a result of changes in airspeed, geometry, etc., the model must be changed as well. In other words, the gains must be scheduled with airspeed, mast angle, and anything else that conventional wisdom holds constant. Scheduling is one means of designing an adaptive control law.

Another method to adapt actually calculates the gains on the fly, pun intended. Dithering the controls and measuring the response is one way in which the plant model can be continuously updated. An interesting technique uses artificial neural networks and the second method of Lyapunov to arrive at a training law for the gains in the network. The network does not attempt to modify handling quality gains.

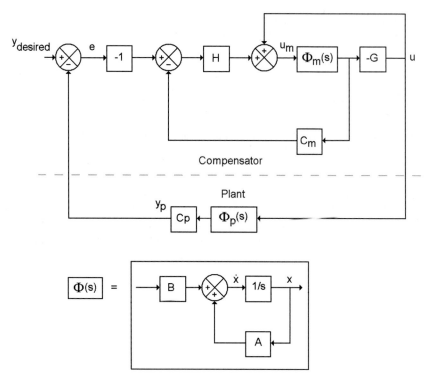

Fig. 15.10   Model-based compensator.

Instead, it attempts to compensate for changes in the plant by adding sufficient extra control input to follow the desires of the basic control law. Rysdyk and Calise [2] describe this technique in detail.

15.5 Conclusions

The chapter explored the intricacies of the control system, presenting fundamental issues in rigging for single main rotor and tandem helicopters, as well as the special washout functions for tiltrotors and tiltwing aircraft by extension. The path from pilot input through additional commands from the SCAS and past the actuator commands and phasing concerns was illuminated. Elastic deflections of the fuselage and rotor masts create unwanted inputs; this chapter discussed these concerns as well. Finally, two popular architectures for a SCAS were presented.

References

[1] Blakelock, J. H., *Automatic Control of Aircraft and Missiles*, Wiley, New York, 1965, pp. 56–106, 137–182, 199–221.

[2]Rysdyk, Rolf, T., and Calise, Anthony, J., "*Adaptive Model Inversion Flight Control for Tiltrotor Aircraft*," Presented at the 54th Annual Forum of the American Helicopter Society, May 1998.

Problems

15.1   Name two methods to achieve yaw moment (heading control) when flying a *tiltrotor* in airplane mode. Name two methods to achieve yaw moment (heading control) when flying a *tiltwing* in helicopter mode.

15.2   Suppose the rudder stops working on a tiltrotor aircraft while flying in airplane mode. Describe how you would detect the failure, and then how you could reconfigure the control laws to regain control. That is, how would you switch from a rudder-based strategy to an xxxxxx-based strategy?

16.1 Introduction

"The second greatest thrill known to mankind is flying. The first is landing" (anonymous). (One cannot invoke that axiom without recalling the equally obvious aviator's rule-of-thumb: "It is far better to be down here wishing you were up there than to be up there wishing you were down here." Either rule reminds the reader that aviation is a contest between gravity and the aircraft, and gravity always wins.) This axiom underscores the point that flying almost always begins and ends on the ground, where the definition of ground is used with some poetic license. Ground can mean literally terra firma, or it can refer to a reference plane in the gravity potential upon which the aircraft takes off and/or lands. Thus, landing pads on tall buildings, ships at sea, the sea itself, and air launches from other aircraft can all serve as ground. For the sake of clarity, ground will mean terra firma unless otherwise specified.

The landing gear supports an aircraft on the ground. Landing gear are usually wheels or skids. (As with any alleged definitive statement, exceptions always arise. Skis, pontoons, and floats are also landing gear. With some imagination, all three are skids.) Wheeled gears attach to simple flexible beams or more complicated spring-damper compressible struts. The wheels can swivel freely as a castor, or they can be actively steered by the pilot, or their spinning axes can be fixed in position, sans any deformation. The wheels can have brakes. The wheels are subject to sliding, rolling, and static friction, and must be able to support fore/aft, lateral, and normal forces. The gear can also be retractable. A V-22 is shown in Fig. 16.1 with wheeled landing gear extended. The nose wheel can be steered; the main gear have fixed-direction spinning axes.

Skid gear are stiff hollow tubes that run parallel with the longitudinal axis of the aircraft, usually with the front end bent slightly up. The tubes are attached to two arching cross-tube members, which are also stiff hollow tubes. The arching members are attached to the bottom of the aircraft, usually with some elastic isolation such as rubber mounts. Floatation devices can be attached to the skids for those aircraft that travel over the water regularly. Figure 16.2 shows a helicopter with skid gear and floats that can be opened very rapidly against the advent of an emergency landing on water.

Fig. 16.1   Bell-Boeing V-22 with landing gear extended. (Courtesy of Bell Helicopter Textron, Inc.)

Fig. 16.2   Bell Helicopter Textron model 412 with floats attached to skid gear. (Courtesy of Bell Helicopter Textron, Inc.)

16.2   Illustrative Linear Model

Most aspects of a landing-gear model are nonlinear. For this reason, a linear model is insufficient for even the simplest of flight simulators. Nevertheless, a

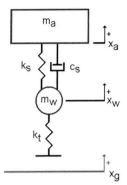

Fig. 16.3   Simple gear model.

simple linear model illustrates basic considerations and provides some insights for the nonlinear problems to come.

Examine Fig. 16.3, which shows a mass representing an aircraft m_a and a mass representing a wheel m_w, connected by a linear spring and a dashpot. The bottom of the wheel also has a spring that represents the tire stiffness and that might or might not be in contact with the ground. The displacement of the wheel (axle) is called x_w, that of the aircraft center of gravity is called x_a, and the ground plane is called x_g. The reader can write the linear equations of motion by inspection:

$$m_a\ddot{x}_a + c_s(\dot{x}_a - \dot{x}_w) + k_s(x_a - x_w) = -m_a g$$
$$m_w\ddot{x}_w + c_s(\dot{x}_w - \dot{x}_a) + k_s(x_w - x_a) + k_t(x_w - x_g) = -m_w g \qquad (16.1)$$

This linear model works well for analyzing the stability of the system, but several details are problematic. Some simple nonlinear devices improve significantly the realism of the model.

First, the tire stiffness term opposes compression, which is good, but it also glues the tire to the ground, which means the aircraft could never take off. This problem is corrected by introducing a nonlinearity that describes the force the tire applies to the axle.

$$F_{\text{tire}} = \begin{cases} -k_t(x_w - R_{\text{tire}} - x_g), & x_g > x_w - R_{\text{tire}} \\ 0, & x_g \leq x_w - R_{\text{tire}} \end{cases} \qquad (16.2)$$

The term R_{tire}, which represents the radius of the tire, appears so that the ground contact test is conducted with the bottom of the tire, not the axle.

Second, note that the ground plane is not always flat or static. For instance, landing on a ship at sea introduces inclined planes and ground motion, landing on the edge of a building means the ground plane could suddenly vanish during a taxi operation, and sliding sideways into a curbstone can lead to dynamic rollover. The model admits such variability by introducing the variable x_g, which can be time dependent.

Third, because strut forces are usually given as a function of stroke and stroke rate, modelers sometimes use the compression of the strut as the second degree of freedom and then define the position of the wheel from the strut. For instance, let the strut compression variable be s, and let it have a value of zero when the strut is extended to its full length of L_{fe}. The wheel states are now defined by the following expressions:

$$x_w = x_a + s - L_{fe}$$

$$\dot{x}_w = \dot{x}_a + \dot{s}$$

$$\ddot{x}_w = \ddot{x}_a + \ddot{s} \tag{16.3}$$

Making these substitutions, the tire force is expressed in the alternate form:

$$F_{tire} = \begin{cases} -k_t(x_a - L_{fe} + s - R_{tire} - x_g), & x_g > x_a - L_{fe} + s - R_{tire} \\ 0, & x_g \le x_a - L_{fe} + s - R_{tire} \end{cases} \tag{16.4}$$

Fourth, the spring term must include the presence of a preload, and the stroke must be limited in travel. In addition, the damper coefficient changes magnitude depending on whether the strut is compressing or extending. The following expressions provide an improved representation of the forces.

$$F_{strut} = \begin{cases} F_{damper} + F_{spring}, & F_{tire} \ge F_0 \\ F_{tire}, & F_{tire} < F_0 \end{cases}$$

$$F_{damper} = \begin{cases} c_{sc}\dot{s}, & \dot{s} > 0 \\ c_{se}\dot{s}, & \dot{s} \le 0 \end{cases}$$

$$F_{spring} = \begin{cases} k_s L_{fe} + F_0, & s > L_{fe} \\ k_s s + F_0, & L_{fe} \ge s > 0 \\ F_0, & s \le 0 \end{cases} \tag{16.5}$$

The damping term has two coefficients, with the compression coefficient being greater than the extension coefficient. This means the strut can resist compressive rates but extend rapidly in preparation for the next compressive stroke. The preload F_0 has the effect of making the strut appear like a rigid link up to the point where the force applied across the endpoints of the strut exceeds the preload. Then the strut behaves like a spring. If one uses the forces so described in lieu of expanding the constitutive equations, the differential equations of motion become those shown next:

$$m_a \ddot{x}_a = F_{strut} - m_a g$$

$$m_w \ddot{x}_w = F_{tire} - F_{strut} - m_w g \tag{16.6}$$

Strut acceleration can replace the wheel acceleration after some algebra. The
alternate equations of motion are expressed in Eqs. (16.7):

$$\ddot{x}_a = \frac{F_{\text{strut}}}{m_a} - g$$

$$\ddot{s} = \frac{F_{\text{tire}}}{m_w} - \left(1 + \frac{m_w}{m_a}\right)\frac{F_{\text{strut}}}{m_w} \qquad (16.7)$$

(The solution to either set of equations yields the same results of course. Physics is
independent of the keyhole through which one looks.) The ratio m_w/m_a is usually
so small that it can be ignored without consequence.

One last detail addresses the motion limits of the strut. When the strut is fully
extended or when it is fully compressed, the stroke rate must go to zero, but
only if the applied force is in the direction that would cause the motion to exceed
limits. Two popular methods drive the stroke rate to zero and ensure the stroke
stays bounded. The first method simply detects the approach of the limit and sets
the stroke rate to zero, but only if the applied force were to cause the derivative
to continue in the direction of the limit. The logic tests are straightforward, but
inelegant. The second method uses the concept of servo control, multiplying the
error between the stroke and the limit by a high gain, and subtracting the product
from the current stroke rate. This has the effect of driving the strut into a stiff, one-
way spring at the limits. The logic tests are simple, and this method will admit other
sophistication if required. The downside of this method is that the stroke will exceed
the limits by minute amounts for a frame or two. In the simple demonstration code
associated with this chapter, the second method is employed. The actual code is

$$\dot{s}_{\text{use}} = \begin{cases} \dot{s}_{\text{act}} - G(s - L_{\text{fe}}), & s > L_{\text{fe}} \\ \dot{s}_{\text{act}}, & L_{\text{fe}} \geq s > 0 \\ \dot{s}_{\text{act}} - Gs & s \leq 0 \end{cases}$$

$$s = s + \int_0^{\Delta t} \dot{s}_{\text{use}}\, dt \qquad (16.8)$$

A sample subroutine, written in BASIC and found at the end of this chapter,
shows one way to implement this procedure. A demonstration program called
LANDGRS5.EXE uses this subroutine. The program has several graphic windows
and a text box. The graphic window on the left shows a square fuselage attached
to a wheel/tire with a strut. The strut has preload, a linear spring, and a damper
that changes value depending on whether the strut is compressing or extending.
The wheel/tire is a simple spring that generates force only when the wheel is
compressed. The other graphic windows present several time histories that include
the height of the bottom of the fuselage, the tire height less the tire radius, and
several force components. The simulation runs for 0.8 s of problem time and begins
with the aircraft held above the ground and then dropped. Notice the final solution
in the text box, which shows that the tire force and the strut force are not equal. This
is because the tire must support the mass of the wheel and aircraft, but the strut only
needs to support the mass of the aircraft. Three command buttons are available. The
button labeled "Linear (Za, s)" executes Eqs. (16.6), while the "Linear (Za, Zw)"

button uses Eqs. (16.7). Another section toward the end of this chapter describes the "Non-Linear (Za, s)" button.

The remainder of this chapter will present fundamental concepts of modeling strut and skid gear, though the emphasis will be on struts. Because the loads that the landing gear generates depend on the relative orientation of the aircraft and the ground plane, a rigorous mathematical definition of several axis systems is paramount. This text, quite literally, develops a basic landing-gear model from the ground up. This is a complex subject worthy of an entire text. Currey [1] presents an excellent description on the principles of landing-gear design.

16.3 Ground Model

The ground model begins with the definition of the datum. The datum is a plane that is tangent to a perfectly smooth, spherical Earth and locally normal to the gravity vector, which is assumed to act toward the center of the Earth. The datum is this plane from which all elevations are measured; it might be mean sea level or some other agreed-upon elevation. The elevation of the datum above the center of the Earth remains constant throughout the analysis. The interchangeable subscripts d or e will identify reference to the datum.

The ground plane is the actual surface of the Earth. The ground (plane) is assumed to be stationary. This restriction relaxes when shipboard operations are explored. The ground can be a smooth, vast plane, or it can be fractal surface with many changes in slope. A longitude and a latitude locate a radial spike that extends outward from the center of the Earth. The longitude and latitude provide two coordinates: local elevation of the ground plane is the third and is a function of the first two. The slope of the ground plane at a given location is also important. Slopes are measured relative to the datum plane. The subscript g will identify reference to the ground plane or surface tangent. Figure 16.4 shows the basic elements of describing the ground for landing-gear problems.

16.3.1 Surface Normal

The elevation, the north-south slope, and the east-west slope describe the ground plane or surface tangent completely. It is not necessary to describe the slope with angles, though that is sometimes the case. A surface normal is sufficient and might be easier to work with. The normal is found easily with the cross product of two vectors that are constructed readily. Given the north and east locations of the point of interest, determine the height of the ground plane above the datum. The triple of north, east, and height above the datum is a point on the actual surface of the Earth. This point, called P_0, is the reference point in the ground plane. Now, move one unit to the north and obtain the height above the datum at this new location. Call this new point P_1. Return to P_0 and then move one unit east and get the height above the datum there. Call this point P_2. Each of the points is a three-dimensional vector, arranged thus:

$$P = \left\{ \begin{array}{c} P_{\text{North}} \\ P_{\text{East}} \\ -(P_{\text{Height}} - P_{\text{Datum}}) \end{array} \right\} \tag{16.9}$$

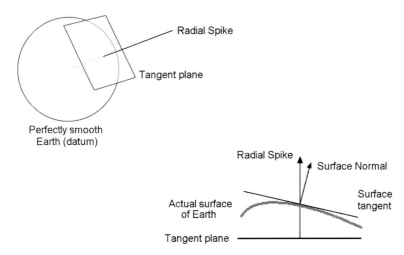

Fig. 16.4 Basic elements of ground description.

Note: The datum and height values are usually given as positive numbers. Expression (16.9) introduces a negative sign in front of the height above the datum so that this triple is in accordance with the right-hand rule and the north-east-down sequence.

To find the normal to the ground plane at P_0, calculate the cross product of the vector $(P_1 - P_0)$ with the vector $(P_2 - P_0)$, and normalize the result for unit magnitude. That is, the normal vector is

$$P_n = \{P_1 - P_0\} \times \{P_2 - P_0\} \tag{16.10}$$

and the *outward unit* normal is

$$n_g = -\frac{P_n}{\|P_n\|} \tag{16.11}$$

Note: The order of the cross product is important. As just shown, the cross product generates a normal that points toward the center of the Earth. The negative sign in expression (16.11) makes the unit vector an outward normal. Because friction forces depend on an accurate accounting of normal forces, calculation of the surface normal, although simple, is profoundly important to a good landing-gear model.

A two-axis rotation matrix is another method to describe the ground surface orientation. Attach an axis system to the ground so that the x axis is parallel to the local line of longitude, the y axis is parallel to the local line of latitude, and the z axis points toward the center of the Earth. Now, rotate those axes about the y axis first through some angle θ_g and then about the new x axis through some angle ϕ_g. The resulting Euler rotation matrix is

$$T_{g-e} = R_x(\phi_g)R_y(\theta_g) = \begin{bmatrix} C_{\theta_g} & 0 & -S_{\theta_g} \\ S_{\phi_g}S_{\theta_g} & C_{\phi_g} & S_{\phi_g}C_{\theta_g} \\ C_{\phi_g}S_{\theta_g} & -S_{\phi_g} & C_{\phi_g}C_{\theta_g} \end{bmatrix}$$

The by-now familiar shorthand for trigonometric functions has been employed. This matrix can be generated from the unit vectors. The transpose of this matrix rotates a vector expressed in the sloped plane back to the tangent plane aforementioned. This means that the following associations hold:

$$n_{g,x} = -C_{\phi_g} S_{\theta_g}$$
$$n_{g,y} = S_{\phi_g}$$
$$n_{g,z} = -C_{\phi_g} C_{\theta_g}$$
$$\theta_g = \arctan(n_{g,x}/n_{g,z}) \tag{16.12}$$

and

$$C_{\phi_g} = \sqrt{1 - n_{g,y}^2}$$

The preceding associations are sufficient to define all elements of the T_{g-e} matrix. (The decision to use roll and pitch angles was not arbitrary. Because a rotorcraft simulation is unlikely to require an inverted landing attitude, roll and pitch angles will always be less than 180 deg in absolute value. This avoids a sign ambiguity that would appear if roll and yaw or pitch and yaw had been used. Such an ambiguity leads to curious behavior, for example, dropped balls bouncing uphill!) This matrix will be used when the ground reaction loads are resolved to body axes.

16.3.2 Minimum Distance to a Plane

Another important calculation determines the minimum distance from a point above the ground plane to the ground plane. References [2] and [3] develop the necessary relationships from first principles. The standard equation of a plane in three-dimensional space is

$$Ax + By + Cz + D = 0 \tag{16.13}$$

Given three noncollinear points, the coefficients in expression (16.13) are found from the following determinants:

$$A = \begin{vmatrix} 1 & y1 & z1 \\ 1 & y2 & z2 \\ 1 & y3 & z3 \end{vmatrix}, \quad B = \begin{vmatrix} x1 & 1 & z1 \\ x2 & 1 & z2 \\ x3 & 1 & z3 \end{vmatrix}, \quad C = \begin{vmatrix} x1 & y1 & 1 \\ x2 & y2 & 1 \\ x3 & y3 & 1 \end{vmatrix},$$

$$D = - \begin{vmatrix} x1 & y1 & z1 \\ x2 & y2 & z2 \\ x3 & y3 & z3 \end{vmatrix} \tag{16.14}$$

If the point P_0 is known to lie in the plane, and the normal to the plane is already known, then the preceding definitions simplify. [This will usually be the case. The available ground model reports the elevation and surface normal as functions of the north and east coordinates, or the surface normal can be constructed at the point named by the north and east coordinates and the associated height using Eqs. (16.9–16.11)].

$$A = n_{g,x}, \quad B = n_{g,y}, \quad C = n_{g,z}, \quad D = -n_g^T P_0 \tag{16.15}$$

The following expression calculates the minimum distance from any point P not on the plane to the plane.

$$d = \left(\{A, \quad B, \quad C\} \cdot P + D\right) / \sqrt{A^2 + B^2 + C^2}$$

or

$$d = \left[n_g^T (P - P_0) \right] \tag{16.16}$$

The point in the plane P_p, coincident with the surface normal that penetrates P, is given by

$$P_p = P - n_g \cdot d \tag{16.17}$$

This result is particularly useful when defining a point in the ground plane that is not the reference point. In that case, $d = 0$, and Eq. (16.16) is written:

$$n_g^T P_g - n_g^T P_0 = 0$$

or

$$n_{g,x} x_g + n_{g,y} y_g + n_{g,z} z_g - n_g^T P_0 = 0 \tag{16.18}$$

where the three coordinates of the ground plane are collected into the vector

$$P_g = \begin{Bmatrix} x_g \\ y_g \\ z_g \end{Bmatrix}$$

Given the x_g and y_g position over the datum, the z_g position on the ground plane is found:

$$z_g = -n_{g,z}^{-1}(-n_g^T P_0 + n_{g,x} x_g + n_{g,y} y_g) \tag{16.19}$$

This result will be used directly in the calculation of the distance and closing rate between the tire and the ground plane.

16.3.3 Contact Point Location

No matter what type of landing gear is modeled, the distance and closing speed between the gear and the ground are required for accurate gear load calculations. The surface of the ground might have a slope, and the aircraft might have an arbitrary angular orientation with respect to the Earth. Through some simple, yet rigorous axis system manipulations, the location of the contact point on the ground and on the wheel or skid is easily found.

Let the location of the aircraft center of gravity with respect to the station-line, butt-line, and water-line axis system be

$$P_{cg-0|0} = \left\{ \begin{matrix} SL \\ BL \\ WL \end{matrix} \right\}_{cg} \tag{16.20}$$

Subscript 0 refers to the reference axes for the station-line, butt-line, and water-line axis system.

Let the location of an axle on a fully extended strut or point on the skid with respect to the same axis system be

$$P_{ax0-0|0} = \left\{ \begin{matrix} SL \\ BL \\ WL \end{matrix} \right\}_{ax} \tag{16.21}$$

These position vectors must be resolved to the body axes, subscript b, which has the z axis pointing down and the x axis pointing forward. This is accomplished with a rotation of 180 deg about the y axis.

$$P_{cg-0|b} = R_y(\pi)P_{cg-0|0}$$

$$P_{ax0-0|b} = R_y(\pi)P_{ax0-0|0} \tag{16.22}$$

From this, the position vector pointing to the axle from the center of gravity, resolved to the body axes, is

$$P_{ax0-cg|b} = P_{ax0-0|b} - P_{cg-0|b} \tag{16.23}$$

The axle is attached to a strut. Let the "moving" end of the fully extended strut (the end at or nearest to the axle) have the position vector $S_{ax0-cg|b}$. The instantaneous position vector $S_{ax-cg|b}$ defines the position of the strut with arbitrary strut deformation. The difference between the two vectors describes the deformation or compression: $S_{cg|b} = S_{ax0-cg|b} - S_{ax-cg|b}$. Therefore, when the strut has some compression, the instantaneous value of the axle position is

$$P_{ax-cg|b} = P_{ax0-cg|b} - S_{cg|b} \tag{16.24}$$

For clarity, shorten the name $S_{cg|b}$ to S, which has elements

$$S = \left\{ \begin{matrix} s_x \\ s_y \\ s_z \end{matrix} \right\}$$

and which represents the compression of the strut in three dimensions with respect to the center of gravity, resolved to body axes. When the strut is parallel to the body z axis, this vector is simply

$$S = \begin{Bmatrix} 0 \\ 0 \\ s \end{Bmatrix}$$

and the stroke is limited to the range $0 < s \le L_{fe}$.

Because the aircraft is situated with arbitrary angular orientation at some point above the datum, the position of the axle with respect to the ground plane, resolved to the Earth, is

$$P_{ax-g|e} = T_{be}^T P_{ax-cg|b} + P_{cg-g|e} \qquad (16.25)$$

The transformation matrix $T_{be} = R_x(\phi)R_y(\theta)R_z(\psi)$ rotates vectors from Earth (datum) to body axes. In the preceding expression, the transpose of T_{be} rotates the axle position from body axes to Earth axes. The additional position vector places the center of gravity above the datum. That is,

$$P_{cg-g|e} = \begin{Bmatrix} North_e \\ East_e \\ Down_e \end{Bmatrix} - \begin{Bmatrix} 0 \\ 0 \\ P_{0,z} \end{Bmatrix} \qquad (16.26)$$

At this point, assume that the landing gear is the wheeled type and that the tire is a wafer-thin disk mounted normal to the axle, which is itself assumed parallel to the body y axis. This assumption is not too restrictive and certainly is at the same level of texture as the rest of the model. The necessary changes to accommodate a skid gear will be described after this development. Refer to Fig. 16.5, which shows a wheel near the ground plane.

The position of any point on the circumference of the tire is

$$P_{t-cg|b} = P_{ax-cg|b} + T_y^T(\tau)L_T \qquad (16.27)$$

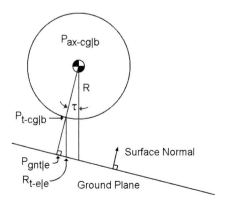

Fig. 16.5 Wheel near a ground plane.

where L_T introduces the tire radius, that is,

$$L_T = \begin{Bmatrix} 0 \\ 0 \\ R \end{Bmatrix}$$

The angle τ measures around the axle. When $\tau = 0$, a ray starting at the axle points in the direction of the positive body z axis. Resolve this position vector to Earth axes:

$$\boldsymbol{P}_{t-\text{cg}|e} = T_{be}^T \left[\boldsymbol{P}_{\text{ax}-\text{cg}|b} + T_y^T(\tau)L_T \right] = T_{be}^T \boldsymbol{P}_{t-\text{cg}|b} \qquad (16.28)$$

The tire point position with respect to the datum is

$$\boldsymbol{P}_{t-g|e} = T_{be}^T \left[\boldsymbol{P}_{\text{ax}-\text{cg}|b} + T_y^T(\tau)L_T \right] + \boldsymbol{P}_{\text{cg}-g|e} = T_{be}^T \boldsymbol{P}_{t-\text{cg}|b} + \boldsymbol{P}_{\text{cg}-g|e} \quad (16.29)$$

Given the tire point position over the ground plane, the point on the ground plane directly beneath the tire point is found using expression (16.19):

$$\boldsymbol{R}_{t-g|e} = \begin{Bmatrix} P_{t-g|e,x} \\ P_{t-g|e,y} \\ -n_{g,z}^{-1}(-n^T P_0 + n_{g,x} P_{t-g|e,x} + n_{g,y} P_{t-g|e,y}) \end{Bmatrix} \qquad (16.30)$$

The distance between $P_{t-g|e}$ and $R_{t-g|e}$ is

$$d_t = \boldsymbol{n}_g^T(\boldsymbol{P}_{t-g|e} - \boldsymbol{R}_{t-g|e}) = n_{g,x} P_{t-g|e,x} + n_{g,y} P_{t-g|e,y} + n_{g,z} P_{t-g|e,z} - \boldsymbol{n}_g^T P_0$$
$$(16.31)$$

The closest part of the tire to the ground plane is found by differentiating d_t with respect to τ, setting the result to zero, and solving for τ:

$$\frac{\partial d_t}{\partial \tau} = 0 = \boldsymbol{n}_g^T \left\{ \frac{\partial \boldsymbol{P}_{t-g|e}}{\partial \tau} - \frac{\partial \boldsymbol{R}_{t-g|e}}{\partial \tau} \right\}$$

At this point, the arithmetic is straightforward, though it is a bit messy. The result is

$$\frac{\partial d_t}{\partial \tau} = 0 = n_{g,x}(T_{11}C_\tau - T_{31}S_\tau) + n_{g,y}(T_{12}C_\tau - T_{32}S_\tau) + n_{g,z}(T_{13}C_\tau - T_{33}S_\tau)$$
$$(16.32)$$

The shorthand notations $T_{11} = T_{be}(1,1)$, $C_\tau = \cos(\tau)$, etc. reduce clutter. Solve for τ, and call the result τ^* to indicate that this is the angle that corresponds to the minimum vertical distance:

$$\tau^* = \tan^{-1}\left[\frac{n_{g,x}T_{11} + n_{g,y}T_{12} + n_{g,z}T_{13}}{n_{g,x}T_{31} + n_{g,y}T_{32} + n_{g,z}T_{33}} \right] \qquad (16.33)$$

With τ^* known, the point on the tire with respect to the Earth, resolved to Earth axes, is

$$P_{t-g|e} = T_{be}^T[P_{ax-cg|b} + T_y^T(\tau^*)L_T] + P_{cg-g|e} \qquad (16.34)$$

From this, the point on Earth directly beneath this point is found from expression (16.30). The vertical distance is found from expression (16.31). The line that is normal to the ground plane and passes through the tire point above also passes through the ground plane. Those coordinates are

$$P_{gnt|e} = P_{t-g|e} - \mathbf{n} \cdot d_t \qquad (16.35)$$

If the landing gear is the skid type, the calculations involving τ are not required. The position vector describing the location of a point on the skid is needed. Let the axle position be the bottom of the skid at the desired station line and butt line. Then,

$$P_{s-g|e} = T_{be}^T P_{ax-cg|b} + P_{cg-g|e} \qquad (16.36)$$

The subscript s (for skid) distinguishes this expression from the subscript t (for tire) expression derived earlier. The point on the Earth directly beneath this point is

$$R_{s-g|e} = \left\{ \begin{array}{c} P_{s-g|e,x} \\ P_{s-g|e,y} \\ -n_{g,z}^{-1}(-n_g^T P_0 + n_{g,x}P_{s-g|e,x} + n_{g,y}P_{s-g|e,y}) \end{array} \right\} \qquad (16.37)$$

The vertical distance is

$$d_s = n_{g,x}P_{s-g|e,x} + n_{g,y}P_{s-g|e,y} + n_{g,z}P_{s-g|e,z} - n_g^T P_0 \qquad (16.38)$$

The point on the ground normal to the ground plane and passing through the skid point is simply

$$P_{gns|e} = P_{s-g|e} - \mathbf{n} \cdot d_s \qquad (16.39)$$

16.3.4 Closing Velocity at Contact Point

Damping forces in the strut are velocity dependent; find the velocity of the tire or axle normal to the ground plane by differentiating d_t or d_s with respect to time:

$$\frac{d(d_t)}{dt} = n_{g,x}\frac{d}{dt}P_{t-g|e,x} + n_{g,y}\frac{d}{dt}P_{t-g|e,y} + n_{g,z}\frac{d}{dt}P_{t-g|e,z} \qquad (16.40)$$

The time derivative of $P_{t-e|e}$ is

$$\dot{P}_{t-g|e} = T_{be}^T[\dot{P}_{ax-cg|b} + \dot{T}_y^T(\tau^*)L_T + \omega_b \times (P_{ax-cg|b} + T_y^T(\tau^*)L_T)] + \dot{P}_{cg-g|e} \qquad (16.41)$$

The derivative of $P_{cg-g|e}$ is

$$\dot{P}_{cg-g|e} = \begin{Bmatrix} \dot{N} \\ \dot{E} \\ \dot{D} \end{Bmatrix} = \begin{Bmatrix} u_g \\ v_g \\ w_g \end{Bmatrix} \tag{16.42}$$

The influence of $\dot{T}_y^T(\tau^*)$ is small; neglect it. The time derivative of the axle position is

$$\dot{P}_{ax-cg|b} = - \begin{Bmatrix} \dot{s}_x \\ \dot{s}_y \\ \dot{s}_z \end{Bmatrix} \tag{16.43}$$

Therefore, the desired velocity is

$$\dot{P}_{t-g|e} = \begin{Bmatrix} \dot{N} \\ \dot{E} \\ \dot{D} \end{Bmatrix} + T_{be}^T \left[\omega_b \times P_{t-cg|b} - \begin{Bmatrix} \dot{s}_x \\ \dot{s}_y \\ \dot{s}_z \end{Bmatrix} \right] \tag{16.44}$$

An analogous expression is readily written for skid gear:

$$\dot{P}_{s-g|e} = \begin{Bmatrix} \dot{N} \\ \dot{E} \\ \dot{D} \end{Bmatrix} + T_{be}^T \left[\omega_b \times P_{ax-cg|b} - \begin{Bmatrix} \dot{s}_x \\ \dot{s}_y \\ \dot{s}_z \end{Bmatrix} \right] \tag{16.45}$$

16.4 Strut Models

In the preceding section, the strut displacement vector was defined generally in three-dimensional space. Struts that are parallel to the body z axis are perhaps the most common, but some aircraft employ angled bracing. In this section, both *z-aligned* and *angle-braced* struts are examined.

16.4.1 Z-Aligned Strut

Figure 16.6 shows a stylized wheel, z-aligned strut and the aircraft center of gravity relative to the ground plane just at the moment of touchdown (A) and after the strut has compressed (B). The same situations are presented in (C) and (D), but now the displacements of interest are highlighted.

In general, the location of the axle is the important parameter. Because the landing gear transmits forces to the aircraft center of gravity, it makes sense to describe the location of the axle relative to body axes and resolve the answer to body axes. As before, the vector $P_{ax0-cg|b}$ represents the position of the axle at the end of the fully extended strut relative to the aircraft center of gravity. $P_{ax0-cg|b}$ is resolved to body axes.

$$P_{ax0-cg|b} = \begin{Bmatrix} x_a \\ y_a \\ z_a \end{Bmatrix}_0 \tag{16.46}$$

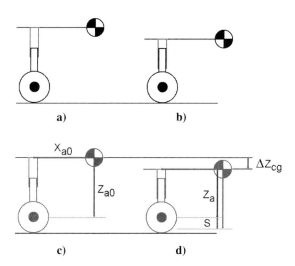

Fig. 16.6   Strut geometry and important displacements.

As the aircraft settles and the landing gear begins to take more of the aircraft weight, the strut compresses. A new vector $\boldsymbol{P}_{ax-cg|b}$ describes the actual position of the axle relative to the center of gravity. Call the difference between $\boldsymbol{P}_{ax0-cg|b}$ and $\boldsymbol{P}_{ax-cg|b}$ the strut deformation vector $\boldsymbol{\Delta P}_a$.

$$\Delta \boldsymbol{P}_{ax} = \boldsymbol{P}_{ax0-cg|b} - \boldsymbol{P}_{ax-cg|b} \qquad (16.47)$$

By convention, a positive stroke compresses the strut. For the strut shown in Fig. 16.6d, the only nonzero element in $\Delta \boldsymbol{P}_a$ is the z-direction displacement, so that

$$s = (P_0 - P)_{ax-cg|b,z} \qquad (16.48)$$

Other gear configurations, such as the angle-braced struts, produce nonzero x and y values as well. An excursion into slightly more complex geometry is instructive and is considered next.

16.4.2   Angle-Braced Strut

   A stylized rendition of an angled strut is pictured in Fig. 16.7. A port-side strut is viewed from behind.
   The position vectors from the center of gravity to hinge points 1 and 2 are fixed. The length and geometry of the support bar 1-3-a is fixed. (The subscript 0 is used in lieu of cg to make the development that follows look less cluttered.) Therefore,

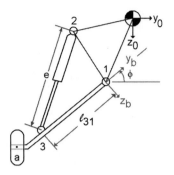

Fig. 16.7   Stylized angled strut.

the following vectors are known:

$$P_{1-0|0} = \begin{Bmatrix} x_{10} \\ y_{10} \\ z_{10} \end{Bmatrix}, \quad P_{2-0|0} = \begin{Bmatrix} x_{20} \\ y_{20} \\ z_{20} \end{Bmatrix}, \quad P_{2-1|0} = \begin{Bmatrix} x_{21} \\ y_{21} \\ z_{21} \end{Bmatrix},$$

$$L_{31|b} = \begin{Bmatrix} 0 \\ -l_{31} \\ 0 \end{Bmatrix}, \quad L_{a3|b} = \begin{Bmatrix} x_{a3} \\ y_{a3} \\ z_{a3} \end{Bmatrix}$$

The notation on vectors $L_{31|b}$ and $L_{a3|b}$ indicates that the measurements are resolved to the b axes; hence the negative sign before l_{31} in the definition of $L_{31|b}$. For a given angle ϕ, vector $P_{3-1|0} = R_x^T(\phi)L_{31|b}$; $R_x(\phi)$ is the rotation matrix about the x axis. Note: Because $L_{31|b}$ is expressed in the bar axes (subscript b) but the desired position vector $P_{3-1|0}$ is resolved to body axes (subscript 0 in this case), the transpose of the $R_x(\phi)$ matrix is used. Also, as seen in Fig. 16.7, the rotation angle ϕ has a negative value. When the unloaded strut extends fully, the position angle has the value ϕ_0, and the fully extended position vector is

$$P_{3-1|0}^0 = R_x^T(\phi_0)L_{31|b} \tag{16.49}$$

The strut deflection is of primary interest because the flexibility and damping are functions of strut deflection and rate. The fully extended strut position, relative to point 2, resolved to point 0 is

$$P_{3-2|0}^0 = P_{3-1|0}^0 - P_{2-1|0} \tag{16.50}$$

and at any position angle is

$$P_{3-2|0} = P_{3-1|0} - P_{2-1|0} \tag{16.51}$$

The location of the axle (point a) at any position angle is

$$P_{a-0|0} = P_{a-3|0} - P_{1-3|0} + P_{1-0|0} = P_{a-3|0} + P_{3-1|0} + P_{1-0|0}$$

or

$$P_{a-0|0} = R_x^T(\phi)\left[L_{a3|b} + L_{31|b}\right] + P_{1-0|0} \tag{16.52}$$

Note that reversing the subscripts on $P_{1-3|0}$ to read $P_{3-1|0}$ changes the subtraction originally indicated to addition in agreement with the vector addition rules discussed in a precceding chapter. The length of the fully extended strut, and the strut at any position angle, are respectively given by

$$e_0 = \sqrt{\left(P_{3-2|0}^0\right)^T \left(P_{3-2|0}^0\right)} \tag{16.53}$$

and

$$e = \sqrt{\left(P_{3-2|0}\right)^T \left(P_{3-2|0}\right)} \tag{16.54}$$

The difference between e_0 and e is called the stroke, and by convention a positive stroke compresses the strut:

$$s = e_0 - e \tag{16.55}$$

Substitute the expressions for $P_{3-1|0}^0$ and $P_{3-2|0}^0$ into the expression for the stroke, expand and rearrange. The resulting expression for stroke is

$$s = e_0 - \sqrt{L_{31|b}^T L_{31|b} + P_{2-1|0}^T P_{2-1|0} - 2P_{2-1|0}^T R_x^T(\phi)L_{31|b}} \tag{16.56}$$

Differentiate the preceding expression for stroke rate:

$$\frac{\mathrm{d}s}{\mathrm{d}t} = \dot{s} = \frac{P_{2-1|0}^T}{e}\frac{\mathrm{d}P_{3-1|0}}{\mathrm{d}t} = \frac{P_{2-1|0}^T}{e_0 - s}\frac{\mathrm{d}P_{3-1|0}}{\mathrm{d}t} \tag{16.57}$$

Employing the usual shorthand convention for trigonometric functions, the position vector and rate vector are defined by

$$P_{3-1|0} = R_x^T(\phi)L_{31|b} = -l_{31}\left\{\begin{array}{c} 0 \\ C_\phi \\ -S_\phi \end{array}\right\} \tag{16.58}$$

$$\dot{P}_{3-1|0} = \dot{R}_x^T(\phi)L_{31|b} = -l_{31}\left\{\begin{array}{c} 0 \\ -S_\phi \\ -C_\phi \end{array}\right\}\dot{\phi} \tag{16.59}$$

The preceding derivation requires an intermediate angular position variable. This angle is not always available or convenient to find. The derivative of the angle is equally inconvenient to find. A better derivation does not require the angle explicitly. Begin with expression (16.53), repeated here:

$$P_{a-0|0} = R_x^T(\phi)\left[L_{a3|b} + L_{31|b}\right] + P_{1-0|0}$$

Subtract $P_{1-0|0}$ from both sides to create a new variable called $P_{a-1|0}$, and rename the constant vectors on the right-hand side to $L_{a1|b}$. Thus,

$$P_{a-1|0} = R_x^T(\phi)L_{a1|b} \tag{16.60}$$

From the definition of the rotation matrix, a 2×2 transformation involving only trigonometric functions of the rotation angle relates the y and z components of $P_{a-1|0}$ to their counterparts in $L_{a1|b}$.

$$\left\{ \begin{matrix} P_y \\ P_z \end{matrix} \right\}_{a-1|0} = \begin{bmatrix} C_\phi & -S_\phi \\ S_\phi & C_\phi \end{bmatrix} \left\{ \begin{matrix} L_y \\ L_z \end{matrix} \right\}_{a1|b} \tag{16.61}$$

The notation was simplified slightly for clarity and ease; the meanings of the new terms should be obvious. This expression is easily rearranged to read:

$$\left\{ \begin{matrix} P_y \\ P_z \end{matrix} \right\}_{a-1|0} = \begin{bmatrix} L_y & -L_z \\ L_z & L_y \end{bmatrix}_{a1|b} \left\{ \begin{matrix} C_\phi \\ S_\phi \end{matrix} \right\} \tag{16.62}$$

whence

$$\left\{ \begin{matrix} C_\phi \\ S_\phi \end{matrix} \right\} = \frac{1}{L_y^2 + L_z^2} \begin{bmatrix} L_y & L_z \\ -L_z & L_y \end{bmatrix}_{a1|b} \left\{ \begin{matrix} P_y \\ P_z \end{matrix} \right\}_{a-1|0} \tag{16.63}$$

In other words, the trigonometric functions of the rotation angle are available without the expense of inverse trigonometry. The trigonometric functions associated with the fully extended strut have an obvious definition. The rotation matrix $R_x^T(\phi)$ is constructed easily, the position vectors $P_{3-1|0}$, $P_{3-2|0}$, $P_{3-1|0}^0$, and $P_{3-2|0}^0$ are calculable, and the strut stroke is found using expressions (16.53–16.55).

The strut stroke rate, which is necessary for damping calculations, requires the time derivative of ϕ. A "nice" expression that does not require inverse trigonometry is desired. Begin with expression (16.63), and differentiate with respect to time:

$$\left\{ \begin{matrix} -S_\phi \\ C_\phi \end{matrix} \right\} \dot{\phi} = \frac{1}{L_y^2 + L_z^2} \begin{bmatrix} L_y & L_z \\ -L_z & L_y \end{bmatrix}_{a1|b} \left\{ \begin{matrix} \dot{P}_y \\ \dot{P}_z \end{matrix} \right\}_{a-1|0} \tag{16.64}$$

But,

$$\left\{ \begin{matrix} -S_\phi \\ C_\phi \end{matrix} \right\} = \begin{bmatrix} 0 & -1 \\ 1 & 0 \end{bmatrix} \left\{ \begin{matrix} C_\phi \\ S_\phi \end{matrix} \right\} \tag{16.65}$$

Substitute expression (16.63) into expression (16.65) then substitute that result into expression (16.64) and, solve for $\dot{\phi}$:

$$\dot{\phi} = \frac{P_y \dot{P}_z - P_z \dot{P}_y}{(P_y^2 + P_z^2)} |_{a-1|0} \tag{16.66}$$

With the angular rate known, the value for $\dot{P}_{3-1|0} = \dot{R}_x^T(\phi)L_{31|b} = -l_{31}$

$\begin{Bmatrix} 0 \\ -S_\phi \\ -C_\phi \end{Bmatrix} \dot{\phi}$ and the value for stroke rate is

$$\dot{s} = \frac{P_{2-1|0}^T}{e}\dot{P}_{3-1|0} = \frac{P_{2-1|0}^T}{e_0 - s}\dot{P}_{3-1|0} \qquad (16.67)$$

Finally, expression (16.52) gives the axle location at any strut deflection because the rotation angle is now known.

Example 16.1

Given the geometry shown in Fig. 16.7, where is the point a relative to the aircraft center of gravity, resolved to body axes? How much has the strut compressed, that is, what is the instantaneous stroke value? Let the length of the bar $l_{31} = 3$, the fully extended strut position angle $\phi_0 = -30$ deg, the instantaneous strut position angle $\phi = -15$ deg, and the other fixed position vectors be

$$P_{1-0|0} = \begin{Bmatrix} x_{10} \\ y_{10} \\ z_{10} \end{Bmatrix} = \begin{Bmatrix} -1.0 \\ -1.0 \\ 1.0 \end{Bmatrix}, \quad P_{2-0|0} = \begin{Bmatrix} x_{20} \\ y_{20} \\ z_{20} \end{Bmatrix} = \begin{Bmatrix} -1.0 \\ -1.5 \\ 0.5 \end{Bmatrix},$$

$$L_{a3|b} = \begin{Bmatrix} x_{a3} \\ y_{a3} \\ z_{a3} \end{Bmatrix} = \begin{Bmatrix} 0.0 \\ -0.5 \\ -0.1 \end{Bmatrix}$$

All linear measurements have units of feet.

Answer: First, calculate the fixed position vector:

$$P_{2-1|0} = P_{2-0|0} - P_{1-0|0} = \begin{Bmatrix} 0.0 \\ -0.5 \\ -0.5 \end{Bmatrix}$$

Next, for the fully extended strut position angle, the position vector is

$$P_{3-1|0}^0 = R_x^T(\phi_0)L_{31|b} = \begin{bmatrix} 1 & 0 & 0 \\ 0 & C_{\phi 0} & -S_{\phi 0} \\ 0 & S_{\phi 0} & C_{\phi 0} \end{bmatrix} \begin{Bmatrix} 0 \\ -3 \\ 0 \end{Bmatrix} = \begin{Bmatrix} 0 \\ -2.598 \\ 1.5 \end{Bmatrix}$$

The instantaneous position vector is given by

$$P_{3-1|0} = R_x^T(\phi)L_{31|b} = \begin{bmatrix} 1 & 0 & 0 \\ 0 & C_\phi & -S_\phi \\ 0 & S_\phi & C_\phi \end{bmatrix} \begin{Bmatrix} 0 \\ -3 \\ 0 \end{Bmatrix} = \begin{Bmatrix} 0 \\ -2.8978 \\ 0.7765 \end{Bmatrix}$$

Thus, the position of the axle at the instantaneous strut angle relative to point 1 is

$$P_{a-1|0} = P_{a-3|0} + P_{3-1|0} = R_x^T(\phi)L_{a3|b} + P_{3-1|0}$$

or

$$P_{a-1|0} = \begin{bmatrix} 1 & 0 & 0 \\ 0 & C_\phi & -S_\phi \\ 0 & S_\phi & C_\phi \end{bmatrix} \begin{Bmatrix} 0 \\ -0.5 \\ -0.1 \end{Bmatrix} + \begin{Bmatrix} 0 \\ -2.8978 \\ 0.7765 \end{Bmatrix} = \begin{Bmatrix} 0 \\ -3.4066 \\ 0.8093 \end{Bmatrix}$$

Relative to the center of gravity and resolved to the body axes, the axle is located at

$$P_{a-0|0} = P_{a-1|0} - P_{0-1|0} = P_{a-1|0} + P_{1-0|0} = \begin{Bmatrix} -1.0 \\ -4.4066 \\ 1.8093 \end{Bmatrix}$$

The position of point 3 relative to point 2 when the strut is fully extended is

$$P_{3-2|0}^0 = P_{3-1|0}^0 - P_{2-1|0} = \begin{Bmatrix} 0 \\ -2.598 \\ 1.5 \end{Bmatrix} - \begin{Bmatrix} 0 \\ -0.5 \\ -0.5 \end{Bmatrix} = \begin{Bmatrix} 0 \\ -2.098 \\ 2.0 \end{Bmatrix}$$

This makes the fully extended length

$$e_0 = \sqrt{\left(P_{3-2|0}^0\right)^T \left(P_{3-2|0}^0\right)} = 2.8986 \text{ ft}$$

The instantaneous length is

$$e = \sqrt{\left(P_{3-2|0}\right)^T \left(P_{3-2|0}\right)} = 2.7164 \text{ ft}$$

Therefore, the stroke is

$$s = e_0 - e = 2.8986 - 2.7164 = 0.1822 \text{ ft}$$

The stroke as a function of axle z displacement is illustrated in Fig. 16.8. The author has elected to display z displacement from the fully extended condition and positive up. The sign convention rigor has not been sacrificed; the displayed results come after all of the calculations. The reader should note that in this example the stroke is almost linear with axle displacement, even with angles as great as 30 deg. This is not always the case—the geometry of the example happens to work out this way.

The point of this exercise is that the stroke displacement and rate are knowable from kinematics alone, but the expressions can get messy. The remaining discussion on strut location and geometry will be limited to struts that deflect only in the body-axis z direction.

Strut Kinematics

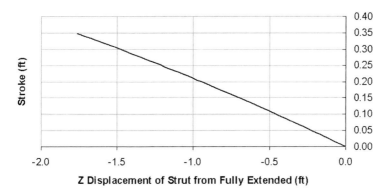

Z Displacement of Strut from Fully Extended (ft)

Fig. 16.8   Relationship of strut stroke with axle displacement for example strut.

16.4.3   Vertical-Displacement-Only Struts

The following Web site teaches that the oleo/pneumatic strut was patented in 1915 as a recoil device for large cannons: http//www.allstar.fiu.edu/aerojava/faq-princ-flight.htm#oleo. Compressed gas such as dry air or nitrogen serves as a spring, and oil forced through a small hole in a piston provides damping. In

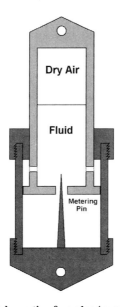

Fig. 16.9   Schematic of an oleo/pneumatic strut.

some cases, a metering pin varies the size of the hole with the amount of compression. Various arrangements of these basic elements have been introduced, but the principle is the same. A schematic of a strut is shown in Fig. 16.9.

Let the lower portion of the strut be driven upward. The upper portion, called the piston, will transmit an upward force equal to some nonlinear function of the strut displacement and strut rate, that is,

$$f_z = F(s, \dot{s}) \tag{16.68}$$

Expression (16.69) is typical of the form that models the spring characteristics:

$$F_{\text{spring}} = \begin{cases} F_0(1 - K_1 s)^{-p}, & s > 0 \\ 0, & s \leq 0 \end{cases} \tag{16.69}$$

Such a model has a preload equal to F_0 and a spring rate given by

$$K_{\text{rate}} = \begin{cases} p K_1 F_0 (1 - K_1 s)^{-(p+1)}, & s > 0 \\ 0, & s \leq 0 \end{cases} \tag{16.70}$$

The exponent p has a value in the range from 1.1 to 1.3. Figure 16.10 shows a typical strut force-stroke curve using this model. Expression (16.71) is one model of strut damping force:

$$F_{\text{damper}} = \frac{D_1 \dot{s} |\dot{s}|}{(D_2 - D_3 s - D_4 s^2)} \tag{16.71}$$

The metering pin makes the damping a function of stroke, so that expression (16.71) generates a family of curves as illustrated in Fig. 16.11. All positive coefficients means that the damping force increases for a given rate as the stroke increases.

The LANDGRS5.EXE program mentioned in the Illustrative Linear Model section shows how the behavior of the pneumatic spring differs from the linear

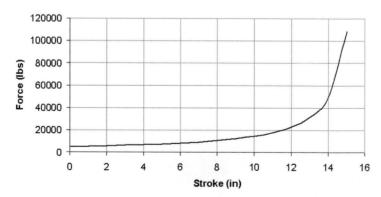

Fig. 16.10   Spring force produced by an oleo strut.

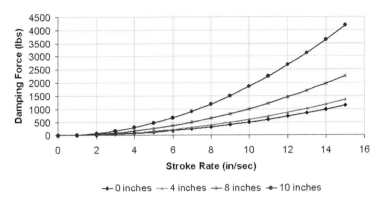

Fig. 16.11   Damping force produced by an oleo strut.

spring. Click on the button labeled "non-linear (Za, s)" to execute the spring model described in this section, then click on either of the other buttons to compare the behavior.

16.5   Wheel and Tire Model

The tire is a rubber bladder that deforms slightly under the weight of the aircraft. The deformation compresses the air inside the tire, creating a pneumatic spring. The rubber itself also adds stiffness. The deformation of the tire causes the contact area between it and the ground to vary. The contact area determines partly the side force and fore/aft force that the tire generates. If the tire is modeled as a torus, then the contact area can be modeled as a spiric section (the intersection of a plane with a torus), which produces an oval-shaped footprint. A second method estimates the contact area assuming a rectangular footprint, some simple geometry, and these assumptions: 1) the tire is circular in cross section, 2) deformation of the tire is small in comparison with its radius, and 3) deformation of the tire is small in comparison with its cross-sectional radius.

Either method gives reasonable results for small deformations, but the second method is less cumbersome mathematically, and so it is developed here. Under the preceding assumptions, the geometry of the undeformed tire is presented in side view and cross section in Fig. 16.12a, and the deformed tire is presented with the same views in Fig. 16.12b.

If the tire flattens by an amount δ when under compression, then from the Pythagorean theorem and Fig. 16.12b,

$$R^2 = h^2 + \left(\frac{c_x}{2}\right)^2 \tag{16.72}$$

But,

$$R = h + \delta \tag{16.73}$$

Substitute expression (16.73) into (16.72), and solve for c_x:

$$c_x = 2D(\bar{\delta}_x - \bar{\delta}_x^2)^{1/2} \qquad (16.74)$$

where the major tire compression is defined as

$$\bar{\delta}_x = \frac{\delta}{D} \qquad \text{and} \qquad D = 2R \qquad (16.75)$$

A similar expression relates the y-direction chord to the tire compression:

$$c_y = 2d(\bar{\delta}_y - \bar{\delta}_y^2)^{1/2} \qquad (16.76)$$

Here, the minor tire compression is defined as

$$\bar{\delta}_y = \frac{\delta}{d} \qquad \text{and} \qquad d = 2r \qquad (16.77)$$

If the diameter of the tire cross section is $d = 2r$, then a fineness ratio f can be defined that compares the tire diameter with the cross-section diameter:

$$f = \frac{d}{D} \qquad (16.78)$$

The area of the compressed tire that is in contact with the ground is the product of the expressions (16.74) and (16.76):

$$A_{\text{contact}} = c_x c_y = 4dD\sqrt{(\bar{\delta}_x - \bar{\delta}_x^2)(\bar{\delta}_y - \bar{\delta}_y^2)}$$

or

$$\frac{A_{\text{contact}}}{D^2} = 4\sqrt{(\bar{\delta}_x - \bar{\delta}_x^2)(f\bar{\delta}_x - \bar{\delta}_x^2)} \qquad (16.79)$$

Figure 16.13 shows how the contact area varies with tire compression for various fineness ratios.

The contact area and tire compression are nondimensional, divided by the tire diameter or its square as appropriate. At a compression ratio of approximately

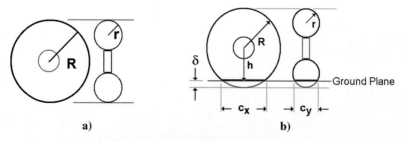

a)   b)

Fig. 16.12   a) Undeformed tire geometry. b) Deformed tire geometry.

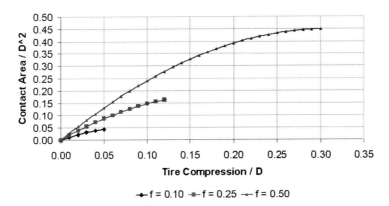

Fig. 16.13 Variation of contact area with tire compression [Eq. (16.15)].

one-half of the fineness ratio, the small compression assumption breaks down, and the area begins an unrealistic decrease. Expression (16.79) should be used with caution.

As the tire deforms, the volume of the torus decreases. One can estimate the decrement in volume by integrating the differential volume formed by the area given in expression (16.77) and the infinitesimal compression $d\delta$.

$$\Delta V = 4D^3 \int_0^{\delta_c/D} \sqrt{\left(\frac{\delta}{D} - \frac{\delta^2}{D^2}\right)\left(f\frac{\delta}{D} - \frac{\delta^2}{D^2}\right)}\, d\frac{\delta}{D} \qquad (16.80)$$

In the undeformed state, the volume of air in the tire is given by

$$V = 2\pi^2 R r^2 \qquad \text{or} \qquad \frac{V}{D^3} = \frac{\pi^2 f^2}{4} \qquad (16.81)$$

Let V_1 and V_2 be the volume of the undeformed tire and the volume of the tire under compression, respectively. They are related by expression (16.78), that is,

$$V_2 = V_1 - \Delta V$$

Then, assuming an isothermal, adiabatic process, $P_1 V_1 = P_2 V_2$, and the pressure rise in the tire is estimated to be

$$\frac{P_2}{P_1} = \frac{V_1}{V_1 - \Delta V} \qquad (16.82)$$

This relationship is shown in Fig. 16.14. Note: Both P_1 and P_2 are absolute pressures. If one has gauge pressure, add the atmospheric pressure to gauge pressure before applying the preceding expression.

Pressure Ratio vs Deformation

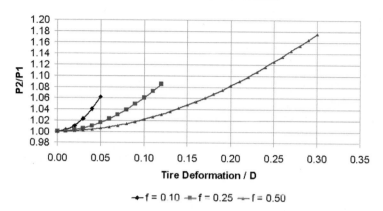

Fig. 16.14   Pressure rise as a function of deformation.

Example 16.2

A tire has a diameter of 12 in., a cross-sectional diameter of 3 in., a gauge pressure of 45 psi, and is supporting a 600-lb load at the axle. Assume ambient pressure is 15 psi. What is the tire deformation neglecting the stiffness of the tire wall?

Answer: The fineness ratio is $f = 3/12 = 0.25$. The gauge pressure multiplied by the contact area supports the 600-lb load. The contact area is given by Eq. (16.79) or Fig. 16.13, and the pressure ratio is given by Fig. 16.14. The deformation is required in its own solution. This implicit relationship requires iteration.

Iteration 1: Begin with an estimate for the deformation. Try $\delta/D = 0.06$. From Figs. 16.13 and 16.14, the contact area and pressure ratio are 0.1014 and 1.02308, respectively. The absolute pressure is $(45 + 15) = 60$ psi, so that the increased absolute pressure is $(60)(1.02308) = 61.3848$ psi $= 46.3848$ psi gauge. The error between the desired support and the actual support is

$$\varepsilon = 600 - (46.3848)(12^2)(0.1014) \approx -77.3$$

That is, the tire is deformed too much—as if it were trying to lift 677.3 lb. Decrease the deformation and try again.

Iteration 2: Try $\delta/D = 0.05$ The contact area and pressure ratio are 0.08718 and 1.016, respectively. The increased absolute pressure is $(60)(1.016) = 60.96$ psi $= 45.96$ psi gauge. The error between the desired support and the actual support is

$$\varepsilon = 600 - (45.96)(12^2)(0.08718) \approx 23$$

Iteration 3: Interpolation between the first two iterations suggests $\delta/D = 0.0523$. The contact area and pressure ratio are 0.09055 and 1.0175, respectively.

The increased absolute pressure is $(60)(1.0175) = 61.05\,\mathrm{psi} = 46.05\,\mathrm{psi}$ gauge. The error between the desired support and the actual support is

$$\varepsilon = 600 - (46.05)(12^2)(0.09055) \approx -0.52$$

The load error is approximately 0.52 lb, or about 0.08%, which is sufficiently accurate for this analysis. The tire has deformed $0.0523^*12 = 0.63$ in. and has a contact area of about $0.09055^*12^*12 = 13.04\,\mathrm{in}^2$. The compression ratio is $0.63/12 = 0.0525$, which is much less than half of the fineness ratio, therefore, these answers are judged reasonable. In more sophisticated models, the load-deformation curves are provided by the tire manufacturers. This analysis was presented for "mental calibration" purposes and to offer a back-of-the-envelope method to estimate load-deformation characteristics.

Up to now, the models that have been presented have had the orientation of the spin axis fixed with respect to the body. That constraint can be relaxed so that the wheel pivots freely or can be steered.

Begin with a definition of the zero angle for the wheel. This is the turning angle that orients the spinning axis of the wheel parallel to the body y axis. A positive wheel angle δ_w will mean the spinning axis has reoriented so that the wheel now points to the right. Figure 16.15 shows a wheel and its caster mount from the side and the wheel from above turned through a positive wheel angle.

Now, if the wheel casters, this means that the wheel turning angle is changing so that the lateral force drives to zero. Pilot input also directs the turning angle when the wheel can be steered. The change in turning angle is not instantaneous. Let the mass of the wheel be m_w, and the action arm be a_c. The wheel is supporting a normal force of N, so that a lateral force equal to $\mu N \cdot \mathrm{sign}(a_c\dot{\delta}_w - v_w)$ develops. The term v_w is the sideward velocity of the wheel parallel to the axle. The wheel resists lateral shearing, which is approximately $K_{yw}(\delta_w - \delta_c)$, where δ_c is the pilot command. K_{yw} is a lateral stiffness of the wheel wall. Summing moments about the caster pivot yields the following second-order differential equation:

$$m_w a_c^2 \ddot{\delta}_w + a_c \mu N \cdot \mathrm{sign}(a_c\dot{\delta}_w) + a_c K_{yw}\delta_w = a_c K_{yw}\delta_c + a_c \mu N \cdot \mathrm{sign}(v_w)$$

$$(16.83)$$

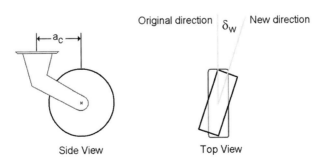

Fig. 16.15   Two views of a castering wheel.

The sign function is presumed to equal zero when the input argument is zero. Normalize this expression with $a_c K_{yw}$:

$$\frac{m_w a_c}{K_{yw}} \ddot{\delta}_w + \frac{\mu N}{K_{yw}} \cdot \text{sign}(a_c \dot{\delta}_w) + \delta_w = \delta_c + \frac{\mu N}{K_{yw}} \cdot \text{sign}(v_w) \qquad (16.84)$$

The coefficient $m_w a_c / K_{yw}$ is much smaller than unity. If one decides to neglect the acceleration altogether, the resulting equation is static because the rate term on the left-hand side is not a proper definition of the time derivative of δ_w and so must be discarded. (The term cannot be moved to the right-hand side of the equation because no definition of the time derivative exists.) The static turning angle equation becomes

$$\delta_w = \delta_c + \frac{\mu N}{K_{yw}} \cdot \text{sign}(v_w) \qquad (16.85)$$

A reasonable range for the rate coefficient is $0.1 < \mu N / K_{yw} < 1$. If δ_P is the pilot input, δ_{P_0} the zero point, and $\partial \delta_w / \partial P$ a gearing ratio, then the steering command is

$$\delta_c - \frac{\partial \delta_w}{\partial \delta_P}(\delta_P - \delta_{P_0}) \qquad (16.86)$$

In some cases, the reader may demand some dynamics. In such a case, Eq. (16.85) can be modified to fit empirical data or the reader's sense of time constant. One possibility is

$$\tau_w \dot{\delta}_w + \delta_w = \delta_c + \frac{\mu N}{K_{yw}} \cdot \text{sign}(v_w) \qquad (16.87)$$

Time constants on the order of 10 to 20 ms are probably reasonable.

16.6   Total Load at Contact Point

The forces at the contact point are caused by friction and the normal force. The normal force, which equals the tire force, is directed along the unit normal vector outward.

The in-plane force, which has components in the x and y directions, is defined by the normal force, some friction coefficients, the steering angle, and the velocity vector at the contact point resolved to steering axes. The friction coefficients are of three types: rolling, sliding, and static. Rolling friction is experienced normally in the x direction of the steering axes and only if the wheel is free to spin as it moves on the surface. If brakes forces are high enough, the wheel is not free to spin. In this case, the wheel may be sliding or the wheel and aircraft may have come to a rest. In the y direction of the steering axes, the wheel experiences only static or sliding friction.

It is important to understand the nature of friction before plunging into the force equations. *Static friction is a potential force.* A block sitting on a level surface is not producing a friction force of $\mu_{static} N$ in a lateral direction. Instead, the block has the potential of resisting an applied lateral force of up to $\mu_{static}N$. Until the applied force reaches that threshold, the block will not move. The block will accelerate in the direction of the force and experience sliding friction only when the applied force exceeds $\mu_{static}N$. The coefficient of sliding friction is generally lower than static friction, so that once sliding motion commences less applied force is required to continue the sliding motion. In the case of rolling motion, the rolling-friction coefficient starts at some level that decreases with forward speed to some minimum value. Basic friction models then behave like this:

$$f_{\text{translate}} = N \begin{cases} f_p \mu_{\text{static}} \cdot \text{sign}(-f_{\text{applied}}), & U = 0 \\ \mu_{\text{sliding}} \cdot \text{sign}(-U), & |U| > 0 \end{cases}$$

$$f_{\text{rolling}} = N \begin{cases} f_p(\mu_{\text{rolling0}} + \mu_{\text{rolling1}}) \cdot \text{sign}(-f_{\text{applied}}), & U = 0 \\ [\mu_{\text{rolling0}} + \mu_{\text{rolling1}}(1 - |U|/U_{\text{break}})] \\ \quad \cdot \text{sign}(-U), & 0 < |U| < U_{\text{break}} \\ \mu_{\text{rolling0}} \cdot \text{sign}(-U), & |U| \geq U_{\text{break}} \end{cases}$$

$$f_p = \frac{f_{\text{applied}}}{\mu_{\text{static}}N} \tag{16.88}$$

The term f_p is a participation factor that lies between -1 and $+1$. It indicates how much potential friction force is actually used.

16.7   Total Load at Aircraft Center of Mass

Each wheel or skid contact point generates three forces. They are the in-plane force normal to the wheel spin axis, the in-plane force parallel to the wheel spin axis, and a force normal to the ground plane. Because the ground plane is not always parallel to the body x-y plane, the forces must be resolved to the body axes. The transpose of the ground orientation matrix resolves the wheel contact point forces to Earth axes, and the familiar Earth–to-body transformation matrix resolves those forces to body axes. Specifically, for the ith wheel, the contact point forces resolved to body axes are given by

$$(\boldsymbol{F}_{\text{wcp}|\text{cg}})_i = T_{\text{be}} T_{g-g0}^T (\boldsymbol{F}_{\text{wcp}|e})_i \tag{16.89}$$

Once the resolution is made, the total loads applied by the gear to the body are easily determined:

$$\boldsymbol{F}_{\text{LG}|\text{cg}} = \sum_{i=1}^{n} (\boldsymbol{F}_{\text{wcp}|\text{cg}})_i \tag{16.90}$$

The forces give rise to moments as well. The moment arm is the distance from the aircraft center of mass to the contact point, and the forces are the contact point forces resolved to body axes.

$$\boldsymbol{M}_{\text{LG}|\text{cg}} = \sum_{i=1}^{n} (\boldsymbol{P}_{t-\text{cg}|\text{cg}} \times \boldsymbol{F}_{\text{wcp}|\text{cg}})_i \tag{16.91}$$

16.8 Special Problems

Those who model landing gear have come across several celebrated problems. Two favorites are the problem of underconstrained systems and the dithering problem. These two problems are introduced here, and potential (though certainly not the only) solutions are also presented.

16.8.1 Dithering

Suppose a block is sliding on a level surface with initial velocity $\dot{x}(0)$. The block has no applied force, so that the only lateral force acting on it is the sliding friction. The block will decelerate. The equation of motion for this system is

$$m\ddot{x} = \begin{cases} \mu_{\text{sliding}}N \cdot \text{sign}(-\dot{x}), & |\dot{x}| > 0 \\ f_p \mu_{\text{static}}N \cdot \text{sign}(-f_{\text{applied}}), & \dot{x} - 0 \end{cases} \qquad (16.92)$$

The problem stipulated no applied force, and so $f_p = f_{\text{applied}} = 0$. Rewrite the surviving equation of motion as

$$\ddot{x} = \frac{\mu_{\text{sliding}}N \cdot \text{sign}(-\dot{x})}{m} = K \cdot \text{sign}(-\dot{x}) \qquad (16.93)$$

Over one interval of integration, the solution to the equation of motion is

$$\dot{x}(t + \Delta t) = \dot{x}(t) + \ddot{x}(t)\Delta t$$

or

$$\dot{x}(t + \Delta t) = \dot{x}(t) + K \cdot \text{sign}[-\dot{x}(t)]\Delta t \qquad (16.94)$$

This system is perfectly well behaved during deceleration up to the moment when $K\Delta t \cdot \text{sign}[-\dot{x}(t)]$ is more negative than $\dot{x}(t)$. (That is, when the decelerating term causes more deceleration than is required to come exactly to rest.) After that, this simple equation becomes an oscillator. For example, let $\dot{x}(t) = 1$ and $K\Delta t = 0.9$. The first five time steps in the numerical solution are shown in Table 16.1.

The block never comes to rest even though friction resists the motion in every frame! The consequences are evident in Fig. 16.16.

Table 16.1   Dithering in the solution of a friction deceleration

Time	$\dot{x}(t)$	$a_{\text{decel}} = K\Delta t \cdot \text{sign}[-\dot{x}(t)]$	$\dot{x}(t + \Delta t)$
0	1	−0.9	0.1
Δt	0.1	−0.9	−0.8
$2\Delta t$	−0.8	0.9	0.1
$3\Delta t$	0.1	−0.9	−0.8
$4\Delta t$	−0.8	0.9	0.1

Skittering Problem Explained

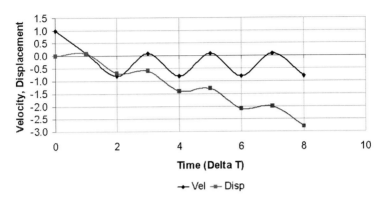

Fig. 16.16 Skittering problem. The velocity exhibits a limit cycle; the displacement of the tire continues ad nauseum.

The astute reader surmises the reason is that the deceleration is not proportional to the speed, but rather is dependent only on the sign of the speed. This suggests a simple solution. Use only as much of the decelerating force as is required to come to rest. That is,

$$a_{\text{decel}} = \begin{cases} K\Delta t \cdot \text{sign}[-\dot{x}(t)], & \text{sign}\{\dot{x}(t) + K\Delta t \cdot \text{sign}[-\dot{x}(t)]\} = \text{sign}[\dot{x}(t)] \\ -\dot{x}(t)/\Delta t, & \text{sign}\{\dot{x}(t) + K\Delta t \cdot \text{sign}[-\dot{x}(t)]\} = -\text{sign}[\dot{x}(t)] \end{cases}$$

$$(16.95)$$

The same problem is solved using the proposed solution. The solution is shown in Table 16.2 and Fig. 16.17.

This technique requires that the sign function is zero for an argument of zero value. Not all computer languages support such logic—it is perhaps best that the reader write a special purpose sign function for use in this application.

Table 16.2 No dithering in the friction deceleration

Time	$\dot{x}(t)$	$a_{\text{decel}} = \begin{cases} K\Delta t \cdot \text{sign}[-\dot{x}(t)] \\ \text{or} \\ -\dot{x}(t)/\Delta t \end{cases}$	$\dot{x}(t + \Delta t)$
0	1	−0.9	0.1
Δt	0.1	−0.1	0.0
$2\Delta t$	0.0	0.0	0.0
$3\Delta t$	0.0	0.0	0.0
$4\Delta t$	0.0	0.0	0.0

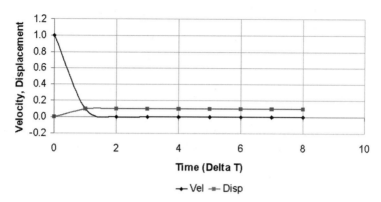

Fig. 16.17   The skittering problem is solved as described in the text using just enough of the potential friction force to stop the motion.

The switching logic presented here is inelegant, but the technique will work for the sliding block. Another approach is to introduce a fictitious damping term that is velocity dependent. However, a fictitious damping term smacks of deus ex machina and is not adaptive, therefore, fictitious damping is not recommended.

16.8.2 Underconstrained Systems

The ubiquitous tricycle landing-gear arrangement presents an interesting problem when trying to calculate an on-the-ground trim condition. A trim means that the summation of forces and moments along and about each of the three body axes must be zero. A total of six equations must be driven to zero simultaneously. Each wheel has associated with it a normal force and two in-plane forces. The normal forces are determined by strut deflection, which in turn are determined by overall z direction settling (plunge) of the aircraft on its gear plus any influence caused by aircraft roll or pitch. Therefore a tricycle landing-gear arrangement has nine independent variables, namely, the plunge displacement, the roll angle, the pitch angle, and two in-plane participation factors for each of the three tires. This is an underconstrained system—no unique solution exists. However, one need only to see that aircraft parked at an airport are not skittering about looking for a solution to realize that some "preferred" solution exists. (Preferred might be too strong a word. "Acceptable" or "tolerated" might be preferred instead.) One approach to finding a trim requires the user to specify the values for three of the nine independent variables so that the resulting system has been made square and invertible. This approach is not desirable because it requires the user to have some preconceived notion of the solution that might not always be correct. An alternative approach is to assume that nature seeks a solution that searches for the minimum amount of friction required to achieve a trim solution. The text presents examples of both alternatives.

First, state the problem precisely. Start with the equations of motion for the six rigid-body degrees of freedom, rearranged so that the accelerations are the only elements on the left-hand side (LHS).

$$M_b \dot{V}_b = -\omega_b \times (mV_b) + T_{be} \begin{Bmatrix} 0 \\ 0 \\ mg \end{Bmatrix} + F_{aero} + F_{LG|cg}$$

$$I_n \dot{\omega}_b = -\omega_b \times (I_n \omega_b) + M_{aero} + M_{LG|cg} \qquad (16.96)$$

The vectors $F_{LG|cg}$ and $M_{LG|cg}$, derived in the preceding section, are the total forces and moments applied by all of the landing gear. In a trim condition, the LHS is zero. The translational and rotational velocities are also zero, so that the problem reduces to this form:

$$F_{LG|cg} = -F_{aero} - T_{be} \begin{Bmatrix} 0 \\ 0 \\ mg \end{Bmatrix} = -F_{aero} - F_{grav}$$

$$M_{LG|cg} = -M_{aero} \qquad (16.97)$$

As is usually the case, the trim technique of choice is to start with an initial guess of the plunge, roll and pitch angles, and the friction participation factors, then build a Taylor series to model small changes near the initial guess:

$$F_{LG|cg} = F_{0LG|cg} + \left[\frac{\partial F_{LG|cg}}{\partial c} \right] \Delta c = -F_{aero} - F_{grav}$$

$$M_{LG|cg} = M_{0LG|cg} + \left[\frac{\partial M_{LG|cg}}{\partial c} \right] \Delta c = -M_{aero} \qquad (16.98)$$

The control column is arranged thus:

$$c_9 = \{ h, \quad \varphi, \quad \theta, \quad f_{p1x}, \quad f_{p1y}, \quad f_{p2x}, \quad f_{p2y}, \quad f_{p3x}, \quad f_{p3y} \}^T \qquad (16.99)$$

Each of the partial derivative matrices in Eq. (16.98) has three rows and nine columns. The two equations in Eq. (16.98) can be combined into one matrix level expression:

$$[P]\Delta c = b \qquad (16.100)$$

where

$$[P] = \begin{bmatrix} \partial F_{LC|cg} / \partial c \\ \partial M_{LG|cg} / \partial c \end{bmatrix}$$

and

$$b = \begin{Bmatrix} -F_{0LG|cg} - F_{aero} - F_{grav} \\ -M_{0LG|cg} - M_{aero} \end{Bmatrix}$$

The P matrix is 6×9 in size; it has no inverse in the usual sense. It is at this point that investigators employ various tricks. Here are two of them.

16.8.3 Defined-Constraint Solution

In this technique, choose six of the nine control candidates as active elements, and define the remaining three with constant values or as functions of the six active control candidates. For instance, if the nose gear is point one, the left main is point two, and the right main is point three, then a reasonable selection for the six active control candidates is

$$c_6 = \{h, \quad \varphi, \quad \theta, \quad f_{p1y}, \quad f_{p2x}, \quad f_{p3x}\} \tag{16.101}$$

These three friction participation factors were selected because 1) the nose wheel typically does not have brakes, so that $f_{p1x} = 0$ and 2) left and right main gear friction potential can be set to some fraction of the nose wheel side potential, $f_{p2y} = f_{p3y} = 0.5 f_{p1y}$ for example. This assignment is probably reasonable if the aircraft is sitting on a level surface and is not suffering any unbalanced lateral force.

The original nine controls are related to Eq. (16.101) via the algebraic statement:

$$c_9 = Dc_6 + c_0 \tag{16.102}$$

The constraint definition matrix and constant value vector are

$$D = \begin{bmatrix} 1 & 0 & 0 & 0 & 0 & 0 \\ 0 & 1 & 0 & 0 & 0 & 0 \\ 0 & 0 & 1 & 0 & 0 & 0 \\ 0 & 0 & 0 & 0 & 0 & 0 \\ 0 & 0 & 0 & 1 & 0 & 0 \\ 0 & 0 & 0 & 0 & 1 & 0 \\ 0 & 0 & 0 & 0.5 & 0 & 0 \\ 0 & 0 & 0 & 0 & 0 & 1 \\ 0 & 0 & 0 & 0.5 & 0 & 0 \end{bmatrix}, \quad c_0 = \begin{Bmatrix} 0 \\ 0 \\ 0 \\ 0 \\ 0 \\ 0 \\ 0 \\ 0 \\ 0 \end{Bmatrix} \tag{16.103}$$

Rewrite expression (16.100) thus

$$PDc_6 = b - Pc_0 = \bar{b} \tag{16.104}$$

The matrix product PD is square and likely invertible. Solve Eq. (16.104) for c_6, and then recover c_9 from Eq. (16.102):

$$c_6 = (PD)^{-1}\bar{b} \tag{16.105}$$

This technique is best suited for trimming an aircraft on a level surface. If the aircraft has four wheels, then more constraint equations will be required in the D matrix. This becomes problematic quickly. If the surface has some elevation and the aircraft is oriented arbitrarily on it, then the following technique *may* offer a workable solution.

16.8.4 Tikhonov Method

Through a series of elementary matrix manipulations, decompose P into three matrices named L, M, and R. That is,

$$P\Delta c = b \tag{16.106}$$

becomes

$$L^{-1}MR\Delta c = b \tag{16.107}$$

As implied, the L and R matrices are guaranteed invertible. The M matrix has the particular form:

$$M = \begin{bmatrix} I & C \end{bmatrix} \tag{16.108}$$

where the C submatrix represents constraints among some of the coefficients. Substitute the definition of M into the expression above it to get

$$L^{-1}\begin{bmatrix} I & C \end{bmatrix} R\Delta c = b \tag{16.109}$$

The appendix on required mathematics develops the solution technique from here. The solution for Δc is

$$\Delta c = R^{-1} \begin{Bmatrix} y_1 \\ y_2 \end{Bmatrix} \tag{16.110}$$

where

$$y_1 = Lb - Cy_2$$

and

$$y_2 = (I + C^T C)^{-1} C^T Lb$$

Update the control column in the usual manner:

$$c_{\text{next}} = c_{\text{current}} - \Delta c \tag{16.111}$$

Apply this improved guess to the equations of motion, and continue until the solution converges or until some maximum iteration count is exceeded. The result is a control vector with the trim values of plunge, Euler roll angle, Euler pitch angle, and x- and y-direction friction participation factors for each wheel.

16.8.5　Error Penalty Method

Another method to solve the underconstrained problem uses optimization techniques. The correction equation is

$$P\Delta c = b \qquad (16.112)$$

Create a new variable that represents the error between the left- and right-hand sides of Eq. (16.112). Call it e.

$$e = P\Delta c - b \qquad (16.113)$$

The goal is to minimize this error while constraining the size of the correction. The solution is to create a quadratic function that represents the square of the error in Eq.(16.113) and adjoin to it a quadratic function that penalizes the size of the correction. Let the total objective function becomes

$$J = e^T Q e + \Delta c^T R \Delta c = (P\Delta c - b)^T Q(P\Delta c - b) + \Delta c^T R \Delta c \qquad (16.114)$$

Set the derivative of this function with respect to Δc equal to zero, and solve for Δc.

$$\Delta c = (P^T Q P + R)^{-1} P^T Q b \qquad (16.115)$$

Update the control column in the usual manner. Apply this improved guess to the equations of motion, and continue until the solution converges or until some maximum iteration count is exceeded.

The Q and R matrices are square and symmetric. In practice, they are often diagonal. A simple method to set the diagonal entries in the Q matrix is this. For the (j,j) entry in Q, decide on the maximum acceptable error for the jth row in Eq. (16.113). Square that error and enter its reciprocal into Q:

$$Q = \begin{bmatrix} \dfrac{1}{E_1^2} & 0 & \cdots & 0 \\ 0 & \dfrac{1}{E_2^2} & \cdots & 0 \\ \vdots & \vdots & \ddots & \vdots \\ 0 & 0 & \cdots & \dfrac{1}{E_n^2} \end{bmatrix} \qquad (16.116)$$

where E_j is the maximum acceptable value of the error e_j. The entries in the R matrix are defined in a similar way, except that one is now penalizing the correction Δc with no regard for the error equation. Decide on a maximum amount of tolerable correction, square it, and place its reciprocal in the corresponding diagonal. Note that the reader will probably want to use all of the available correction for the plunge, roll, and pitch (theoretically infinite), so that the first three entries in the R matrix are zero!

Two items concerning the Tikhonov and error-penalty methods bear discussion. First, the author has used the Tikhonov and error-penalty methods with some success, but the solution is often not what was expected. For instance, if the initial guesses on the friction participation factors are not zero, then the final values might not be zero, even if the aircraft is sitting on a perfectly level field. The reason for this is that the solution surface can be likened to a bowl with a flat bottom. If the initial guess is on the side of the bowl, then an acceptable zero is the first moment when the bottom of the bowl is reached. In all likelihood, that first moment will not be at the center of the bowl.

Second, at no time was the value for any of the participation factors limited to $+/-1$ as they should have been. During the iteration, checks should be performed on these values. The analyst can then choose to take either of these actions:

1) Let the participation factors take on any value required to trim. At the end of the trim, report any factors that are out of range, and declare the trim invalid.

2) After every update during the iteration, limit the participation factors to $+/-1$. To build a partial derivative matrix numerically, the differentiation subroutine must detect a participation factor that is near to or against a limit, and then direct the numerical differentiation into backward differencing or forward differencing as would be appropriate to prevent perturbation past the limit. This ensures a valid derivative near or at the limits.

16.9 Sample Code to Model Coupled Landing Gear/Aircraft Dynamics

```
Sub gear (v() As Single, vd() As Single, dt As Single, icycle As Integer)
'
'     This is a simple gear dynamics model for a vertically
'     aligned strut and an aircraft sitting on top of it.
'     The tire has stiffness, and the strut has stiffness and
'     damping. The damping is a function of direction.
'
'     The strut uses a servo to limit it at the top and the
'     bottom of its stroke.
'
'     The sign convention in this simple example is positive up.
'
Dim s As Single
Dim sd As Single
Dim sdd As Single
Dim zwg As Single

glimit = 2000#
'
'     Calculate the motion of the wheel given the aircraft motion
'     and the strut motion, or calculate the strut motion given the
'     aircraft motion and the wheel motion. The term lfe is the
```

```
'    length of the strut fully extended. The term s is the amount
'    of strut compression. It will always be a value between 0 and
'    lfe.
'
za = v(1)
zad = v(2)
If imethod = 1 Or imethod = 3 Then
    s = v(3)
    sd = v(4)
    zw = s + za − lfe
    zwd = sd + zad
Else
    zw = v(3)
    zwd = v(4)
    s = zw − za + lfe
    sd = zwd − zad
End If
'
'    Calculate the force the tire generates. This is the force
'    transmitted to the axle from the tire.
'
zwg = (zw − radius) − zg
If zwg < 0 Then
    ftire = −kt * zwg
Else
    ftire = 0
End If
'
'    Calculate the force that the spring and damper generate.
'    Together these are the strut force. The strut has a preload.
'    The preload must be exceeded by an external force before
'    it compresses.
'
'    When the strut is compressing, sd>0. Use the compression
'    coefficient for the damper. When sd<0 then use the extension
'    coefficient.
'
'    When the strut is compressed, 0<s<lfe. Use the spring
'    constant and add it to the preload. When the strut is at
'    one of its limits, initiate an error signal that will
'    be used in a high stiffness servo equation that drives the
'    strut to its limit. Then calculate the spring value.
'
If imethod = 1 Then

    If s >= lfe Then                              'fully compressed
        er = s − lfe
        sd = sd − glimit * er
        zwd = sd + zad
        fspring = ks * lfe + preload
```

```
      ElseIf s <= 0 Then                        'fully extended
          er = s
          sd = sd − glimit * er
          zwd = sd + zad
          fspring = preload

      Else
          fspring = ks * s + preload

      End If
  ElseIf imethod = 2 Then

      If s >= lfe Then                          'fully compressed
          er = s − lfe
          zwd = zwd − glimit * er
          sd = zwd − zad
          fspring = ks * lfe + preload

      ElseIf s <= 0 Then                        'fully extended
          er = s
          zwd = zwd − glimit * er
          sd = zwd − zad
          fspring = preload

      Else
          fspring = ks * s + preload

      End If
  Else

      If s >= lfe Then                          'fully compressed
          er = s − lfe
          sd = sd − glimit * er
          s = lfe
          v(3) = s
          sd = amin (sd, 0#)
          zwd = sd + zad
          fspring = 3 * preload / (1 − 0.5 * s) ^ 1.2

      ElseIf s <= 0 Then                        'fully extended
          er = s
          sd = sd − glimit * er
          s = 0
          v(3) = s
          sd = amax (sd, 0#)
          zwd = sd + zad
          fspring = 3 * preload

      Else
          fspring = 3 * preload / (1 − 0.5 * s) ^ 1.2

      End If
  End If
'
```

```
If sd > 0 Then
    fdamper = csc * sd
Else
    fdamper = cse * sd
End If
'
If ftire >= preload Then
    fstrut = fdamper + fspring
Else
    fstrut = ftire
End If
'
If icycle = 1 Then
    fstrut0 = fstrut
    fspring0 = fspring
    fdamper0 = fdamper
    ftire0 - ftire
End If
'
'       Apply the forcing function.
'
If imethod = 1 Or imethod = 3 Then
    zadd = -grav + (fstrut) / ma + thrust / ma * 0
    sdd = ftire / mw - (1 + mw / ma) * fstrut / mw
Else
    zadd = fstrut / ma - grav
    zwdd = (ftire - fstrut) / mw - grav
End If
'
vd(1) = zad
vd(2) = zadd
If imethod = 1 Or imethod = 3 Then
    vd(3) = sd
    vd(4) = sdd
Else
    vd(3) = zwd
    vd(4) = zwdd
End If
'
End Sub
```

16.10   Conclusions

Landing-gear models always seem to get the least amount of attention in a full-up simulation model. This chapter attempted to introduce the reader to the common problems associated with landing-gear models. When possible, we employed rigorous mathematics with vectors to describe the approach and contact of a wheel to an arbitrarily oriented ground plane. Two strut arrangements were presented with a polynomial model of the nonlinear stiffness and damping characteristics of an oleo strut. Some effort was spent describing the stiffness of a crushing tire. Finally, two common problems were presented: the skittering problem and the underconstrained trimming problem. Possible methods to solve them were presented as well.

References

[1]Currey, N. S., *Aircraft Landing Gear Design: Principles and Practices*, AIAA, New York, 1988.

[2]Bourke, P., *"Minimum Distance Between a Point and a Plane,"* [Retrieved 4 Dec. 2003] http://astronomy.swin.edu.au/~pbourke/geometry/pointplane/1996.

[3]Bourke, P., *"Equation of a Plane,"* [Retrieved 4 Dec. 2003] http://astronomy.swin. edu.au/~pbourke/geometry/planeeq/1989.

[4]Rysdyk, Rolf T., and Calise, Anthony J., *"Adaptive Model Inversion Flight Control for Tiltrotor Aircraft,"* Presented at the 54th Annual Forum of the American Helicopter Society, May 1998.

[5]Williamson, D. R., Hoffman, J. A., and Henninger, W. C., *"Mathematical Methods Incorporated in the Wind Energy System Coupled Dynamics Analysis Methodology: Wind Turbine Linear Analysis Software System (WINDLASS),"* Paragon Pacific, Inc., Rept. PPI-1018-7, El Segundo, CA, Sept. 1977.

Problems

16.1   Spanky and his gang have invented a wagon that always goes downhill, and therefore does not require an engine. Does this idea work? Explain your answer in terms of the equations of motion for the wagon and how gravity and the reaction loads on the wheels force the equation.

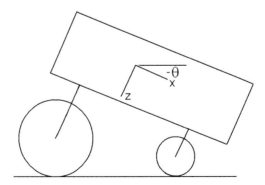

16.2   Place a wagon on two steps of a staircase as shown in the illustration. Does it move anywhere? Explain your answer in terms of the equation of motion for the wagon and how gravity and the reaction loads on the wheels force the equation.

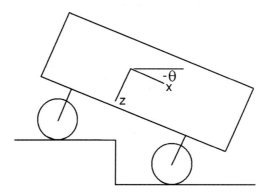

16.3   Place a wagon on an inclined plane as shown in the illustration. Does it move anywhere? Explain your answer in terms of the equation of motion for the wagon and how gravity and the reaction loads on the wheels force the equation.

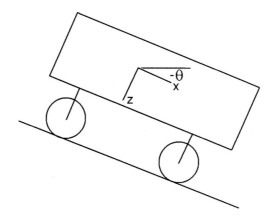

16.4   A tire has a diameter of 12 in., a cross-sectional diameter of 3 in., a gauge pressure of 90 psi, and is supporting a 2000-lb load at the axle. Assume ambient pressure is 15 psi. Estimate the tire deformation.

16.5   Consider the illustrative linear gear model and the equations that describe it. Let the mass of the aircraft be 200 slugs, the mass of the wheel be 1 slug, the stiffness of the strut be 1000 lb/in., and the stiffness of the tire be 10000 lb/in. What are the steady-state solutions for the strut deflection and the tire compression?

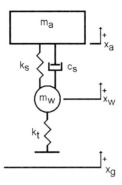

$$m_a \ddot{x}_a + c_s \left(\dot{x}_a - \dot{x}_w \right) + k_s \left(x_a - x_w \right) = -m_a g$$
$$m_w \ddot{x}_w + c_s (\dot{x}_w - \dot{x}_a) + k_s (x_w - x_a) + k_t (x_w - x_g) = -m_w g$$

17
Trimming

17.1 Introduction

In 1912, Wilbur Wright testified in a patent infringement case brought against Herring-Curtiss and Glenn Curtiss. His testimony is an eloquent recapitulation of the history of the development of manned flight. As reported in [1], at one point in the testimony, Wilbur Wright remarked,

> "As to the state of experimental knowledge at the time we began our experiments, we reached the conclusion that the problem of constructing wings sufficiently strong to carry the weight of the machine itself, along with that of the motor and of the aviator, and also that of constructing sufficiently light motors were sufficiently worked out to present no serious difficulty; but that the problem of equilibrium had been the real stumbling block in all serious attempts to solve the problem of human flight, and that this problem of equilibrium in reality constituted the problem of flight itself. *We, therefore, decided to give our special attention to inventing means of retaining equilibrium, and as this was a field where mere speculation was of no value at all, we made a careful study of the state of the experimental knowledge ...".*

When flight simulation programmers speak of trim, they refer to the process of manipulating Euler angles and pilot controls to cause the sum of the forces along each of the body axes and the sum of the moments about each body axis to go to zero while observing all bounds on the independent variables and all constraints on the output variables. In other words, trimming a vehicle is the process of finding equilibrium. There are several reasons the simulation engineer desires this unaccelerated state.

1) Performance is evaluated in steady-state flight. Power absorbed by the airframe and rotors is a function of velocity. If the aircraft simulation is not trimmed to zero acceleration, then the performance of the aircraft may be exaggerated. For instance, it is not likely that a Cessna 152 can fly at 300 kn, yet one can specify that flight condition and analyze all of the forces and moments. Given the limited amount of installed power, the thrust would never balance the drag. The result would be a nonzero sum of forces in the x direction leading to a decelerated flight condition.

2) Steady-state flight is interesting to the handling-qualities (HQ) engineer, whose task it is to evaluate the stability and controllability of an aircraft. Stability

and control derivatives provide the HQ engineers with a linear model of the aircraft at a specific set point.

3) Man-in-the-loop simulations often start midmission. One does not always want to start from the ground, take off, climb to 20,000 f, and then search for the tanker to practice refueling techniques. Trimming one mile behind the tanker at altitude and speed is much faster and cheaper.

There are other reasons for determining the trim condition as well. The point is that trimming is an integral part of the simulation problem and helicopters and tiltrotors present some very interesting problems above and beyond the usual six-degrees-of-freedom trim.

17.2   Trim Requirements and Options

In the most general sense, a trim problem satisfies these conditions:

1) Control settings and initial conditions on one or more coupled differential equations must be found that drive to zero the highest-order derivatives of all equations, or achieve a periodic solution when a periodic forcing function is applied.

2) Control settings must lie in the physical range available. Derived physical values such as power from throttle must lie in the physical range available. Thought of as a search problem, the independent arguments must lie within their bounds.

3) The trim problem must be well formed; the user must specify a sufficient number of initial conditions on the aircraft states. Sometimes the specification can be in the form of a constraint that combines several states. Other times, the specification can be an assumed default. An example of the former is, "the total velocity must be 200 f/s." The solution can mean all 200 f/s is directed along the x direction, or some of that velocity vector can include rate of climb and sideslip. An example of an assumed default is "establish a hover in zero wind." To do this, the helicopter pilot must accept a small amount of roll angle because sideslip velocity is zero.

4) The independent variables that are chosen to solve the trim problem must span the degrees of freedom. In control theory, this trim assignment problem means the dependent degrees of freedom are reachable from the independent variables. For instance, one is ill advised to select lateral cyclic, pedal, or roll angle when trying to trim the longitudinal degrees of freedom. Selecting a sufficient number of independent controls is equally important. The full six-degrees-of-freedom trim problem looks like it is being solved with just four pilot controls at first. Euler angles contribute two additional controls by directing the gravity vector and/or the magnitude and direction of the sideslip velocity.

5) Candidate trim variables that are not selected must be given constraint values. That statement demonstrates that trim is not a unique problem. A helicopter flying at constant speed and altitude can have zero roll and some sideslip, or zero sideslip and some roll, or any combination between these conditions. If the acceleration in body axes is zero, all of these conditions are valid trim points. But, as soon as the user specifies level flight for instance, then roll angle has been constrained to zero and sideslip has been chosen as a trim variable.

Table 17.1   Six rigid-body degrees of freedom requiring trim

Degree of freedom	Description
$\dot{u}_b$	Acceleration directed along the body x axis. Principle contributors are drag, thrust, and rotor H-force.
$\dot{v}_b$	Acceleration along the body y axis; typically rotor Y-force, fuselage side force, thrust of an antitorque rotor, vertical stabilizer/rudder force.
$\dot{w}_b$	Acceleration directed along the body z axis; thrust of rotors in typical helicopter configuration, wing lift, fuselage download, and weight contribute.
$\dot{p}_b$	Roll acceleration is directed about the body x axis. Rotors, propellers, wings, and stabilizers all generate rolling moments.
$\dot{q}_b$	Pitch acceleration is directed about the body y axis. Rotors, horizontal stabilizer/elevator, and fuselage are the major contributors.
$\dot{r}_b$	Yaw acceleration is directed about the body z axis. Vertical stabilizers/rudders, rotors through flapping and torque absorption contribute here.

Tables 17.1 and 17.2 list the degrees of freedom of the rigid aircraft body and additional degrees of freedom for rotors. Table 17.3 lists available trim variables. Table 17.3 is based on the list in the chapter on controls. It is expanded here to include some additional candidates.

17.3   Organizing the Trim Problem

The chapter on kinematics and dynamics provided the best tool to organize the trim problem. Repeated next, Eqs. (17.1) present the rigid-body equations of motion in body axes, along with motion over the Earth and angular orientation with respect to the inertial system. Table 17.4 describes every term in the four vector equations:

$$\dot{P}_e = T_{\mathrm{BE}}^{-1}(\varphi, \theta, \psi)V_b = T_{\mathrm{BE}}^{-1}(\alpha_e)V_b$$

$$\dot{V}_b = \mathrm{M}_b^{-1}\left[F_{\mathrm{total}} - \omega_b \times (mV_b)\right]$$

$$\dot{\omega}_b = I_n^{-1}\left[M_{\mathrm{total}} - \omega_b \times (I_n\omega_b)\right]$$

$$\dot{\alpha}_e = E^{-1}(\phi, \theta)\omega_b = E^{-1}(\alpha_e)\omega_b \qquad (17.1)$$

Table 17.2   Optional degrees of freedom requiring trim

Degree of freedom	Description
$\dot{\Omega}_{xmsn}$	Transmission acceleration is determined by the difference between the torque supplied by the engine(s) and the torque absorbed by the rotors, generators, airconditioners, etc. Transmission speed is often characterized by a single value called the reference speed. From the transmission speed the various rotor speeds are determined by gearing. At steady state, this value is zero.
$\dot{e}_0, \dot{e}_1, \dot{e}_2, \dot{e}_3$	Quaternion rates are the four degrees of freedom associated with quaternions. These rates are driven by body-axis angular rates and a constraint equation.
$a_{1|1}, b_{1|1}$	Longitudinal and lateral flapping of rotor number one. If the rotor model is the simple rigid beam with flapping hinge like the type presented in the rotor chapter, then these degrees of freedom are available. Often, they are not retained as independent degrees of freedom. Instead, the rotor dynamics are *residualized*; the rotor is treated as nothing more than a force and moment generator, and the flapping is solved algebraically.
$\dot{a}_{1|1}, \dot{b}_{1|1}$	Longitudinal and lateral flapping rates of rotor number one. If the rotor flapping degrees of freedom are retained as independent states, then flapping angles and rates will be used in the definition of flapping acceleration.
$a_{1|2}, b_{1|2}$	Longitudinal and lateral flapping of rotor number two; same description as for rotor number one.
$\dot{a}_{1|2}, \dot{b}_{1|2}$	Longitudinal and lateral flapping rates of rotor number two; same description as for rotor number one.
$[\beta(0), \dot{\beta}(0)]_{,m,b}$	For a more sophisticated rotor model, several elastic degrees of freedom (subscript m) are modeled for each blade (subscript b).

Table 17.3   Conceptual list of controls available to the pilot

Pilot control	Operation
Collective	The collective lever is the principle means of controlling collective blade pitch on main rotor of a single main rotor (SMR) helicopter, or both rotors of a tandem helicopter or tiltrotor.
Fore/aft cyclic	The fore/aft cyclic stick controls longitudinal cyclic blade pitch of an SMR helicopter or tiltrotor and differential collective blade pitch of a tandem helicopter. In airplane mode of a tiltrotor, this control also affects the elevator angle.

Continued

Table 17.3   Conceptual list of controls available to the pilot (*Continued*)

Pilot control	Operation
Lateral cyclic	The lateral cyclic stick controls lateral cyclic blade pitch of an SMR helicopter or the forward rotor of a tandem helicopter and differential collective blade pitch of a tiltrotor in helicopter mode and differential flaperon deflection of a tiltrotor in airplane mode.
Pedal	The pedals control collective blade pitch on the tail rotor of an SMR helicopter, lateral cyclic blade pitch on the aft rotor of a tandem helicopter, differential longitudinal cyclic blade pitch on a tiltrotor in helicopter mode, and differential collective blade pitch and/or rudder displacement on a tiltrotor in airplane mode.
Power lever	In tiltrotor aircraft, this lever is the collective/power lever. It commands collective blade-pitch angle in helicopter mode and power in airplane mode.
Throttle	Usually ganged with collective or power lever, the throttle controls fuel flow to the engines, thereby regulating potential power.
Mast angle	Unique to tiltrotor aircraft, the pylons (and therefore the masts) can be tilted forward from 90 to 0 deg, or aft to 95 deg. The mast angle is a very powerful pilot control. Control phasing, mixing, and washout are all governed by mast angle and airspeed.
Wing angle	Unique to tiltwing aircraft, the entire wing can be tilted forward from 90 deg to 0 deg. Rotor downwash helps maintain the wing at small angles of attack despite the apparent large geometric angles. In tiltwing aircraft, the angle of the wing governs control mixing, phasing, and washout.
Rotor rpm	The pilot has limited control over the rotor rpm, usually restricted to some nominal speed plus or minus a small range. Tiltrotors and tiltwings have two nominal values, one for helicopter mode and one for airplane mode. The pilot's control over these values is limited.
Flaps	Tiltrotors and tiltwings are equipped with flaps or flaperons on the main wing. The flaps are controlled by a lever in the cockpit, or sometimes by the control laws that depend on airspeed and mast angle.
LTM	Lateral translation mode is sometimes provided in tiltrotor aircraft. This is nothing more than lateral cyclic blade pitch introduced by the pilot via a small thumbwheel mounted on the collective lever head.
φ	Euler roll angle moves a component of the gravity vector along the body y axis.
θ	Euler pitch angle moves a component of the gravity vector along the body x axis.
$\beta_{sideslip}$	The sideslip angle resolves a component of forward velocity in to a sideward velocity. Note, this angle is opposite in direction from Euler yaw angle.

Table 17.4　Description of the terms in the equations of motion

Vector	Description
$P_e = \left\{ \begin{matrix} N \\ E \\ D \end{matrix} \right\}$	The position vector of the aircraft center of gravity in inertial (Earth) axes. The elements are the north, east, and down position.
$\alpha_e = \left\{ \begin{matrix} \phi \\ \theta \\ \psi \end{matrix} \right\}$	The vector of angular position of the aircraft body axes with respect to the Earth, resolved to the earth. The elements are roll, pitch, and yaw angles. They are usually called the Euler angles. The NASA convention for body axes is this: the origin is located at the center of gravity. The x axis points to the nose of the aircraft, the y axis points toward the right, and the z axis points down, consistent with a right-hand coordinate system.
$V_e = \left\{ \begin{matrix} \dot{N} \\ \dot{E} \\ \dot{D} \end{matrix} \right\}$	The velocity of the aircraft with respect to the Earth, resolved to the Earth. The elements are north-dot, east-dot, and down-dot. Down-dot is usually called the rate of descent.
$\dot{\alpha}_e = \omega_e = \left\{ \begin{matrix} \dot{\phi} \\ \dot{\theta} \\ \dot{\psi} \end{matrix} \right\}$	The time rate of change of the Euler angles.
$T_{BE}(\phi, \theta, \psi) = R_x(\phi)R_y(\theta)R_z(\psi)$	Transformation matrix from Earth to body axes, used for linear velocity terms. This matrix is orthonormal.
$R_x(\cdot), R_y(\cdot), R_z(\cdot)$	Rotation matrices about the x, y, and z axes, respectively. They are built with the rules discussed earlier. These matrices are orthonormal.
$E(\phi, \theta)$ $= \begin{bmatrix} 1 & 0 & -\sin(\theta) \\ 0 & \cos(\phi) & \sin(\phi)\cos(\theta) \\ 0 & -\sin(\phi) & \cos(\phi)\cos(\theta) \end{bmatrix}$	Transformation matrix from Earth to body axes for angular velocity terms. This matrix is not orthonormal, and its inverse is singular at $+/-90$ deg of pitch.
$V_b = T_{BE}V_e = \left\{ \begin{matrix} u \\ v \\ w \end{matrix} \right\}$	Inertial linear velocity of the aircraft, resolved to body axes. The elements are u, v, and w along the x, y, and z axes, respectively.

Continued

Table 17.4   Description of the terms in the equations of motion (*Continued*)

Vector	Description
$\boldsymbol{\omega}_b = E\boldsymbol{\omega}_e = \begin{Bmatrix} p \\ q \\ r \end{Bmatrix}$	Inertial angular velocity of the aircraft, resolved to body axes. The elements are the roll rate p, the pitch rate q, and the yaw rate r.
$c = \{Coll, Cyclic, Pedal, Throttle, \ldots\}$	A general collection of trim variable candidates that the pilot can manipulate.
$F_g = \begin{Bmatrix} -\sin(\theta) \\ \sin(\phi)\cos(\theta) \\ \cos(\phi)\cos(\theta) \end{Bmatrix} mg$	The gravity load applied to the aircraft center of gravity in body axes.
$F_{cg}(c) = \begin{Bmatrix} Fx \\ Fy \\ Fz \end{Bmatrix}$	The three-element force vector applied to the aircraft center of gravity, resolved to body axes.
$M_{\text{total}}(c) = \begin{Bmatrix} Mx \\ My \\ Mz \end{Bmatrix} = \begin{Bmatrix} L \\ M \\ N \end{Bmatrix}$	The three-element moment vector applied to the aircraft center of gravity, resolved to body axes.
$\dot{V}_b = M_b^{-1}\left[F_{\text{total}}(c) - \boldsymbol{\omega}_b \times mV_b\right]$	The body-axis acceleration vector. M_b is the mass matrix, and m is the mass. $F_{\text{total}}(c) = F_g + F_{cg}(c)$.
$\dot{\boldsymbol{\omega}}_b = I_n^{-1}\left[M_{\text{total}}(c) - \boldsymbol{\omega}_b \times (I_n\boldsymbol{\omega}_b)\right]$	The body-axis angular acceleration vector. I_n is the inertia matrix.

17.4   Specifying the Trim Problem

The problem must be specified with enough constraints and available trim controls so that the potential for a solution is possible. This means the simulation engineer must specify how many degrees of freedom the problem has; specify the flight regime with values for airspeed, rate of climb, rate of turn, etc.; specify the trim variables that will trim the degrees of freedom; and specify constraint values for the unused variables.

In the simplest case, the model has six degrees of freedom composed of three linear accelerations and three angular accelerations. All six accelerations must be driven to zero. The engineer-user must specify the airspeed, rate of climb, etc. For example, let the problem be to seek the controls and Euler angles needed to trim a six-degrees-of-freedom (DOF) aircraft in a 1.5-g turn at 100 kn with no rate of climb or descent. The first bullet has been covered—the aircraft has six degrees of freedom. The second bullet has been addressed, albeit indirectly. This point will be covered in greater detail a little later. The controls that will be used are the collective, fore/aft cyclic, lateral cyclic, pedal, Euler roll angle and Euler pitch angle. Naming the controls satisfies the third bullet. Finally, the variables that were not selected as trim candidates must have a value. So, set the yaw angle to zero, the rpm to some nominal operating speed, etc. All four bullets have been addressed, and so a trim problem with a unique solution has been specified provided the independent variables reach all of the dependent variables.

17.5 Selecting a Trim Method

Several methods are available to trim the aircraft model or dynamic subsystems. The most popular have names like sequential-correction, fly-to-trim, and Newton–Raphson or Jacobian method. Each is described in this section beginning with sequential correction.

17.5.1 Sequential Correction

Imagine the aircraft mounted on a sting in a wind tunnel. The attachment point is at the center of gravity. The sting prevents the aircraft from translating but does permit angular orientation with respect to the oncoming wind. The trim problem becomes one of finding the controls and angular orientation so that the three forces and three moments measured at the top of the sting are zero.

The usual implementation, which is inspired by piloting technique, is to find a solution for each degree of freedom sequentially, using a single control mapped to a single degree of freedom, then repeating the sequence in the hope that the sequence and the aircraft configuration do not lead to a nonconverging cycle of iterative guesses.

As an example, look at the problem of finding the trim solution for an American-made helicopter in hover, equipped with a single main rotor. Gross approximations of the effects of manipulating a particular control are given in Table 17.5. Notice the cross-control effects, especially of the collective. Raising the collective has predictable effects on the variables that are classically reserved for longitudinal dynamics alone. However, raising the collective also couples the longitudinal and lateral degrees of freedom by introducing a significant yaw moment.

In Table 17.6, the various degrees of freedom are paired with the trim variable most effective at controlling them. This table constitutes a *control strategy*. Also, the degrees of freedom are attacked in the order given in Table 17.6.

Let the initial guesses for the controls and Euler angles be 1) full down for collective, 2) center position for both cyclic controls and the pedals, and 3) zero for the Euler roll and pitch angles.

Now imagine a single pass using the sequential correction method. The X-force and Y-force are easily dispatched using the Euler pitch and roll angles in that order. The collective stick is raised to drive the Z-force to zero, which also introduces a large yawing moment. The lateral cyclic and longitudinal cyclic are manipulated to drive the roll and pitch moments to zero. Unfortunately, the cyclic application also generates significant force in the X and Y directions, upsetting the null that was achieved a few steps back. The pedal is used to zero the yaw moment, but this also generates a Y-force and a roll moment. So, the process must start again.

Obviously, a solution exists. Helicopters fly. But this technique chases its tail and can take a long time to converge. The reason is that the independent controls

Table 17.5 Example of control effectiveness

Force or moment	Collective (up)	Fore/aft (forward)	Lateral (right)	Pedal (right)	Roll (right)	Pitch (up)	Sideslip (nose left)
X-force	Small positive	Big positive	—	—	—	Big negative	—
Y-force	—	—	Big positive	Moderate negative	Big positive	—	Moderate negative
Z-force	Big negative	Small positive	—	—	Small positive	Small positive	—
Roll moment	—	—	Big positive	Moderate negative	—	—	Moderate negative
Pitch moment	Small negative	Big negative	—	—	—	—	—
Yaw moment	Big positive	—	Small negative	Big positive	—	—	Moderate negative

Table 17.6   Control mapping

Degree of freedom	Controlled by
X-force	Pitch
Y-force	Roll
Z-force	Collective
Roll moment	Lateral cyclic
Pitch moment	Fore/aft cyclic
Yaw moment	Pedal

Table 17.7   Demonstrating the effects of strong off-diagonal terms on the sequential-correction method

Plant 1	Plant 2
$$\begin{bmatrix} 4 & 1 \\ 1 & 4 \end{bmatrix} \begin{Bmatrix} x \\ y \end{Bmatrix} = \begin{Bmatrix} 3 \\ -3 \end{Bmatrix}$$	$$\begin{bmatrix} 4 & 4 \\ -4 & 4 \end{bmatrix} \begin{Bmatrix} x \\ y \end{Bmatrix} = \begin{Bmatrix} 0 \\ -8 \end{Bmatrix}$$
Assign x as the control for the top row and y as the control for the bottom row. Rewrite the equations to show the diagonal solution.	Assign x as the control for the top row and y as the control for the bottom row. Rewrite the equations to show the diagonal solution.
$x = 3/4 - 1/4y$ $y = -3/4 - 1/4x$	$x = 0 - y$ $y = -2 + x$
Start the solution with $y = 0$; solve for x using 1st equation.	Start the solution with $y = 0$, solve for x using 1st equation.
$x = 3/4$	$x = 0$
Using this value for x, solve for y using 2nd equation.	Using this value for x, solve for y using 2nd equation.
$y = -3/4 - 3/16 = -15/16$	$y = -2 + 0 = -2$
So, the solution after one complete pass through the equations is ...	The sequence thus far is represented by the ordered pairs ...
$x = 0.75$ $y = -0.938$	$x = 0$ $y = -2$
Go back to solve for x with the newest y value, and then solve for y with the newest x value. The solution after two complete passes through the equations is ...	Go back to solve for x with the newest y value, and then solve for y with the newest x value. The solution after two complete passes through the equations is ...
$x = 0.984$ $y = -0.996$	$x = 2$ $y = 0$
One more pass yields:	One more pass yields:
$x = 0.999$ $y = -1.000$	$x = 0$ $y = -2$

exercise very strong off-diagonal influence. A simple example illustrates the off-diagonal problem. Table 17.7 shows two 2×2 plants. Each plant has the same diagonal strength, and each plant has the same solution, namely, $x = 1, y = -1$. However, the plant on the left converges in only a few cycles while the plant on the right enters into a nonconverging cycle of estimation.

Obviously, the sequence on the left in Table 17.7 is converging to the correct answer $\{1, -1\}$. The sequence on the right in the table is oscillating with undiminished strength between two equally close/distant estimates to the solution.

If one knows that the plant has strong diagonal terms and weak off-diagonal terms, then the sequential-correction method, which is also known as the Gauss–Seidel method [2], will converge to the correct solution in a few iterations. Unfortunately, helicopters are rarely so cooperative.

17.5.2 Fly to Trim

It is tempting to try to do in a trim loop what pilots seemingly do with utter ease. Coding a robust fly-to-trim routine is difficult for airplanes and nearly impossible for helicopters. (Some readers will protest immediately that they have accomplished such a feat and that it was not difficult to do. In the author's experience, the protestor fails to point out that the trim procedure is tuned only for straight and level flight or climbing flight or turning flight, in other words, for a specific problem, not a general case. Furthermore, the trim tool is good only for that one aircraft or simple derivatives of it. Selective memory almost always plays a part—successes are more easily remembered than failures.) The attempt usually proceeds along these lines. As with the sequential-correction method, imagine that the aircraft is mounted on a sting in a wind tunnel. The attachment point is at the center of gravity. The sting constrains the aircraft from translating but permits angular orientation with respect to the oncoming wind. The trim problem becomes one of finding the controls and angular orientation so that the three forces and three moments measured at the top of the sting are zero.

Now, instead of zeroing the forces and moments one at a time, they are all driven to zero simultaneously. One of the Euler angles (roll or yaw) is constrained. The other angle, along with the pitch angle, is found by letting the dynamic equations of angular motion drive the Euler angles. In other words, four controls are being used to drive six degrees of freedom. The other two control "knobs" come from the gravity vector, which is being directed by two Euler angles. The angles come from some combination of the solution of the roll, pitch, and yaw equations of motion.

This technique requires a control law of sorts—one in which the nonzero accelerations are the error signal. As a first pass, one is tempted to arrange the process as shown in Fig. 17.1.

The initial guess on the controls C_{IC}, produces accelerations in body axes. These accelerations are passed through gains and generate derivatives of controls. Integration in time produces corrections to the controls that are added (or subtracted) to the initial guesses. In this simple scheme there would be 24 gains that the user would have to estimate.

Sometimes the fly-to-trim idea is employed for some inner-loop dynamics, whereas the outer loop is solved using an algebraic scheme. A popular application

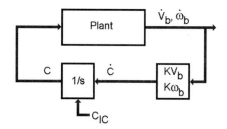

Fig. 17.1   Fly-to-trim scheme.

is finding the periodic solution for the rotor degrees of freedom. The rotor is simply permitted to spin around the azimuth some number of times with the hope that the transients decay to zero.

Fly-to-trim has several problems. The first problem is the need for the feedback gains before the trim process starts. A priori knowledge is hard to come by, especially when the gains are in unfamiliar units of control units per second per acceleration units, for example, (in./s)/(f/s²), as one surmises from Fig. 17.1. The second problem is the lack of damping in the feedback path. This problem is sometimes corrected one of two ways. A proportional-plus-integral feedback block is employed where just the integrator now shows, or a proportional-plus-derivative feedback block is employed with the more conventional stability and control derivatives. In either case, a stable closed-loop system is not guaranteed. A third problem is the unknown performance of the aircraft dynamics. Even with artificial damping, the time to settle on a solution can be great. Knowing how long to let the aircraft "fly" becomes a matter of "by guess and by golly."

This technique is not very good for coupled multiple-degrees-of-freedom systems. It is not even that good for single-degree-of-freedom-systems. However, it is often employed because it seems to be easier than finding an algebraic solution. It is not easier, as will be shown later in this chapter.

17.5.3 Jacobian

The preferred method of finding a trim for an n-degree-of-freedom system is the Jacobian method. This method comes from the same general technique that finds a solution x such that two functions $f(x)$ and $g(x)$ equal each other. The concept is simplicity itself. Let each function be represented by a Taylor series evaluated at an estimated root x_i and truncated after the linear term:

$$f(x_i + \Delta x) = f(x_i) + \frac{\partial f(x_i)}{\partial x} \Delta x$$

$$g(x_i + \Delta x) = g(x_i) + \frac{\partial g(x_i)}{\partial x} \Delta x$$

(17.2)

Set the two function series equal to each other, and solve for the correction:

$$\Delta x = -\left[\frac{\partial f(x_i)}{\partial x} - \frac{\partial g(x_i)}{\partial x}\right]^{-1} \left[f(x_i) - g(x_i)\right]$$

(17.3)

The astute reader recognizes the similarity to the redoubtable Newton–Raphson method. If the function $f(x_i)$ is the desired acceleration or error, which is zero in this case, then it is a constant, and there is no partial derivative of $f(x_i)$ with respect to x_i. Therefore, setting $f(x_i)$ and $\partial f(x_i)/\partial x$ to zero, Eq. (17.3) reduces to

$$\Delta x = -\left[\frac{\partial g(x_i)}{\partial x}\right]^{-1} g(x_i) \qquad (17.4)$$

The next guess for x is just $x_{i+1} = x_i + \Delta x$.

Continuing, here is how the Jacobian method is applied to the trim problem. Consider the six rigid-body equations of motion in vector form:

$$m\dot{V}_b + \omega_b \times (mV_b) = F_g + F_{cg} = F_t$$
$$I_n\dot{\omega}_b + \omega_b \times (I_n\omega_b) = M_{cg} = M_t \qquad (17.5)$$

The angular rates are usually zero, though they will contribute significant nonzero forces when trimming in a turn. Rearrange the preceding expressions, and solve for the highest derivatives.

$$\dot{V}_b = m^{-1}[F_t - \omega_b \times (mV_b)]$$
$$\dot{\omega}_b = I_n^{-1}[M_t - \omega_b \times (I_n\omega_b)] \qquad (17.6)$$

When the aircraft is in trim, the accelerations are zero:

$$\dot{V}_b = 0$$
$$\dot{\omega}_b = 0 \qquad (17.7)$$

The forces and moments applied at the center of gravity are functions of velocity, control settings, and Euler angles. A control column that contains the controls and Euler angles that are to be used as independent variables constitutes a control strategy. The trim problem becomes finding the values of the control strategy that satisfy expressions 17.7. The process proceeds this way.

Guess the values for the control strategy, and evaluate expressions (17.6). Unless the initial guesses were truly inspired or lucky, the accelerations will not be zero. So, build a Taylor series in the dependent and independent variables for each of the equations in (17.6):

$$\dot{V}_{b|0} + \Delta\dot{V}_b = m^{-1}\left[F_{t|0} - \omega_b \times (mV_b)\right] + m^{-1}\left(\frac{\partial F_t}{\partial c}\Delta c\right)$$
$$\dot{\omega}_{b|0} + \Delta\dot{\omega}_b = I_n^{-1}\left[M_{t|0} - \omega_b \times (I_n\omega_b)\right] + I_n^{-1}\left(\frac{\partial M_t}{\partial c}\Delta c\right) \qquad (17.8)$$

The partial derivatives on the RHS are a linear model of how a small change in a control variable will change a dependent variable. For instance, the first row in the preceding force equation looks like this if expanded:

$$\dot{u}_0 + \Delta \dot{u} = -(q_0 w_0 - r_0 v_0)$$

$$+ m^{-1} \left(\begin{array}{c} F_{x|0} + \dfrac{\partial F_x}{\partial \theta_0} \Delta \theta_0 + \dfrac{\partial F_x}{\partial A_1} \Delta A_1 + \dfrac{\partial F_x}{\partial B_1} \Delta B_1 \\[2ex] + \dfrac{\partial F_x}{\partial \theta_{\text{ped}}} \Delta \theta_{\text{ped}} + \dfrac{\partial F_x}{\partial \phi} \Delta \phi + \dfrac{\partial F_x}{\partial \theta} \Delta \theta \end{array} \right) \quad (17.9)$$

At trim, all subzero terms balance, that is,

$$\dot{u}_0 = -(q_0 w_0 - r_0 v_0) + m^{-1} F_{x|0} \quad (17.10)$$

Because this is the goal, subtract Eq. (17.10) from Eq. (17.9). The result is a linear model of the untrimmed aircraft:

$$\Delta \dot{u} = m^{-1} \left(\begin{array}{c} \dfrac{\partial F_x}{\partial \theta_0} \Delta \theta_0 + \dfrac{\partial F_x}{\partial A_1} \Delta A_1 + \dfrac{\partial F_x}{\partial B_1} \Delta B_1 + \dfrac{\partial F_x}{\partial \theta_{\text{ped}}} \Delta \theta_{\text{ped}} \\[2ex] + \dfrac{\partial F_x}{\partial \phi} \Delta \phi + \dfrac{\partial F_x}{\partial \theta} \Delta \theta \end{array} \right) \quad (17.11)$$

Carrying out the multiplication by the inverse of the mass as indicated in Eq. (17.11), the change in longitudinal acceleration is knowable as a function of any change to a control input or Euler angle:

$$\Delta \dot{u} = \left[\dfrac{\partial \dot{u}}{\partial \theta_0} \quad \dfrac{\partial \dot{u}}{\partial A_1} \quad \dfrac{\partial \dot{u}}{\partial B_1} \quad \dfrac{\partial \dot{u}}{\partial \theta_{\text{ped}}} \quad \dfrac{\partial \dot{u}}{\partial \phi} \quad \dfrac{\partial \dot{u}}{\partial \theta} \right] \left\{ \begin{array}{c} \Delta \theta_0 \\ \Delta A_1 \\ \Delta B_1 \\ \Delta \theta_{\text{ped}} \\ \Delta \phi \\ \Delta \theta \end{array} \right\} \quad (17.12)$$

Equation (17.12) was put into the inner product form to emphasize the vector arithmetic about to come. Expand similarly the other five equations of motion, and collect the partial derivatives in a square matrix, which is called the Jacobian, shown in expression (17.13).

$$J = \begin{bmatrix} \dfrac{\partial \dot{u}}{\partial \theta_0} & \dfrac{\partial \dot{u}}{\partial A_1} & \dfrac{\partial \dot{u}}{\partial B_1} & \dfrac{\partial \dot{u}}{\partial \theta_p} & \dfrac{\partial \dot{u}}{\partial \phi} & \dfrac{\partial \dot{u}}{\partial \Theta} \\[2mm] \dfrac{\partial \dot{v}}{\partial \theta_0} & \dfrac{\partial \dot{v}}{\partial A_1} & \dfrac{\partial \dot{v}}{\partial B_1} & \dfrac{\partial \dot{v}}{\partial \theta_p} & \dfrac{\partial \dot{v}}{\partial \phi} & \dfrac{\partial \dot{v}}{\partial \Theta} \\[2mm] \dfrac{\partial \dot{w}}{\partial \theta_0} & \dfrac{\partial \dot{w}}{\partial A_1} & \dfrac{\partial \dot{w}}{\partial B_1} & \dfrac{\partial \dot{w}}{\partial \theta_p} & \dfrac{\partial \dot{w}}{\partial \phi} & \dfrac{\partial \dot{w}}{\partial \Theta} \\[2mm] \dfrac{\partial \dot{p}}{\partial \theta_0} & \dfrac{\partial \dot{p}}{\partial A_1} & \dfrac{\partial \dot{p}}{\partial B_1} & \dfrac{\partial \dot{p}}{\partial \theta_p} & \dfrac{\partial \dot{p}}{\partial \phi} & \dfrac{\partial \dot{p}}{\partial \Theta} \\[2mm] \dfrac{\partial \dot{q}}{\partial \theta_0} & \dfrac{\partial \dot{q}}{\partial A_1} & \dfrac{\partial \dot{q}}{\partial B_1} & \dfrac{\partial \dot{q}}{\partial \theta_p} & \dfrac{\partial \dot{q}}{\partial \phi} & \dfrac{\partial \dot{q}}{\partial \Theta} \\[2mm] \dfrac{\partial \dot{r}}{\partial \theta_0} & \dfrac{\partial \dot{r}}{\partial A_1} & \dfrac{\partial \dot{r}}{\partial B_1} & \dfrac{\partial \dot{r}}{\partial \theta_p} & \dfrac{\partial \dot{r}}{\partial \phi} & \dfrac{\partial \dot{r}}{\partial \Theta} \end{bmatrix} \tag{17.13}$$

Obviously, the Jacobian relates small changes in trim variables to small changes in acceleration. That is,

$$\Delta a = (J)\,\Delta c \tag{17.14}$$

The acceleration and control perturbation vectors are ordered thus:

$$\Delta a = \{\Delta \dot{u} \quad \Delta \dot{v} \quad \Delta \dot{w} \quad \Delta \dot{p} \quad \Delta \dot{q} \quad \Delta \dot{r}\}^T$$
$$\Delta c = \{\Delta \theta_0 \quad \Delta A_1 \quad \Delta B_1 \quad \Delta \theta_{\text{ped}} \quad \Delta \varphi \quad \Delta \theta\}^T \tag{17.15}$$

As suggested earlier, the initial acceleration vector a_0

$$a_0 = \{\dot{u} \quad \dot{v} \quad \dot{w} \quad \dot{p} \quad \dot{q} \quad \dot{r}\}_0^T \tag{17.16}$$

will probably not be zero, based on poor initial guesses for the trim variables in c_0.

$$c_0 = \{\theta_0 \quad A_1 \quad B_1 \quad \theta_{\text{ped}} \quad \varphi \quad \theta\}_0^T \tag{17.17}$$

The guesses are improved by expanding the Taylor series and setting the result to the desired value, in this case zero:

$$0 = a_0 + \Delta a = a_0 + J\Delta c \tag{17.18}$$

Invert the J matrix, and solve for the correction:

$$\Delta c = -J^{-1} a_0 \tag{17.19}$$

This correction scheme is carried out until the acceleration error is acceptably small (good trim) or until the trim column is not changing (which might or might not mean a good trim has been achieved).

The Jacobian is not always known. Most often, the Jacobian must be calculated numerically, rather than analytically. Here is one method.

Given an initial guess at the trim column c_0, the accelerations are computed and placed in the vector a_0. Now, repeat the following steps for every variable in the trim column.

1) Set $k = 0$. The index k points to the kth element in c_0.

2) Increment $k(k = k + 1)$.

3) Add a small value $\varepsilon/2$ to the kth element in c_0, and put the result into the column c.

4) Evaluate the accelerations using this new c column. Put the accelerations into a column called a_p.

5) Subtract a small value $\varepsilon/2$ from the kth element in c_0, and put the result into the column c.

6) Evaluate the accelerations using this new c column. Put the accelerations into a column called a_m.

7) Subtract the a_m column from the a_p column, and divide each of those answers by ε. Place the result, which is a central difference approximation to the derivative of the acceleration with respect to c, into the kth column of J.

8) If k is less than 6, go back to step 2; otherwise, stop. At this point, J will now be filled with 36 partial derivatives.

This algorithm is the central-difference-derivative calculation of the Jacobian. Forward and backward difference derivatives are also possible. The best approach mixes all three derivatives. When a trim variable is near its lower limit and a negative perturbation would push it outside its physical limit, then a forward difference derivative should be calculated. Likewise, a backward difference derivative should be used if a forward perturbation would push a trim variable past its upper limit. Central difference derivatives should be used in all other cases.

17.5.4   Periodic Shooting

Let a dynamic system like the one described by Eq. (17.20) have a periodic, but otherwise mean-spirited forcing function, perhaps like that shown in Fig. 17.2:

$$\ddot{\beta} + 2\omega\varsigma\dot{\beta} + \omega^2\beta = u(t) \tag{17.20}$$

The dotted lines in Fig. 17.2 indicate the start of a period in the forcing function $u(t)$. In state-space notation, Eq. (17.20) is expressed as shown in Eq. (17.21):

$$\begin{Bmatrix} \dot{\beta} \\ \ddot{\beta} \end{Bmatrix} = \begin{bmatrix} 0 & 1 \\ -\omega^2 & -2\omega\varsigma \end{bmatrix} \begin{Bmatrix} \beta \\ \dot{\beta} \end{Bmatrix} + \begin{bmatrix} 0 \\ 1 \end{bmatrix} u(t) \tag{17.21}$$

or

$$\dot{x}(t) = Ax(t) + Bu(t) \tag{17.22}$$

Often, one is required to find the periodic solution to such a driven system. When one seeks a periodic solution, one requires the state vector at time zero to equal

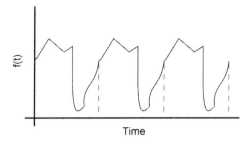

Fig. 17.2 **Periodic, but very jagged forcing function.**

the state vector at time T.

$$x(T) = x(0) \quad (17.23)$$

The time T is the period of the forcing function. If the system is thought of as a process, then the functional form is

$$x(T) = g[x(0)] \quad (17.24)$$

In other words, given the state vector at time zero, the process generates the state vector at time T, plus all intermediate times. If $x(T) = x(0)$, then the solution is periodic. If not, then imagine a small correction added to the initial condition so that the final result also has the same small change:

$$x(T) + \Delta x = g[x(0) + \Delta x] \quad (17.25)$$

Now expand the RHS in a Taylor series:

$$x(T) + \Delta x = g[x(0)] + G[x(0)]\Delta x \quad (17.26)$$

where

$$G[x(0)] = \left. \frac{\partial g(x)}{\partial x} \right|_{x=x(0)}$$

Because the desired solution is $x(T) = x(0)$, make this substitution to the LHS of Eq. (17.24), and solve the resulting equation for Δx:

$$\Delta x = \{1 - G[x(0)]\}^{-1}\{g[x(0)] - x(0)\} \quad (17.27)$$

Finally, substitute Eq. (17.24) into Eq. (17.27) to get

$$\Delta x = \{1 - G[x(0)]\}^{-1}[x(T) - x(0)] \quad (17.28)$$

One sees that the preceding expression is just a variation on the theme introduced by Eq. (17.3). This update equation is the so-called periodic-shooting technique, and it has a remarkable, though certainly not unexpected, strength. If the dynamic system is linear, as Eq. (17.20) is, and the forcing function is independent of the state vector and its derivative, then this technique will find the periodic solution in just one iteration. Even if the system is slightly nonlinear, or the forcing function has some dependence on the state vector (damping in the blade flapping equation due to modal rate is one example), this technique will perform well, finding the periodic solution and a linear correction model at the same time in just a few iterations.

All that is left is to determine the partial derivative matrix $G(x)$. What follows is a straightforward numerical technique that has served the author well over the years:

1) Guess values for the elements of the state vector $x_0(0)$ at time $= 0$. The null vector is often as good as any other guess.

2) Integrate this equation through one full period of the forcing function, and store the state vector at the end of the integration in a vector called $x_0(2\pi)$. That is, integrate $\dot{x}(t) = Ax(t) + Bu(t)$ with the initial condition on $x(0) = x_0(0)$. If $x_0(2\pi) = x_0(0)$, then the initial conditions are correct, and a periodic solution exists; skip to step eight. If not, proceed to step three.

3) Set an index $j = 1$.

4) Create a new initial guess vector by perturbing element j of the $x_0(0)$ vector with a small quantity ε:

$$x_j(0) = x_0(0) + E(j)\varepsilon \qquad \text{with} \quad E(1) = \begin{Bmatrix} 1 \\ 0 \\ \vdots \\ 0 \end{Bmatrix}, \quad E(2) = \begin{Bmatrix} 0 \\ 1 \\ \vdots \\ 0 \end{Bmatrix}, \text{ etc.}$$

$E(j)$ is a column of zeros, except the jth element, which is unity.

5) Integrate this equation through one full period, and store the state vector at the end of the integration in a vector called $x_j(2\pi)$. In other words, integrate $\dot{x}(t) = Ax(t) + Bu(t)$ with the initial condition on $x(0) = x_j(0)$.

6) Load the jth column of an $n \times n$ matrix G with the quantity

$$G(1 : n, j) = \frac{\left[x_j(T) - x_j(0)\right]}{\varepsilon}$$

The notation $G(1 : n, j)$ refers to elements in rows 1 to n of column j. The term n is the number of states in the x vector.

7) If j is less than n, increment j by one, and repeat steps four to six. If j equals n, then the calculation of G is finished.

8) End algorithm.

At the end of this chapter, the reader will find an example of code written in BASIC that trims a second-order system using the periodic-shooting technique.

17.6 Two Special Trim Problems

17.6.1 Special Case of Trimming in a Turn

In the section labeled **Specifying the Trim Problem**, the problem of indirect specification was mentioned. The example was the problem of finding a trim in a turn at a given airspeed and at a desired load factor. Ideally, the user specifies values for the states directly. However, it is sometimes much easier to specify values for a derived parameter and then solve for the states using the equations of motion in static equilibrium. For instance, start again with the equations of linear motion and formal definitions of the state vectors.

$$M\dot{V}_b + \omega_b \times MV_b = F_{\text{grav}} + F_a \tag{17.29}$$

where

$$V_b = \begin{Bmatrix} u \\ v \\ w \end{Bmatrix}_b = \begin{bmatrix} T_{11} & T_{12} & T_{13} \\ T_{21} & T_{22} & T_{23} \\ T_{31} & T_{32} & T_{33} \end{bmatrix} \begin{Bmatrix} \dot{N} \\ \dot{E} \\ \dot{D} \end{Bmatrix}_e \tag{17.30}$$

$$\omega_b = \begin{Bmatrix} p \\ q \\ r \end{Bmatrix}_b = \begin{bmatrix} 1 & 0 & -\sin\theta \\ 0 & \cos\phi & \sin\phi\cos\theta \\ 0 & -\sin\phi & \cos\phi\cos\theta \end{bmatrix} \begin{Bmatrix} \dot{\phi} \\ \dot{\theta} \\ \dot{\psi} \end{Bmatrix} \tag{17.31}$$

$$F_{\text{grav}} = \begin{Bmatrix} F_{\text{gx}} \\ F_{\text{gy}} \\ F_{\text{gz}} \end{Bmatrix} = \begin{Bmatrix} -\sin\theta \\ \sin\phi\cos\theta \\ \cos\phi\cos\theta \end{Bmatrix} mg = \begin{Bmatrix} T_{13} \\ T_{23} \\ T_{33} \end{Bmatrix} mg \tag{17.32}$$

$$F_a = \begin{Bmatrix} F_{\text{ax}} \\ F_{\text{ay}} \\ F_{\text{az}} \end{Bmatrix} \tag{17.33}$$

Now, define load factors as the ratio of aerodynamic force to aircraft weight:

$$N_x = \frac{F_{\text{ax}}}{mg}$$
$$N_y = \frac{F_{\text{ay}}}{mg} \tag{17.34}$$
$$N_z = -\frac{F_{\text{az}}}{mg}$$

Note the negative sign in the N_z expression. This sign makes N_z positive (a historical requirement) because F_{az} is negative in trim. In trim, the accelerations are zero. For a turn as seen from Earth, the only nonzero Euler angle rate is $\dot{\psi}$. Substitute

Eqs. (17.30)–(17.34) into Eq. (17.29), and set $\dot{V}_b = 0$. The result is

$$\dot{\psi}\left(T_{12}\dot{N} - T_{11}\dot{E}\right) = g\left(T_{13} + N_x\right)$$
$$\dot{\psi}\left(T_{22}\dot{N} - T_{31}\dot{E}\right) = g\left(T_{23} + N_y\right) \qquad (17.35)$$
$$\dot{\psi}\left(T_{32}\dot{N} - T_{31}\dot{E}\right) = g\left(T_{33} - N_z\right)$$

In a coordinated turn, a desired N_z is achieved while $N_y = 0$. The sideslip velocity in Earth axes is $\dot{E}$, which is set to zero for this discussion. The expressions that follow are easily adapted for the case of a nonzero $\dot{E}$. Substitute the desired value for N_z into the third of Eqs. (17.35), and set $N_y = 0$ in the second of Eq. (17.34):

$$\dot{\psi} = \frac{gT_{23}}{U_e T_{22}}$$
$$\dot{\psi} = \frac{g\left(T_{33} - N_{z\text{-desired}}\right)}{U_e T_{32}} \qquad (17.36)$$

Set the two preceding expressions equal to each other, and solve for N_z:

$$N_{z\text{-desired}} = T_{33} - \frac{T_{23}T_{32}}{T_{22}} = \frac{T_{11}}{T_{22}} \qquad (17.37)$$

Expression (17.37) is a nonlinear constraint equation on the Euler roll and pitch angles. However, it is sufficient to find the necessary roll angle to achieve the desired load factor in the z direction and maintain a zero load factor in the y direction. To see this, expand Eq. (17.37) in a Taylor series about the roll angle:

$$N_{z\text{-desired}} = N_{z0} + \frac{\partial N_z}{\partial \phi}\Delta\phi = N_{z0} - \frac{T_{11}T_{32}}{T_{22}^2}\Delta\phi \qquad (17.38)$$

Now solve for the change in roll angle:

$$\Delta\phi = \frac{-T_{22}^2\left(N_{z\text{-desired}} - N_{z0}\right)}{T_{11}T_{32}} \qquad (17.39)$$

If one starts with the classical definition of the roll angle for a desired load factor, namely,

$$\phi_0 = \cos^{-1}\left(\frac{1}{N_{z\text{-desired}}}\right) \qquad (17.40)$$

and one applies the correction of Eq. (17.39) at the bottom of a trim loop, *after* the other updates from the standard trim method, then the trim will be driven to the desired load factor in the z direction and zero lateral load factor.

17.6.2 Special Case of Trimming in a Pull-up

When one desires a wings level load factor other than unity, use a pull-up or pushover. Start with Eq. (17.29) and rearrange to isolate the angular rates:

$$\boldsymbol{\omega}_b \times M\boldsymbol{V}_b = \boldsymbol{F}_{\text{grav}} + \boldsymbol{F}_a - M\dot{\boldsymbol{V}}_b \qquad (17.41)$$

Trim means the body-axis acceleration is zero. Substitute Eqs. (17.30–17.34) into Eq. (17.41), and solve for the body-pitch rate q. The result is

$$q = \frac{(N_{z\text{-desired}} - T_{33})\, g + (\dot{\phi} + T_{13}\dot{\psi})(T_{21}\dot{N} + T_{22}\dot{E} + T_{23}\dot{D})}{(T_{11}\dot{N} + T_{12}\dot{E} + T_{13}\dot{D})} \qquad (17.42)$$

If $\dot{E} = \dot{D} = \dot{\phi} = \dot{\psi} = \phi = \theta = \psi = 0$, then the result is the well-known expression:

$$q = \frac{(N_{z\text{-desired}} - 1)\, g}{\dot{N}} \qquad (17.43)$$

This chapter shows that classical results are subsets of expressions of greater rigor and that with some simple notation greater rigor is achieved without any appreciable increase in effort. The reader is encouraged to find other expressions that relate load factor to angular rates and also to find methods to trim to desired nonzero acceleration.

17.7 Example Code for Periodic Shooting

```
DECLARE SUB rotor (x!(), a!(), b!(), dt!, nt!, ns!, om!, iplot)
DECLARE SUB trimrot (a!(), b!(), x0!(), x!(), x2pi!(), xe(), jac!(), dt, nt, ns, om)
'
'    This routine demonstrates periodic shooting. We will use it
'    to find the initial conditions for a rotor equation given a
'    strange forcing function.
'

DIM a(2, 2)
DIM b(2)
DIM x0(2)
DIM x2pi(2)
DIM x(2)
DIM xe(2)
DIM jac(2, 2)
'
CLS
ns = 2                          'Number of states
nt = 24                         '# of azimuth positions
om = 30!                        'Rotor speed
p = 1.05                        'Non-dimensional modal freq.
wn = p * om                     'Modal frequency
```

```
a(1, 1) = 0!                          'Dynamic matrix
a(1, 2) = 1!                          '
a(2, 1) = -wn * wn                    '
a(2, 2) = 0!                          '
b(1) = 0!                             'Control power matrix
b(2) = wn * wn                        '
period = 2 * 3.141592654# / om        'Period of rotor revolution
dt = period / nt                      'Integration step size
'
x0(1) = 0!                            'Guess initial conditions
x0(2) = 0!                            '
CALL trimrot (a(), b(), x0(), x(), x2pi(), xe(), jac(), dt, nt, ns, om)
'
'       Demonstrate the trim.
'
FOR j = 1 TO ns                       'Load the initial conditions
    x(j) = x0(j)                      'into the state vector.
NEXT j                               '
nt = nt * 3                          'Show several periods.
CALL rotor(x(), a(), b(), dt, nt, ns, om, 1)   'Run rotor for 1 revolution
PRINT USING "####.### "; x0(1), x0(2)          'Print azimuth 0
PRINT USING "####.### "; x(1), x(2)            'Print azimuth 2 pi.


SUB rotor (x(), a(), b(), dt, nt, ns, om, iplot)
'
'       Create a dummy rotor model.
'
IF iplot = 1 THEN
    SCREEN 8
    LINE (0, 100) – (600, 100), 4
    LINE (0, 0) – (0, 199), 4
END IF
'
ffl = 4
daz = om * dt
FOR i = 1 TO nt
    az = (i – 1) * daz
    ff = 3 * COS(az) – 2 * SIN(2 * az) ^ 2 + COS(3 * az) ^ 3
    xd1 = a(1, 1) * x(1) + a(1, 2) * x(2) + b(1) * ff
    xd2 = a(2, 1) * x(1) + a(2, 2) * x(2) + b(2) * ff
    x1 = x(1) + xd1 * dt
    x2 = x(2) + xd2 * dt
    IF iplot = 1 THEN
        ix1 = (i – 1) * 8
        ix2 = ix1 + 8
        iy1 = 100 – x(1) * 5
        iy2 = 100 – x1 * 5
        LINE (ix1, iy1) – (ix2, iy2), 14
```

```
        iy1 = 100 – ffl * 5
        iy2 = 100 – ff * 5
        LINE (ix1, iy1) – (ix2, iy2), 12
      END IF
      x(1) = x1
      x(2) = x2
      ffl = ff
  NEXT i
  END SUB
  SUB trimrot (a(), b(), x0(), x(), x2pi(), xe(), jac(), dt, nt, ns, om)
  '
  '       Use the periodic shooting technique to find the initial conditions
  '       for the rotor state variables.
  '
  eps = .1                                    'Perturbation on state
  DO                                          'Begin trim loop
  '
      FOR j = 1 TO ns                         'Load the initial conditions
        x(j) = x0(j)                          'into the state vector.
      NEXT j                                  '
      CALL rotor(x(), a(), b(), dt, nt, ns, om, 0)   'Run rotor for 1 revolution
      FOR j = 1 TO ns                         'Read the final conditions
        x2pi(j) = x(j)                        'from the state vector.
        xe(j) = x2pi(j) – x0(j)               'Get error column for this
      NEXT j                                  'sub-zero pass.

      FOR k = 1 TO ns                         'Now build the Jacobian
        x0(k) = x0(k) + eps                   'Perturb the kth state
        FOR i = 1 TO ns                       'Load the initial conditions
          x(i) = x0(i)                        'into the state vector.
        NEXT i                                '
        CALL rotor(x(), a(), b(), dt, nt, ns, om, 0) 'Run rotor for 1 revolution
        FOR i = 1 TO ns                       'Read the final conditions
        jac(i, k) = (x(i) – x2pi(i)) / eps    'Get error column for this
        NEXT i                                'perturbation pass.
        x0(k) = x0(k) – eps                   'Recover initial value of kth state
      NEXT k                                  '
  '
  '       The jacobian matrix represents a linear model of the change in
  '       a state at azimuth 2 pi due to a change at azimuth 0, i.e.,
  '       dx(2pi) = J * dx(0). We want x(2pi) = x(0). Expand both sides
  '       in a Taylor series, to first terms. Then
  '
  '       x(2pi) + dx(2pi) = x(0) + dx(0).
  '
  '       But, since dx(2pi) = J * dx(0), then then expression above can be
  '       written as
  '
```

> x(2pi) + J * dx(0) = x(0) + dx(0)
>
> Solving for dx(0) yields:
>
> dx(0) = inv(1 – J) * (x(2pi) – x(0))
>
> Calculate the inverse of 1 – Jac.
>

```
jac(1, 1) = 1! – jac(1, 1)
jac(1, 2) = –jac(1, 2)
jac(2, 1) = –jac(2, 1)
jac(2, 2) = 1! – jac(2, 2)
det = jac(1, 1) * jac(2, 2) – jac(2, 1) * jac(1, 2)
tmp = jac(1, 1)
jac(1, 1) = jac(2, 2) / det
jac(2, 2) = tmp / det
jac(1, 2) = –jac(1, 2) / det
jac(2, 1) = –jac(2, 1) / det
```

>
> Get the correction
>

```
FOR i = 1 TO ns
  sum = 0!
  FOR j = 1 TO ns
    sum = sum + jac(i, j) * xe(j)
  NEXT j
  x0(i) = x0(i) + sum
NEXT i
```

>
> Get the magnitude of the error.
>

```
sum = 0!
FOR i = 1 TO ns
  sum = sum + xe(i) * xe(i)
NEXT i
magxe = SQR(sum)
icnt = icnt + 1
```

>

```
LOOP UNTIL icnt = 5 OR magxe < .0001
END SUB
```

17.8 Conclusions

After discussing the requirements and organization of the problem of trim, this chapter described several methods to manipulate independent variables so that dependent variables could be driven to some desired values, usually zero. These Jocobian and periodic-shooting methods are easily used in problems other than flight simulations, and so this is a generic discussion once the reader gets past the flight references. The reader is also discouraged from using the fly-to-trim method because it consumes much time and cannot positively guarantee a solution will ever be achieved. The chapter ends with two special flight problems: trimming in a turn and trimming in a pull-up or pushover.

References

[1] Geibert, Ronald R., and Nolan, Patrick B., *Kitty Hawk and Beyond, the Wright Brothers and the Early Years of Aviation*, Roberts Rinehart Publishers, Lanham, MD, 1990, p. 27.

[2] Beckett, Royce, and Hurt, James, *Numerical Calculations and Algorithms*, McGraw–Hill, New York, 1967, pp. 101–107.

Problems

17.1 You desire to find a trim condition for a helicopter simulation. The trim condition is 100 kn, wings level (meaning there is no roll angle). Knowing that the tail rotor is mounted above the center of gravity and generates significant y-force directed toward the right because of its antitorque job, how are you going to achieve wings-level trim?

17.2 You desire to trim a tiltrotor for straight and level flight at 165 kn using 2000 hp. Unfortunately 2000 hp is insufficient to maintain altitude. What do you do? How many dependent degrees of freedom are required for this trim problem? What are they? How many independent degrees of freedom do you need to do the trim? What are they? Create a table similar to Table 17.5, which maps the influence of each independent control to one or more dependent variables. Indicate the strength of the influence, e.g., "strong," "moderate," or "weak."

17.3 Use the Jacobian method to find u and v such that x and y are both zero in the two simultaneous nonlinear equations shown next. Use $\begin{Bmatrix} u \\ v \end{Bmatrix} = \begin{Bmatrix} 1 \\ 1 \end{Bmatrix}$ as the initial guess.

$$x = 10u^2 - 2uv - 2v^2 - 34$$

$$y = -5u^2 + 12uv + 10v^2 + 2$$

How many iterations were required to achieve a solution?

17.4 Repeat problem three, but now use $\begin{Bmatrix} u \\ v \end{Bmatrix} = \begin{Bmatrix} 1 \\ 0 \end{Bmatrix}$ as the initial guess. Did your solution converge? If not, why not? If so, how many iterations were required to achieve a solution?

17.5 Repeat problem three, but now use $\begin{Bmatrix} u \\ v \end{Bmatrix} = \begin{Bmatrix} 0 \\ 1 \end{Bmatrix}$ as the initial guess. Did your solution converge? If not, why not? If so, how many iterations were required to achieve a solution?

17.6 Repeat problem three, but now use $\begin{Bmatrix} u \\ v \end{Bmatrix} = \begin{Bmatrix} 0 \\ 0 \end{Bmatrix}$ as the initial guess. Did your solution converge? If not, why not? If so, how many iterations were required to achieve a solution?

18
Assembly

18.1 Introduction

All of the best tools and elemental models in the world do no good if they cannot be organized into a sensible simulation. A sensible simulation comes from a well-written mathematical model that is easy to read, easy to navigate, easy to modify, easy to maintain, and uses variable names that are familiar to the industry and consistent throughout the model. The computer code that expresses the model should have those same features and also include nice features such as computer variable names that resemble the mathematical model names and obvious functional divisions like subroutines that perform a single, specific function such as matrix inversion or modeling a wing. One can never include too many comments—making a code self-documenting will help you and the people that follow you when modifications to the code are needed. (The author takes some pride in the fact that a particular piece of FORTRAN code he wrote in the mid-1970s actually caused one compiler to choke. The error reported by the compiler was that there were too many comments!) These requirements are obvious, but are important enough to mention.

The distinction between a mathematical model and a computer code has not been made before now, but the difference is important. A mathematical model is a collection of the equations that describe the physics of a problem. That is, if one wishes to describe the lift on a wing, one uses Eq. (18.1).

$$L = \frac{1}{2}\rho V^2 S C_L \tag{18.1}$$

That is an example of a statement from a mathematical model. Now, if one wishes for a computer to solve this equation, the following FORTRAN code fragment will suffice:

```
REAL*4   LIFT
LIFT = 0.5 * RHO * V ** 2 * S * CL
```

A BASIC fragment might read:

```
DIM LIFT AS SINGLE
LIFT = 0.5 * RHO * V^2 * S * CL
```

393

Both of the code fragments calculate the lift, though subtle differences exist in the grammar and syntax of the language. In other words, the mathematical model is the same, but the expression in the computer code is different. Many professionals are often careless about the distinction. Do not emulate them.

There are other, less obvious requirements on mathematical models and the computer codes that support them. The structure of the model and code, how one initializes the model and the code, and how one constructs an interface between the code and other software and hardware comprise questions that this chapter answers.

18.2   Structure

Consider the dynamic equations of motion of the six rigid-body degrees of freedom. From the chapter on kinematics and dynamics, the fuselage-state equations are

$$\dot{P}_e = T_{\mathrm{BE}}^{-1}(\Phi, \Theta, \Psi)V_b = T_{\mathrm{BE}}^{-1}(\alpha_e)V_b$$

$$\dot{V}_b = M_b^{-1}[F_{\mathrm{ext}} - \omega_b \times (M_b V_b)]$$

$$\dot{\omega}_b = I_n^{-1}[M_{\mathrm{ext}} - \omega_b \times (I_n \omega_b)]$$

$$\dot{\alpha}_e = E^{-1}(\Phi, \Theta)\omega_b = E^{-1}(\alpha_e)\omega_b \qquad (18.2)$$

Recall, each vector equation represents three degrees of freedom, and so the preceding collection represents a total of 12 differential equations. The first remarkable point about these equations is that, except for the forces and moments named in the middle two equations, all of this information is easily modeled on one page, and one can argue, in one subroutine. Figures 18.1 and 18.2 show one way in which the equations are expressed schematically.

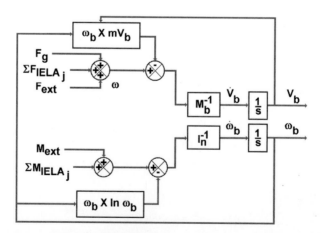

Fig. 18.1   Schematic of the linear and angular acceleration equations.

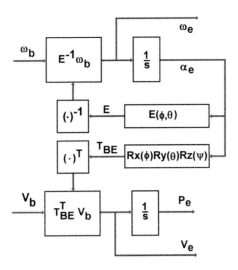

Fig. 18.2   Origin of the Euler angles and Earth-to-body transformation equations.

Modelers who are new to the process of simulation are often confused about where to break the equations to start the simulation. That confusion is sometimes because a trim problem is specified in Earth axes, whereas the fuselage states are expressed in body axes. To make the transformation, Euler angles are required. But Euler angles, which measure with respect to the Earth, are the integrated output of rates expressed in body axes. It seems that a never-ending loop is formed. Ratiocination has taken a holiday. In effect, an infinite loop has been formed; Figs. 18.1 and 18.2 support this assertion, but logical reasoning has not been abandoned.

The goal of this section is to describe one approach to organize a flight simulation. If one takes the time to write and organize before programming, then the code will practically write itself.

Step 1: Obtain a clear and concise copy of the mathematical model.   Without an unambiguous description of the physics and mathematics, the reader will not create a simulation. Instead, the simulation engineer will generate a complex plate of "spaghetti code" that bears only a passing resemblance to flight dynamics. (So-called spaghetti code is computer code that uses "go to" statements that meander throughout a routine, backtracking sometimes, forming loops that exit with clumsy condition tests, etc. It is called spaghetti code because a flow chart of the code cannot be drawn in one plane without many information paths that cross over or tangle with other paths—the flowchart resembles a plate of spaghetti.) This cannot be stressed enough. Review the mathematical model. Look for consistency on variable name usage. Look for dynamic loops, and identify all integrations so that the number of initial conditions that must be specified or found is known. Look for algebraic loops, and ascertain their need. For instance, the thrust/induced velocity loop is an algebraic loop that must be solved at every time step. Identify constants and variables, and determine which of the constants are low-level user-defined data and which are derived from user-defined data. Be brutal in your inquisition.

Step 2: Determine the end use of the simulation.   Determine if the simulation is to operate in non real time, for instance, by a user sitting at a desk, or is the simulation to be part of a larger man-in-the-loop effort with hardware interfaces that must also be driven. Asking and answering this question early will help to organize the input and output to the program. In several programs with which the author is intimate, the same code is used for batch and real-time processing. The code was written so that control inputs were introduced to the program either through an interface to hardware such as the pilot's cyclic stick, or though a time history of control input that could be read from an input file. End use also helps determine what method(s) should be used to solve the mathematical model. For instance, should an all-digital solution technique be employed, or should an analog computer be used for integration, or should some hybrid combination be employed?

Step 3: Decide on operation or execution features.   If the simulation is a batch process, the end-user might not have a need for re-initialization (RE-IC) or execution hold. However, if the simulation is to operate in real time, then trim at arbitrary points, reset to those trim points; normal operation and freeze execution (HOLD) are all likely to be desired. Be certain to consider control over all dynamic states collectively and separately. Be certain also that algebraic loop implicit "states" are initialized properly.

Step 4: Choose the programming language.   If one is fortunate enough to start a project with a clean sheet of paper, then the choice of language is yours. When choosing the language, you will consider the ease of coding, readability, maintainability, transportability, intended use, ease of interface with other languages, and your own familiarity and comfort with a programming language. On the other hand, if you are modifying or extending the capability of an extant code, the vast majority of legacy code is written in FORTRAN of various ages, and this language will continue because business cases for rewriting a code into a new language just because the original language is old just do not exist. Worse yet, rewriting is a superlative method to introduce errors. (The author does not want to proselytize on the selection of computer languages, but some defense of FORTRAN is called for because many engineering schools have stopped teaching FORTRAN, opting instead to instruct in C or C++. The fact is, both languages are fine. FORTRAN, which stands for formula translation, was designed to let the scientist/engineer use the power of the computer without having to become a computer scientist to do it. With FORTRAN and ASSEMBLY, man went to the moon. Those who argue that C or C++ is faster than FORTRAN are eliciting an appeal to elitism more than stating fact. The author once demonstrated that point by writing two programs that multiplied two 10×10 matrices together 1000 times. The first was written in tight C code; the second was written in FORTRAN. Both were compiled and executed on the same computer. The C code took 2% *more* time to execute than the FORTRAN code! Code speed is a function of the compiler as much as anything else. But more to the point, the great strength of C is not its speed in mathematics, but rather its ability to work with memory so that, for instance, clever user interface programming is possible. If the language you know is C, then by all means use it, but do not "poo poo" a language without cause.)

Step 5: Decide on names of variables, indexing and subscripting rules. All variables that represent physical properties or specific ideas in the mathematical model should be given names that resemble the mathematical model names as closely as possible. Variables that perform the function of place-keeper should be given simple names. For instance, the names of vectors that will be added together in a subroutine designed to perform this generic function should use problem-independent variable names. Do not get cute. The author is reminded of a colleague who used to name subroutines after his many girlfriends. This did not endear him to either his girlfriends or his coworkers.

In some cases, the mathematical model may specify that a particular set of arithmetic functions be performed on many similar devices. For instance, a generic landing-gear model only needs to be written for one gear. Then a loop that calls the generic model with an appropriate subscript solves the loads problem for each gear. The mathematical model may specify G_L, G_R, G_N for left, right, and nose gear. The code will require integers, not characters for subscripts. Comments in the code do the trick.

Sometimes a variable can have more than one subscript. An example might be a force vector that stores the X, Y, and Z direction forces for 15 different elements on the aircraft. High-level languages permit multiple indices, but which index should come first? That is, should the force vector be declared as F(3,15) or F(15,3)? The author favors the first option because the columns will most likely be premultiplied by transformation matrices. Certain economies of coding are possible if the storage technique is kept in mind.

Another consideration is the use of structures. High-level languages such as C, FORTRAN, and Visual BASIC® permit, and even encourage, the use of structures and classes.

Step 6: Decide on the types of trims or program initializations that are required. In the real world, a pilot climbs into a "cold, dark" cockpit and runs through a specific process to bring systems on line, start engines, taxi, and fly. That is, in the real world, the aircraft usually starts on the ground, not moving.

In the simulator world, the end-user might wish to trim the aircraft on the ground. More likely, the end-user will want to trim the aircraft in a steady-state flight condition. It is also possible that the user will want to trim only a subsystem on the aircraft. A carefully thought-out program will enable the end-user to specify a trim assignment with all of the following features:

1) What degrees of freedom are to be trimmed?
2) To what constraints (type and value) are the dependent variables subjected?
3) What candidate variables (controls) can be applied to the trim problem?
4) To what bounds are the candidate variables subjected?
5) What are the initial guesses for the candidates.
6) If a candidate locks itself to a bound, can another variable be used in its place so that the trim can continue? If so, how does one specify that?

To see how these questions are answered, consider this trim assignment. "Trim the six degree of freedom aircraft to a total velocity of 60 knots at a constant power of 100 horsepower. The rigid body is to be unaccelerated and have zero sideslip angle. The usual fore/aft and lateral stick, pedals, and collective can be employed within their physical limits. If the collective reaches a limit, freeze the collective at the limit, and use rotor speed as an alternative independent variable. Use the center position of all controls and zero rate of descent, pitch angle, and roll angle as the initial guess." The reader can argue that this assignment was embellished, and that common usage implies many of the things that were stated. The fact is, if a shorter script, say, "Trim the helicopter at 60 kn and 100 hp," was specified, then the end-user either had the other constraints in mind, or had asked the simulation code to solve an underconstrained problem.

Step 7: List the elements that require models.   The mathematical model should make this step easy. Examine the model for elements that require detailed modeling. Elemental models can include fuselage, wings, rotors, propellers, landing gear, control laws, control mixing, geometry, mass properties, fuel system, etc. Each elemental model will have its own preferred reference axes, position vectors, and orientation vectors that position it relative to some overall aircraft reference axes. Once the models are known, look for obvious duplications so that a generic piece of code works for many elemental models. For instance, a vertical stabilizer/ rudder is not different from a wing with a flap, only the orientation and operating environment changed. Consider coding one generic wing module.

Step 8: List the mathematical operations that appear with regularity.   This text has repeatedly used vector and matrix representation to do most of the work. A set of algebra routines will reduce coding errors and debug effort by an order of magnitude. Consider writing routines to do the following: matrix inversion; matrix multiplication; matrix addition/subtraction; matrix Transposition; matrix copy; vector addition/subtraction; inner product; cross product; outer product; vector copy; matrix-vector multiplication; quaternion operations; rotations about X, Y, and Z individually; speciality transformation for linear velocities from Earth to body using Euler angles; speciality transformation for angular velocities from Euler rates to body angular rates; and numerical integration, both definite and open.

Step 9: Decide on a top level for the code.   The code is probably most easily organized as a driver code that does little more than call all of the elemental models in some logical sequence. The output of the code should be the time derivatives of the dynamic states in the model. This concept is so important that it will be expanded in a separate section.

Step 10: Incorporate the code into a global wrapper.   A global wrapper or driver code provides easy access to peripheral functions such as file manipulation, data storage and retrieval, and so on. Such a wrapper is call a simulation executive, and it also is described in detail in an upcoming section.

18.3   Model to Code Structure

Equations (18.2), repeated next, will serve as the road map for the model-to-code structure:

$$\dot{P}_e = T_{\mathrm{BE}}^{-1}(\Phi, \Theta, \Psi)V_b = T_{\mathrm{BE}}^{-1}(\boldsymbol{\alpha}_e)V_b$$

$$\dot{V}_b = M_b^{-1}[F_{\mathrm{ext}} - \boldsymbol{\omega}_b \times (M_b V_b)]$$

$$\dot{\boldsymbol{\omega}}_b = I_n^{-1}[\boldsymbol{M}_{\text{ext}} - \boldsymbol{\omega}_b \times (I_n\boldsymbol{\omega}_b)]$$

$$\dot{\boldsymbol{\alpha}}_e = E^{-1}(\Phi, \Theta)\boldsymbol{\omega}_b = E^{-1}(\boldsymbol{\alpha}_e)\boldsymbol{\omega}_b$$

The first and fourth vector equations describe the time derivative of fuselage position and orientation over the Earth. Specifically, the expression $\dot{\boldsymbol{P}}_e = T_{\text{BE}}^{-1}(\Phi, \Theta, \Psi)V_b = T_{\text{BE}}^{-1}(\boldsymbol{\alpha}_e)V_b$ is a definition of the velocity of the aircraft in Earth axes. The elements of the Earth velocity vector are $\dot{\boldsymbol{P}}_e = \{Vnorth, Veast, Vdown\}^T$, which means $\boldsymbol{P}_e = \{North, East, Down\}^T$. Generally, these three position values are specified; they do not need to be iterated upon. The one exception is when a ground trim is desired. In that case, *Down* will be manipulated as one of the independent trim variables.

The Euler rates are defined from the body-axis rates and the Euler angles themselves. The expression $\dot{\boldsymbol{\alpha}}_e = E^{-1}(\Phi, \Theta)\boldsymbol{\omega}_b = E^{-1}(\boldsymbol{\alpha}_e)\boldsymbol{\omega}_b$ leads to $\boldsymbol{\alpha}_e = \{\phi, \theta, \psi\}^T$. Generally, two of the three Euler angles are used as independent trim variables. The third must be constrained.

If one accepts for the moment that angular rates and translational rates in body axes exist, then the schematic for the position and orientation equations are shown in Figs. 18.3 and 18.4.

In the chapter on landing gear, the reader was reminded that aviation is a contest between the aircraft and gravity, and that gravity always wins. Now is as good a time as any to introduce the calculation of gravity forces.

Because mass was used in the definition of the gravity forces, the top-level view of mass calculations is shown next in Fig. 18.5. Mass is not a constant; fuel burns and dropping or retrieving of stores change the mass and inertia properties. The pilot has limited command of the configuration of the aircraft as well. Pylons can be tilted, and wings can be swept. This moves the center of gravity about. All of these actions must be considered in the code that goes into the schematic shown in Fig. 18.6.

Pilot controls and center-of-gravity location have a direct bearing on the location of some aircraft elements relative to the center of gravity. This is important because the moment arm from the center of gravity to the element influences the inertial velocity and acceleration at the element. The moment arm also influences the force and moments sent back to the center of gravity.

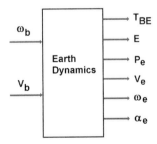

Fig. 18.3   Top-level view of position and velocity schematic.

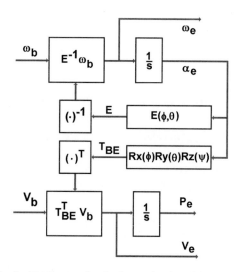

Fig. 18.4   Inside the top-level schematic of position and velocity.

The geometry operations shown in Figs. 18.7 and 18.8 do the work portrayed in Fig. 18.9.

With the geometry defined, the velocity and acceleration in individual element local axes (IELA) are found using some simple arithmetic. Figure 18.10 shows the top-level schematic, and Fig. 18.11 shows a detailed look at the process.

The "Mux" operation combines two input vectors into one output vector; "Demux" is the opposite operation.

The aerodynamic velocity at the IELA is next. Figures 18.12 and 18.13 show the top-level and detailed view of this calculation.

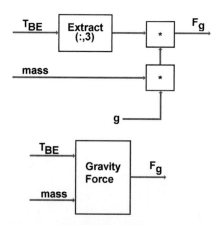

Fig. 18.5   Exploded view and top-level schematic view of gravity force vector.

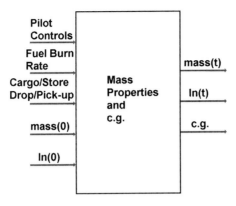

Fig. 18.6   Top-level schematic of mass properties calculations.

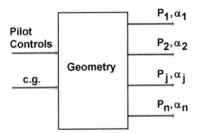

Fig. 18.7   Top-level schematic of geometry operation. For each element, a position and angular orientation vector are generated.

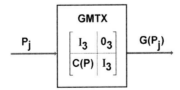

Fig. 18.8a   Detail of the geometry operator. The schematic shows a 6 × 1 vector P generating a 6 × 6 matrix $G(P)$. The I_3 are 3 × 3 identity matrices; the $C(P)$ is the cross product operator.

$$C(P) \rightarrow \begin{bmatrix} 0 & -z & y \\ z & 0 & -x \\ -y & x & 0 \end{bmatrix}$$

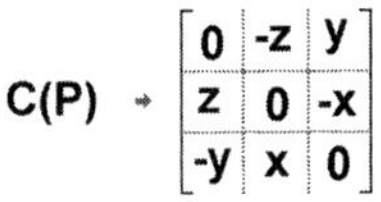

Fig. 18.8b   Detail of the cross-product operator.

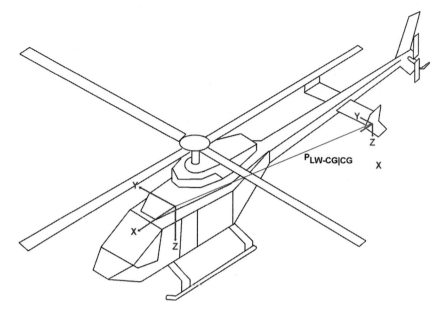

Fig. 18.9   Position vector from center of gravity to some element.

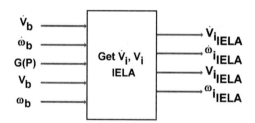

Fig. 18.10   Top-level schematic of the calculation of IELA velocity and acceleration.

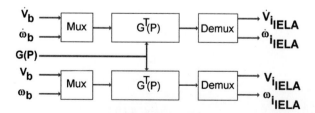

Fig. 18.11   More detail into the calculation of IELA velocity and acceleration.

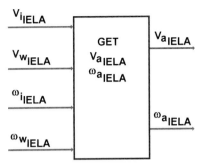

Fig. 18.12   Top-level view of calculation of aerodynamic velocity at IELA.

The inertial velocity, inertial acceleration, and aerodynamic velocity must now be oriented to axes attached to the element. That is, the action of Fig. 18.14 is desired.

The first step in that orientation is the calculation of the orientation matrices. Each element has three orientation angles. They are used to construct the orientation matrix as shown in Fig. 18.15.

With the orientation matrices known, the three vectors aforementioned can now be resolved to their IERA. Figure 18.16 shows the top-level schematic; Fig. 18.17 shows more detail.

Everything that is needed to calculate the forces and moments generated by individual elements has been assembled and is ready in the IERA for that element. At this point, use the detailed models of the past chapters to generate three forces and three moments. These will be in IERA. They must be reoriented to the IELA. Figures 18.18 and 18.19 illustrate this action.

Each element that generates an aerodynamic force or moment also generates an aerodynamic wash. It matters not what wash model is used; the upper-level schematic in Fig. 18.20 admits them all.

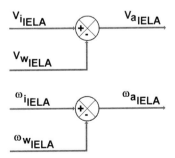

Fig. 18.13   Detailed view of calculation of aerodynamic velocity at IELA.

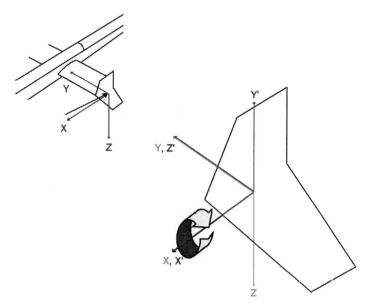

Fig. 18.14   Reorientation of vectors from IELA to IERA.

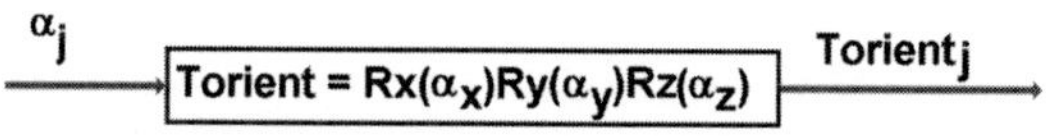

$$\alpha_j \longrightarrow \boxed{\text{Torient} = R_x(\alpha_x)R_y(\alpha_y)R_z(\alpha_z)} \xrightarrow{\text{Torient}_j}$$

Fig. 18.15   Construct the orientation matrix for each element.

The simulation flowchart has come full circle. The wash velocities of Fig. 18.20 feed back to Fig. 18.13. The forces and moments of Fig. 18.19 feed forward to Fig. 18.20 and back to Fig. 18.1. Other connections are easily discerned. The flow

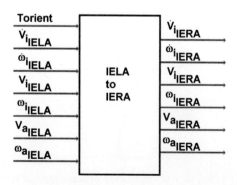

Fig. 18.16   Top-level schematic of transformation from IELA to IERA.

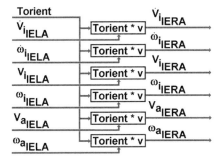

Fig. 18.17   Detailed view of transformation from IELA to IERA.

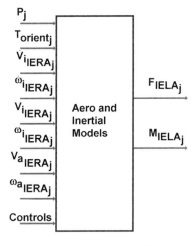

Fig. 18.18   Top-level schematic of the generation of forces and moments in the IELA. Note the inclusion of controls vector and position vector.

of information is as follows:

1) Figures 18.3 and 18.4: When trimming, initial estimates and iterated values for the Euler angles and controls are needed, as well as Earth-based velocities. An inverse calculation gives body-based velocities. When running, the Euler angles are the output of the Euler rate integrators, and the body velocities are the output of the integrated body-axis accelerations. Earth velocities and position follow.

2) Figure 18.6: Starting with initial values for mass and inertia tensor, the instantaneous values of mass, inertia tensor, and center-of-gravity position are found.

3) Figure 18.5: Knowing the mass and the angular orientation, the gravity forces are calculated.

4) Figures 18.7 and 18.8: Knowing the pilot controls and the center-of-gravity position, the position vectors for all of the individual elements are found.

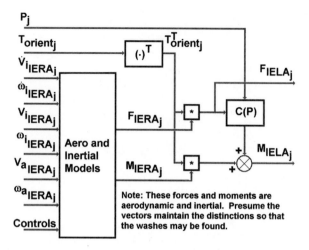

Fig. 18.19 Detailed look at the transformation of forces from IERA to IELA.

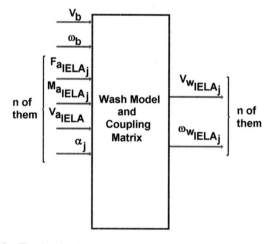

Fig. 18.20 Top-level schematic of the calculation of the wash velocities.

5) Figures 18.10 and 18.11: The inertial velocity and acceleration of the individual elements, resolved to IELA, are found.

6) Figures 18.12 and 18.13: The aerodynamic velocity at each IELA is found.

7) Figure 18.15: Each element has three orientation angles that are used to make the orientation matrix from IELA to IERA.

8) Figures 18.16 and 18.17: All of the individual element velocities and accelerations are oriented from the IELA to the IERA.

9) Figures 18.18 and 18.19: Forces and moments at each individual element are generated and resolved back to IELA.

10) Figure 18.20: The aerodynamic wash velocity for each element is calculated.

11) Figure 18.1: The loop is completed.

Apply the trimming techniques discussed in a preceding chapter to initialize the dynamic states of the aircraft and find the starting control positions. For the six-degrees-of-freedom aircraft, four control positions and two Euler angles are usually specified.

18.4   Simulation Executives

A simulation executive (SE) has several goals. The SE organizes the model execution into obvious execution options. The SE provides links to peripheral devices. The SE forms links to hardware that is used in man-in-the-loop (MITL) simulation. The SE can provide portability across platforms. The SE can provide "ride-along" capability so that the simulation program and the computer that executes it mount in the actual aircraft and execute in real time with the flying vehicle. In other words, the mathematical model does not and should not have to deal with an interface to the real world. The SE provides the shell and interfaces that the mathematical model code does not have. Some of the actions of the SE are spelled out in this section.

18.4.1   Organize Model Execution into Obvious Actions

This list of obvious actions is not comprehensive; the intent is to illustrate the kinds of problems that the SE might need to address.

1) *Full trim*: This is the usual six-degrees-of-freedom trim problem. However, this does not always mean straight and level trim. Trims in a turn, climbing and descending flight, and trims on the ground are all required. The mathematical model must be able to do these trims, but the SE must be able to detect and organize the trim type and specify the trim assignment. Trim sweeps are another option under the SE.

2) *Subsystem trim*: Sometimes the end-user might only want to trim the rotor for a desired flapping or force condition so that comparisons can be made to a wind-tunnel test or other analysis. The SE must be able to specify this type of trim assignment as well.

3) *Maneuver*: After a trim has been achieved, the end-user might want to perform some transient analysis. This is a maneuver option. Depending on whether the program is being executed in batch mode or MITL mode, the inputs to the code must be properly read and directed by the SE.

18.4.2   Select Data-Input Features

No matter if the simulation executes in batch or MITL mode, constant data such as physical descriptions of the aircraft and data tables must find their way into the code. The SE must oversee initial data loads and provide a simple-to-use method to modify scalar data and data tables.

Input data files will likely include time histories of control inputs if a batch execution of a transient analysis is desired. However, if MITL execution is desired, the SE must provide the links to the hardware that the pilot will use to fly the aircraft. This means that the SE must perform hardware initialization with product-specific software, open hardware communication channels, and synchronize the hardware to the simulation frames.

18.4.3   Select Data Display Features For Non-Real-Time Execution

If the simulation is executed in batch mode, the transient data that are generated are most likely desired as plots of the dependent variables vs time. In some cases, phase-plane analysis, which plots one state against another, might be required. The SE must provide easy storage, retrieval, and manipulation of the data. Links to plotters and operating system file manipulation commands are a minimum requirement.

18.4.4   Select Data-Output Features for Real-Time Execution

Face it, the great attraction for the majority of users is the sensation of flight that simulation offers. The "willing suspension of disbelief" is the goal of MITL simulation. The simulation approaches this goal by using superior visual systems, cockpit instruments, sound systems, control loader, or force-feel systems and switches in a simulation cockpit that resembles the actual aircraft. Of course, all of this hardware must also be initialized using product-specific software, and the communication channels must be opened and synchronized with the simulation. Besides the pilot-stimulating devices, real-time data must be collected and directed so that it can be observed in real time on strip chart recorders, oscilloscopes, and monitors. The data must be available in analog and digital formats. The data must also be written to files for postflight analysis.

18.4.5   Ride-Along Capability

The space shuttle astronauts train for landing the shuttle in a specially modified jet aircraft. That jet is a so-called variable-stability aircraft. Control inputs from the pilot-trainee do not go to the usual control laws. Instead, the signals go to a computer with a math model that simulates a space shuttle (in control parlance, a model). The output of the model represents the desired response of the jet aircraft. A second level of control laws then uses the desired response and actual jet states to determine the surface deflections, throttle positions, etc. that will make the jet follow the desired response. The result is that the jet flies just like the shuttle. A simulation executive organizes this override and also permits immediate reversion back to the usual characteristics of the jet.

18.5   Alpha-to-Omega Example Simulation

Even with the flowchart just presented, organizing a simulation is a daunting task. This section offers an example of a simulation of a single main rotor helicopter.

Many of the important features that the reader will need when writing a simulation are presented here. This is a working simulation, written in Microsoft's Visual Basic®. You will probably use a different language—so be it. The structure is the important lesson here. The code is presented in functional units with a short discussion following each unit.

18.5.1 Main Routines

```
'
'     Load the data.
'
load_data
'
'     Define the trim problem
'
usephi = True
roc_fpm = 0#
For ivinf = 0 To 28
   vinf_kts = ivinf * 5
'
   problem_def
'
'     Trim the aircraft and manufacture a summary
'
   actrim
   trim_summary msg$
'
'     Make spreadsheet-friendly file of interesting results.
'
   write_data ifile1
'
Next ivinf

Sub load_data ( )
'
'     This is the routine you would use to load the model
'     with data from a data file.
'
'     Note:    The example aircraft does not represent any particular
'     aircraft - and no resemblance should be inferred.
'
Dim span As Single
Dim a0 As Single
Dim r As Single
Dim c As Single
Dim dmass As Single
Dim e As Single
Dim khub As Single
Dim nb As Integer
Dim del3 As Single
Dim sigma As Single
Dim iflap As Single
```

```
Dim gamma As Single

Call atmos
'
'     Mass properties
'
gw = 6700#
ixx = 4180#
ixy = 0
ixz = 0
iyy = 10700#
iyz = 0
izz = 10300#
slcg0 = 10#
blcg0 = 0#
wlcg0 = 5#
mass = gw / grav
'
'     Fuselage constants
'
fuse.sl = 10#
fuse.bl = 0#
fuse.wl = 5#
fuse.phii = 0#
fuse.thetai = 0#
fuse.psii = 0#
fuse.carea = 49#
fuse.clen = 37.3
fuse.cxu = 0.377
fuse.cxv = 0#
fuse.cxw = 0.233
fuse.cyu = -0.035
fuse.cyv = 1.78
fuse.cyw = 0#
fuse.czu = 0.0715
fuse.czv = 0#
fuse.czw = 0.755
fuse.cmu = 0.00822
fuse.cmv = 0#
fuse.cmw = 0.518
fuse.cnu = 0.00274
fuse.cnv = -0.144
fuse.cnw = 0#
fuse.a11 = 0.0163
fuse.a22 = 0.0183
fuse.a33 = 0.0183
'
'     Horizontal stabilizer constants
'
span = 9.33
wings(1).sl = 26.9
wings(1).bl = 0#
wings(1).wl = 5.25
```

```
wings(1).phii = 0#
wings(1).thetai = 0#
wings(1).psii = 0#
wings(1).a0 = 5.73
wings(1).span = span
wings(1).chord = 2.54
wings(1).area = 23.6
wings(1).cd0 = 0.0105
wings(1).cd1 = 0#
wings(1).cd2 = 0.01325
wings(1).cm0 = 0#
wings(1).cma = 0#
wings(1).dihedral = 0#
wings(1).taper = 1#
wings(1).a11 = 4 / (3.14159 * span * span)
wings(1).a22 = 4 / (3.14159 * span * span)
wings(1).a33 = 4 / (3.14159 * span * span)
nwings = 1
'
'      Vertical stabilizer constants
'
span = 5.51
fins(1).sl = 34.8
fins(1).bl = 0#
fins(1).wl = 9.06
fins(1).phii = 90# / 57.295
fins(1).thetai = 0# / 57.295
fins(1).psii = 0#
fins(1).a0 = 5.73
fins(1).span = span
fins(1).chord = 2.9
fins(1).area = 16#
fins(1).cd0 = 0.0105
fins(1).cd1 = 0#
fins(1).cd2 = 0.01325
fins(1).cm0 = 0#
fins(1).cma = 0#
fins(1).dihedral = 0#
fins(1).taper = 0#
fins(1).a11 = 4# / (3.14159 * span * span)
fins(1).a22 = 4# / (3.14159 * span * span)
fins(1).a33 = 4# / (3.14159 * span * span)
nfins = 1
'
'      Main Rotor constants
'
a0 = 5.73
r = 22
c = 2.25
dmass = 0.395
e = 0#
nb = 2
khub = 0#
```

```
del3 = 0#
rotors(1).sl = 10
rotors(1).bl = 0#
rotors(1).wl = 11.6
rotors(1).phii = 0#
rotors(1).thetai = −0.0523
rotors(1).psii = 0#
rotors(1).nb = nb
rotors(1).radius = r
rotors(1).chord = c
rotors(1).dmass = dmass
rotors(1).bt = 0.97

rotors(1).precone = 1.875 / 57.295
rotors(1).a0 = a0
rotors(1).del0 = 0.0105
rotors(1).del1 = 0#
rotors(1).del2 = 0.01325
rotors(1).del3 = del3
rotors(1).eps0 = rotors(1).del0 / rotors(1).a0
rotors(1).omega = 32.5
rotors(1).twist = −10# / 57.295
rotors(1).e = e
rotors(1).khub = khub
rotors(1).m1 = rotors(1).dmass * rotors(1).radius ^ 2 / 2#
rotors(1).iflap = rotors(1).dmass * rotors(1).radius ^ 3 / 3#
rotors(1).e = e
rotors(1).hubtype = 0
sigma = nb * c / pi / r
iflap = rotors(1).iflap
gamma = rho * c * a0 * r ^ 4 / iflap
rotors(1).p = Sqr(1# + 3 * e / 2 / (r − e) + khub / iflap + gamma * Tan(del3) / 8#)
rotors(1).gamma = gamma
rotors(1).sigma = sigma
rotors(1).a11 = 1# / (3.14159 * r * r)
rotors(1).a22 = 1# / (3.14159 * r * r)
rotors(1).a33 = 1# / (3.14159 * r * r)
'
'     Main rotor initial guesses
'
rotors(1).cont(1) = 0.2476
rotors(1).cont(2) = 0#
rotors(1).cont(3) = 0#
rotors(1).vw(3) = 10#
'
'     Tail rotor constants
'
a0 = 5.73
r = 4.25
c = 0.702
dmass = 0.08
e = 0#
```

```
nb = 2
khub = 0#
del3 = 45# / 57.295
rotors(2).sl = 36.7
rotors(2).bl = −1.2
rotors(2).wl = 10.6
rotors(2).phii = −1.57078
rotors(2).thetai = 0#
rotors(2).psii = 0#
rotors(2).nb = 2
rotors(2).radius = r
rotors(2).chord = c
rotors(2).dmass = dmass
rotors(2).bt = 0.97

rotors(2).precone = 0#
rotors(2).a0 = 5.73
rotors(2).del0 = 0.0105
rotors(2).del1 = 0#
rotors(2).del2 = 0.01325
rotors(2).del3 = del3
rotors(2).eps0 = rotors(2).del0 / rotors(2).a0
rotors(2).omega = 172#
rotors(2).twist = 0#
rotors(2).e = e
rotors(2).hubtype = 0
rotors(2).khub = khub
rotors(2).m1 = rotors(2).dmass * rotors(2).radius ^ 2 / 2#
rotors(2).iflap = rotors(2).dmass * rotors(2).radius ^ 3 / 3#
sigma = nb * c / pi / r
gamma = rho * c * a0 * r ^ 4 / iflap
rotors(2).p = Sqr(1# + 3 * e / 2 / (r − e) + khub / iflap + gamma * Tan(del3) / 8#)
rotors(2).gamma = gamma
rotors(2).sigma = sigma
rotors(2).a11 = 1# / (3.14159 * r * r)
rotors(2).a22 = 1# / (3.14159 * r * r)
rotors(2).a33 = 1# / (3.14159 * r * r)
'
'      Tail rotor initial guesses
'
rotors(2).cont(1) = 5# / 57.295
rotors(2).cont(2) = 0#
rotors(2).cont(3) = 0#
rotors(2).vw(2) = −10#
'
nrotors = 2
End Sub

Sub problem_def( )
'
'      This routine defines the trim problem and sets constraints
'      or initial conditions on some aircraft states.
```

```vb
'
'       In this routine, the user would connect to some GUI or
'       data file to get the initial problem definition. In this
'       simple example program, the problem will simply be to find
'       the trim for an SMR helicopter at 20 knots. 20 knots is
'       chosen because it is a low enough velocity that the fuselage
'       will not be able to develop enough side force due to yaw
'       to use yaw as one of the independent trim variables. Instead,
'       roll angle will be required.
'
Dim phi As Single
Dim theta As Single
Dim psi As Single
Dim i As Integer
'
pe(1) = 0#
pe(2) = 0#
pe(3) = 0#
vearth(1) = vinf_kts * 1.6878
vearth(2) = 0#
vearth(3) = -roc_fpm / 60#
omearth(1) = 0#
omearth(2) = 0#
omearth(3) = 0#
phi = 0# / 57.295
theta = 0# / 57.2905
psi = 0# / 57.295
alphae(1) = phi
alphae(2) = theta
alphae(3) = psi
'
make_t3 phi, theta, psi, tbe( )
make_emtx phi, theta, emtx( )
mtxvecmpy tbe( ), vearth( ), vib( ), 3, 3
mtxvecmpy emtx( ), omearth( ), omb( ), 3, 3
'
sv(1) = pe(1)              'North
sv(2) = pe(2)              'East
sv(3) = pe(3)              'Down
sv(4) = vib(1)            'u
sv(5) = vib(2)            'v
sv(6) = vib(3)            'w
sv(7) = omb(1)           'p
sv(8) = omb(2)           'q
sv(9) = omb(3)           'r
sv(10) = alphae(1)       'phi
sv(11) = alphae(2)       'theta
sv(12) = alphae(3)       'psi
'
'       We have 7 candidate trim variables:
'
'       CFA             Fore/Aft cyclic
```

```
'      CLAT          Lateral cyclic
'      CPED          Pedal
'      CCOL          Collective
'      PHI           Roll angle
'      THETA         Pitch angle
'      PSI           Yaw angle
'
'      We will choose the first six and constrain the yaw
'      angle to be 0.0 radians. Some initial guesses for
'      some of the controls have already been declared in
'      the load_data routine. Load those values in the
'      cont vector now. Then, build the trim vector using
'      the initial values.
'
For i = 1 To 3
   cont(i) = rotors(1).cont(i)
   cont(3 + i) = rotors(2).cont(i)
Next i
For i = 1 To 4
   trimv(i) = cont(i)
Next i
trimv(5) = phi
trimv(6) = theta
'
End Sub

Sub trim_summary(msg$)
'
'      Pretty display of aircraft forces and moments and
'      other trim parameters.
'
Dim fmtot(7, 6) As Single
Dim fmname(7) As String
Dim Value As String * 12
Dim power_total As Single
'
fmname(1) = "Fuselage"
For i = 1 To 3
   fmtot(1, i) = fuse.force_cg(i)
   fmtot(1, i + 3) = fuse.moment_cg(i)
Next i
fmname(2) = "Main Rotor"
For i = 1 To 3
   fmtot(2, i) = rotors(1).force_cg(i)
   fmtot(2, i + 3) = rotors(1).moment_cg(i)
Next i
fmname(3) = "Tail Rotor"
For i = 1 To 3
   fmtot(3, i) = rotors(2).force_cg(i)
   fmtot(3, i + 3) = rotors(2).moment_cg(i)
Next i
fmname(4) = "Hor Stab"
```

```
For i = 1 To 3
   fmtot(4, i) = wings(1).force_cg(i)
   fmtot(4, i + 3) = wings(1).moment_cg(i)
Next i
fmname(5) = "Vert Stab"
For i = 1 To 3
   fmtot(5, i) = fins(1).force_cg(i)
   fmtot(5, i + 3) = fins(1).moment_cg(i)
Next i
fmname(6) = "Gravity"
For i = 1 To 3
   fmtot(6, i) = tbe(i, 3) * gw
   fmtot(6, i + 3) = 0#
Next i
fmname(7) = "Total"
For i = 1 To 6
   fmtot(7, i) = 0#
   For j = 1 To 6
      fmtot(7, i) = fmtot(7, i) + fmtot(j, i)
   Next j
Next i
'
msg$ = "Trim assignment:" + vbCrLf
msg$ = msg$ + "Vinf (knots) : " + Format$(vinf_kts, "#0.000") + vbCrLf
msg$ = msg$ + "R/C (fpm) : " + Format$(roc_fpm, "###0.000;\- ###0.000") + vbCrLf +
vbCrLf
'
msg$ = msg$ + "Element" + Space(8) + "X Force" + Space(5) + "Y Force" + Space(5) +
"Z Force" + Space(4)
msg$ = msg$ + "L Moment" + Space(4) + "M Moment" + Space(4) + "N Moment" +
vbCrLf
msg$ = msg$ + Space(16) + "(Lbs)" + Space(7) + "(Lbs)" + Space(7) + "(Lbs)" +
Space(5)
msg$ = msg$ + "(Ft-Lbs)" + Space(4) + "(Ft-Lbs)" + Space(4) + "(Ft-Lbs)" + vbCrLf
For i = 1 To 7
   msg$ = msg$ + fmname(i) + ":"
   For j = 1 To 6
      RSet Value = Format$(fmtot(i, j), "\ 0.0000E + 00\ ;\ -0.0000E + 00\ ")
      msg$ = msg$ + Value
      If j Mod 10 = 0 Then msg$ = msg$ + vbCrLf
   Next j
   msg$ = msg$ + vbCrLf
Next i
msg$ = msg$ + vbCrLf
'
msg$ = msg$ + "Flapping      Coning      Fore/aft      Lateral" + vbCrLf
msg$ = msg$ + fmname(2) + ":"
For j = 1 To 3
   RSet Value = Format$ (rotors(1).flap( j) * 57.295, "\0.0000E + 00\ ;\-0.0000E + 00 ")
   msg$ = msg$ + Value
Next j
msg$ = msg$ + vbCrLf
msg$ = msg$ + fmname(3) + ":"
```

```
For j = 1 To 3
    RSet Value = Format$ (rotors(2).flap( j) * 57.295, "\ 0.0000E + 00\ ;\ −0.0000E+00\ ")
    msg$ = msg$ + Value
Next j
msg$ = msg$ + vbCrLf
msg$ = msg$ + vbCrLf
'
power_total = 0#
For i = 1 To 2
    power_total = power_total + rotors(i).power
Next i

msg$ = msg$ + "Power (Hp)" + vbCrLf
msg$ = msg$ + fmname(2) + ":" + Format$(rotors(1).power, "\ 0.0000E + 00\ ;
\ −0.0000E + 00\ ")
msg$ = msg$ + vbCrLf
msg$ = msg$ + fmname(3) + ":" + Format$(rotors(2).power, "\ 0.0000E + 00\ ;
\ −0.0000E + 00\ ")
msg$ = msg$ + vbCrLf
msg$ = msg$ + "Total : " + Format$(power_total, "\ 0.0000E + 00\ ;\ −0.0000E + 00\ ")
msg$ = msg$ + vbCrLf + vbCrLf
'
msg$ = msg$ + "Phi : " + Format$ (alphae(1) * 57.295, "\ 00.0000\ ;\ −00.0000\ ") +
vbCrLf
msg$ = msg$ + "Theta : " + Format$ (alphae(2) * 57.295, "\ 00.0000\ ;\ −00.0000\ ") +
vbCrLf
msg$ = msg$ + "Psi : " + Format$ (alphae(3) * 57.295, "\ 00.0000\ ;\ −00.0000\ ") +
vbCrLf
msg$ = msg$ + vbCrLf
'
msg$ = msg$ + "Controls" + Space(5) + "Theta0 (MR)" + Space(2) + "A1 (MR)" +
Space(5) + "B1(MR)" + Space(3) + "Theta0 (TR)" + vbCrLf
msg$ = msg$ + Space(15) + "(Deg)" + Space(7) + "(Deg)" + Space(7) + "(Deg)" +
Space(7) + "(Deg)" + vbCrLf
msg$ = msg$ + Space(12)
For j = 1 To 4
    RSet Value = Format$ (cont( j) * 57.295, "\ 0.0000E + 00\ ;\ −0.0000E + 00\ ")
    msg$ = msg$ + Value
Next j
msg$ = msg$ + vbCrLf + vbCrLf
msg$ = msg$ + Space(13) + "Collective" + Space(2) + "Lat Cyclic" + Space(2) + "F/A
Cyclic" + Space(4) + "Pedal" + vbCrLf
msg$ = msg$ + Space(16) + "(In)" + Space(8) + "(In)" + Space(8) + "(In)" + Space(8) +
"(In)" + vbCrLf
msg$ = msg$ + Space(12)
For j = 1 To 4
    RSet Value = Format$ (pcont(j), "\ 0.0000E + 00\ ;\ −0.0000E + 00\ ")
    msg$ = msg$ + Value
Next j
msg$ = msg$ + vbCrLf + vbCrLf
'
msg$ = msg$ + "Self-induced wash velocity" + vbCrLf
msg$ = msg$ + "Element" + Space(8) + "U wash" + Space(6) + "V wash" + Space(6) +
```

```
"W wash" + vbCrLf
msg$ = msg$ + Space(14) + "(Ft/sec)" + Space(4) + "(Ft/sec)" + Space(4) +
"(Ft/sec)" + vbCrLf
msg$ = msg$ + fmname(1) + ":"
For j = 1 To 3
   washvel = fuse.d(j)
   RSet Value = Format$ (washvel, "\ 0.0000E + 00\ ;\ -0.0000E + 00\ ")
   msg$ = msg$ + Value
Next j
msg$ = msg$ + vbCrLf
msg$ = msg$ + fmname(2) + ":"
For j = 1 To 3
   washvel = rotors(1).d(j)
   RSet Value = Format$ (washvel, "\ 0.0000E + 00\ ;\ -0.0000E + 00\ ")
   msg$ = msg$ + Value
Next j
msg$ = msg$ + vbCrLf
msg$ = msg$ + fmname(3) + ":"
For j = 1 To 3
   washvel = rotors(2).d(j)
   RSet Value = Format$ (washvel, "\ 0.0000E + 00\ ;\ -0.0000E + 00\ ")
   msg$ = msg$ + Value
Next j
msg$ = msg$ + vbCrLf
msg$ = msg$ + fmname(4) + ":"
For j = 1 To 3
   washvel = wings(1).d(j)
   RSet Value = Format$ (washvel, "\ 0.0000E + 00\ ;\ -0.0000E + 00\ ")
   msg$ = msg$ + Value
Next j
msg$ = msg$ + vbCrLf
msg$ = msg$ + fmname(5) + ":"
For j = 1 To 3
   washvel = fins(1).d(j)
   RSet Value = Format$ (washvel, "\ 0.0000E + 00\ ;\ -0.0000E + 00\ ")
   msg$ = msg$ + Value
Next j
msg$ = msg$ + vbCrLf
msg$ = msg$ + vbCrLf
'
msg$ = msg$ + "Full wash velocity - includes interferences" + vbCrLf
msg$ = msg$ + "Element" + Space(8) + "U wash" + Space(6) + "V wash" + Space(6) +
"W wash" + vbCrLf
msg$ = msg$ + Space(14) + "(Ft/sec)" + Space(4) + "(Ft/sec)" + Space(4) +
"(Ft/sec)" + vbCrLf
msg$ = msg$ + fmname(1) + ":"
For j = 1 To 3
   washvel = fuse.vw(j)
   RSet Value = Format$ (washvel, "\ 0.0000E + 00\ ;\ -0.0000E + 00\ ")
   msg$ = msg$ + Value
Next j
msg$ = msg$ + vbCrLf
```

```
msg$ = msg$ + fmname(2) + ":"
For j = 1 To 3
  washvel = rotors(1).vw(j)
  RSet Value = Format$ (washvel, "\ 0.0000E + 00\ ;\ −0.0000E + 00\ ")
  msg$ = msg$ + Value
Next j
msg$ = msg$ + vbCrLf
msg$ = msg$ + fmname(3) + ":"
For j = 1 To 3
  washvel = rotors(2).vw(j)
  RSet Value = Format$ (washvel, "\ 0.0000E + 00\ ;\ −0.0000E + 00\ ")
  msg$ = msg$ + Value
Next j
msg$ = msg$ + vbCrLf
msg$ = msg$ + fmname(4) + ":"
For j = 1 To 3
  washvel = wings(1).vw(j)
  RSet Value = Format$ (washvel, "\ 0.0000E + 00\ ;\ −0.0000E + 00\ ")
  msg$ = msg$ + Value
Next j
msg$ = msg$ + vbCrLf
msg$ = msg$ + fmname(5) + ":"
For j = 1 To 3
  washvel = fins(1).vw(j)
  RSet Value = Format$ (washvel, "\ 0.0000E + 00\ ;\ −0.0000E + 00\ ")
  msg$ = msg$ + Value
Next j
msg$ = msg$ + vbCrLf
msg$ = msg$ + vbCrLf
'
End Sub

Sub write_data(ifile As Integer)
'
'     Write a spreadsheet-friendly data file.
'
Dim msg$
'
msg$ = " "
msg = msg$ + Str$ (vinf_kts) + ", "
msg = msg$ + Str$ (rotors(1).power) + ", "
msg = msg$ + Str$ (rotors(2).power) + ", "
msg = msg$ + Str$ (rotors(1).power + rotors(2).power) + ", "
msg = msg$ + Str$ (alphae(1) * 57.295) + ", "
msg = msg$ + Str$ (alphae(2) * 57.295) + ", "
msg = msg$ + Str$ (alphae(3) * 57.295) + ", "
msg = msg$ + Str$ (cont(1) * 57.295) + ", "
msg = msg$ + Str$ (cont(2) * 57.295) + ", "
msg = msg$ + Str$ (cont(3) * 57.295) + ", "
msg = msg$ + Str$ (cont(4) * 57.295) + ", "
```

```
msg = msg$ + Str$ (rotors(1).flap(1) * 57.295) + ", "
msg = msg$ + Str$ (rotors(1).flap(2) * 57.295) + ", "
msg = msg$ + Str$ (rotors(1).flap(3) * 57.295) + ", "
msg = msg$ + Str$ (rotors(2).flap(2) * 57.295) + ", "
msg = msg$ + Str$ (rotors(2).flap(3) * 57.295) + ", "
msg = msg$ + Str$ (rotors(1).force(1)) + ", "
msg = msg$ + Str$ (rotors(1).force(2)) + ", "
msg = msg$ + Str$ (rotors(1).force(3)) + ", "
msg = msg$ + Str$ (rotors(1).d(1)) + ", "
msg = msg$ + Str$ (rotors(1).d(2)) + ", "
msg = msg$ + Str$ (rotors(1).d(3)) + ", "
msg = msg$ + Str$ (rotors(2).force(1)) + ", "
msg = msg$ + Str$ (rotors(2).force(2)) + ", "
msg = msg$ + Str$ (rotors(2).force(3)) + ", "
msg = msg$ + Str$ (rotors(2).d(1)) + ", "
msg = msg$ + Str$ (rotors(2).d(2)) + ", "
msg = msg$ + Str$ (rotors(2).d(3))
'

Print #ifile, msg$
End Sub
```

18.5.2 Discussion of Main Routines

The main routine first calls subroutine LOAD_DATA, which loads the physical description of the aircraft being modeled. A data file or other executive system method can be employed as easily. Next, a loop is established that increments the true airspeed so that a velocity sweep is possible. Inside the loop, call subroutine PROBLEM_DEF first. This routine uses the gross characterization of the trim problem, that is, zero rate of climb and speed of thus and so, and sets the initial conditions and/or makes the initial guesses for the trim routine. Subroutine ACTRIM calculates the trim condition for each problem presented to it, and subroutine TRIM_SUMMARY prepares neat output of the forces and moments that each element generates, along with induced velocity, power requirements, rotor flapping, control inputs, and the trim Euler angles. Subroutine WRITE_DATA writes the data to a flat file for later postprocessing.

18.5.3 Declaration Section

```
Global Const pi = 3.1415926538
Global Const grav = 32.174
Global Const MainCaption$ = "SMR Helicopter Simulation Example"
'

Global sv(12) As Single
Global svd(12) As Single
Global acc0(6) As Single
Global pe(3) As Single
Global vib(3) As Single
Global omb(3) As Single
```

```
Global alphae(3) As Single
Global ped(3) As Single
Global vibd(3) As Single
Global ombd(3) As Single
Global vearth(3) As Single
Global omearth(3) As Single
Global alphaed(3) As Single
Global tbe(3, 3) As Single
Global teb(3, 3) As Single
Global emtx(3, 3) As Single
Global einv(3, 3) As Single
Global fcg(3) As Single
Global mcg(3) As Single
Global fg(3) As Single
Global Inmtx(3, 3) As Single
Global Inmtxi(3, 3) As Single
Global gw As Single
Global mass As Single
Global ixx As Single
Global ixy As Single
Global ixz As Single
Global iyy As Single
Global iyz As Single
Global izz As Single
Global slcg0 As Single
Global blcg0 As Single
Global wlcg0 As Single
Global slcg As Single
Global blcg As Single
Global wlcg As Single
Global usephi As Boolean
'
Global ff(3) As Single
Global mf(3) As Single
Global fr1(3) As Single
Global mr1(3) As Single
Global fr2(3) As Single
Global mr2(3) As Single
Global fw1(3) As Single
Global mw1(3) As Single
Global ff1(3) As Single
Global mf1(3) As Single
Global fext(3) As Single
Global mext(3) As Single
'
Global cont(6) As Single
Global trimv(6) As Single
Global pcont(6) As Single
'
Global rho As Single
Global vinf_kts As Single
Global roc_fpm As Single
```

,

```
Type body
  sl As Single
  bl As Single
  wl As Single
  phii As Single
  thetai As Single
  psii As Single
  va(3) As Single
  vw(3) As Single
  d(3) As Single
  omw(3) As Single
  carea As Single
  clen As Single
  cxu As Single
  cxw As Single
  cxv As Single
  cyu As Single
  cyv As Single
  cyw As Single
  czu As Single
  czv As Single
  czw As Single
  cmu As Single
  cmv As Single
  cmw As Single
  cnu As Single
  cnv As Single
  cnw As Single
  a11 As Single
  a22 As Single
  a33 As Single
  force(3) As Single
  moment(3) As Single
  force_cg(3) As Single
  moment_cg(3) As Single
End Type

Type rotor
  sl As Single
  bl As Single
  wl As Single
  phii As Single
  thetai As Single
  psii As Single
  va(3) As Single
  vw(3) As Single
  d(3) As Single
  omw(3) As Single
  nb As Integer
  radius As Single
  chord As Single
```

```
    dmass As Single
    m1 As Single
    iflap As Single
    gamma As Single
    sigma As Single
    bt As Single
    precone As Single
    a0 As Single
    del0 As Single
    del1 As Single
    del2 As Single
    eps0 As Single
    del3 As Single
    omega As Single
    twist As Single
    e As Single
    khub As Single
    p As Single
    flap(3) As Single
    cont(3) As Single
    a11 As Single
    a22 As Single
    a33 As Single
    force(3) As Single
    moment(3) As Single
    force_cg(3) As Single
    moment_cg(3) As Single
    power As Single
    hubtype As Integer
End Type

Type wing
    sl As Single
    bl As Single
    wl As Single
    phii As Single
    thetai As Single
    psii As Single
    a0 As Single
    span As Single
    chord As Single
    cd0 As Single
    area As Single
    cd1 As Single
    cd2 As Single
    cm0 As Single
    cma As Single
    dihedral As Single
    sweep As Single
    incid As Single
    taper As Single
    va(3) As Single
```

```
    vw(3) As Single
    d(3) As Single
    omw(3) As Single
    cont As Single
    a11 As Single
    a22 As Single
    a33 As Single
    force(3) As Single
    moment(3) As Single
    force_cg(3) As Single
    moment_cg(3) As Single
End Type

Type fin
    sl As Single
    bl As Single
    wl As Single
    phii As Single
    thetai As Single
    psii As Single
    a0 As Single
    span As Single
    chord As Single
    cd0 As Single
    area As Single
    cd1 As Single
    cd2 As Single
    cm0 As Single
    cma As Single
    dihedral As Single
    sweep As Single
    incid As Single
    taper As Single
    va(3) As Single
    vw(3) As Single
    d(3) As Single
    omw(3) As Single
    cont As Single
    a11 As Single
    a22 As Single
    a33 As Single
    force(3) As Single
    moment(3) As Single
    force_cg(3) As Single
    moment_cg(3) As Single
End Type

Global fuse As body
Global rotors(2) As rotor
Global wings(1) As wing
Global fins(1) As fin
Global nwings As Integer
```

Global nfins As Integer
Global nrotors As Integer

18.5.4 *Discussion of Declaration Section*

The declaration section identifies and sizes certain vectors that most element model routines use. This section also defines the structure for the rotor, wing, fin, and fuselage models.

18.5.5 *Trimming Section*

```
Sub actrim( )
'
'       This routine trims the aircraft to zero accelerations
'       in accordance with the problem definition.
'
Dim acc0(6) As Single
Dim accp(6) As Single
Dim accm(6) As Single
Dim jacob(6, 6) As Single
Dim deltt(6) As Single
Dim det As Single
Dim anorm As Single
Dim i As Integer
Dim iter As Integer
Dim ijac As Integer
Dim jjac As Integer
Dim eps As Single
'
aircraft1
make_derivs fext( ), mext( )
'
anorm = 0#
For i = 1 To 6
    acc0(i) = svd(i + 3)
    anorm = anorm + acc0(i) * acc0(i)
Next i
anorm = Sqr(anorm)
'
iter = 1
While (anorm > 0.001 And iter < 20)
'
'       Now, build the Jacobian. Perturb the elements
'       of the trimv vector.
'
    eps = 0.01
    For jjac = 1 To 6
'
```

```
'      Fwd perturbation
'
       trimv(jjac) = trimv(jjac) + eps
       For i = 1 To 4
           cont(i) = trimv(i)
       Next i
       If usephi Then
           sv(10) = trimv(5)        'alphae(1)
       Else
           sv(12) = trimv(5)        'alphae(3)
       End If
       sv(11) = trimv(6)            'alphae(2)
       aircraft1
       make_derivs fext( ), mext( )
       For i = 1 To 6
           accp(i) = svd(i + 3)
       Next i
'
'      Bkwd perturbation
'
       trimv(jjac) = trimv(jjac) − 2 * eps
       For i = 1 To 4
           cont(i) = trimv(i)
       Next i
       If usephi Then
           sv(10) = trimv(5)        'alphae(1)
       Else
           sv(12) = trimv(5)        'alphae(3)
       End If
       sv(11) = trimv(6)            'alphae(2)
       aircraft1
       make_derivs fext( ), mext( )
       For i = 1 To 6
          accm(i) = svd(i + 3)
       Next i
'
'      Return trim column to starting value in this
'      iteration
'
       trimv(jjac) = trimv(jjac) + eps
       For i = 1 To 4
           cont(i) = trimv(i)
       Next i
       If usephi Then
           sv(10) = trimv(5)        'alphae(1)
       Else
           sv(12) = trimv(5)        'alphae(3)
       End If
```

```
        sv(11) = trimv(6)              'alphae(2)
'
'        Build the derivative column.
'
        For ijac = 1 To 6
            jacob(ijac, jjac) = (accp(ijac) − accm(ijac)) / 2 / eps
        Next ijac
'
    Next jjac
'
'        Invert the Jacobian and postmultiply by the acceleration
'        error.
'
    mtxinv jacob( ), 6, det
    mtxvecmpy jacob( ), acc0( ), deltt( ), 6, 6
'
    For i = 1 To 6
        trimv(i) = trimv(i) − deltt(i)
    Next i
    For i = 1 To 4
        cont(i) = trimv(i)
    Next i
    If usephi Then
        sv(10) = trimv(5)              'alphae(1)
    Else
        sv(12) = trimv(5)              'alphae(3)
    End If
    sv(11) = trimv(6)                  'alphae(2)
'
'        Evaluate the newest iteration
'
    aircraft1
    make_derivs fext( ), mext( )
'
    anorm = 0#
    For i = 1 To 6
        acc0(i) = svd(i + 3)
        anorm = anorm + acc0(i) * acc0(i)
    Next i
    anorm = Sqr(anorm)
    iter = iter + 1
    msg$  = MainCaption$ & ":" + Str$ (iter) & ":"& rformat(anorm)
    BaseSimForm.Caption = msg$
    BaseSimForm.Refresh
'
Wend
'
End Sub
```

18.5.6 Discussion of Trimming Section

The subroutine ACTRIM comprises the trimming section. The aircraft model, represented by subroutine AIRCRAFT1, generates the forces and moments that the individual elements produce. The MAKE_DERIVS subroutine uses those loads to calculate the unbalanced accelerations along and about three body axes. These are the accelerations that the trimming routine drives to zero. The ACTRIM routine begins by evaluating the initial aircraft accelerations with the current set of control settings and Euler angles. Then, ACTRIM systematically computes the Jacobian matrix using a central-difference-derivative estimation. Postmultiply the inverse of the Jacobian by the initial accelerations; the result is the correction to the initial control settings and Euler angles. Repeat this process until the accelerations are acceptably small or until the iteration count exceeds the maximum allowable number of iterations.

18.5.7 Aircraft Model Section

```
Sub aircraft1( )
'
'     Call the model elements, including the atmosphere,
'     the controls and the wash model
'
Dim i As Integer
'
atmos
make_mass_prop
make_vi
control_system
fuselagemodel
wingmodel 1
finmodel 1
rotormodel 1
rotormodel 2
washmodel
'
'     Sum the external forces and moments applied to the
'     c.g.
'
fext(1) = 0#
fext(2) = 0#
fext(3) = 0#
mext(1) = 0#
mext(2) = 0#
mext(3) = 0#
For i = 1 To 3
    fext(i) = fext(i) + fuse.force_cg(i)
    mext(i) = mext(i) + fuse.moment_cg(i)
Next i
For i = 1 To 3
    fext(i) = fext(i) + wings(1).force_cg(i)
    mext(i) = mext(i) + wings(1).moment_cg(i)
```

```
Next i
For i = 1 To 3
   fext(i) = fext(i) + fins(1).force_cg(i)
   mext(i) = mext(i) + fins(1).moment_cg(i)
Next i
For i = 1 To 3
   fext(i) = fext(i) + rotors(1).force_cg(i)
   mext(i) = mext(i) + rotors(1).moment_cg(i)
Next i
For i = 1 To 3
   fext(i) = fext(i) + rotors(2).force_cg(i)
   mext(i) = mext(i) + rotors(2).moment_cg(i)
Next i

End Sub
```

18.5.8 Discussion of Aircraft Model Section

The AIRCRAFT1 subroutine calls all of the element models in almost arbitrary order. The atmosphere model is called ATMOS and is simply a statement of the air density in this example. Subroutine MAKE_MASS_PROP makes the mass properties such as mass, inertia tensor, and center-of-gravity location. Subroutine MAKE_VI resolves the inertial velocity to body axes. Subroutine CONTROL_SYSTEM distributes values in the global control column to individual element structures. It also calculates the pilot stick values given the actuator values. Subroutine FUSELAGEMODEL uses the simple equation model. Subroutines WINGMODEL and FINMODEL use the point-load method to calculate the forces and moments at the local axes and at the center of gravity. The index that follows the call selects which wing or fin in the case of multiple wings or fins. Subroutine ROTORMODEL uses the quasi-static rotor model. Two significant differences exist between the equations in this routine and those presented in the chapter on rotor models. First, the thrust-induced-velocity (TIV) loop calculates an analytical derivative to aid in convergence. Second, because the TIV loop is closed in the rotor model instead of the wash model, the interference velocities from all other elements must be isolated and added to the inertial velocity so that TIV loop does not double dip on induced velocity. The indices 1 and 2, which follow the first and second calls refer to the main and tail rotor, respectively. The WASHMODEL uses the modified Glauert method to calculate the self-influence of each element and then combines these results to make the total wash velocity that is passed to the individual elements.

Subroutines MAKE_DERIVS, MAKE_EMTX, and MAKE_EINV support the calculation of the aircraft body-axis accelerations. Notice how compact the code is when vectors and linear algebra are used. Subroutine MAKE_T3 is a utility routine that builds the three-axis rotation matrix.

18.5.9 Element Model Section

```
Sub atmos( )
rho = 0.002378
End Sub
```

```
Sub control_system( )
'
'        Put the control column values into the
'        appropriate elements. The addition of a
'        simple velocity-dependent term to adjust
'        the incidence angle of the horizontal
'        tail keeps the fuselage close to level
'        over the entire flight envelop. The
'        price you pay is significant fore/aft
'        flapping.
'
rotors(1).cont(1) = cont(1)
rotors(1).cont(2) = cont(2)
rotors(1).cont(3) = cont(3)
rotors(2).cont(1) = cont(4)
'wings(1).cont = −8# / 57.295 * (vinf_kts / 140#)
'
'        Calculate what pilot controls would be using
'        the following rigging:
'
'        Coll          10 to 25 deg;          0−8 in
'        F/A          −10 to 10 deg;          −4 to 4 in
'        Lat          −10 to 10 deg;          −4 to 4 in
'        ped          −12 to +1 deg;          −2 to 2 in
'
pcont(1) = (cont(1) * 57.295 − 10#) / (25# − 10#) * (8# − 0#) + 0#
pcont(2) = (cont(2) * 57.295 − (−10#)) / (10# − (−10#)) * (4# − (−4#)) − 4#
pcont(3) = (cont(3) * 57.295 − (−10#)) / (10# − (−10#)) * (4# − (−4#)) − 4#
pcont(4) = (cont(4) * 57.295 − (−12#)) / (1# − (−12#)) * (2# − (−2#)) − 2#

End Sub

Sub finmodel(ifin As Integer)
'
'        This routine calculated the forces and moments produced
'        by the ifin'th fin. Use the point-load method.
'
Dim a0 As Single
Dim a03d As Single
Dim aoa As Single
Dim ar As Single
Dim b As Single
Dim cbar As Single
Dim cd As Single
Dim cd0 As Single
Dim cd1 As Single
Dim cd2 As Single
Dim cl As Single
Dim cm As Single
Dim cm0 As Single
Dim cma As Single
Dim croot As Single
```

```
Dim delf As Single
Dim dihedral As Single
Dim drag As Single
Dim incid As Single
Dim lift As Single
Dim momy As Single
Dim phii As Single
Dim psii As Single
Dim qtots As Single
Dim s12 As Single
Dim slambda As Single
Dim stot As Single
Dim sweep As Single
Dim smac As Single
Dim thetai As Single
Dim v2 As Single
Dim xmac As Single
Dim ymacLw As Single
Dim ymacRw As Single
Dim zmac As Single
Dim i As Integer
'
Dim fc(3) As Single
Dim mc(3) As Single
Dim omcr(3) As Single
Dim vw(3) As Single
Dim omw(3) As Single
Dim rrwiera(3) As Single
Dim rwing_cg(3) As Single
Dim viela(3) As Single
Dim omiela(3) As Single
Dim va(3) As Single
Dim oma(3) As Single
Dim t3(3, 3) As Single
Dim t3t(3, 3) As Single
Dim ta3(3, 3) As Single
Dim ta3t(3, 3) As Single
Dim viera(3) As Single
Dim omiera(3) As Single
Dim vmac_iera(3) As Single
Dim ommac_iera(3) As Single
Dim vmac_wra(3) As Single
Dim ommac_wra(3) As Single
Dim tma(3, 3) As Single
Dim tmat(3, 3) As Single
Dim pfwra(3) As Single
Dim pmwra(3) As Single
Dim pfiela(3) As Single
Dim pmiela(3) As Single
Dim pfiera(3) As Single
Dim pmiera(3) As Single
Dim rcf(3) As Single
```

```
Dim pfwingb(3) As Single
Dim pmwingb(3) As Single
'
'       Unload structure into local variables:
'
'       Orientation angles
'
phii = fins(ifin).phii
thetai = fins(ifin).thetai
psii = fins(ifin).psii
'
'       Wash velocities in local axes
'
For i = 1 To 3
    vw(i) = fins(ifin).vw(i)
    omw(i) = fins(ifin).omw(i)
Next i
'
'       Geometry and simple aero constants
'
a0 = fins(ifin).a0
b = fins(ifin).span
croot = fins(ifin).chord
slambda = fins(ifin).taper
dihedral = fins(ifin).dihedral
sweep = fins(ifin).sweep
incid = fins(ifin).incid
cd0 = fins(ifin).cd0
cd1 = fins(ifin).cd1
cd2 = fins(ifin).cd2
cm0 = fins(ifin).cm0
cma = fins(ifin).cma
delf = fins(ifin).cont
'
'       Calculate some intermediate wing constants. Note:
'       stot = 2 * s12 because b/2 in the wing model is now
'       b in the fin model. This also affects smac, which
'       now needs to be multiplied by 2.
'
s12 = b * croot * (1 + slambda) / 4#
stot = s12 * 2
cbar = 2 * croot * (slambda ^ 2 + slambda + 1) / 3 / (slambda + 1)
smac = b * (2 * slambda + 1) / 6 / (slambda + 1) * 2
xmac = −Sin(sweep) * Cos(−dihedral) * smac
ymacRw = Cos(sweep) * Cos(−dihedral) * smac
ymacLw = −Cos(sweep) * Cos(−dihedral) * smac
zmac = Sin(−dihedral) * smac
ar = b * b / stot
a03d = a0 * ar / (ar + 2 * (ar + 4) / (ar + 2))
'
'       Translate cg velocities to iela.
'
```

```
rwing_cg(1) = −(fins(ifin).sl − slcg)
rwing_cg(2) = (fins(ifin).bl − blcg)
rwing_cg(3) = −(fins(ifin).wl − wlcg)
'
cross omb( ), rwing_cg( ), omcr( )
vecadd vib( ), omcr( ), viela( ), 3, 1
veceql omiela( ), omb( ), 3
'
'       Subtract wash to get aerodynamic velocities
'
vecadd viela( ), vw( ), va( ), 3, 2
vecadd omiela( ), omw( ), oma( ), 3, 2
'
'       Translate and rotate velocities to iera
'
make_t3 phii, thetai, psii, t3( )
mtxtranspose t3t( ), t3( ), 3, 3
mtxvecmpy t3( ), va( ), viera( ), 3, 3
mtxvecmpy t3( ), oma( ), omiera( ), 3, 3
'
rrwiera(1) = xmac
rrwiera(2) = ymacRw
rrwiera(3) = zmac
'
cross omiera( ), rrwiera( ), omcr( )
vecadd viera( ), omcr( ), vmac_iera( ), 3, 1
veceql ommac_iera( ), omiera( ), 3
'
make_t3 (−dihedral), incid, sweep, ta3( )
mtxtranspose ta3t( ), ta3( ), 3, 3
'
mtxvecmpy ta3( ), vmac_iera( ), vmac_wra( ), 3, 3
mtxvecmpy ta3( ), ommac_iera( ), ommac_wra( ), 3, 3
'
'       Calculate aerodynamic loads in WRA
'
aoa = vbatan4((vmac_wra(3)), (vmac_wra(1))) * pi / 180#
'
cd = cd0 + aoa * (cd1 + aoa * cd2)
cl = a03d * aoa
cm = cm0 + cma * aoa
'
innerp vmac_wra( ), vmac_wra( ), v2, 3
qtots = rho * v2 / 2# * stot
drag = qtots * cd
lift = qtots * cl
momy = qtots * cbar * cm
fc(1) = −drag
fc(2) = 0#
fc(3) = −lift
mc(1) = 0#
mc(2) = momy
```

```
mc(3) = 0#
'
'       Rotate loads back to IELA, then translate to cg.
'
make_t3 0, (−aoa), 0, tma( )
mtxtranspose tmat( ), tma( ), 3, 3
mtxvecmpy tmat( ), fc( ), pfwra( ), 3, 3
mtxvecmpy tmat( ), mc( ), pmwra( ), 3, 3
mtxvecmpy ta3t( ), pfwra( ), pfiera( ), 3, 3
mtxvecmpy ta3t( ), pmwra( ), pmiera( ), 3, 3
cross rrwiera( ), pfiera( ), rcf( )
vecadd pmiera( ), rcf( ), pmiera( ), 3, 1
mtxvecmpy t3t( ), pfiera( ), pfiela( ), 3, 3
mtxvecmpy t3t( ), pmiera( ), pmiela( ), 3, 3
veceql pfwingb( ), pfiela( ), 3
cross rwing_cg( ), pfiela( ), rcf( )
vecadd pmiela( ), rcf( ), pmwingb( ), 3, 1
'
'       Load results into structure.
'
For i = 1 To 3
    fins(ifin).force(i) = pfiela(i)
    fins(ifin).moment(i) = pmiela(i)
    fins(ifin).force_cg(i) = pfwingb(i)
    fins(ifin).moment_cg(i) = pmwingb(i)
    fins(ifin).va(i) = va(i)
Next i

End Sub

Sub fuselagemodel( )
'
'       Calculate the forces and moments that the fuselage generates.
'
Dim rfuse_cg(3) As Single
Dim viela(3) As Single
Dim omiela(3) As Single
Dim vdiela(3) As Single
Dim omdiela(3) As Single
Dim vaiera(3) As Single
Dim omaiera(3) As Single
Dim omcr(3) As Single
Dim omdcr(3) As Single
Dim va(3) As Single
Dim oma(3) As Single
Dim vw(3) As Single
Dim omw(3) As Single
Dim t3(3, 3) As Single
Dim t3t(3, 3) As Single
Dim tmp(3) As Single
Dim tmp2(3) As Single
Dim phii As Single
```

```
Dim thetai As Single
Dim psii As Single
Dim fiela(3) As Single
Dim miela(3) As Single
Dim fmb(6) As Single
Dim coef(6, 3) As Single
Dim i As Integer
Dim fact1 As Single
Dim fact2 As Single
'
'       Unload structure into local variables:
'
'       Orientation angles
'
phii = fuse.phii
thetai = fuse.thetai
psii = fuse.psii
'
'       Wash velocities in local axes
'
For i = 1 To 3
    vw(1) = fuse.vw(i)
    omw(i) = fuse.omw(i)
Next i
'
'       Geometry and simple aero constants
'
coef(1, 1) = −fuse.cxu
coef(1, 2) = −fuse.cxv
coef(1, 3) = −fuse.cxw
coef(2, 1) = −fuse.cyu
coef(2, 2) = −fuse.cyv
coef(2, 3) = −fuse.cyw
coef(3, 1) = −fuse.czu
coef(3, 2) = −fuse.czv
coef(3, 3) = −fuse.czw
coef(4, 1) = 0#
coef(4, 2) = 0#
coef(4, 3) = 0#
coef(5, 1) = fuse.cmu
coef(5, 2) = fuse.cmv
coef(5, 3) = fuse.cmw
coef(6, 1) = fuse.cnu
coef(6, 2) = fuse.cnv
coef(6, 3) = fuse.cnw
'
'       Construct transformation matrices to move
'       velocities from cg to iera.
'
make_t3 phii, thetai, psii, t3( )
mtxtranspose t3t( ), t3( ), 3, 3
'
```

```
'      Translate cg velocities to iela.
'
rfuse_cg(1) = −(fuse.sl − slcg)
rfuse_cg(2) = (fuse.bl − blcg)
rfuse_cg(3) = −(fuse.wl − wlcg)
'
cross omb( ), rfuse_cg( ), omcr( )
cross ombd( ), rfuse_cg( ), omdcr( )
vecadd vib( ), omcr( ), viela( ), 3, 1
veceql omiela( ), omb( ), 3
vecadd vibd( ), omdcr( ), vdiela( ), 3, 1
veceql omdiela( ), ombd( ), 3
'
'      Subtract wash to get aerodynamic velocities
'
vecadd viela( ), vw( ), va( ), 3, 2
vecadd omiela( ), omw( ), oma( ), 3, 2
'
'      Rotate velocities to iera
'
mtxvecmpy t3( ), va( ), vaicra( ), 3, 3
mtxvecmpy t3( ), oma( ), omaiera( ), 3, 3
'
'      Calculate the aerodynamic forces and moments.
'
fact1 = 0.5 * rho * fuse.carea * vaiera(1)
fact2 = fact1 * fuse.clen
mtxvecmpy coef( ), vaiera( ), fmb( ), 6, 3
'
'      Load vectors with aero loads and rotate to iela
'
For i = 1 To 3
     tmp2(i) = fact1 * fmb(i)
Next i
mtxvecmpy t3t( ), tmp2( ), fiela( ), 3, 3
For i = 1 To 3
     tmp2(i) = fact2 * fmb(i + 3)
Next i
mtxvecmpy t3t( ), tmp2( ), miela( ), 3, 3
'
'      Do rxf to get moments at cg, then put into structure
'
cross rfuse_cg( ), fiela( ), tmp( )
For i = 1 To 3
     fuse.force(i) = fiela(i)
     fuse.moment(i) = miela(i)
     fuse.force_cg(i) = fiela(i)
     fuse.moment_cg(i) = miela(i) + tmp(i)
     fuse.va(i) = va(i)
Next i
'
End Sub
```

```
Sub make_derivs(fext( ) As Single, mext( ) As Single)
'
'       Generate the derivatives of the states.
'
Dim phie As Single
Dim thetae As Single
Dim psie As Single
Dim omcv(3) As Single
Dim h(3) As Single
Dim omch(3) As Single
Dim tmp(3) As Single
'
'       Unload the state vector into easy to use sub-vectors.
'
For i = 1 To 3
    pe(i) = sv(i)
    vib(i) = sv(i + 3)
    omb(i) = sv(i + 6)
    alphae(i) = sv(i + 9)
Next i
'
phie = alphae(1)
thetae = alphae(2)
psie = alphae(3)
make_t3 phie, thetae, psie, tbe( )
mtxtranspose teb( ), tbe( ), 3, 3
make_emtx phie, thetae, emtx( )
make_einv phie, thetae, einv( )
'
For i = 1 To 3
    fcg(i) = tbe(i, 3) * gw + fext(i)
    mcg(i) = mext(i)
Next i
'
cross omb( ), vib( ), omcv( )
For i = 1 To 3
    vibd(i) = fcg(i) / mass − omcv(i)
Next i
'
mtxvecmpy Inmtx( ), omb( ), h( ), 3, 3
cross omb( ), h( ), omch( )
For i = 1 To 3
    tmp(i) = mcg(i) − omch(i)
Next i
mtxvecmpy Inmtxi( ), tmp( ), ombd( ), 3, 3
'
mtxvecmpy teb( ), vib( ), ped( ), 3, 3
'
mtxvecmpy einv( ), omb( ), alphaed( ), 3, 3
'
For i = 1 To 3
    svd(i) = ped(i)
```

```
      svd(i + 3) = vibd(i) ' * mass
      svd(i + 6) = ombd(i) ' * Inmtx(i, i)
      svd(i + 9) = alphaed(i)
Next i

End Sub

Sub make_einv(phie As Single, thetae As Single, einv( ) As Single)
'
'     Make the inverse of the E matrix.
'
Dim cfe As Single
Dim sfe As Single
Dim cth As Single
Dim sth As Single
'
cfe = Cos(phie)
sfe = Sin(phie)
cth = Cos(thetae)
sth = Sin(thetae)
tth = sth / cth
'
einv(1, 1) = 1#
einv(1, 2) = sfe * tth
einv(1, 3) = cfe * tth
einv(2, 1) = 0#
einv(2, 2) = cfe
einv(2, 3) = −sfe
einv(3, 1) = 0#
einv(3, 2) = sfe / cth
einv(3, 3) = cfe / cth
'
End Sub

Sub make_emtx(phie As Single, thetae As Single, emtx( ) As Single)
'
'     Make the E matrix.
'
Dim cfe As Single
Dim sfe As Single
Dim cth As Single
Dim sth As Single
Dim tth As Single
'
cfe = Cos(phie)
sfe = Sin(phie)
cth = Cos(thetae)
sth = Sin(thetae)
tth = sth / cth
'
emtx(1, 1) = 1#
emtx(1, 2) = 0
```

```
emtx(1, 3) = −sth
emtx(2, 1) = 0#
emtx(2, 2) = cfe
emtx(2, 3) = sfe * cth
emtx(3, 1) = 0#
emtx(3, 2) = −sfe
emtx(3, 3) = cfe * cth
'
End Sub

Sub make_mass_prop( )
'
'      This routine makes/updates the mass and inertia matrices.
'      In this simple example, the mass and inertia matrices are
'      static.
'
Dim det As Single
'
mass = gw / grav
Inmtx(1, 1) = ixx
Inmtx(1, 2) = −ixy
Inmtx(1, 3) = −ixz
Inmtx(2, 1) = −ixy
Inmtx(2, 2) = iyy
Inmtx(2, 3) = −iyz
Inmtx(3, 1) = −ixz
Inmtx(3, 2) = −iyz
Inmtx(3, 3) = izz
mtxeql Inmtxi( ), Inmtx( ), 3, 3
mtxinv Inmtxi( ), 3, det
slcg = slcg0
blcg = blcg0
wlcg = wlcg0

End Sub

Sub make_t3(phi As Single, theta As Single, psi As Single, t3( ) As Single)
'
'      Make the transformation matrix from inertial to body axes.
'
Dim rotx(3, 3) As Single
Dim roty(3, 3) As Single
Dim rotz(3, 3) As Single
Dim tmp(3, 3) As Single
'
rotatex phi, rotx( )
rotatey theta, roty( )
rotatez psi, rotz( )
mtxmpy rotx( ), roty( ), tmp( ), 3, 3, 3
mtxmpy tmp( ), rotz( ), t3( ), 3, 3, 3
End Sub
```

```
Sub make_vi( )
'
'      This routine makes the body axis inertial velocities
'      and accelerations from the earth axis velocities and
'      accelerations.
'
Dim phie As Single
Dim thetae As Single
Dim psie As Single
Dim tmp(3) As Single
Dim i As Integer
'
'      Unload the state vector into easy to use sub-vectors.
'
For i = 1 To 3
      alphae(i) = sv(i + 9)
Next i
'
phie = alphae(1)
thetae = alphae(2)
psie = alphae(3)
make_t3 phie, thetae, psie, tbe( )
make_emtx phie, thetae, emtx( )
mtxvecmpy tbe( ), vearth( ), vib( ), 3, 3
mtxvecmpy emtx( ), omearth( ), omb( ), 3, 3
'
sv(1) = pe(1)               'North
sv(2) = pe(2)               'East
sv(3) = pe(3)               'Down
sv(4) = vib(1)              'u
sv(5) = vib(2)              'v
sv(6) = vib(3)              'w
sv(7) = omb(1)              'p
sv(8) = omb(2)              'q
sv(9) = omb(3)              'r
sv(10) = alphae(1)          'phi
sv(11) = alphae(2)          'theta
sv(12) = alphae(3)          'psi

End Sub

Sub rotormodel(irot As Integer)
'
'      This routine calculated the forces and moments produced
'      by the irot'th rotor.
'
Dim rrot_cg(3) As Single
Dim viela(3) As Single
Dim omiela(3) As Single
Dim vdiela(3) As Single
Dim omdiela(3) As Single
Dim vaiera(3) As Single
Dim omaiera(3) As Single
```

```
Dim viera(3) As Single
Dim omiera(3) As Single
Dim vwiera(3) As Single
Dim vdiera(3) As Single
Dim omdiera(3) As Single
Dim omcr(3) As Single
Dim omdcr(3) As Single
Dim va(3) As Single
Dim oma(3) As Single
Dim vw(3) As Single
Dim d(3) As Single
Dim vif(3) As Single
Dim omw(3) As Single
Dim vawm(3) As Single
Dim omawm(3) As Single
Dim viwm(3) As Single
Dim omiwm(3) As Single
Dim vidwm(3) As Single
Dim omidwm(3) As Single
'
Dim t3(3, 3) As Single
Dim t3t(3, 3) As Single
Dim twm(3, 3) As Single
Dim twmt(3, 3) As Single
Dim tmp(3) As Single
Dim tmp2(3) As Single
Dim fiela(3) As Single
Dim miela(3) As Single
Dim fmbwm(6) As Single
Dim fmb(6) As Single
Dim cont(3) As Single
Dim flap(3) As Single
Dim acmtx(3, 7) As Single
Dim rmtx(3, 3) As Single
Dim fmtx(3, 3) As Single
Dim cmtx(3, 4) As Single
Dim cvec(4) As Single
Dim rvec(3) As Single
Dim acvec(7) As Single
Dim phii As Single
Dim thetai As Single
Dim psii As Single
Dim bt As Single
Dim hubtype As Integer
Dim precone As Single
Dim lamwold As Single
Dim lamw As Single
Dim det As Single
Dim i As Integer
Dim a0 As Single
Dim del0 As Single
Dim del1 As Single
Dim del2 As Single
```

```
Dim del3 As Single
Dim eps0 As Single
Dim nb As Integer
Dim radius As Single
Dim chord As Single
Dim dmass As Single
Dim omega As Single
Dim omegap As Single
Dim omegaa As Single
Dim twist As Single
Dim prev As Single
Dim m1 As Single
Dim iflap As Single
Dim sigma As Single
Dim gamma As Single
Dim um As Single
Dim vm As Single
Dim vmtot2 As Single
Dim cchi As Single
Dim schi As Single
'
'       Unload structure into local variables:
'
'       Orientation angles
'
phii = rotors(irot).phii
thetai = rotors(irot).thetai
psii = rotors(irot).psii
'
'       Wash velocities in local axes. A small trick must
'       be employed here. The vw vector that comes from the
'       wash model contains the self-influence wash and the
'       sum of all of the interference washes. Since the
'       rotor model closes the thrust-induced velocity loop
'       here instead of in the wash model, and that wash is
'       only the self-influence part, the sum of all of the
'       interferences must be extracted, then added to the
'       inertial terms as if they were gust terms. Then,
'       induced velocity may be found. After that, it is
'       added back in the wash model.
'
For i = 1 To 3
    vw(i) = rotors(irot).vw(i)
    d(i) = rotors(irot).d(i)
    omw(i) = rotors(irot).omw(i)
    vif(i) = vw(i) − d(i)
Next i
'
'       Geometry and simple aero constants
'
a0 = rotors(irot).a0
del0 = rotors(irot).del0
```

```
del1 = rotors(irot).del1
del2 = rotors(irot).del2
del3 = rotors(irot).del3
eps0 = rotors(irot).eps0
precone = rotors(irot).precone
nb = rotors(irot).nb
radius = rotors(irot).radius
chord = rotors(irot).chord
dmass = rotors(irot).dmass
bt = rotors(irot).bt
omega = rotors(irot).omega
twist = rotors(irot).twist
prev = rotors(irot).p
m1 = rotors(irot).m1
iflap = rotors(irot).iflap
sigma = rotors(irot).sigma
hubtype = rotors(irot).hubtype
khub = rotors(irot).khub
'
'       Calculate some intermediate rotor constants.
'
gamma = rho * chord * a0 * radius ^ 4 / iflap
'
For i = 1 To 3
    flap(i) = rotors(irot).flap(i)
    cont(i) = rotors(irot).cont(i)
Next i
'
'       Construct transformation matrices to move
'       velocities from cg to iera.
'
make_t3 phii, thetai, psii, t3( )
mtxtranspose t3t( ), t3( ), 3, 3
'
'       Translate cg velocities to iela.
'
rrot_cg(1) = −(rotors(irot).sl − slcg)
rrot_cg(2) = (rotors(irot).bl − blcg)
rrot_cg(3) = −(rotors(irot).wl − wlcg)
'
cross omb( ), rrot_cg( ), omcr( )
cross ombd( ), rrot_cg( ), omdcr( )
vecadd vib( ), omcr( ), viela( ), 3, 1
vecadd viela( ), vif( ), viela( ), 3, 2
veceql omiela( ), omb( ), 3
vecadd vibd( ), omdcr( ), vdiela( ), 3, 1
veceql omdiela( ), ombd( ), 3
'
'       Subtract wash to get aerodynamic velocities
'
vecadd viela( ), vw( ), va( ), 3, 2
vecadd omiela( ), omw( ), oma( ), 3, 2
```

```
'
'      Rotate velocities to iera
'
mtxvecmpy t3( ), va( ), vaiera( ), 3, 3
mtxvecmpy t3( ), oma( ), omaiera( ), 3, 3
mtxvecmpy t3( ), viela( ), viera( ), 3, 3
mtxvecmpy t3( ), omiela( ), omiera( ), 3, 3
mtxvecmpy t3( ), vdiela( ), vdiera( ), 3, 3
mtxvecmpy t3( ), omdiela( ), omdiera( ), 3, 3
'
'      Rotate controls, flapping and velocities to wind-mast axes.
'
um = vaiera(1)
vm = vaiera(2)
vmtot2 = um * um + vm * vm
If vmtot2 < 0.00001 Then
     cchi = 1#
     schi = 0#
Else
     cchi = um / Sqr(um * um + vm * vm)
     schi = vm / Sqr(um * um + vm * vm)
End If
twm(1, 1) = cchi
twm(1, 2) = schi
twm(1, 3) = 0#
twm(2, 1) = -schi
twm(2, 2) = cchi
twm(2, 3) = 0#
twm(3, 1) = 0#
twm(3, 2) = 0#
twm(3, 3) = 1#
mtxtranspose twmt( ), twm( ), 3, 3
mtxvecmpy twm( ), vaiera( ), vawm( ), 3, 3
mtxvecmpy twm( ), omaiera( ), omawm( ), 3, 3
mtxvecmpy twm( ), viera( ), viwm( ), 3, 3
mtxvecmpy twm( ), omiera( ), omiwm( ), 3, 3
mtxvecmpy twm( ), vdiera( ), vidwm( ), 3, 3
mtxvecmpy twm( ), omdiera( ), omidwm( ), 3, 3
omegap = omega - omiwm(3)
omegaa = omega - omawm(3)
'
'      Calculate the aerodynamic forces and moments.
'      Since the induced velocity and thrust are so
'      tightly coupled, that loop is solved first,
'      then the flapping is solved, then the other
'      loads are found.
'
theta0 = cont(1)
ca1 = cchi * cont(2) - schi * cont(3)
cb1 = schi * cont(2) + cchi * cont(3)
beta0 = (flap(1) - precone) * hubtype + precone
a1 = cchi * flap(2) - schi * flap(3)
```

```
b1 = schi * flap(2) + cchi * flap(3)
'
vtipa = omegaa * radius
fact1 = (rho * pi * radius * radius * vtipa * vtipa)
lambdi = viwm(3) / vtipa
'
mu = vawm(1) / vtipa
mu2 = mu * mu
mu3 = mu2 * mu
lambda = vawm(3) / vtipa
lamwold = lambdi - lambda
pahat = omawm(1) / omega
qahat = omawm(2) / omega
pihat = omiwm(1) / omega
qihat = omiwm(2) / omega
pid = omidwm(1) * 0
qid = omidwm(2) * 0
ax = vidwm(1)
ay = vidwm(2)
az = vidwm(3)
'
'      Close thrust-induced velocity loop
'
For i = 1 To 10
    bt2 = bt * bt
    bt3 = bt2 * bt
    bt4 = bt3 * bt
    bt5 = bt4 * bt
    czth0 = bt3 / 3# + mu2 * bt / 2#
    cztht = bt4 / 4# + mu2 * bt2 / 4#
    czlam = (bt2 / 2# + mu2 / 4#) * (1 + eps0)
    czcb1 = bt2 * mu / 2# + mu3 / 8#
    czpa = bt2 * mu / 4# * (1 + eps0)

    cz0 = czth0 * theta0 + cztht * twist + czcb1 * cb1 + czpa * pahat
    cz0 = -sigma * a0 / 2 * cz0
    cz1 = cz0 - sigma * a0 / 2 * czlam * lambdi
    cz = cz0 - sigma * a0 / 2 * czlam * lambda
    fact2 = Sqr(mu2 + lambda * lambda)
    lamw = -cz1 / 2 / (fact2 + sigma * a0 * czlam / 4)
    lamw = 0.8 * lamw + 0.2 * lamwold
    lamwold = lamw
    lambda = lambdi - lamw
    bt = 1 - Sqr(2 * Abs(cz)) / nb
    bt = amax(amin(bt, 1#), 0.9)
    clbar = -6 * cz / sigma
    cdavg = del0 + clbar * (del1 + clbar * del2)
    eps0 = cdavg / a0
Next i
vawm(3) = lambda * vtipa
rotors(irot).bt = bt
rotors(irot).eps0 = eps0
```

```
'
'    Find the flapping
'
fom = omegaa / omegap
fom2 = fom * fom
f0 = (bt4 / 4 + bt2 * mu2 / 4) * fom2
ft = (bt5 / 5 + bt3 * mu2 / 6) * fom2
fla = (bt3 / 3) * (1 + eps0) * fom2
fcb1 = (bt3 * mu / 3) * fom2
fp = (bt3 * mu / 6) * (1 + eps0) * fom2
fa1 = (bt3 * mu / 6 / fom) * (1 + eps0) * (1 − fom) * fom2
'
aa0 = (2 * bt3 * mu / 3) * fom2
aat = (bt4 * mu / 2) * fom2
aala = (bt2 * mu / 2 − mu3 / 8) * (1 + eps0) * fom2
aacb1 = (bt4 / 4 + 3 * bt2 * mu2 / 8) * fom2
aap = (bt4 / 4) * (1 + eps0) * fom2
aa1 = (bt4 / 4 / fom − bt2 * mu2 / 8) * (1 + eps0) * fom2
'
bb0 = (bt3 * mu / 3) * (1 + eps0) * fom2
bca1 = (bt4 / 4 + bt2 * mu2 / 8) * fom2
bq = (bt4 / 4) * (1 + eps0) * fom2
bb1 = (bt4 / 4 / fom + bt2 * mu2 / 8) * (1 + eps0) * fom2
'
fmtx(1, 1) = prev * prev
fmtx(1, 2) = gamma * fa1 / 2
fmtx(1, 3) = 0
fmtx(2, 1) = 0
fmtx(2, 2) = gamma * aa1 / 2
fmtx(2, 3) = 1 − prev * prev
fmtx(3, 1) = gamma * bb0 / 2
fmtx(3, 2) = 1 − prev * prev
fmtx(3, 3) = −gamma * bb1 / 2
'
cmtx(1, 1) = gamma * f0 / 2
cmtx(1, 2) = gamma * ft / 2
cmtx(1, 3) = 0
cmtx(1, 4) = gamma * fcb1 / 2
cmtx(2, 1) = gamma * aa0 / 2
cmtx(2, 2) = gamma * aat / 2
cmtx(2, 3) = 0
cmtx(2, 4) = gamma * aacb1 / 2
cmtx(3, 1) = 0
cmtx(3, 2) = 0
cmtx(3, 3) = gamma * bca1 / 2
cmtx(3, 4) = 0
'
rmtx(1, 1) = gamma * fla / 2
rmtx(1, 2) = gamma * fp / 2
rmtx(1, 3) = 0
rmtx(2, 1) = gamma * aala / 2
rmtx(2, 2) = gamma * aap / 2
```

```
rmtx(2, 3) = 0
rmtx(3, 1) = 0
rmtx(3, 2) = 0
rmtx(3, 3) = gamma * bq / 2
'
acmtx(1, 1) = 0
acmtx(1, 2) = 0
acmtx(1, 3) = 0
acmtx(1, 4) = 0
acmtx(1, 5) = −m1 * radius * a1 / 2 / iflap
acmtx(1, 6) = m1 * radius * b1 / 2 / iflap
acmtx(1, 7) = m1 * radius / iflap
acmtx(2, 1) = 0
acmtx(2, 2) = −2
acmtx(2, 3) = 1
acmtx(2, 4) = 0
acmtx(2, 5) = 0
acmtx(2, 6) = −m1 * radius * beta0 / iflap
acmtx(2, 7) = 0
acmtx(3, 1) = 2
acmtx(3, 2) = 0
acmtx(3, 3) = 0
acmtx(3, 4) = 1
acmtx(3, 5) = m1 * radius * beta0 / iflap
acmtx(3, 6) = 0
acmtx(3, 7) = 0
'
cvec(1) = theta0
cvec(2) = twist
cvec(3) = ca1
cvec(4) = cb1
rvec(1) = lambda
rvec(2) = pahat
rvec(3) = qahat
acvec(1) = pihat
acvec(2) = qihat
acvec(3) = pid / (omegap ^ 2)
acvec(4) = qid / (omegap ^ 2)
acvec(5) = ax / (radius * omegap ^ 2)
acvec(6) = ay / (radius * omegap ^ 2)
acvec(7) = az / (radius * omegap ^ 2)
'
'      Solve for flapping in wind-mast axes
'
mtxvecmpy acmtx( ), acvec( ), tmp2( ), 3, 7
mtxvecmpy rmtx( ), rvec( ), tmp( ), 3, 3
vecadd tmp( ), tmp2( ), tmp( ), 3, 1
mtxvecmpy cmtx( ), cvec( ), tmp2( ), 3, 4
vecadd tmp( ), tmp2( ), tmp( ), 3, 1
mtxinv fmtx( ), 3, det
mtxvecmpy fmtx( ), tmp( ), flap( ), 3, 3
flap(1) = (flap(1) − precone) * hubtype + precone
```

```
beta0 = flap(1)
a1 = flap(2)
b1 = flap(3)
'
'     Find x-force
'
cxeps = bt2 * mu / 2#
cxth0 = bt * mu * lambda / 2# − bt3 * a1 / 3#
cxtht = bt2 * mu * lambda / 4# − bt4 * a1 / 4#
cxa1b1 = bt3 * beta0 / 6#
cxb1 = bt2 * lambda / 4# − bt2 * mu * a1 / 4#
cxlaa1 = 3# * bt2 / 4#
cxb02a12 = bt2 * mu / 4#
cxpa = bt3 * theta0 / 6# + bt4 * twist / 8# + bt2 * lambda / 2#
cxpa = cxpa + 3# * bt2 * mu * cb1 / 16# + bt2 * mu * a1 / 16#
cxqa = bt3 * beta0 / 6# + bt2 * mu * ca1 / 16# + bt2 * mu * b1 / 16#
cx = −cxeps * eps0 + cxth0 * theta0 + cxtht * twist + cxa1b1 * (ca1 + b1)
cx = cx + cxb1 * cb1 − cxlaa1 * lambda * a1 − cxb02a12 * (beta0 * beta0 + a1 * a1)
cx = cx + cxpa * pahat + cxqa * qahat
cx = sigma * a0 / 2 * cx
'
'     Find y-force
'
cyth0 = (bt3 / 3# + bt * mu2 / 2#) * b1 − 3# * bt2 * mu * beta0 / 4#
cytht = (bt4 / 4# + bt2 * mu2 / 4#) * b1 − bt3 * mu * beta0 / 2#
cyca1 = bt2 * lambda / 4# + bt2 * mu * a1 / 4#
cycb1 = −(bt3 / 6# + bt * mu2 / 2#) * beta0 + bt2 * mu * b1 / 2#
cyla = 3# * bt2 * b1 / 4# − 3# * bt * mu * beta0 / 2#
cya1 = bt3 * beta0 / 6# + bt2 * mu * b1 / 4# − bt * mu2 * beta0
cypa = bt2 * mu * ca1 / 16# − bt3 * beta0 / 6# + 5# * bt2 * mu * b1 / 16#
cyqa = bt3 * theta0 / 6# + bt4 * twist / 8# + bt2 * lambda / 2# + bt2 * mu * cb1 / 16 + 7
      * bt2 * mu * a1 / 16#
cy = cyth0 * theta0 + cytht * twist + cyca1 * ca1 + cycb1 * cb1
cy = cy + cyla * lambda + cya1 * a1 + cypa * pahat + cyqa * qahat
cy = sigma * a0 / 2 * cy
'
'     Find torque
'
cq0eps = bt4 / 4# + bt2 * mu2 / 4#
cq0la = bt3 * theta0 / 3# + bt4 * twist / 4# + bt2 * lambda / 2#
cq0b02 = bt2 * mu2 / 4#
cq0a12 = bt4 / 8# + 3# * bt2 * mu2 / 16#
cq0b12 = bt4 / 8# + bt2 * mu2 / 16#
cq0b0b1 = bt3 * mu / 3#
cq0a1la = bt2 * mu / 2#
cq0 = cq0eps * eps0 − cq0la * lambda − cq0b02 * beta0 * beta0
cq0 = cq0 − cq0a12 * a1 * a1 − cq0b12 * b1 * b1 + cq0b0b1 * beta0 * b1
cq0 = cq0 − cq0a1la * a1 * lambda
cq0 = sigma * a0 / 2 * cq0
'
cqcb1a1 = bt4 / 8# − bt2 * mu2 / 16#
cqcb1la = bt2 * mu / 4#
```

```
cqca1b0 = bt3 * mu / 6#
cqca1b1 = bt4 / 8# + bt2 * mu2 / 16#
cqcyc = cqcb1a1 * cb1 * a1 − cqcb11a * cb1 * lambda + cqca1b0 * ca1 * beta0
cqcyc = cqcyc − cqca1b1 * ca1 * b1
cqcyc = sigma * a0 / 2 * cqcyc
'
cqpa = −bt4 * cb1 / 8# − bt3 * mu * theta0 / 6# − bt4 * mu * twist / 8#
cqpa = cqpa − bt4 * pahat / 8# + bt4 * a1 / 4#
cqqa = −bt4 * ca1 / 8# + bt3 * mu * beta0 / 3# − bt4 * qahat /8# − bt4 * b1 / 4#
cqpq = cqpa * pahat + cqqa * qahat
cqpq = sigma * a0 / 2 * cqpq
'

cq = cq0 + cqcyc + cqpq
'
'       Get the hub loads
'
xforce = cx * fact1
yforce = cy * fact1
thrust = cz * fact1
torque = cq * fact1 * radius
'
fmbwm(1) = cx * fact1
fmbwm(2) = cy * fact1
fmbwm(3) = cz * fact1
fmbwm(4) = khub * b1
fmbwm(5) = khub * a1
fmbwm(6) = cq * fact1 * radius
For i = 1 To 3
    tmp2(i) = fmbwm(i + 3)
Next i
mtxvecmpy twmt( ), fmbwm( ), fmb( ), 3, 3
mtxvecmpy twmt( ), tmp2( ), tmp( ), 3, 3
For i = 1 To 3
    fmb(i + 3) = tmp(i)
Next i
'
'       Load vectors with aero loads and rotate to iela
'
mtxvecmpy t3t( ), fmb( ), fiela( ), 3, 3
For i = 1 To 3
    tmp2(i) = fmb(i + 3)
Next i
mtxvecmpy t3t( ), tmp2( ), miela( ), 3, 3
flap(2) = cchi * a1 + schi * b1
flap(3) = −schi * a1 + cchi * b1
'
'       Since induced velocity is calculated here,
'       it must be resolved from wind-mast axes back
'       to local axes. This means the induced velocity
'       and the aerodynamic velocity must both be
'       rotated.
'
```

```
mtxvecmpy twmt( ), vawm( ), vaiera( ), 3, 3
mtxvecmpy t3t( ), vaiera( ), va( ), 3, 3
vecadd viela( ), va( ), vw( ), 3, 2
'
'      Do rxf to get moments at cg, then put into structure
'
cross rrot_cg( ), fiela( ), tmp( )
For i = 1 To 3
    rotors(irot).force(i) = fiela(i)
    rotors(irot).moment(i) = miela(i)
    rotors(irot).force_cg(i) = fiela(i)
    rotors(irot).moment_cg(i) = miela(i) + tmp(i)
    rotors(irot).d(i) = vw(i)
    rotors(irot).va(i) = va(i)
    rotors(irot).flap(i) = flap(i)
Next i
rotors(irot).power = torque * omega / 550#
rotors(irot).bt = bt
'
End Sub

Sub washmodel( )
'
'      This routine calculates the wash velocity produced by
'      each element, then combines them according to some
'      basic rules.
'
'      Fuselage self-influence
'
rtworho = 1# / (2 * rho)
vatot = 0#
For i = 1 To 3
    vatot = vatot + fuse.va(i) * fuse.va(i)
Next i
vatot = Sqr(vatot)
If vatot < 0.1 Then
    fuse.d(1) = 0#
    fuse.d(2) = 0#
    fuse.d(3) = 0#
Else
    fuse.d(1) = -rtworho * fuse.a11 * fuse.force(1) / vatot
    fuse.d(2) = -rtworho * fuse.a22 * fuse.force(2) / vatot
    fuse.d(3) = -rtworho * fuse.a33 * fuse.force(3) / vatot
End If
'
'      Wing self-influence
'
For iwing = 1 To nwings
    vatot = 0#
    For i = 1 To 3
        vatot = vatot + wings(iwing).va(i) * wings(iwing).va(i)
    Next i
    vatot = Sqr(vatot)
```

```
        If vatot < 0.1 Then
           wings(iwing).d(1) = 0#
           wings(iwing).d(2) = 0#
           wings(iwing).d(3) = 0#
        Else
           wings(iwing).d(1) = −rtworho * wings(iwing).a11 * wings(iwing).force(1) / vatot
           wings(iwing).d(2) = −rtworho * wings(iwing).a11 * wings(iwing).force(2) / vatot
           wings(iwing).d(3) = −rtworho * wings(iwing).a11 * wings(iwing).force(3) / vatot
        End If
   Next iwing
'
'     Fin self-influence
'
   For ifin = 1 To nfins
        vatot = 0#
        For i = 1 To 3
           vatot = vatot + fins(ifin).va(i) * fins(ifin).va(i)
        Next i
        vatot = Sqr(vatot)
        If vatot < 0.1 Then
           fins(ifin).d(1) = 0#
           fins(ifin).d(2) = 0#
           fins(ifin).d(3) = 0#
        Else
           fins(ifin).d(1) = −rtworho * fins(ifin).a11 * fins(ifin).force(1) / vatot
           fins(ifin).d(2) = −rtworho * fins(ifin).a22 * fins(ifin).force(2) / vatot
           fins(ifin).d(3) = −rtworho * fins(ifin).a33 * fins(ifin).force(3) / vatot
        End If
   Next ifin
'
'     Rotor self-influence
'
   For irotor = 1 To nrotors
        vatot = 0#
        For i = 1 To 3
           vatot = vatot + rotors(irotor).va(i) * rotors(irotor).va(i)
        Next i
        vatot = Sqr(vatot)
        If vatot < 0.1 Then
           rotors(irotor).d(1) = 0#
           rotors(irotor).d(2) = 0#
           rotors(irotor).d(3) = 0#
        Else
           rotors(irotor).d(1) = −rtworho * rotors(irotor).a11 * rotors(irotor).force(1) / vatot
           rotors(irotor).d(2) = −rtworho * rotors(irotor).a22 * rotors(irotor).force(2) / vatot
           rotors(irotor).d(3) = −rtworho * rotors(irotor).a33 * rotors(irotor).force(3) / vatot
        End If
   Next irotor
'
'     Mutual interferences:
'
'     F(x) on HS(x)
'     F(z) on MR(z)
```

```
'     MR(z) on F(z)
'     MR(z) on HS(z)
'     TR(y) on VS(y)
'     VS(y) on TR(y)
'
For i = 1 To 3
    fuse.vw(i) = fuse.d(i)
    rotors(1).vw(i) = rotors(1).d(i)
    rotors(2).vw(i) = rotors(2).d(i)
    wings(1).vw(i) = wings(1).d(i)
    fins(1).vw(i) = fins(1).d(i)
Next i
'
'     Main rotor on fuselage
'
dx = rotors(1).sl − fuse.sl
dy = rotors(1).bl − fuse.bl
dz = rotors(1).wl − fuse.wl
dist = Sqr(dx * dx + dy * dy + dz * dz)
zor = dist / rotors(1).radius
coef1 = 1 + zor / Sqr(1 + zor * zor)
fuse.vw(3) = fuse.vw(3) + coef1 * rotors(1).d(3)
'
'     Main rotor on horizontal stabilizer - assumes
'     the horizontal stabilizer is always in the wake.
'
dx = wings(1).sl - rotors(1).sl
dy = wings(1).bl - rotors(1).bl
dz = wings(1).wl - rotors(1).wl
dist = Sqr(dx * dx + dy * dy + dz * dz)
zor = dist / rotors(1).radius
coef1 = 1 + zor / Sqr(1 + zor * zor)
wings(1).vw(3) = wings(1).vw(3) + coef1 * rotors(1).d(3)
'
'     Fuselage on main rotor
'
rotors(1).vw(3) = rotors(1).vw(3) + fuse.d(3)
'
'     Vertical fin on tail rotor
'
rotors(2).vw(2) = rotors(2).vw(2) + fins(1).d(2)
'
'     Tail rotor on vertical fin
'
fins(1).vw(2) = fins(1).vw(2) + rotors(2).d(2)
'
'     Fuselage on horizontal stabilizer
'
wings(1).vw(1) = wings(1).vw(1) + fuse.d(1)
'
End Sub
```

```
Sub wingmodel(iwing As Integer)
'
'       This routine calculates the forces and moments produced
'       by the iwing'th wing. Use the point-load method. The
'       wing is modeled as two half-wings symmetrically constructed
'       in the x-z plane.
'
Dim a0 As Single
Dim a03d As Single
Dim aoa As Single
Dim ar As Single
Dim b As Single
Dim bo2 As Single
Dim cbar As Single
Dim cd As Single
Dim cd0 As Single
Dim cd1 As Single
Dim cd2 As Single
Dim cl As Single
Dim cm As Single
Dim cm0 As Single
Dim cma As Single
Dim croot As Single
Dim delf As Single
Dim dihedral As Single
Dim drag As Single
Dim incid As Single
Dim lift As Single
Dim momy As Single
Dim phii As Single
Dim psii As Single
Dim qtots12 As Single
Dim s12 As Single
Dim slambda As Single
Dim stot As Single
Dim sweep As Single
Dim smac As Single
Dim thetai As Single
Dim v2 As Single
Dim xmac As Single
Dim ymacLw As Single
Dim ymacRw As Single
Dim zmac As Single
Dim i As Integer
'
Dim fc(3) As Single
Dim mc(3) As Single
Dim omcr(3) As Single
Dim vw(3) As Single
Dim omw(3) As Single
Dim rlwiera(3) As Single
```

```
Dim rrwiera(3) As Single
Dim rwing_cg(3) As Single
Dim viela(3) As Single
Dim omiela(3) As Single
Dim va(3) As Single
Dim oma(3) As Single
Dim t3(3, 3) As Single
Dim t3t(3, 3) As Single
Dim ta3(3, 3) As Single
Dim ta3t(3, 3) As Single
Dim viera(3) As Single
Dim omiera(3) As Single
Dim vmac_iera(3) As Single
Dim ommac_iera(3) As Single
Dim vmac_wra(3) As Single
Dim ommac_wra(3) As Single
Dim tma(3, 3) As Single
Dim tmat(3, 3) As Single
Dim pfwra(3) As Single
Dim pmwra(3) As Single
Dim pfriela(3) As Single
Dim pmriela(3) As Single
Dim pfliela(3) As Single
Dim pmliela(3) As Single
Dim pfiera(3) As Single
Dim pmiera(3) As Single
Dim rcf(3) As Single
Dim pfrwingb(3) As Single
Dim pmrwingb(3) As Single
Dim pflwingb(3) As Single
Dim pmlwingb(3) As Single
'
'       Unload structure into local variables:
'
'       Orientation angles
'
phii = wings(iwing).phii
thetai = wings(iwing).thetai
psii = wings(iwing).psii
'
'       Wash velocities in local axes
'
For i = 1 To 3
    vw(i) = wings(iwing).vw(i)
    omw(i) = wings(iwing).omw(i)
Next i
'
'       Geometry and simple aero constants
'
a0 = wings(iwing).a0
b = wings(iwing).span
bo2 = b / 2#
```

```
croot = wings(iwing).chord
delf = wings(iwing).cont
slambda = wings(iwing).taper
dihedral = wings(iwing).dihedral
sweep = wings(iwing).sweep
incid = wings(iwing).incid + delf
cd0 = wings(iwing).cd0
cd1 = wings(iwing).cd1
cd2 = wings(iwing).cd2
cm0 = wings(iwing).cm0
cma = wings(iwing).cma
'
'       Calculate some intermediate wing constants.
'
s12 = b * croot * (1 + slambda) / 4#
stot = s12 * 2
cbar = 2 * croot * (slambda ^ 2 + slambda + 1) / 3 / (slambda + 1)
smac = b * (2 * slambda + 1) / 6 / (slambda + 1)
xmac = −Sin(sweep) * Cos(−dihedral) * smac
ymacRw = Cos(sweep) * Cos(−dihedral) * smac
ymacLw = −Cos(sweep) * Cos(−dihedral) * smac
zmac = Sin(−dihedral) * smac
ar = b * b / stot
a03d = a0 * ar / (ar + 2 * (ar + 4) / (ar + 2))
'
'       Translate cg velocities to iela.
'
rwing_cg(1) = −(wings(iwing).sl − slcg)
rwing_cg(2) = (wings(iwing).bl − blcg)
rwing_cg(3) = −(wings(iwing).wl − wlcg)
'
cross omb( ), rwing_cg( ), omcr( )
vecadd vib( ), omcr( ), viela( ), 3, 1
veceql omiela( ), omb( ), 3
'
'       Subtract wash to get aerodynamic velocities
'
vecadd viela( ), vw( ), va( ), 3, 2
vecadd omiela( ), omw( ), oma( ), 3, 2
'
'       Translate and rotate velocities to iera
'
make_t3 phii, thetai, psii, t3( )
mtxtranspose t3t( ), t3( ), 3, 3
mtxvecmpy t3( ), va( ), viera( ), 3, 3
mtxvecmpy t3( ), oma( ), omiera( ), 3, 3
'
'       Start with right wing.
'
rrwiera(1) = xmac
rrwiera(2) = ymacRw
rrwiera(3) = zmac
```

```
'

cross omiera( ), rrwiera( ), omcr( )
vecadd viera( ), omcr( ), vmac_iera( ), 3, 1
veceql ommac_iera( ), omiera( ), 3
'

make_t3 (−dihedral), incid, sweep, ta3( )
mtxtranspose ta3t( ), ta3( ), 3, 3
'

mtxvecmpy ta3( ), vmac_iera( ), vmac_wra( ), 3, 3
mtxvecmpy ta3( ), ommac_iera( ), ommac_wra( ), 3, 3
'

'     Calculate aerodynamic loads in WRA
'

aoa = vbatan4((vmac_wra(3)), (vmac_wra(1))) * pi / 180#
'

cd = cd0 + aoa * (cd1 + aoa * cd2)
cl = a03d * aoa
cm = cm0 + cma * aoa
'

innerp vmac_wra( ), vmac_wra( ), v2, 3
qtots12 = rho * v2 / 2# * s12
drag = qtots12 * cd
lift = qtots12 * cl
momy = qtots12 * cbar * cm
fc(1) = −drag
fc(2) = 0#
fc(3) = −lift
mc(1) = 0#
mc(2) = momy
mc(3) = 0#
'

'     Rotate loads back to IELA, then translate to cg.
'

make_t3 0, (−aoa), 0, tma( )
mtxtranspose tmat( ), tma( ), 3, 3
mtxvecmpy tmat( ), fc( ), pfwra( ), 3, 3
mtxvecmpy tmat( ), mc( ), pmwra( ), 3, 3
mtxvecmpy ta3t( ), pfwra( ), pfiera( ), 3, 3
mtxvecmpy ta3t( ), pmwra( ), pmiera( ), 3, 3
cross rrwiera( ), pfiera( ), rcf( )
vecadd pmiera( ), rcf( ), pmiera( ), 3, 1
mtxvecmpy t3t( ), pfiera( ), pfriela( ), 3, 3
mtxvecmpy t3t( ), pmiera( ), pmriela( ), 3, 3
veceql pfrwingb( ), pfriela( ), 3
cross rwing_cg( ), pfriela( ), rcf( )
vecadd pmriela( ), rcf( ), pmrwingb( ), 3, 1
'

'     Now, the left wing panel.
'

rlwiera(1) = xmac
rlwiera(2) = ymacLw
rlwiera(3) = zmac
'
```

```
cross omiera( ), rlwiera( ), omcr( )
vecadd viera( ), omcr( ), vmac_iera( ), 3, 1
veceql ommac_iera( ), omiera( ), 3
'
make_t3 (dihedral), incid, (−sweep), ta3( )
mtxtranspose ta3t( ), ta3( ), 3, 3
'
mtxvecmpy ta3( ), vmac_iera( ), vmac_wra( ), 3, 3
mtxvecmpy ta3( ), ommac_iera( ), ommac_wra( ), 3, 3
'
'      Calculate aerodynamic loads in WRA
'
aoa = vbatan4((vmac_wra(3)), (vmac_wra(1))) * pi / 180#
'
cd = cd0 + aoa * (cd1 + aoa * cd2)
cl = a03d * aoa
cm = cm0 + cma * aoa
'
innerp vmac_wra( ), vmac_wra( ), v2, 3
qtots12 = rho * v2 / 2# * s12
drag = qtots12 * cd
lift = qtots12 * cl
momy = qtots12 * cbar * cm
fc(1) = −drag
fc(2) = 0#
fc(3) = −lift
mc(1) = 0#
mc(2) = momy
mc(3) = 0#
'
'      Rotate loads back to IELA, then translate to cg.
'
make_t3 0, (−aoa), 0, tma( )
mtxtranspose tmat( ), tma( ), 3, 3
mtxvecmpy tmat( ), fc( ), pfwra( ), 3, 3
mtxvecmpy tmat( ), mc( ), pmwra( ), 3, 3
mtxvecmpy ta3t( ), pfwra( ), pfiera( ), 3, 3
mtxvecmpy ta3t( ), pmwra( ), pmiera( ), 3, 3
cross rlwiera( ), pfiera( ), rcf( )
vecadd pmiera( ), rcf( ), pmiera( ), 3, 1
mtxvecmpy t3t( ), pfiera( ), pfliela( ), 3, 3
mtxvecmpy t3t( ), pmiera( ), pmliela( ), 3, 3
veceql pflwingb( ), pfliela( ), 3
cross rwing_cg( ), pfliela( ), rcf( )
vecadd pmliela( ), rcf( ), pmlwingb( ), 3, 1
'
'      Load results into structure.
'
For i = 1 To 3
    wings(iwing).force(i) = pfriela(i) + pfliela(i)
    wings(iwing).moment(i) = pmriela(i) + pmliela(i)
    wings(iwing).force_cg(i) = pfrwingb(i) + pflwingb(i)
    wings(iwing).moment_cg(i) = pmrwingb(i) + pmlwingb(i)
```

```
    wings(iwing).va(i) = va(i)
Next i

End Sub
```

18.5.10   Discussion on Element Models

Details about each of the models are unnecessary. The chapters on the elements do a good job of documenting them. However, it is instructive to see how vectors and linerar algebra can preserve the fidelity of a model while maintining a compact presentation. In particular, examine the WINGMODEL just shown. Notice that results from the scalar equations load vectors that are easily manipulated by matric and vector subroutines. Notice also how this correlates well with the math model presented in the chapter on wings.

18.5.11   Math Package

```
Option Explicit
Global Const pi = 3.1415926538

Function amax(a As Single, b As Single) As Single
'
'       This function returns the maximum of a or b.
'
'       Author: Mark E. Dreier
'
'       Copyright 1991
'       Bell Helicopter Textron, Inc.
'       Unpublished - All Rights Reserved
'
If a > b Then
      amax = a
Else
      amax = b
End If
End Function

Function amin(a As Single, b As Single) As Single
'
'       This function returns the minimum of a or b.
'
'       Author: Mark E. Dreier
'
'       Copyright 1991
'       Bell Helicopter Textron, Inc.
'       Unpublished - All Rights Reserved
'
If a < b Then
      amin = a
Else
      amin = b
```

End If
End Function

Sub cross(a( ) As Single, b( ) As Single, axb( ) As Single)
'
'   The cross product of A and B is returned
'   in AXB.
'
'   Author: Mark E. Dreier
'
'   Copyright 2001
'   Bell Helicopter Textron, Inc.
'
'   Unpublished - All Rights Reserved
'
axb(1) = a(2) * b(3) − a(3) * b(2)
axb(2) = a(3) * b(1) − a(1) * b(3)
axb(3) = a(1) * b(2) − a(2) * b(1)
End Sub

Sub innerp(x( ) As Single, y( ) As Single, z As Single, n As Integer)
'
'   This routine calculates the inner product of two
'   vectors x and y, and places the result in z. The
'   length of the vectors is assumed to be n.
'
'   Author: Mark E. Dreier
'
'   Copyright 1991
'   Bell Helicopter Textron, Inc.
'   Unpublished - All Rights Reserved
'
Dim i As Integer
'
z = 0#
For i = 1 To n
        z = z + x(i) * y(i)
Next i
End Sub

Sub mtxadd(a( ) As Single, b( ) As Single, c( ) As Single, nr As Integer, nc As Integer, iop
As Integer)
'
'   This if iop = 1, then this routine adds the upper left
'   nr x nc matrix in A to the upper left nr x nc matrix
'   in B to generate the upper left nr x nc matrix in c.
'   If iop = 2, then this routine subtracts the b matrix
'   from the a matrix and puts the result in c. If iop = 3,
'   then this routine subtracts a from b and puts the
'   result in c. If iop = 4, then c = −a − b.
'
'   Author: Mark E. Dreier
'

```
'     Copyright 1991
'     Bell Helicopter Textron, Inc.
'     Unpublished - All Rights Reserved
'
Dim i As Integer
Dim j As Integer
'
Select Case iop
Case 1
    For i = 1 To nr
      For j = 1 To nc
        c(i, j) = a(i, j) + b(i, j)
      Next j
    Next i
Case 2
    For i = 1 To nr
      For j = 1 To nc
        c(i, j) = a(i, j) - b(i, j)
      Next j
    Next i
Case 3
    For i = 1 To nr
      For j = 1 To nc
        c(i, j) = b(i, j) - a(i, j)
      Next j
    Next i
Case 4
    For i = 1 To nr
      For j = 1 To nc
        c(i, j) = -(a(i, j) + b(i, j))
      Next j
    Next i
Case Else
    For i = 1 To nr
      For j = 1 To nc
        c(i, j) = 0#
      Next j
    Next i
End Select
End Sub


Sub mtxeql(copyofa( ) As Single, a( ) As Single, nr As Integer, nc As Integer)
'
'     This routine copies a into copyofa. The matrix a is
'     of size nr x nc.
'
'     Author: Mark E. Dreier
'
'     Copyright 1991
'     Bell Helicopter Textron, Inc.
'     Unpublished - All Rights Reserved
'
```

```
Dim i As Integer
Dim j As Integer
'
For i = 1 To nr
    For j = 1 To nc
        copyofa(i, j) = a(i, j)
    Next j
Next i
End Sub

Sub mtxinv(x( ) As Single, n As Integer, det As Single)
'
'       This routine calculates the inverse of the upper
'       N x N submatrix of X in place. It also calculates
'       the determinant and places it in DET.
'
'       The author is unknown. This QuickBASIC implementation
'       was coded by:
'       Mark E. Dreier
'
ReDim irow(n) As Integer
ReDim icol(n) As Integer
ReDim b1(n)
ReDim c1(n)
Dim am As Single
Dim ar As Single
Dim epsilon As Single
Dim i As Integer
Dim j As Integer
Dim k As Integer
Dim ik As Integer
Dim ikk As Integer
Dim ki As Integer
Dim kj As Integer
Dim kc As Integer
Dim sf As Single
Dim temp2 As Single
'
'       Determine the machine precision.
'
epsilon = 1#
While 1# + epsilon > 1#
    epsilon = epsilon / 2
Wend
sf = Sqr(epsilon)
'
det = 1#
'
'       Locate pivot
'
For k = 1 To n
    am = 0#
```

```
For j = k To n
   For i = k To n
      ar = x(i, j) * x(i, j)
      If ar > am Then
         am = ar
         irow(k) = i
         icol(k) = j
      End If
   Next i
Next j
If am <= sf Then
   det = 0#
   irow(k) = k
   icol(k) = k
Else
   If irow(k) <> k Then
      det = -det
      For j = 1 To n
         temp2 = x(irow(k), j)
         x(irow(k), j) = x(k, j)
         x(k, j) = temp2
      Next j
   End If
   If icol(k) <> k Then
      det = -det
      For i = 1 To n
         temp2 = x(i, icol(k))
         x(i, icol(k)) = x(i, k)
         x(i, k) = temp2
      Next i
   End If
   temp2 = x(k, k)
   det = det * temp2
   For j = 1 To n
      If j = k Then
         b1( j) = 1# / temp2
         c1( j) = 1#
      Else
         b1( j) = -x(k, j) / temp2
         c1( j) = x( j, k)
         x( j, k) = 0#
      End If
      x(k, j) = 0#
   Next j
   For j = 1 To n
      For i = 1 To n
         x(i, j) = x(i, j) + b1(j) * c1(i)
      Next i
   Next j
End If
Next k
'
```

```
'      Now rearrange the matrix into final form
'
For kc = 1 To n
    k = n - kc + 1
    If irow(k) <> k Then
      ikk = irow(k)
      ik = k
      For i = 1 To n
         temp2 = x(i, ik)
         x(i, ik) = x(i, ikk)
         x(i, ikk) = temp2
      Next i
    End If
    If icol(k) <> k Then
      kj = icol(k)
      ki = k
      For j = 1 To n
         temp2 = x(kj, j)
         x(kj, j) = x(ki, j)
         x(ki, j) = temp2
      Next j
    End If
Next kc
End Sub


Sub mtxmpy(a( ) As Single, b( ) As Single, c( ) As Single, nra As Integer, nca As Integer,
ncb As Integer)
'
'      This routine post-multiplies matrix a by matrix b
'      and places the result in matric c. The number of
'      rows in a is NRA, the number of columns in a is
'      NCA and the number of columns in b is ncb. The
'      number of rows in b is assumed to be the number of
'      columns in a. The c matrix is of size nra x ncb.
'
'      Author: Mark E. Dreier
'
'      Copyright 1991
'      Bell Helicopter Textron, Inc.
'      Unpublished - All Rights Reserved
'
Dim i As Integer
Dim j As Integer
Dim k As Integer
Dim sum As Single
'
For i = 1 To nra
    For j = 1 To ncb
      sum = 0#
      For k = 1 To nca
         sum = sum + a(i, k) * b(k, j)
      Next k
```

```
        c(i, j) = sum
    Next j
Next i
End Sub

Sub mtxtranspose(at( ) As Single, a( ) As Single, nra As Integer, nca As Integer)
'
'       This routine returns the transpose of matrix a( )
'       in at( ). Matrix a is nra x nca.
'
'       Author: Mark E. Dreier
'
'       Copyright 2002
'       Bell Helicopter Textron, Inc.
'       Unpublished - All Rights Reserved
'
Dim i As Integer
Dim j As Integer
'
For i = 1 To nra
    For j = 1 To nca
        at( j, i) = a(i, j)
    Next j
Next i
End Sub

Sub mtxvecmpy(a( ) As Single, b( ) As Single, c( ) As Single, nra As Integer, nca As Integer)
'
'       This routine post-multiplies matrix a by vector b
'       and places the result in vector c. The number of
'       rows in a is NRA, the number of columns in a is
'       NCA.
'
'       Author: Mark E. Dreier
'
'       Copyright 1996
'       Bell Helicopter Textron, Inc.
'       Unpublished - All Rights Reserved
'
Dim i As Integer
Dim j As Integer
Dim sum As Single
'
For i = 1 To nra
    sum = 0#
    For j = 1 To nca
        sum = sum + a(i, j) * b(j)
    Next j
    c(i) = sum
Next i
End Sub
```

```
Function rformat(x As Single) As String
'
'      Formats the variable x into a nice string.
'
If Abs(x) >= 10000# Then
    rformat = Format$ (x, "0.0000E + 00;-0.0000E + 00;0.0")
Else
    rformat = Format$ (x, "####.0000;-####.0000;0.0")
End If
End Function

Sub rotatex(arg As Single, mtx( ) As Single)
'
'      Make the x-axis rotation matrix.
'
Dim carg As Single
Dim sarg As Single
'
carg = Cos(arg)
sarg = Sin(arg)
'
mtx(1, 1) = 1#
mtx(1, 2) = 0#
mtx(1, 3) = 0#
mtx(2, 1) = 0#
mtx(2, 2) = carg
mtx(2, 3) = sarg
mtx(3, 1) = 0#
mtx(3, 2) = -sarg
mtx(3, 3) = carg
'
End Sub

Sub rotatey(arg As Single, mtx( ) As Single)
'
'      Make the y-axis rotation matrix.
'
Dim carg As Single
Dim sarg As Single
'
carg = Cos(arg)
sarg = Sin(arg)
'
mtx(1, 1) = carg
mtx(1, 2) = 0#
mtx(1, 3) = -sarg
mtx(2, 1) = 0#
mtx(2, 2) = 1#
mtx(2, 3) = 0#
mtx(3, 1) = sarg
mtx(3, 2) = 0#
```

```
mtx(3, 3) = carg
'
End Sub

Sub rotatez(arg As Single, mtx( ) As Single)
'
'      Make the z-axis rotation matrix.
'
Dim carg As Single
Dim sarg As Single
'
carg = Cos(arg)
sarg = Sin(arg)
'
mtx(1, 1) = carg
mtx(1, 2) = sarg
mtx(1, 3) = 0#
mtx(2, 1) = -sarg
mtx(2, 2) = carg
mtx(2, 3) = 0#
mtx(3, 1) = 0#
mtx(3, 2) = 0#
mtx(3, 3) = 1#
'
End Sub

Function vbatan4(n As Single, d As Single) As Single
'
'      This routine calculates the 4 quadrant phase angle
'      given the n(umerator) and d(enomenator) components.
'      The phase angle is returned in degrees from -180 to
'      180.
'
Dim ans As Single                       '
'
If d > 0# Then                          '1st or 4th
    If n > 0# Then                      '1st
        ans = Atn(n / d)               '
    ElseIf n = 0# Then                  '0
        ans = 0#                        '
    Else                                '4th
        ans = Atn(n / d)               '
    End If                              '
ElseIf d = 0# Then                      '+90 or -90
    If n > 0# Then                      '+90
        ans = pi / 2#                   '
    ElseIf n = 0# Then                  'Indeterminant, set to 0.
        ans = 0#                        '
    Else                                '-90
        ans = -pi / 2#                  '
    End If                              '
Else                                    '2nd or 3rd or 180 deg
    ans = pi + Atn(n / d)              '
```

```
End If                         '
vbatan4 = ans * 180# / pi         'Convert to degrees.
End Function

Sub vecadd(a( ) As Single, b( ) As Single, ab( ) As Single, n As Integer, iop As Integer)
'
'    This if iop = 1, then this routine adds the vector
'    A to the vector B to produce vector AB. If iop = 2,
'    then this routine subtracts the B vector from the
'    A vector and puts the result in AB. If iop = 3,
'    then this routine subtracts A from B and puts the
'    result in AB. If iop = 4, then AB = −A − B.
'
'    Author: Mark E. Dreier
'
'    Copyright 1995
'    Bell Helicopter Textron, Inc.
'    Unpublished - All Rights Reserved
'
Dim i As Integer
'
Select Case iop
Case 1
    For i = 1 To n
        ab(i) = a(i) + b(i)
    Next i
Case 2
    For i = 1 To n
        ab(i) = a(i) − b(i)
    Next i
Case 3
    For i = 1 To n
        ab(i) = b(i) − a(i)
    Next i
Case 4
    For i = 1 To n
        ab(i) = −(a(i) + b(i))
    Next i
Case Else
    For i = 1 To n
        ab(i) = 0#
    Next i
End Select
End Sub

Sub veceql(copyofa( ) As Single, a( ) As Single, n As Integer)
'
'    This routine copies the vector a into copyofa.
'    The vector is n elements long.
'
'    Author: Mark E. Dreier
'
```

'   Copyright 1995
'   Bell Helicopter Textron, Inc.
'   Unpublished - All Rights Reserved
'

Dim i As Integer
'

For i = 1 To n
    copyofa(i) = a(i)
Next i
End Sub

18.5.12   Discussion of Math Package

This is not a complete mathematical package, but it does contain all of the supporting math routines that this simulation requires. The names of the routines and the comments in them should suffice to explain their operation.

18.5.13   Results of this Simulation Program

The CD that accompanies this text includes the VisualBASIC® source and an executable of this program. The program is set to perform a sweep from hover to 140 kn. The first and last trim cases from an execution of this program are presented next.

Trim assignment:
Vinf (knots) : 0.000
R/C (fpm)   : 0.000

Element	X Force (Lbs)	Y Force (Lbs)	Z Force (Lbs)	L Moment (Ft-Lbs)	M Moment (Ft-Lbs)	N Moment (Ft-Lbs)
Fuselage :	−3.4348E + 01	3.1888E + 00	−6.5143E + 00	0.0000E + 00	2.7935E + 01	9.3116E + 00
Main Rotor :	1.8736E + 02	−2.4160E + 02	−6.7522E + 03	−2.1057E + 03	−1.2366E + 03	9.7632E + 03
Tail Rotor :	0.0000E + 00	3.8351E + 02	6.2466E − 03	2.1477E + 03	1.1790E + 02	−1.0240E + 04
Hor Stab :	2.4467E + 02	0.0000E + 00	7.5049E + 01	0.0000E + 00	1.2072E + 03	0.0000E + 00
Vert Stab :	5.2504E + 01	−1.8845E + 01	−4.0294E − 04	−4.1898E + 01	−1.1674E + 02	4.6735E + 02
Gravity :	−4.5018E + 02	−1.2624E + 02	6.6837E + 03	0.0000E + 00	0.0000E + 00	0.0000E + 00
Total :	1.0834E − 02	1.0040E − 02	−5.3711E − 03	1.0237E − 01	−3.4834E − 01	1.1987E − 01

Flapping	Coning	Fore/aft	Lateral
Main Rotor :	1.8750E + 00	1.4079E + 00	−2.0524E + 00
Tail Rotor :	0.0000E + 00	0.0000E + 00	0.0000E + 00

Power (Hp)
Main Rotor : 5.7771E + 02
Tail Rotor : 3.6819E + 01
Total   : 6.1453E + 02

Phi   : −01.0821
Theta   : 03.8526
Psi   : 00.0000

Controls	Theta0 (MR) (Deg)	A1 (MR) (Deg)	B1 (MR) (Deg)	Theta0 (TR) (Deg)
	1.4908E + 01	2.0777E + 00	1.4334E + 00	−7.9765E + 00

Collective (In)	Lat Cyclic (In)	F/A Cyclic (In)	Pedal (In)
2.6174E + 00	8.3110E − 01	5.7334E − 01	−7.6201E − 01

Self-induced wash velocity

Element	U wash (Ft/sec)	V wash (Ft/sec)	W wash (Ft/sec)
Fuselage :	2.9769E + 00	−3.1028E − 01	6.3385E − 01
Main Rotor :	−8.3873E − 01	1.0815E + 00	3.0226E + 01
Tail Rotor :	0.0000E + 00	−3.9940E + 01	−6.5054E − 04
Hor Stab :	−1.6232E + 01	0.0000E + 00	−4.9790E + 00
Vert Stab :	−1.2292E + 01	4.4117E + 00	9.4332E − 05

Full wash velocity - includes interferences

Element	U wash (Ft/sec)	V wash (Ft/sec)	W wash (Ft/sec)
Fuselage :	2.9769E + 00	−3.1028E − 01	3.9545E + 01
Main Rotor :	−8.3873E − 01	1.0815E + 00	3.0860E + 01
Tail Rotor :	0.0000E + 00	−3.5528E + 01	−6.5054E − 04
Hor Stab :	−1.3255E + 01	0.0000E + 00	4.4421E + 01
Vert Stab :	−1.2292E + 01	−3.5528E + 01	9.4332E − 05

Trim assignment:
Vinf (knots) : 140.000
R/C (fpm) : 0.000

Element	X Force (Lbs)	Y Force (Lbs)	Z Force (Lbs)	L Moment (Ft-Lbs)	M Moment (Ft-Lbs)	N Moment (Ft-Lbs)
Fuselage :	−1.0956E + 03	8.6233E + 01	2.3786E + 01	0.0000E + 00	−5.3418E + 03	2.4961E + 02
Main Rotor :	4.4874E + 02	−3.9139E + 02	−7.1508E + 03	−3.3689E + 03	−2.9617E + 03	1.5010E + 04
Tail Rotor :	−6.9890E + 01	6.2735E + 02	2.6336E + 00	3.5100E + 03	4.5403E + 02	−1.6834E + 04
Hor Stab :	3.3007E + 01	0.0000E + 00	4.6448E + 02	0.0000E + 00	7.8415E + 03	0.0000E + 00
Vert Stab :	−3.3226E + 00	−6.3494E + 01	−1.3576E − 03	−1.4117E + 02	7.3537E + 00	1.5747E + 03
Gravity :	6.8706E + 02	−2.5871E + 02	6.6597E + 03	0.0000E + 00	0.0000E + 00	0.0000E + 00
Total :	4.8828E − 03	−7.1106E − 03	−2.0020E − 01	−7.2510E − 02	−6.3119E − 01	9.2651E − 02

Flapping	Coning	Fore/aft	Lateral
Main Rotor :	1.8750E + 00	−3.6572E + 00	−2.7344E + 00
Tail Rotor :	0.0000E + 00	−5.4734E + 00	2.0223E − 01

Power (Hp)
Main Rotor : 8.8817E + 02
Tail Rotor : −2.3979E + 00
Total : 8.8577E + 02

Phi : −02.2246
Theta : −05.8857
Psi : 00.0000

Controls	Theta0 (MR) (Deg)	A1 (MR) (Deg)	B1 (MR) (Deg)	Theta0 (TR) (Deg)
	1.9610E + 01	3.6875E + 00	−1.0698E + 01	−6.1230E + 00

Collective (In)	Lat Cyclic (In)	F/A Cyclic (In)	Pedal (In)
5.1251E + 00	1.4750E + 00	−4.2792E + 00	−1.9169E − 01

Self-induced wash velocity

Element		U wash (Ft/sec)	V wash (Ft/sec)	W wash (Ft/sec)
Fuselage	:	1.6170E + 01	−1.4289E + 00	−3.9414E − 01
Main Rotor	:	−2.6190E − 01	2.2843E − 01	4.1734E + 00
Tail Rotor	:	1.1004E + 00	−9.8773E + 00	−4.1464E − 02
Hor Stab	:	−4.5916E − 01	0.0000E + 00	−6.4614E + 00
Vert Stab	:	1.2398E − 01	2.3692E + 00	5.0658E − 05

Full wash velocity - includes interferences

Element		U wash (Ft/sec)	V wash (Ft/sec)	W wash (Ft/sec)
Fuselage	:	1.6170E + 01	−1.4289E + 00	4.9785E + 00
Main Rotor	:	−2.6190E − 01	2.2843E − 01	3.7793E + 00
Tail Rotor	:	1.1004E + 00	−7.5081E + 00	−4.1464E − 02
Hor Stab	:	1.5711E + 01	0.0000E + 00	3.5948E − 01
Vert Stab	:	1.2398E − 01	−7.5081E + 00	5.0658E − 05

18.6   Conclusions

Considerably more can be written about simulation, but because the purpose of this text is to introduce the reader to the modeling aspects of flight simulation, the discussion closes here. If the reader decides that flight simulation is his/her cup of tea, he or she will find that each simulation facility has its closely guarded simulation secrets and corporate mandated methods. The author hopes that this text has demystified the art and science of flight simulation, especially as applied to helicopters and tiltrotors, and that it will serve as a foundation for their professional pursuits.

Problem

18.1 You have been asked to write a simulation of a helicopter that has two rotors and a fuselage. No fins, wings, or stabilizers are present. You will need a large sheet of paper or several notebook-size sheets of paper to do this problem. Draw the complete flowchart of the time-domain simulation using the individual blocks as described in the text. Your diagram should make clear (a) where axis system transformations must take place, (b) what signals are passing from one block to another, (c) to which axis system the signals are resolved, and (d) what assumptions have been made about the control laws, the pilot interface, aerodynamic interference, etc.

Appendix A
Units

There are few things that can grasp defeat from the jaws of victory faster than errors in units. Units errors are embarrassing at the least, usually costly, and potentially dangerous in some cases. One infamous example is the crash of Air Canada Flight 143, a Boeing 767 that ran out of fuel because of the confusion between pounds, kilograms, and liters! Air Canada's pilots were accustomed to computing the fuel load in pounds, but the fuel consumption on the 767 was expressed in kilograms, in order to meet the new requirements of the Canadian government, which was introducing metric units nationwide. To compound the problem, the fuel gauge on this particular aircraft was inoperative, and so a visual inspection method with a "drip stick" was employed. This method told the pilots how much fuel was already in the aircraft, but it expressed the answers in centimeters. A table in the flight manual then converted the linear measurement to liters. One person involved in the refueling thought he recalled some conversion factor that would convert from pounds to liters (or pounds to kilograms, or liters to gallons, you get the idea) and suggested they use that number to compute how many liters of fuel would have to be loaded on the aircraft to make the planned journey. Their answer was 5000 liters. They were 15,000 liters short! The accident that followed was inevitable. At 29,000 ft over Red Lake, both engines flamed out because of fuel starvation. The commander, a skilled glider pilot, flew the aircraft to a dead-stick landing at an abandoned airfield named Gimli. No one was seriously injured. Nearly $1,000,000 damage was done to the aircraft when the nose wheel collapsed. The comic-relief finish to this incident is that the rescue crew that raced to Gimli field left without topping off the tanks in the rescue truck. They ran out of gas on their way to the rescue!

Another embarrassing recent example is the Mars Climate Orbiter, which was to have entered an orbit around Mars, but instead dove steeply into the Martian atmosphere and crashed, perhaps even burning up during the final plunge. The navigational error was attributed to a mix-up over the use of English and metric units between NASA and Lockheed Martin, the contractor that built the orbiter. This mix-up compounded itself in the dozens of small maneuver calculations during the journey. The result was an expensive lesson.

A consistent set of units is a cornerstone of simulation. Consistent misuse is the Achilles heel. A couple of decades ago, the United States attempted to convert from the English system, which uses pounds, slugs, feet, and seconds, to SI (System International, often called metric) units, which uses newtons, kilograms, meters,

471

and seconds. It did not catch on in mainstream America, though NASA continues with SI units, despite the potentially expensive problems (Mars Climate Orbiter) associated with them. This text uses the English system as the primary system of units, but includes SI units so that the reader can calibrate himself or herself. Conversions from one system to another are inevitable. The tables that follow are not exhaustive, but they should help you navigate the conversion quagmire.

A.1 Unit Prefixes

Use Table A.1 to convert orders of magnitude. For example, if a measurement is given in centimeters and meters are required, multiply the centimeter value by 10^{-2}. The SI units use these magnitude conversion prefixes often. In electronics, capacitance is often expressed in microfarads, or picofarads, power in kilowatts, etc. In mechanical engineering, one speaks of microstrain in defining shear displacement. And, of course, the standard unit of measurement in beauty is the millihelen, a face pretty enough to launch one ship.

Table A.1   Unit prefixes

Magnitude	Prefix	Symbol
10^9	giga-	G
10^6	mega-	M
10^3	kilo-	k
10^2	hecto-	h
10^1	deka-	da
10^{-1}	deci-	d
10^{-2}	centi-	c
10^{-3}	milli-	m
10^{-6}	micro-	μ
10^{-9}	nano-	n
10^{-12}	pico-	p

A.2 Displacement

Table A.2 converts feet to several popular units. From this table, one sees that a foot is 12 in., but only 1/660 of a furlong.

Table A.3 is the inverse of Table A.2. To get back to feet from inches, multiply inches by 0.083333.

A.3 Area

Certainly, there are more different types of area measurements than these. Star-Trek fans will want to know where square parsecs are, and civil engineers will

Table A.2   Convert feet to other units

Multiply this	By this	To get this
Feet	0.3048	Meters
Feet	0.001515	Furlongs
Feet	0.000189	Miles (statute)
Feet	0.000165	Miles (nautical)
Feet	0.33333	Yards
Feet	12	Inches
Feet	0.0003048	Kilometers
Feet	0.1666667	Fathoms

Table A.3   Convert other units to feet

Multiply this	By this	To get this
Meters	3.28084	Feet
Kilometers	3280.84	Feet
Furlongs	660	Feet
Yards	3.0	Feet
Inches	0.0833333	Feet
Miles (statute)	5280	Feet
Miles (nautical)	6076.115	Feet
Fathoms	6.0	Feet

demand a definition of hectares. This text is focused on rotorcraft and aircraft, and so the usual dimensions for area will be square feet and/or square meters. Pressure is often expressed in pounds per square inch, so Table A.4 or A.5 will give you the necessary factors to convert from one to the other. Or, you can wait for the table on pressure conversion.

Use Table A.5 to convert units other than square feet to square feet.

Table A.4   Convert ft^2 to other units

Multiply this	By this	To get this
Square feet	144	Square inches
Square feet	0.1111111	Square yards
Square feet	0.000023	Acres
Square feet	0.092903	Square meters
Square miles (statute)	0.755123	Square miles (nautical)

Table A.5   Convert other units to ft^2

Multiply this	By this	To get this
Square inches	0.006944	Square feet
Square yards	9	Square feet
Acres	43560	Square feet
Square meters	10.764	Square feet
Square miles (nautical)	1.324288	Square miles (statute)

A.4   Volume

Most often, volumes will be expressed in units other than cubic feet, requiring the inverse conversion. For the sake of consistency, Table A.6 is presented first. Table A.7 will take you back to cubic feet.

Table A.6   Convert ft^3 to other units

Multiply this	By this	To get this
Cubic feet	1728	Cubic inches
Cubic feet	0.028317	Cubic meters
Cubic feet	7.4805	Gallons (liquid)
Cubic feet	28.3168	Liter
Cubic feet	29.922	Quarts

Table A.7   Convert other units to ft^3

Multiply this	By this	To get this
Cubic inches	0.000579	Cubic feet
Cubic meters	35.3147	Cubic feet
Gallons (liquid)	0.13368	Cubic feet
Liter	0.035315	Cubic feet
Quarts	0.03342	Cubic feet

A.5   Rate

If there was ever a conversion more misunderstood, or simply forgotten, it is the conversion of velocities to correct units. Again, Table A.8 is most useful to convert the engineering answer of feet/second to units with which most people are familiar.

Use Table A.9 to convert familiar units of speed to English engineering-friendly units.

Table A.8   Convert engineering units to familiar units

Multiply this	By this	To get this
feet/second	0.68182	miles/hour
feet/second	0.59248	knots
feet/second	1.09728	kilometer/hour
feet/second	0.3048	meters/second
miles/hour	0.86898	knots
miles/hour	1.60935	kilometer/hour
miles/hour	0.44704	meters/second
knots	1.852	kilometer/hour
knots	0.51444	meters/second

Table A.9   Inverse of Table A.8

Multiply this	By this	To get this
miles/hour	1.46666	feet/second
knots	1.68781	feet/second
kilometer/hour	0.91134	feet/second
meters/second	3.28084	feet/second
knots	1.15078	miles/hour
kilometer/hour	0.62137	miles/hour
meters/second	2.23694	miles/hour
kilometer/hour	0.53996	knots
meters/second	1.94385	knots

A.6   Acceleration

There are not too many ways in which acceleration is expressed. Use Table A.10 to go from feet/second/second to other units, such as Gauss.

Table A.10   Convert engineering units to other units

Multiply this	By this	To get this
feet/second^2	0.031081	Gauss
feet/second^2	0.000305	kilometer/second^2
feet/second^2	0.3048	meters/second^2

Use Table A.11 to go from familiar units of acceleration to English-friendly engineering units.

Table A.11   Inverse of Table A.10

Multiply this	By this	To get this
Gauss	32.174	feet/second^2
kilometer/second^2	3280.84	feet/second^2
meters/second^2	3.28084	feet/second^2

A.7 Mass/Inertia

Because of indiscriminant use of the language, the term pound has been used for both force and mass. In this text, the slug is the preferred unit of mass because its definition is consistent with the SI concept of relating unit force to unit mass and unit acceleration. To wit, 1 pound-force = 1 slug $*$ 1 ft/s^2. Table A.12 converts slugs or slug-ft^2 to SI units.

More often, you will be given units of pound-mass or kilograms. Use Table A.13 to convert to slugs or slug-feet^2.

Table A.12   Convert English mass units to SI units

Multiply this	By this	To get this
Slug	32.174	lbm
Slug	14.60592	kgm
Slug-feet^2	32.174	lbm-sec^2
Slug-feet^2	1.35693	kgm-m^2

Table A.13   Convert SI mass units to English units

Multiply this	By this	To get this
lbm	0.031081	slug
kgm	0.068465	slug
lbm-s^2	0.031081	slug-feet^2
kgm-m^2	0.73696	slug-feet^2

A.8 Force/Moment

Force is measured in pounds or newtons. A kilogram is not a unit of force; it is a unit of mass. Therefore, a conversion from pounds to kilograms is not shown because it does not make sense. Table A.14 will convert lb or lb-ft to SI units and a familiar force unit. Table A.15 provides the inverse conversions.

Table A.14 Convert English force and moment units to SI units

Multiply this	By this	To get this
lb	4.44822	newton
lb	0.00100	kip
lb-ft	12.0	pounds-inch
lb-ft	1.35582	newton-meter

Table A.15 Convert SI force and moment units to English units

Multiply this	By this	To get this
newton	0.22481	lb
kip	1000	lb
pounds-inch	0.083333	lb-ft
newton-meter	0.73756	lb-ft

At this point, it is instructive to relate force, mass, and acceleration. Newton's observation that force equals the rate of change of linear momentum is often shortened to the familiar mantra $F = m * a$. In keeping with that definition, a force of 1 lb accelerates a mass of one slug 1 ft/s^2. In the SI, a force of 1 N accelerates a mass of 1 kg 1 m/s^2.

$$1\,\text{lbf} = 1\,\text{slug} * 1\,\text{ft/s}^2$$

$$1\,\text{N} = 1\,\text{kgm} * 1\,\text{m/s}^2$$

A.9 Pressure

Though you will most often encounter pressure in pounds per square inch (psi), most areas you will calculate will be in square feet. Multiplying one by the other to get force would actually produce pound square feet per square inch, requiring a factor of 144 somewhere. Inches of mercury (Hg) are shown in Table A.16 because altimeters are set with these units. Table A.17 provides the inverse of the conversions in Table A.16.

A.10 Power

Power is the rate of change of energy, and so Table A.18 has units of force times a distance divided by a time interval. We are perhaps most familiar with horsepower, which is defined as 33,000 ft-lb/min, or 550 ft-lb/s. Watts is a units often used for electrical and sound measurement. Table A.19 provides the inverse of the conversions in Table A.18.

Table A.16   Convert English pressure units to familiar units

Multiply this	By this	To get this
lbf/ft^2 (psf)	0.006944	lbf/in.^{2} (psi)
lbf/ft^2 (psf)	0.014179	in. Hg (60 °F)
lbf/ft^2 (psf)	0.000473	atm
lbf/ft^2 (psf)	47.88026	n/m^2 (Pascal)
lbf/ft^2 (psf)	0.000479	bar

Table A.17   Convert familiar pressure units to English units

Multiply this	By this	To get this
lbf/in.^{2} (psi)	144	lbf/ft^2 (psf)
in. Hg (60 °F)	70.527	lbf/ft^2 (psf)
atm	2116.21	lbf/ft^2 (psf)
n/m^2 (Pascal)	0.020885	lbf/ft^2 (psf)
bar	2088.54	lbf/ft^2 (psf)

Table A.18   Convert English power units to familiar units

Multiply this	By this	To get this
ft-lb/s	0.001817	horsepower
ft-lb/s	0.001356	kilowatts
ft-lb/s	4.6293	BTU/hour
ft-lb/s	1.3558	watts (joules/second)

Table A.19   Convert familiar power units to English units

Multiply this	By this	To get this
horsepower	550	ft-lbs/s
kilowatts	737.562	ft-lbs/s
BTU/hour	0.216014	ft-lbs/s
watts (joules/second)	0.737652	ft-lbs/s

Table A.20   Convert ft-lb of energy to familiar units

Multiply this	By this	To get this
ft-lb	12	inch-pound
ft-lb	0.323832	calorie
ft-lb	1.355818	joule
ft-lb	1.355818	newton-meter
ft-lb	0.000377	watt-hour
ft-lb	0.001285	BTU

Table A.21   Convert familiar energy units to ft-lb

Multiply this	By this	To get this
inch-pound	0.083333	ft-lb
calorie	3.08803	ft-lb
joule	0.737562	ft-lb
newton-meter	0.737562	ft-lb
watt-hour	2655.224	ft-lb
BTU	778.17	ft-lb

A.11   Energy

The area under a curve of power vs time is the energy expended, that is, energy is the integral of power. Energy has units of force times a distance. We are all familiar with the terms BTU and calories, especially as they pertain to the pathetic attempts of air conditioners to keep up with the brutal summer heat of Texas. In flight, we will use the notion of potential energy in autorotations. Tables A.20 and A.21 provide conversions from ft-lbs to familiar energy units and back.

A.12   Angles

Angles are commonly measured in degrees, and many of the aerodynamic tables you will encounter use that unit. However, in many developments, the

Table A.22   Convert familiar angular units to radians

Multiply this	By this	To get this
degrees	0.017453	radians
minutes	0.000291	radians
seconds	0.000005	radians
Full circle	6.283185	radians

Table A.23 Convert radians to familiar angular units

Multiply this	By this	To get this
radians	57.29578	degrees
radians	3437.747	minutes
radians	206264.8	seconds
radians	0.159155	Full circle

radian is used. The radian is the angular displacement obtained by moving around the circumference of a circle the arclength distance equal to the circle radius. One clear advantage of using radians is that small-angle assumptions are easy to make. Specifically, the sine of an angle measured in radians is equal to the angle in radians for angles up to nearly 15 deg (about 0.25 radians) with only a 1% error in the answer. Likewise, the cosine of an angle measured in radians is unity for angles up to nearly 15 deg, again with only a 4.5% error. Tangents display a similar grace, with only 3% error for angles up to 15 deg. Tables A.22 and A.23 provide angular conversions to and from radians respectively.

A.13 Frequency

Frequency refers to the angular speed of motion, or the rate at which a periodic event takes place. Commonly, frequency is measured in hertz (Hz), or some multiple such as kilohertz (kHz), or megahertz (mHz) as in the frequency of your favorite radio station. When talking about how fast the rotor or propeller is spinning on a rotorcraft, the speed is usually given in rpm or radians/second. To convert from rpm to radians/sec, remember this method:

$$1\,\text{revolution/minute} = 1\,\text{revolution/minute} \times 6.283185\,\text{radians/revolution}$$
$$\times \text{minute}/60\,\text{seconds}$$

That is, if you are given rpm, dividing by 10 will get you radians per second with only 5% error. Tables A.24 and A.25 will help you convert familiar frequency units to rad/sec and back again.

Table A.24 Convert familiar frequency units to radians/sec

Multiply this	By this	To get this
hertz	6.283185	rad/sec
cycle/second	6.283185	rad/sec
deg/second	0.017453	rad/sec
rpm	0.10472	rad/sec

Table A.25 Convert radians/sec to familiar frequency units

Multiply this	By this	To get this
rad/sec	0.159155	hertz
rad/sec	0.159155	cycle/second
rad/sec	57.295	degrees/second
rad/sec	9.5493	rpm

Table A.26 Temperature conversions

If you have	Use this formula	To get this
Fahrenheit	R = F + 459.67	Rankine
Fahrenheit	C = (5/9)(F − 32)	Celsius
Fahrenheit	K = (5/9)F + 255.37	Kelvin
Celsius	F = (9/5)C + 32	Fahrenheit
Celsius	K = C + 273.15	Kelvin
Celsius	R = (9/5)(C + 273.15)	Rankine
Rankine	F = R − 459.67	Fahrenheit
Rankine	K = (5/9)R	Kelvin
Rankine	C = (5/9)R − 273.15	Celsius
Kelvin	F = (9/5)(K − 273.15) + 32	Fahrenheit
Kelvin	R = (9/5)K	Rankine
Kelvin	C = K − 273.15	Celsius

A.14 Temperature

Temperature is one of the few conversions that requires a formula, not just a factor (Table A.26). That is because the "zero" for different temperature scales is located at different points in the range of kinetic energy. You will run across every one of these units of temperature, and so this is the complete list of conversions from one to the other. In any given formula, R refers to the temperature in Rankine, F refers to Fahrenheit, K for Kelvin, and C for centigrade or Celsius.

You can make most units conversions that you encounter in flight simulation with the preceding tables. Of course, there is always someone who insists on the classic screwy conversion, and so to satisfy them here is the speed of light in standard units and a few others:

$$c = 186,000 \, \text{miles/s}$$

$$c = 186,000 \, \text{miles/s} \times 5280 \, \text{ft/mile} = 982,080,000 \, \text{ft/s}$$

$$c = 186,000 \, \text{miles/s} \times 5280 \, \text{ft/mile} \times 60 \, \text{s/min} \times 60 \, \text{min/h} \times \text{km}/3280.84 \, \text{ft}$$

$$= 1,077,616,708 \, \text{km/h}$$

$c = 186{,}000 \, \text{miles/s} \times 5280 \, \text{ft/mile} \times \text{furlong/660 ft} \times 60 \, \text{s/min} \times 60 \, \text{min/h}$

$\times 24 \, \text{h/day} \times 14 \, \text{days/fortnight}$

$= 1{,}799{,}984{,}800{,}000 \, \text{furlongs/fortnight}$

For other conversion values, a convenient Web site is www.onlineconversion.com.

Problems

A.1 You are running in a subway car at 10 ft/s in the direction the car is moving. The car is moving at 40 miles/h past an observer on a fixed platform. How fast are you moving past him? Express your answer in feet per second, miles per hour, knots, and furlongs per fortnight.

A.2 Your helicopter is flying on a calm day with an indicated airspeed of 70 kn. Your rate of climb is 500 ft/min. What is your forward speed over the ground in miles per hour? Hint: The indicated airspeed is measured on the hypotenuse of a right triangle. The height of the triangle is the rate of climb, and the base is the desired speed in this problem.

Appendix B
Integration Techniques

B.1   Open Integration

In the late 1600s, Newton, Liebnitz, and the Bernoullis were about the only people in Europe that understood the recent mathematical invention known today as the calculus. These scientists used the calculus to understand how dependent variables changed with continuous changes in independent variables. This is still the focus of the calculus of elementary functions today. The two branches of calculus with which most work in this text is solved are integral calculus and differential calculus of a single variable. Integral calculus will be applied most often when looking for a sum of infinitesimals (the area under a curve) as an independent variable runs from one endpoint to another. Differential calculus will be used most often to express the relationship between applied forces and the motion those forces generate. The goal of this appendix is to present a few techniques that will reduce the sting of calculus, so that the problems set up in the rest of the text can be solved with a minimum of discomfort.

The solution to a differential calculus problem of course requires integration. If the differential equation is to be solved over a closed domain, that is, if the integration goes from one specific point to another specific point in the domain of the independent variable, then closed-integration techniques provide the complete solution. On the other hand, if the integration has no specific endpoints, or if it proceeds from a specific beginning point (initial conditions) and marches toward an indefinite value in the domain of the independent variable, then open-integration methods provide the complete solution. A third class of problem involves boundary values at both the beginning and end of the domain of the independent variable. They are a form of the closed-integration technique, with a special provision to match boundary values.

B.1.1   Linearity/Nonlinearity

If the coefficients of the differential equations describing the behavior of a system are constant, the equations are linear. On the other hand, if the coefficients are functions of the independent and dependent variables, the equations are non-linear. Although the real world rarely fits the simple linear mold, many nearly linear problems can be adequately simulated with linear equations. Therefore, this chapter focuses primarily on integration techniques that apply to linear problems.

B.1.2 Order of an Equation and State-Space Notation

The order of a differential equation is simply the difference between the order indices of the highest and lowest derivatives in the equation. For example, a second-order differential equation describes the classical mass, spring, damper system because the highest derivative is the second, representing acceleration, and the lowest derivative is the zero derivative, representing displacement. Filters often have even higher orders of derivatives and can include derivatives in the forcing function. Equations can be coupled, leading to high-order systems. Fear not. All linear multi-degrees-of-freedom systems can be expressed as a series of coupled first-order equations, which implies that learning the method to solve a first-order equation will cover a multitude of problems. To illustrate how a higher-order system is reduced to a set of coupled first-order equations, consider the mass-spring-damper system with an arbitrary forcing function:

$$m\ddot{x}(t) + b\dot{x}(t) + kx(t) = f(t) \tag{B.1}$$

The states of the system are x and $\dot{x}$. If these states are mapped to a *state vector* of length 2,

$$z_1 = x$$
$$z_2 = \dot{x} \tag{B.2}$$

so that the column vector z is defined as

$$z = \begin{Bmatrix} z_1 \\ z_2 \end{Bmatrix} \tag{B.3}$$

then the time derivative of z is

$$\dot{z} = \begin{Bmatrix} \dot{z}_1 \\ \dot{z}_2 \end{Bmatrix} = \begin{Bmatrix} \dot{x} \\ \ddot{x} \end{Bmatrix} \tag{B.4}$$

Now, the differential equation can be expressed in the *state-space* form:

$$\dot{z} = Az + Bu$$
$$y = Cz + Du \tag{B.5}$$

where z is the *state vector*, the *input vector* $u = \{f\}$, and the four matrices are as follows:

1) The *dynamic* matrix

$$A = \begin{bmatrix} 0 & 1 \\ -\dfrac{k}{m} & -\dfrac{b}{m} \end{bmatrix} \text{ of size } n \times n \tag{B.6}$$

2) The *control* matrix

$$B = \begin{bmatrix} 0 \\ 1 \end{bmatrix} \text{ of size } \quad n \times m \tag{B.7}$$

3) The *observability* matrix

$$C = \begin{bmatrix} 1 & 0 \\ 0 & 1 \end{bmatrix} \text{ of size } \quad p \times n \tag{B.8}$$

4) The *feedforward* matrix

$$D = \begin{bmatrix} 0 \\ 1 \end{bmatrix} \text{ of size } \quad p \times m \tag{B.9}$$

The number of states is n, m is the number of control inputs, and p is the number of items one wishes to observe. Expanding the equations indicated by the preceding matrix-vector math, the two first-order equations are

$$\dot{z}_1 = z_2$$
$$\dot{z}_2 = -\frac{k}{m}z_1 - \frac{b}{m}z_2 + \frac{1}{m}f \tag{B.10}$$

Substituting the original variable names for the state vector names gives

$$\dot{x} = \dot{x}$$
$$\ddot{x} = -\frac{k}{m}x - \frac{b}{m}\dot{x} + \frac{1}{m}f \tag{B.11}$$

The first equation is hardly controversial—it seems as though it came from the department of redundancy department. It is simply a consequence of collapsing the second-order equation to a system of coupled first-order equations. The second equation is simply a restatement of the original differential equation.

Higher-order dynamics are accommodated with longer state vectors that store all but the highest derivative. In addition, input signals that admit the forcing function and its derivatives can also be modeled in this way.

In general, the differential equation

$$a_n x^{(n)} + a_{n-1} x^{(n-1)} + \cdots + a_2 \ddot{x} + a_1 \dot{x} + a_0 x = \text{RHS} \tag{B.12}$$

where

$$\text{RHS} = b_m f^{(m)} + \cdots + b_1 \dot{f} + b_0 f \tag{B.13}$$

can also be expressed in transfer function notation as

$$\frac{X(s)}{F(s)} = \frac{b_m s^{(m)} + \cdots + b_1 s + b_0}{a_n s^{(n)} + \cdots + a_1 s + a_0} \qquad m \leq n \tag{B.14}$$

The differential equation can also be modeled in state space in this way. First, express all but the highest derivative of the dependent variable as elements of a state vector z. Organize the dynamic matrix and control matrix as shown here:

$$z = \left\{ \begin{array}{c} x \\ \dot{x} \\ \ldots \\ x^{(n-1)} \end{array} \right\} \tag{B.15}$$

$$A = \begin{bmatrix} 0 & 1 & 0 & \ldots & 0 \\ 0 & 0 & 1 & \ldots & 0 \\ 0 & 0 & 0 & \ldots & \ldots \\ \ldots & \ldots & \ldots & \ldots & 1 \\ -\dfrac{a_0}{a_n} & -\dfrac{a_1}{a_n} & -\dfrac{a_2}{a_n} & \ldots & -\dfrac{a_{n-1}}{a_n} \end{bmatrix} \quad \text{and} \quad B = \begin{bmatrix} 0 \\ 0 \\ \ldots \\ 0 \\ 1 \\ a_n \end{bmatrix} \tag{B.16}$$

A is $n \times n$ in size, and B is $n \times 1$ in size. To make the bookkeeping easier, make the number of b coefficients equal to the number of a coefficients, setting $b_j = 0$, if $j > m$. Now, the number of b coefficients is $m = n$. This permits the RHS to be written:

$$\text{RHS} = b_n f^{(n)} + b_{n-1} f^{(n-1)} + \cdots + b_1 \dot{f} + b_0 f \tag{B.17}$$

With this manipulation, the C and D matrices are expressed:

$$C = \left[\left(b_0 - a_0 \frac{b_n}{a_n} \right) \quad \left(b_1 - a_1 \frac{b_n}{a_n} \right) \quad \left(b_2 - a_2 \frac{b_n}{a_n} \right) \quad \cdots \quad \left(b_{n-1} - a_{n-1} \frac{b_n}{a_n} \right) \right] \tag{B.18}$$

and

$$D = \left[\frac{b_n}{a_n} \right] \tag{B.19}$$

The C matrix is $1 \times n$, and the D matrix is 1×1.

With this admittedly brief description to state-space modeling, techniques for solving these systems are the next objective.

B.1.3 Open-Integration Techniques

Consider the first-order system with the following constant coefficients:

$$\dot{x}(t) = ax(t) + bu(t) \tag{B.20}$$

The independent variable is time (assumed throughout this text unless otherwise stated), the dependent variable is x, and u is an input function that is independent of x. In simulation, the solution that is most often sought is one in which an initial condition is specified and the solution marches in time. Very often, these equations can be solved in stepwise fashion. That is, solve the equation over just one increment of time, using the answer as the initial condition for the next step. (This is called a Markov process.) Many different schemes are available to solve the differential equation. References [1–3] describe the methods and discuss their strengths and weaknesses. Some of the most commonly used methods are presented next. Note: Just because they are common does not mean that they are best. In fact, simple Euler integration should almost never be used, but it almost always is!

B.1.3.1 Exact Solution

Referring to the preceding first-order equation, if the analytic expression for $u(t)$ is known for all time, and the initial conditions $x(0)$ are specified, then Green's theorem provides the exact solution.

$$x(t) = e^{at}x(0) + \int_0^t e^{a(t-\lambda)}bu(\lambda)\,d\lambda \qquad (B.21)$$

The variable λ is a dummy variable of integration, used as a placeholder for the time argument. The t is the integration interval. This solution is perfectly general and admits an input function that changes over the integration interval. Although the preceding expression is the solution to a scalar problem, this technique applies to higher-order equations as well. The method to exponentiate a matrix A is discussed later. The only assumption this method makes, aside from linearity, is that the coefficients are constant.

B.1.3.2 Exact Solution with Constant Forcing Function

The exact solution leads to a very nice, easy-to-use time-marching algorithm if one further assumption is imposed. If the value of the forcing function is held constant over the interval of integration, then $u(t)$ is a constant as far as the exact solution is concerned, and the integral can be evaluated exactly over a small time step. The exact solution with the assumption of constant coefficients and a constant forcing function value over the step is

$$x_{k+1} = e^{at}x_k + \left(\frac{1}{a}\right)(e^{at} - 1)bu_k$$

$$x_{k+1} = \Phi x_k + \Gamma u_k \qquad (B.22)$$

The subscripts k and $k+1$ refer to the current time point and next time point respectively and are introduced here to emphasize the stepwise marching nature of the algorithm. Once the solution has stepped from k to $k+1$, with initial conditions x_k and forcing function u_k, another step begins with the initial conditions set equal to the final values of the preceding step. The forcing function starts at the point where the preceding one ended.

The second equation is the more common expression and illustrates that this method is applicable equally to scalar and matrix-level equations. This equation is probably the most well known of the "exact" solutions—you will see it everywhere.

B.1.3.3   Numerical Solutions   An analytical expression for the forcing function is rarely known in piloted simulation. Likewise, the coefficients in the differential equations are usually nonlinear and not known a priori. Cases like these call for numerical techniques. There are a number of numerical solutions that work well. Their success is dependent on proper selection of the step size in comparison to the forcing function frequency, the admittance coefficient b, and the dynamics coefficient a. Here are some of the best and worst.

B.1.3.3.1   Euler Integration   Given the differential equation, march to the next value of x using rectangular integration. The technique is demonstrated next for one time step. If the original differential equation is

$$\dot{x}(t) = ax(t) + bu(t) \tag{B.23}$$

then the value of x after one time step using Euler integration is

$$x(t + \Delta t) = x(t) + \dot{x}(t)\Delta t$$
$$x(t + \Delta t) = x(t) + [ax(t) + bu(t)]\Delta t$$
$$x(t + \Delta t) = (1 + a\Delta t)x(t) + (b\Delta t)u(t) \tag{B.24}$$

or

$$x(t + \Delta t) = \tilde{\Phi}x(t) + \tilde{\Gamma}u(t) \tag{B.25}$$

The tilde over the Φ and Γ coefficients indicates that these are numerically derived and only approximate. The Euler method is the easiest method to implement but is also the worst method because error builds rapidly. Reducing the size of the time step helps a little, but the fundamental fact is that the method is no better than first-order accurate. This method should only be used for gross "sanity checks."

B.1.3.3.2   Corrected Euler Integration   A simple trick improves the Euler-integration method, making it second-order accurate. The corrected method is also easy to implement, because it is just the Euler-integration method applied twice for a given time step.

Once again, start with Eq. (B.23), and perform an Euler-integration step. Call the result p. Use p as the value of the state in the differential equation. Calculate the derivative again with the forcing function evaluated at the end of the time step. Average the two derivatives, and perform an Euler step with the average.

$$\dot{x}(t) = ax(t) + bu(t)$$
$$p = x(t) + \dot{x}(t)\Delta t$$
$$\dot{x}_p(t + \Delta t) = ap + bu(t + \Delta t)$$
$$x(t + \Delta t) = x(t) + [\dot{x}(t) + \dot{x}_p(t + \Delta t)]\frac{\Delta t}{2} \tag{B.26}$$

Incidentally, the selection of the name p for the state after the first Euler step is not arbitrary. The p is a mnemonic device to emphasize that the intermediate result is a prediction. The prediction is corrected with another equation. A pseudocode fragment that solves the scalar differential equation (B.23) with the improved Euler scheme looks like this:

```
!**********************************
!          Initialization
!**********************************

X = Initial condition on X
T = 0.

!**********************************
!          Run time section
!**********************************

DO

          U = some function at time t
          XDOT = A * X + B * U
          P = X + XDOT * DT

          UP = same function at time t+dt
          XPDOT = A * P + B * UP

          X = X + (XDOT + XPDOT) * DT/2.
          T = T + DT

LOOP UNTIL (SOME END CONDITION IS MET)
```

In fact, the corrected Euler method is the simplest example of a class of methods called predictor Corrector. There are many others.

B.1.3.3.3 Adams–Bashforth   The Adams–Bashforth method is a fifth-order predictor-corrector algorithm. The prediction uses a sliding curve, fit through the current value of the dependent variable, and the current and last three values of the derivative of the dependent variable. The correction uses the current value of the dependent variable, the current and last two values of the derivative, and the derivative one step ahead in time, based on the prediction.

Start with Eq. (B.23). For the moment, assume that the solution has been going for quite some time, and that the past values of the dependent variable and its derivative have been stored in a first-in, first-out (FIFO) stack. The formula for the predictor is

$$p = x(t) + [55\dot{x}(t) - 59\dot{x}(t - \Delta t) + 37\dot{x}(t - 2\Delta t) - 9\dot{x}(t - 3\Delta t)]\frac{\Delta t}{24} \quad (B.27)$$

Previous steps have already evaluated past values of the derivative. The only new evaluation of the derivative is the current one—the first on the right-hand side (RHS) of the prediction equation.

Estimate the derivative of the function at the predicted value using an Euler step:

$$\dot{x}_p(t + \Delta t) = ap + bu(t + \Delta t) \quad (B.28)$$

With the prediction and its derivative estimated, the correction and new value of the dependent variable one step ahead is given by the formula:

$$x(t + \Delta t) = x(t) + [9\dot{x}_p(t + \Delta t) + 19\dot{x}(t) - 5\dot{x}(t - \Delta t) + \dot{x}(t - 2\Delta t)]\frac{\Delta t}{24}$$

$$(B.29)$$

A pseudocode fragment that solves the scalar differential equation (B.23) with the AB method looks like this:

```
!**********************************
!          Initialization
!**********************************

X = Initial condition on X
XDOTL = 0. [or some other calculation]
XDOTLL = 0. [or some other calculation]
XDOTLLL = 0. [or some other calculation]
T = 0.

!**********************************
!          Run time section
!**********************************

DO

            U = some function at time t
            XDOT = A * X + B * U
            P = X + (55 * XDOT-59 * XDOTL+37 * XDOTLL-9 * XDOTLLL) * DT/24

            UP = same function at time t+dt
            XPDOT = A * P + B * UP

            X = X + (9 * XPDOT+19 * XDOT-5 * XDOTL+XDOTLL) * DT/24

            XDOTLLL = XDOTLL
            XDOTLL = XDOTL
            XDOTL = XDOT
            T = T + DT

LOOP UNTIL (SOME END CONDITION IS MET)
```

The Adams–Bashforth is fifth-order accurate, but requires only two evaluations of the RHS of the differential equation for each time step. The objectionable property of this method is the history requirement—three past values of the derivative. This requirement is not an overwhelming problem. If the solution starts from some steady state, the derivatives are known—they are zero! However, if this technique is to be applied to an equation that has a periodic (but not necessarily harmonic) solution, the derivatives are not so easily declared. In fact, some other integrating technique might be required to "start" the A-B method. One such method is the Runge–Kutta technique.

B.1.3.3.4 Runge–Kutta   Runge–Kutta is the name applied to an entire family of integrating algorithms. The most well known in the family are of orders two through four. Of those, the one that almost everyone thinks of is the so-called Kutta-Simpson formula. It is fourth order accurate, but it requires four evaluations of the derivative expression for every time step. This is disastrous for real time work, but is good for batch processing.

As always, begin with the differential equation:

$$\dot{x}(t) = \text{RHS}[x(t), u(t)] \tag{B.30}$$

where

$$\text{RHS}[x(t), u(t)] = ax(t) + bu(t) \tag{B.31}$$

Calling the forcing function RHS (for right-hand side) makes the bookkeeping easier and the entire presentation neater. Starting at time t, predict the *change* to the dependent variable over an entire time step with an Euler step, that is, calculate the derivative and multiply it by the time step. Call that predicted change p:

$$p = \text{RHS}[x(t), u(t)]\Delta t \tag{B.32}$$

Evaluate the RHS again, this time adding half the predicted change from the preceding step to the dependent variable, and evaluating the forcing function one half-step into the future. Name this result q:

$$q = \text{RHS}\left[x(t) + \frac{p}{2}, u\left(t + \frac{\Delta t}{2} \right) \right] \Delta t \tag{B.33}$$

Now, reevaluate the RHS again, this time adding half the predicted change from the preceding step to the dependent variable, and evaluating the forcing function one half-step into the future. Call this prediction r:

$$r = \text{RHS}\left[x(t) + \frac{q}{2}, u\left(t + \frac{\Delta t}{2} \right) \right] \Delta t \tag{B.34}$$

Once more, evaluate the RHS, this time adding all of the predicted change from the preceding step to the dependent variable, and evaluating the forcing function one full step into the future. This last prediction is named s:

$$s = \text{RHS}\left[x(t) + r, u(t + \Delta t) \right] \Delta t \tag{B.35}$$

Four different shots, not quite in the dark, have been taken at the change of the dependent variable. A weighted average of these added to the current value gives the solution at the next time point. There is some liberty in selecting the coefficients that weight the p, q, r, and s predicted changes. One popular choice is shown in the following update equation:

$$x(t + \Delta t) = x(t) + \frac{(p + 2q + 2r + s)}{6} \tag{B.36}$$

A pseudocode fragment that solves the scalar differential equation (B.23) with the RK-4 scheme looks like this:

```
!**********************************
!          Initialization
!**********************************

X = Initial condition on X
T = 0.

!**********************************
!          Run time section
!**********************************

DO

          U = some function at time t
          P = (A*X + B*U)*DT

          UP2 = same function at time t+dt/2
          Q = (A*(X+P/2) + B*UP2)*DT
          R = (A*(X+Q/2) + B*UP2)*DT

          UP = same function at time t+dt
          S = (A*(X+R) + B*UP)*DT

          X = X + (P + 2*Q + 2*R + S)/6
          T = T + DT

LOOP UNTIL (SOME END CONDITION IS MET)
```

As stated before, predictor-corrector algorithms use the RK4 method as a starter. However, because RK4 is self-starting, Markov, fourth-order accurate, and straightforward to implement, it is often used for the entire solution. The downside is it is very expensive timewise, especially if the RHS is a complex function with hundreds of table look-ups, thousands of equations, etc.

B.1.3.3.5 Difference Equation   Difference-equation methods include Z-transforms and Tustin or bilinear transforms. In both cases, discrete differences are incorporated in a definition of the Laplace domain variable s. The resulting equation is manipulated to yield the next value of the dependent variable based on previous value(s) of it and current and past values of the input signal. The bilinear transformation is a bit more intuitive, and so it is used to explain the concepts.

First, express the differential equation in Laplace notation, and move all dependent variable references to the left-hand side (LHS) and all independent variable references to the RHS:

$$\dot{x}(t) = ax(t) + bu(t)$$
$$sX(s) = aX(s) + bU(s) \qquad (B.37)$$
$$(s - a)X(s) = bU(s)$$

Substitute the following expression for the Laplacian operator s. The z is a one-step-forward operator, and so by definition z^{-1} is a one-step-backward operation:

$$s = \frac{2(1 - z^{-1})}{\Delta t (1 + z^{-1})} \tag{B.38}$$

This expression is akin to a backward-difference derivative:

$$\dot{x}(t) \approx \frac{(1 - z^{-1})x}{\Delta t} = \frac{[x(t) - x(t - \Delta t)]}{\Delta t} \tag{B.39}$$

taken over a time average of the input

$$\frac{1}{u_{\text{avg}}} = \left[\frac{2}{u(t) + u(t - \Delta t)} \right] \tag{B.40}$$

Making this substitution yields

$$\left[\frac{2(1 - z^{-1})}{\Delta t (1 + z^{-1})} - a \right] X(z) = bU(z) \tag{B.41}$$

The operation of z^{-1} on a variable, say $X(z)$, creates a reference to that variable one time step ago, X_L. That is,

$$X_L = X(t - \Delta t) = z^{-1}X(z) \tag{B.42}$$

The L is a mnemonic for "last pass." The difference equation in marching form emerges after some algebraic manipulation:

$$\begin{aligned} X &= C_1 X_L + C_2 U + C_3 U_L \\ X_L &= z^{-1}X \\ U_L &= z^{-1}U \end{aligned} \tag{B.43}$$

and

$$\begin{aligned} C_1 &= \left(1 - \frac{a\Delta t}{2} \right)^{-1} \left(1 + \frac{a\Delta t}{2} \right) \\ C_2 &= \left(1 - \frac{a\Delta t}{2} \right)^{-1} \left(\frac{b\Delta t}{2} \right) \\ C_3 &= C_2 \end{aligned}$$

or

$$\begin{aligned} C_1 &= \left(I - A\frac{\Delta t}{2} \right)^{-1} \left(I + A\frac{\Delta t}{2} \right) \\ C_2 &= \left(I - A\frac{\Delta t}{2} \right)^{-1} \left(B\frac{\Delta t}{2} \right) \\ C_3 &= C_2 \end{aligned} \tag{B.44}$$

The A, B, and I are matrices, whereas a and b are scalars. The inverse notation, rather than the solidus, emphasizes the fact that the same formulae are good for matrices as well as scalars. A pseudocode fragment that solves the scalar differential equation (B.23) with the difference equation method looks like this:

```
!**********************************
!          Initialization
!**********************************

C1 = (1+A*DT/2.)/(1−A*DT/2.)
C2 = (B*DT/2.)/(1−A*DT/2.)
C3 = C2

XL = Initial condition on X
UL = Initial value of U
T = 0.

!**********************************
!          Run time section
!**********************************

DO

          U = some function at time t
          X = C1*XL + C2*U + C3*UL

          XL = X
          UL = U
          T = T + DT


LOOP UNTIL (SOME END CONDITION IS MET)
```

B.1.3.3.6 State Transition   Time and again, you will be required to solve (numerically) the second-order differential equation given here:

$$\ddot{x} + \omega^2 x = f \qquad (B.45)$$

or, in its state-space representation,

$$\dot{z} = Az + Bu \qquad (B.46)$$

where

$$z = \begin{Bmatrix} x \\ \dot{x} \end{Bmatrix}, \quad u = \{f\} \qquad (B.47)$$

and

$$A = \begin{bmatrix} 0 & 1 \\ -\omega^2 & 0 \end{bmatrix}, \quad B = \begin{bmatrix} 0 \\ 1 \end{bmatrix} \qquad (B.48)$$

Using Green's theorem and assuming the solution is constant during one time step, the solution is

$$z(t) = e^{At}z(0) + \int_0^t e^{A(t-\lambda)} B(\lambda) u(\lambda) \, d\lambda$$

$$z(t) = e^{At}z(0) + e^{At} \int_0^t e^{-A\lambda} \, d\lambda B u(0) \tag{B.49}$$

$$z(t) = e^{At}z(0) + A^{-1} \left[e^{At} - 1 \right] B u(0)$$

That last step is possible because $e^{At}A^{-1} = A^{-1}e^{At}$.

So, the question becomes, how does one calculate the exponential of a matrix? One answer is to calculate the eigenvalues of the $n \times n$ A matrix, then make use of a corollary of the Cayley–Hamilton theorem, which states that the exponential of the A matrix can be expressed as an expansion with a finite number of terms.

$$e^{At} = \alpha_0(t)I + \alpha_1(t)A + \alpha_2(t)A^2 + \cdots + \alpha_{n-1}(t)A^{n-1} \tag{B.50}$$

The unknown coefficients, $\alpha_i(t)$ are found from the n algebraic equations:

$$\alpha_0 + \alpha_1\lambda_1 + \alpha_2\lambda_1^2 + \cdots + \alpha_{n-1}\lambda_1^{n-1} = e^{\lambda_1 t}$$

$$\alpha_0 + \alpha_1\lambda_2 + \alpha_2\lambda_2^2 + \cdots + \alpha_{n-1}\lambda_2^{n-1} = e^{\lambda_2 t}$$

$$\vdots \tag{B.51}$$

$$\alpha_0 + \alpha_1\lambda_n + \alpha_2\lambda_n^2 + \cdots + \alpha_{n-1}\lambda_n^{n-1} = e^{\lambda_n t}$$

A modification is required if some of the eigenvalues are repeated. Complex arithmetic is the norm, and this becomes messy. There is another way that makes use of the series expansion of an exponential. Multiply the A matrix with the time step t.

$$At = \begin{bmatrix} 0 & 1 \\ -\omega^2 & 0 \end{bmatrix} t \tag{B.52}$$

Recall the series expansion for e^x:

$$e^x = 1 + x + \frac{x^2}{2!} + \frac{x^3}{3!} + \frac{x^4}{4!} + \cdots \tag{B.53}$$

Now substitute At for x, and perform the indicated matrix multiplication:

$$e^{At} = \begin{bmatrix} 1 & 0 \\ 0 & 1 \end{bmatrix} + \begin{bmatrix} 0 & 1 \\ -\omega^2 & 0 \end{bmatrix} t + \begin{bmatrix} 0 & 1 \\ -\omega^2 & 0 \end{bmatrix} \begin{bmatrix} 0 & 1 \\ -\omega^2 & 0 \end{bmatrix} \frac{t^2}{2!}$$

$$+ \begin{bmatrix} 0 & 1 \\ -\omega^2 & 0 \end{bmatrix} \begin{bmatrix} 0 & 1 \\ -\omega^2 & 0 \end{bmatrix} \begin{bmatrix} 0 & 1 \\ -\omega^2 & 0 \end{bmatrix} \frac{t^3}{3!} + \cdots \tag{B.54}$$

Carrying this out to four terms yields

$$e^{At} \cong \begin{bmatrix} \left(1 - \dfrac{\omega^2 t^2}{2} + \dfrac{\omega^4 t^4}{24}\right) & \left(t - \dfrac{\omega^2 t^3}{6}\right) \\[2ex] \left(-\omega^2 t + \dfrac{\omega^4 t^3}{6}\right) & \left(1 - \dfrac{\omega^2 t^2}{2} + \dfrac{\omega^4 t^4}{24}\right) \end{bmatrix} \tag{B.55}$$

Recalling the series expansions for $\sin(x)$ and $\cos(x)$, namely,

$$\sin(x) = x - \frac{x^3}{3!} + \frac{x^5}{5!} - \cdots$$

$$\cos(x) = 1 - \frac{x^2}{2!} + \frac{x^4}{4!} - \cdots \tag{B.56}$$

then it is easy to see that the exponential of this At is

$$e^{At} = \begin{bmatrix} \cos(\omega t) & \dfrac{\sin(\omega t)}{\omega} \\[2ex] -\omega \sin(\omega t) & \cos(\omega t) \end{bmatrix} \tag{B.57}$$

Using this exact definition of the exponential of At, the equation for $y(t)$ is exact over the interval of integration provided the forcing function does not change in the interval.

More often than not, the second-order system you will be asked to solve also has some damping.

$$\ddot{x} + 2\omega\varsigma\dot{x} + \omega^2 x = f \tag{B.58}$$

The associated state space equation is

$$\dot{z} = Az + Bu$$

where

$$z = \begin{Bmatrix} x \\ \dot{x} \end{Bmatrix}, \quad \dot{z} = \begin{Bmatrix} \dot{x} \\ \ddot{x} \end{Bmatrix}, \quad A = \begin{bmatrix} 0 & 1 \\ -\omega^2 & -2\omega\varsigma \end{bmatrix}, \quad B = \begin{bmatrix} 0 \\ 1 \end{bmatrix} \quad \text{and} \quad u = \{f\} \tag{B.59}$$

The solution using Green's theorem is exactly the same, namely,

$$z(t) = e^{At}z(0) + A^{-1}[e^{At} - 1]Bu(0) \tag{B.60}$$

or

$$z(t) = \Phi z(0) + \Gamma u(0)$$

The difference is that the exponential of the product At is now

$$e^{At} = e^{-\omega_n \varsigma t} \left\{ \begin{array}{cc} \left[\cos(\omega_d t) + \dfrac{\omega_n \varsigma}{\omega_d} \sin(\omega_d t)\right] & \left[\dfrac{1}{\omega_d} \sin(\omega_d t)\right] \\[2ex] \left[\dfrac{-\omega_n^2}{\omega_d} \sin(\omega_d t)\right] & \left[\cos(\omega_d t) - \dfrac{\omega_n \varsigma}{\omega_d} \sin(\omega_d t)\right] \end{array} \right\}$$

$$\text{(B.61)}$$

where

$$\omega_n = \omega \tag{B.62}$$

and

$$\omega_d = \omega_n \sqrt{1 - \varsigma^2} \tag{B.63}$$

From this, the so-called Φ and Γ matrices are

$$\Phi = e^{At} = \begin{bmatrix} \Phi_{1,1} & \Phi_{1,2} \\ \Phi_{2,1} & \Phi_{2,2} \end{bmatrix} \tag{B.64}$$

and

$$\Gamma = \begin{bmatrix} (1 - \Phi_{2,2})/\omega_n^2 - 2\varsigma\Phi_{1,2}/\omega_n \\ \Phi_{1,2} \end{bmatrix} = \begin{bmatrix} (1 - \Phi_{1,1})/\omega_n^2 \\ \Phi_{1,2} \end{bmatrix} \tag{B.65}$$

From the expression for the state transition matrix, it is easy to see that the exponential coefficient $e^{-\omega_n \varsigma t}$ defines an envelope that governs how rapidly the system damps out or blossoms.

Before leaving this integration technique, there are two important points to be made about the evaluation of the matrices Φ and Γ. First, telescoping the series expansion for exponentiation saves computation time and accuracy. Rewrite the exponentiation series this way:

$$e^{At} = I + At \left[I + \frac{At}{2} \left(I + \frac{At}{3} I + \frac{At}{4} \left[I + \frac{At}{5} (\ldots) \right] \right) \right] \tag{B.66}$$

A simple algorithm that evaluates the exponentiation of the A matrix is expressed in pseudocode here:

```
PHI = I + A*DT/N
For J = N To 2 Step − 1
    PHI = I + A*DT*PHI/(J − 1)
Next J
```

Here, I is the identity matrix, and details of matrix multiplication are left to the reader. Please notice that the time variable t has been replaced with the variable DT. The state transition matrix steps the states from one moment to the next over an interval of DT. The algorithm is trivial to code, it preserves significant figure accuracy, and if the elements in the A matrix are constant, the series needs to be evaluated only once.

The other point concerns the evaluation of the Γ matrix. From expression (B.60), the definition of the Γ matrix requires the inverse of the A matrix. However, the A matrix may be singular if the dynamic system has free zeros. The solution is to form an augmented matrix F partitioned as shown next:

$$F = \begin{bmatrix} A & B \\ 0 & 0 \end{bmatrix} \tag{B.67}$$

The A matrix has n rows and n columns, the B matrix has n rows and p columns, and the null matrices in F should have p rows. This makes the F matrix $(n + p) \times (n + p)$ in size. Now, simply calculate the exponential of Ft using the same techniques as just shown. The result is partitioned thus:

$$e^{Ft} = S = \begin{bmatrix} \Phi & \Gamma \\ ? & ? \end{bmatrix} \tag{B.68}$$

The size of the matrices Φ and Γ are $n \times n$ and $n \times p$, respectively. The bottom p rows of the S matrix are discarded. This method completely bypasses the need to invert the A matrix.

A pseudocode fragment that solves the scalar differential equation (B.23) with the state-transition-matrix method looks like this:

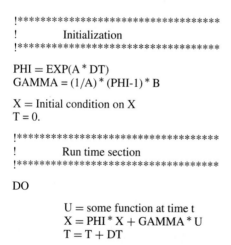

```
!*********************************
!          Initialization
!*********************************

PHI = EXP(A * DT)
GAMMA = (1/A) * (PHI-1) * B

X = Initial condition on X
T = 0.

!*********************************
!          Run time section
!*********************************

DO

        U = some function at time t
        X = PHI * X + GAMMA * U
        T = T + DT

LOOP UNTIL (SOME END CONDITION IS MET)
```

B.1.3.3.7 Harmonic Solutions   Harmonic solutions depend on the assumption that the differential equation is linear and that the forcing function is periodic. Harmonic solutions give you the infinite-time or steady-state solution to a problem after all transients are presumed to have died off. These solutions are sometimes also called the quasi-static solution because they are the rigorous solution to a differential equation, but they ignore the transient part of the solution. If the transient behavior of the system is desired, a different solution technique must be used. If one knows in advance that the transient solution is highly damped and has little influence on the answer, then the dynamic behavior is accurately modeled, provided the forcing function is periodic and harmonic. This technique has an insidious downside; it will be perfectly happy to suggest a periodic solution to a system that is unstable and by rights should blow up. In spite of these problems, the technique is very useful in the simulation of rotating machinery, including rotors, propellers, etc.

To employ this method, express the expected solution and the presumed form of the forcing function as a Fourier series:

$$x(t) = \beta_0 + \beta_c \cos(\Omega t) + \beta_s \sin(\Omega t)$$
$$\dot{x}(t) = -\Omega \beta_c \sin(\Omega t) + \Omega \beta_s \cos(\Omega t)$$
$$u(t) = u_0 + u_c \cos(\Omega t) + u_s \sin(\Omega t) \tag{B.69}$$

The derivative $\dot{x}(t)$ is found from straight differentiation. Substitute these expressions into the differential equation (B.23). The result is

$$-\Omega \beta_c \sin(\Omega t) + \Omega \beta_s \cos(\Omega t) = a\beta_0 + a\beta_c \cos(\Omega t) + a\beta_s \sin(\Omega t)$$
$$+ bu_0 + bu_c \cos(\Omega t) + bu_s \sin(\Omega t) \tag{B.70}$$

Now, create three separate equations by gathering all elements that are constant and all elements that are multiplied by cosine and all elements that are multiplied by sine. The constant terms are

$$0 = a\beta_0 + bu_0$$
$$\therefore \beta_0 = -a^{-1} bu_0 \tag{B.71}$$

The sine and cosine equations are

$$-\Omega \beta_c = a\beta_s + bu_s$$
$$\Omega \beta_s = a\beta_c + bu_c \tag{B.72}$$

These equations can be arranged into a 2×2 matrix equation:

$$\begin{bmatrix} -\Omega & -a \\ -a & \Omega \end{bmatrix} \begin{Bmatrix} \beta_c \\ \beta_s \end{Bmatrix} = b \begin{bmatrix} 1 & 0 \\ 0 & 1 \end{bmatrix} \begin{Bmatrix} u_s \\ u_c \end{Bmatrix} \tag{B.73}$$

Premultiplying both sides of the equation by the inverse of the matrix on the LHS yields

$$\begin{Bmatrix} \beta_c \\ \beta_s \end{Bmatrix} = \frac{-b}{(\Omega^2 + a^2)} \begin{bmatrix} -\Omega & a \\ a & -\Omega \end{bmatrix} \begin{Bmatrix} u_s \\ u_c \end{Bmatrix} \tag{B.74}$$

whence

$$x(t) = -a^{-1}bu_0 - \frac{b}{(\Omega^2 + a^2)}[(\Omega u_s + au_c)\cos(\Omega t) + au_s - \Omega u_c \sin(\Omega t)]$$
(B.75)

This formula can be verified by direct substitution back into the original differential equation of motion.

A second-order differential equation is solved in the same way, but with a bit more elbow grease.

$$\beta(t) = \beta_0 + \beta_c \cos(\Omega t) + \beta_s \sin(\Omega t)$$

$$\dot{\beta}(t) = -\Omega\beta_c \sin(\Omega t) + \Omega\beta_s \cos(\Omega t)$$

$$\ddot{\beta}(t) = -\Omega^2\beta_c \cos(\Omega t) - \Omega^2\beta_s \sin(\Omega t) = \Omega^2[\beta_0 - \beta(t)]$$

$$f(t) = f_0 + f_c \cos(\Omega t) + f_s \sin(\Omega t)$$
(B.76)

Substitute these expressions into the linear, second-order differential equation with constant coefficients:

$$\ddot{\beta}(t) + 2\omega\varsigma\dot{\beta}(t) + \omega^2\beta(t) = f(t)$$
(B.77)

The result is

$$-\Omega^2\beta_c C - \Omega^2\beta_s S - 2\omega\varsigma\Omega\beta_c S + 2\omega\varsigma\Omega\beta_s C + \omega^2\beta_0 + \omega^2\beta_c C + \omega^2\beta_s S$$
$$= f_0 + f_c C + f_s S$$
(B.78)

The C and S terms just shown are shorthand for cosine and sine of Ωt. Gather up the constant, cosine, and sine terms into three separate equations.

$$\omega^2\beta_0 = f_0$$

$$\begin{bmatrix} (\omega^2 - \Omega^2) & 2\omega\Omega\varsigma \\ -2\omega\Omega\varsigma & (\omega^2 - \Omega^2) \end{bmatrix} \begin{Bmatrix} \beta_c \\ \beta_s \end{Bmatrix} = \begin{Bmatrix} f_c \\ f_s \end{Bmatrix}$$
(B.79)

The solution is

$$\begin{Bmatrix} \beta_c \\ \beta_s \end{Bmatrix} = \frac{1}{(\omega^2 - \Omega^2)^2 + 4\omega^2\Omega^2\varsigma^2} \begin{bmatrix} (\omega^2 - \Omega^2) & -2\omega\Omega\varsigma \\ 2\omega\Omega\varsigma & (\omega^2 - \Omega^2) \end{bmatrix} \begin{Bmatrix} f_c \\ f_s \end{Bmatrix}$$
(B.80)

Often, the ratio of the forcing function frequency to the natural frequency is given as r. Thus, the preceding equation can be cleaned up to give

$$\begin{Bmatrix} \beta_c \\ \beta_s \end{Bmatrix} = \frac{1}{\omega^2} \begin{bmatrix} \frac{1}{(1 - r^2)^2 + 4r^2\varsigma^2} \end{bmatrix} \begin{bmatrix} (1 - r^2) & -2r\varsigma \\ 2r\varsigma & (1 - r^2) \end{bmatrix} \begin{Bmatrix} f_c \\ f_s \end{Bmatrix}$$
(B.81)

where

$$r = \frac{\Omega}{\omega}$$

Before leaving this equation, look at the solution if the forcing function frequency equals the natural frequency ($r = 1$):

$$\begin{Bmatrix} \beta_c \\ \beta_s \end{Bmatrix} = \frac{1}{\omega^2} \left(\frac{1}{4\varsigma^2} \right) \begin{bmatrix} 0 & -2\varsigma \\ 2\varsigma & 0 \end{bmatrix} \begin{Bmatrix} f_c \\ f_s \end{Bmatrix} \tag{B.82}$$

or

$$\beta_c = \frac{-f_s}{2\omega^2 \varsigma}$$

$$\beta_s = \frac{f_c}{2\omega^2 \varsigma}$$

In other words, the cosine response β_c is generated by the sine input f_s, and the sine response β_s is generated by the cosine input f_c. If the damping ς is zero, the response of this system in resonance is infinite. A famous example of a lightly damped system responding catastrophically to a resonant forcing function is the Tacoma Narrows Bridge, also known as Galloping Gertie, which shook itself apart in the wind just four months after opening. The interested reader can learn more at this Web site: www.pbs.org/wgbh/buildingbig/wonder/structure/tacoma_narrows.html

B.1.4   Open-Integration Potpourri

Before leaving the open-integration techniques, two methods that do not quite fit the molds just introduced are described.

B.1.4.1   Ersatz AB2
The first is often, wrongly, called AB2, implying it is part of the Adams–Bashforth family of predictor-corrector integrators. It mixes two different integration schemes to produce a specialized solution to the following second-order equation:

$$\ddot{x} + 2\omega\varsigma\dot{x} + \omega^2 x = f \tag{B.83}$$

Presuming interest in both the displacement and its first derivative, find the first derivative with the expression:

$$\dot{x}(t + \Delta t) = \dot{x}(t) + [3\ddot{x}(t) - \ddot{x}(t - \Delta t)]\frac{\Delta t}{2} \tag{B.84}$$

The displacement is found with

$$x(t + \Delta t) = x(t) + [\dot{x}(t + \Delta t) + \dot{x}(t)]\frac{\Delta t}{2} \tag{B.85}$$

If the acceleration is a constant, then these expressions give the exact result for displacement and velocity over the interval of integration.

A pseudocode fragment that solves the scalar differential equation (B.83) with the ersatz AB2 scheme looks like this:

```
!*********************************
!        Initialization
!*********************************

XL = Initial condition on X
XDL = Initial condition on XD
XDDL = Past value of highest derivative
T = 0.

!*********************************
!        Run time section
!*********************************

DO

        F = some function at time t
        XDD = F - 2 * OM * ZETA * XD-OM * OM * X
        XD = XDL + (3 * XDD - XDDL) * DT/2
        X = XL + (XD + XDL) * DT/2

        XDDL = XDD
        XDL = XD
        XL = X
        T = T + DT


LOOP UNTIL (SOME END CONDITION IS MET)
```

B.1.4.2 Scalar Bilinear

The second method produces a difference equation, but in scalar form. Start with a transfer function of order m over n ($m \leq n$):

$$\frac{X(s)}{U(s)} = \frac{b_m s^m + b_{m-1} s^{m-1} + \cdots + b_0}{a_n s^n + a_{n-1} s^{n-1} + \cdots + a_0} \qquad (B.86)$$

Arrange the equation with $X(s)$ on the LHS and $U(s)$ on the RHS:

$$\left(a_n s^n + a_{n-1} s^{n-1} + \cdots + a_0\right) X(s) = \left(b_m s^m + b_{m-1} s^{m-1} + \cdots + b_0\right) U(s)$$
$$(B.87)$$

Substitute the approximation for the Laplacian operator s, next:

$$s = \frac{2(1 - z^{-1})}{\Delta t(1 + z^{-1})} \qquad (B.88)$$

into the differential equation. This produces

$$
\text{LHS} = \left[a_n \left(\frac{\Delta t}{2} \right)^n \left(\frac{1 - z^{-1}}{1 + z^{-1}} \right)^n + a_{n-1} \left(\frac{\Delta t}{2} \right)^{n-1} \left(\frac{1 - z^{-1}}{1 + z^{-1}} \right)^{n-1} \right.
$$

$$
\left. + \cdots + a_0 \right] X(z)
$$

(B.89)

$$
\text{RHS} = \left[b_m \left(\frac{\Delta t}{2} \right)^m \left(\frac{1 - z^{-1}}{1 + z^{-1}} \right)^m + b_{m-1} \left(\frac{\Delta t}{2} \right)^{m-1} \left(\frac{1 - z^{-1}}{1 + z^{-1}} \right)^{m-1} \right.
$$

$$
\left. + \cdots + b_0 \right] U(z)
$$

Of course, the LHS equals the RHS. Clear the denominator by multiplying by $(2/\Delta t)^n (1 + z^{-1})^n$ to get

$$
\text{LHS} = \left[\begin{array}{c} a_n \left(1 - z^{-1} \right)^n + a_{n-1} \left(\dfrac{2}{\Delta t} \right) \left(1 - z^{-1} \right)^{n-1} \left(1 + z^{-1} \right) \\[2ex] + \cdots + a_0 \left(\dfrac{2}{\Delta t} \right)^n \left(1 + z^{-1} \right)^n \end{array} \right] X(z)
$$

$$
\text{RHS} = \left[\begin{array}{c} b_m \left(\dfrac{\Delta t}{2} \right)^{m-n} \left(1 - z^{-1} \right)^m \left(1 + z^{-1} \right)^{n-m} \\[2ex] + b_{m-1} \left(\dfrac{\Delta t}{2} \right)^{m-1-n} \left(1 - z^{-1} \right)^{m-1} \left(1 + z^{-1} \right)^{n-m+1} \\[2ex] + \cdots + b_0 \left(\dfrac{\Delta t}{2} \right)^{-n} \left(1 + z^{-1} \right)^n \end{array} \right] U(z)
$$

(B.90)

Expand every polynomial in z. Some of the expansions are shown here:

$$
(1 - z^{-1})^1 = (1 - z^{-1})
$$

$$
(1 - z^{-1})^2 = (1 - 2z^{-1} + z^{-2})
$$

$$
(1 - z^{-1})^3 = (1 - 3z^{-1} + 3z^{-2} - z^{-3})
$$

$$
(1 - z^{-1})^4 = (1 - 4z^{-1} + 6z^{-2} - 4z^{-3} + z^{-4})
$$

$$
\cdots
$$

$$
(1 - z^{-1})(1 + z^{-1}) = (1 - z^{-2})
$$

etc.   (B.91)

Note: This is a *very* tedious step. The clever reader can write a simple program that expands these polynomials symbolically. For instance, expansion of the $(1 - z^{-1})^n$ and $(1 + z^{-1})^n$ polynomials involves building a Pascal triangle.

Gather coefficients in like powers of z^{-1}:

$$\text{LHS} = \left[C_0 + C_1 z^{-1} + C_2 z^{-2} + \cdots + C_n z^{-n} \right] X(z)$$

$$\text{RHS} = \left[D_0 + D_1 z^{-1} + D_2 z^{-2} + \cdots + D_n z^{-n} \right] U(z) \qquad \text{(B.92)}$$

Finally, the difference equation and support equations that solve the original differential equation are

$$X = -\frac{C_1}{C_0} X_L - \frac{C_2}{C_0} X_{LL} \cdots - \frac{C_n}{C_0} X_{L^n} + \frac{D_0}{C_0} U + \frac{D_1}{C_0} U_L + \cdots + \frac{D_n}{C_0} U_{L^n} \quad \text{(B.93)}$$

$$X_{L^n} = X_{L^{n-1}}$$

$$X_{L^{n-1}} = X_{L^{n-2}}$$

$$\cdots$$

$$X_{LL} = X_L$$

$$X_L = X$$

$$U_{L^n} = U_{L^{n-1}}$$

$$U_{L^{n-1}} = U_{L^{n-2}}$$

$$\cdots$$

$$U_{LL} = U_L$$

$$U_L = U \qquad \text{(B.94)}$$

The L subscript means the last-pass value of the variable, LL means the value two frames ago, and L^n means the value of the variable n frames ago.

A pseudocode fragment that solves the scalar differential equation (B.83) with the scalar bilinear scheme looks like this:

```
!************************************
!          Initialization
!************************************

C0 = 1+2 * OM * ZETA * DT/2 + (OM * DT/2)^2
C1 = 2 * (OM * DT/2)^2 - 2
C2 = 1 - 2 * OM * ZETA * DT/2+(OM * DT/2)^2
D0 = (DT/2)^2
D1 = 2 * (DT/2)^2
D2 = (DT/2)^2

X = Initial condition on X
XL = X
FL = some function at time t = t0 - dt
FLL = same function at time t = t0 - 2dt
T = 0.
```

```
!************************************
!          Run time section
!************************************
DO

        F = some function at time t
        X = (−C1 * X − C2 * XL + D0 * F + D1 * FL + D2 * FLL)/C0

        XL = X
        FLL = FL
        FL = F
        T = T + DT

LOOP UNTIL (SOME END CONDITION IS MET)
```

B.1.5 Comparison and Summary

Each of the methods described are suitable for open integration. Some methods are better suited in a particular application than others. Table B.1 summarizes the relative advantages and lists some significant disadvantages of each method.

B.2 Closed Integration

To find the "area under a curve" is to find the antiderivative, which is the integral calculus. Integral calculus is necessary when looking for the sum of infinitesimals as an independent variable runs from one endpoint to another. As always, exact solutions are preferable, and a great many standard texts are available to find the exact solution to the indefinite integral. Reference 4 is an excellent general source of indefinite integrals.

Usually, the function that is to be integrated either does not have an antiderivative, or it is not known in analytical form but can be evaluated and tabulated. In such cases, the definite integral is approximated through quadrature. Quadrature is the process of substituting a definite integral with a finite summation using coefficients designed to smoothly pass an interpolating polynomial through the function points with a minimum of curvature (waviness). This chapter presents a few well-known quadrature formulas. In all cases, the number of function evaluations in the interval of integration is known a priori and have already been performed.

B.2.1 Rectangular Integration

The grossest approximation to an integral is to draw a horizontal line halfway between the function evaluation at the left (or lower) point of integration and the function evaluation at the right (or upper) point. This average value multiplied by the distance between the left and right values of the independent variable is the approximation of the integral:

$$\int_a^b f(x)\,dx \approx \frac{[f(b) + f(a)]}{2}(b - a) \tag{B.95}$$

Table B.1   Comparison of open integration schemes

Technique	Advantages	Disadvantages
Exact solution	Exact solution Minimal numeric error	Significant amount of work No solution sometimes Not well suited to arbitrary forcing functions
Exact solution with constant forcing function	Exact solution over a small step Minimal numeric error Works well with arbitrary forcing functions	Best applied to single- degree-of-freedom systems Piecewise linear systems only Piecewise constant coefficient systems only
Euler	Simplest of numerical methods One function evaluation per time step	Excessive error buildup Many small time steps required to minimize error build up
Corrected Euler	Simple to implement Second-order accurate	Second-order accurate Two function evaluations required per time step
Adams–Bashforth	Fifth-order accuracy Two function evaluations per step size	Requires history vector of function and derivatives Requires starting algorithm
Runge–Kutta	Popular Self-starting, Markov process Fourth-order accurate	Requires four function evaluations per time step
Difference equation	Second-order accuracy Integrating algorithm requires just one initialization—after that, it is just a cascade of previous solutions.	Linear systems only
State transition matrix	Exact solution with a constant forcing function STM can be found analytically or nume- rically	Forcing function is constant over integration step—phase is introduced. Analytical solution requires significant amount of work.
Harmonic balance	Easy to implement Exact solution to steady- state problem No sensitivity to step size	Discards transient solution Requires significant work to find solution
Ersatz AB2	Exact solution to second- order differential equation	Requires history of past values and past derivatives

Continued

Table B.1   **Comparison of open integration schemes** *(Continued)*

Technique	Advantages	Disadvantages
	with constant force over time step and constant coefficients	Not suitable for coupled differential equations
Scalar bilinear	Accurate difference equation solution to *m*th over *n*th order transfer function	Tedious to set up, though it could be automated with difficulty
		Constant coefficient system only
		Linear system only

As the distance between the lower and upper limits of integration shrinks, this formula becomes more and more accurate. (The accuracy increases only to a point. After that, roundoff error becomes an important player because of the finite number of bits in a computer word.)

If the integration is to be performed over several evaluations, then this summation is carried out with a simple cascade:

$$\int_{x_1}^{x_n} f(x)\,dx \approx \int_{x_1}^{x_2} f(x)\,dx + \int_{x_2}^{x_3} f(x)\,dx + \cdots + \int_{x_{n-1}}^{x_n} f(x)\,dx \quad \text{(B.96)}$$

Each of the integrals on the right-hand side is carried out using the approximation:

$$\int_{x_1}^{x_n} f(x)\,dx \approx \frac{[f(x_1)+f(x_2)]}{2}(x_2 - x_1) + \frac{[f(x_2)+f(x_3)]}{2}(x_3 - x_2)+\cdots$$

$$+ \frac{[f(x_{n-1})+f(x_n)]}{2}(x_n - x_{n-1}) \quad \text{(B.97)}$$

It is convenient to express this approximation in standard summation notation. A slight rearrangement gives

$$\int_{x_1}^{x_n} f(x)\,dx \approx \sum_{i=1}^{n} c_i f(x_i) = \sum_{i=1}^{n} c_i f_i \quad \text{(B.98)}$$

where

$$c_i = \begin{cases} \dfrac{(x_2 - x_1)}{2}, & i = 1 \\ \dfrac{(x_{i+1} - x_{i-1})}{2}, & i = 2, n-1 \\ \dfrac{(x_n - x_{n-1})}{2}, & i = n \end{cases} \quad \text{(B.99)}$$

and the notation f_i is introduced as shorthand for $f(x_i)$ for convenience.

This method is easy to implement and surprisingly good. For integration of smooth functions over some span, this method is "good enough for ...," well, you know. Here is some pseudocode that shows one way to implement this algorithm:

```
SUM = 0.
FOR I = 1 TO N-1
   SUM = SUM + (F(I+1)+F(I)) * (X(I+1)-X(I))/2.
NEXT I
```

B.2.2 Simpson Integration

An inexpensive improvement to second-order accuracy comes with two conditions: that the number of function evaluations is odd, and that the evaluations are evenly spaced along the domain of the independent variable. If this is the case, then Simpson's rule for integration can be used. In the case of three function evaluations, the rule is given by

$$\int_{x_1}^{x_3} f(x)\, dx \approx \frac{h}{3}[f(x_1) + 4f(x_2) + f(x_3)] \qquad (B.100)$$

where $h = (x_2 - x_1) = (x_3 - x_2)$. If the function has been evaluated five or more times (always an odd number), over the interval, then the integration is approximated with a cascade summation:

$$\int_{x_1}^{x_n} f(x)\, dx \approx \int_{x_1}^{x_3} f(x)\, dx + \int_{x_3}^{x_5} f(x)\, dx + \cdots + \int_{x_{n-2}}^{x_n} f(x)\, dx \qquad (B.101)$$

where

$$\int_{x_1}^{x_3} f(x)\, dx \approx \frac{h}{3}[f(x_1) + 4f(x_2) + f(x_3)]$$

$$\int_{x_3}^{x_5} f(x)\, dx \approx \frac{h}{3}[f(x_3) + 4f(x_4) + f(x_5)]$$

$$\int_{x_{n-2}}^{x_n} f(x)\, dx \approx \frac{h}{3}[f(x_{n-2}) + 4f(x_{n-1}) + f(x_n)] \qquad (B.102)$$

Because the values of the independent argument are equally spaced, the endpoints of the interior integrations can add directly to their neighbors. The result is

$$\int_{x_1}^{x_n} f(x)\, dx \approx \frac{h}{3}[f_1 + 4f_2 + 2f_3 + 4f_4 + 2f_5 + \cdots + 4f_{n-1} + f_n] \qquad (B.103)$$

Again, it is convenient to express this approximation in standard summation notation:

$$\int_{x_1}^{x_n} f(x)\, dx \approx \sum_{i=1}^{n} c_i f(x_i) = \sum_{i=1}^{n} c_i f_i \qquad (B.104)$$

where

$$c_i = \begin{cases} \dfrac{h}{3}, & i = 1 \\[2mm] \dfrac{4h}{3}, & i = 2, 4, \ldots n - 2 \\[2mm] \dfrac{2h}{3}, & i = 3, 5, \ldots n - 1 \\[2mm] \dfrac{h}{3}, & i = n \end{cases} \tag{B.105}$$

Here is some pseudocode that shows one way to implement the Simpson integration algorithm:

```
!*********************************
!          Initialization
!*********************************
    SUM = F(1)
    FOR I = 2 TO N-1
     S = S + 2 * F(I)
      IF I MOD 2 = 0 THEN S = S + 2 * F(I)
    NEXT I
    S = S + F(N)
    S = S* H/3
```

A multitude of other methods is available. References [1–3] discuss them in detail.

B.2.3 Comparison and Summary

Rectangular integration, Simpson integration, and exact solutions are suitable for open integration. Some methods are better suited in a particular application than others. Table B.2 summarizes the relative advantages and lists some significant disadvantages of each method.

B.3 Important Integrals

Trigonometric identities reduce powers of trigonometric functions to functions of a base argument and higher harmonics, which makes the evaluation of integrals of trigonometric functions very easy. Commonly used trigonometric identities can be found in [4]. From them, the following useful integrals were produced. The integrals are presented twice, first as a definite integral evaluated from 0 to 2π and then as an indefinite integral. The list of functions that follows is in no way comprehensive, but it does cover the most frequently used trigonometric integrals in rotor analysis. For a comprehensive list, consult [4].

Table B.2   Comparison of closed integration schemes

Technique	Advantages	Disadvantages
Exact solution	Exact solution Minimal numeric error	Analytical function required Analytical antiderivative may not exist
Rectangular integration	Easy to implement Does not require analytical function	First-order accurate Small amount of additional logic to set up coefficients
Simpson integration	Easy to implement Does not require analytical function Second-order accuracy	Small amount of additional logic to set up coefficients Must have an odd number of points

B.3.1   Definite Integrals

B.3.1.1   First Harmonic

$$\int_0^{2\pi} \cos(\Theta)\, d\Theta = 0 \quad \int_0^{2\pi} \sin(\Theta)\, d\Theta = 0$$

B.3.1.2   Second Harmonic

$$\int_0^{2\pi} \cos^2(\Theta)\, d\Theta = \pi \quad \int_0^{2\pi} \cos(\Theta)\sin(\Theta)\, d\Theta = 0 \quad \int_0^{2\pi} \sin^2(\Theta)\, d\Theta = \pi$$

B.3.1.3   Third Harmonic

$$\int_0^{2\pi} \cos^3(\Theta)\, d\Theta = 0 \quad \int_0^{2\pi} \cos^2(\Theta)\sin(\Theta)\, d\Theta = 0 \quad \int_0^{2\pi} \cos(\Theta)\sin^2(\Theta)\, d\Theta = 0$$

$$\int_0^{2\pi} \sin^3(\Theta)\, d\Theta = 0$$

B.3.1.4   Fourth Harmonic

$$\int_0^{2\pi} \cos^4(\Theta)\, d\Theta = \frac{3\pi}{4} \quad \int_0^{2\pi} \cos^3(\Theta)\sin(\Theta)\, d\Theta = 0 \quad \int_0^{2\pi} \cos^2(\Theta)\sin^2(\Theta)\, d\Theta = \frac{\pi}{4}$$

$$\int_0^{2\pi} \cos(\Theta)\sin^3(\Theta)\, d\Theta = 0 \quad \int_0^{2\pi} \sin^4(\Theta)\, d\Theta = \frac{3\pi}{4}$$

B.3.1.5   Fifth Harmonic

$$\int_0^{2\pi} \cos^5(\Theta)\,d\Theta = 0 \quad \int_0^{2\pi} \cos^4(\Theta)\sin(\Theta)\,d\Theta = 0 \quad \int_0^{2\pi} \cos^3(\Theta)\sin^2(\Theta)\,d\Theta = 0$$

$$\int_0^{2\pi} \cos^2(\Theta)\sin^3(\Theta)\,d\Theta = 0 \quad \int_0^{2\pi} \cos(\Theta)\sin^4(\Theta)\,d\Theta = 0 \quad \int_0^{2\pi} \sin^5(\Theta)\,d\Theta = 0$$

B.3.1.6   Sixth Harmonic

$$\int_0^{2\pi} \cos^6(\Theta)\,d\Theta = \frac{5\pi}{8} \quad \int_0^{2\pi} \cos^5(\Theta)\sin(\Theta)\,d\Theta = 0 \quad \int_0^{2\pi} \cos^4(\Theta)\sin^2(\Theta)\,d\Theta = \frac{\pi}{8}$$

$$\int_0^{2\pi} \cos^3(\Theta)\sin^3(\Theta)\,d\Theta = 0 \quad \int_0^{2\pi} \cos^2(\Theta)\sin^4(\Theta)\,d\Theta = \frac{\pi}{8} \quad \int_0^{2\pi} \cos(\Theta)\sin^5(\Theta)\,d\Theta = 0$$

$$\int_0^{2\pi} \sin^6(\Theta)\,d\Theta = \frac{5\pi}{8}$$

B.3.2   Indefinite Integrals

B.3.2.1   First Harmonic

$$\int \cos(\Theta)\,d\Theta = \sin(\Theta) + C$$

$$\int \sin(\Theta)\,d\Theta = -\cos(\Theta) + C$$

B.3.2.2   Second Harmonic

$$\int \cos^2(\Theta)\,d\Theta = \frac{\Theta}{2} + \frac{\sin(2\Theta)}{4} + C$$

$$\int \cos(\Theta)\sin(\Theta)\,d\Theta = -\frac{\cos(2\Theta)}{4} + C$$

$$\int \sin^2(\Theta)\,d\Theta = \frac{\Theta}{2} - \frac{\sin(2\Theta)}{4} + C$$

B.3.2.3   Third Harmonic

$$\int \cos^3(\Theta)\,d\Theta = \frac{3\sin(\Theta)}{4} + \frac{\sin(3\Theta)}{12} + C$$

$$\int \cos^2(\Theta)\sin(\Theta)\,d\Theta = -\frac{\cos(\Theta)}{4} - \frac{\cos(3\Theta)}{12} + C$$

$$\int \cos(\Theta)\sin^2(\Theta)\,d\Theta = \frac{\sin(\Theta)}{4} - \frac{\sin(3\Theta)}{12} + C$$

$$\int \sin^3(\Theta)\,d\Theta = -\frac{3\cos(\Theta)}{4} + \frac{\cos(3\Theta)}{12} + C$$

B.3.2.4 Fourth Harmonic

$$\int \cos^4(\Theta) \, d\Theta = \frac{3\Theta}{8} + \frac{\sin(2\Theta)}{4} + \frac{\sin(4\Theta)}{32} + C$$

$$\int \cos^3(\Theta) \sin(\Theta) \, d\Theta = -\frac{\cos(2\Theta)}{8} - \frac{\cos(4\Theta)}{32} + C$$

$$\int \cos^2(\Theta) \sin^2(\Theta) \, d\Theta = \frac{\Theta}{8} - \frac{\sin(4\Theta)}{32} + C$$

$$\int \cos(\Theta) \sin^3(\Theta) \, d\Theta = -\frac{\cos(2\Theta)}{8} + \frac{\cos(4\Theta)}{32} + C$$

$$\int \sin^4(\Theta) \, d\Theta = \frac{3\Theta}{8} - \frac{\sin(2\Theta)}{4} + \frac{\sin(4\Theta)}{32} + C$$

B.3.2.5 Fifth Harmonic

$$\int \cos^5(\Theta) \, d\Theta = \frac{10\sin(\Theta)}{16} + \frac{5\sin(3\Theta)}{48} + \frac{\sin(5\Theta)}{80} + C$$

$$\int \cos^4(\Theta) \sin(\Theta) \, d\Theta = -\frac{2\cos(\Theta)}{16} - \frac{5\cos(3\Theta)}{80} - \frac{\cos(5\Theta)}{80} + C$$

$$\int \cos^3(\Theta) \sin^2(\Theta) \, d\Theta = \frac{2\sin(\Theta)}{16} - \frac{\sin(3\Theta)}{48} - \frac{\sin(5\Theta)}{80} + C$$

$$\int \cos^2(\Theta) \sin^3(\Theta) \, d\Theta = -\frac{2\cos(\Theta)}{16} - \frac{\cos(3\Theta)}{48} + \frac{\cos(5\Theta)}{80} + C$$

$$\int \cos(\Theta) \sin^4(\Theta) \, d\Theta = \frac{2\sin(\Theta)}{16} - \frac{5\sin(3\Theta)}{80} + \frac{\sin(5\Theta)}{80} + C$$

$$\int \sin^5(\Theta) \, d\Theta = -\frac{10\cos(\Theta)}{16} + \frac{5\cos(3\Theta)}{48} - \frac{\cos(5\Theta)}{80} + C$$

B.3.2.6 Sixth Harmonic

$$\int \cos^6(\Theta) \, d\Theta = \frac{10\Theta}{32} + \frac{15\sin(2\Theta)}{64} + \frac{6\sin(4\Theta)}{128} + \frac{\sin(6\Theta)}{192} + C$$

$$\int \cos^5(\Theta) \sin(\Theta) \, d\Theta = -\frac{5\cos(2\Theta)}{64} - \frac{4\cos(4\Theta)}{128} - \frac{\cos(6\Theta)}{192} + C$$

$$\int \cos^4(\Theta) \sin^2(\Theta) \, d\Theta = \frac{2\Theta}{32} + \frac{\sin(2\Theta)}{64} - \frac{2\sin(4\Theta)}{128} - \frac{\sin(6\Theta)}{192} + C$$

$$\int \cos^3(\Theta) \sin^3(\Theta) \, d\Theta = -\frac{3\cos(2\Theta)}{64} + \frac{\cos(6\Theta)}{192} + C$$

$$\int \cos^2(\Theta)\sin^4(\Theta)\,d\Theta = \frac{2\Theta}{32} - \frac{\sin(2\Theta)}{64} - \frac{2\sin(4\Theta)}{128} + \frac{\sin(6\Theta)}{192} + C$$

$$\int \cos(\Theta)\sin^5(\Theta)\,d\Theta = -\frac{5\cos(2\Theta)}{64} + \frac{4\cos(4\Theta)}{128} - \frac{\cos(6\Theta)}{192} + C$$

$$\int \sin^6(\Theta)\,d\Theta = \frac{10\Theta}{32} - \frac{15\sin(2\Theta)}{64} + \frac{6\sin(4\Theta)}{128} - \frac{\sin(6\Theta)}{192} + C$$

References

[1] Carnahan, B., Luther, H. A., and Wilkes, J. O., *Applied Numerical Methods*, Wiley, New York, 1969, pp. 69–140, 341–428.

[2] Press, W. H., Teukolsky, S. A., Vetterling, W. T., and Flannery, B. P., *Numerical Recipes in Fortran, The Art of Scientific Computing*, 2nd ed., Cambridge, Press Syndicate of the Univ. of Cambridge, MA, 1992, pp. 123–158, 701–744.

[3] Beckett, R., and Hurt, J., *Numerical Calculations and Algorithms*, McGraw–Hill, 1967, pp. 146–176, 178–221.

[4] Selby, Samuel M., and Weast, Robert C., *CRC Standard Mathematical Tables*, 21st ed., The Chemical Rubber Co., Cleveland, OH, 1973, pp. 225–231, 435–447.

Problems

B.1 A parachutist jumps from an airplane at 10,000 ft. If W is the vertical speed, the equation of vertical motion for the parachutist is

$$\dot{W} = 32.2 - (0.001585)W^2$$

The vertical distance the parachutist drops is

$$D = \int_0^T W\,dt$$

Terminal velocity is that speed at which there is no more acceleration and the parachutist is falling at constant speed. Find the exact solution for terminal velocity, then use any open-integration method you want except simple Euler to answer the following questions. How much time was required for the parachutist to get to within 1% of the terminal velocity? How far did the parachutist fall before reaching that velocity?

B.2 Use rectangular (also known as trapezoidal) integration to estimate the area under the following curve between the indicated limits and above the x axis:

$$\text{Area} = \int_0^1 \sqrt{1 - x^2}\,dx$$

Start with just two points in the domain. Then use four points, then eight, etc. Continue doubling the number of points until you are satisfied the answer has converged. Compare this answer to the exact answer.

Appendix C
Linear Algebra

Problem:

$$\text{Find } x \text{ such that } Ax = b$$

Solution:

$$x = A^{-1}b$$

Unlike the calculus, history credits no single person with the invention of algebra; the web site http://www.newton.dep.anl.gov/newton/askasci/1995/math/MATH010.HTM suggests algebra appears to have "grown up." Egyptians, Chinese, Hindus, and Babylonians all contributed to the understanding of various aspects of finding the hidden number that would cause two things to equal each other. The wisdom of the ages was collected and published by the Arab mathematician Muhammed ibn Musa al-Khowarizmi, whose celebrated description of reduction, "Hisab al-jabr w'al muqabalah," which roughly translated means "the science of reunion and reduction," greatly influenced Western mathematicians and coincidentally provided us with the word "algebra" (al-jabr). (It is not a stretch to see that the name al-Khowarizm also gives us the word algorithm.)

From the simple algebra of al-Khowarizmi to the linear algebra of today required hundreds of years of incremental "ah-hah!" moments, but look what that effort yielded. Simultaneous equations, either static or dynamic, are efficiently manipulated with the tools of linear algebra. Linear algebra uses vectors as objects and matrices as collections of coefficients or operators. Although the list of tools that are available in linear algebra is extensive, the basic techniques can be described with a small number of well-defined rules. It is not the intent of this chapter to justify those rules. A better source for the proper mathematical foundations can be found in [1]. This chapter provides an overview and demonstrates the use of some of the more useful tools.

C.1 Vectors

Engineering purists insist that vectors are constructs that present displacement, motion, forces, and so forth as arrows with definite direction, resolution, and origin. When expressed in a form that is convenient for mathematical manipulation, a vector is an array. In mechanics, the vector is often 3×1 in size.

In mathematics, a vector is any well-ordered collection of information. The information can be numerical, such as a list of the room temperature measured at evenly spaced increments of time. The information can be symbolic, such as a list of the variable names used to describe the dynamic state of an aircraft. This text uses both interpretations; the broader meaning applies to the discussion that follows.

Often, a letter with an overarrow, for example, $\vec{a}$, expresses a vector symbolically, though just as often the context is sufficient to identify the vector without the use of the overarrow. (AIAA style denotes vectors using boldface, italic type.) This text uses lowercase letters for vectors, and uppercase letters for matrices. Subscripts provide additional information about the nature of the information in the vector.

Unless otherwise specified, a vector is a collection placed in a *column*. For instance, if a Cartesian coordinate system is attached to one corner of a room, then any point in that room can be located relative to that corner (more properly, the origin) given three measurements along the three mutually perpendicular axes commonly called width, depth, and height. Numeric values locate a specific point; symbolic names locate a general point:

$$s = \begin{Bmatrix} 5 \\ 3 \\ 7 \end{Bmatrix}$$

or

$$s = \begin{Bmatrix} \text{width} \\ \text{depth} \\ \text{height} \end{Bmatrix}$$

A vector with n elements, or of length n, is written:

$$v = \begin{Bmatrix} v_1 \\ v_2 \\ \dots \\ v_n \end{Bmatrix}$$

This vector is said to have dimensions $n \times 1$, read n by 1. The n indicates the number of rows, and the 1 indicates the number of columns. If the vector must be expressed as a row vector, use the *transpose* operation:

$$w = v^T = \begin{Bmatrix} v_1 & v_2 & \dots & v_n \end{Bmatrix}$$

This is read $w = v$ transpose and has dimensions $1 \times n$, read 1 by n. Observe now that the dimension statement indicates one row and n columns. *Transposing a vector switches the numbers that indicate row and column length.* Keeping track of the number of rows and columns is vitally important.

C.1.1 Vector Addition and Subtraction

Vectors follow the usual rules of arithmetic when it comes to addition and subtraction, provided that the vectors are the same length, and both vectors are either column or row vectors. The individual elements of two vectors are added or subtracted as indicated in the notation:

$$c_i = a_i + b_i$$

or

$$c_i = a_i - b_i$$

For example, if vector

$$a = \begin{Bmatrix} 1 \\ 2 \\ 3 \end{Bmatrix}$$

and vector

$$b = \begin{Bmatrix} 7 \\ 1 \\ 8 \end{Bmatrix}$$

then the sum

$$c = a + b = \begin{Bmatrix} 1 \\ 2 \\ 3 \end{Bmatrix} + \begin{Bmatrix} 7 \\ 1 \\ 8 \end{Bmatrix} = \begin{Bmatrix} (1+7) \\ (2+1) \\ (3+8) \end{Bmatrix} = \begin{Bmatrix} 8 \\ 3 \\ 11 \end{Bmatrix}$$

and the difference

$$d = a - b = \begin{Bmatrix} 1 \\ 2 \\ 3 \end{Bmatrix} - \begin{Bmatrix} 7 \\ 1 \\ 8 \end{Bmatrix} = \begin{Bmatrix} (1-7) \\ (2-1) \\ (3-8) \end{Bmatrix} = \begin{Bmatrix} -6 \\ 1 \\ -5 \end{Bmatrix}$$

The *commutative law* for addition and subtraction holds for vectors. That is,

$$a + b = b + a$$

and

$$a - b = -b + a$$

The *associative law* for addition and subtraction also holds:

$$a + (b + c) = (a + b) + c$$

C.1.2 Vector Multiplication

Vector multiplication seems to follow unusual rules. There are three different ways in which vectors can be multiplied. Each method produces a different type of result.

C.1.2.1 Inner product The *inner product* of two vectors, sometimes called the *dot product*, requires that both vectors be the same length. The inner product produces a scalar. The formal manipulation is

$$s = a^T \cdot b = b^T \cdot a = \sum_{i=1}^{n} a_i b_i = a_1 b_1 + a_2 b_2 + \cdots + a_n b_n$$

Both vectors in the preceding description are n-length column vectors, and the transpose operation has been performed on the leading vector. The reason for this formality becomes clear in the general case of matrix multiplication. There is no limit on the length of the vectors.

Example C.1

If vector

$$a = \begin{Bmatrix} 1 \\ 2 \\ 3 \\ 4 \end{Bmatrix}$$

and vector

$$b = \begin{Bmatrix} 5 \\ -4 \\ 3 \\ -2 \end{Bmatrix},$$

then the dot product is

$$s = a^T \cdot b = \{1 \quad 2 \quad 3 \quad 4\} \cdot \begin{Bmatrix} 5 \\ -4 \\ 3 \\ -2 \end{Bmatrix}$$

$$= (1)(5) + (2)(-4) + (3)(3) + (4)(-2) = -2$$

The *norm* of a vector is the square root of the sum of the squares of the individual elements in the vector. It is the Pythagorean theorem generalized to n dimensions. The norm of vector a is

$$s = \sqrt{a^T \cdot a} = \sqrt{ \{1 \quad 2 \quad 3 \quad 4\} \cdot \begin{Bmatrix} 1 \\ 2 \\ 3 \\ 4 \end{Bmatrix} } = \sqrt{30}$$

C.1.2.2 Cross product The vector cross product is an operation performed on two three-element vectors. The operation produces a vector of length three. The cross product is found in the calculation of torque, which is a force multiplied by a distance, and tangential velocity, which is an angular speed multiplied by a distance. The formal manipulation is

$$c = a \times b = \begin{Bmatrix} a_x \\ a_y \\ a_z \end{Bmatrix} \times \begin{Bmatrix} b_x \\ b_y \\ b_z \end{Bmatrix} = \begin{Bmatrix} a_y b_z - a_z b_y \\ a_z b_x - a_x b_z \\ a_x b_y - a_y b_x \end{Bmatrix}$$

For example, if vector

$$a = \begin{Bmatrix} 1 \\ 2 \\ 3 \end{Bmatrix}$$

and vector

$$b = \begin{Bmatrix} 7 \\ 1 \\ 8 \end{Bmatrix}$$

then the cross product is

$$c = a \times b = \begin{Bmatrix} 1 \\ 2 \\ 3 \end{Bmatrix} \times \begin{Bmatrix} 7 \\ 1 \\ 8 \end{Bmatrix} = \begin{Bmatrix} 2*8 - 3*1 \\ 3*7 - 1*8 \\ 1*1 - 2*7 \end{Bmatrix} = \begin{Bmatrix} 13 \\ 13 \\ -13 \end{Bmatrix}$$

The cross product is also represented by a matrix-vector multiplication. The first vector is represented in a cross-product operator, and the second vector postmultiplies it:

$$c = a \times b = C(a) * b = \begin{bmatrix} 0 & -a_z & a_y \\ a_z & 0 & -a_x \\ -a_y & a_x & 0 \end{bmatrix} \begin{Bmatrix} b_x \\ b_y \\ b_z \end{Bmatrix} = \begin{Bmatrix} a_y b_z - a_z b_y \\ a_z b_x - a_x b_z \\ a_x b_y - a_y b_x \end{Bmatrix}$$

$$c = a \times b = \begin{bmatrix} 0 & -3 & 2 \\ 3 & 0 & -1 \\ -2 & 1 & 0 \end{bmatrix} \begin{Bmatrix} 7 \\ 1 \\ 8 \end{Bmatrix} = \begin{Bmatrix} 13 \\ 13 \\ -13 \end{Bmatrix}$$

Reversing the order of the vectors changes the sign of the result, but not the magnitude:

$$a \times b = -b \times a$$

It is also clear that the cross product of a vector with itself is the null vector:

$$c = a \times a = \left\{ \begin{matrix} 0 \\ 0 \\ 0 \end{matrix} \right\}$$

The cross product, coupled with the square root of an inner product, is an easy way to determine the unit norms of the plane defined by the two intersecting lines represented by vectors a and b (defined earlier):

$$c = a \times b = \left\{ \begin{matrix} 13 \\ 13 \\ 13 \end{matrix} \right\}$$

Thus,

$$\|c\| = \sqrt{c^T \cdot c} = 22.517$$

and

$$\left\{ \begin{matrix} n_x \\ n_y \\ n_z \end{matrix} \right\} = \left\{ \begin{matrix} 13/22.517 \\ 13/22.517 \\ -13/22.517 \end{matrix} \right\} = \left\{ \begin{matrix} 0.57735 \\ 0.57735 \\ -0.57735 \end{matrix} \right\}$$

C.1.2.3 Outer product   The outer product of two vectors produces a two-dimensional result called a matrix. The two vectors do not need to be the same length. If vector a has m elements in it, and vector b has n elements in it, then the outer product of a and b is a matrix with m rows and n columns. Formally, if

$$a = \left\{ \begin{matrix} a_1 \\ a_2 \\ \dots \\ a_m \end{matrix} \right\}$$

and

$$b = \left\{ \begin{matrix} b_1 \\ b_2 \\ \dots \\ b_n \end{matrix} \right\}$$

then the outer product is

$$C_{i,j} = a_i b_j$$

or

$$C = ab^T$$

or

$$C = \begin{bmatrix} a_1 b_1 & a_1 b_2 & \cdots & a_1 b_n \\ a_2 b_1 & a_2 b_2 & \cdots & a_2 b_n \\ \cdots & \cdots & \cdots & \cdots \\ a_m b_1 & a_m b_2 & \cdots & a_m b_n \end{bmatrix}$$

If a and b are the same length, then the outer product is a square matrix. If a and b are the same vector, then the outer product is a square and symmetric matrix.

If c is an $m \times n$ matrix, read m by n, then the transpose of that matrix is an $n \times m$ matrix in which every element $C_{i,j}$ has swapped positions with every element $C_{j,i}$. That is,

$$C_{i,j}^T = C_{j,i}$$

The following numerical examples make these fundamental operations clear: If

$$a = \begin{Bmatrix} 2 \\ 3 \end{Bmatrix}$$

and

$$b = \begin{Bmatrix} -4 \\ 5 \\ -6 \end{Bmatrix}$$

then the outer product is

$$C = ab^T = \begin{Bmatrix} 2 \\ 3 \end{Bmatrix} \{-4 \quad 5 \quad -6\}$$

$$= \begin{bmatrix} (2)(-4) & (2)(5) & (2)(-6) \\ (3)(-4) & (3)(5) & (3)(-6) \end{bmatrix} = \begin{bmatrix} -8 & 10 & -12 \\ -12 & 15 & -18 \end{bmatrix}$$

and the transpose of C is

$$C^T = \begin{bmatrix} -8 & -12 \\ 10 & 15 \\ -12 & -18 \end{bmatrix}$$

In general, if the order of the two vectors is reversed, the resulting matrix is the transpose of the original matrix.

$$C = ab^T \neq ba^T$$

but

$$C^T = ba^T = (ab^T)^T$$

In the preceding example, the vector a is a 2×1 vector. The vector b is a 3×1 vector. The matrix resulting from the outer product of a and b^T is a 2×3 matrix.

C.2 Matrices

C.2.1 Matrix Addition

Two matrices C and D can be added or subtracted using the usual rules of addition and subtraction. The commutative and associative laws hold for matrix addition and subtraction. For this operation to be defined, the matrices must be compatible with each other for the addition operation. This means that C and D must have the same number of rows *and* columns. If this is so, then the resulting matrix is the same size as the original matrices, and its elements are simply the sum or difference of an element-wise operation. The compact way of stating this is

$$A = C + D$$

which means

$$A_{i,j} = C_{i,j} + D_{i,j}$$

Similarly,

$$B = C - D$$

means

$$B_{i,j} = C_{i,j} - D_{i,j}$$

The *commutative law* holds:

$$A + B = B + A$$

and

$$A - B = -B + A$$

The *associative law* also holds:

$$A + (B + C) = (A + B) + C$$

The *transpose* of a sum is the sum of the transposes:

$$A = B + C$$

implies

$$A^T = B^T + C^T$$

C.2.2 Matrix/Vector and Matrix/Matrix Multiplication

The general product C of A times B is

$$C_{i,j} = \sum_{k=1}^{p} A_{i,k} B_{k,j}$$

where the A matrix is of size $m \times p$, the B matrix is of size $p \times n$, and the product matrix C is of size $m \times n$. Note that the number of columns in the A matrix must equal the number of rows in the B matrix for this operation to take place. That is, A and B must be conformable for multiplication. In this operation, the A matrix is said to *premultiply* the B matrix, or the B matrix is said to *postmultiply* the A matrix.

Example C.2

$$A = \begin{bmatrix} 1 & 2 & 3 \\ 4 & 5 & 6 \end{bmatrix}$$

$$B = \begin{bmatrix} 2 & -1 \\ 6 & -4 \\ 7 & 7 \end{bmatrix}$$

$$C = AB = \begin{bmatrix} 1 & 2 & 3 \\ 4 & 5 & 6 \end{bmatrix} \begin{bmatrix} 2 & -1 \\ 6 & -4 \\ 7 & 7 \end{bmatrix} = \begin{bmatrix} 35 & 12 \\ 80 & 18 \end{bmatrix}$$

where, for instance, $C_{2,1} = $ the inner product of row 2 in matrix A and column 1 in matrix B, or $C_{2,1} = (4)(2) + (5)(6) + (6)(7) = 80$.

The *associative law* in multiplication gives

$$A(BC) = (AB)C$$

Likewise, the *distributive law* in multiplication gives

$$A(B + C) = AB + AC$$

However, the *commutative law* in multiplication does not hold in general:

$$AB \neq BA$$

It is easy to see that the general definition of matrix multiplication defines the special case of a matrix postmultiplied by a column vector because a column vector can be thought of as a matrix with n rows and one column. In a similar way, a row vector (the transpose of a column vector) premultiplying a matrix is also defined because the row vector can be thought of as a $1 \times m$ matrix. In these cases, the answer is always a column vector or row vector as shown in the following example. Let

$$A = \begin{bmatrix} 1 & 2 \\ 3 & 4 \\ 5 & 6 \end{bmatrix}$$

$$x = \begin{Bmatrix} 7 \\ 8 \end{Bmatrix}$$

$$y = \begin{Bmatrix} 9 \\ 10 \\ 11 \end{Bmatrix}$$

Then,

$$Ax = b$$

yields

$$\begin{bmatrix} 1 & 2 \\ 3 & 4 \\ 5 & 6 \end{bmatrix} \begin{Bmatrix} 7 \\ 8 \end{Bmatrix} = \begin{Bmatrix} 1*7+2*8 \\ 3*7+4*8 \\ 5*7+6*8 \end{Bmatrix} = \begin{Bmatrix} 23 \\ 53 \\ 83 \end{Bmatrix}$$

and

$$y^T A = d^T$$

yields

$$\begin{Bmatrix} 9 & 10 & 11 \end{Bmatrix} \begin{bmatrix} 1 & 2 \\ 3 & 4 \\ 5 & 6 \end{bmatrix} = \begin{Bmatrix} (9*1+10*3+11*5) & (9*2+10*4+11*6) \end{Bmatrix}$$

$$= \begin{Bmatrix} 94 & 124 \end{Bmatrix}$$

where

$$d = \begin{Bmatrix} 94 \\ 124 \end{Bmatrix}$$

C.2.3 Matrix Inversion

Matrix division is an undefined process except for the trivial case of a matrix of size 1×1, which is a scalar. Instead, the operation called inversion is defined. Formally, inversion can only be performed on a square matrix of size $n \times n$ and *rank n*. That is, the square matrix must be nonsingular. The inverse of a matrix, when premultiplied or postmultiplied by the original matrix, will yield the identity matrix, which is a diagonal matrix with unity on the diagonal. The symbol A^{-1} denotes the inverse of a matrix A and is read "A inverse." Thus,

$$A^{-1}A = AA^{-1} = I$$

If one writes algebraic statement

$$Ax = b$$

then the vector x can be found by premultiplying both sides of the expression by A^{-1}, to wit:

$$Ax = b$$

$$A^{-1}Ax = A^{-1}b$$

$$Ix = A^{-1}b$$

$$x = A^{-1}b$$

The procedure for calculating the inverse of the 2×2 matrix A is this. Given A,

$$A = \begin{bmatrix} a_{1,1} & a_{1,2} \\ a_{2,1} & a_{2,2} \end{bmatrix}$$

The inverse is

$$A^{-1} = \frac{1}{(a_{1,1}a_{2,2} - a_{2,1}a_{1,2})} \begin{bmatrix} a_{2,2} & -a_{1,2} \\ -a_{2,1} & a_{1,1} \end{bmatrix}$$

The term in the preceding parentheses is called the *determinant*. If the determinant is nonzero, then the matrix is nonsingular, and the inverse of A exists. If the determinant is zero, the matrix is singular, and the inverse is not defined.

The inversion of matrices larger than 2×2 is a difficult procedure by hand. Several well-known algorithms are available on-line; others can be found in linear algebra texts. At the end of this appendix, the reader will find an algorithm that features full pivoting for numerical precision. The author has used this program for many years, and it has performed without flaw.

C.2.4 *Matrix Partitioning*

A vector or matrix can be subdivided into smaller units called submatrices or subvectors. This process is called partitioning. For instance, if a vector has m rows, the first p of them may make up one subvector, while the remaining m-p elements make up a second subvector:

$$a_{mx1} = \begin{Bmatrix} a_{(1,1)} \\ \cdots \\ a_{(p,1)} \\ a_{(p+1,1)} \\ \cdots \\ a_{(m,1)} \end{Bmatrix} = \begin{Bmatrix} \hat{a}_1 \\ \hat{a}_2 \end{Bmatrix}$$

In the more general case of the $m \times n$ matrix A, it can be partitioned into submatrices of sizes $p \times q$, $(m - p) \times q$, $p \times (n - q)$, and $(m - p) \times (n - q)$. For example, let A be the 3×4 matrix shown here:

$$A = \begin{bmatrix} 1 & 2 & 3 & 4 \\ 5 & 6 & 7 & 8 \\ 9 & 10 & 11 & 12 \end{bmatrix}$$

If $p = 2$ and $q = 3$, then the four submatrices are

$$A_{11} = \begin{bmatrix} 1 & 2 & 3 \\ 5 & 6 & 7 \end{bmatrix}$$

$$A_{12} = \begin{bmatrix} 4 \\ 8 \end{bmatrix}$$

$$A_{21} = \begin{bmatrix} 9 & 10 & 11 \end{bmatrix}$$

$$A_{22} = \begin{bmatrix} 12 \end{bmatrix}$$

and the completely equivalent definition of A becomes

$$A = \begin{bmatrix} A_{11} & A_{12} \\ A_{21} & A_{22} \end{bmatrix}$$

Note the subtle difference between defining the elements of a matrix and defining submatrices. The elements of a matrix are specified with lowercase letters, and the first and second indices are separated with commas. Submatrices are still matrices and so use an uppercase letter. Furthermore, commas do not separate the indices. Obviously, one can subdivide a matrix into any number of submatrices, which might require commas to separate indices if the partitioning becomes excessive.

C.3   What Can You Do with Linear Algebra?

The techniques of linear algebra are used throughout the text to solve simultaneous equations, to find initial conditions for differential equations, and to minimize or maximize a function. Several types of problem are regarded in this section to illustrate the use of the techniques.

C.3.1   Solution of Simultaneous Equations—A Square System

If n simultaneous linear equations exist with n unknown variables, then the easiest method to solve for the unknowns uses the inverse of the coefficient matrix. For example, consider the equation of a plane in three-dimensional space:

$$Ax + By + Cz = D$$

Suppose three measurements from a plane give the following results:

X	Y	Z	D
1	2	3	4
3	2	1	4
1	3	1	5

What are the coefficients (A, B, C) of the plane equation? The answer is easily determined by arranging the problem in the form of a linear algebra problem. Let the coefficient matrix be called E, the vector of unknowns be called w, and the vector of required results be called b. Then

$$E = \begin{bmatrix} 1 & 2 & 3 \\ 3 & 2 & 1 \\ 1 & 3 & 1 \end{bmatrix}, \quad w = \begin{Bmatrix} A \\ B \\ C \end{Bmatrix}, \quad \text{and} \quad b = \begin{Bmatrix} 4 \\ 4 \\ 5 \end{Bmatrix}$$

This matrix and these vectors, written as shown next, express the problem at hand:

$$Ew = b$$

The solution is

$$w = E^{-1}b$$

The numerical results are

$$E^{-1} = \begin{bmatrix} -0.0625 & 0.4375 & -0.2500 \\ -0.1250 & -0.1250 & 0.5000 \\ 0.4375 & -0.0625 & -0.2500 \end{bmatrix}$$

whence

$$w = \begin{Bmatrix} 0.25 \\ 1.5 \\ 0.25 \end{Bmatrix} = \begin{Bmatrix} A \\ B \\ C \end{Bmatrix}$$

These results are easily verified by substitution into the original equation.

This is the most basic problem that the reader will face—a square system in which the number of equations equals the number of unknowns and the equations are linearly independent. The next example considers the overconstrained problem, which has many more equations than unknowns.

C.3.2 Solution of Simultaneous Equations—More Equations Than Unknowns

C.3.2.1 Left Pseudoinverse The situation in which many more equations than unknowns are available arises when many experiments are performed on a problem in the hope that the "strong law of large numbers" will yield a consensus value for unknowns. The reader may recall the venerable least-squares technique, also called regression, for curve fitting. The least-squares method solves the problem of more equations than unknowns. For example, suppose that the following measurements were made of an engine on a test stand. The engine speed, manifold pressure, and power were measured, and we desire a linear equation of the form

$$\text{hp} = C_1(\text{rpm}) + C_2(\text{MAP})$$

The test data are shown in Table C.1.

Call the coefficient matrix A, the result vector b, and the unknown vector x. That is,

$$A = \begin{bmatrix} 1900 & 25 \\ 1800 & 20 \\ 2300 & 23 \\ 2000 & 21 \\ 2100 & 22 \\ 2200 & 19 \end{bmatrix}, \quad b = \begin{Bmatrix} 220 \\ 190 \\ 230 \\ 205 \\ 215 \\ 205 \end{Bmatrix} \quad \text{and} \quad x = \begin{Bmatrix} C_1 \\ C_2 \end{Bmatrix}$$

The problem is now expressed concisely as

$$Ax = b$$

The vector x is $n(=2) \times 1$ in length, the vector b is $m(=6) \times 1$ in length, and the matrix A is rectangular with size $m(=6) \times n(=2)$. Because A is not square, an inverse cannot be calculated directly. However, if one premultiplies both sides of the preceding expression by the transpose of A, one obtains

$$A^T A x = A^T b$$

The left-hand side now has a square matrix $A^T A$, which may be nonsingular. If it is nonsingular, then its inverse exists, and both sides of the equation can be multiplied by the inverse of $A^T A$:

$$(A^T A)^{-1}(A^T A)x = (A^T A)^{-1} A^T b$$

Table C.1   Test data

rpm	MAP	hp
1900	25	220
1800	20	190
2300	23	230
2000	21	205
2100	22	215
2200	19	205

or

$$x = (A^T A)^{-1} A^T b$$

The grouping $(A^T A)^{-1} A^T$ is called the left pseudoinverse of A. Thus the solution is written in the concise form:

$$x = Pb$$

where

$$P = (A^T A)^{-1} A^T$$

In the problem just presented, the left pseudoinverse of A is

$$P = \begin{bmatrix} -0.0011 & -0.0002 & 0.0004 & 0.0001 & 0.0001 & 0.0010 \\ 0.1129 & 0.0248 & -0.0252 & 0.0003 & -0.0008 & -0.0910 \end{bmatrix}$$

This leads to the coefficients

$$x = \begin{Bmatrix} C_1 \\ C_2 \end{Bmatrix} = \begin{Bmatrix} 0.05 \\ 5.0 \end{Bmatrix}$$

Again, these results can be verified by using them with the original measurements.

No guarantee exists that $A^T A$ is nonsingular. If the left pseudoinverse still cannot be calculated, then singular value decomposition is the next method of choice.

C.3.2.2 Singular value decomposition

Singular value decomposition proceeds by representing the A matrix as a product of three matrices:

$$A = UWV^T$$

$$U^T U = I$$

$$VV^T = I$$

A is the original $m \times n$ matrix, U is an $m \times n$ column-orthogonal matrix, W is a semidefinite $n \times n$ diagonal matrix with positive or zero-value elements on the diagonal, and V^T is a $n \times n$ orthogonal matrix. One can find the algorithm to decompose A on the Internet or in [2]. To solve for x from $Ax = b$, decompose A into its special three matrix representation, and substitute this expansion into the original equation:

$$UWV^T x = b$$

Premultiply both sides by U^T. From the definition of U^T, the product $U^T U$ is the identity matrix, and so the problem changes to

$$(U^T U) WV^T x = U^T b$$

$$IWV^T x = U^T b$$

$$WV^T x = U^T b$$

For the moment, assume all of the diagonal elements of W are nonzero. If this is the case, then the inverse is a diagonal matrix with the reciprocals of the diagonal elements of W. Premultiply both sides of the equation by W^{-1}. This changes the equation to

$$W^{-1}WV^Tx = W^{-1}U^Tb$$

$$V^Tx = W^{-1}U^Tb$$

Finally, premultiply both sides of the expression by V. From the definition of V, the product VV^T is the identity matrix, leaving the final solution for x:

$$VV^Tx = VW^{-1}U^Tb$$

$$x = VW^{-1}U^Tb$$

One should object that if W has diagonal elements that are zero then the inverse of W is not defined. Here is the one time when childhood fantasies of dividing by zero are permitted. When $w_i = 0$, then substitute 0 for $1/w_i$ in the inverse of W. The reasons for this are beyond the scope of this text.

C.3.2.3 Optimal best guess
The example problems have been designed to have "nice" solutions so that the method is not obfuscated by discussion of correlation coefficients. Furthermore, no attention was paid to the magnitude of the values in the solution vector. However, a time will come when the solution vector must be *constrained*, that is, the values must be required to lie between some upper and lower limits. Many methods are available; here is one in which the constraints are "soft," but active.

Imagine that the original problem is transformed into an error minimization statement. That is, rewrite the original problem:

$$Ax = b$$

into an error statement such that a perfect answer yields zero error:

$$\varepsilon = Ax - b$$

Obviously the vector ε is $m \times 1$, where m is the length of the b vector. It is helpful to look at the error equation in an expanded form:

$$\begin{Bmatrix} \varepsilon_1 \\ \vdots \\ \varepsilon_i \\ \vdots \\ \varepsilon_m \end{Bmatrix} = \begin{bmatrix} a_{1,1} & \cdots & a_{1,n} \\ \vdots & \ddots & \vdots \\ a_{i,1} & \cdots & a_{i,n} \\ \vdots & \ddots & \vdots \\ a_{m,1} & \cdots & a_{m,n} \end{bmatrix} \begin{Bmatrix} x_1 \\ \vdots \\ x_n \end{Bmatrix} - \begin{Bmatrix} b_1 \\ \vdots \\ b_i \\ \vdots \\ b_m \end{Bmatrix}$$

The ith equation is

$$\varepsilon_i = a_{i,1}x_1 + a_{i,2}x_2 + \cdots + a_{i,n}x_n - b_i$$

Real-world effects such as measurement error, sensor error, and so forth conspire to make some measurements not as useful as others. If one has a sense of the relative worth of one measurement to another, then one can weight each measurement with some factor. Let the positive-definite diagonal matrix Q be the weighting factor for the error equations. If the measurement error (standard deviation) is known, then the Q matrix can be set to the inverses of the squared standard deviations:

$$Q = \begin{bmatrix} \dfrac{1}{\sigma_1^2} & & & & \\ & \ddots & & & \\ & & \dfrac{1}{\sigma_j^2} & & \\ & & & \ddots & \\ & & & & \dfrac{1}{\sigma_m^2} \end{bmatrix}$$

Calculate the square of the error and call that e^2:

$$e^2 = \varepsilon^T Q \varepsilon = (x^T A^T - b^T) Q (Ax - b)$$

At this point, the process is proceeding just like the least-squares method. But now, the constraints on the solution variables are introduced. If one knows that the maximum value of the ith solution variable is $x\,\text{max}_i$, then a weighting matrix for soft constraints is the positive-definite diagonal matrix R, given by

$$R = \begin{bmatrix} \dfrac{1}{x\,\text{max}_1^2} & & & & \\ & \ddots & & & \\ & & \dfrac{1}{x\,\text{max}_i^2} & & \\ & & & \ddots & \\ & & & & \dfrac{1}{x\,\text{max}_n^2} \end{bmatrix}$$

The penalty for large values of a solution variable is thus

$$p^2 = x^T R x$$

The total objective function to minimize is given by the addition of the error function and the penalty function:

$$J = e^2 + p^2 = (x^T A^T - b^T) Q (Ax - b) + x^T R x$$

Calculate the derivative of J with respect to x, set the derivative to zero, and then solve for x. The result is

$$x = (A^T Q A + R)^{-1} A^T Q b$$

Using the engine data of the preceding example, presuming the measurement errors to have unity value, and declaring that the maximum value (in a soft sense) is 0.1 and 4.0 for C_1 and C_2, then the best guesses for C_1 and C_2 are

$$x = \begin{Bmatrix} C_1 \\ C_2 \end{Bmatrix} = \begin{Bmatrix} 0.0501 \\ 4.9930 \end{Bmatrix}$$

One sees that the soft constraint of 4.0 for C_2 was violated. Nevertheless, this technique did attempt to rein in the value for C_2.

The preceding techniques work with any A matrix, though they are most strongly associated with a system that has more equations than unknowns, that is, $m > n$. If one has more unknowns than equations, then the method of Tikhonov is suggested.

C.3.3   Solution of Simultaneous Equations—More Unknowns Than Equations

Suppose one is given a matrix of observations A, which is $m \times n$, $m < n$, where each row represents a single observation and each column contains an observed value that is multiplied by an as-yet-undetermined coefficient x. A column x, $n \times 1$, contains the undetermined coefficients, and a column b, $m \times 1$, is a vector of desired results. This matrix and these columns form the following expression:

$$Ax = b$$

The column of coefficients x is desired such that $e = Ax - b$ minimizes some norm of e. The solution is straightforward using the Tikhonov method.

Through a series of elementary matrix manipulations, A decomposes into three matrices that are named L, M, and R. That is,

$$Ax = b$$

becomes

$$L^{-1}MRx = b$$

As implied, the L matrix is guaranteed invertible. The R matrix is also guaranteed to be invertible. The M matrix partitions into the particular form:

$$M = \begin{bmatrix} I & C \end{bmatrix}$$

The C submatrix represents constraints among some of the coefficients. Substitute the definition of M into the expression above it to get

$$L^{-1}\begin{bmatrix} I & C \end{bmatrix}Rx = b$$

I is the $m \times m$ identity matrix, and C is of size $m \times (n - m)$. Define a new variable $y = Rx$, and partition y into y_1 and y_2, where y_1 is an $m \times 1$ vector, and y_2 is an $(n - m) \times 1$ vector. Multiply each side of the preceding equation by L to get

$$[I \quad C] \begin{Bmatrix} y_1 \\ y_2 \end{Bmatrix} = Lb$$

From this, y_2 defines y_1:

$$y_1 = Lb - Cy_2$$

Now, find the norm of the y vector

$$\|y\| = \left[\begin{pmatrix} y_1 \\ y_2 \end{pmatrix}^T \begin{pmatrix} y_1 \\ y_2 \end{pmatrix} \right]^{1/2} = \left[\begin{pmatrix} Lb - Cy_2 \\ y_2 \end{pmatrix}^T \begin{pmatrix} Lb - Cy_2 \\ y_2 \end{pmatrix} \right]^{1/2}$$

$$= \left[(Lb - Cy_2)^T (Lb - Cy_2) + y_2^T y_2 \right]^{1/2}$$

To minimize the norm, differentiate the norm with respect to y_2, set the result to zero, and solve for y_2:

$$\frac{\partial \|y\|}{\partial y_2} = \frac{1}{2} \|y\|^{-1} [2C^T C y_2 - 2C^T Lb + 2y_2] = 0$$

$$\therefore$$

$$y_2 = (I + C^T C)^{-1} C^T Lb$$

Recover y_1 from its definition:

$$y_1 = Lb - Cy_2 = [I - C(I + C^T C)^{-1} C^T] Lb$$

Finally, recover x from y:

$$x = R^{-1} \begin{Bmatrix} y_1 \\ y_2 \end{Bmatrix}$$

The expression for y_2 is Tikhonov-esque. Without the identity matrix, this would simply be the left pseudoinverse. In Tikhonov's development, the identity matrix is replaced with a diagonal matrix of weights W, selected to make $(W + C^T C)$ strongly diagonal and therefore nonsingular.

C.3.4 Core Set of Matrix and Vector Functions

A well-formed set of computer routines that do the matrix and vector manipulations described in this chapter will pay off in spades. Table C.2 suggests a minimum set of useful functions. Code for each of the routines is supplied in a form of BASIC™ for your help. Of course, different languages have different capabilities. For instance, Visual BASIC™ does not require the user to pass the declared size of an array when it is used as an argument. That information is part of the array header. On the other hand, the column-major language FORTRAN requires the column length when a two-dimensional array is passed. Without that information, hideous scrambling of data will surely ruin your day. So, here are three very good pieces of advice. First, use a given routine listed here as a "go-by." Consider the code you see here to be PDL (program design language) or pseudocode. Second, code to a broad standard. That is, do not code to take advantage of some obscure capability of a language unless you never intend to make the code transportable. Further, when passing arrays for instance, always pass the declared size of the array (number of rows and number of columns dimensioned or declared) as well as the number of rows and columns to be used in the current operation. Third, test the routines with many examples of various sizes and problems (like singularities, zero lengths, incompatible lengths, etc.). The greater the number of problems you catch early on, the greater will be your success later on.

```
Sub cross(a( ) As Single, b( ) As Single, c( ) As Single)
'
'      The cross-product of A and B is returned
'      in C.
'
'      Copyright 1991
'      Mark E. Dreier
'      Unpublished - All Rights Reserved
'
c(1) = a(2) * b(3) − a(3) * b(2)
c(2) = a(3) * b(1) − a(1) * b(3)
c(3) = a(1) * b(2) − a(2) * b(1)
End Sub
Sub mtxeql (asv( ) As Single, a( ) As Single, nr As Integer, nc As Integer)
'
'      This routine copies a into asv. The matrix a is
'      of size nr × nc.
'
'      Copyright 1991
'      Mark E. Dreier
'      Unpublished - All Rights Reserved
'
Dim i As Integer
Dim j As Integer
'
For i = 1 To nr
  For j = 1 To nc
    asv(i, j) = a(i, j)
  Next j
Next i
End Sub

Sub mtxmpy(a( ) As Single, b( ) As Single, c( ) As Single, nra As Integer, nca
As Integer, ncb As Integer)
'
'      This routine post-multiplies matrix a by matrix b
```

Table C.2   Recommended set of linear algebra routines

Function name	Symbolic action	Description
MTXCLEAR	$C = \text{NULL}$	Simple initialization for a matrix. This routine places zero into each cell in the $m \times n$ matrix C.
MTXMPY	$C = A * B$	Matrix-matrix multiply—this routine multiplies matrices A and B together to get C. If A is $m \times n$, and B is $p \times q$, then C is $m \times q$, and n must equal p for the operation to be defined.
MTXVECMPY	$w = A * v$	Matrix-vector multiply—this routine postmultiplies matrix A by vector v to produce vector w. If A is $m \times n$, then v must be $n \times 1$, and w will be $m \times 1$.
MTXADD	$C = A(+ \text{ or } -)B$	Matrix add/subtract—this routine adds matrix B to matrix A, or subtracts matrix B from matrix A. A user-option flag determines which action is desired. If A is $m \times n$, then B and C must also be $m \times n$.
MTXPLACE	$B_{k,l} = A_{i,j}$	Submatrix placement—this routine places the $m \times n$ matrix A into the larger matrix B, such that element i,j in A is located at element k,l in B. Special care must be taken to ensure that A will fit in the boundaries of B.
VECCLEAR	$W = \text{NULL}$	Simple initialization for a vector. This routine places zero into each cell in the n length vector w.
VECADD	$w = u(+ \text{ or } -)v$	Vector add/subtract—this routine adds vector v to vector u, or subtracts vector v from vector u. A user-option flag determines which action is desired. If u is $m \times 1$, then v and w must also be $m \times 1$.
INNERPROD	$w = u^T * v$	Inner product—this routine calculates the inner product of two $n \times 1$ vectors u and v. The scalar result is w.
CROSSPROD	$w = u \times v$	Cross product—this routine calculates the cross product of two 3×1 vectors u and v. The result is a 3×1 vector w.
OUTERPROD	$W = u * v^T$	Outer product—this routine calculates the outer product of the $m \times 1$ vector u and the $n \times 1$ vector v to produce the $m \times n$ matrix W.
TRANSPOSE	$B = A^T$	Transpose—this routine places in matrix B the $n \times m$ transpose of the $m \times n$ matrix A.
MTXINV	$B = A^{-1}$	Matrix inversion—this routine produces the $n \times n$ inverse of the $n \times n$ matrix A, if it exists. If A is singular, a flag indicating failure should be returned, and the output should be regarded as poison.

```
'    and places the result in matric c. The number of
'    rows in a is NRA, the number of columns in a is
'    NCA and the number of columns in b is ncb. The
'    number of rows in b is assumed to be the number of
'    columns in a. The c matrix is of size nra × ncb.
'
'    Copyright 1991
'    Mark E. Dreier
'    Unpublished - All Rights Reserved
'
Dim i As Integer
Dim j As Integer
Dim k As Integer
Dim sum As Single
'
For i = 1 To nra
   For j = 1 To ncb
      sum = 0#
      For k = 1 To nca
         sum = sum + a(i, k) * b(k, j)
      Next k
      c(i, j) = sum
   Next j
Next i
End Sub

Sub mtxtranspose(at( ) As Single, a( ) As Single, nra As Integer, nca As Integer)
'
'    This routine returns the transpose of matrix a( )
'    in matrix at( ). Matrix a( ) is nra by nca big.
'    The transpose is nca by nra of course.
'
'    Copyright 1991
'    Mark E. Dreier
'    Unpublished - All Rights Reserved
'
Dim i As Integer
Dim j As Integer
'
For i = 1 To nra
   For j = 1 To nca
      at( j, i) = a(i, j)
   Next j
Next i
End Sub

Sub mtxadd(a( ) As Single, b( ) As Single, c( ) As Single, nr As Integer, nc As Integer,
iop As Integer)
'
'    This if iop = 1, then this routine adds the upper left
'    nr × nc matrix in A to the upper left nr × nc matrix
'    in B to generate the upper left nr × nc matrix in c.
```

```
'       If iop = 2, then this routine subtracts the b matrix
'       from the a matrix and puts the result in c. If iop = 3,
'       then this routine subtracts a from b and puts the
'       result in c. If iop = 4, then c = −a − b.
'
'       Copyright 1991
'       Mark E. Dreier
'       Unpublished - All Rights Reserved
'
Dim i As Integer
Dim j As Integer
'
Select Case iop
Case 1
   For i = 1 To nr
      For j = 1 To nc
         c(i, j) = a(i, j) + b(i, j)
      Next j
   Next i
Case 2
   For i = 1 To nr
      For j = 1 To nc
         c(i, j) = a(i, j) − b(i, j)
      Next j
   Next i
Case 3
   For i = 1 To nr
      For j = 1 To nc
         c(i, j) = b(i, j) − a(i, j)
      Next j
   Next i
Case 4
   For i = 1 To nr
      For j = 1 To nc
         c(i, j) = −(a(i, j) + b(i, j))
      Next j
   Next i
Case Else
   For i = 1 To nr
      For j = 1 To nc
         c(i, j) = 0#
      Next j
   Next i
End Select
End Sub

Sub mtxinv(x( ) As Single, n As Integer, det As Single)
'
'       This routine calculates the inverse of the upper
'       N × N submatrix of X in place. It also calculates
'       the determinant and places it in DET.
'
```

```
'     The author is unknown. This QuickBASIC implementation
'     was coded by Mark E. Dreier.
'
ReDim irow(n) As Integer
ReDim icol(n) As Integer
ReDim b1(n)
ReDim c1(n)
Dim am As Single
Dim ar As Single
Dim epsilon As Single
Dim i As Integer
Dim j As Integer
Dim k As Integer
Dim ik As Integer
Dim ikk As Integer
Dim ki As Integer
Dim kj As Integer
Dim kc As Integer
Dim sf As Single
Dim temp2 As Single
'
'     Determine the machine precision.
'
epsilon = 1#
While 1# + epsilon > 1#
    epsilon = epsilon/2
Wend
sf = Sqr(epsilon)
'
det = 1#
'
'     Locate pivot
'
For k = 1 To n
    am = 0#
    For j = k To n
        For i = k To n
            ar = x(i, j) * x(i, j)
            If ar > am Then
                am = ar
                irow(k) = i
                icol(k) = j
            End If
        Next i
    Next j
    If am <= sf Then
        det = 0#
        irow(k) = k
    icol(k) = k
Else
  If irow(k) <> k Then
      det = -det
```

```
  For j = 1 To n
      temp2 = x(irow(k), j)
      x(irow(k), j) = x(k, j)
      x(k, j) = temp2
  Next j
 End If
 If icol(k) <> k Then
   det = −det
   For i = 1 To n
      temp2 = x(i, icol(k))
      x(i, icol(k)) = x(i, k)
      x(i, k) = temp2
   Next i
 End If
 temp2 = x(k, k)
 det = det * temp2
 For j = 1 To n
   If j = k Then
      b1( j) = 1# / temp2
      c1( j) = 1#
   Else
      b1( j) = −x(k,  j) / temp2
      c1( j) = x(j,  k)
      x( j,  k) = 0#
   End If
   x(k, j) = 0#
 Next j
 For  j = 1 To n
   For  i = 1 To n
      x(i, j) = x(i, j) + b1(j) * c1(i)
   Next i
 Next j
 End If
Next k
'
' Now rearrange the matrix into final form
'
For kc = 1 To n
   k = n − kc + 1
   If irow(k) <> k Then
      ikk = irow(k)
      ik = k
      For i = 1 To n
         temp2 = x(i, ik)
         x(i, ik) = x(i, ikk)
         x(i, ikk) = temp2
      Next i
   End If
   If icol(k) <> k Then
      kj = icol(k)
      ki = k
      For j = 1 To n
```

```
            temp2 = x(kj, j)
            x(kj, j) = x(ki, j)
            x(ki, j) = temp2
         Next j
      End If
   Next kc
End Sub


Sub mtxplace(a( ) As Single, nra As Integer, nca As Integer, b( ) As Single, ib As Integer,
jb As Integer, iopt As Integer)
'
'     This routine places the nra x nca matrix a in
'     the matrix b at location ib, jb. The option
'     flag iopt has this effect:
'
'     IOPT   Action
'       1      A overwrites B.
'       2     −A overwrites B.
'       3      A is added to B.
'       4     −A is added to B.
'
'     Copyright 1991
'     Mark E. Dreier
'     Unpublished - All Rights Reserved
'
Dim i As Integer
Dim j As Integer
Dim k As Integer
Dim sum As Single
'
Select Case iopt
Case 1
   For i = 1 To nra
      For j = 1 To nca
         b(ib + i − 1, jb + j − 1) = a(i, j)
      Next j
   Next i
Case 2
   For i = 1 To nra
      For j = 1 To nca
         b(ib + i − 1, jb + j − 1) = −a(i, j)
      Next j
   Next i
Case 3
   For i = 1 To nra
      For j = 1 To nca
         b(ib + i − 1, jb + j − 1) = b(ib + i − 1, jb + j − 1) + a(i, j)
      Next j
   Next i
Case 4
   For i = 1 To nra
```

```
    For j = 1 To nca
        b(ib + i − 1, jb + j − 1) = b(ib + i − 1, jb + j − 1) − a(i, j)
    Next j
  Next i
Case Else
End Select
End Sub

Sub mtxvecmpy(a( ) As Single, b( ) As Single, c( ) As Single, nra As Integer,
nca As Integer)
'
'    This routine post-multiplies matrix a by vector b
'    and places the result in vector c. The number of
'    rows in a is NRA, the number of columns in a is
'    NCA.
'
'    Copyright 1991
'    Mark E. Dreier
'    Unpublished - All Rights Reserved
'
Dim i As Integer
Dim j As Integer
Dim sum As Single
'
For i = 1 To nra
  sum = 0#
  For j = 1 To nca
    sum = sum + a(i, j) * b( j)
  Next j
  c(i) = sum
Next i
End Sub

Sub outerp(x( ) As Single, y( ) As Single, z( ) As Single, n As Integer)
'
'    This routine calculates the outer product of two
'    vectors x and y, and places the result in matrix z.
'    The length of the vectors is assumed to be n.
'
'    Copyright 1991
'    Mark E. Dreier
'    Unpublished - All Rights Reserved
'
Dim i As Integer
Dim j As Integer
Dim xi As Single
'
For i = 1 To n
  xi = x(i)
  For j = 1 To n
    z(i, j) = xi * y( j)
  Next j
```

```
Next i
End Sub

Sub vecadd(a( ) As Single, b( ) As Single, c( ) As Single, n As Integer, iop As Integer)
'
'    This if iop = 1, then this routine adds the vector
'    A to the vector B to produce vector C. If iop = 2,
'    then this routine subtracts the B vector from the
'    A vector and puts the result in C. If iop = 3,
'    then this routine subtracts A from B and puts the
'    result in C. If iop = 4, then C = −A − B.
'
'    Copyright 1991
'    Mark E. Dreier
'    Unpublished - All Rights Reserved
'
Dim i As Integer
'
Select Case iop
Case 1
    For i = 1 To n
        c(i) = a(i) + b(i)
    Next i
Case 2
    For i = 1 To n
        c(i) = a(i) − b(i)
    Next i
Case 3
    For i = 1 To n
        c(i) = b(i) − a(i)
    Next i
Case 4
    For i = 1 To n
        c(i) = − (a(i) + b(i))
    Next i
Case Else
    For i = 1 To n
        c(i) = 0#
    Next i
End Select
End Sub

Sub veceql(a( ) As Single, b( ) As Single, n As Integer)
'
'    This routine copies the vector b into a. The vector
'    is n elements long.
'
'    Copyright 1991
'    Mark E. Dreier
'
'    Unpublished - All Rights Reserved
'
```

```
Dim i As Integer
'
For i = 1 To n
    a(i) = b(i)
Next i
End Sub
```

References

[1] Shields, Paul C., *Elementary Linear Algebra*, Worth Publishers, Inc., New York, 1968.
[2] Press, W. H., Teukolsky, S. A., Vetterling, W. T., and Flannery, B. P., *Numerical Recipes in FORTRAN, The Art of Scientific Computing*, 2nd ed., Press Syndicate of the Univ. of Cambridge, Cambridge, MA, 1992, pp. 51–63.

Problems

C.1 Given vectors A and B, find the following quantities:

$$A = \begin{Bmatrix} 1 \\ 2 \\ 3 \end{Bmatrix}, \quad B = \begin{Bmatrix} 3 \\ -2 \\ 1 \end{Bmatrix}$$

(a) $A + B$
(b) $A - B$
(c) $B - A$
(d) $A^\mathrm{T}B$
(e) AB^T
(f) BA^T
(g) $B^\mathrm{T}A$

C.2 Given the vectors C and D, tell which operations are permitted and what the result is if permitted. If the operation is not permitted, tell why.

$$C = \begin{Bmatrix} 1 \\ 2 \end{Bmatrix}, \quad D = \begin{Bmatrix} 3 \\ 4 \\ 5 \end{Bmatrix}$$

(a) CD^T
(b) $C^\mathrm{T}D$
(c) $C + D$
(d) $C^{-1}D$
(e) DC^T

C.3 Given the matrices E, F, and G, find the result of the indicated operation or tell why it is not possible:

$$E = \begin{bmatrix} 1 & -1 \\ 2 & -2 \\ 3 & -3 \end{bmatrix}, \quad F = \begin{bmatrix} 1 & 3 & 5 \\ -5 & -3 & -1 \end{bmatrix}, \quad G = \begin{bmatrix} 2 & 0 \\ 0 & 3 \end{bmatrix}$$

(a) EF
(b) FE
(c) $E + G$
(d) $F + G$
(e) $EF + G$
(f) $FE - G$

C.4 What is the inverse of each of the matrices given here?

$$A = \begin{bmatrix} \cos\theta & \sin\theta \\ \sin\theta & -\cos\theta \end{bmatrix}, \quad B = \begin{bmatrix} 1 & 0 & 0 \\ 0 & \cos\theta & \sin\theta \\ 0 & -\sin\theta & \cos\theta \end{bmatrix}$$

C.5 Solve the following linear algebra problems for the unknowns a, b, and c:

(a)

$$\begin{bmatrix} 1 & 1 & 1 \\ 2 & 0 & 2 \\ 0 & 3 & 1 \\ 1 & 2 & 3 \end{bmatrix} \begin{Bmatrix} a \\ b \\ c \end{Bmatrix} = \begin{Bmatrix} 2 \\ 8 \\ -3 \\ 6 \end{Bmatrix}$$

(b)

$$\begin{bmatrix} 1 & 2 & 3 \\ 3 & 2 & 1 \\ 1 & 3 & 1 \end{bmatrix} \begin{Bmatrix} a \\ b \\ c \end{Bmatrix} = \begin{Bmatrix} 5 \\ 7 \\ 7 \end{Bmatrix}$$

C.6 Solve the following linear algebra problem for $x1$ and $x2$ symbolically:

$$\begin{bmatrix} a_{11} & a_{12} \\ a_{21} & a_{22} \end{bmatrix} \begin{Bmatrix} x_1 \\ x_2 \end{Bmatrix} = \begin{Bmatrix} b_1 \\ b_2 \end{Bmatrix}$$

Appendix D
Useful Mathematical Tools

This appendix is a potpourri of mathematical techniques especially useful when working rotor aerodynamics and dynamics problems.

D.1 Methods to Find the Real Roots of a Polynomial

Very often, the solution to a problem one poses is one of the roots of a function. That is, one is often faced with the task of finding a value for x such that

$$f(x) = 0$$

The degree of difficulty of finding a root is determined by the degree of nonlinearity of the function, the number of roots, the distribution of the roots, etc. In many cases, imaginary or complex roots can be mixed with real roots. The interested reader will find a warehouse full of information on root finding in the literature. For a good cross section of techniques, the reader is encouraged to seek and read [1]. Two tried-and-true techniques are presented here to get the reader started.

The first technique is called the Newton–Raphson technique. This technique relies on a good initial guess for the root and the ability to evaluate a derivative of the function, even if its analytical form is unknown. Suppose that a function $f(x)$ is continuous and has a continuous first derivative $F(x) = \partial f(x)/\partial x$. (The derivative is indicated as a partial because one might encounter a need to find the roots of two functions simultaneously, each being a function of the same two independent variables. In that case, the Newton–Raphson technique is still applicable on a matrix and linear algebra level, but the name is more popularly know as the Jacobian technique then.) If the value for x is near a root, then the function is nearly zero. A small correction to x might be enough to zero the function. How do you find the correction? Begin by constructing a Taylor series for the function:

$$f(x_{i+1}) = f(x_i + \Delta x) = f(x_i) + F(x_i)\Delta x$$

The subscript on the independent variable indicates which iteration is being evaluated. Because a value for x is sought such that the next evaluation of the function is zero, proceed by setting $f(x_{i+1}) = 0$, and solve for Δx, which is the correction that is desired:

$$\Delta x = -F^{-1}(x_i)f(x_i)$$

Table D.1   Demonstration of Newton–Raphson method

Solution using analytical derivative	Solution using numerical derivative
First guess: $x = 0$.	First guess: $x = 0$. Use $\varepsilon = 0.1$ for numerical differentiation.
$f(0) = -5.0$	$f(0) = -5.0$
$F(0) = 2.0$	$f(0.1) = -4.77$
	$f(-0.1) = -5.17$
	$F(0) \cong \dfrac{-4.77 - (-5.17)}{0.2} = 2.0$
First correction	First correction
$\Delta x = -(2.0)^{-1}(-5.0) = 2.5$	$\Delta x = -(2.0)^{-1}(-5.0) = 2.5$
$x_{new} = x_{old} + \Delta x$	$x_{new} = x_{old} + \Delta x$
$x_{new} = 0.0 + 2.5 = 2.5$	$x_{new} = 0.0 + 2.5 = 2.5$
Second guess: $x = 2.5$	Second guess: $x = 2.5$
$f(2.5) = 18.75$	$f(2.5) = 18.75$
$F(2.5) = 17$	$f(2.6) = 20.48$
	$f(2.4) = 17.08$
	$F(2.5) \cong \dfrac{20.48 - (17.08)}{0.2} = 17.0$
Second correction	Second correction
$\Delta x = -(17.0)^{-1}(18.75) = -1.103$	$\Delta x = -(17.0)^{-1}(18.75) = -1.103$
$x_{new} = x_{old} + \Delta x$	$x_{new} = x_{old} + \Delta x$
$\therefore$	
$x_{new} = 2.5 - 1.103 = 1.397$	$x_{new} = 2.5 - 1.103 = 1.397$
Third guess: $x = 1.397$	Third guess: $x = 1.397$
$f(1.397) = 3.649$	$f(1.397) = 3.649$
$F(1.397) = 10.382$	$f(1.497) = 4.71703$
	$f(1.297) = 2.64063$
	$F(1.397) \cong \dfrac{4.71703 - (2.64063)}{0.2}$
	$= 10.382$
Third correction	Third correction
$\Delta x = -(10.382)^{-1}(3.649) = -0.3515$	$\Delta x = -(10.382)^{-1}(3.649) = -0.3515$
$x_{new} = x_{old} + \Delta x$	$x_{new} = x_{old} + \Delta x$
$\therefore$	
$x_{new} = 1.397 - 0.3515 = 1.0455$	$x_{new} = 1.397 - 0.3515 = 1.0455$
One more iteration brings the guess to 1.007, which is close enough to the exact answer of 1.0.	One more iteration brings the guess to 1.007, which is close enough to the exact answer of 1.0.

The improved value for x is:

$$x_{i+1} = x_i + \Delta x$$

If the function is linear, this technique will find the root in one iteration no matter what initial guess was used. Nonlinear functions require a few more iterations to find the dominant root. If one does not have the function explicitly expressed, the derivative can be estimated using numerical differentiation:

$$F(x) = \frac{f(x + \varepsilon) - f(x - \varepsilon)}{2\varepsilon}$$

Consider this example function solved using analytical differentiation and numerical differentiation:

Given:

$$f(x) = 3x^2 + 2x - 5, \quad F(x) = 6x + 2$$

Find:

$$x \qquad \text{so that} \qquad f(x) = 0$$

Table D.1 shows how the Newton–Raphson technique works with analytic and numerical derivatives. Using the so-called central-difference numerical derivative, coupled with the fact that the function is "nice," the technique converged to nearly the solution in just four iterations.

The second technique is called interval halving. This technique finds the root by pinching tighter and tighter the region where a root is known to lie. A root is

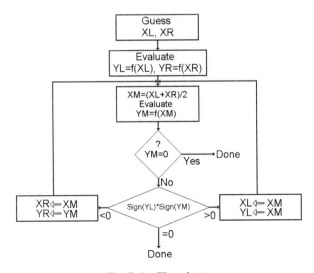

Fig. D.1   Flowchart.

known to lie between two brackets if the sign of the function for the left bracket is opposite that for the right bracket. The algorithm then proceeds this way. Choose a point exactly halfway between the two brackets, and evaluate the function there. If the function is zero, stop—the root has been found. If the function has the same sign as the function evaluated with the left bracket (call it the *left function*), then the root must be to the right of the midpoint. Replace the left bracket with the midpoint guess, and compute a new midpoint guess. A similar process is executed if the function has the same sign as the function evaluated with the right bracket (call it the *right function*). Continue this process until the function is zero when evaluated with the midpoint guess, or until the difference between the left function and the right function is acceptably small. The flowchart in Fig. D.1 makes this algorithm clear.

Other techniques are available. Again, the reader is directed to [1] for lucid explanations of various methods.

D.2 Buckingham Pi Theorem

The Buckingham pi theorem is a method to estimate the functional form of a relationship. At its simplest, it is a dimensional analysis tool. It does not (and cannot) give you the exact equation you seek, but it does point out some expected relationships. The entire theorem is not presented here. However, the technique of dimensional analysis is demonstrated through an example.

The Buckingham pi theorem requires that basic metrics of mass M, length L, and time T balance on both sides of an equation. Specific units such as slugs for mass, or meters for length, are not important here. Powers of metrics must also balance on each side of an equation. Derived metrics are expressed in terms of basic metrics. For instance, pounds force is expressed as slug-feet/second^2. With this as a starting point, consider the induced (wash) velocity coming from a fan.

From personal experience, the wash velocity seems to be related to the area of the rotor disk. Certainly, it is related to some properties of the air. Density and temperature are two possible properties. The force with which the fan pushes the air must also be a factor in wash strength. So, with a "gut" feel for the dependence of wash velocity on force, area, density and temperature, propose the following expression:

$$w = F^a * \rho^b * A^c * \tau^d$$

Now, force is the product of a mass and acceleration, or M(ass) times L(ength)$/T$(ime)^2. Density is M(ass) per volume or L(ength)^3. Area is L(ength)^2, of course, and temperature is in degrees, represented by τ. That is, the dimensional relations are

$$w = \frac{L}{T}$$

$$F = \frac{M \cdot L}{T^2}$$

$$\rho = \frac{M}{L^3}$$

$$A = L^2$$

$$\tau = \mathrm{Deg}$$

Making the substitutions, one gets

$$\frac{L}{T} = \left(\frac{M \cdot L}{T^2}\right)^a \left(\frac{M}{L^3}\right)^b \left(L^{2c}\right)(\tau)^d$$

Expanding, and gathering powers of like physical quantities, yields

$$L = L^a \cdot L^{-3b} \cdot L^{2c} = L^{a-3b+2c}$$

$$T^{-1} = T^{-2a}$$

$$M^0 = M^a \cdot M^b = M^{a+b}$$

$$\tau^0 = \tau^d$$

From this, the powers are found:

$$1 = a - 3b + 2c$$

$$1 = 2a$$

$$0 = a + b$$

$$0 = d$$

which leads to

$$a = \frac{1}{2}$$

$$b = -\frac{1}{2}$$

$$c = -\frac{1}{2}$$

$$d = 0$$

or

$$w \approx \sqrt{\frac{F}{\rho A}}$$

From this analysis, the wash is expected to rise as the square root of the disk-loading F/A and the square root of the inverse of the density. Temperature, as a strong independent variable, does not influence wash directly, though it is known that temperature does modify the density. This does not invalidate the analysis; it merely reinforces the need for the analyst to take care in the selection of the independent variables that are used on the RHS.

Rotor wash in forward flight is also dependent on flight speed. If one drops the temperature but includes a velocity term on the RHS of the original supposition and then performs the same type of dimensional analysis, one ends up with four unknown powers, but only three equations. In this case, assume one of them is unity, for instance, the exponent for force. Now, the resultant functional form is

$$w \approx \frac{F}{\rho A V}$$

Both expressions are correct, and in fact one comes from the other. In general, the induced velocity is proportional to force and inversely proportional to density, the area over which the force acts, and some velocity.

The point of introducing the Buckingham pi theorem is this. Dimensional analysis is important. It can help when deriving long, complicated expressions, by enforcing the need for a balance of metrics on both sides of an equation. Also, the Buckingham pi theorem can lead the analyst to an understanding and even an expectation of a functional form. This will aid in experiments down the road. At the very least, the Buckingham pi theorem is a useful sanity check. For more examples of the use of the Buckingham pi theorem, see [2].

D.3 Estimating Damping Ratio

There is an easy-to-remember rule of thumb for estimating the damping ratio of a second-order system. Examine the system in free vibration. Measure the time to half-amplitude; call it $T_{1/2}$. If the natural frequency of the system is known, then the period of the system is $T = 2\pi/\omega_n$, or solving for the frequency, $\omega_n = 2\pi/T$. The envelope defining the amplitude of the vibration of a second-order system is $e^{-\omega_n \varsigma t}$. If $T_{1/2}$ is substituted for t and if $e^{-\omega_n \varsigma T_{1/2}}$ is set equal to $1/2$, the resulting expression can be solved for the damping ratio:

$$e^{-\omega_n \varsigma T_{1/2}} = 0.5$$

or

$$-\omega_n \varsigma T_{1/2} = \ell n(0.5) = -0.693$$

or

$$\varsigma = \left[\frac{0.693}{\omega_n T_{1/2}} \right]$$

But

$$\omega_n = \frac{2\pi}{T}$$

so

$$\varsigma = \left[\frac{0.693}{2\pi T_{1/2}/T} \right] = \left[\frac{0.11}{T_{1/2}/T} \right]$$

In other words, look at the trace of the solution, and determine how many cycles were required to damp to half-amplitude. Call that number N. If cycles are difficult to count, then measure the time to half-amplitude, and calculate the ratio $T_{1/2}/T$. The damping ratio is estimated by

$$\varsigma = \left[\frac{0.11}{N} \right]$$

or

$$\varsigma = \left[\frac{0.11}{T_{1/2}/T} \right]$$

Simple, n'est pas?

D.4 Trigonometric Identities

Easy manipulation of trigonometric functions is important in most engineering disciplines. It is imperative in simulation and modeling. In the study of rotating machinery, products of these functions are frequently encountered. Very often, the lowest harmonic is the only item of interest. Therefore, the following conversions are written in terms of the lowest possible harmonic. The list of functions that follows is in no way comprehensive, but it does cover the most frequently used conversions. For a comprehensive list of trigonometric identities, consult [3].

D.4.1 First-Order-Expansion

$$\cos(\theta) = \cos(\theta)$$
$$\sin(\theta) = \sin(\theta)$$

D.4.2 Second-Order-Expansion

$$\cos^2(\Theta) = \frac{[1 + \cos(2\Theta)]}{2}$$
$$\sin(\Theta) * \cos(\Theta) = \frac{\sin(2\Theta)}{2}$$
$$\sin^2(\Theta) = \frac{[1 - \cos(2\Theta)]}{2}$$

D.4.3 Third-Order-Expansion

$$\cos^3(\Theta) = \frac{3 * \cos(\Theta) + \cos(3\Theta)}{4}$$

$$\cos^2(\Theta) * \sin(\Theta) = \frac{\sin(\Theta) + \sin(3\Theta)}{4}$$

$$\cos(\Theta) * \sin^2(\Theta) = \frac{\cos(\Theta) - \cos(3\Theta)}{4}$$

$$\sin^3(\Theta) = \frac{3 * \sin(\Theta) - \sin(3\Theta)}{4}$$

D.4.4 Fourth-Order-Expansion

$$\cos^4(\Theta) = \frac{3 + 4 * \cos(2\Theta) + \cos(4\Theta)}{8}$$

$$\cos^3(\Theta) * \sin(\Theta) = \frac{2 * \sin(2\Theta) + \sin(4\Theta)}{8}$$

$$\cos^2(\Theta) * \sin^2(\Theta) = \frac{1 - \cos(4\Theta)}{8}$$

$$\cos(\Theta) * \sin^3(\Theta) = \frac{2 * \sin(2\Theta) - \sin(4\Theta)}{8}$$

$$\sin^4(\Theta) = \frac{3 - 4 * \cos(2\Theta) + \cos(4\Theta)}{8}$$

D.4.5 Fifth-Order-Expansion

$$\cos^5(\Theta) = \frac{10 * \cos(\Theta) + 5 * \cos(3\Theta) + \cos(5\Theta)}{16}$$

$$\cos^4(\Theta) * \sin(\Theta) = \frac{2 * \sin(\Theta) + 3 * \sin(3\Theta) + \sin(5\Theta)}{16}$$

$$\cos^3(\Theta) * \sin^2(\Theta) = \frac{2 * \cos(\Theta) - \cos(3\Theta) - \cos(5\Theta)}{16}$$

$$\cos^2(\Theta) * \sin^3(\Theta) = \frac{2 * \sin(\Theta) + \sin(3\Theta) - \sin(5\Theta)}{16}$$

$$\cos(\Theta) * \sin^4(\Theta) = \frac{2 * \cos(\Theta) - 3 * \cos(3\Theta) + \cos(5\Theta)}{16}$$

$$\sin^5(\Theta) = \frac{10 * \sin(\Theta) - 5 * \sin(3\Theta) + \sin(5\Theta)}{16}$$

D.4.6 Sixth-Order-Expansion

$$\cos^6(\Theta) = \frac{[10 + 15 * \cos(2\Theta) + 6 * \cos(4\Theta) + \cos(6\Theta)]}{32}$$

$$\cos^5(\Theta) * \sin(\Theta) = \frac{[5 * \sin(2\Theta) + 4 * \sin(4\Theta) + \sin(6\Theta)]}{32}$$

$$\cos^4(\Theta) * \sin^2(\Theta) = \frac{[2 + \cos(2\Theta) - 2 * \cos(4\Theta) - \cos(6\Theta)]}{32}$$

$$\cos^3(\Theta) * \sin^3(\Theta) = \frac{[3 * \sin(2\Theta) - \sin(6\Theta)]}{32}$$

$$\cos^2(\Theta) * \sin^4(\Theta) = \frac{[2 - \cos(2\Theta) - 2 * \cos(4\Theta) + \cos(6\Theta)]}{32}$$

$$\cos(\Theta) * \sin^5(\Theta) = \frac{[5 * \sin(2\Theta) - 4 * \sin(4\Theta) + \sin(6\Theta)]}{32}$$

$$\sin^6(\Theta) = \frac{[10 - 15 * \cos(2\Theta) + 6 * \cos(4\Theta) - \cos(6\Theta)]}{32}$$

Higher-order expansions can be derived using the four following relationships:

$$\sin(\alpha) * \sin(\beta) = \frac{\cos(\alpha - \beta) - \cos(\alpha + \beta)}{2}$$

$$\cos(\alpha) * \cos(\beta) = \frac{\cos(\alpha - \beta) + \cos(\alpha + \beta)}{2}$$

$$\sin(\alpha) * \cos(\beta) = \frac{\sin(\alpha + \beta) + \sin(\alpha - \beta)}{2}$$

$$\cos(\alpha) * \sin(\beta) = \frac{\sin(\alpha + \beta) - \sin(\alpha - \beta)}{2}$$

References

[1] Press, W. H., Teukolsky, S. A., Vetterling, W. T., and Flannery, B. P., *Numerical Recipes in FORTRAN, The Art of Scientific Computing*, 2nd ed., Cambridge Univ. Press, New York, 1992, pp. 340–375.

[2] Dommasch, D. O., Sherby, S. S., and Connolly, T. F., *Airplane Aerodynamics*, Pitman, New York, 1967, pp. 106–110.

[3] Selby, Samuel M., and Weast, Robert C., *CRC Standard Mathematical Tables*, 21st ed., The Chemical Rubber Co., Cleveland, OH, 1973, pp. 225–231.

Appendix E
Nondimensional Coefficients

Nondimensional coefficients are an economical way to organize data and scale results. Instead of a multivariant table of lift, drag, and moment values for a full-size wing that was operated at various speeds, angles and values of density in some wind tunnel, one table of nondimensional coefficients suffices. What's more, that table allows the aerodynamicist to estimate wing performance of many different-sized wings. To see how this is done, consider the simple experiment described next.

Construct a wing, and test it in a wind tunnel at various values of wind speed and angle of attack. Measure the lift and place the values into a table. The result is a multivariable table for lift as a function of angle of attack and airspeed that can look like Table E.1.

Plot the lift as a function of angle of attack for various speeds (Fig. E.1).

Now plot the data sweeping velocity for various angles of attack (Fig. E.2).

One observes that higher speeds and higher angles of attack lead to higher values of lift. But, can these data be collapsed to find a convenient functional relationship between lift, angle of attack, and velocity? Furthermore, what if the density changes because of altitude or temperature? Does that fact make this table completely invalid to describe the performance of the wing? The answer is yes because these data are presented with dimensional quantities. However, the hard work expended to gather these data is not all for naught.

The remedy for this problem is to make the data nondimensional. Divide every lift value by the product of the dynamic pressure $\rho V^2/2$ and the wing area S. The result is the lift coefficient:

$$C_L = \frac{\text{Lift}}{1/2\rho V^2 S}$$

Dividing by the dynamic pressure effectively removes the variation with density and airspeed. Dividing by the wing area frees the data of scaling effects as well. The product of dynamic pressure and wing area has units of force, the same units as the measured lift. If that product divides the lift, the data collapse on itself as shown in Fig. E.3.

Most aerodynamic tables are presented in dimensionless form for just these reasons. Normally, the product of a dynamic pressure and a characteristic area normalizes forces. Likewise, the product of a dynamic pressure, a characteristic area, and a characteristic length normalizes moments. In some cases, forces are

Table E.1   Wing lift as a function as angle of attack and airspeed

Angle/ velocity, deg	10.0 fps	20.0 fps	30.0 fps	40.0 fps	50.0 fps	60.0 fps	70.0 fps
0.00	1.189	4.756	10.701	19.024	29.725	42.804	58.261
1.00	2.378	9.512	21.402	38.048	59.450	85.608	116.522
2.00	3.567	14.268	32.103	57.072	89.175	128.412	174.783
3.00	4.756	19.024	42.804	76.096	118.900	171.216	233.044
4.00	5.945	23.780	53.505	95.120	148.625	214.020	291.305
5.00	7.134	28.536	64.206	114.144	178.350	256.824	349.566

Lift vs Angle of Attack for Various Speeds

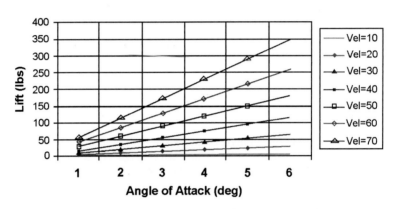

Fig. E.1   Lift vs angle of attack for various speeds.

Lift vs Speed for Various Angles of Attack

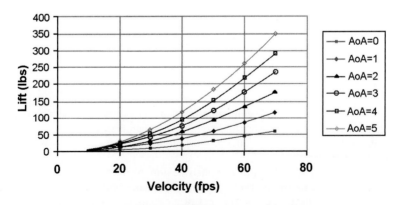

Fig. E.2   Lift vs speed for various angles of attack.

Normalized Lift

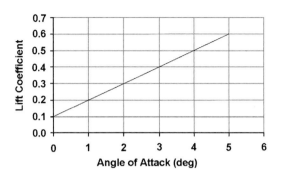

Fig. E.3   Lift coefficient vs angle of attack.

not made dimensionless. Instead, the forces are presented as equivalent flat-plate drag areas. This will be covered in greater detail elsewhere in the main body of the text.

Reference

[1]Abbott, I. H., and Von Doenhoff, A. E., *Theory of Wing Sections, Including a Summary of Airfoil Data*, Dover, New York, 1959, pp. 449–687.

Problem

E.1 Go to a good text on aerodynamics [1], find the lift and drag curves for a NACA 0012 airfoil, and plot them. (Use the standard roughness curves if available, or else use the highest Reynolds-number data.) Observe the linear region of the lift curve near the origin. How far does this linear region extend? What shape does the drag coefficient take in the corresponding range of angle of attack? Use any method available to you to derive the coefficients for a second-order polynomial describing the drag coefficient as a function of the angle of attack.

Appendix F
Solution of the Biot–Savart Law for a Straight-Line Segment

Vorticity is not a mathematical abstraction. It is a very real physical phenomenon, and its presence causes, among other things, a drag penalty from lift called *induced drag*. Vorticity is also responsible for so-called *wake turbulence*. Vorticity lends itself to mathematical representation through an expression called the Biot–Savart law. With a change of constants, this is the same law that relates magnetism and current flow. In the general case the Biot–Savart law is intractable. However, in some very specific cases an exact solution is possible. Before presenting the solution, a practical example of vortices can be instructive.

One who has ever flown commercially into an airport where the humidity is high has probably seen the white streamers emanating from the tips of the wings during final approach. Those streamers are vortices made visible by local condensation. The picture of a Bell Helicopter model 214 (Fig. F.1) taken during a pipe-laying operation shows the same thing, though these streamers leave the blade in helical fashion. Notice also that the cylinder defined by the helical vortex system seems to contract as the downwash transports the vortices away from the plane of the rotor. The momentum principle readily explains this.

Many excellent references [1, 2] develop vortex theory well. The interested reader is encouraged to go there for more information. The intention of this appendix is to acquaint the reader with vortex theory, provide the reader with a simple, yet rigorous solution to the mathematical model of vorticity, and demonstrate its use.

F.1 Biot–Savart Law

The Biot–Savart law is used to describe the induced velocity in the vicinity of an idealized vortex filament. There are four points the reader should know about vortices:

1) A vortex cannot simply begin and end anywhere. A vortex filament must go to $+/-$ infinity, or it must close on itself, or it must begin or end at a wall. This is called Helmholtz's law.

2) An ideal vortex maintains its strength along the entire length of the filament. That strength has the symbol γ and has the units of (length^2/time).

559

Fig. F.1 Bell Helicopter Textron, Inc., model 214ST lifting a pipe. Note the contraction of the wake. (Courtesy of Bell Helicopter Textron, Inc.)

3) A vortex filament lies in R^3 space and so is parametrically defined with an arclength s and a R^3 position vector that is a function of s. This also means that the vortex filament is directed. That is, a segment has a head and a tail.

4) A vortex is a miniature tornado. The very strong wind it produces in its neighborhood is inversely proportional to the distance from the filament. That wind is the induced velocity.

In Fig. F.2, a straight black arrow labeled ds marks a differential element of the directed vortex filament. The square dot removed a distance r from the filament marks the point where one wishes to calculate the induced velocity, a differential amount of which is called dv_i. Please notice that the vector r measures from the point of interest to ds. In keeping with the right-hand rule, the direction of the spin

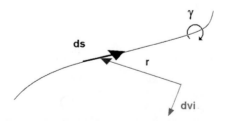

Fig. F.2　The geometry found in the Biot–Savart law.

is indicated with the arrow wrapping around the filament. The Biot–Savart law concisely relates all of these elements:

$$d\mathbf{vi} = \frac{\gamma}{4\pi} \frac{\mathbf{r} \times d\mathbf{s}}{|\mathbf{r}|^3}$$

The vectors $d\mathbf{vi}$, $d\mathbf{s}$, and $\mathbf{r}$ are all three-element column vectors.

By far the most useful filament to analyze is a straight line that goes to plus and minus infinity. A bit more interesting is the segment that runs from one point to another on the infinite length filament (Fig. F.3). (This is not a violation of Helmholtz's law. If the vortex filament made a sharp turn, to the right for instance, then another sharp turn to the right after some distance, the influence of the segment found between the two turns is a perfectly valid thing to seek. In fact, the so-called horseshoe vortex thus formed is a mainstay of aerodynamics.) Let the filament run along the x axis, from x_1 (to the left of the origin) to x_2 (to the right of the origin) and at the origin measure along the positive y axis a distance h from the filament. This marks the point $(x = 0, y = h)$ at which we wish to know the velocity. From this information, the following vectors are defined:

$$d\mathbf{s} = \begin{Bmatrix} dx \\ 0 \\ 0 \end{Bmatrix} \quad \text{and} \quad \mathbf{r} = \begin{Bmatrix} x \\ -h \\ 0 \end{Bmatrix}$$

Substitute the vector expression for $\mathbf{r} \times d\mathbf{s}$ and the magnitude of $\mathbf{r}$, raised to the third power, and perform the indicated integration. The final result is

$$\mathbf{r} \times d\mathbf{s} = \begin{Bmatrix} 0 \\ 0 \\ h \cdot dx \end{Bmatrix} \quad \text{then} \quad vi = \frac{\gamma}{4\pi} \int_{x_1}^{x_2} \frac{\mathbf{r} \times d\mathbf{s}}{|\mathbf{r}|^3}$$

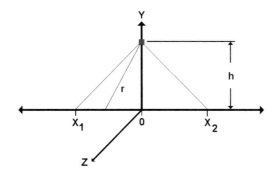

Fig. F.3   An infinite length straight-line vortex filament.

This yields

$$vi(x) = 0$$

$$vi(y) = 0$$

$$vi(z) = \frac{\gamma}{4\pi h}\left[\frac{x_2}{\left(x_2^2 + h^2\right)^{1/2}} - \frac{x_1}{\left(x_1^2 + h^2\right)^{1/2}}\right]$$

That is, the induced velocity is in the positive z direction in this case. Two special cases come out of this expression. If x_2 is located at positive infinity and x_1 is located at negative infinity, then the induced velocity is

$$vi(z) = \frac{\gamma}{2\pi h}$$

This is the expression for the two-dimensional case. If x_1 starts at the origin and x_2 goes to positive infinity, then the induced velocity is

$$vi(z) = \frac{\gamma}{4\pi h}$$

This makes sense because only half of an infinite length of filament was used (if the reader can imagine such a thing!).

F.2 General Solution to the Straight-Line Vortex Segment

In general, the straight-line vortex segments will not oblige the reader by falling conveniently on the x axis.

The general case involves two points on the segment, $s1$ and $s2$, and a point p not on the segment (Fig. F.4). The induced velocity in three dimensions is desired.

The general solution begins by defining a continuous vector from point

$$S_1 = \begin{Bmatrix} x_1 \\ y_1 \\ z_1 \end{Bmatrix}$$

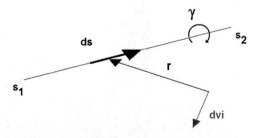

Fig. F.4   A general, straight-line vortex segment.

to point

$$S_2 = \begin{Bmatrix} x_2 \\ y_2 \\ z_2 \end{Bmatrix}$$

using the arclength parameter s. S_1 and S_2 are R^3 vectors measured from the origin. Any point

$$S = \begin{Bmatrix} x \\ y \\ z \end{Bmatrix}$$

on the straight-line filament is

$$S = S_1 + (S_2 - S_1)s = S_1 + S_{21}s$$

where

$$S_{21} = \begin{Bmatrix} x_2 - x_1 \\ y_2 - y_1 \\ z_2 - z_1 \end{Bmatrix}$$

The position vector of the point of interest is also measured from the origin:

$$P = \begin{Bmatrix} x_p \\ y_p \\ z_p \end{Bmatrix}$$

The vector measuring from P to an arbitrary point on the filament is

$$r = S - P = S_1 - P + (S_2 - S_1)s = S_{1P} + S_{21}s$$

Obviously,

$$S_{1P} = \begin{Bmatrix} x_1 - x_P \\ y_1 - y_P \\ z_1 - z_P \end{Bmatrix}$$

The differential filament element is

$$dS = S_{21} \, ds$$

Expanding the cross product

$$r \times dS = \begin{vmatrix} i & j & k \\ (S_{1Px} + S_{21x}s) & (S_{1Py} + S_{21y}s) & (S_{1Pz} + S_{21z}s) \\ S_{21x}ds & S_{21y}ds & S_{21z}ds \end{vmatrix}$$

$$= \begin{Bmatrix} (S_{1Py}S_{21z} - S_{1Pz}S_{21y})i \\ (S_{1Pz}S_{21x} - S_{1Px}S_{21z})j \\ (S_{1Px}S_{21y} - S_{1Py}S_{21x})k \end{Bmatrix} ds$$

The cube of the magnitude of the r vector is

$$|r|^3 = \left[\sqrt{(S_{1Px} + S_{21x}s)^2 + (S_{1Py} + S_{21y}s)^2 + (S_{1Pz} + S_{21z}s)^2} \right]^3$$

Expand the preceding expression, and recombine terms to get

$$|r|^3 = (A + Bs + Cs^2)^{3/2}$$

where

$$A = S_{1Px}^2 + S_{1Py}^2 + S_{1Pz}^2$$
$$B = 2(S_{1Px}S_{21x} + S_{1Py}S_{21y} + S_{1Pz}S_{21z})$$
$$C = S_{21x}^2 + S_{21y}^2 + S_{21z}^2$$

Making the indicated substitutions, the induced velocity in the x direction is

$$\Delta v_x = \frac{\gamma}{4\pi} \int_0^1 \frac{(S_{1Py}S_{21z} - S_{1Pz}S_{21y})}{(\sqrt{A + Bs + Cs^2})^{3/2}} \, ds$$

$$\Delta v_x = \frac{\gamma}{4\pi}(S_{1Py}S_{21z} - S_{1Pz}S_{21y}) \left\{ \frac{4C + 2B}{(4AC - B^2)\sqrt{A + B + C}} - \frac{2B}{(4AC - B^2)\sqrt{A}} \right\}$$

Following a similar process, the induced velocities in the y and z directions are

$$\Delta v_y = \frac{\gamma}{4\pi}(S_{1Pz}S_{21x} - S_{1Px}S_{21z}) \left\{ \frac{4C + 2B}{(4AC - B^2)\sqrt{A + B + C}} - \frac{2B}{(4AC - B^2)\sqrt{A}} \right\}$$

$$\Delta v_z = \frac{\gamma}{4\pi}(S_{1Px}S_{21y} - S_{1Py}S_{21x}) \left\{ \frac{4C + 2B}{(4AC - B^2)\sqrt{A + B + C}} - \frac{2B}{(4AC - B^2)\sqrt{A}} \right\}$$

The three preceding expressions are the general solution (with one caveat) to the Biot–Savart law as applied to a straight-line vortex of arbitrary length. The point of interest must not lie on the line containing the vortex filament because this leads to an infinite velocity as might be surmised from the expression for the z-direction velocity given earlier, for if $h = 0$, then

$$vi(z) = \frac{\gamma}{4\pi h} \left[\frac{x_2}{(x_2^2 + h^2)^{1/2}} - \frac{x_1}{(x_1^2 + h^2)^{1/2}} \right] = \frac{\gamma}{4\pi \cdot 0} \left[\frac{x_2}{x_2} - \frac{x_1}{x_1} \right] = \infty$$

F.3   Another General Solution to the Straight-Line Vortex Segment

A second method calculates the induced velocity using the special case of a filament lying on the x axis and a point that is not collinear. The solution begins as before, defining the filament in a parametric sense and constructing the normal from the point of interest to the filament:

$$S = S_1 + (S_2 - S_1)s = S_1 + S_{21}s$$

The position vector of the point of interest also measures from the origin:

$$P = \begin{Bmatrix} x_p \\ y_p \\ z_p \end{Bmatrix}$$

Find the normal from P to the filament by constructing a general position vector from P to the filament and then minimizing the length:

$$r = S - P = S_1 - P + (S_2 - S_1)s = S_{1P} + S_{21}s$$

Again,

$$S_{1P} = \begin{Bmatrix} x_1 - x_P \\ y_1 - y_P \\ z_1 - z_P \end{Bmatrix}$$

The length is $d^2 = \bar{r}^T \bar{r}$. Take the derivative of d^2 with respect to s, set this to zero, and solve for s:

$$\frac{\partial d^2}{\partial s} = 2(S_{1p} + S_{21}s)^T (S_{21}) = 0$$

Thus

$$s = - \left(S_{21}^T S_{21} \right)^{-1} S_{21}^T S_{1p}$$

and

$$S_i = S_1 + S_{21}s$$

The normal intersects the extended filament line beyond S_2 if $s > 1$. If $s < 0$, then the normal intersects the extended filament line before S_1. Imagine that the filament lies on the x axis, and the point P lies on the y axis, which intersects the x axis at point S_i, which is now the origin. The distance from the origin to S_2 corresponds to X_2 and similarly for S_1 and X_1. Accounting for filament extensions, the definitions for X_1 and X_2 become

$$X_2 = \sqrt{(S_i - S_2)^T (S_i - S_2)} \, \text{sign}(1 - s)$$

$$X_1 = \sqrt{(S_i - S_1)^T (S_i - S_1)} \, \text{sign}(0 - s)$$

The simple expression for induced velocity parallel to the z axis is

$$V_z = \frac{\gamma}{4\pi d} \left[\frac{x_2}{\left(x_2^2 + d^2\right)^{1/2}} - \frac{x_1}{\left(x_1^2 + d^2\right)^{1/2}} \right]$$

This vector must be resolved to the original axis system. Crossing the vector from P to S_1, into the vector from S_1 to S_2, then normalizing the resulting vector by its magnitude finds the unit norms:

$$c = (S_1 - P) \times (S_2 - S_1)$$

$$n = \frac{c}{|c|}$$

The induced velocity from the irrotational part is thus:

$$v_i = nV_z$$

F.4   Refinement for Rotational Core

An important refinement to the irrotational vortex model comes from measurements and observation of real-world phenomenon. Rather than infinite velocity at the center of a vortex, the velocity reduces smoothly and continuously to zero. A discontinuous first-order approximation of this vortex model introduces a rotational core in which the induced velocity varies according to the simple expression:

$$v_i = p_{\text{core}}r$$

At the edge of the core, the rotational value must equal the irrotational value, that is,

$$p_{\text{core}}r_{\text{core}} = \frac{\Gamma}{Kr_{\text{core}}}$$

But, at any point d from the center of the irrotational vortex filament, the tangential velocity is given by

$$V_z = \frac{\Gamma}{Kd}$$

Solving for K, then the core rotational rate, and finally the tangential velocity in the rotational core yields

$$V_z' = V_z \frac{d^2}{r_{\text{core}}^2}$$

Finally, the induced velocity from the rotational part is

$$v_i = nV_z'$$

Sample code, written in BASIC and found at the end of this appendix, shows one way to implement this procedure.

F.5 Practical Applications of Vortex Theory

Though strictly not part of the general solution, a most practical application of the solution to the Biot–Savart law comes in the analysis of so-called wake turbulence. The wake behind a wing that produces lift is not turbulent. A very well-defined structure can be discerned. In a lay explanation, when an airplane generates lift, the pressure above the wing is lower than the pressure below the wing. The pressure imbalance is relieved when the air below the wing curls around the tips of the wings. Combined with the forward motion of the wing, the swirling wind approximates a vortex. One speaks of the two counter-rotating trailing vortices and the bound vortex that joins them at the wing tips as a horseshoe vortex system. Such a system is shown in Fig. F.5.

Measurements with a laser velocimeter have recorded the flowfield behind an aircraft, Reference [3]. Figure F.6 shows the typical signature of so-called *wake turbulence*, though one sees that the well-defined flowfield has only a small turbulent velocity component.

Notice the magnitude of the velocities. Also, notice that near station 150 and station 270, the velocities suddenly reverse sign. An aircraft penetrating such a flowfield at one of these two stations would experience differential lift deltas that generate a rolling moment that can easily exceed the restoring moment available

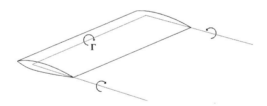

Fig. F.5   Horseshoe vortex system.

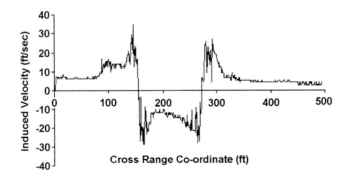

Fig. F.6   Induced velocity measured behind an aircraft.

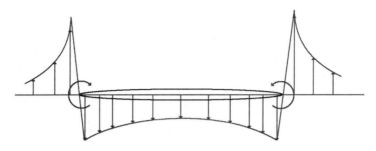

Fig. F.7   Biot–Savart model of induced velocity behind an aircraft.

from full opposite aileron. It is this strong rolling moment that causes the moniker wake turbulence to persist.

If one applies the Biot–Savart law to a horseshoe vortex model, an induced velocity map similar to the flowfield in Fig. F.7 is modeled easily.

The downwash between the two trailing tip vortices has an effect on the fuselage and horizontal stabilizer. It is easy to imagine that this wind pushes down on the horizontal tail and the fuselage behind the wing. Designers account for this by introducing an incidence angle to the horizontal stabilizer. In some cases, the incidence angle might even be controllable.

Readers interested in learning more about this are encouraged to visit the references.

F.6   Sample Code to Solve Biot–Savart Law with Rotational Core

```
Sub biot_savart(s1() As Single, s2() As Single, p() As Single, gamma As Single, v() As
Single, rcore As Single)
'
'    This subroutine calculates the induced velocity generated by a vortex
'    filament using the biot-savart law.
'
'    S1 and S2 are the starting and ending points of a directed vortex
'    filament segment. P is the point at which we wish to know the
'    velocity. Gamma is the strength of the irrotational part of the
'    vortex. V is the induced velocity vector. rcore is the radius
'    of the rotational core in a more realistic vortex model.
'
'    Author: Mark E. Dreier
'    Copyright 2004
'    Bell Helicopter Textron, Inc.
'    All Rights Reserved
'
Dim d As Single
Dim denom As Double
Dim fact As Single
Dim nt As Single
```

```
Dim numer As Double
Dim pi As Single
Dim rxds(3) As Single
Dim si(3) As Single
Dim sip(3) As Single
Dim si1(3) As Single
Dim si2(3) As Single
Dim s1p(3) As Single
Dim s21(3) As Single
Dim t As Double
Dim threshold As Single
'
pi = 4# * Atn(1)
fact = gamma / (4# * pi)
threshold = 0.0001
'
'   Find normal from point to vortex filament,
'   and calculate the point on the line. In
'   the process, check if the point is on the
'   line. If it is, the velocity is zero.
'
fvecadd s2(), s1(), s21(), 3, 2
fvecadd s1(), p(), s1p(), 3, 2
fcross s1p(), s21(), rxds()
nt = fvecmag(rxds(), 3)
numer = finnerp(s21(), s1p(), 3)
denom = finnerp(s21(), s21(), 3)
t = −numer / denom
For i = 1 To 3
    si(i) = s1(i) + s21(i) * t
Next i
'
'   Get the induced velocity from an irrotational
'   vortex at the point using plane geometry.
'
fvecadd si(), p(), sip(), 3, 2
fvecadd si(), s1(), si1(), 3, 2
fvecadd si(), s2(), si2(), 3, 2
d = fvecmag(sip(), 3)
If d <= threshold Or nt <= threshold Then
    For i = 1 To 3
        v(i) = 0#
    Next i
Else
    x2 = fvecmag(si2(), 3) * Sgn(1 − t)
    x1 = fvecmag(si1(), 3) * Sgn(0 − t)
    vz = fact / d * (x2 / Sqr(x2 * x2 + d * d) − x1 / Sqr(x1 * x1 + d * d))
    v(1) = vz * rxds(1) / nt
```

```
    v(2) = vz * rxds(2) / nt
    v(3) = vz * rxds(3) / nt
End If
'

'   Adjust for rotational core.
'

If d < rcore Then
    For i = 1 To 3
        v(i) = v(i) * (d / rcore) ^ 2
    Next i
End If
'

End Sub


Sub fcross(a() As Single, b() As Single, c() As Single)
'

'   The cross product of A and B is returned
'   in C.
'   Author: Mark E. Dreier
'   Copyright 2001
'   Unpublished - All Rights Reserved
'

c(1) = a(2) * b(3) − a(3) * b(2)
c(2) = a(3) * b(1) − a(1) * b(3)
c(3) = a(1) * b(2) − a(2) * b(1)
End Sub


Sub fvecadd(a() As Single, b() As Single, c() As Single, n As Integer, iop As Integer)
'

'   This if iop = 1, then this routine adds the vector A to the vector B to produce
'   vector C. If iop = 2, then this routine subtracts the B vector from the A vector
'   and puts the result in C. If iop = 3, then this routine subtracts A from B and puts
'   the result in C. If iop = 4, then C = −A − B.
'   Author: Mark E. Dreier
'   Copyright 1995
'   Unpublished - All Rights Reserved
'

Dim i As Integer
Select Case iop
Case 1
    For i = 1 To n
        c(i) = a(i) + b(i)
    Next i
Case 2
    For i = 1 To n
        c(i) = a(i) − b(i)
    Next i
Case 3
```

```
    For i = 1 To n
        c(i) = b(i) − a(i)
    Next i
Case 4
    For i = 1 To n
        c(i) = −(a(i) + b(i))
    Next i
Case Else
    For i = 1 To n
            c(i) = 0#
    Next i
End Select
End Sub


Function fvecmag(a() As Single, n As Integer) As Single
'
'    This routine returns the magnitude of the vector A, which is n long.
'    Author: Mark E. Dreier
'    Copyright 1995
'    Unpublished - All Rights Reserved
'
Dim i As Integer
Dim sum As Double
sum = 0#
For i = 1 To n
    sum = sum + a(i) * a(i)
Next i
fvecmag = Sqr(sum)
End Function


Function finnerp(x() As Single, Y() As Single, n As Integer) As Single
'
'    This routine calculates the inner product of two vectors x and y, and places the
'    result in z. The length of the vectors is assumed to be n. The vectors are assumed
'    to have starting pointers. IPX points to the 1st element of X(), and ipy points to
'    the first element of Y().
'    Author: Mark E. Dreier
'    Copyright 1991
'    Unpublished - All Rights Reserved
'
Dim i As Integer
Dim z As Double
z = 0#
For i = 1 To n
    z = z + x(i) * Y(i)
Next i
finnerp = z
End Function
```

References

[1] McCormick, B. W., *Aerodynamics of V/STOL Flight*, Academic Press, New York, 1967, pp. 25–29.

[2] Karamcheti, Krishnamurty, Principles of Ideal-Fluid Aerodynamics, John Wiley & Sons, Inc., New York/London/Sydney, 1966, pp. 523–530.

[3] Ferguson, S., and Dreier, M. E., "Empirical Wake Turbulence Model for Tiltrotor Aircraft," Society of Automotive Engineers, paper 2005-01-3182, Aug. 2005.

Appendix G
Momentum Principles

The momentum principle relates applied force to the rate of change of momentum. In problems involving fluid, often what is sought is the mean velocity of the fluid after some force has been applied to the fluid, though one can also calculate the force a moving stream of fluid applies as it impinges upon a body. In either case, from [1] the integral expression relating the sum of all of the forces acting on the fluid particle to the flux of momentum and rate of change of momentum of the inviscid fluid is

$$F = -\iint_S (pn)\, dS + B$$

$$= \iint_S \rho V(V \cdot n)\, dS + \frac{\partial}{\partial t} \iiint_{\text{Vol}} \rho V\, d\tau$$

The left-hand side of the equation is the force applied to the fluid particles. The right-hand side is the momentum flux and the rate of change of fluid momentum.

This is a formidable equation, both in its capability and in the arithmetic required to solve it in the general case. However, two examples given next demonstrate its usefulness for the kinds of problems that you will encounter in the main text.

Example G.1

This example is taken from [2]. Direct a stream of water from a garden hose at a sheet of plywood supported vertically. To hold the plywood in place, some force will be required. Why? The sheet of plywood is a surface that the water cannot penetrate. The water must change direction. Any time the velocity of a mass is changed, either in magnitude or direction, a force is responsible. This is Newton's second law paraphrased. One can calculate easily the amount of force if the flow rate of the fluid is known, even if the exact shape of the splash is not known. The formal arithmetic is shown in the box.

573

Water issues horizontally from a hose at $60\,\text{ft/s}$, through a nozzle opening of $2\,\text{in}^2$. The density of the water is $1.94\,\text{slugs/ft}^3$. What force does the water exert as it splashes on the wall?

From the momentum principle, the negative of the area integral of the pressure directed normally out from the surface (the wall in this case) equals the area integral of the moving fluid, directed normally to the surface. In the absence of other body forces, the momentum principle concisely states this in symbols in this way:

$$-\iint\limits_{S} (p\boldsymbol{n})\,\mathrm{d}s = \iint\limits_{S} \rho V(V\cdot \boldsymbol{n})\,\mathrm{d}s$$

The normal of the wall opposes the normal of the fluid, and both are along the x axis (the horizon). Using the values provided,

$$F_{\text{wall}} = \iint\limits_{S_{\text{wall}}} (p\boldsymbol{n})\,\mathrm{d}s$$

$$-F_{\text{wall}} = F_{\text{water}} = \iint\limits_{S_{\text{nozzle}}} \rho V(V\cdot \boldsymbol{n})\,\mathrm{d}s$$

$$-F_{\text{wall}} = F_{\text{water}} = \iint\limits_{2/144} 1.94 \cdot 60i \cdot (-60)\cdot \mathrm{d}s = -97i$$

So, even though the exact nature of the pressure distribution over the wall is unknown, it is known that it must equal the momentum force of 97 lb coming from the hose.

The development of the momentum equation is beyond the scope of this text. Interested readers are encouraged to consult [1–3]. In particular, [3] also provides several more lucid examples of the application of the momentum equation. What is important is that with very little information reliable results are available. For instance, consider the thrusting rotor in forward flight.

Example G.2

The classical treatment for thrust produced by a rotor uses the momentum theory and some keen insight. Several assumptions make the model tractable for gross performance estimates. Those assumptions are as follows:

1) The thrust loading is uniform over the rotor disk. This implies an infinite number of infinitely narrow blades—the definition of an "actuator" disk.

2) Uniform induced velocity over the face of the rotor disk is another assumption.

3) Rotation of the wake is not permitted; therefore, no energy is lost to that motion.

4) A well-defined slipstream differentiates the flow through the rotor from the flow outside of the rotor.

5) Far ahead and far behind the rotor, the static pressure equals the freestream static pressure.

6) The fluid is inviscid.

Recall the continuity equation, which states the amount of mass entering a streamtube, minus the amount of mass leaving a streamtube must equal the amount of mass accumulating in the streamtube. Now, if no mass is accumulating in the system, then with a bit more rigor we state

$$\rho_1 A_1 V_1 = \rho_2 A_2 V_2$$

If the density is constant, then the product of the area and velocity is a constant. As [4] suggests, think about a pitcher of syrup. At the top, the cross-sectional area of the syrup stream is wide, and it pours slowly out of the pitcher. At the waffle, the cross-sectional area has shrunk, but the syrup is pouring faster. However, the amount leaving the pitcher must equal the amount hitting the waffle. Thus, a narrowing slipstream means the fluid must speed up if no fluid leaves or enters the system.

Now look at a thrusting rotor, and draw a streamtube such that the walls of it just touch the rotor. Experience with a fan indicates that wind is generated at the plane of the rotor. This is induced velocity. Far upstream of this rotor, the air velocity is greatly diminished. Therefore, the mouth of the streamtube must widen. Far downstream, the streamtube narrows, though it is not easy to see why immediately, except for the syrup analogy.

Now, around the whole system, draw a control volume of some gigantic radius R. The system looks like that shown in Fig. G.1.

The amount of air entering the control volume in unit time on the left side is just the density of the air ρ times the area of the control volume face πR^2 times the freestream velocity V_0, or

$$Q_{\text{in}} = \rho \pi R^2 V_0$$

If r is the radius of the streamtube far downstream, flow values Q_{out1} and Q_{out2} comprise the amount of air leaving the control volume in unit time on

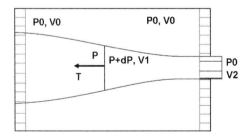

Fig. G.1   The streamtube and control volume that surround an actuator disk.

the right side:

$$Q_{out1} = \rho\pi(R^2 - r^2)V_0$$

$$Q_{out2} = \rho\pi r^2 V_2$$

These two mass flow rates represent the fluid flowing out of the annular area surrounding the narrowed streamtube and the fluid flowing out of the narrowed streamtube, respectively. Obviously, the sum of the fluid flow out of the right face of the control volume is greater than the fluid flowing into the left face. Therefore, there must be some flow coming in from the side walls. Its value is $Q_{out1} + Q_{out2} - Q_{in}$, or

$$Q_{side} = Q_{out1} + Q_{out2} - Q_{in} = \rho\pi(R^2 - r^2)V_0 + \rho\pi r^2 V_2 - \rho\pi R^2 V_0$$

or

$$Q_{side} = \rho\pi r^2(V_2 - V_0)$$

The term called momentum flux is the product of the mass flow through a face and its associated velocity. Therefore, the total momentum flux is

$$\text{Flux} = Q_{out1}V_0 + Q_{out2}V_2 - Q_{in}V_0 - Q_{side}V_0$$

Q_{side} is multiplied by V_0 because, even though the side flow is directed radially inward, it is being transported downstream at velocity V_0. The flux is equal to T, the thrust of the actuator disk. Doing the algebra,

$$T = \rho\pi r^2 V_2(V_2 - V_0)$$

Now, the thrust is also expressed easily by

$$T = A \cdot dP$$

where A is the area of the actuator disk, and dP is the discontinuous increase in static pressure across the disk. Bernoulli's equation cannot be applied across the disk because of the discontinuous jump in energy indicated by dP. However, Bernoulli's equation can be applied just in front of and just behind the disk:

$$p0 + \frac{1}{2}\rho V_0^2 = p + \frac{1}{2}\rho V_1^2$$

$$p0 + \frac{1}{2}\rho V_2^2 = p + \frac{1}{2}\rho V_1^2 + dP$$

$$\therefore$$

$$dP = \frac{1}{2}\rho(V_2^2 - V_0^2) = \frac{1}{2}\rho(V_2 - V_0)(V_2 + V_0)$$

Also, from the diagram, and applying the continuity equation,

$$\rho A V_1 = \rho\pi r^2 V_2$$

So, by combining the two expressions for thrust, eliminating r, and expressing dP in terms of the velocity far upstream and far downstream, the velocity at the disk plane is found to be the average of the velocity in the slipstream far upstream and far downstream of the rotor:

$$V_1 = \frac{V_2 + V_0}{2}$$

The increment that is added to the freestream velocity at the rotor disk is called the induced velocity w:

$$w = V_1 - V_0$$

With a bit more algebra, the thrust can be expressed in terms of the induced velocity and the freestream velocity; thus,

$$T = \rho A (V_0 + w) 2w$$

This expression relates how much induced velocity thrust produces when acting over an area A. When the rotor is in hover, the freestream velocity is zero, and the induced velocity is given by

$$w = \sqrt{\frac{T}{2\rho A}}$$

Because helicopter rotors fly with the thrust axis pointing nearly normal to the direction of flight, the inflow and forward speed are not simply additive, except in the vector sense. The following expression gives a better representation of the induced velocity.

$$w_{\text{ind}} = \frac{-F_z}{2\rho A \left(u_a^2 + v_a^2 + w_a^2 \right)^{\frac{1}{2}}}$$

$$u_a = u_b - u_{\text{ind}}$$

$$v_a = v_b - v_{\text{ind}}$$

$$w_a = w_b - w_{\text{ind}}$$

The negative sign is introduced because induced velocity is always directed opposite to the force that generates it.

This result of momentum theory serves the helicopter community well. Every helicopter manufacturer has its extra refinements to this model in order to make the result fit experiment. The main text explores these refinements.

A nice feature of the momentum model is that it also applies to any and all aerodynamic force generators—bodies, wings, etc. In general, if an aerodynamic body has associated with it a characteristic area A_j normal to the jth direction, the body generates aerodynamic force F_j, and tuning parameter K introduces empirical correction, and then the following model expresses the induced linear velocity concisely:

$$w_j = \frac{-K \cdot F_j}{2\rho A_j V_a}$$

$$u_a = u_b - u_{\text{ind}}$$

$$v_a = v_b - v_{\text{ind}}$$

$$w_a = w_b - w_{\text{ind}}$$

$$V_a = \sqrt{u_a^2 + v_a^2 + w_a^2}$$

V_a is the aerodynamic velocity at the reference point of the element The tuning parameter K is also called a correlation coefficient, or for the hard-core cynic, a fudge factor. As already shown, the characteristic area for a rotor is the disk area. For a wing, a good estimate is $A_{\text{wing}} = \pi(b^2/4)$, where b is the wing span. For a fuselage, try $A_{\text{fuselage}} = \pi(L^2/4)$, where L is the length or width of the fuselage as appropriate to the direction under consideration.

References

[1]McCormick, B. W., *Aerodynamics of V/STOL Flight*, Academic Press, New York, 1967, pp. 12–14.

[2]McCormick, B. W., *Aerodynamics, Aeronautics and Flight Mechanics*, Wiley, New York, 1979, pp. 29–31.

[3]Kuethe, A. M., and Chow, C. Y., *Foundations of Aerodynamics: Bases of Aerodynamic Design*, 3rd ed., Wiley, New York, 1976, p. 297.

[4]Prouty, R. W., *Helicopter Performance, Stability and Control*, Krieger, Malabar, FL, 1995, pp. 3–5.

Appendix H
Propeller1 Program User's Guide

H.1   Data Preparation

This text provides a simple computer program that performs a propeller analysis. The analysis is based on the momentum theory or blade-element theory; the user selects the option at run time. Furthermore, both on-axis performance and analysis of off-axis behavior are possible. Again, the user selects the option at run time. A sample propeller is provided as internal data, but the user can override this internal table with his/her own data. A sample input data file provides a "go-by." Table H.1 describes the data that goes into the input file line by line. This appendix describes the preparation of the data file.

The sample input data in the file named Userdat.dat are shown in Table H.2. Note: The line numbers are shown to the left so that the reader can easily compare the data with the descriptions in Table H.1. The actual data file does not have the line numbers.

H.2   Operating the Program

The Propeller1 program operates in the Windows environment. Double clicking the icon in the Windows Explorer, or using any shortcut the reader might have established, starts the program. The startup page looks like Fig. H.1.

The menu bar across the top of the page leads the user through the options as shown in Table H.3.

After making the selections from the menu bar, click on the Execute button at the lower left of the form. The caption bar will indicate the progress. The results are displayed graphically and as a table in the text box. The performance results in Fig. H.2 through H.4 were obtained using the example data.

The thrust coefficient, Fig. H.2, increases with increased blade pitch—no surprise there. The term dTheta is the increment added to the root pitch. The thrust coefficient decreases with forward speed for a given blade pitch. At first, this might seem surprising, but with reflection one realizes that the velocity of the oncoming wind can be so high that the propeller is actually coming close to windmilling. In such a case, the angle of attack goes negative, and so does the thrust.

The power coefficient behavior is a bit more complex, Fig. H.3. For a given speed, it increases with increased blade pitch. This is because increased thrust means increased induced velocity at a given forward speed, but as forward speed

Table H.1   Description of input data

Line number	Item	Description/units
1	Nb	Number of blades; nondimensional.
2	R, Xhub	Two values on this line separated by a comma. The first is the propeller radius, in units of feet.
		The second is the ratio of hub cutout to rotor radius to account for spinner. A value of 0.2 means the inner 20% of the propeller is not to be used in the calculation of rotor thrust. Nondimensional.
3	rpm	Rotational speed of the rotor. rpm.
4–14	$r(i), \theta(i), c(i)$	Eleven lines, each with three values on them separated by commas.
		The first value is the radial station on the blade, measuring from the centerline of the propeller to the blade tip in units of feet. The stations are not necessarily evenly spaced.
		The second value on a line is the blade-pitch angle, measured in radians. A positive angle means the propeller station is screwing into the wind. In general, a blade root has a value near 1.57 (90 deg) while the tip has a smaller value near 0.2 (11 deg or so).
		The third value on a line is the chord, measured in feet.
15	a0, cd0, cd1, cd2	This line has four values on it, separated by commas. The first is the slope of the airfoil lift curve in the linear range. It has units of CL/radian. The second, third, and fourth coefficients are the terms in the quadratic drag polar equation: $Cd = Cd0 + Cl * (Cd1 + Cl * Cd2)$.
16	Vinf1, Vinf2, dV	This line has three values on it, separated by commas. Those values represent the starting, ending, and increment values of the freestream velocity used in the speed sweep. They have units of feet/second.
17	Ntheta	Number of root pitch increments to use in the blade-pitch sweep. Each increment is 5 deg.

increases, the induced velocity decreases. As thrust goes negative, the power will go negative. Again, this is windmilling.

The efficiency of the propeller is the ratio of induced (ideal) power to total power or $\eta = JC_T/C_P$. One sees in Fig. H.4 that propellers are remarkably efficient

Table H.2   Sample data found in Userdat.dat

Line number	Input data
1	3
2	4.0, 0.2
3	1800.
4	0.0, 1.571, 0.150
5	0.4, 0.961, 0.150
6	0.8, 0.633, 0.155
7	1.2, 0.547, 0.205
8	1.6, 0.465, 0.254
9	2.0, 0.382, 0.304
10	2.4, 0.323, 0.269
11	2.8, 0.279, 0.234
12	3.2, 0.246, 0.200
13	3.6, 0.220, 0.165
14	4.0, 0.198, 0.130
15	6.00, 0.006225, −0.003, 0.01
16	0.0, 600.0, 20.0
17	7

Fig. H.1   Startup page for Propeller1 program.

devices over a wide range of advance ratios; however, they do require quite a bit of power to turn.

One of the strengths of simulation is the estimation of behavior as well as performance. The preceding results are performance estimates. The results in Fig. H.5 are behavior estimates of the example propeller at a single pitch angle, but at various values of vertical velocity, as one might encounter during climbout.

Table H.3   Menu options

Options	Description
File/Simple Test Data	Click this option to load the internal data.
File/Open	Click this option to open a file input dialog box. From there, read an input file. The example Userdat.dat is available as a go-by.
File/Save	Click this option to save the results of an analysis.
File/Exit	Click this option to end the execution.
Analysis/Performance	Click this option to select on-axis (axial) performance calculations.
Analysis/Off-Axis	Click this option to select off-axis behavior calculations.
Method/Blade Element—Simple	Click this option to select the closed-form solutions.
Method/Blade Element—Momentum	Click this option for the more rigorous blade-element solution.

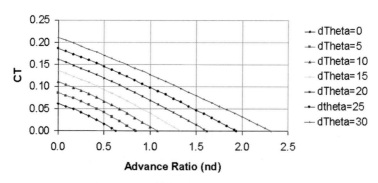

Fig. H.2   Advance ratio effect on thrust coefficient.

The thrust, X-force resolved to the IERA and X-moment (i.e., p-factor) resolved to the IERA are shown.

One sees that the thrust coefficient is relatively unaffected by off-axis velocity. This should probably not be too much of a surprise. The ratio of vertical velocity to tip speed ranges from 0 to 0.2, and the effects of such an in-plane velocity affect the thrust coefficient by the square of that ratio.

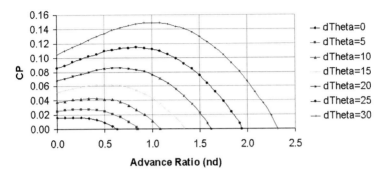

Fig. H.3   Advance ratio effect on power coefficient.

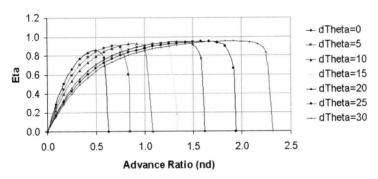

Fig. H.4   Advance ratio effect on efficiency.

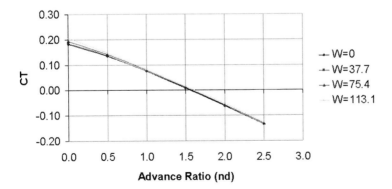

Fig. H.5   Effect of cross flow on thrust coefficient.

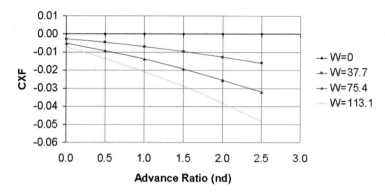

Fig. H.6   Effect of cross flow on vertical force.

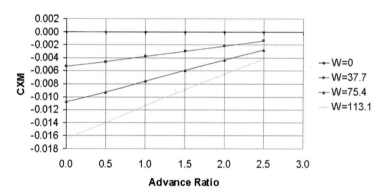

Fig. H.7   Effect of cross flow on yaw moment.

The effect of off-axis velocity on X-force is more interesting. First, be certain what force is being discussed. Recall, the IERA is the axis system with z axis along the propeller shaft. The x axis is generally pointing to the ground. Thus, Fig. H.6 shows that as the vertical component of freestream wind increases (from the bottom), the X-force becomes increasingly negative, that is, the X-force is pointing up, in the direction opposite the in-plane direction of motion.

The effect of off-axis velocity on X-moment is what was described earlier as p-factor. From Fig. H.7, one sees that during a climbout, when the vertical component of the freestream is pointing up, the rotor is developing a nose-left moment. This moment decreases with increased speed.

Appendix I
Pearls of Wisdom

Some of the wisdom of the flying ages is presented here, partly for your amusement, partly because pilots that will fly your simulators all know these pearls, and partly because you will want to learn them the easy way if you intend to learn to fly:

- Flying is the second greatest thrill known to man. Landing is the first.
- It is far better to be down here wishing you were up there than up there wishing you were down here.
- Taking off is optional; landing is mandatory.
- From Paul F. Crickmore (test pilot): "You've never been lost until you've been lost at Mach 3."
- The only time you have too much fuel is when you're on fire.
- From an old carrier sailor: There are more planes in the ocean than submarines in the sky.
- If the wings are traveling faster than the fuselage, it's probably a helicopter—and therefore, unsafe.
- When one engine fails on a twin-engine airplane, the other engine has enough power to fly you to the scene of the crash.
- Without ammunition, the USAF would be just another expensive flying club.
- What is the similarity between air traffic controllers and pilots? If a pilot screws up, the pilot dies; If ATC screws up . . . the pilot dies.
- Never trade luck for skill.
- The three most common expressions (or famous last words) in aviation are: Why is it doing that? Where are we? and "Oh %#&@!."
- Weather forecasts are horoscopes with numbers.
- Airspeed, altitude, and brains. Two are always needed to successfully complete the flight.
- A smooth landing is mostly luck; two in a row is all luck; three in a row is prevarication.
- I remember when sex was safe and flying was dangerous.
- Mankind has a perfect record in aviation; we never left one up there!

- Flashlights are tubular metal containers kept in a flight bag for the purpose of storing dead batteries.
- Flying the airplane is more important than radioing your plight to a person on the ground incapable of understanding or doing anything about it.
- When a flight is proceeding incredibly well, something was forgotten.
- Just remember, if you crash because of weather, your funeral will be held on a sunny day.
- Advice given to RAF pilots during WWII: "When a prang (crash) seems inevitable, endeavor to strike the softest, cheapest object in the vicinity as slow and gently as possible."
- Attributed to Max Stanley (Northrop test pilot): "The Piper Cub is the safest airplane in the world; it can just barely kill you."
- From Jon McBride, astronaut: "A pilot who doesn't have any fear probably isn't flying his plane to its maximum."
- From Bob Hoover (renowned aerobatic and test pilot): "If you're faced with a forced landing, fly the thing as far into the crash as possible."
- From sign over squadron ops desk at Davis-Monthan Air Force Base, AZ, 1970: "There is no reason to fly through a thunderstorm in peacetime."
- If something hasn't broken on your helicopter, it's about to.
- Basic Flying Rules: "Try to stay in the middle of the air. Do not go near the edges of it. The edges of the air can be recognized by the appearance of ground, buildings, sea, trees and interstellar space. It is much more difficult to fly there."
- You know that your landing gear is up and locked when it takes full power to taxi to the terminal.
- Attributed to Ray Crandell (Lockheed test pilot): As the test pilot climbs out of the experimental aircraft, having torn off the wings and tail in the crash landing, the crash truck arrives, the rescuer sees a bloodied pilot and asks, "What happened?" The pilot's reply: "I don't know, I just got here myself!"
- When flying at night, remember the aircraft doesn't know it's night and there are certain aircraft sounds that can only be heard at night.
- The most useless things to a pilot are (pick any three) the following: runway behind you; sky above you; three seconds ago; air in the fuel tank; salesman in the other front seat; fuel in the gas truck; approach plates in the car; airspeed you don't have; and running out of airspeed, altitude, and ideas at the same time.

Appendix J
Details of Simple Rotor Model

J.1 Introduction

This appendix presents the details of the expansion of the thrust and flapping equation for a paddle blade rotor model. The development of a simple rotor model involves a considerable amount of algebraic manipulation, and expansion of the equations of flapping motion is error prone. Furthermore, when one is finished developing the model, the result is still just an approximation. Nevertheless, the knowledge one gains from the details is valuable and can lead to other insights.

J.2 Mechanical Properties of the Paddle Blade Rotor

The paddle blade rotor has these mechanical properties. The rotor has b paddles. Each paddle has mass m and is mounted at the end of a zero-thick, weightless rod that is infinitely stiff in tension, torsion, and bending. The rod runs along the quarter-chord line of the paddle. The center of pressure of the paddle is at a radial distance R from the center of rotation and located at the quarter-chord. Each paddle has area S. The root end of the paddle is equipped with a lever coming off of the leading or trailing edge. This lever, called a *pitch horn*, is attached by a ball and socket joint to a *pitch rod*. By pushing and pulling on the pitch rod, the geometric pitch of the paddle is made to increase or decrease. The other end of the pitch rod is attached to the moving portion of a swashplate mechanism, which permits the pilot to introduce steady and cyclic blade pitch from the nonrotating system to the rotating system. Figure J.1, based on the work of Reference [1], is a schematic of the swashplate, the linkage to the pilot's controls, and the linkage to the pitch rods, pitch horn, and paddle.

The root end of the rod connecting the paddle to the rotating shaft, also called the mast, is attached to a hinge that permits the blade to "flap" out of the plane of rotation. The reason for this hinge or any flexure permitting out-of-plane flapping will become clear directly. No means for in-plane lead-lag motion is provided. Such an attachment is called *simply articulated* and is the arrangement used for the remainder of this appendix. Other hub configurations are presented in the main text. Figure J.2 shows an overhead and schematic side view of a simply articulated blade attachment.

587

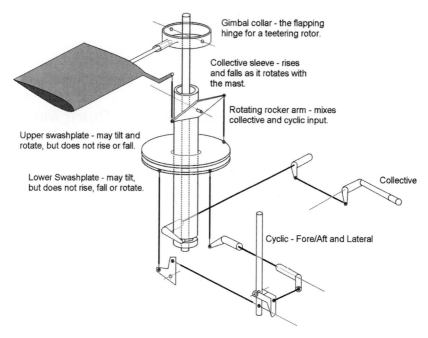

Fig. J.1   Schematic of swashplate and control linkage for a teetering rotor.

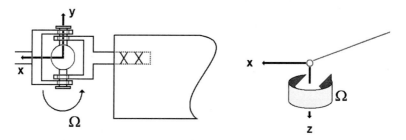

Fig. J.2   Simply articulated rotor with hinge offset seen from above and schematically from the side. The blade is shown flapped up out of the plane of rotation. The X symbol indicates the location of a pitch (also called feathering) bearing.

J.3   Aerodynamic Properties of the Simple Rotor

The paddle blade has these aerodynamic characteristics. The airfoil section is presumed to be symmetric; the pitch change axis pierces the quarter-chord point of the section, and in the case of the full-span blade lies along the loci of quarter-chord points. The lift coefficient of an airfoil is a function of angle of attack, flap deflection, Mach number, and the Reynolds number, which is a dimensionless ratio of dynamic forces to viscous forces. Figure J.3 shows a typical plot of lift coefficient vs angle of attack for various Mach numbers for the NACA 0015 airfoil.

Mach Effect on Lift Coefficient

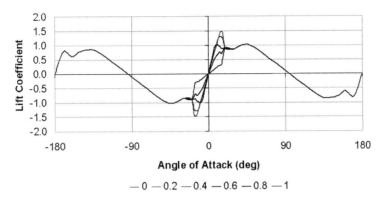

Fig. J.3   **Lift coefficient vs angle of attack for various Mach numbers for the NACA 0015 airfoil.**

Figure J.4 shows the detail in the range between $+/-20$ deg. The variation in drag coefficient with Mach number and angle of attack is shown in Fig. J.5, and a detail from that figure is presented in Fig. J.6.

The linear character of the Mach = 1 curve in Fig. J.6 warrants skepticism. Such detailed representation of the lift and drag exceeds the "texture" of the rest of the simple model being developed here. Instead, linear aerodynamics are employed. Examine the coefficients of lift and drag between -14 and $+14$ deg of angle of attack as shown in Figs. J.7 and J.8.

The data in Fig. J.7 clearly shows that the lift coefficient can be modeled as a constant multiplied by the angle of attack in the range -12 to $+12$ deg, that is,

$$C_l = a_0 \alpha$$

Mach Effect on Lift Coefficient

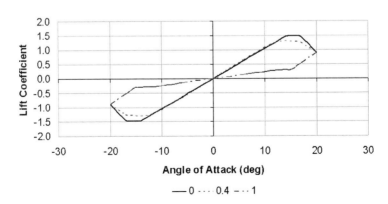

Fig. J.4   **Detail of the preceding figure.**

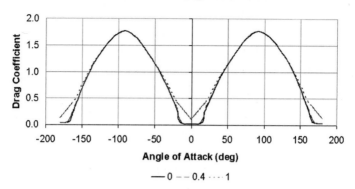

Fig. J.5 Drag coefficient vs angle of attack for various Mach numbers for the NACA 0015 airfoil.

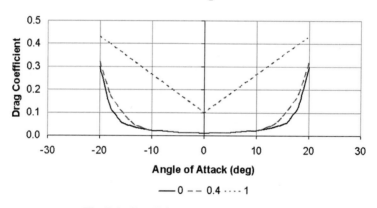

Fig. J.6 Detail from the preceding figure.

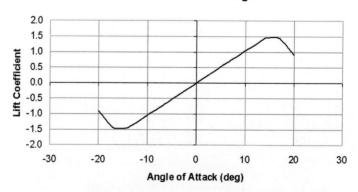

Fig. J.7 Lift coefficient in the approximately linear range.

Drag Coefficient in Linear Lift Region

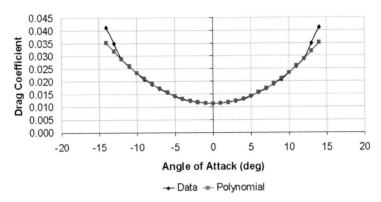

Fig. J.8   Drag coefficient in the angle-of-attack range corresponding to the approximately linear lift region.

This is the linear lift region, and the constant slope is called the linear lift-curve slope. A typical value for a_0, which is the symbol used industry wide for this constant is 0.1 CL/radian or 5.73 CL/deg.

From Fig. J.8, one sees that the drag coefficient might be fitted well with the quadratic polynomial

$$C_d = \delta_0 + \delta_1 \alpha + \delta_2 \alpha^2$$

Using the tabulated data between -12 and $+12$ deg of angle of attack, the drag coefficients are

$$\delta_0 = 0.0113$$
$$\delta_1 = 0.0$$
$$\delta_2 = 0.400$$

Note: The angle of attack must be expressed in radians.

A symmetric airfoil shows no pitching moment about the quarter-chord line in the linear region, and so $C_m = 0.0$.

Linear aerodynamics implies the use of small angles. In this development, a small angle lies approximately between $+/-12$ deg. The angle of attack violates significantly the small-angle assumption under certain conditions. Methods to account for the large angles are presented in the main text.

When a rotor generates lift, it pushes air. The breeze one feels from a fan is an example of air being pushed by a rotor. This breeze is called *induced velocity*. In fact, whenever an aerodynamic force is generated, the air in the vicinity of the body generating the force is pushed in a direction opposed to the direction of generated force. In the general case, the air that is being pushed is called *wash*. Therefore, the literature speaks of *downwash* when describing the induced velocity of a rotor situated so that the thrust vector points up. Wash velocities can be translational and rotational, and they add in a vector sense to the inertial velocity to produce aerodynamic velocity. Of this, more will be written later.

One large angle called the azimuth angle describes the location of the paddle as it is projected in the plane of rotation, which is also called the shaft-normal plane. The azimuth angle is measured positively in the direction of rotation of the paddles, which is counterclockwise when viewed from above for American-made rotors (see Fig. J.9). The reference line of a paddle at zero azimuth points in the negative x-body-axis direction or roughly over the tailboom for a single main rotor helicopter.

The time derivative of the azimuth angle is the rotor spin rate Ω. The center of rotation is at the top of the rotating shaft, which is called the mast.

Now, imagine a point of light attached to the tips of the blades during night flight. Call the visible plane described by the path of the blade tips the tip-path plane. The view in Fig. J.10 is of the tip-path plane as seen from the left side of the aircraft. The hub axes are fixed to the aircraft and do not spin. Though it is certainly true that the aircraft experiences angular motion, we say the axes are attached to the nonrotating frame.

The tip-path plane is tipped aft through an angle a_1, which is called the longitudinal or fore/aft flapping angle. By convention, aft flapping is positive. As a first approximation, one can imagine that the thrust vector is normal to the tip-path

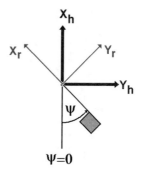

Fig. J.9   Relationship between hub axes, rotor axes, and azimuth angle showing sign convention.

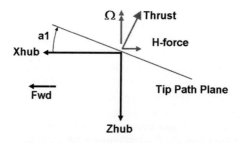

Fig. J.10   Left side view of tip-path plane.

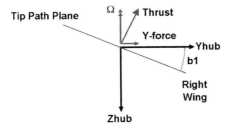

Fig. J.11   Aft view of tip-path plane.

plane, and so the horizontal component of thrust, called H-force, can be estimated quickly by multiplying thrust by the sine of the longitudinal flapping angle. For small angles, the sine of the angle is equal to the angle in radians.

The same tip-path plane can also be tilted to one side or the other. In Fig. J.11, the reader views the tip-path plane from behind the aircraft, looking forward. Here, the tip-path plane is tilted such that the thrust vector has a component pointing to the right. By convention, this is the direction of positive lateral flapping, which the symbol b_1 denotes. Again, by multiplying the thrust by the sine of the lateral flapping angle, the lateral force, called Y-force, is approximated.

Although the hub axes do not spin with the rotor, they can be installed with some tilt, or, as in the case of tiltrotors, they can be moved to some other angular orientation, but they are considered to be part of the fixed system. In the next two diagrams, the axes are labeled Xr, Yr, and Zr, where the r is meant to indicate rotor or rotating.

In Fig. J.12, the reader views the rotating system axes from a point on the negative Yr axis looking toward the origin, which is the center of the hub. One sees the trailing edge of the paddle a distance R from the center of rotation. When the blade flaps up out of the plane of rotation, it is called positive flapping. The literature uses the symbol β for the flapping angle. The figure also clearly shows the positive direction of the time derivatives of β. Three fundamental forces that act on the paddle blade are also shown. Aerodynamic action generates the first of these, called lift L, which is normal to the blade element in this side view. Positive lift pulls the paddle up out of the shaft normal plane. The second fundamental force is centrifugal force $mR\Omega^2$, which puts the rod attaching the paddle to the mast in

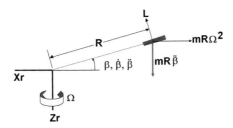

Fig. J.12   Rotating axes with important forces shown acting on a paddle or blade element.

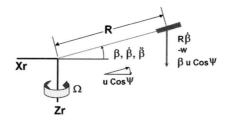

Fig. J.13   **Rotating axes with important velocities and states shown.**

tension. Centrifugal force, acting over a small moment arm, $R\sin(\beta) \approx R\beta$, pulls the paddle into the shaft normal plane. The third force is an inertial load $mR\ddot{\beta}$, which is caused by flapping acceleration. Any attempt to accelerate the paddle in some direction is met with opposing inertial resistance.

Several velocity vectors are presented in Fig. J.13. Let the forward velocity of the hub (nonrotating) axes be called u. The component of u resolved to the rotating system and lying along the Xr axis has magnitude and direction given by $u\cos\psi$. The component of this velocity normal to the flapped paddle is $\beta u\cos\psi$, assuming small angles. An upward-flapping paddle feels wind striking its upper surface at a speed equal to $R\beta$ in the downward direction. Finally, the vertical aerodynamic velocity w is induced velocity added to any vertical inertial velocity.

This breakdown is the classical approach describing the genesis of the various velocities and forces. This appendix will develop the various velocities and forces with greater ease using a more rigorous approach later.

Figure J.14 is a view of the blade section as seen by an observer placed just outside of the blade section looking in toward the center of rotation. The blade section is at a geometric pitch angle θ, which is under pilot control. The arctangent of the ratio of vertical velocity to in-plane velocity is called the inflow angle ϕ. The angle of attack is clearly the sum of the geometric and inflow angles:

$$\alpha = \theta + \phi$$

The lift and drag forces are also visible. Note that the lift is perpendicular to the total velocity vector and drag is parallel to it.

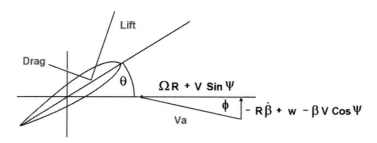

Fig. J.14 End view of blade section showing forces and important velocity components.

Two of the three axes of the paddle section axes are visible in Fig. J.14. The origin of the paddle section axes is attached to the blade reference line or BRL. The positive x_b axis lies on the BRL and points generally toward the hub. The positive y_b axis points from the BRL to the leading edge and lies on or parallel to the chord. The positive z_b axis is normal to the y_b axis, in the plane of the page, and oriented to complete a right-handed system.

J.4 Rotor Math Model

The math model for a rotor divides into two pieces called dynamics and aerodynamics. The dynamics part is written without regard to the atmosphere—a paddle in a vacuum chamber can generate dynamic loads. The aerodynamics part is written without regard to the mass properties of the paddle. However, each part affects the other, and so as each part is developed lip service will be paid to the other until the two parts are joined. The dynamics model is developed first.

J.4.1 Simplified Dynamics of a Paddle Blade Rotor

The center of mass of the paddle is located a distance R from the center of rotation. The quarter-chord line of the paddle blade is coincident with this rod. The instantaneous position of the mass is located in three dimensions if the flapping angle is known. The flapping angle and the distance R completely define the blade reference line. Refer to Fig. J.15.

The BRL is given by the following vector. The velocity and acceleration of the position are found by direct differentiation:

$$s = \left\{ \begin{array}{c} -R\cos(\beta) \\ 0 \\ -R\sin(\beta) \end{array} \right\} \cong \left\{ \begin{array}{c} -R \\ 0 \\ -R\beta \end{array} \right\}$$

The first derivative with respect to time is

$$\dot{s} = \left\{ \begin{array}{c} R\sin(\beta)\dot{\beta} \\ 0 \\ -R\cos(\beta)\dot{\beta} \end{array} \right\} \cong \left\{ \begin{array}{c} 0 \\ 0 \\ -R\dot{\beta} \end{array} \right\}$$

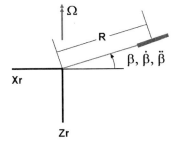

Fig. J.15 Blade-reference-line geometry.

The second derivative with respect to time is

$$\ddot{s} = \left\{ \begin{array}{c} R\cos(\beta)\dot{\beta}^2 + R\sin(\beta)\ddot{\beta} \\ 0 \\ R\sin(\beta)\dot{\beta}^2 - R\cos(\beta)\ddot{\beta} \end{array} \right\} \cong \left\{ \begin{array}{c} 0 \\ 0 \\ -R\ddot{\beta} \end{array} \right\}$$

Products of the flapping angle with itself or any of its derivatives are considered higher order and are discarded. Note that the BRL vector uses the spatial measure s instead of r, which seems a more likely candidate because r suggests an association with radial position. The reasons for this are these: the symbol s reminds the reader that the position on the BRL measures along the BRL in an arclength sense, and the symbol r already represents the angular rotation rate of the hub axes.

The rotor spins with constant speed Ω about the negative z axis. For this simple model, the rotor hub can translate in space along the x and z axes, but it might not rotate about any axis. (Note: This does not mean that the rotor is not spinning. *Rotor* axes do spin, but the *hub* axes, from which the spin is measured, do not.) In a more rigorous treatment to follow, these constraints will be lifted.

The acceleration of the paddle mass with respect to inertial space is found by twice differentiating the position vector expressed in rotor axes while accounting for the rotation of the rotor axes. That is,

$$\frac{ds}{dt} = \frac{\partial s}{\partial t} + \omega_{\text{rotor}|\text{rotor}} \times s$$

followed by

$$\frac{d}{dt}\left(\frac{ds}{dt}\right) = \frac{\partial}{\partial t}\left(\frac{\partial s}{\partial t} + \omega_{\text{rotor}|\text{rotor}} \times s\right) + \omega_{\text{rotor}|\text{rotor}} \times \left(\frac{\partial s}{\partial t} + \omega_{\text{rotor}|\text{rotor}} \times s\right)$$

Employing the conventional shorthand for time derivatives, the acceleration is

$$a = \ddot{s} + 2\omega_{\text{rotor}|\text{rotor}} \times \dot{s} + \dot{\omega}_{\text{rotor}|\text{rotor}} \times s + \omega_{\text{rotor}|\text{rotor}} \times (\omega_{\text{rotor}|\text{rotor}} \times s)$$

The rotor angular velocity and acceleration vectors are simply

$$\omega_{\text{rotor}|\text{rotor}} = \left\{ \begin{array}{c} 0 \\ 0 \\ -\Omega \end{array} \right\} \quad \text{and} \quad \dot{\omega}_{\text{rotor}|\text{rotor}} = \left\{ \begin{array}{c} 0 \\ 0 \\ 0 \end{array} \right\}$$

respectively.

Expanding, the acceleration is

$$a = \left\{ \begin{array}{c} R\Omega^2 \\ 0 \\ -R\ddot{\beta} \end{array} \right\}$$

The acceleration causes an inertial load:

$$f_i = -ma$$

The variable m is the paddle mass given in units of slugs for instance. The inertial forces give rise to inertial moments, which are found by crossing the position vector into the force:

$$M_i = s \times f_i$$

Expand this expression to find the inertial moment about the y (flapping hinge) axis:

$$My_i = -(R\beta)fx_i + (R)fz_i$$

After expansion and dropping higher-order terms, the simplified dynamic model of the flapping paddle is

$$My_i = I_b(\ddot{\beta} + \Omega^2\beta)$$

The term $I_b = mR^2$ is the flapping inertia.

J.4.2 Simplified Aerodynamic Model of a Paddle Blade Rotor

The elements of the velocity triangle pictured in Fig. J.14 are now derived with a bit of formality using position vectors and axis system transformation matrices. The aerodynamic velocity at the blade section is the prize. It is easiest to begin with the inertial velocity, adding the wash velocity later.

The hub axis velocity is

$$V_{hub} = \begin{Bmatrix} u_i \\ 0 \\ w_i \end{Bmatrix}$$

Resolve this vector to the rotating system using the azimuthal transformation $T_z(-\psi)$:

$$T_z(-\psi) = \begin{bmatrix} \cos(\psi) & -\sin(\psi) & 0 \\ \sin(\psi) & \cos(\psi) & 0 \\ 0 & 0 & 1 \end{bmatrix}$$

Then, resolve the result to the flapped axes using the small-angle approximation for flapping about the y axis:

$$T_y(-\beta) = \begin{bmatrix} 1 & 0 & \beta \\ 0 & 1 & 0 \\ -\beta & 0 & 1 \end{bmatrix}$$

to get

$$V_{hub}^{blade} = T_y(-\beta)T_z(-\psi)V_{hub} = \begin{Bmatrix} u_i\cos(\psi) + w_i\beta \\ u_i\sin(\psi) \\ -u_i\beta\cos(\psi) + w_i \end{Bmatrix}$$

The paddle has velocity as a result of its flapping motion and its angular motion with respect to inertial space. This velocity is added to the hub velocity, now expressed in paddle axes:

$$V_i = V_{hub}^{blade} + \dot{s} + \omega \times s = \left\{ \begin{array}{c} u_i \cos(\psi) + w_i \beta \\ u_i \sin(\psi) \\ -u_i \beta \cos(\psi) + w_i \end{array} \right\} + \left\{ \begin{array}{c} 0 \\ 0 \\ -R\dot{\beta} \end{array} \right\} + \left\{ \begin{array}{c} 0 \\ R\Omega \\ 0 \end{array} \right\}$$

so that

$$V_i = \left\{ \begin{array}{c} u_i \cos(\psi) + w_i \beta \\ u_i \sin(\psi) + R\Omega \\ -u_i \beta \cos(\psi) + w_i - R\dot{\beta} \end{array} \right\}$$

Aerodynamic velocity is sum of the inertial velocity and the wash velocity. A negative sign precedes the wash velocity because of the sign convention applied to the wash.

$$V_a = V_i - V_w$$

V_w is the wash velocity. In general, the rotorcraft community uses only the axial wash velocity, and in particular, this paddle model will consider only the axial wash velocity. However, the subscript a will be retained as a reminder that aerodynamic velocity is to be used when talking about aerodynamic forces and moments. Thus,

$$u_a = u_i$$
$$v_a = v_i$$
$$w_a = w_i - w_w$$

The same azimuthal transformations applied to the inertial velocities are also applied to the wash velocities, and so the result is easily written:

$$V_a = \left\{ \begin{array}{c} u_a \cos(\psi) + w_a \beta \\ u_a \sin(\psi) + R\Omega \\ -u_a \beta \cos(\psi) + w_a - R\dot{\beta} \end{array} \right\} = \left\{ \begin{array}{c} U_r \\ U_t \\ U_p \end{array} \right\}$$

The subscripts r, t, and p on the velocity elements on the right-hand side stand for radial, tangential, and perpendicular. These names are used often in the literature.

The industry uses several velocity ratios with regularity. Among them, the most common are as follows:

$$\mu = \frac{u_i}{V_T} \approx \frac{u_a}{V_T}$$

$$\lambda_i = \frac{w_i}{V_T}$$

$$\lambda_w = \frac{w_w}{V_T}$$

$$\lambda_a = \frac{w_a}{V_T} = \lambda_i - \lambda_w$$

where

$$V_T = \Omega R$$

The new nondimensional parameter μ is called the advance ratio, which is the ratio of the forward speed to the tip speed. Typical advance ratio values lie between 0 (hover) and 0.3 to 0.4 for high-speed flight. The other three ratios are the inflow caused by inertial velocity, the inflow caused by downwash, and the total inflow ratio. Using these expressions and factoring out the tip speed, the tangential and perpendicular velocities at the paddle are given by

$$U_t = V_a(y) = V_T[1 + \mu \sin(\psi)]$$

$$U_p = V_a(z) = V_T \left[-\mu\beta \cos(\psi) + \lambda_a - \frac{\dot{\beta}}{\Omega} \right]$$

Therefore, the inflow angle is given by

$$\phi = \arctan\left(\frac{U_p}{U_t}\right) \approx \frac{U_p}{U_t} \approx \frac{[-\mu\beta \cos(\psi) + \lambda_a - (\dot{\beta}/\Omega)]}{[1 + \mu \sin(\psi)]}$$

It was stated earlier that the pilot had control over the geometric pitch of the paddle. This control is accomplished with the cyclic stick and the collective. The pitch of the paddle as a function of azimuth angle is given by

$$\theta = \theta_0 + A_1 \cos(\psi) + B_1 \sin(\psi)$$

The fore/aft or longitudinal cyclic feathering angle has the name B_1. This term is not to be confused with b_1, which is the lateral flapping angle. Static displacement of the cyclic stick forward or rearward (longitudinal cyclic) introduces a once-per-revolution (one-per-rev or one-P are the jargon of the industry) variation in the pitch of the blades such that the tip-path plane will tip forward or rearward, pointing the thrust vector slightly forward or rearward. Figure J.1 shows that by pushing the stick forward the geometric pitch of the blade decreases as it advances toward the right side of the aircraft and then increases as it retreats toward the tail. This seems counterintuitive; one expects that the maximum pitch should occur where maximum lift is desired, over the tail boom for instance, not a quarter of a revolution before. The reason why the cyclic is rigged this way becomes apparent shortly.

The name for lateral cyclic feathering is A_1, which should not be confused with a_1, the longitudinal flapping angle. Pushing the cyclic stick to one side or the other (lateral cyclic) introduces lateral cyclic feathering, another one-P variation in blade pitch that causes the tip-path plane to tip to one side or the other, with attendant pointing of the thrust vector. Again, the cyclic stick presents the change to geometric pitch 90 deg before the desired blade-flapping response.

When the geometric pitch angle and inflow angle are known, the paddle angle of attack is

$$\alpha = \theta + \phi \approx \theta_0 + A_1 \cos(\psi) + B_1 \sin(\psi) + \frac{[-\mu\beta \cos(\psi) + \lambda_a - (\dot{\beta}/\Omega)]}{[1 + \mu \sin(\psi)]}$$

It is not unreasonable to assume that the tangential velocity is much greater than the perpendicular velocity, that is, $U_t \gg U_p$, so that the magnitude of the aerodynamic velocity vector can be approximated by

$$\|V_a\| = \sqrt{U_t^2 + U_p^2} \cong U_t$$

Putting this all together, the lift of the paddle is the product of the dynamic pressure, the area, the linear lift-curve slope, and the angle of attack:

$$L = \underbrace{\frac{1}{2}\rho V_T^2 [1 + \mu \sin(\psi)]^2 Sa_0}_{\text{Dynamic Pressure}}$$

$$\times \underbrace{\left\{\theta_0 + A_1 \cos(\psi) + B_1 \sin(\psi) + \left[\frac{-\mu\beta \cos(\psi) + \lambda_a - x(\dot{\beta}/\Omega)}{1 + \mu \sin(\psi)}\right]\right\}}_{\text{Angle of Attack}}$$

The drag is given by a similar function:

$$D = \frac{1}{2}\rho V_T^2 [\mu \sin(\psi) + x]^2 Sa_0\varepsilon_0$$

where

$$\varepsilon_0 = \frac{\overline{C}_D}{a_0}$$

and $\overline{C}_D$ is the average drag coefficient around the azimuth. The aerodynamic forces are resolved to the rotor axes by rotating them about the x_b axis through the inflow angle, and then about the y_b axis through the flapping angle. Small angles can be used in the transformation matrices:

$$Fa_r = \begin{bmatrix} 1 & 0 & -\beta \\ 0 & 1 & 0 \\ \beta & 0 & 1 \end{bmatrix} \begin{bmatrix} 1 & 0 & 0 \\ 0 & 1 & -\phi \\ 0 & \phi & 1 \end{bmatrix} \begin{Bmatrix} 0 \\ -D \\ -L \end{Bmatrix} = \begin{Bmatrix} \beta L \\ -D + \phi L \\ -\phi D - L \end{Bmatrix} = \begin{Bmatrix} Fxa_r \\ Fya_r \\ Fza_r \end{Bmatrix}$$

The aerodynamic moments at the top of the mast are found by crossing the BRL into the force vector:

$$Ma_r = s \times Fa_r$$

Expanding this expression,

$$Ma_r = \begin{vmatrix} i & j & k \\ -R & 0 & -R\beta \\ Fxa_r & Fya_r & Fza_r \end{vmatrix} = \left\{ \begin{array}{c} R\beta(Fya_r) \\ -R\beta(Fxa_r) + R(Fza_r) \\ -R(Fya_r) \end{array} \right\}$$

The y component is the flapping moment. Substituting the expressions for Fxa_r and Fya_r into the flapping moment gives

$$Mya_r = -R\beta(\beta L) + R(-\phi D - L) \cong R(-\phi D - L)$$

Higher-order terms have been cast aside. Substitute the expressions for L, D, and ϕ into the preceding equation. After some algebra and factoring, the aerodynamic flapping moment becomes

$$Mya_r = -\frac{1}{2}\rho V_T^2 RSa_0[1 + \mu \sin(\psi)]^2 \left\{ \theta_0 + A_1 \cos(\psi) + B_1 \sin(\psi) \right.$$
$$\left. + \left[\frac{-\mu\beta \cos(\psi) + \lambda_a - x(\dot{\beta}/\Omega)}{1 + \mu \sin(\psi)} \right](1 + \varepsilon_0) \right\}$$

The term $(1 + \varepsilon_0)$, which amplifies the inflow ratio, is very nearly unity. If the average drag coefficient is 0.015 and the lift-curve slope is 5.73, then this term has a value of 1.00262. That is to say, this term will change the flapping moment by no more than a few tenths of a percent over what would be calculated if we ignored the drag contribution. For this reason, it is safe to ignore ε_0 and set the term $(1 + \varepsilon_0)$ to unity in the flapping moment above. Expand the preceding expression, and retain all harmonics for the moment:

$$Mya_r = -\frac{1}{2}\rho V_T^2 RSa_0 \left\{ \begin{array}{l} [1 + 2\mu \sin(\psi) + \mu^2 \sin^2(\psi)]\theta_0 \\ +[1 + 2\mu \sin(\psi) + \mu^2 \sin^2(\psi)]A_1 \cos(\psi) \\ +[1 + 2\mu \sin(\psi) + \mu^2 \sin^2(\psi)]B_1 \sin(\psi) \\ -[1 + \mu \sin(\psi)](\mu\beta C - \lambda_a) \\ \\ -[1 + \mu \sin(\psi)]\left(\dfrac{\dot{\beta}}{\Omega}\right) \end{array} \right\}$$

Add Myi and $Myar$, and set the sum to zero. Divide the result by the flapping inertia I_b. Define the nondimensional factor:

$$\gamma = \frac{\rho a_0 SR^3}{I_b}$$

Factor the sum and rearrange:

$$\ddot{\beta} + \frac{\overline{\gamma}\Omega}{2}[1 + \mu\sin(\psi)]\dot{\beta} + \Omega^2\left\{1 + \frac{\overline{\gamma}}{2}[1 + \mu\sin(\psi)]\mu\cos(\psi)\right\}\beta$$

$$= \frac{\overline{\gamma}\Omega^2}{2}\left\{\begin{array}{l}[1 + 2\mu\sin(\psi) + \mu^2\sin^2(\psi)]\theta_0 \\ +[1 + 2\mu\sin(\psi) + \mu^2\sin^2(\psi)]A_1\cos(\psi) \\ +[1 + 2\mu\sin(\psi) + \mu^2\sin^2(\psi)]B_1\sin(\psi) \\ +[1 + \mu\sin(\psi)]\lambda_a\end{array}\right\}$$

This is the flapping equation, which is linear with time-varying, periodic coefficients. In general, this is a very messy equation to solve analytically. However, a quasi-static approach can be employed to arrive at some useful results. This technique is described next.

J.5 Quasi-Static Solution of the Flapping Equation

The quasi-static solution begins with several assumptions:

1) The paddle flaps in simple harmonic motion, limited to the first harmonic and a steady term.

2) The coefficients describing the simple harmonic motion are constant.

3) The quasi-static solution assumes that the system operates at a high enough frequency and with enough damping that all transients decay rapidly and that the so-called infinite time solution is acceptable even in the presence of time-varying inputs.

4) The quasi-static solution presumes that the periodic coefficients in the equation do not affect the stability of the system appreciably. Floquet or root-perturbation methods confirm this assumption.

The proposed solution to the flapping equation is

$$\beta = \beta_0 - a_1\cos(\psi) - b_1\sin(\psi)$$

The three constants in the assumed flapping response, namely, β_0, a_1, and b_1 represent the coning angle, the fore/aft or longitudinal flapping angle, and the lateral flapping angle, respectively. The derivatives are

$$\dot{\beta} = [a_1\sin(\psi) - b_1\cos(\psi)]\frac{d\psi}{dt} = [a_1\sin(\psi) - b_1\cos(\psi)]\Omega$$

$$\ddot{\beta} = [a_1\cos(\psi) + b_1\sin(\psi)]\Omega^2$$

Substitute these expressions into the flapping equation and expand. There just is not an easy way to reduce the arithmetic involved short of spending money on a symbolic manipulation package or writing your own program to do that. The author wrote a simple text substitution program to assist in the expansions and then checked the results against known solutions. (Beware hand expansions. A friend once said of a well-known computer program that all one had to do was open the listing to any page, flip a dime on the page, and that dime would cover a sign error. That friend is a cynic and a curmudgeon, but he was also right about that code.) The result includes several terms with complex products of trigonometric functions. Use the following formulas to reduce the complex products to steady and harmonic terms:

$$\sin^2(\psi) = \frac{1}{2} - \frac{\cos(2\psi)}{2}$$

$$\cos^2(\psi) = \frac{1}{2} + \frac{\cos(2\psi)}{2}$$

$$\sin(\psi)\cos(\psi) = \frac{1}{2}\sin(2\psi)$$

$$\sin^2(\psi)\cos(\psi) = \frac{\cos(\psi)}{4} - \frac{\cos(3\psi)}{4}$$

$$\sin(\psi)\cos^2(\psi) = \frac{\sin(\psi)}{4} + \frac{\sin(3\psi)}{4}$$

$$\sin^3(\psi) = \frac{3\sin(\psi)}{4} - \frac{\sin(3\psi)}{4}$$

Retain only the steady and first harmonic elements, and write three algebraic equations. The first equation has only the steady terms, the second equation has only the sine terms, and the third equation has only the cosine terms. The three equations are conveniently gathered into a matrix level expression, given next:

$$\begin{bmatrix} 1 & 0 & 0 \\ 0 & \frac{\bar{\gamma}}{2}A_{a_1} & 0 \\ \frac{\bar{\gamma}}{2}B_{\beta_0} & 0 & -\frac{\bar{\gamma}}{2}B_{b_1} \end{bmatrix} \begin{Bmatrix} \beta_0 \\ a_1 \\ b_1 \end{Bmatrix} = \begin{bmatrix} \frac{\bar{\gamma}}{2}F_0 & 0 & \frac{\bar{\gamma}}{2}F_{B_1} & \frac{\bar{\gamma}}{2}F_\lambda \\ \frac{\bar{\gamma}}{2}A_0 & 0 & \frac{\bar{\gamma}}{2}A_{B_1} & \frac{\bar{\gamma}}{2}A_\lambda \\ 0 & \frac{\bar{\gamma}}{2}B_{A_1} & 0 & 0 \end{bmatrix} \begin{Bmatrix} \theta_0 \\ A_1 \\ B_1 \\ \lambda_a \end{Bmatrix}$$

The coefficients are defined next:

$$F_0 = \left(1 + \frac{\mu^2}{2}\right) \quad F_{B_1} = (\mu) \quad F_\lambda = 1$$

$$A_0 = (2\mu) \quad A_{B_1} = \left(1 + \frac{3\mu^2}{4}\right) \quad A_\lambda = (\mu) \quad A_{a_1} = \left(1 - \frac{\mu^2}{4}\right)$$

$$B_{\beta_0} = (\mu) \quad B_{A_1} = \left(1 + \frac{\mu^2}{4}\right) \quad B_{b_1} = \left(1 + \frac{\mu^2}{4}\right)$$

The coning angle, longitudinal-flapping angle, and lateral-flapping angle, are found by solving the preceding simultaneous equations.

$$
\begin{Bmatrix} \beta_0 \\ a_1 \\ b_1 \end{Bmatrix} = \begin{bmatrix} \dfrac{\bar{\gamma}}{2}F_0 & 0 & \dfrac{\bar{\gamma}}{2}F_{B_1} & \dfrac{\bar{\gamma}}{2}F_\lambda \\[2ex] \dfrac{A_0}{A_{a_1}} & 0 & \dfrac{A_{B_1}}{A_{a_1}} & \dfrac{A_\lambda}{A_{a_1}} \\[2ex] \dfrac{\bar{\gamma}}{2}\dfrac{B_{\beta_0}}{B_{b_1}}F_0 & -\dfrac{B_{A_1}}{B_{b_1}} & \dfrac{\bar{\gamma}}{2}\dfrac{B_{\beta_0}}{B_{b_1}}F_{B_1} & \dfrac{\bar{\gamma}}{2}\dfrac{B_{\beta_0}}{B_{b_1}}F_\lambda \end{bmatrix} \begin{Bmatrix} \theta_0 \\ A_1 \\ B_1 \\ \lambda_a \end{Bmatrix}
$$

From this simple analysis, these statements can be made:

1) Coning is strongly influenced by application of collective and by inflow ratio.

2) As airspeed increases, increased longitudinal cyclic increases coning.

3) At hover, a one-to-one correspondence exists between longitudinal flapping and longitudinal cyclic. This is the so-called equivalence of flapping and feathering.

4) As airspeed increases, the flapping-to-feathering ratio is amplified.

5) Forward flight causes aft flapping.

6) Lateral flapping and lateral cyclic are in one-to-one correspondence over the entire velocity range.

7) Increased coning causes increased lateral flapping.

8) Longitudinal flapping, which is a cosine term, is produced by a sine term in the forcing function. Likewise, lateral flapping, which is a sine term, is produced by a cosine term in the forcing function. The flapping **LAGS** the forcing function by 90 deg.

These results agree surprisingly well with more sophisticated results and so can be used as a sanity check. Statement 8 speaks to the reason why manufacturers rig the cyclic pitch control in such a funny way. Because the rotor has mass, it behaves as a gyroscope. The response of a gyroscope lags an applied torque by 90 deg. So, in order to introduce flapping in a given direction, the blade pitch must be altered maximally 90 deg before the desired response!

This appendix modeled a rotor with a paddle for the blade. Whereas the physical model is simplistic, the method that was used is applicable to a full-span blade with additional features such as hub restraint, blade twist, hub motion, and hub acceleration. The reader is encouraged to consult References [2] and [3] for more information on quasi-static models.

References

[1] Gessow, A., and Myers, G. C., JR., *Aerodynamics of the Helicopter*, Frederick Ungar Publishing Co., New York, 1978, p. 27.

[2] McCormick, Barnes W., *Aerodynamics of V/STOL Flight*, Academic Press, New York, 1967, pp. 124–145.

[3] Dreier, Mark E., "*The Influence of a Trailing Tip Vortex on a Thrusting Rotor*," Master's Thesis, Dept. of Aerospace Engr., Univ. of Pennsylvania, University Park, PA, March 1977.

Appendix K
Improvement of the Quasi-Static
Rotor Model

K.1 Introduction

The quasi-static solution to the flapping equation is the so-called infinite-time or steady-state solution. It is the solution that would be achieved by time-integration methods after all transients have died away. For static performance analysis, this is quite acceptable. For maneuvering flight simulation, the quasi-static solution would be much too "snappy" in response to pilot input. Several authors of helicopter simulation have attempted to preserve the dynamics by employing the time-dependent coefficients in the harmonic solution. See in particular [1] and [2]. This appendix discusses that method.

K.2 Improved Quasi-Static Solution

The classical flapping equation, extended for angular rates, was developed in the main text. It is repeated here:

$$
\ddot{\beta} + \frac{\gamma \Omega_a^2}{2} \left(\frac{B_T^4}{4} + \frac{\mu B_T^3 S}{3} \right) (1 + \varepsilon_0) \frac{\dot{\beta}}{\Omega_a}
$$

$$
+ \left[\omega^2 + \frac{\gamma \Omega_a^2}{2} \left(\frac{B_T^3}{3} + \frac{\mu B_T^2 S}{2} \right) (1 + \varepsilon_0) \mu C + \frac{M_1}{I_b} \left(a_x C - a_y S \right) \right] \beta
$$

$$
= \frac{\gamma \Omega_a^2}{2} \left[\left(\frac{B_T^4}{4} + \frac{2\mu B_T^3 S}{3} + \frac{\mu^2 B_T^2 S^2}{2} \right) \Theta_0 \right.
$$

$$
+ \left(\frac{B_T^5}{5} + \frac{2\mu B_T^4 S}{4} + \frac{\mu^2 B_T^3 S^2}{3} \right) \Theta_T + \left(\frac{B_T^4}{4} + \frac{2\mu B_T^3 S}{3} + \frac{\mu^2 B_T^2 S^2}{2} \right) A_1 C
$$

$$
+ \left(\frac{B_T^4}{4} + \frac{2\mu B_T^3 S}{3} + \frac{\mu^2 B_T^2 S^2}{2} \right) B_1 S + \left(\frac{B_T^3}{3} + \frac{\mu B_T^2 S}{2} \right) (1 + \varepsilon_0) \lambda_a
$$

605

$$+ \left(\frac{B_T^4}{4} + \frac{\mu B_T^3 S}{3} \right)(1 + \varepsilon_0)\hat{p}_a S + \left(\frac{B_T^4}{4} + \frac{\mu B_T^3 S}{3} \right)(1 + \varepsilon_0)\hat{q}_a C \Bigg]$$

$$+ \dot{p}_i S - 2q_i \Omega' S + \dot{q}_i C + 2p_i \Omega' C + \frac{M_1}{I_b} a_z \tag{K.1}$$

The Lock number is defined as

$$\gamma = \frac{\rho c a_0 R^4}{I_b} \tag{K.2}$$

The quasi-static solution method presumes a harmonic solution to the flapping equation, which when differentiated and substituted into the flapping equation yields three algebraic equations. The algebraic equations are solved for the three coefficients that represent the displacement and angular orientation of the tip path plane relative to the top of the mast. That is, the solution of the equation of motion of the blade in the rotating system is represented by three coefficients in the fixed system. In vibration analysis, this is called a demodulation problem, and it leads to another problem that brings to mind the phrase "jumping from the frying pan into the fire." This leap is explained in a moment, but first, it is instructive to examine the quasi-static method in a little more detail.

The quasi-static solution relies on several assumptions:

1) The blade flaps in simple harmonic motion, limited to the first harmonic and a steady term.

2) The coefficients describing the simple harmonic motion are constant.

3) The quasi-static solution assumes that the system operates at a high enough frequency and with high enough damping that all transients decay rapidly and that the so-called infinite-time solution is acceptable even in the presence of time-varying inputs.

4) The quasi-static solution presumes that the periodic coefficients in the equation do not affect the stability of the system appreciably.

The expressions for flapping, flapping rate, and flapping acceleration shown next embody these assumptions. The expressions that follow employ shorthand for the trigonometric functions, namely, $C = \cos(\psi)$, $S_2 = \sin(2\psi)$, and so forth:

$$\beta = \beta_0 - a_1 C - b_1 S$$

$$\dot{\beta} = (a_1 S - b_1 C)\frac{d\psi}{dt} = (a_1 S - b_1 C)\,\Omega'$$

$$\ddot{\beta} = (a_1 C + b_1 S)\left(\Omega'\right)^2 \tag{K.3}$$

The following trigonometric identities are also employed in the quasi-static solution:

$$S^2 = \frac{1}{2} - \frac{C_2}{2}$$

$$C^2 = \frac{1}{2} + \frac{C_2}{2}$$

$$SC = \frac{1}{2}S_2$$

$$S^2C = \frac{C}{4} - \frac{C_3}{4}$$

$$SC^2 = \frac{S}{4} + \frac{S_3}{4}$$

$$S^3 = \frac{3S}{4} - \frac{S_3}{4} \tag{K.4}$$

The first, second, and third assumptions just listed can be successfully challenged. In the case of the first assumption, simple harmonic motion can be extended to higher harmonics if one is willing to do the arithmetic. As is easily demonstrated, forward flight introduces a second harmonic to the aerodynamic forcing function that can be solved with a presumed second harmonic in the solution. An expansion to second harmonics is shown in Eq. (K.5):

$$\beta = \beta_0 - a_1 C_1 - b_1 S_1 - a_2 C_2 - b_2 S_2$$

$$\dot{\beta} = (a_1 S_1 - b_1 C_1)\frac{d\psi}{dt} + 2(a_2 S_2 - b_2 C_2)\frac{d\psi}{dt}$$

$$= (a_1 S_1 - b_1 C_1)\Omega' + 2(a_2 S_2 - b_2 C_2)\Omega'$$

$$\ddot{\beta} = (a_1 C_1 + b_1 S_1)(\Omega')^2 + 4(a_2 C_2 + b_2 S_2)(\Omega')^2 \tag{K.5}$$

The first assumption also implies the use of a rigid blade with but a single flapping hinge at or near the center of rotation. This assumption flies in the face of measurement—blades are known to exhibit significant elastic deformation rather than simple harmonic motion. The analysis of such behavior, called *aeroelastic rotor analysis*, is touched on briefly in the main text.

The benefit of the presumed higher harmonic solution is not certain. The magnitude of the higher harmonic forcing functions decreases rapidly, and the action would always be directed on the rigid-body motion. In an aeroelastic analysis, the higher harmonic forcing functions can force an elastic mode that is very lightly damped and thus stimulate a vigorous response. But because this first look at rotors concentrates only on the rigid-body motion of the flapping blade, the presumption of second harmonic motion will not be discussed further. (The author hates himself for suggesting this—extending the presumed solution to second, third, and fourth harmonics is left as an exercise for the interested reader.)

Assuming the coefficients are themselves functions of time challenges the second assumption. Now the solution is no longer quasi static. The dynamics are preserved, and the transient response is improved. Once again, begin with the first harmonic presumption, but now presume that the coefficients are also differentiable. Thus,

$$\beta = \beta_0 - a_1 C - b_1 S$$

$$\dot{\beta} = \dot{\beta}_0 - \dot{a}_1 C - \dot{b}_1 S + (a_1 S - b_1 C)\Omega'$$

$$\ddot{\beta} = \ddot{\beta}_0 - \ddot{a}_1 C - \ddot{b}_1 S + 2(\dot{a}_1 S - \dot{b}_1 C)\Omega' + (a_1 C + b_1 S)(\Omega')^2 \tag{K.6}$$

Substitute these expressions into the flapping equation, and separate them into equations with like harmonics. This is a tiresome exercise. Fortunately, the right-hand side of the flapping equation is unaffected; only the left-hand side is shown here:

$$
\begin{bmatrix} 1 & 0 & 0 \\ 0 & 0 & -1 \\ 0 & -1 & 0 \end{bmatrix} \begin{Bmatrix} \ddot{\beta}_0 \\ \ddot{a}_1 \\ \ddot{b}_1 \end{Bmatrix} + \Omega' \begin{bmatrix} \dfrac{\gamma}{2} D_{\beta_0 \dot{\beta}_0} & 0 & -\dfrac{\gamma}{2} D_{\beta_0 \dot{b}_1} \\ \dfrac{\gamma}{2} D_{a_1 \dot{\beta}_0} & 2 & -\dfrac{\gamma}{2} D_{a_1 \dot{b}_1} \\ 0 & -\dfrac{\gamma}{2} D_{b_1 \dot{a}_1} & -2 \end{bmatrix} \begin{Bmatrix} \dot{\beta}_0 \\ \dot{a}_1 \\ \dot{b}_1 \end{Bmatrix}
$$

$$
+ (\Omega')^2 \begin{bmatrix} P^2 & \dfrac{\gamma}{2} F_{a_1} & 0 \\ 0 & \dfrac{\gamma}{2} A_{a_1} & (1-P^2) \\ \dfrac{\gamma}{2} B_{\beta_0} & (1-P^2) & -\dfrac{\gamma}{2} B_{b_1} \end{bmatrix} \begin{Bmatrix} \beta_0 \\ a_1 \\ b_1 \end{Bmatrix} = \text{RHS} \qquad (K.7)
$$

The coefficients are

$$
D_{\beta_0 \dot{\beta}_0} = F_\Omega \left(\frac{B_T^4}{4} \right) \qquad D_{\beta_0 \dot{b}_1} = F_\Omega \left(\frac{\mu B_T^3}{6} \right)
$$

$$
D_{a_1 \dot{\beta}_0} = F_\Omega \left(\frac{\mu B_T^3}{3} \right) \qquad D_{a_1 \dot{b}_1} = F_\Omega \left(\frac{B_T^4}{4} \right)
$$

$$
D_{b_1 \dot{a}_1} = F_\Omega \left(\frac{B_T^4}{4} \right) \qquad (K.8)
$$

$$
F_0 = F_\Omega^2 \left(\frac{B_T^4}{4} + \frac{B_T^2 \mu^2}{4} \right) \qquad F_T = F_\Omega^2 \left(\frac{B_T^5}{5} + \frac{B_T^3 \mu^2}{6} \right)
$$

$$
F_\lambda = F_\Omega^2 \left(\frac{B_T^3}{3} \right)(1+\varepsilon_0) \qquad F_{B1} = F_\Omega^2 \left(\frac{B_T^3 \mu}{3} \right)
$$

$$
F_p = F_\Omega^2 \left(\frac{B_T^3 \mu}{6} \right)(1+\varepsilon_0) \qquad F_{a1} = F_\Omega^2 \left(\frac{\mu B_T^3}{6 F_\Omega} \right)(1+\varepsilon_0)(1-F_\Omega) \qquad (K.9)
$$

$$
A_0 = F_\Omega^2 \left(\frac{2 B_T^3 \mu}{3} \right) \qquad A_T = F_\Omega^2 \left(\frac{B_T^4 \mu}{2} \right)
$$

$$
A_\lambda = F_\Omega^2 \left(\frac{B_T^2 \mu}{2} - \left\langle \frac{\mu^3}{8} \right\rangle \right)(1+\varepsilon_0) \qquad A_{B1} = F_\Omega^2 \left(\frac{B_T^4}{4} + \frac{3 B_T^2 \mu^2}{8} \right)
$$

$$
A_p = F_\Omega^2 \left(\frac{B_T^4}{4} \right)(1+\varepsilon_0) \qquad A_{a1} = F_\Omega^2 \left(\frac{B_T^4}{4 F_\Omega} - \frac{B_T^2 \mu^2}{8} \right)(1+\varepsilon_0) \qquad (K.10)
$$

$$B_{\beta_0} = F_\Omega^2 \left(\frac{B_T^3 \mu}{3} \right) (1 + \varepsilon_0) \qquad B_{A_1} = F_\Omega^2 \left(\frac{B_T^4}{4} + \frac{B_T^2 \mu^2}{8} \right)$$

$$B_q = F_\Omega^2 \left(\frac{B_T^4}{4} \right) (1 + \varepsilon_0) \qquad B_{b_1} = F_\Omega^2 \left(\frac{B_T^4}{4 F_\Omega} + \frac{B_T^2 \mu^2}{8} \right) (1 + \varepsilon_0) \qquad \text{(K.11)}$$

and

$$P = \frac{\omega}{\Omega'}$$

$$F_\Omega = \frac{\Omega_a}{\Omega'}$$

$$\hat{p}_i = \frac{p_i}{\Omega'}$$

$$\hat{q}_i = \frac{q_i}{\Omega'} \qquad \text{(K.12)}$$

The static or steady-state solution is identical to that shown in the main text. However, the transformation of the flapping equation from the rotating system to the fixed system actually increases the natural frequency of the flapping equation and triples the number of second-order differential equations. The frequency increase is a simple fact of trigonometry—multiply the nth harmonic of some signal by the sine or cosine of the first harmonic, and observe that the new signal has frequency content in the $n + 1$st and $n - 1$st harmonics:

$$\sin(\psi) [A \sin(n\psi)] = \frac{A}{2} \cos [(n - 1)\psi] - \frac{A}{2} \cos [(n + 1)\psi]$$

$$\cos(\psi) [A \sin(n\psi)] = \frac{A}{2} \sin [(n - 1)\psi] + \frac{A}{2} \sin [(n + 1)\psi]$$

What this means to a simulation is demonstrated by an example. Consider a simple rotor with these properties at hover:

$$P = 1.05$$
$$F_\Omega = 1$$
$$\Omega = 32.5$$
$$\gamma = 2$$
$$\varepsilon_0 = 0$$
$$\mu = 0$$

The left-hand side of the original flapping equation of motion becomes

$$\ddot{\beta} + (8.125)\dot{\beta} + (1164.5)\beta = \cdots$$

This oscillator has eigenvalues of $-4.0625 +/- 33.8823$i. Substitute the preceding rotor parameters into Eq. (K.7), and the eigenvalues are $-4.0625 +/- 33.8823$i, $-4.0625 +/- 66.3823$i, and $-4.0625 +/- 1.3823$i. The reader sees immediately that the new system of equations has frequencies approximately double the original system. In other words, in an attempt to make the flapping equation of motion easier to solve, the amount of work has been tripled and made numerically worse because of the higher frequency of the coupled system! This is a dubious improvement.

K.3   Modified Improved Quasi-Static Solution

In light of the preceding analysis, one might be tempted to conclude that the time-domain integration of the original flapping equation is the only alternative to the quasi-static solution. Investigators have introduced a variation on the method given earlier. Start with Eq. (K.7), but discard the second derivative. The result is

$$
\Omega'
\begin{bmatrix}
\dfrac{\gamma}{2}D_{\beta_0\dot{\beta}_0} & 0 & -\dfrac{\gamma}{2}D_{\beta_0\dot{b}_1} \\[2mm]
\dfrac{\gamma}{2}D_{a_1\dot{\beta}_0} & 2 & -\dfrac{\gamma}{2}D_{a_1\dot{b}_1} \\[2mm]
0 & -\dfrac{\gamma}{2}D_{b_1\dot{a}_1} & -2
\end{bmatrix}
\begin{Bmatrix}
\dot{\beta}_0 \\[1mm] \dot{a}_1 \\[1mm] \dot{b}_1
\end{Bmatrix}
$$

$$
+ (\Omega')^2
\begin{bmatrix}
P^2 & \dfrac{\gamma}{2}F_{a_1} & 0 \\[2mm]
0 & \dfrac{\gamma}{2}A_{a_1} & (1-P^2) \\[2mm]
\dfrac{\gamma}{2}B_{\beta_0} & (1-P^2) & -\dfrac{\gamma}{2}B_{b_1}
\end{bmatrix}
\begin{Bmatrix}
\beta_0 \\ a_1 \\ b_1
\end{Bmatrix} = \text{RHS}
\qquad (\text{K.13})
$$

The original problem has been changed from a single second-order differential equation to three first-order differential equations. The eigenvalues of this system are $-143.3, -4.21 +/- 1.14$. Now the transformed system responds almost instantly in coning β_0 and at a highly damped, moderate rate in the two orientation angles. Casual observation of the tip-path plane response to step inputs on the cyclic confirms this behavior. Engineering justification for dropping the second derivative is difficult to come by; [3] has some observations. Further justification comes from a time-domain simulation. Values typical of a medium-sized single main rotor helicopter were used in the quasi-static, first-order, and second-order solutions to the flapping equations. A step input to the longitudinal cyclic perturbed the system. The response of the longitudinal flapping appears in Fig. K.1 for all three orders. One sees that the quasi-static response is unrealistically crisp, but that the first-order and second-order solutions track each other closely. The amount of damping in the flapping equation defines how well the second-order system tracks the first-order system, but even the lightly damped system shown here ($\varsigma = 0.31$) shows that the first-order system provides realistic and usable flapping response.

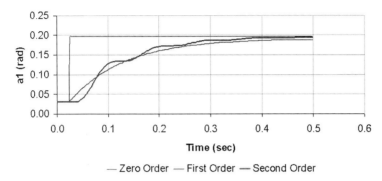

Fore/Aft Flapping Response as a Function of System Order

— Zero Order — First Order — Second Order

Fig. K.1   Comparison of the fore/aft flapping response to a step input for various representations of the flapping equation.

References

[1]Chen, R. T. N., *"A Simplified Rotor System Mathematical Model for Piloted Flight Dynamics Simulation,"* NASA TM-78575, 1979.

[2]Langston, J., *"A Generic Simulation Model for Tiltrotor Aircraft,"* Bell Helicopter Textron, Rept. 901-985-002, Rev. D., Bell-Boeing Joint Program Office, Arlington, VA, 2003, Sept. 30, 2003.

[3]Talbot, P. D., Tinling, B. E., Decker, W. A., and Chen, R. T., *"A Mathematical Model of a Single Main Rotor Helicopter for Piloted Simulation,"* NASA TM 84281, Sept. 1982.

Appendix L
Rotor Tutor Program User's Guide

L.1   Introduction

A rotor simulation program comes with this text. The program, titled Rotor Tutor, gives the user an opportunity to test many of the concepts that the chapter and appendix on rotor models presents. A few words about the assumptions that were made in the program are in order before describing the input:

1) The rotor can have from two to four blades.

2) The blades are infinitely stiff on either side of the flapping hinge.

3) The blades have a rectangular planform; the chord is constant.

4) The blades employ linear twist.

5) The blades have a uniformly distributed mass.

6) The pitch change axis is on the quarter-chord line of the airfoil sections.

7) Each blade has 21 evenly spaced radial stations.

8) The blades employ the same blade-section aerodynamics along their entire length—either linear aerodynamics or table look-up is available.

9) Rotor speed is constant.

10) The downwash is based on the Glauert momentum model, modified with a speed-sensitive time constant for dynamic effects.

11) The downwash can be uniform or triangular.

12) The flapping hinge can be offset.

13) The flapping hinge can be restrained with a spring.

14) Positive and negative pitch-flap coupling (delta-3) can be introduced.

15) The blades can flap independently, or they can be attached to a teetering hub.

16) Prandtl's tip loss factor is a constant.

Despite this formidable list of assumptions, the user can acquire a significant appreciation of the dynamics and aerodynamic problems associated with a rotor in hover and forward flight.

L.2   Operating the Code

The user starts the code in the directory in which it was installed. The flash screen gives way to the main screen when the user presses any key or clicks the flash screen with the mouse.

The main screen has a large picture area on the left and a smaller text box on the right. One also finds a scroll bar in the lower-right corner. The menu bar across

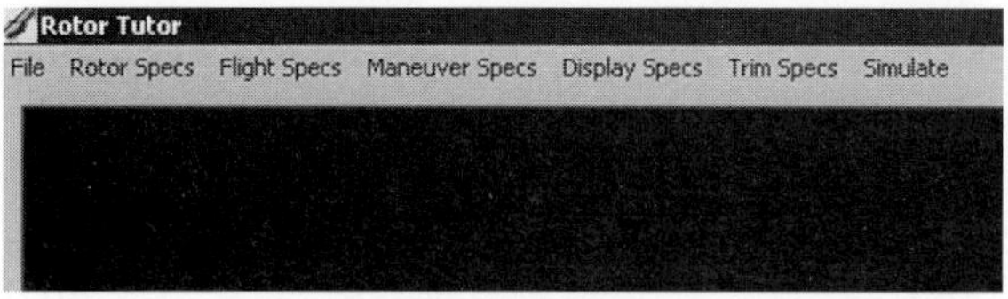

Fig. L.1   Menu.

the top of the screen leads the user through the options and operation of the code (see Fig. L.1).

Proceeding from left to right, these are the menu options.

L.2.1   File/Open Rotor Spec

The Rotor Tutor program can save and read a file with rotor specifications. Rotor specifications describe the physical attributes of the rotor that the user is modeling. A specification file with the default data is shown here:

clalfa =	5.73
cd0 =	0.0105
cd1 =	0
cd2 =	0.01325
clmax =	1.4
rpm =	310.3521
radius =	22
cord =	2
nb =	2
kbeta =	0
ehf =	0
th0deg =	15
twistdeg =	−11
A1sdeg =	0
B1sdeg =	0
delta3 =	0
hubtype =	1
waketype =	1
ar_correction =	0
iblade =	1403.059
Btip =	0.97
hub_cutout =	0
thrust =	6000

Invoking the Open Rotor Spec command causes the Rotor Tutor to open a dialog box that prompts the user for the name of the specification file. Enter the name and click "OK" to read the file. The meaning of the variables is provided in a later section.

L.2.2 File/Save Rotor Spec

Once a user has defined a rotor, the user can save the specifications. Select the Save Rotor Spec option to open a dialog box that prompts the user for the file name the user wants to use to save the specifications.

L.2.3 File/About

The About option offers basic information about the Rotor Tutor program and provides a System Information inquiry for user interest.

L.2.4 File/Exit

The Exit option closes all open files, ends the program, and returns system resources.

L.2.5 Rotor Specs

The physical attributes of the rotor are assigned with this option. A form presents numerous text boxes and option switches. The meaning of each attribute, and its keyword in the rotor specification file, is presented in Table L.1. The form is seen in the screen print after the table (Fig. L.2).

In the frame titled "Enter Flapping Inertia," one sees reference to Lock number. The user cannot change this value directly. One sees from the expression for Lock number, $\gamma = \rho c a_0 R^4 / I_b$, that this parameter is a function of several other variables on this form. It is printed in its own text box for informational purposes only and is updated with every change to the other parameters in its definition.

The AR_correction flag is an option that attempts to adjust the slope of the lift curve in the linear region for three-dimensional effects. The correction this program uses is

$$a_{0|3-D} = a_{0|2-D} \frac{A}{A + 2(A + 4/A + 2)}$$

where the aspect ratio for a rectangular blade is given by

$$A = \frac{R}{c}$$

The user can elect to use a table of lift and drag coefficients vs angle of attack to define the aerodynamics of the blade sections. Click on the "Press to use aero table" button to call a dialog box that requests the file name. A file for the NACA 0012 airfoil is included with the code to serve as a go-by.

L.2.6 Flight Specs

Invoke the Flight Specs form to input the airspeed, rate of climb, aerodynamic and inertial roll rate, pitch rate, yaw rate, and density ratio. The user can also input the blade-pitch controls. In another option, the controls can be iterated upon to drive the rotor to user-set values for thrust or power, flapping angles, H-force, and Y-force. The Flight Specs screen is shown in Fig. L.3.

Table L.1   Rotor specifications the user may change

Name on form	Spec file name	Description
Radius	radius	Rotor radius from center of mast to blade tip, ft
Chord	cord	Thrust-weighted chord, ft
Twist	twistdeg	Linear twist value; negative is washout, deg
Number of blades	nb	Number of blades, nd
Rotor speed	rpm	Rotor speed, rpm
Kbeta	kbeta	Flapping hinge spring strength, ft-lb/deg
Flapping hinge offset	ehf	Flapping hinge offset, ft
Delta 3	Delta3	Parameter couples blade pitch and flapping; positive value means pitch angle decreases with increased flapping, deg
Root cutout	Hub_cutout	Blade aerodynamics ignored inboard of this blade station, ft
Tip loss factor	Btip	Lift is set to zero from this station to the blade tip, nd
Ib	iblade	Blade flapping inertia, slug-ft^2
a0	clalfa	Blade-section lift-curve slope in linear range, CL/radian
Clmax	clmax	Maximum (absolute) value of blade-section lift, CL
Cd0	Cd0	Minimum drag in blade-section drag polar, CD
Cd1	Cd1	Variation of blade-section drag with lift coefficient, CD/CL
Cd2	Cd2	Variation of blade-section drag with square of lift coefficients, CD/CL^2
AR correction	ar_correction	Switch to turn on or off a correction to the blade-section lift-curve slope; suggest value is OFF (0), nd
Hub type	hubtype	Switch to select hub type; articulated (0) means each blade is independent of all others; teetering (1) means flapping moments are transmitted to a common ring, nd
Wake type	waketype	Switch to select wake distribution; uniform (0) means the wake has no azimuthal or radial variation; triangular (1) means the wake has radial variation, nd
Not on this form	thrust	The value of thrust desired in the trim option
Not on this form	Th0deg	Collective pitch angle, deg
Not on this form	A1sdeg	Lateral cyclic angle; a positive value produces a negative lateral flapping angle in hover, deg
Not on this form	B1sdeg	Longitudinal cyclic angle; a positive value produces a positive longitudinal flapping angle in hover, deg

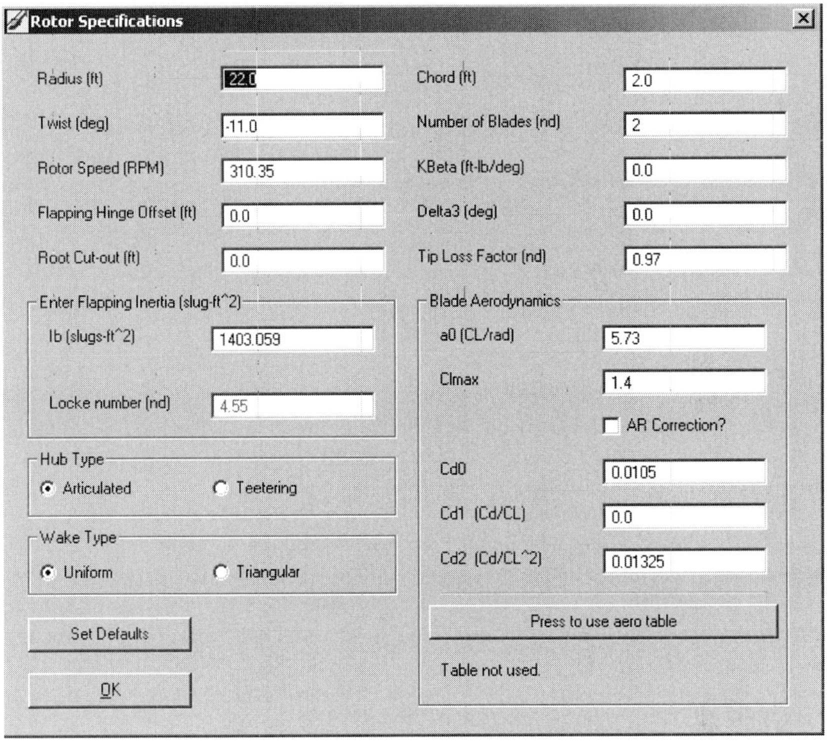

Fig. L.2 Rotor specifications form.

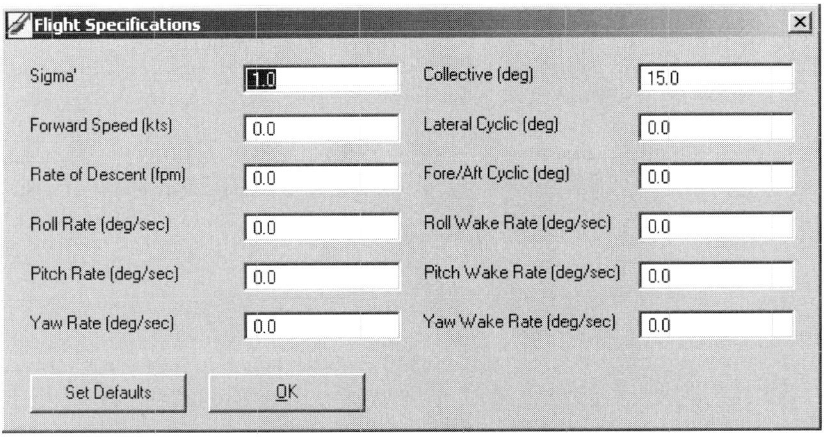

Fig. L.3 Flight specs form.

L.2.7 Maneuver Specs

When the simulation executes, the rotor spins around the azimuth for 14 revolutions. The Maneuver Specification dialog box lets the user introduce a step change to the collective, lateral cyclic, and longitudinal cyclic at the beginning of the eighth revolution. The amount of the change is specified on this form, which is shown in Fig. L.4. If no change is desired, set the change values to zero.

L.2.8 Display Specs

The user selects the nature of the graphical output with the form shown in Fig. L.5.

The *Show Blade* display presents a blade section at the 3/4-radius station. The user will observe the blade change pitch and move in response to the flapping information coming from the transient solution. A yellow line represents the relative wind coming at the blade section, and the two blue lines represent the distributed lift and drag at that station. Figure L.6 provides an example.

The *Show Disc* display presents a color map of the azimuthally varying lift, drag, angle of attack and out-of-plane displacement of each blade station. A small yellow dot, chased by a fading series of yellow dots, marks the azimuth location of blade number one. An example of this display is shown in Fig. L.7.

The *Show Time History* display plots blade-flapping parameter, thrust, and induced velocity as a function of azimuth angle of blade number one. One should note that the distance between tick marks along the abscissa is one revolution. Figure L.8 shows one such time history of the transient solution to the flapping equations for a two-bladed, articulated rotor in forward flight. A collective step down at the beginning of the eighth revolution excites transient behavior.

The *Show Rotor Loads* display, which is the default, shows the most information. As the transient solution is calculated, a stylized blade, seen in perspective, revolves around a center point. The distributed lift, drag, and resultant are plotted along the blade at each azimuth, according to the selections made by the user on the Display Specifications form. Other information is shown as well, including blade

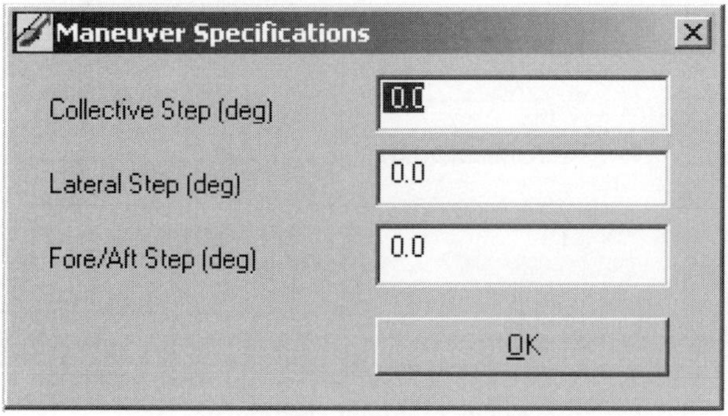

Fig. L.4 Maneuver specification form.

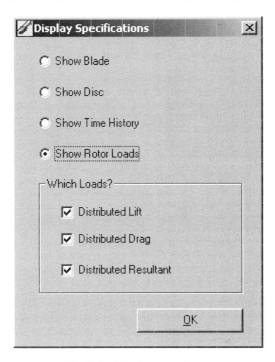

Fig. L.5   Display specs form.

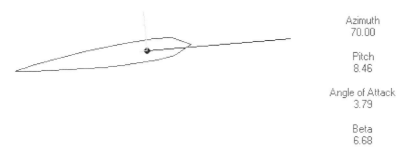

Fig. L.6   Example screen from Show Blade option.

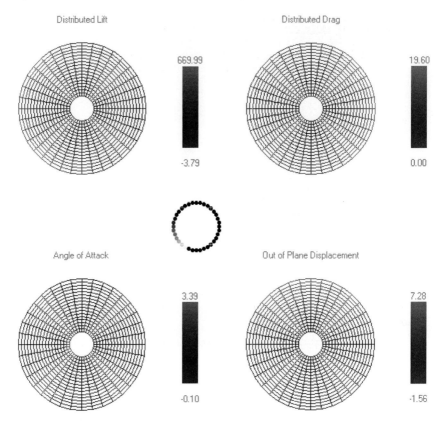

Fig. L.7   Show Disk option clearly identifies the reverse-flow region of a rotor in forward flight.

flapping as in the rotating system, and the relative wind and distributed lift and drag of the zero-lift line of the blade sections at the 1/10 and 3/4 radial stations. Fixed-system tip-path plane is also shown. The state of the rotor when the blade is at azimuth station 270 is seen in Fig. L.9.

L.2.9   Trim Specs

With this option the user tells Rotor Tutor what type of trim analysis is desired (see Fig. L.10). The user might wish to require that the rotor always trim to a given fore/aft flapping or a given H-force. If so, the user should check the Longitudinal Trim box, then select from the two options, and provide the desired value. A similar process holds for the Lateral Trim and for Collective Trim. Please note that each of these trim options is independent, so that any or all three can be selected. Clicking on the Trim Analysis causes the program to use the Periodic Shooting technique to trim flapping and at the same time drive the solution to the desired flapping, power, or loads. Once the trim has been achieved, the solution is

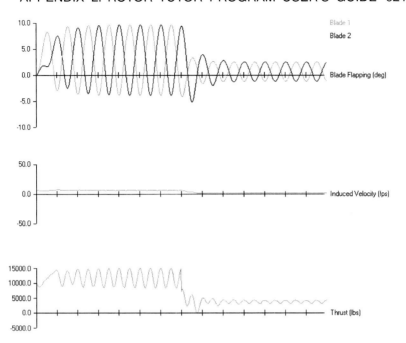

Fig. L.8   Show Time History display.

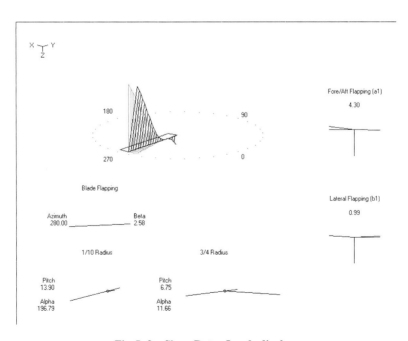

Fig. L.9   Show Rotor Loads display.

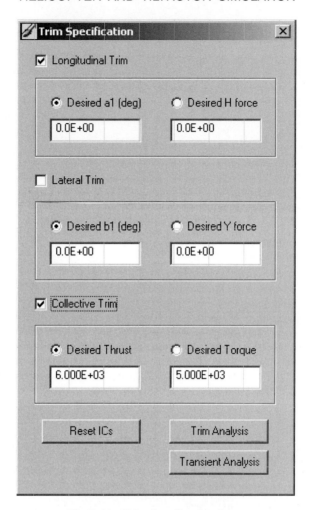

Fig. L.10   Trim Specification form.

displayed in the text box to the right of the screen. If the Transient Analysis button is clicked, this form closes, and the user is then ready for the final main-menu option button.

L.2.10   Simulate/Start

This option starts the time-domain simulation of the rotor. According to the selections made on the Display Specs form, the program will display the solution using the format of Figs. L.6, L.7, L.8, or L.9. If the user selected Trim Analysis on the previous form, then the flapping solution begins from a trim condition, that is, one will not observe any transients. If the user selected Transient

Analysis, the time-domain solution begins from an initial flapping angle and rate of zero.

L.2.11   Simulate/Stop

This option stops the time-domain simulation.

L.3   Other Options

The program has two other useful options. The first is the horizontal scroll bar at the bottom right of the main screen. When the scroll "thumb" is all the way to the right, the time-domain simulation operates at its highest speed. As the user drags the thumb to the left, the time-domain solution will slow, allowing the user to take lingering looks at the display. The slowest speed is approximately 1 s per azimuth cut.

The other option allows the user to shrink or expand the displayed information. Right click on the picture area, and a dialog box opens.

L.4   Comparisons

When a simulation or a trim is complete, the average values of several rotor output variables are printed in the text box on the right side of the screen. One will also observe that some average values are printed twice—one set comes from numerical integrations and large angle manipulations, and the other set is generated from the simple closed-form solutions in the main text. The reader might be surprised, and misled, by the seeming excellent correlation as demonstrated in the following comparisons. In all figures, the "be" designation means "blade element," the numerical integration answer. The "txt" designator means these answers were calculated using the closed-form solutions in the text. The "nlbe" label implies lift and drag coefficients that come from table look-up.

In Figs. L.11a and L.11b, the thrust is shown as a function of collective angle at two different advance ratios. One sees excellent correlation at hover. However, at higher forward speed the realistic lift and drag representation from the tables cause blade stall and a dramatic departure from what linear aerodynamics estimates.

In Fig. L.12, the torque is shown as a function of advance ratio for a constant value of thrust. One observes that the table-driven answers show that the rotor requires less torque than the linear predictions and that the linear predictions become questionable at high advance ratio.

Figures L.13a and L.13b show the correlation of longitudinal flapping with longitudinal cyclic at hover and at high advance ratio. Again, the results are surprisingly good.

Do not be fooled into thinking that the simple closed-form, quasi-static rotor model equations in the main text will be adequate for all flight regimes. Obviously blade stall is not well handled, and power (torque) shows a significant difference over the entire range of advance ratio. The simple model is just that. But, such a model can serve the reader well for initial performance and behavior estimates.

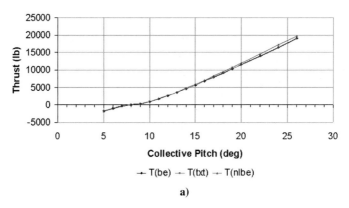

a)

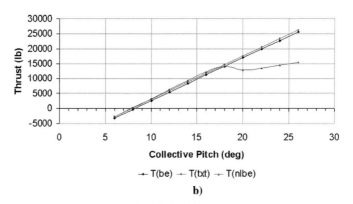

b)

Fig. L.11   Thrust vs collective for two values of advance ratio.

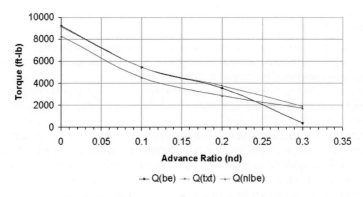

Fig. L.12   Torque as a function of advance ratio.

Longitudinal Flapping vs Fore/Aft Cyclic (mu=0.0)

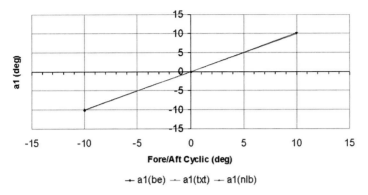

— a1(be) — a1(txt) — a1(nlb)

Fig. L.13a   The a1 at hover.

Longitudinal Flapping vs Fore/Aft Cyclic (mu=0.3)

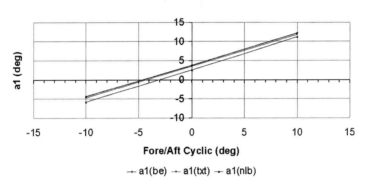

— a1(be) — a1(txt) — a1(nlb)

Fig. L.13b   The a1 at high advance ratio.

L.5 Useful Hints

Each blade in the Rotor Tutor program has 21 radial stations and 24 azimuth stations. Each blade has its own flapping angle and associated derivatives. In the time-domain solution, the forces, moments, and forcing function for the flapping equation are calculated by radial integration. If the blades are independent, then the program proceeds to the azimuthal integration. If the blades communicate with each other via a gimbal ring or teetering hub, then the moments are summed appropriately, and the states of the gimbal degrees of freedom are calculated.

In the time-domain step to the next azimuth, the solution to the flapping equation for each blade is applied, and the axial force, thrust, is used as the forcing function to a first-order differential equation for the wake model as described in the main text. This process continues for 14 complete revolutions.

Occasionally, especially at high advance ratios or high descent rates, a trim analysis will fail. One reason this happens is because the linear aerodynamics introduces instability reminiscent of resonance in the integrating algorithm. One way to get beyond that problem is to select Transient Analysis after setting up the rotor model. (This is also a good time to suggest that when you have set up the rotor model on the Rotor Specs page, go back to the main menu, and save the Rotor Specification file. This saves you from having to retype all of the rotor inputs.) If that fails, it might be that you have selected a flight condition that is physically unreasonable or unattainable. If that is not the case, then you have likely run into the limits of this simple program. The Rotor Tutor program is designed to demonstrate some basic principles only.

Index